James Halliday's
AUSTRALIAN
WINE
GUIDE

To Ron

Good on yor, sport!

With love

Meppi

16.11.91

James Halliday's
AUSTRALIAN
WINE
GUIDE

1990
EDITION

ANGUS
& ROBERTSON
PUBLISHERS

ANGUS & ROBERTSON PUBLISHERS

Unit 4, Eden Park Estate, 31 Waterloo Road,
North Ryde, NSW, Australia 2113; and
16 Golden Square, London W1R 4BN,
United Kingdom

First published in Australia
by Angus & Robertson Publishers in 1989
First published in the United Kingdom
by Angus & Robertson (UK) in 1990

Copyright © James Halliday 1989

ISSN 0 817 0215

Typeset in Baskerville
Printed and bound by Griffin Press,
South Australia

Contents

How to Use This Guide

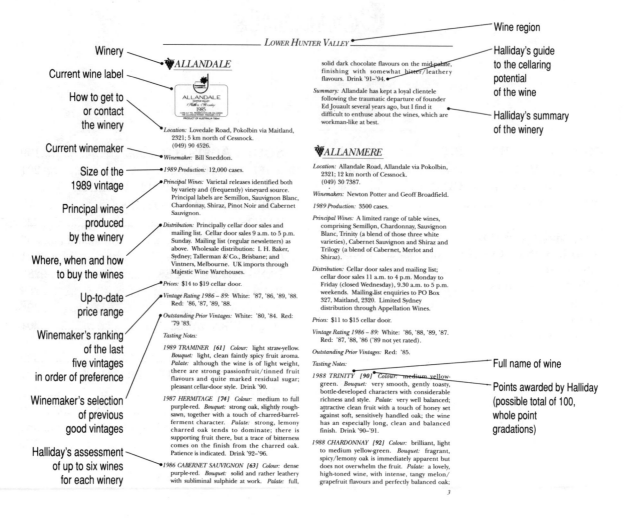

Winery

Current wine label

How to get to
or contact
the winery

Current winemaker

Size of the
1989 vintage

Principal wines
produced
by the winery

Where, when and how
to buy the wines

Up-to-date
price range

Winemaker's ranking
of the last
five vintages
in order of preference

Winemaker's selection
of previous
good vintages

Halliday's assessment
of up to six wines
for each winery

Wine region

Halliday's guide
to the cellaring
potential
of the wine

Halliday's summary
of the winery

Full name of wine

Points awarded by Halliday
(possible total of 100,
whole point
gradations)

LOWER HUNTER VALLEY

ALLANDALE

Location: Lovedale Road, Pokolbin via Maitland, 2321; 5 km north of Cessnock. (049) 90 4526.

Winemaker: Bill Sneddon.

1989 Production: 12,000 cases.

Principal Wines: Varietal releases identified both by variety and (frequently) vineyard source. Principal labels are Semillon, Sauvignon Blanc, Chardonnay, Shiraz, Pinot Noir and Cabernet Sauvignon.

Distribution: Principally cellar door sales and mailing list. Cellar door sales 9 a.m. to 5 p.m. Sunday. Mailing list (regular newsletters) as above. Wholesale distribution: I. H. Baker, Sydney; Tallerman & Co., Brisbane; and Vintners, Melbourne. UK imports through Majestic Wine Warehouses.

Prices: $14 to $19 cellar door.

Vintage Rating 1986 – 89: White: '87, '86, '89, '88. Red: '86, '87, '89, '88.

Outstanding Prior Vintages: White: '80, '84. Red: '79 '83.

Tasting Notes:

1989 TRAMINER [61] Colour: light straw-yellow. *Bouquet:* light, clean faintly spicy fruit aroma. *Palate:* although the wine is of light weight, there are strong passionfruit/tinned fruit flavours and quite marked residual sugar; pleasant cellar-door style. Drink '90.

1987 HERMITAGE [74] Colour: medium to full purple-red. *Bouquet:* strong oak, slightly rough-sawn, together with a touch of charred-barrel-ferment character. *Palate:* strong, lemony charred oak tends to dominate; there is supporting fruit there, but a trace of bitterness comes on the finish from the charred oak. Patience is indicated. Drink '92–'96.

1986 CABERNET SAUVIGNON [63] Colour: dense purple-red. *Bouquet:* solid and rather leathery with subliminal sulphide at work. *Palate:* full,

solid dark chocolate flavours on the mid-palate, finishing with somewhat bitter/leathery flavours. Drink '91–'94.

Summary: Allandale has kept a loyal clientele following the traumatic departure of founder Ed Jouault several years ago, but I find it difficult to enthuse about the wines, which are workman-like at best.

ALLANMERE

Location: Allandale Road, Allandale via Pokolbin, 2321; 12 km north of Cessnock. (049) 30 7387.

Winemakers: Newton Potter and Geoff Broadfield.

1989 Production: 3500 cases.

Principal Wines: A limited range of table wines, comprising Semillon, Chardonnay, Sauvignon Blanc, Trinity (a blend of those three white varieties), Cabernet Sauvignon and Shiraz and Trilogy (a blend of Cabernet, Merlot and Shiraz).

Distribution: Cellar door sales and mailing list; cellar door sales 11 a.m. to 4 p.m. Monday to Friday (closed Wednesday), 9.30 a.m. to 5 p.m. weekends. Mailing list enquiries to PO Box 327, Maitland, 2320. Limited Sydney distribution through Appellation Wines.

Prices: $11 to $15 cellar door.

Vintage Rating 1986 – 89: White: '86, '88, '89, '87. Red: '87, '88, '86 ('89 not yet rated).

Outstanding Prior Vintages: Red: '85.

Tasting Notes:

1988 TRINITY [90] Colour: medium yellow-green. *Bouquet:* very smooth, gently toasty, bottle-developed characters with considerable richness and style. *Palate:* very well balanced; attractive clean fruit with a touch of honey set against soft, sensitively handled oak; the wine has an especially long, clean and balanced finish. Drink '90–'91.

1988 CHARDONNAY [92] Colour: brilliant, light to medium yellow-green. *Bouquet:* fragrant, spicy/lemony oak is immediately apparent but does not overwhelm the fruit. *Palate:* a lovely, high-toned wine, with intense, tangy melon/grapefruit flavours and perfectly balanced oak;

3

Grape Varieties

Albillo: An incorrect name for the grape variety chenin blanc.

Aleatico: A grape of the muscat family from Italy and grown in Australia chiefly in the Mudgee region. Produces red or fortified wine.

Alicante Bouschet (or **Bouchet**): A French hybrid red grape grown extensively in France and, to a lesser degree, California. High-yielding but inferior quality grapes are produced. Limited plantings in Australia, chiefly north-east Victoria.

Alvarelhao: A Portuguese grape variety once propagated in tiny quantities in southern New South Wales and nothern Victoria. Has little or no future.

Aubun: An extremely rare red-grape variety from the Mediterranean region of France; a few vines still exist at Bests Great Western Vineyards.

Aucerto: Incorrect name for montils.

Barbera: The principal red-wine grape of Italy, grown in tiny quantities in Australia, chiefly in Mudgee but also in the Murrumbidgee Irrigation Area. Noted for its high acidity and pH.

Bastardo: A red-grape variety from Spain, incorrectly called cabernet gros in South Australia. Of minor importance.

Biancone: A white grape of Corsica; the highest-yielding variety in commercial propagation in Australia, regularly achieving 30 tonnes per hectare in the relatively small plantings in South Australia's Riverland area.

Blanquette: Synonym for clairette.

Blue Imperial: Synonym for cinsaut.

Bonvedro: A red grape of Portugal, grown principally in South Australia with a little in New South Wales and Victoria. Produces a relatively light-bodied wine; not an important variety.

Bourboulenc: A white-grape variety from the Mediterranean region of France, included in the Busby importation of 1832 but now restricted to a few wines in central and northern Victoria. Unlikely ever to be of significance in Australia.

Brown frontignac: Incorrect name for muscat à petits grains.

Brown muscat: Incorrect name for muscat à petits grains.

Cabernet: In Australia, simply an abbreviation for cabernet sauvignon; also used to denote the cabernet family (see below).

Cabernet franc: An important red-grape variety in Bourdeaux and the Loire Valley in France; also extensively propagated in Italy. Until recently, little attention was paid to the variety in Australia but it is now assuming greater importance for top-quality reds. Produces a wine similar to but slightly softer than cabernet sauvignon.

Cabernet gros: Incorrect name for bastardo.

Cabernet sauvignon: The great red grape of Bordeaux and, with pinot noir, one of the two most noble red varieties in the world. It has become the most important top-quality red-wine grape in Australia only during the last two decades; prior to that time it was grown in small quantities.

Carignan, Carignane: A grape variety of Spanish origin but very widely propagated in the south of France to produce *vin ordinaire*. Also extensively grown in California for similar purposes. Some South Australian plantings of an unidentified grape are incorrectly called carignane; the grape is not commercially propagated in Australia.

Chardonnay: The greatest white grape of France (Burgundy and Champagne), grown extensively throughout the world and in particular in California. All but unknown in Australia before 1970, it has since had a meteoric rise. As elsewhere, it provides rich table wines and fine sparkling wines.

Chasselas: The principal white-wine grape of Switzerland, and also extensively propagated in France and Italy. In Europe and in Australia it is used both for wine-making and as a table grape. In the last century it was called sweet-water; the principal area of propagation in Australia is at Great Western in Victoria.

Chenin blanc: The principal white grape of the Loire Valley in France, grown in relatively small quantities in Western Australia, South Australia and Victoria and for long incorrectly identified variously as semillon and albillo. Seldom produces wines of the same character as in the Loire Valley, but the plantings have recently shown a modest increase. Can produce great botrytised wines.

Cinsaut: A red-grape variety from the Mediterranean region of France. Frequently called blue imperial in north-east Victoria, black prince in Great Western and confused with oeillade in

South Australia. Produces agreeable soft wines with good colour but low in tannin.

Clairette: A once very important white-grape variety in the south of France, grown in relatively small quantities in Australia where it is often called blanquette (particularly in the Hunter Valley). A difficult wine to make and of no great merit.

Clare riesling: Incorrect name for crouchen.

Colombard: A white grape extensively grown in France, used both for table-winemaking and also in the production of brandy. Extensively propagated in California where it is known as French colombard. Has been planted extensively in Australia's warm irrigated regions because of its excellent acid-retention capacity. Used both in blends and in varietal white wines.

Crouchen: A white grape originally from France but now propagated only in South Africa and Australia. The substantial plantings in this country have been consistently incorrectly identified for a century, being called Clare riesling in the Clare Valley, semillon in the Barossa Valley, and firstly Clare riesling and then semillon in South Australia's Riverland, before being finally identified as crouchen. A relatively high-yielding variety, producing wines of modest quality; of declining importance.

Dolcetto: A red grape from Piedmont in Italy, grown in tiny quantities in South Australia and Victoria. Many of the old classic Saltram reds contained small quantities of the variety.

Doradillo: An extremely important white grape in Australia but of little significance elsewhere, which was brought to Australia by James Busby from Spain. Grown principally in the Riverland areas for distillation

into brandy and for the production of sherry.

Durif: A variety first propagated in the Rhône Valley only a century ago, and called petite sirah in California. Grown in tiny amounts in Australia, notably in north-eastern Victoria by Morris.

Esparte: Synonym for mataro.

Farana: A white grape from the Mediterranean region grown in tiny quantities in the Barossa Valley, where it was previously confused with trebbiano.

Fetayaska: A white grape grown in tiny quantities in north-east Victoria and South Australia to make a white table wine of no great significance.

Folle blanche: A still important white-grape variety used in the production of brandy in France. The supposed Australian plantings have now been identified as ondenc.

Frontignac: Incorrect name for muscat à petits grains.

Furmint: The white grape used to make the famous Hungarian tokay. Introduced into Australia by James Busby; a few vines exist at Great Western and one or two boutique wineries have experimental plantings.

Gamay: Gamay is the red grape which produces beaujolais in France; it is also grown extensively in the Loire Valley. Two attempts to introduce the variety into Australia from California have failed. The first introduction turned out to be pinot noir, the second valdigue. Still grown only in tiny quantities; it seems inevitable that further attempts to propagate it in the future will be made.

Gewurztraminer: Synonym for traminer

Glory of Australia: A black grape from the Burgundy region of France, from which it

disappeared after phylloxera; frequently mentioned in the nineteenth-century accounts of the vineyards of Geelong. A few vines survive at Great Western. Also called liverdun, la gloire, but correctly called troyen.

Gouais: A minor white-grape variety from the centre of France, extensively propagated in Victoria in the nineteenth century but now largely disappeared except from areas around Rutherglen.

Graciano: A red variety of importance in Spain's Rioja area. Called morrastel in France, but unrelated to the variety once called thus in South Australia (which is in fact mataro). Grown in small quantities in north-eastern Victoria. Produces strongly coloured wines, rich in tannin and extract, which age well.

Hárslevelü: A white grape of Hungary used in making Hungarian tokay. Tiny plantings in Australia.

Hermitage: An incorrect name for shiraz.

Hunter River riesling: Incorrect name for semillon.

Irvine's white: Incorrect name for ondenc.

Jacquez: An American variety thought to be a naturally occurring hybrid between the species *Vitis aestivalis* and *Vitis vinifera*. Small quantities grown in the Murrumbidgee Irrigation Area and the Hunter Valley where it is usually called troia. It has a strong, unusual flavour less unpleasant than those of the species *Vitis labrusca*.

Malbec: A red-grape variety grown chiefly in and around Bordeaux and also in the Loire Valley where it is known as cot. Grown on a vast scale in Argentina and in a minor way throughout Australia. Has been confused with dolcetto and tinta amarella. Ideal for blending with cabernet sauvignon which it softens and fills out.

Mammolo: A red-grape variety once of minor importance in Tuscany, Italy; a few vines exist in Mudgee, and there have apparently been some other isolated recent plantings. The wine is said to have an aroma resembling the scent of violets.

Marsanne: A white-grape variety of declining importance in the Rhône Valley of France, grown in relatively small quantities in the Goulburn Valley, north-east Victoria and the Hunter Valley. Once famous in the Yarra Valley, where tiny plantings also still exist.

Mataro: A red grape of major importance in Spain, where it is called morastell or monastrell. Once one of Australia's most important red grapes in terms of production, but now declining. Called balzac at Corowa and esparte at Great Western. Yields well and produces a neutrally flavoured but astringent wine which is best blended with other varieties.

Melon: A white grape which originated in Burgundy but is now propagated principally in the Loire Valley, where it is known as muscadet. Significant plantings in California are called pinot blanc. Only small quantities are propagated in Australia, chiefly in South Australia.

Merlot: One of the most important red-grape varieties in the Bordeaux region, dominant in St Emilion and Pomerol. A relatively recent arrival in California and even more recent in Australia, where the small commercial plantings to date have been disappointing from a viticultural viewpoint. Poor fruiting has caused some experimental plantings to be abandoned. However, others are persevering and plantings are on the increase.

Meunier: A red grape almost invariably known under its synonym pinot meunier in Australia. Also called Miller's burgundy at Great Western. A naturally occurring derivative of pinot noir and grown principally in France in Champagne. The upsurge in interest in sparkling wine in Australia may see the increase in the presently small and isolated plantings, chiefly in Victoria.

Miller's burgundy: Incorrect name for meunier.

Monbadon: A white variety of declining importance in Bordeaux and Cognac; grown on a small scale in the Corowa–Wahgunyah area of north-east Victoria.

Mondeuse: A red grape of minor importance in the east of France, grown chiefly by Brown Brothers at Milawa in north-eastern Victoria. Introduced to Australia at the suggestion of Francois de Castella in the aftermath of phylloxera. Produces a very strong, tannic wine ideal for blending with softer varieties.

Montils: A white grape grown in small quantities in Cognac. Small plantings in the Hunter Valley where it is also known as aucerot; the aucerot of north-eastern Victoria is a separate and, as yet, unidentified variety. Produces a wine with low pH and high acidity, and would appear to have at least as much potential as colombard, but little commercial interest has so far been demonstrated.

Moschata paradisa: A white-grape variety grown in tiny quantities in Mudgee, but so far its overseas source has not been identified. Australia's most unusual grape.

Müller-Thurgau: A cross, bred by Dr Müller in 1882 and put into commercial propagation in 1920 in Germany; now that country's most important grape.

Originally thought to be a riesling–silvaner cross, but now believed to be a cross of two riesling grapes. Propagated in limited quantities in Australia; produces a fairly uninteresting wine. The most important white grape in New Zealand, where it is generally known as riesling sylvaner.

Muscadelle: The white grape which is the third and least important component of the wines of Sauternes. Grown across Australia, and usually known as tokay. The largest plantings are in South Australia, but in north-east Victoria extremely ripe, raisined grapes are used to make the famous fortified tokay of that region. The grape is not used for this purpose anywhere else in the world.

Muscadet: Synonym for melon.

Muscat à petits grains: A grape variety grown over much of Europe and which is called by a wide variety of names both there and in Australia, not surprising given that it appears in three colour variants—white, rosé and red. The coloured forms mutate readily from one to the other, while chimeras, in which the genetic make-up of the skin differs from that of the flesh, also exist. It is grown principally in South Australia and New South Wales and Victoria (most frequently called white, red or brown frontignac). The white variety is common in South Australia, the red in north-eastern Victoria, where it is known as brown muscat (or brown frontignac) and used to make the great fortified wines of that region. The white variant is used to make table wine of very high flavour, often used in small percentages with other more noble varieties such as rhine riesling.

Muscat gordo blanco: A white-grape variety, originating in Spain but grown in many countries. A very important variety in Australia for winemaking, drying and table-grape use. Widely called muscat of Alexandria, it is a high-yielding multi-purpose grape. For winemaking it is used for fortified sweet wines such as cream sherry and also in cask and flagon wines, often in combination with sultana.

Muscat of Alexandria: Synonym for muscat gordo blanco.

Oeillade: Incorrect name for cinsaut.

Ondenc: An obscure white grape from France, travelling both there and in Australia under a confusingly large number of names. Probably brought to this country by James Busby as piquepoule, but then became known as sercial in South Australia and Irvine's white in Victoria at Great Western. In France it is used for brandy-making; in Australia for sparkling wine (because of its neutrality), chiefly by Seppelt at Great Western and Drumborg.

Orange muscat: A highly aromatic white-grape variety, also known in France as muscat fleur d'orange; grown chiefly in north-eastern Victoria.

Palomino: A white grape from Spain providing virtually all the raw material for sherry. Grown on a very large scale in South Africa and an important variety in Australia. Very similar to pedro ximinez. Used chiefly for fortified wine in Australia, and in particular dry sherry.

Pedro ximinez: Another Spanish variety used to produce both dry and sweet fortified wines. Extensively propagated in Argentina and important in Australia (although decreasing). Grown chiefly in the Riverland areas, it is used in the making of sherry, but also to provide flagon and cask white wine.

Peloursin: An ancient grape variety from the east of France but of little or no commercial significance. Survives in Australia and California interplanted with durif, which it resembles.

Petit meslier: An extremely obscure, although still permitted, white-grape variety in Champagne in France; a few vines survive amongst ondenc plantings at Great Western.

Petit verdot: A minor red grape of Bourdeaux of declining importance in that region. The once significant Hunter Valley plantings have disappeared since 1930, but a few tiny plantings have since been established elsewhere in Australia by those seeking to emulate the great wines of Bordeaux.

Petite sirah: Incorrect name for durif used throughout America.

Pinot blanc: The true pinot blanc is a white variant of pinot noir, seemingly grown only in Alsace, Germany and Italy. Varieties grown elsewhere and called pinot blanc are variously chardonnay, chenin blanc or melon.

Pinot chardonnay: Incorrect name for chardonnay.

Pinot de la Loire: French synonym for chenin blanc.

Pinot gris: Another colour variant of pinot noir similar to pinot blanc. Grown in Alsace, Germany (where it is called rulander) and northern Italy.

Pinot meunier: Synonym for meunier.

Pinot noir: The classic red grape of Burgundy, grown in practically every country in the world but only producing wine of real quality in cool climates. Plantings in Australia are expected to increase substantially with increasing use of the variety for sparkling wine.

Piquepoule noir: A minor red-

grape variety from the Chateauneuf-du-Pape region of France, surviving as a few vines at Great Western.

Rhine riesling: Simply known as riesling in its native Germany, where it is the most highly regarded white grape. Grown extensively around the world; known as white riesling or Johannisberg riesling in California and by a host of names in other countries. While it has fallen from public favour in Australia, it still remains the most important high-quality wine grape. The widespread advent of botrytis has meant that both dry and very sweet wines of excellent quality can be made from it.

Riesling: (i) Preferred for rhine riesling. (ii) A dry white wine which may or may not be made from or contain a percentage of rhine riesling in it.

Rkatitseli: A Russian white grape propagated chiefly in the Murrumbidgee Irrigation Area by McWilliam's and others.

Roussane: A white grape grown in the Rhône Valley and usually blended with marsanne. Also a minor component of some (red) Chateauneuf-du-Pape wines. Experimental plantings at Yeringberg in Yarra Valley.

Rubired: An American-bred red hybrid producing wines of startlingly intense colour and very useful for blending in small quantities for this purpose. Propagated on a limited scale in Australia.

Ruby cabernet: Another red hybrid bred by Professor Olmo at the University of California. Grown on a very limited scale in Australia.

Rulander: German synonym for pinot gris.

Sauvignon blanc: A white grape which is the most important component of the sweet (sauternes) and dry white wines of Bordeaux (where it is blended with semillon and muscadelle), and which is also grown extensively in the Loire Valley where it provides crisp, dry wines, Sancerre and Pouilly Fumé being the best known. It is of rapidly increasing popularity in Australia, chiefly in dry white wines which are often wood-aged and marketed as Fumé Blanc (although there is no legal requirement that Fumé Blanc contain any particular grape variety or varieties). It flourishes in New Zealand, producing wines with razor-sharp grassy/gooseberry/asparagus varietal aroma and flavour.

Semillon: The major white grape of Bordeaux and the second most widely grown in the whole of France. Outside France it is propagated chiefly in the southern hemisphere, particularly in Chile. Has been confused with chenin blanc in Western Australia and crouchen in South Australia; Barnawartha pinot of north-eastern Victoria is semillon. The classic white grape of the Hunter Valley; produces wines which are extremely long-lived and often need five or 10 years to reach their peak. Now also matured in new oak to produce a different style, and increasingly used for the production of sauternes-style wines in South Australia.

Sercial: Incorrect name for ondenc.

Shepherd's riesling: An incorrect (and no longer used) name for semillon.

Shiraz: A red grape coming from the Hermitage area of the Rhône Valley, the origins of which are obscure and hotly debated. Frequently called hermitage in Australia (particularly in New South Wales and Victoria). For long the mainstay of the Australian red-wine industry, and still the most widely propagated red

grape. The fact it can produce wines of the very highest quality is frequently forgotten; a very versatile variety which can do well in all climates and soil types. Also useful for blending with cabernet sauvignon.

Silvaner, Sylvaner: A vigorous, high-yielding white grape extensively grown in Germany, producing rather neutral-flavoured wines. Even in cool-climate areas such as Drumborg and Keppoch it produces an unexciting wine. The modest plantings are not likely to increase.

Souzão: A minor red grape grown in the Douro Valley of Portugal.

Sultana: A white grape which originated in Asia Minor or the Middle East, and which is principally used both in Australia and elsewhere as a table grape. In California, where it is known as Thompson's seedless, it is grown on a very large scale and significant quantities are used for white-winemaking. In Australia it is produced primarily for drying, but a considerable amount is used in winemaking and some for table-grape purposes. It produces a very neutral wine with quite good acidity.

Sylvaner: See **Silvaner**.

Syrah: Synonym for shiraz.

Tarrango: A red hybrid grape bred by the CSIRO. Chiefly used in the production of nouveau-style reds by Brown Bros and others; has considerable promise.

Tempranillo: The most highly regarded of the red-grape varieties grown in Spain's Rioja, and known as valdepenas in California. A small planting by that name in the Upper Hunter Valley is presumably tempranillo. The wine matures extremely quickly.

Terret noir: A grape grown in

the Languedoc area of France. Appearing in three colour combinations—white, grey and black. A small planting of the latter type exists in the Barossa Valley.

Thompson's seedless: American synonym for sultana.

Tinta amarélla: A red grape widely grown in the Douro Valley of Portugal and used in vintage port. There is a small amount in South Australia, where the variety is known as portugal. It has from time to time been confused with malbec.

Tinta Cão: A red grape grown in the Douro Valley in Portugal and important in the making of vintage port.Only experimental plantings in Australia.

Tokai friulano: A white grape closely related to sauvignon blanc and grown extensively in the Friuli-Venezia-Giulia region of north Italy. Grown on a large scale in Argentina where it is called sauvignon. Isolated vines exist in Mudgee, the Goulburn Valley and Great Western, sometimes in surprisingly large numbers. The wine has a definite bouquet and a slight bitterness, as its sauvignon blanc heritage would suggest.

Tokay: See **Muscadelle**.

Touriga: The most important red grape in the Douro Valley in Portugal, used extensively in vintage port. Small plantings have been grown for many years in the Corowa region, and there have been small recent plantings on the floor of the Barossa Valley. It is used to make high-quality vintage port, and a modest increase in plantings can be expected.

Traminer: An ancient white-grape variety derived from the primitive wild grapes of Europe. The main European plantings are in Alsace and Germany, and also northern Italy. Produces a highly aromatic wine which can quickly become overbearing and over-blown. Contrary to popular belief, there is no viticultural or other distinction between traminer and gewurztztraminer, although the latter is supposedly more spicy in aroma and taste.

Trebbiano: The leading white grape of Italy, and now dominant in the Cognac region of France where it is known as St Emilion, although the official French name is ugni blanc. It is known by both these names in Australia and also (incorrectly) as white shiraz or white hermitage. It is grown in virtually all Australian wine regions, bearing well to produce a neutral and rather hard table wine and an excellent distillation base for brandy.

Ugni blanc: French synonym for trebbiano.

Valdepenas: California synonym for tempranillo.

Verdelho: A white grape from Portugal, grown on the island of Madeira where it is used to make fortified wine, and in small quantities in the Douro Valley. The Australian plantings of under 100 hectares are divided between Western Australia, South Australia and New South Wales. Produces a very distinctive full-bodied table wine, and can also be used to make fortified wine.

Viognier: A white grape grown chiefly at the northern end of the Rhône Valley to produce distinctive and highly flavoured although relatively quick-maturing wine. Experimental plantings in Australia show some promise.

White frontignac: Synonym for muscat à petits grains.

White hermitage: Incorrect name for trebbiano.

Zinfandel: A grape variety grown chiefly in California, but may be related to the widely propagated primitivo variety of Italy. Grown in small quantities in Australia, chiefly in Western Australia and South Australia. Can produce a wine deep in colour and rich in soft, spicy flavour.

Wine-producing Regions

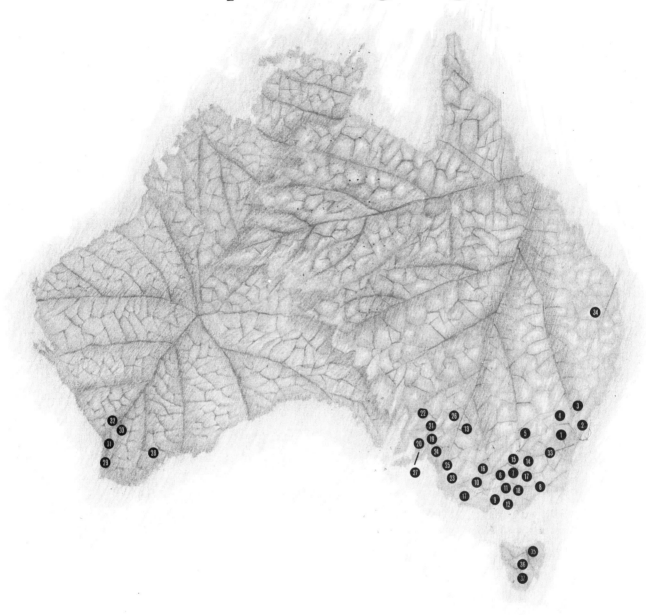

New South Wales
1 Hilltops
2 Lower Hunter Valley
3 Upper Hunter Valley
4 Mudgee
5 Murrumbidgee Irrigation Area

Victoria
6 Bendigo and District
7 Central Goulburn Valley
8 Gippsland
9 Geelong
10 Great Western and District
11 Macedon
12 Mornington Peninsula
13 Murray River
14 North-East Victoria
15 North Goulburn River
16 Pyrenees
17 Southern and Central Victoria
18 Yarra Valley

South Australia
19 Adelaide Hills
20 Adelaide Metropolitan Area/
   Adelaide Plains
21 Barossa Valley
22 Clare Valley
23 Coonawarra
24 Langhorne Creek
25 Padthaway/Keppoch
26 Riverland
27 Southern Vales

Western Australia
28 Lower Great Southern Area
29 Margaret River
30 Perth Hills
31 South-West Coastal Plain
32 Swan Valley

Canberra District
33

Queensland
34 Granite Belt

Tasmania
35 Pipers Brook
36 Tamar Valley
37 Derwent

Introduction

This book is written as a companion to my *Australian Wine Compendium*. The Compendium covers the history of the wine regions and the wineries which populate those regions; it gives a detailed description of the vineyards; and it tells you much about the winemakers and their winemaking philosophies.

Here I cover rather different ground. On the one hand there are all the hard facts: precise addresses; telephone numbers; where, when and how the wines may be purchased; up-to-date (1989 vintage) production details; and current prices. Then follows a relative rating of the last four vintages ('86 – '89 inclusive), and in some instances a one-line listing of outstanding prior vintages. These vintage ratings are those of the winemaker and, even if I disagree with them, I have left them unaltered.

Most conspicious are my tasting notes of the wines. Up to this point the book is self-explanatory, but I believe the tasting notes require explanation and—if you wish—justification.

WINE SELECTION

Firstly, except where otherwise indicated the wines were tasted (and the notes made) in July and August 1989, specifically for the purposes of this book. I in fact tasted many more wines (over 5000 in all), but for a variety of reasons have not included all the notes. The primary reason for exclusion was the limits necessarily imposed by the size of this book. Thus the (somewhat arbitrary) maximum number of wines for any one winery is six, while that for small or less important wineries is significantly lower.

For all that, it should be borne in mind that between four and five months will elapse between the time the wines were tasted and this book is published. It may be substantially longer again before you, the reader, assimilate my tasting notes. Accordingly, where I suggest that a wine either needs time to fill out, or should develop well in bottle, bear in mind that this transformation may have already occurred.

Furthermore, not all of the 1989 white wines nor all of the 1989 and 1988 red wines tasted were bottled samples. In other words, some have been drawn from barrel or tank. Where such a wine appeared to me to be ready for bottling, I treated it as if it were already bottled and pointed (and described it) in the usual fashion. In the majority of instances, however, I show it as *[CS]*, meaning cask sample, or *[TS]*, meaning tank sample. I have then given a more general description of the wine, and hazarded a guess about the points it might eventually gain. Please be aware, however, that more wines are spoilt during bottling than at any other stage of their production. What is more, single cask samples of oak-matured wines can be utterly unrepresentative of the finished wine in the bottle. Usually they are better, but sometimes an over-oaked wine can be brought back into balance by the final blending.

More than ever before, I have tried to select wines which are likely to reflect favourably the quality and style of the winery—in other words, those wines which I would be most likely to choose to drink from the output of the winery concerned. This may give a somewhat rosy overall picture, but in the end I decided that this book should be a book about wines to buy, rather than wines to avoid. In these circumstances, readers are encouraged to draw their own conclusions from silence.

Finally, I have endeavoured to focus on wines which are likely to be available for sale in 1990. With some of the more fashionable small wineries this may prove a vain hope— although the "sold out" sign is an increasingly rare phenomenon, it is still not extinct.

TASTING JARGON

There are as many schools of thought about the language of tasting notes as there are wine-lovers (or critics). At one extreme there are those who poke fun at the inevitably odd language of even the most restrained tasting note, reaching the ultimate in asking "how can a wine have a nose?" At the other end there are those who argue that if the taster is restricted to a prescribed series of defined technical terms, tasting notes will be of very limited use. They will be able to convey certain basic impressions, but will fail utterly to come to grips with the myriad differing sensations and tastes which one constantly comes face to face with in the world of wine.

The very reason that so much is written about wine is its endless complexity and subtlety. It is trite in the extreme to observe that no two wines are precisely the same; more significantly, one can find the most unexpected flavours and sensations in a high-quality wine, let alone one which exhibits a

winemaking fault.

So the liberals say that if a wine smells of truffles, wood violets, salami, hazelnuts (or whatever) you should say so; if its texture seems voluptuous (in other words, generous, rounded, fleshy and soft) you should likewise say so. Above all else, the initial impression should be captured and recorded. It is often the most accurate: repeated visits to the glass tend to blur the impact of the initial sensation. All agree it is impossible to measure a taste or a colour scientifically or objectively. It is all a matter of comparison, of imagery.

Those who are most prone to criticise the language of tasting notes are those who have never attempted the exercise of writing them in the first place.

THE FALLIBILITY OF TASTING NOTES

In any event, I believe the limitations of tasting notes go far deeper that the clothing of language which surrounds them.

First and foremost, they are one person's views at a given time of the highly subjective impact of the taste of a wine. They have no universal or immutable validity. No matter how skilled the taster or how perfect the tasting conditions, there will inevitably be some difference in two successive tasting notes by the same taster of the same wine completed (say) at an interval of one week. Most probably, there will be what seems to the untutored eye a substantial difference.

The wine has not changed in this time, but its effect on the taster has. There are an infinite number of variables which interface with the tasting process. Is the tasting conducted in the morning, afternoon or night? Is the taster tired or alert? Has he or she eaten within the previous hour or two? Is the wine tasted as part of a comparative line-up, or on its own? Was there any prior knowledge of the wine (district, water, grape variety or vintage)? Was the tasting conducted with others present? If so, was there any discussion about the wine?

Let me explain a little more about just a few of these factors, all of which are quite clearly important and all of which will impact on the tasting note which is ultimately produced.

I have absolutely no doubt that the comparative tasting is the most reliable method of tasting wines, and of putting them into perspective. The opposite extreme is the tasting of a wine drawn from a barrel in the dim recesses of a winery you know and love by a winemaker you respect. It is nearly certain you will think the wine is magnificent.

Tasted in a comparative line-up in the cold light of the following day , in the glare of the colour-corrected neon lights of a winemaker's laboratory, it is very probable you will detect a shortcoming, if not a positive fault (possibly remediable), in the wine which so impressed you the day before.

There can be no better example of this than the elementary procedure of the three-way trial which should be—but unhappily frequently is not—part of a winemaker's repertoire. Young red (and sometimes white) wines frequently suffer from hydrogen sulphide problems. At high levels the fault is readily detectable, but in small concentrations it can be very difficult to tell whether the wine is simply showing the after-effects of fermentation or whether indeed it has hydrogen sulphide. (I should add that, if untreated, hydrogen sulphide ultimately produces mercaptan.)

Hydrogen sulphide is readily removed by the addition of small quantities of copper. So one or two of the three glasses are treated (the taster does not know if it is one or two) and the three glasses are then placed in random order (marked on their under-base, if needs be). Even the slightest contami-nation is immediately detectable to the skilled taster once the comparison is available. Yet this technique works as well as it does because the three wines are of basically identical composition and style.

Once wines of differing parentage, age and weight are placed next to each other, the picture becomes more confused. A light-bodied, fragrant and delicate red which follows a blockbuster—a strong cabernet high in tannin and from a warm vintage—may easily be lost or unfairly downpointed. So the comparative system, while still the best, is not foolproof. At the very least, it requires considerable skills on the part of the taster.

Another factor worth looking at in a little more detail is the question of whether the taster knows anything of the origin of the wine. An English wine writer once observed that a quick glance at the label is worth 20 years in the wine trade.

Closer to home I have seen the following exercise practised with devastating results. Each guest at a dinner party (or wine-tasting) is asked to bring a bottle of his or her favourite wine. All the bottles are then lined up and each person lists the wines in expected order of preference. The wines are then masked, and each is tasted and assessed without knowledge of its identity. Once again each taster ranks the wine (this time by glass number) in order of preference. It is not uncommon to find the initial "consensus" order reversed by the blind tasting. Certainly it is rare to find that any one taster's two lists correspond to any marked degree.

Indeed, even the most skilled taster cannot help but be influenced by knowledge of the label. It is for this reason that wherever practicable (and for logistical reasons it is not always possible) I conduct "blind" comparative tastings.

WHEN TO DRINK

There is no doubt that the most difficult task for someone learning about wine is to foresee what is likely to happen to a particular wine in the years to come. I am asked the "cellar-ing potential" question more frequently than any other. So I have attempted to forestall those questions by providing a "drink '90–'92" type of guide. The most obvious feature of this guide is that (with a few exceptions) it does not say "drink '91". More particularly, it does not say "drink 14 July 1991". Contrary to widespread belief, there is no particular point in the development of a wine which either human or computer can identify as the perfect moment for consumption.

The reason is simple enough; the process of wine development is a leisurely one. Obviously, the life span (and development potential) of a beaujolais nouveau will be decidedly shorter and more rapid than that of a great cabernet. But such exceptions to one side, at any given point in the maturity (or drink) span I have given, someone is going to regard the wine as at its most perfect, someone not.

The development of wine in bottle is an extremely complex one; while many of the chemical changes are far better understood and recorded than in years gone by, their relevance to the flavour and style of the wine is still hotly debated and imperfectly understood.

The overall result of cellaring, however, is not in dispute: from the day the wine is put into the bottle there is an inexorable progression as the wine loses primary fruit aroma and flavour, and in its place—and up to a certain point—gains in complexity.

How one relates to the wine during this initial development phase is an intensely personal (and subjective) matter. Some look to fruit freshness, life and lift of a young wine; others to the more mellow and rounded depths of complexity of the same wine 3, 10 or 15 years later.

The spans I have given in the tasting notes are deliberately conservative, particularly at their outer end. There is no doubt that a significant number of the wines will still be in first-class condition 10 or 20 years after the end of the span I have stipulated. On the other hand, many Australian wines made in the 1960s and the first half of the 1970s which promised so much when young are now found wanting. This is due to two things: firstly, an inherent lack of fruit durability in the wine; and, secondly, to changes in winemaking techniques and styles which have since altered the public's perception of just what is desirable in a top quality red wine.

In other words, in the mid-1960s there were virtually no straight cabernet sauvignons available on the market; by mid-1975 they had started to appear in numbers, but most were made from grapes grown in warm climates, and the cabernet flavour tended to be chocolatey and somewhat burnt; in the latter part of the 1970s the first of the herbaceous/cool climate cabernets started to appear in quantity; and finally, by 1985 the pendulum had swung back somewhat from the ultra-green/grassy unripe cabernet flavour to a fuller and more modulated flavour profile. Thus it is that a perfectly cellared bottle of 1973 Cabernet Sauvignon, which has done everything its maker could have expected or hoped of it, and which (when first released) was highly regarded, will now seem passé and old fashioned.

In fact, the overwhelming number of Australian reds have really failed to live up to expectations, even if one discounts the impact of the style change. For all of these reasons I have been conservative in stipulating the outer limit of the cellaring span; from this time onwards you would be well advised to keep a close watch on the development of the wine. It may continue to develop complexity and richness for decades and you will have chosen well.

A brief word on cellaring white wines. So far, at least, Australian white wines have defied conventional wisdom. All but a handful of Australian chardonnays have bloomed all too briefly; luscious when young, they tend to become tired and flabby in the third or fourth year after vintage. On the other hand, well-made semillon and a considerable number of the traditional rhine rieslings (particularly those from the Eden and Clare Valleys) can improve in bottle for as long as many red wines. A quick visit to a Lindemans Classic Wine stockist and the purchase of a 1970 Hunter River Riesling (in other words, semillon) or a 1975 Leo Buring White Label Rhine Riesling will prove the point.

The one word of warning here is that one should carefully inspect the bottle. The quality of Australian bottles, and the quality of the corks used by the majority of the major wine companies, leave a very great deal to be desired. Whereas a 15-year-old French wine is likely to be at the same level in the bottle as the day it was filled, that of an Australian wine will have receded down the neck and probably part-way down the shoulders of the bottle. Ullage, as it is known, is the chief problem confronting those who wish to have and enjoy fully mature Australian wine. It is not too much to say that the major Australian winemakers should be condemned for their penny-pinching and short-sighted views about wine bottles and the corks which go into them.

POINTS SCORE AND SUMMARY

In this and the previous edition I have used a 100-point scale, similar to that used by American wine writers, and in particular the redoubtable Robert M. Parker. There are, however, critical differences: for a start I have absolutely no desire that my tasting notes(or points) should be granted the status of holy writ as are those of Mr Parker. I cannot emphasise too strongly that I see my tasting notes as an indication, a guide, and that they have no absolute, unvarying infallibility. Wines change in bottle and, what is more, I have not had the opportunity of tasting and retasting the wines over a six- to nine-month period as does Mr Parker.

The other difference lies in the gradation I have used. Rober Parker finds it necessary to use, in effect, half points within a 100-point scale. If the same fine judgment were used on a 20-point scale, it would give rise to points such as 17.05 or 18.35. Those statisticians who have considered the results of tasting notes by the world's most experienced tasters would say that such incredibly fine gradations have no statistical validity.

Without becoming involved in that argument, I have presumed to use whole-point gradations on the 100-point scale. Within that system I have constructed the following groups of classification.

Any wine pointed at 95 or above (and there are very few of these) is a rare, absolutely outstanding wine destined to become (if not already) a classic. Price should be no consideration.

A wine given between 85 and 94 points inclusive is an exceptional wine of the best quality, which should be expensive, by which I mean falling in the $20 to $50 or above price range. A wine given between 75 and 84 points inclusive is of premium quality, and one would normally expect to find it in the middle-to-upper price range of $12 to $19.

Between 65 and 74 points inclusive come good commercial wines, with plenty of positive characters and style; these should fall in the lower-to-middle price range of $6 to $11. Between 50 and 64 points inclusive one finds wines of basic marketable quality; at the lower end winemaking faults may be apparent, but are not of such magnitude as to render the wine unsuitable for sale. Any wine pointed in this range should be at the lower end of the market, that is, below $6.

I have avoided providing notes for wines with points below 50. I have previously explained that this is intended to be a book about wines to buy, rather than about wines to avoid.

PRICES

Prices quoted should in most instances be current at the time of publication in December 1989. Equally, they will become increasingly outdated as 1990 wears on. Please do not berate the winemaker or the retailer if you are asked to pay more, for the sharp increases in grape prices over the 1988 and 1989 vintages are still to work their way through the system. And before you complain too much, do remember that the reason why Australian wine is doing so well in export markets is that the rest of the world perceives it as offering unequalled value for money. That is so even when the additional costs and duties of imported products are taken into account, and the wine is competing (for example) on the American market against American-produced wine. When you look at the prices prevailing in Australia, and judge those against our average weekly earnings, there is no arguing the proposition that we enjoy the cheapest wine (relative to quality) in the world today.

New South Wales

Lower Hunter Valley

1988 VINTAGE

The cycle of reasonably wet winter–spring weather continued, and, as with 1987, the season got away to a very good start. Flowering and set were not interrupted, and yields were abundant. Indeed, the high yields meant a late start to the vintage, and it was here that trouble began.

Around 125 centimetres of rain fell between 7 February and 21 February, causing great problems in both vineyard and winery alike. Quality varied greatly, being affected by two factors: whether or not the vigneron elected to delay picking, and the type of soil on which the vineyard was situated.

In the outcome, the white wines suffered less than the reds, mainly because the bulk was picked before the rain became too serious. Those who delayed picking their whites paid the price, however, as did those vineyards with dense canopies on the more sandy, fertile soils. Chardonnay probably did best, with some quite lovely wines being made, but semillon also performed well.

The greatest variation occurred with the red wines: some vignerons claimed outstanding success with very late picked wines harvested after the soil had dried out and the excess water had departed from the vines' system, but those who harvested early or during the rain produced light, inconsequential wines.

1989 VINTAGE

Once again, near perfect conditions got the vintage away to a flying start after 100 centimetres of rain fell between July and September. However, a burst of unseasonably hot and very windy weather in October interrupted flowering, savagely reducing the yields of some varieties. Thus the chardonnay and cabernet sauvignon were down by as much as 75 per cent in some vineyards; the bunches appeared to be there, but many berries were missing or undersized, with the result that bunch weights were very low.

Favourable weather conditions in November and December were followed by 175 centimetres of rain in January. At the end of that month the portents were for a disastrous year of the kind not seen since 1971. However, just when all appeared lost, the rains stopped, and vineyards commenced to dry out.

Those on the tougher, harder soils did best, partly because of less dense canopies; those on the wetter, sandier soils suffered from bunch rot.

Once again, there was a mixed approach to picking dates, some preferring to pick early and avoid the spectre of rot, while others decided that alcohol (and hopefully early structure) was more important. Once again, the feeling is that chardonnay fared marginally better than semillon, while the lower yielding vineyards with open canopies were able to pick some high baume shiraz in late February.

Despite the outspoken optimists of the region who see a classic vintage in every year, neither 1988 nor 1989 will go down in the long term as anything more than average years bedevilled by the vintage rain which haunts the Hunter like Hamlet's Ghost.

THE CHANGES

Eight new entries, although one of these is a complicated name-change fallout of the trials and tribulations of Murray Robson. The new arrivals are Briar Holme, Peacock Hill, Peppers Creek, Pokolbin Estate, Pothana, Murray Robson Wines, Richmond Grove and Thalgara Estate.

Briar Holme and Murray Robson Wines have split, like parts of an amoeba, from what was previously called The Robson Vineyard. It has now become Briar Holme, while Murray Robson Wines has adopted something of a hermit crab-like existence, with winemaking carried out in one place and the vineyard cellar door sales at another. The appearance of Peacock Hill is also a sign of changed circumstances. Its production was originally earmarked exclusively for export markets, and principally the United States. A turndown in that market has meant the wines, made under contract by Rothbury Estate on a vineyard re-established in 1985–86, are now sparingly available on the local market.

Peppers Creek is part of an ambitious tourist development by Pam and Peter Ireland. Antiques and not-so-antique wine are both available at the complex. Peter Ireland is an industrial chemist, but has added the skills of a master builder through renovating a series of old houses and finally a church, before building the lovely house they have at Peppers Creek. Pam Ireland has been an antique dealer for many years, and is said to be no mean hand with a pick and shovel.

Perhaps the most significant new arrival is Richmond Grove, translocated from the Upper Hunter (where the Richmond Grove vineyard remains). A state-of-the-art winery has been built with significant input from Ian Scarborough: it is designed to handle premium parcels of grapes in relatively small batches, and the flag bearers (in quality and price terms) for the entire Wyndham group are likely to originate from here.

Pothana Vineyard has been in existence for some little time now, with production slowly increasing to its present level of 1200 cases under the direction of winemaker David Hook. Pokolbin Estate has also been on MacDonalds Road for some years; originally owned by the MacDougall family, it now acts as a retailer (through cellar door) for its own and a number of other brands (including Pothana, Peacock Hill, Lakes Folly and Lowe Family, the last from Mudgee) and as a wholesaler through its corporate owner, Efficiency Displays Pty Ltd. Finally, Steve Lamb and Phillipa Treadwell have established Thalgara Estate in Debeyers Road, Pokolbin, selling most of their production through the cellar door and mailing list.

Overall, the Hunter continues to flourish, with new developments of every shape and size opening their doors day by day. The range of facilities for tourists and conventions is second to none, and the wineries (which started it all) are reaping their just desserts. Wine quality is, quite frankly, variable. That old enemy of the district, which in days gone by used to be euphemistically (and I must say picturesquely) called sweaty saddle, and which is nothing other than sulphide (or mercaptan), is still distressingly common among the reds. Semillon and chardonnay are robust white varieties, but in this day and age it is not good enough that these be made as if they were red wines – in other words, using red wine techniques and red winemaking equipment. In so much of Australia, the gulf between the professionally run winery staffed by qualified winemakers (usually but not invariably the larger wineries) and the weekend hobbyist is immense. True, wineries such as Allanmere and Marsh Estate have done very well, but most of the smaller wineries have succeeded thanks to either a full time winemaker on staff or through expert consultancy advice.

ALLANDALE

Location: Lovedale Road, Pokolbin via Maitland, 2321; 5 km north of Cessnock.
(049) 90 4526.

Winemaker: Bill Sneddon.

1989 Production: 12,000 cases.

Principal Wines: Varietal releases identified both by variety and (frequently) vineyard source. Principal labels are Semillon, Sauvignon Blanc, Chardonnay, Shiraz, Pinot Noir and Cabernet Sauvignon.

Distribution: Principally cellar door sales and mailing list. Cellar door sales 9 a.m. to 5 p.m. Sunday. Mailing list (regular newsletters) as above. Wholesale distribution: I. H. Baker, Sydney; Tallerman & Co., Brisbane; and Vintners, Melbourne. UK imports through Majestic Wine Warehouses.

Prices: $14 to $19 cellar door.

Vintage Rating 1986 – 89: White: '87, '86, '89, '88. Red: '86, '87, '89, '88.

Outstanding Prior Vintages: White: '80, '84. Red: '79 '83.

Tasting Notes:

1989 TRAMINER [61] Colour: light straw-yellow. *Bouquet:* light, clean faintly spicy fruit aroma. *Palate:* although the wine is of light weight, there are strong passionfruit/tinned fruit flavours and quite marked residual sugar; pleasant cellar door style. Drink '90.

1987 HERMITAGE [74] Colour: medium to full purple-red. *Bouquet:* strong oak, slightly rough-sawn, together with a touch of charred-barrel-ferment character. *Palate:* strong, lemony charred oak tends to dominate; there is supporting fruit there, but a trace of bitterness comes on the finish from the charred oak. Patience is indicated. Drink '92–'96.

1986 CABERNET SAUVIGNON [63] Colour: dense purple-red. *Bouquet:* solid and rather leathery with subliminal sulphide at work. *Palate:* full,

solid dark chocolate flavours on the mid-palate, finishing with somewhat bitter/leathery flavours. Drink '91–'94.

Summary: Allandale has kept a loyal clientele following the traumatic departure of founder Ed Jouault several years ago, but I find it difficult to enthuse about the wines, which are workman-like at best.

ALLANMERE

Location: Allandale Road, Allandale via Pokolbin, 2321; 12 km north of Cessnock.
(049) 30 7387.

Winemakers: Newton Potter and Geoff Broadfield.

1989 Production: 3500 cases.

Principal Wines: A limited range of table wines, comprising Semillon, Chardonnay, Sauvignon Blanc, Trinity (a blend of those three white varieties), Cabernet Sauvignon and Shiraz and Trilogy (a blend of Cabernet, Merlot and Shiraz).

Distribution: Cellar door sales and mailing list; cellar door sales 11 a.m. to 4 p.m. Monday to Friday (closed Wednesday), 9.30 a.m. to 5 p.m. weekends. Mailing list enquiries to PO Box 327, Maitland, 2320. Limited Sydney distribution through Appellation Wines.

Prices: $11 to $15 cellar door.

Vintage Rating 1986 – 89: White: '86, '88, '89, '87. Red: '87, '88, '86 ('89 not yet rated).

Outstanding Prior Vintages: Red: '85.

Tasting Notes:

1988 TRINITY [90] Colour: medium yellow-green. *Bouquet:* very smooth, gently toasty, bottle-developed characters with considerable richness and style. *Palate:* very well balanced; attractive clean fruit with a touch of honey set against soft, sensitively handled oak; the wine has an especially long, clean and balanced finish. Drink '90–'91.

1988 CHARDONNAY [92] Colour: brilliant, light to medium yellow-green. *Bouquet:* fragrant, spicy/lemony oak is immediately apparent but does not overwhelm the fruit. *Palate:* a lovely, high-toned wine, with intense, tangy melon/grapefruit flavours and perfectly balanced oak;

as with the Trinity, the wine has a notably long finish. Drink '90–'92.

1988 TRILOGY [81] Colour: dense purple-red. *Bouquet:* very youthful, clean and concentrated red berry/dark plum fruits. *Palate:* masses of lushly ripe plum/cherry fruit flavours with soft tannins; oak plays a carefully judged support role. Drink '93–'98.

1987 HERMITAGE [63] Colour: medium red-purple. *Bouquet:* soft, velvety/gamey aromas with a touch of the dreaded sweaty saddle. *Palate:* soft red berry fruits under a gamey/ meaty influence. Drink '90–'92.

Summary: In the space of only five vintages, Dr Newton Potter has produced some of the Hunter Valley's loveliest white wines, and more than his fair share of very good reds. Allanmere is slightly off the beaten track, but the rewards are ample for those who find their way to his front door.

❦ BELBOURIE

Location: Branxton Road, Rothbury via Branxton, 2330; 24 km north of Cessnock. (049) 38 1556.

Winemaker: Bob Davies.

Principal Wines: Belah Semillon, Semillon, Traminer Nectar, Bungan Hermitage, Cabernet Sauvignon and Champagne Quartz.

Distribution: Exclusively mailing list and cellar door sales. Cellar door sales 10 a.m. to 5 p.m. weekends and holidays.

Prices: $10 to $24 cellar door.

Summary: John Roberts, son of the late Jim Roberts, summarises the Belbourie style and tradition better than I can. "We continue to experiment with our new plantings and our making techniques, comprehending local and French tradition as much as possible, while experimenting radically in our own self-defined marginal zone of process and flavours."

❦ BRIAR RIDGE VINEYARD
(Formerly The Robson Vineyard)

Location: Mount View Road, Mount View, 2325; 9 km west of Cessnock. (049) 90 3670; Fax (049) 90 7802

Winemaker: Kees van de Scheur.

1989 Production: 7500 cases.

Principal Wines: Chardonnay, Traditional Semillon, Early Harvest Semillon, Oak-Matured Semillon, Traminer, Sauvignon Blanc, Cabernet Sauvignon, Pinot Noir, Malbec, Hermitage, Cabernet Merlot, Muscat and Cabernet Port.

Distribution: Cellar door sales, mailing list, selected fine wine retailers in all eastern States and restaurants. Cellar door sales 9 a.m. to 5 p.m. Monday to Saturday, 10.30 a.m. to 5 p.m. Sunday. Regular mailing list bulletins (address as above). UK imports through Victon Ross.

Prices: $12.50 to $14 cellar door.

Vintage Rating 1986–89: White: '88, '89, '87, '86. Red: '87, '86, '89, '88.

Outstanding Prior Vintages: White: '83, '85. Red: '81, '83, '85.

Tasting Notes:

1989 CHARDONNAY [CS] Colour: light straw-yellow. *Bouquet:* complex, stylish barrel-ferment characters with tangy fruit and oak; outstanding winemaking and handling. *Palate:* the fruit is as yet of light to medium weight, but extraordinarily stylish oak handling has invested the wine with loads of potential. If this is a truly representative sample, and the wine makes it safely to bottle, it will rate 90 or more points.

1988 CHARDONNAY [59] Colour: light to medium yellow-green. *Bouquet:* clean, slightly plain vanillan oak and fruit; muted varietal character. *Palate:* plain, light fruit with a touch of sorbate character; lacks varietal flavour. A dramatic contrast to the '89. Drink '90.

1988 PINOT NOIR [55] Colour: very good purple-red. *Bouquet:* light, clean with a hint of strawberry varietal aroma. *Palate:* very light and thin, and dominated by pencilly oak, with a slightly leathery finish. Drink '90.

1987 HERMITAGE [67] Colour: medium to full purple-red. *Bouquet:* dense, solid and extractive with slightly burnt characters. *Palate:* big, old style extractive/leather/gamey wine needing a great deal of patience. Drink '94–'97.

Summary: Briar Ridge is establishing its own quite distinct personality in the aftermath of the departure of Murray Robson. The beautifully situated winery and vineyard in that most enchanting part of the Hunter Valley (the Mount View sub-district) should be a compulsory stop on any first-time tour.

BROKENWOOD

1988
BROKENWOOD
cabernet sauvignon
'graveyard vineyard'
750 ml   WINE OF AUSTRALIA   13.5% A.V.C.VOL

Location: McDonalds Road, Pokolbin, 2321; 11 km north-west of Cessnock. (049) 98 7559.

Winemaker: Iain Riggs.

1989 Production: 12,500 cases.

Principal Wines: Varietal releases comprise Semillon, Chardonnay, Pinot Noir, Hermitage and Cabernet Sauvignon. Special Graveyard releases; also Hunter/ Coonawarra Cabernet Sauvignon.

Distribution: Substantial cellar door and mailing list sales. Also fine wine retailers and significant exports to UK and USA. cellar door sales 10 a.m. to 5 p.m. 7 days. Mailing list, regular newsletters. Wholesale distributors: Sydney, Brisbane and Perth, Tucker & Co; Melbourne, Rutherglen Wine Company; Adelaide, Chace Agencies; Hobart, Tasmanian Fine Wine Distributors. UK imports through Gullen & Co.

Prices: $15 to $22 cellar door.

Vintage Rating 1986–89: White: '86, '87, '88, '89. Red: '86, '88, '87, '89.

Outstanding Prior Vintages: White: '83, '84, '85. Red: '80, '83, '85.

Tasting Notes:

1989 SEMILLON [80] Colour: light green-yellow. *Bouquet:* clean, light, grassy, spotlessly clean varietal character. *Palate:* youthful, green/grassy semillon style with considerable length; a flick of residual sugar fills out the flavour; admirable fresh seafood style. Drink '90.

1988 GRAVEYARD CHARDONNAY [90] Colour: medium to full yellow. *Bouquet:* very sophisticated spicy/charred oak, rich and full. *Palate:* has excellent mouth-feel and viscosity; intense fruit stands up to the strong oak; a wine with great length and generosity of flavour. Drink '90–'93.

1988 GRAVEYARD HERMITAGE [89] Colour: opaque purple-red. *Bouquet:* hugely concentrated, rich, dark velvety berries with a touch of marzipan oak; spotlessly clean. *Palate:* exceptionally concentrated and rich, with strong supporting oak; tannins run through the palate but do not dominate the dark chocolate/dark berry fruit flavours. Drink '95–2005.

1988 HUNTER/ COONAWARRA/ LANGHORNE CREEK CABERNET SAUVIGNON [87] Colour: dense purple-red. *Bouquet:* rich, clean and fleshy red berry fruit with some charred oak. *Palate:* full, dark berry fruits with very strong charred oak flavours; needs much time to come together. Drink '95–2001.

Summary: Brokenwood is now firmly established as one of the finest and most consistent small producers in the Hunter Valley, demonstrating amongst other things that mercaptan (or sulphide) is not necessarily part of regional character.

CALAIS ESTATES

Location: Palmers Lane, Pokolbin, 2321; 12 km north of Cessnock. (049) 98 7654.

Winemaker: Colin Peterson.

1989 Production: 10,000 cases.

Principal Wines: A range of varietal table wines and the occasional fortified wine, including Semillon, Chardonnay, Traminer, Pinot Noir, Shiraz and Cabernet Sauvignon and Sauternes.

Distribution: Principally cellar door and mailing list; cellar door sales 10 a.m. to 5 p.m. 7 days. Mailing list as above. Also available in selected restaurants and fine wine retailers in Sydney through Calais Estate Wholesale, Unit 8/55 Willowong Road, Caringbah, 2229, telephone (02) 540 2555.

Prices: $8 to $15 cellar door.

Vintage Rating 1987–89: White: '89, '88, '87. Red: '89, '88, '87.

Tasting Notes:

1989 RESERVE CHARDONNAY [CS] *Colour:* medium yellow-green. *Bouquet:* of medium weight, with slightly stalky/herbaceous fruit and some charred oak. *Palate:* light and tangy; quite intense and really comes into its own with a very long finish, augmented by a nice touch of oak. If the wine successfully makes the transition to bottle should rank in the 80's.

1988 CHARDONNAY [64] *Colour:* medium yellow-green. *Bouquet:* rather raw and unintegrated vanillan/oily oak, with a suspicion of volatility. *Palate:* rather common oily/vanillan oak, clean varietal chardonnay of light to medium weight lurking under that oak. Drink '90–'92.

1987 PINOT NOIR [73] *Colour:* good red-purple. *Bouquet:* clean; light to medium weight but entirely regional, and showing almost no discernible varietal character whatsoever. *Palate:* pleasant red berry/cherry flavours; has some vinosity, with good length and balance. An attractive red wine which just happens to be made from pinot noir. Drink '90–'92.

1987 RESERVE CABERNET SAUVIGNON [68] *Colour:* medium to full red-purple. *Bouquet:* slightly muffled and dull, with some leathery overtones. *Palate:* full, ripe red berry fruits dulled by slightly bitter/leathery mercaptans; the fruit has the weight to fight through the shackles. Drink '91–'94.

Summary: Calais Estates is run by Colin Peterson as a quite separate venture from his parents'

winery, Petersons. Situated on the site of the old Wollundry winery, it has a substantial production from the fully mature vineyard. In the tasting for this edition it out-pointed Petersons.

CHATEAU FRANCOIS

Location: Off Broke Road, Pokolbin, 2321; 13 km north-west of Cessnock. (049) 98 7548.

Winemaker: Don Francois.

1989 Production: 1000 cases.

Principal Wines: Varietal releases comprising Semillon, Chardonnay, and a blend of Pinot Noir and Shiraz.

Distribution: Principally mailing list, to Broke Road, Pokolbin, 2321. Cellar door sales and tasting 9 a.m. to 5 p.m. weekends; other times by appointment.

Prices: $9 to $11 cellar door.

Vintage Rating 1986–89: White: '87, '86, '89, '88. Red: '89, '87, '86, '88.

Outstanding Prior Vintages: White: '74, '77, '79, '82. Red: '73, '75, '79, '81, '82.

Tasting Notes:

1987 MALLEE SEMILLON [65] *Colour:* medium to full yellow-green. *Bouquet:* strong, slightly oily/sulphidic bottle-developed characters, but plenty of depth. *Palate:* a real throw-back to old style Hunter winemaking, with green apple/camphor flavours; the type of semillon which will live for ever, becoming increasingly idiosyncratic but also increasingly enjoyable as it ages. Drink '91–'95.

1987 CHARDONNAY [58] *Colour:* medium yellow. *Bouquet:* fruit aroma stripped by hot fermentation. *Palate:* some aged, bottle-developed characters, but varietal fruit sadly lacking; because of the making methods, will slowly improve with age as a Hunter white burgundy style. Drink '90–'94.

Summary: The Chateau Francois wines mature slowly; mercaptan intrudes into the young wines, both white and red, but seems to soften and blend into the style with age.

CHATEAU PATO

Location: Thompson's Road, Pokolbin, 2321; 11 km north-west of Cessnock. (049) 98 7634.

Winemaker: David Paterson.

Principal Wines: Only Gewurztraminer and Hermitage made and marketed.

Distribution: Exclusively mailing list and by direct sales to selected restaurants. Cellar door sales by appointment only. Mailing list enquiries as above.

Tasting Notes:

1989 TRAMINER [65] Colour: light green-yellow. _Bouquet:_ full, floral pungent varietal character; well made. _Palate:_ pronounced lychee flavours on the fore-palate; the mid-palate dips slightly and there is a slight phenolic bitterness on the back-palate which is so difficult to avoid with this variety. Nonetheless, an impressive effort. Drink '90–'91.

1987 HERMITAGE [65] Colour: medium to full purple-red. _Bouquet:_ dense, deep, dark velvety fruit with a touch of sulphide. _Palate:_ a huge, extractive wine with deep fruit and mouth-ripping tannins. May conceivably soften with time and merit substantially higher points. Drink '94–2000.

Summary: A tiny operation with 500 or less cases produced each year; the wines have always been huge, slow maturing styles, and seem to be growing bigger as each new vintage is released. A gentler hand at the press might pay dividends.

DAWSON ESTATE

Location: Londons Road, Lovedale via Nulkaba, 2325; 5 km north of Cessnock. (049) 90 2904.

Winemaker: David Lowe (contract) 1988; Ian Scarborough (contract) 1989.

1989 Production: Approximately 4000 cases.

Principal Wines: Exclusively Chardonnay (400 cases Traminer released through cellar door each year).

Distribution: Principally cellar door sales and mailing list; cellar door sales 9 a.m. to 5 p.m. 7 days. Mailing list as above. Limited wholesale distribution through Fesq & Co., Sydney and Canberra; Victorian Wine Consultants, Melbourne.

Prices: $9 (Traminer) and $12 (Chardonnay).

Vintage Rating 1986–89: '86, '87, '89, '88.

Outstanding Prior Vintages: '80, '83.

Tasting Notes:

1989 CHARDONNAY [CS] Colour: light straw-yellow. _Bouquet:_ of light to medium intensity, with slight condensed-milk characters, probably oak derived. _Palate:_ full flavoured, with some spicy oak and rather bitter phenolics showing early in its life; has the flavour, and with Ian Scarborough as contract winemaker, should come into bottle looking far better than it does now.

Summary: A full range of Dawson Estate Chardonnays back to 1982 was tasted for this edition; of the mature wines, the '87 was the best, followed by the '85, '82 and '86.

DRAYTON'S

Location: Oakey Creek Road, Cessnock, 2321;
7 km west of Cessnock.
(049) 98 7513.

Winemaker: Trevor Drayton.

Principal Wines: Main varietal releases are of Semillon,
Chardonnay, Rhine Riesling, Traminer, Shiraz and
Cabernet Sauvignon, some additionally identified
by vineyard names and others by bin number. Also
occasional brand name releases.

Distribution: Substantial cellar door sales 9 a.m. to
5 p.m. Monday to Saturday. Retail distribution
through Halloran & Manton, Sydney.

Prices: $5.99 to $15 retail.

Vintage Rating 1986–89: White: '87, '88, '89, '86.

Tasting Notes:

1988 CHARDONNAY [91] Colour: light to medium
green-yellow. *Bouquet:* complex charred oak showing
barrel-ferment characters and excellent tangy fruit.
Palate: superb oak handling with spicy/charred
barrel-ferment flavours; pronounced tangy fruit with
excellent length; the oak contribution is substantial,
but the fruit is there to carry it. Drink '90–'94.

1987 SEMILLON [57] Colour: bright, light green-yellow.
Bouquet: fruit spoilt by pronounced bitter sulphides.
Palate: again, attractive semillon fruit is spoilt by
sulphide bitterness. May soften marginally with
further age. Drink '90–'92.

1987 HERMITAGE BIN 5555 [70] Colour: medium
to full red. *Bouquet:* clean, fairly ripe fruit with
slight hay/straw oxidation characters. *Palate:* very
big, very ripe fruit; is clean, but slightly clumsy;
will undoubtedly improve with cellaring as the
ripe fruit flavours subside. Drink '91–'94.

Summary: A long-established family winery with
traditional making and marketing methods and a
somewhat lower profile and reputation than it once
had. The wines are honest enough but variable in
quality; I have assumed the '88 Chardonnay was
bottled mid '89, and if so, it is one of the
outstanding whites of the vintage.

EVANS FAMILY

Location: Palmers Lane, Pokolbin, 2321;
12 km north-north-west of Pokolbin.
(02) 27 4413.

Winemakers: David Lowe (consultant), Len Evans.

1989 Production: Uncertain; the wine may not be
released under the Evans Family label.

Principal Wines: Chardonnay only estate release;
pinot noir planted. Occasional past botrytised
Rhine Riesling releases from Coonawarra,
made at Petaluma.

Distribution: Chiefly mailing list; also available
through Len Evans Wine Club. UK imports
through Geoffrey Roberts & Associates.

Prices: $16.50 retail.

Vintage Rating 1986–89: '86, '87, '88, '89.

Outstanding Prior Vintages: '82, '84.

Summary: According to their creator, the Evans
Family Chardonnays need between two and
five years in bottle to show their best. However,
they have sold out each year long before
reaching this point. Indeed, this edition fell
between two vintages: the '88 has all been sold,
while the '89 has a very uncertain future
thanks to the vicissitudes of the '89 vintage.

FRASER VINEYARD

Location: Lot 5, Wilderness Road, Rothbury, 2321;
3 km east of Main Branxton Road.
(049) 30 7594.

Winemaker: Peter Fraser.

1989 Production: 2500 cases

Principal Wines: Chenin Blanc, Semillon Sauvignon Blanc, Chardonnay and Shiraz.

Distribution: Largely cellar door sales and mailing list; limited retail distribution through Brands Regional Vintners. Cellar door sales 9 a.m. to 5 p.m. 7 days.

Prices: $10 to $15 cellar door.

Vintage Rating 1987–89: White: '89, '87, '88. Red: '87, '88 ('89 not yet rated).

Tasting Notes:

1989 SEMILLON SAUVIGNON BLANC [73] Colour: light to medium yellow-green. *Bouquet:* quite full and tangy, with full fruit. *Palate:* once again, there is good fruit intensity and considerable mid-palate weight; a touch of residual sugar seems an unnecessary sophistication. Drink '90–'92.

1989 CHENIN BLANC [82] Colour: medium yellow-green. *Bouquet:* light, soft, honeyed aromas with what appears to be a distinct touch of toasty oak. *Palate:* lively, tangy fruit flavours and, once again, what appears to be input from oak; unusual handling of the variety; in any event, a wine with both flavour and length. Drink '90–'91.

1989 SEMILLON [70] Colour: light green-yellow. *Bouquet:* light, crisp and grassy, with a slightly charred/bitter edge, possibly from oak. *Palate:* much better with considerable length, and a hint of residual sugar which is not overdone; somewhat incomplete, and could come together in bottle very well indeed. Drink '91–'93

Summary: Peter Fraser's small and very new winery produced wonderful wines in its first (1987) vintage. Quality slipped in 1988 with all sorts of problems encountered in the samples submitted for this edition, but there is a convincing return to form with the '89 whites. Another winery slightly off the beaten track on the Wilderness Road side of the valley which is worth the effort of a detour.

🍇 *GOLDEN GRAPE ESTATE*

Location: Oakey Creek Road, Pokolbin, 2321; 6 km west of Cessnock.
(049) 89 7588.

Principal Wines: A most unusual range of wines, unashamedly reflecting the Pieroth Group philosophy concerning wine styles and labelling.

Distribution: Cellar door sales, through the Pieroth mailing list and Pieroth's own door-to-door sales force. Cellar door sales 9 a.m. to 5 p.m. April to September 7 days, and 10 a.m. to 6 p.m. October to March 7 days.

Summary: Golden Grape Estate is owned by the huge German wine company Pieroth, and was previously part of the Saxonvale Group operations, and, prior to that, it was owned by Barrie Drayton. Wine marketing takes precedence over wine quality; a safe haven for tourist coaches but not wine buffs.

🍇 *HUNGERFORD HILL*

Location: Corner McDonalds Road and Broke Road, Pokolbin, 2321; 11 km north-west of Cessnock.
(049) 98 7666.

Winemaker: Adrian Sheridan.

1989 Production: The equivalent of 55,000 cases.

Principal Wines: Top of the range are vineyard varietals, comprising Hunter Valley Chardonnay, Hunter Valley Pinot Noir, Hunter Valley Semillon Sauvignon Blanc and Hunter Valley Cabernet Merlot. Other varietal releases sold at cellar door, only in much smaller quantities, including specials under the Collection and Show Reserve ranges, including Pinot Noir, Verdelho, Traminer, Semillon and Shiraz.

Distribution: National retail distribution. Also cellardoor sales at the first-class Pokolbin Wine Village, 9 a.m. to 5 p.m. Monday to Saturday, 10 a.m. to 5 p.m. Sunday. The Pokolbin Wine Village offers a wide range of restaurant, tasting and barbecue facilities for the whole family; there are none better in Australia. Special releases also available only at cellar door. UK imports through Corney & Barrow Ltd.

Prices: $5 to $20 cellar door.

Vintage Rating 1986–89: White: '86, '88, '87, '89. Red: '89, '86, '87, '88.

Outstanding Prior Vintages: White: '84. Red: '82, '84.

Tasting Notes:

1988 HUNTER VALLEY CHARDONNAY [64] Colour: medium to full yellow-green. *Bouquet:*

slightly sweet vanillan oak and fruit, together with a touch of volatility. *Palate:* rather cosmetic oak flavours; an excessively sweet wine, again showing a touch of volatility. Drink '90–'91.

1987 SHOW RESERVE CHARDONNAY [61] *Colour:* medium to full yellow-green. *Bouquet:* strong, sweet oak lifted by a degree of volatility. *Palate:* an excessively sweet wine which cloys on the finish. Drink '90.

1987 HUNTER VALLEY CABERNET MERLOT [70] *Colour:* medium to full red-purple. *Bouquet:* strong, clean and full briary/berry aromas. *Palate:* lively leafy/ berry fruit flavours, but just a fraction light and green on the finish. An elegant wine nonetheless. Drink '90–'93.

Summary: Notwithstanding a change in the winemaking team, the variability which I have previously encountered in quality and style continues to plague Hungerford Hill. There were appalling problems with the 1989 white samples submitted; I cannot believe that these were even vaguely representative of the finished wines. Perhaps I am becoming intolerant in my old age, but I also found the chardonnays terribly sweet. Hungerford Hill remains a focal point of the Hunter Valley scene, and has produced some very fine wines over the years. It gives me no pleasure to be so critical of the current releases.

HUNTER ESTATE

Location: Hermitage Road, Pokolbin, 2321. (049) 98 7521.

Winemaker: Neil McGuigan.

1989 Production: 20,000 cases.

Principal Wines: Chardonnay, Fumé Blanc, Pinot Noir and Cabernet Sauvignon.

Distribution: Primarily through Diner's Club and some limited retail distribution. UK imports through Masons of Holbrook.

Prices: $9.99 to $11.50.

Vintage Rating 1986–89: '89, '87, '88, '86.

Outstanding Prior Vintages: White: '79 Red: '79.

Tasting Notes:

1988 CHARDONNAY [69] *Colour:* light green-yellow. *Bouquet:* smooth and clean, with light to medium peachy fruit and light oak. *Palate:* quite aromatic fruit with jujube/lychee characters, not at all what one normally expects to find with chardonnay; of light to medium weight with only slight oak influence. Drink '90–'91.

1987 PINOT NOIR [60] *Colour:* very light red. *Bouquet:* light and clean, with faintly sappy/ stalky aromas. *Palate:* light, clean and relatively simple wine with slightly stewed fruit flavour; there is consistent evidence of a real attempt to make a silk purse out of a sow's ear, but the Hunter Valley is not a kind place in which to make a varietal pinot. Drink '90.

1987 GOLD MEDAL SHIRAZ [77] *Colour:* medium purple-red. *Bouquet:* fruit aromas of light to medium intensity, with some spicy oak and a faint glue paste edge. *Palate:* shows much more flavour and style; spicy/plummy fruit, with slightly jumpy acid on the finish; a wine which has still not entirely come together, but which does score on total flavour. Drink '90–'93.

Summary: A new entry to this edition, even though the label has been around for a considerable time. The winery is of course part of the Wyndham operation, and the wines are largely marketed through direct mail avenues. Over the years, I have tasted some quite astonishing wines under the Hunter Estate label; it is always best to taste these wines masked before prejudice overtakes one.

KINDRED'S LOCHLEVEN ESTATE

Location: Palmers Lane, Pokolbin, 2321; 13 km north-north-west of Cessnock.

Winemakers: Various contract makers over the years.

Principal Wines: A range of varietal wines, many vintages available cellar door only.

Distribution: Cellar door only; open one weekend in two; look for signs on nearby roads which indicate whether it is open or closed.

Summary: So far as I know, the Kindred operation still remains low key, although there was some suggestion that winemaking would recommence from the quite extensive and very excellent vineyards on the Kindred Estate. Over the past decade Kindred has basically been a grape grower.

LAKE'S FOLLY

Location: Broke Road, Pokolbin, 2321; 8 km north of Cessnock. (049) 87 7507.

Winemaker: Stephen Lake.

1989 Production: Approximately 3000 cases.

Principal Wines: Chardonnay and Cabernet Sauvignon.

Distribution: Principally mailing list; also cellar door sales 10 a.m. to 4 p.m. weekdays. Limited fine wine retail distribution and clubs. UK imports through Lay and Wheeler Limited.

Prices: $13. 50 to $16.50 cellar door.

Vintage Rating 1986–89: White: '86, '89, '87, '88. Red: '89, '87, '88, '86.

Outstanding Prior Vintages: White: '74, '76, '82, '83. Red: '66, '69, '72, '78, '81, '85.

Tasting Notes:

1988 CHARDONNAY [85] Colour: light yellow-green. *Bouquet:* light to medium fruit intensity, with smooth French oak, possibly vosges; it is slightly muted by some free SO_2, which will, however, dissipate with a little more time in bottle. *Palate:* a tangy wine with good length, balance and intensity; progressively came up each time it was tasted, underlining its class. Drink '90–'93.

1987 CABERNET SAUVIGNON [80] Colour: light to medium red-purple. *Bouquet:* typically restrained, light and elegant fruit with a touch of spicy/lemony oak. *Palate:* a stylish, light bodied cabernet which has surprising length and intensity; soft, fine tannins linger; like the chardonnay, a wine which grows in the glass. Drink '91–'97.

Summary: The most famous of all the small wineries in Australia, with a reputation stretching to the furthest corner of the globe. It is a matter of opinion whether wine quality always lives up to that reputation. The wines reviewed for this edition certainly can do it no harm, although I was not impressed with the 1988 Cabernet Sauvignon.

LESNIK FAMILY WINES

Location: Branxton Road, Pokolbin, 2321; 7 km north of Cessnock. (049) 98 7755.

Winemaker: Josef Lesnik.

Principal Wines: Wood Matured Semillon, Riesling, Chardonnay, Traminer Riesling, Lake Picked Semillon, Botrytis Semillon, Kiewa (Sauternes), Shiraz, Cabernet Sauvignon, Liqueur Muscat and Vintage Port.

Distribution: Principally cellar door sales and mailing list. Mailing list enquiries to Lesnik Family Wines, PO Box 367, Cessnock, 2325. Cellar door sales 9 a.m. to 5 p.m. 7 days.

Summary: The Lesnik Winery is a massive, modern building which simply cannot be missed as you drive along the Branxton Road. It is, however, simply an insulated warehouse, used by other wineries in the district to store wine in, and the Lesnik Family wine is made under contract at various wineries. The main business of the Lesnik family is grape-growing, with only 50 tonnes of the annual 250 tonnes turned into wine. Wine quality leaves much to be desired.

LINDEMANS

Lindemans
1988
HUNTER RIVER
SEMILLON

BIN 7255

750 ml
LINDEMAN WINES PTY LTD McDONALDS ROAD POKOLBIN NSW 2321
PRODUCE OF AUSTRALIA 10.5% ALC/VOL

Location: McDonalds Road, Pokolbin, 2321;
9 km north-west of Cessnock.
(049) 98 7501.

Winemaker: Gerry Sissingh; cellar door sales,
Richard Woods.

1989 Production: Not stated.

Principal Wines: Reserve bin range (with annually
changing bin numbers) of Semillon, Chablis,
White Burgundy, Semillon/Chardonnay,
Chardonnay and Verdelho. Burgundy and
Steven Hermitage both made from Shiraz.
Older vintages under "Classic" release label.

Distribution: National retail distribution, cellar
door sales 8.30 a.m. to 4.30 p.m. Monday to
Friday and 10 a.m. to 4.30 p.m. Saturday and
Sunday. Winemaking museum. UK imports
through I.D.V., Gilbey House.

Prices: $10 to $13 retail for current release wines;
significantly more for classic releases.

Vintage Rating 1986–89: White: '86, '87, '88, '89.
Red: '87, '86, '88, '89.

Outstanding Prior Vintages: White: '66, '68, '70,
'79. Red: '65, '70, '80, '83.

Tasting Notes:

1989 SEMILLON CHARDONNAY BIN 7472 [80]
Colour: light yellow-green. *Bouquet:* a touch of
vanillan oak; textured, with good fruit richness
and intensity. *Palate:* pleasant spicy/vanillan
oak; a potent grassy tang on the finish, possibly
deriving from relatively early picked fruit; has
length and style, and is a worthy successor to
the much praised '88. Drink '90–'95.

1988 SEMILLON BIN 7255 [74] Colour: light
green-yellow. *Bouquet:* light, clean and soft, yet
to build depth. *Palate:* light, clean and crisp;
well made wine, with slight green fruit
characters; it presently lacks richness, but will at
least partially remedy this with time. Drink
'92–'95.

1988 BURGUNDY RESERVE BIN 7600 [87] Colour:
very good purple-red. *Bouquet:* youthful, with
remarkably intense sweet berry fruit aromas.
Palate: strong and youthful; like the bouquet,
spotlessly clean, with full, sweet berry fruit
flavours; soft tannins in a perfectly structured
wine. Drink '93–2000.

1987 BURGUNDY RESERVE BIN 7400 [90] Colour:
medium purple-red. *Bouquet:* very smooth and
clean, with lovely berry/vanillan flavours,
showing both style and balance. *Palate:* complex
dark berry/dark cherry fruit flavours with
smooth vanillan oak; a beautifully structured
wine, with lingering, soft tannins. Will age with
extreme grace. Drink '95–2005.

1987 BURGUNDY RESERVE BIN 7403 [89] Colour:
medium to full purple-red. *Bouquet:* spotlessly
clean, fragrant cherry/berry aromas with
remarkable balance and style. *Palate:* clean,
rich, full and deep; superb balance and
structure; flavours of dark cherry on the mid-
palate, with excellent balancing fruit and oak
tannins. Drink '93–2000.

1986 BURGUNDY RESERVE BIN 7210 [86] Colour:
medium purple-red. *Bouquet:* clean, fresh berry
fruit with a light touch of lemony French oak; very
good style. *Palate:* remarkable fresh with strong
fruit and pronounced French oak; it has very good
length, and the wine an even longer future. Drink
'92–2000.

Summary: Lindemans has hit a purple patch with its
shiraz-based red wines; those reviewed were
simply the best out of an outstanding collection,
none of which rated below 75 points. It may well
be that all the semillons need is time to show the
same class. Whether or not that is so, Gerry
Sissingh has returned home with a vengeance.

LITTLE'S

Location: Lot 3, Palmers Lane, Pokolbin, 2321;
12 km north of Cessnock.
(049) 98 7626.

Winemaker: Ian Little.

Principal Wines: Varietal releases comprising Semillon, Chardonnay, Traminer, Shiraz, Pinot Noir, Cabernet Sauvignon and Vintage Port.

Distribution: Principally cellar door sales and mailing list; cellar door sales 10 a.m. to 5 p.m. 7 days. Limited wholesale in Sydney through Southern Districts Wine Merchants. UK imports through Chalcott Wines, London.

Prices: $11 to $18.

Vintage Rating 1986–89: White: '86, '89, '88, '87. Red: '86, '89, '88, '87.

Outstanding Prior Vintages: White: '84, '85. Red: '85.

Tasting Notes:

1989 TRAMINER [73] Colour: light to medium green-yellow. *Bouquet:* striking spicy/floral lychee aromas come first, followed by a slightly oily/cosmetic farewell. *Palate:* very high flavoured, strong lychee fruit, followed by a trace of bitterness on the finish. A difficult variety which has been handled with more than a little competence, and will be extremely well received at cellar door. Drink '90.

1988 CHARDONNAY [63] Colour: medium yellow-green. *Bouquet:* honeyed/ buttery fruit and oak, but then some bitter sulphides. *Palate:* full flavoured, but the wine becomes progressively harder on the back palate and finish. Will possibly soften and become more attractive with bottle age. Drink '90–'92.

1988 PINOT NOIR [74] Colour: very good red-purple. *Bouquet:* clean, and quite weighty, but strong lemony oak obscures whatever varietal character is present. *Palate:* oak-driven from start to finish, with strong, spicy/lemony oak; the fruit flavour is there with a touch of sweet strawberry; a good warm area pinot if you like lots of oak in your wine. Drink '90–'91.

Summary: A small, modern and well-equipped winery which produces clean, soft and fruity table wines, and from time to time an excellent vintage port; the latter is testimony to winemaker Ian Little's apprenticeship at Chateau Reynella.

McWILLIAM'S MOUNT PLEASANT

Location: Marrowbone Road, Pokolbin, 2321; 7 km west of Cessnock. (049) 98 7505.

Winemaker: Phillip Ryan.

Principal Wines: Semillon, Chardonnay, Traminer, Pinot Noir, Hermitage and Cabernet Sauvignon. Releases include popular lines such as Elizabeth and Philip, to rarer releases like OP and OH Hermitage and Rosehill Hermitage. Special releases are offered in limited quantities through the 'Homestead' cellar door sales area.

Distribution: National distribution through own distribution channels. Cellar door sales 8.30 a.m. to 4.30 p.m. Monday to Friday, 10 a.m. to 4.30 p.m. Saturday and Sunday and public holidays, offering special releases not available elsewhere. UK imports through McWilliam's Wines (UK) Limited, 41– 43 High Street, Lutterworth, Leicestershire.

Prices: $8 to $25.

Vintage Rating 1986–89: White: '86, '87, '88, '89. Red: '86, '87, '88, '89.

Outstanding Prior Vintages: White: '79, '81, '82, '83, '85. Red: '75, '79, '83, '84, '85.

Tasting Notes:

1986 MOUNT PLEASANT CHARDONNAY [80] Colour: medium full yellow-green. *Bouquet:* developed; full of regional/toasty character. *Palate:* full, soft honeyed, bottle-developed flavours, in Australian white burgundy style rather than varietal; the overall balance is good, and, if oak has been used, it does not make any particular statement. Drink '90–'91.

1984 MOUNT PLEASANT SEMILLON [75] Colour: brilliant yellow-green of light to medium depth. *Bouquet:* very smooth, clean, bottle-developed lemony fruit. *Palate:* spotlessly clean old style, early picked, low alcohol wine with lemony/green apple fruit flavours; will live for many years. Drink '90–'95.

1983 MOUNT PLEASANT HUNTER SEMILLON [82] Colour: bright yellow-green of medium depth. *Bouquet:* smooth and clean, gently honeyed, harmonious bottle-developed characters, still retaining freshness in typical McWilliam style. *Palate:* clean and youthful, still gaining weight, and if anything a fraction light; fresh, crisp finish. Drink '90–'94.

1983 MOUNT PLEASANT ELIZABETH [90] Colour: medium yellow with just a hint of straw. *Bouquet:* soft, clean, honeyed fruit in glorious Hunter traditional style; smooth and has weight. *Palate:* soft, rounded honey fruit of medium weight; an immaculately clean wine with wonderful balance, and which leaves the mouth fresh and asking for more. Drink '90–'95.

1979 MOUNT PLEASANT RHINE RIESLING [85] Colour: glowing yellow-green. *Bouquet:* extremely rich, toasty bottle-developed characters. It is difficult to tell whether the wine is riesling or semillon, but it really does not matter particularly. *Palate:* riesling varietal flavour does come through on a soft full flavoured and fleshy mid-palate, followed by a distinctly soft but ever so pleasant finish. Drink '90–'91.

1983 MOUNT PLEASANT PHILIP [70] Colour: brick-red. *Bouquet:* developed tarry bouquet in absolutely unmistakable McWilliam red wine style. *Palate:* similarly, ultra-stylised wine with very pronounced tarry, regional flavour; the wine does have vinosity, but I would like to see it conform far more to conventional red wine flavour. Drink '90–'94.

Summary: McWilliam's has well and truly thrown off its lethargy of the past 20 years or so. It finds itself in a most interesting position: reaping the rewards of a conservative, traditional approach to white wine making (and in particular the irreplaceable asset of its aged semillons) while simultaneously moving away from its traditional red wine styles. The latter move is yet to materialise, but will become increasingly apparent once the 1985 and 1986 vintages start finding their way onto the market. In the meantime, Elizabeth Riesling stands unchallenged in this book as the outstanding value white wine from the Hunter Valley.

🍇 MARSH ESTATE

Location: Deasey Road, Pokolbin, 2321; 18 km north-west of Pokolbin. (049) 98 7587.

Winemaker: Peter Marsh.

1989 Production: Approximately 5000 cases.

Principal Wines: Varietal wines comprise Semillon, Chardonnay, Traminer, Champagne, Sauternes, Hermitage Vat S and Vat R, Private Bin Hermitage, Cabernet Shiraz, Cabernet Sauvignon Vat N. Also Vintage Port.

Distribution: Entirely cellar door and mailing list. Cellar door sales 10 a.m. to 4.30 p.m. Monday to Friday, 10 a.m. to 5 p.m. Saturday and public holidays, 10 a.m. to 5 p.m. Sunday. Mailing list enquiries: address as above.

Prices: $10.50 to $14.50 cellar door.

Vintage Rating 1986–89: White: '86, '89, '87, '88. Red: '86, '89, '87, '88.

Outstanding Prior Vintages: White: '79. Red: '79, '83, '85.

Tasting Notes:

1989 SEMILLON WHITE BURGUNDY [85] Colour: medium green-yellow. *Bouquet:* light, clean and crisp fruit with a pleasant touch of lemony oak. *Palate:* very good fruit and oak handling; crisp, spicy/lemony oak does not overwhelm quite intense semillon fruit. Judged as a very complete wine, but I am uncertain whether it was finally blended and bottled. Drink '90–'93.

1989 SEMILLON CHABLIS STYLE [CS] Colour: very pale green-straw. *Bouquet:* smoky/tangy youthful fruit with good potential, but distinct fermentation characters lingering. *Palate:* plenty of flavour, but early picking seems to have been counter-balanced by a touch of residual sugar; the wine did not appear to be finished, but should rate somewhere between 70 and 75.

1988 HERMITAGE VAT R *[59]* *Colour:* medium red, with a touch of purple. *Bouquet:* lifted and fragrant, with light to medium spicy oak and light fruit. *Palate:* a light, lemony wine at the start of the palate falls away with a rather bitter, astringent finish. Drink '90–'91.

1988 CABERNET SAUVIGNON VAT N *[84]* *Colour:* medium to full purple-red. *Bouquet:* clean and full, with complex, charred oak set against weighty, ripe fruit. *Palate:* a very big, rich and indeed heavy wine, with masses of flavour, but a trace of worrying bitterness on the finish. A wine which could go either way in the cellar. Drink '92–'97.

Summary: Peter and Robin Marsh have worked unremittingly over the past 10 years on what was at one time intended as a retirement hobby, but which is now a substantial business. Their trophy for Most Successful Exhibitor (Small Winemaker) at the 1987 Hunter Valley Wine Show was no flash in the pan.

❦MILLSTONE WINES

Location: Talga Road, Allandale, 2321; 20 km north-east of Cessnock. (049) 30 7317.

Winemakers: Michael and Rae Tait.

1989 Production: 2000 cases.

Principal Wines: Varietal releases comprise Sauvignon Blanc, Chardonnay, Shiraz, Cabernet Sauvignon, Ruby Cabernet, Pinot Noir and Champagne.

Distribution: Principally cellar door and mailing list. Cellar door sales weekdays (except Wednesday) 10 a.m. to 4 p.m., weekends 10 a.m. to 5 p.m. Mailing list as above.

Prices: $12 to $19 cellar door.

Vintage Rating 1988–89: White: '89, '88. Red: '89, '88. (Change of ownership)

Tasting Notes:

1989 SAUVIGNON BLANC *[CS]* *Colour:* very light green-yellow. *Bouquet:* distinct burnt/medicinal fermentation yeast characters hide any varietal fruit. *Palate:* tangy and long; comes good after a distinctly uncertain start; if it can throw off the burnt fermentation characters it will be headed to 75 points or more.

1989 CHARDONNAY *[CS]* *Colour:* light green-straw. *Bouquet:* strong, burnt/medicinal fermentation characters which may subside and be cleaned up prior to bottling. *Palate:* shows some of the same burnt characters, but there is fruit depth and length; impossible to tell how the wine will finish up, except to say that there is some good material present.

1987 FINESSE SPARKLING ROSE *[15.4]* *Colour:* pale salmon pink. *Bouquet:* powdery/dusty/slightly smelly wet dog aromas. *Palate:* dusty/powdery flavours which, strangely, have some appeal; mercifully, does not rely upon residual sugar. Drink '90.

Summary: The Taits have acquired a winery which has always stood apart from the rest in the Valley, both in terms of its physical location and in terms of its wine styles. Finesse is part of the inherited stock; the 1989 whites have some worrying burnt fermentation characters, but both had good fruit underneath.

❦MOLLY MORGAN

Location: Talga Road, Allandale via Pokolbin, 2321; 5 km west of Lovedale Road, Talga Road junction and 20 km north of Cessnock. (049) 30 7695.

Winemaker: Neil Sutherland (contract).

1989 Production: 500 cases.

Principal Wines: Semillon is the only commercial release.

Distribution: Almost exclusively cellar door sales and mailing list; mailing list enquiries to PO Box 15, Willoughby, 2068; cellar door sales 9 a.m. to 5 p.m. weekends and public holidays. Also available through Arnolds Restaurant, Pokolbin.

Prices: $10 cellar door.

Tasting Notes:

1988 SEMILLON (UNWOODED) *[67]* *Colour:* light

green-yellow. *Bouquet:* clean, soft slightly cosmetic/jujube fruit characters. *Palate:* again, strange fruit flavours manifest themselves in a soft, traminer/jujube spectrum; while non-varietal, by no means unpleasant. Drink '90–'91.

Summary: A tiny and remote vineyard owned by two very engaging characters; some lovely wines were made in 1986 and 1987, but the '88 wines seem a little wobbly to say the least. I did not like the wood matured wine at all.

 MOUNT VIEW ESTATE

Location: Mount View Road, Mount View, 2325; 5 km west of Cessnock. (049) 90 3307.

Winemaker: Harry Tulloch.

1989 Production: 2500 cases.

Principal Wines: Varietal releases of several vintages comprising Chardonnay, Verdelho-Semillon, Verdelho, Traminer, Shiraz, Cabernet Sauvignon, Pinot Noir, Shiraz Port, Liqueur Verdelho and Liqueur Muscat.

Distribution: Cellar door sales and mailing list. Open 9 a.m. to 5 p.m. Friday to Monday; 10 a.m. to 4 p.m. Tuesday, Wednesday and Thursday during school holidays only. Weekday appointments welcome. Mailing list enquiries to PO Box 220, Cessnock, 2325.

Prices: $10 to $16 cellar door.

Vintage Rating 1986–89: White: '86, '89, '87, '88. Red: '87, '86, '88, '89.

Outstanding Prior Vintages: Red: '81, '83.

Tasting Notes:

1989 VERDELHO SEMILLON [64] Colour: light straw-yellow. *Bouquet:* quite clean; of light to medium intensity, with some soft honey evident. *Palate:* very light and still building fruit weight, which is not surprising; a slightly stalky/harsh finish should soften with bottle age. Drink '91–'93.

1987 LIQUEUR VERDELHO [72] Colour: light onionskin/pink. *Bouquet:* strong spirit with crisp, very slightly stalky fruit. *Palate:* intense spirit tends to come first on the palate, but then luscious grapy flavours take over; very clean, and well made in its idiosyncratic style–a lightly fortified wine. Drink '90–'92.

1986 CABERNET SAUVIGNON [64] Colour: medium red-purple. *Bouquet:* complex, tarry, regional sweaty saddle aromas. *Palate:* the tarry/regional flavours overwhelm the fruit; bottle age has given some credibility to the wine, but it could have been so much better. Drink '90–'92.

Summary: Mount View Estate handles its fortified wines (made variously from verdelho and muscat) very well, and produces some pleasant traditional white wines. Sulphide stalks the red wines to a lesser or greater degree.

 MURRAY ROBSON WINES

Location: Debeyers Road, Pokolbin, 2321; 10 km north-west of Cessnock. (049) 98 7539; Fax (049) 98 7746.

Winemaker: Murray Robson.

1989 Production: Not for publication.

Principal Wines: Semillon Early Harvest, Semillon Traditional, Chardonnay, Traminer, Light Cabernet, Hermitage and Cabernet Sauvignon.

Distribution: Through cellar door sales, mailing list and national fine wine distribution. Cellar door sales 9 a.m. to 5 p.m. 7 days; mailing list enquiries as above. National retail distribution through National Wine Brokers. UK imports through Australian Wineries, Ashestead, Surrey.

Prices: $13 to $25 cellar door.

Tasting Notes:

1988 SEMILLON [74] Colour: medium yellow. *Bouquet:* distinct medicinal overtones to rich, sweet fruit. *Palate:* solid, with plenty of weight and length, and a touch of herbaceous varietal fruit which will build to honeyed flavours with age. Drink '90–'94.

1988 CHARDONNAY [72] Colour: light to medium yellow-green. *Bouquet:* some similar friars-balsam/medicinal fermentation aromas over light fruit. *Palate:* pleasant, light, crisp melon fruit; like the Semillon, the problems lie much more with the bouquet than the palate; may develop quite well. Drink '90–'92.

1987 HERMITAGE [73] Colour: medium purple-red. *Bouquet:* fresh, berry aromas with some meaty/spicy carbonic maceration-type aromas. *Palate:* pleasant fresh cherry/berry fruit with some gamey maceration flavours; soft tannins. Drink '90–'92.

1987 CABERNET SAUVIGNON [85] Colour: medium red-purple. *Bouquet:* a wine which progressively came up in the glass, initially showing rough-sawn oak and then spicy oak characters; likewise, the fruit, which was light initially, came up to show strong dark berry characters. *Palate:* spotlessly clean red berry fruit with a hint of cassis and a nice, light touch of spicy oak; finishes with soft tannins. Stylish wine. Drink '92–'96.

Summary: Murray Robson Wines has been established with the old Audrey Wilkinson/Oakdale Vineyard as its base; the wines are being made under contract at Richmond Grove but under the day to day supervision of Murray Robson. As the tasting notes indicate, the quality of the wines is impressive.

OAKVALE

Location: Broke Road, Pokolbin, 2321; 11 km north-west of Cessnock. (049) 98 7520.

Winemaker: Barry Shields.

1989 Production: 5000 cases.

Principal Wines: Semillon, Semillon Chardonnay, Chardonnay, Shiraz and Cabernet Sauvignon.

Distribution: Principally cellar door sales and mailing list; limited retail and restaurant distribution through Carol-Anne Martin Classic Wines, Sydney. Cellar door sales 9 a.m. to 5 p.m. Monday to Saturday 9 a.m. to 1 p.m. Sunday.

Prices: $10 to $15 cellar door.

Vintage Rating 1986–89: White: '88, '89, '87, '86. Red: '87, '89, '88 ('89 not yet rated).

Tasting Notes:

1989 SEMILLON [CS] Colour: light to medium yellow-green. *Bouquet:* of medium fruit intensity, with some fermentation characters subsisting. *Palate:* already very good, with balance, intensity, and already showing some honeyed weight; gives every indication it will be superb, and if it lives up to its potential, will rate 90.

1989 CHARDONNAY [CS] Colour: very light green-straw. *Bouquet:* light, tangy citric/ grapefruit aroma with a whisper of sulphide. *Palate:* quite potent fruit with good length and intensity; if cleaned up, as it no doubt will be, it is headed towards the middle 80's.

1989 SEMILLON CHARDONNAY [84] Colour: brilliant green-yellow. *Bouquet:* light, clean and crisp with a slight herbaceous overtone from the semillon. *Palate:* much softer and more forward; very good mid-palate flavours already apparent, with a fine fruit/acid balance and very appealing fruit flavours. Already complete. Drink '90–'94.

1988 OAKED SEMILLON VAT 2 [CS] Colour: light to medium yellow-green. *Bouquet:* quite pronounced lemony, slightly rough-sawn, oak. *Palate:* over-oaked with lemony/sawdusty flavours; if the oak is fined down by back-blending, could be very good; otherwise will simply improve somewhat with time in bottle.

1989 HERMITAGE [CS] Colour: youthful purple-red. *Bouquet:* soft, clean, slightly squashy berry aromas, quite advanced. *Palate:* fresh, light peppery spicy fruit with jumpy acids; still to settle down from fermentation, but at least to this point shows considerable promise.

Summary: The restored Oakvale Winery, once famous for the wines of Doug Elliott, continues to flourish under the care of former solicitor Barry Shields. The 1989 wines all show considerable promise. I must say I was somewhat disappointed with the way the 1988's went to bottle; either at the latter stages of oak and/or tank maturation (or at bottling) some rather stale, tired characters intruded.

PEACOCK HILL

Location: Corner Palmers Lane and Branxton Road, Pokolbin, 2325 (vineyard only).

Winemaker: David Lowe.

1989 Production: 2700 cases.

Principal Wines: Chardonnay, Shiraz, Cabernet Merlot and Cabernet Sauvignon; Pinot Noir planned for the future.

Distribution: Was initially intended to be entirely devoted to export. However, the failure of the export market to fully develop has led to some local distribution through Pokolbin Estate, acting both as retailers through its cellar door operation in MacDonalds Road, Pokolbin, and as a wholesaler. Also available through mailing list, enquiries to PO Box 239, Cessnock, 2325.

Price: $12.50 retail.

Tasting Notes:

1988 CHARDONNAY [87] Colour: medium to full yellow-straw. *Bouquet:* medium to full, with quite complex melon/fig/honeyed fruit and just a touch of hessiany oak. *Palate:* high-toned grapefruit flavours with strong barrel-fermentation characters and, again, oak-derived complexity. Has masses of flavour without excessive sweetness. Drink '90–'91.

1988 CABERNET MERLOT [72] Colour: medium red. *Bouquet:* light and clean, with soft lemony oak and a touch of minty fruit. *Palate:* leafy/minty/lemony flavours, showing the softening and lightening influence of merlot; low tannin finish. Drink '90–'91.

1987 SHIRAZ [75] Colour: medium red-purple. *Bouquet:* clean, with quite pronounced lemony

oak and fruit of light to medium intensity. *Palate:* fresh and clean red berry fruit flavours with spicy/lemony oak; simply lacks final structure/richness for highest points. Drink '90–'93.

1986 CABERNET SAUVIGNON [75] Colour: medium red, still with just a touch of purple remaining. *Bouquet:* faintly leathery/tarry regional style, with good vinosity underneath. *Palate:* a high flavoured, ultra-regional cabernet but at least has flavour, and certainly will appeal to Hunter afficionados. Drink '90–'94.

Summary: The wines of Peacock Hill have done consistently well in Australian wine shows, which is not surprising. The quality of the fruit from this part of the old Rothbury Herlston Vineyard is obviously very good.

PEPPERS CREEK

Location: Corner Ekerts and Broke Roads, Pokolbin, 2321; 12 km north-west of Cessnock. (049) 98 7532.

Winemaker: Peter Ireland.

1989 Production: 600 cases.

Principal Wines: Semillon, Chardonnay, Shiraz and Merlot.

Distribution: Through cellar door sales Wednesday to Sunday 10 a.m. to 5 p.m. Mail order enquiries welcome.

Prices: $12.50 to $16 cellar door.

Vintage Rating 1987–89: White: '87, '88, '89. Red: '87, '89, '88.

Tasting Notes:

1987 SEMILLON CHARDONNAY [70] Colour: medium-full yellow. *Bouquet:* pleasant, smooth, toasty developed characters of medium intensity and good style. *Palate:* oaky/toasty flavours are strong, but need a little more fruit flesh; good food wine. Drink '90–'91.

1987 CHARDONNAY [64] Colour: medium straw-yellow. _Bouquet:_ most unusual caramel-chew oak on the far side of vanillan. _Palate:_ toffee/caramel flavours sit on top of fruit; truly, a weird wine, though not unpleasant. Drink '90.

1988 SHIRAZ [75] Colour: medium to full red-purple. _Bouquet:_ clean fruit but with some slightly burnt/charred characters which may come from oak or could possibly be fermentation-associated. _Palate:_ of medium to full weight with lots of sweet berry fruit flavour, some charred oak, and again an echo of that slightly medicinal/burnt character which appears on the bouquet. Drink '92–'97.

Summary: Peppers Creek makes an auspicious start; if Peter Ireland is learning on the job, as I gather is the case, I look forward to future vintages. The winery/antique shop complex is an obligatory (and easy to reach) visit.

᪅PETERSONS

Location: Mount View Road, Mount View, 2325; 9 km west of Cessnock.
(049) 90 1704.

Winemaker: Gary Reed.

1989 Production: 6000 cases.

Principal Wines: A limited range of high-quality table wines and the occasional fortified wine, including Semillon, Chardonnay, Traminer, Pinot Noir, Malbec, Hermitage, Cabernet Sauvignon, Sauternes and Vintage Port.

Distribution: Principally cellar door sales and mailing list; cellar door sales 9 a.m. to 5 p.m. Monday to Saturday, noon to 5 p.m. Sunday. Limited fine-wine distribution Sydney and Melbourne. Mailing list enquiries to PO Box 182, Cessnock, 2325.

Prices: $9 to $15 cellar door.

Vintage Rating 1986–89: White: '88, '89, '87, '86. Red: '89, '88, '87, '86.

Outstanding Prior Vintages: White: '83, '84. Red: '82, '83, '85.

Tasting Notes:

1988 SEMILLON [77] Colour: brilliant, light green-yellow. _Bouquet:_ crisp, tangy/lemony fruit and light oak; a faint matchbox character also evident. _Palate:_ very good, intense, crisp semillon, but that touch of matchbox comes to haunt the palate; terrific fruit slightly flawed. Drink '90–'93.

1987 CHARDONNAY [55] Colour: brilliant light medium green-yellow. _Bouquet:_ decidedly curious; very youthful, with powdery/matchbox aromas obliterating whatever fruit is there. _Palate:_ undeveloped, with similar strong matchbox flavours; a major disappointment. Drink '90–'91.

1987 HERMITAGE [59] Colour: medium red-purple. _Bouquet:_ soft, quite ripe red berry fruit with squashy/gamey characters. _Palate:_ soft fruit is surrounded by gamey/meaty flavours which lead to bitterness on the finish. Mercaptans at work. Drink '90–'92.

Summary: A winery which has swept all before its 1984, 1985 and 1986 vintages, but which slumped dramatically in 1987.

᪅POKOLBIN ESTATE

Location: MacDonalds Road, Pokolbin, 2321; 10 km north-west of Cessnock.
(049) 938 7524; Fax (049) 905 7765.

Winemaker: David Hook.

Principal Wines: White Burgundy, Semillon Chardonnay, Traminer Riesling, Hermitage.

Distribution: Pokolbin Estate acts both as a cellar door sales retail operation for its own brands and for Peacock Hill, Lakes Folly and Pothana, 10 a.m. to 5 p.m. 7 days. It also then acts as a wholesaler into the Sydney retail trade through its owner, Efficiency Displays Pty Ltd.

Prices: $10.95 retail.

Tasting Notes:

1988 TRAMINER RIESLING [62] Colour: medium full yellow. _Bouquet:_ soft and light, with just a hint of traminer varietal spice. _Palate:_ pleasant, light commercial wine with light traminer flavour; fault-free, and a very adequate cellar door style. Drink '90.

Summary: Pokolbin Estate, previously owned by the MacDougall Family, is in truth a cellar door operation with all wines (both its own and those it represents) being made elsewhere, either by the producers or under contract. Two other 1988 white wines tasted had mould/taint problems, possibly from faulty corks. The building itself constitutes a very attractive cellar door sales area, and is a convenient tasting point for otherwise inaccessible Hunter labels.

POTHANA VINEYARD

Location: Carramar, Belford, 2335 (065) 74 7164.

Winemaker: David Hook.

1989 Production: 1200 cases.

Principal Wines: Chardonnay and Semillon.

Distribution: Cellar door sales by appointment; otherwise, wine available through Pokolbin Estates.

Prices: $9 to $12 cellar door.

Vintage Rating 1987–89: White: '88, '87, '89.

Tasting Notes:

1989 SEMILLON [CS] Colour: light green-yellow. *Bouquet:* clean, of medium to full weight, with quite intense herbaceous varietal aroma. *Palate:* crisp and tangy; there are definite fermentation characters subsisting, but the fruit is there. On the assumption the wine settles down and makes it safely to bottle, should rate in the mid to high 70's.

1989 CHARDONNAY [CS] Colour: very light straw-green. *Bouquet:* light, clean barrel-fermentation characters linger; stylish fruit and oak balance. *Palate:* still very light, but the signs are all there for a good wine given time. If bottled successfully, will rate in the 80's.

1988 CHARDONNAY [70] Colour: medium yellow-green. *Bouquet:* solid, slightly biscuity oak; honeyed fruit of fair weight. *Palate:* smooth, honeyed fruit with slightly hot/hard alcohol on the finish. Could conceivably soften with time. Drink '90–'91.

1987 SEMILLON [66] Colour: medium full yellow-green. *Bouquet:* strong, positive bottle-developed characters with pronounced herbaceous fruit. *Palate:* tangy/lemony/slightly stalky bottle-developed flavours; really needs greater fruit flesh to carry those characters, and does finish somewhat bitter. Drink '90–'92.

1987 CHARDONNAY [73] Colour: medium to full yellow-green. *Bouquet:* quite full and rich, with complex oak, but the fruit is drying slightly. *Palate:* full, strong fruit comes on entry to the mouth, but then breaks up slightly finishing with rather hot, slightly sweet, high alcohol flavours. A wine of generous proportions which will appeal to many. Drink '90–'91.

Summary: Pothana has already established something of a following for its full blown, rich white wines.

RICHMOND GROVE

Location: Hermitage Road, Pokolbin, 2321. (049) 98 7792.

Winemakers: Mark Cashmore (executive winemaker) and Ian Scarborough (winemaker).

1989 Production: 175,000 cases.

Principal Wines: Oak Matured Chablis, French Cask Chardonnay, Fumé Blanc, Nouvelle Chardonnay, White Bordeaux, White Burgundy, Cabernet Merlot, Nouvelle Cabernet Merlot and Cabernet Sauvignon. A new premium range of varietal wines is expected to be launched late in 1989.

Distribution: Marketed on a national retail basis through Wyndham Estate subsidiary, Australian Vintners Pty Ltd.

Prices: $7.65 to $11.03 cellar door.

Vintage Rating 1986–89: '89, '87, '88, '86.

Outstanding Prior Vintages: White: '79. Red: '78.

Tasting Notes:

1989 CHABLIS [75] Colour: medium to full yellow-green. *Bouquet:* soft, complex with well integrated fruit and oak; quite rich overall. _Palate:_ high flavoured, with full fruit and some quite attractive spicy/chippy oak; a very peculiar idea of chablis, but a very good commercial white wine. Drink '90–'91.

1988 CHARDONNAY [85] Colour: medium to full yellow-green. _Bouquet:_ extremely rich and complex, with superb oak handling and very good fruit. _Palate:_ oak is the dominant contributor to both flavour and complexity, and the fruit is a fraction light on; happily, however, the wine is not sweet, and the oak may settle down with a little more time in bottle. Drink '90–'91.

1988 CABERNET SAUVIGNON [70] Colour: light purple-red. _Bouquet:_ faint smoked bacon/oaked characters with light, fresh fruit underneath the oak. _Palate:_ identical smoked bacon flavours quite evident; the next compartment is smooth fruit; the final compartment is tangy acid. A wine which has by no means come together and I am not sure it will ever do so. The bacon characters undoubtedly come from some form of oak. Drink '92–'95.

1987 BLUE RIBBON CLASSIC CABERNET MERLOT [78] Colour: medium purple-red. _Bouquet:_ clean, with complex leafy/berry fruit, and oak appropriately in restraint. _Palate:_ full and sweet, with smooth plum/berry flavours and very soft tannin; there is an echo of carbonic maceration-type flavours lurking in the wine. Drink '91–'94.

Summary: At the risk of sounding repetitive, if prejudice is cast to one side (and tasting wines blind is the only way I know of doing this) some very good and very serious wines are made by the Wyndham Group. That Richmond Grove should produce excellent wines from its new winery is not the least bit surprising, even less so given the immense skills of Ian Scarborough.

🍇 THE ROTHBURY ESTATE

Location: Broke Road, Pokolbin, 2321; 10 km north of Cessnock. (049) 98 7555.

Winemaker: David Lowe.

1989 Production: 120,000 cases.

Principal Wines: Recent moves have seen a substantial change in the Rothbury product range, labelling and distribution. The wines are now small- and medium-batch bottlings, released under a variety of labels for licensed trade, export, mail order and cellar door, with the emphasis on varietal Individual Vineyard bottlings. Principal varieties are Chardonnay, Semillon, Hermitage and Pinot Noir. Also other much cheaper wines purchased in bulk from other producers and released under the Dove Crag range.

Distribution: Through The Rothbury Estate Society and cellar door; members receive bulletins and special wine offers. Retail distribution of Silver Label range through Thomas Hardy & Sons Wines, and rapidly increasing exports, with UK imports through Geoffrey Roberts & Associates. Unequalled tasting facilities in splendid winery. Open 9.30 a.m. to 4.30 p.m. 7 days.

Prices: $10 to $19.50 retail.

Vintage Rating 1986–89: White: '86, '89, '87, '88. Red: '89, '86, '87, '88.

Outstanding Prior Vintages: White: '72, '74, '76, '79, '84. Red: '73, '75, '79, '83.

Tasting Notes:

1989 INDIVIDUAL PADDOCK SEMILLON [84] Colour: light to medium yellow. _Bouquet:_ very clean; of medium to full intensity, with excellent young varietal fruit. _Palate:_ full flavoured forward and rich; will develop reasonably quickly into a marvellously soft and fleshy white burgundy style, and could very

well rate substantially higher points. Drink
'90–'93.

1989 COWRA CHARDONNAY [84] Colour: light
green-yellow. *Bouquet:* spotlessly clean
citric/grapefruit/melon aromas; excellent
winemaking and good potential. *Palate:* tangy,
rich and intense flavours with very good fruit
and a markedly long finish. Drink '90–'94.

1988 HUNTER VALLEY SEMILLON [79] Colour:
medium to full yellow, with a touch of green.
Bouquet: clean and soft, starting to develop
some pleasing honey aromas; light to medium
intensity. *Palate:* soft, clean and easy drinking
style with a touch of honey, and finishing with
good acid; once again, looks set to develop
reasonably quickly. Drink '90–'93.

*1988 HUNTER VALLEY CHARDONNAY RESERVE
[90] Colour:* medium to full yellow. *Bouquet:*
exceedingly complex, rich, textured/honeyed
barrel-ferment fruit and oak. *Palate:* full
flavoured, rich and complex with strong barrel-
ferment characters again evident; mouth filling
and luscious. Dolly Parton style. Drink '90–
'92.

*1987 HUNTER VALLEY CHARDONNAY RESERVE
[85] Colour:* medium to full yellow, even with a
touch of orange, and showing rapid
development. *Palate:* full, complex buttery/
oaky/toasty aromas, very regional in character.
Palate: riotous oaky/buttery/toasty flavours,
showing marked bottle development; the
balance is good and the wine finishes clean; it
does support Len Evans' contention that these
wines can carry protracted cellaring. Drink
'90–'91.

1986 RESERVE HERMITAGE [80] Colour:
youthful, deep purple-red. *Bouquet:* strong,
dark berry ripe fruit with a touch of charred
oak. *Palate:* rich and full bodied; very ripe,
generous fruit with a similar touch of charred
oak evident in the bouquet; another very
fleshy, luscious wine. Drink '90–'95.

Summary: In recent years The Rothbury Estate has
shown considerable dexterity in meeting the
demands and needs of the marketplace,
particularly by sharply increasing its production
of chardonnay from both the Hunter Valley and
from Cowra, but I still retain a marked affection
for its semillons. As the tasting notes indicate,
wine quality is exemplary.

SAXONVALE

Location: Fordwich Estate, Broke Road, Broke,
2330.
(065) 79 1009.

Winemaker: John Baruzzi.

1989 Production: 200,000 cases.

Principal Wines: There are two distinct ranges of wines:
first, the Premium Bin Range, consisting of Bin 1
Chardonnay, Bin 1 Semillon, Bin 1 Hermitage and
Bin 1 Cabernet Sauvignon; and second, the
cheaper Spring Mountain Varietal Range.

Distribution: Direct marketing through American
Express, Cellarmasters and restaurant
representation through Mark Fesq. UK
imports through Victon Ross Shepherd. USA
imports Touton Selections.

Prices: $9.90 to $14.90 retail.

Vintage Rating 1986–89: '89, '88, '87, '86.

Outstanding Prior Vintages: '80.

Tasting Notes:

1988 CHARDONNAY BIN 1 [83] Colour: full yellow,
suggesting the use of skin contact. *Bouquet:* very
advanced soft, butterscotch/honey fruit. *Palate:*
precisely as the bouquet suggests, very advanced
soft sweet butter/butterscotch flavours; a one or
two glass style, but that is enough to complete the
seduction. Drink '90.

1987 BIN 1 HERMITAGE [60] Colour: medium to
full red, with a touch of purple. *Bouquet:* rather
plain, slightly dull and leathery, with a faint touch
of mint. *Palate:* strong lemony oak submerges
the fruit, which lacks flesh. Drink '90.

1987 BIN 1 CABERNET SAUVIGNON [88] Colour:
medium red, with a touch of purple. *Bouquet:*
spotlessly clean with exemplary cedary/
briary/berry varietal character, astonishing for
the Hunter Valley. *Palate:* very good weight,
balance and style; a chewy, chocolatey wine with
great flavour augmented by the clever use of
sweet, vanillan American oak. Drink '90–'94.

Summary: Yet another limb of the Wyndham octopus; once again, it is essential these wines be tasted blind to circumvent widely held prejudice amongst so-called wine experts.

🍇 SCARBOROUGH WINES

Location: Gillards Road, Pokolbin, 2321. (049) 98 7563.

Winemaker: Ian Scarborough.

1989 Production: Limited, with final quantities for release under the Scarborough label not yet determined.

Principal Wines: Initially only Chardonnay; limited Pinot Noir releases possible for the future; ultimately, likewise Merlot and Verdelho.

Distribution: Initially will be by mailing list and by direct distribution to local restaurants and selected retailers. Cellar door sales by appointment only; telephone as above.

Prices: Approximately $20 cellar door.

Tasting Notes:

1987 CHARDONNAY [88] Colour: medium to full yellow. *Bouquet:* very complex, with some charred/lemony oak evident and excellent bottle development. *Palate:* a wine with real style and complexity, showing superb handling of oak; the wine avoids the sweetness which seems to mar so many of the fuller-bodied Hunter chardonnays. Drink '90–'94.

Summary: Scarborough is in its infancy, and will start to become slightly more obvious as from 1990. Owner/winemaker Ian Scarborough and wife Merrelea have vast industry experience, and I have the highest possible admiration for Scarborough's skills as a winemaker (and formerly as a consultant). I can see no reason why quality should not be exceptional.

🍇 SIMON WHITLAM

Location: Wollombi Brook Vineyard, Broke, 2330; on outskirts of town (vineyard only).

Winemaker: Simon Gilbert, Arrowfield Wines.

1989 Production: In excess of 3500 cases.

Principal Wines: Semillon, Show Reserve Semillon, Late Harvest Semillon, Chardonnay and Cabernet Sauvignon. Second label of Wollombi Brook introduced in 1987.

Distribution: Through mailing list and reasonably extensive fine wine retailers; wholesale distributors De Bono Fine Wine Merchants, Sydney. Mailing list enquiries to Simon Whitlam & Co., 52 Grosvenor Street, Woollahra, 2025, (02) 387 8622.

Prices: $11.10 to $14.50 retail.

Tasting Notes:

1988 CHARDONNAY [87] Colour: medium yellow-green. *Bouquet:* strong, complex, bottle-developed honeyed/oaky aromas with varietal character taking second place. *Palate:* very rich, honeyed/peachy/butter fruit with very good oak handling; it is somewhat sweet, but ultra-commercial. Drink '90–'91.

1988 SEMILLON [69] Colour: medium yellow-green. *Bouquet:* very pronounced oak, with some evidence of volatility. *Palate:* high-toned, oaky, lifted fruit flavours; I have some technical problems with the wine, but the average consumer would in all probability not have the same difficulties. Drink ' 90–'91.

1988 SEMILLON CHARDONNAY [62] Colour: medium yellow-green. *Bouquet:* clean, neutral and slightly skinny fruit characters. *Palate:* plain, slightly skinny/coarse fruit flavours and some green fruit characters. Drink '90.

1988 HERMITAGE [76] Colour: very good red-purple. *Bouquet:* clean and stylish, with pleasant lemony oak and fruit of medium intensity. *Palate:* once again, very clean; the wine does rely quite heavily on lemony/vanillan oak, but there is sufficient fruit there. Drink '91–'94.

1988 CABERNET SAUVIGNON [85] Colour: medium purple-red. *Bouquet:* full and clean, with very well handled charred oak giving richness and complexity. *Palate:* spotlessly clean, with fresh red berry fruit set against strong, quite sweet vanillan American oak. Sophisticated winemaking. Drink '93–'97.

Summary: The Simon Whitlam wines will continue largely unchanged by the acquisition of Arrowfield by interests closely associated with the Simon Whitlam owners (Andrew Simon and Nicholas Whitlam being the chief protagonists). As has been the case in earlier vintages, wine quality is all one could wish for.

❦ SOBELS WINERY

Location: McDonalds Road, Pokolbin, 2321; 12 km north-west of Cessnock. (049) 98 7585.

Winemaker: Kevin Sobels.

Principal Wines: Wines on offer include Rhine Riesling, Semillon Chardonnay, Chablis, Hermitage and Cabernet Sauvignon.

Distribution: Principally cellar door sales; mailing list to be established, with enquiries to above address. Cellar door sales 9 a.m. to 5 p.m. 7 days.

Summary: I know nothing of the present operations of Sobels.

❦ SUTHERLAND WINES

Location: Deasey's Road, Pokolbin, 2321; 14 km north-west of Cessnock. (049) 98 7650.

Winemaker: Neil Sutherland.

1989 Production: 7000 cases.

Principal Wines: Varietal white and red table wines. Labels comprise Chenin Blanc, Semillon, Chardonnay, Shiraz, Pinot Noir and Cabernet Sauvignon.

Distribution: Cellar door sales and mailing list. Cellar door sales 10 a.m. to 5 p.m Monday to Sunday. Mailing list as above. Distribution through Appellation Wines & Spirits.

Prices: $9 to $14 cellar door.

Vintage Rating 1986–89: White: '88, '86, '87 ('89 not rated). Red: '87, '86 ('88 and '89 not rated).

Outstanding Prior Vintages: White: '83, '85.

Tasting Notes:

1989 SHIRAZ [CS] Colour: medium red. *Bouquet:* fresh, full berry fruit, not surprisingly with fermentation characters lingering. *Palate:* youthful, pungent spicy/berry fruit; has obvious potential.

1988 SHIRAZ [60] Colour: medium red-purple. *Bouquet:* light, faintly spicy fruit dulled by leathery sulphides. *Palate:* very light indeed, with faintly spicy/leathery fruit flavours. Drink '90–'91.

1987 SHIRAZ [83] Colour: medium red, with a touch of purple still remaining. *Bouquet:* clean and full, with complex, ripe berry fruits, bordering on the over-ripe. *Palate:* clean, full, ripe red berry fruit with a nice touch of charred oak; an amply proportioned wine which will age well. Drink '91–'96.

Summary: Not for the first time, I encountered tremendous problems with the Sutherland white wines. The now sold-out '87 Chardonnay covered itself in glory at the 1989 Smallmakers Wine Competition, but it is something of a lighthouse among dark and stormy seas.

❦ TAMBURLAINE WINES

Location: McDonalds Road, Pokolbin, 2321; 10 km north-west of Cessnock. (049) 98 7570.

Winemakers: Mark Davidson, Greg Silkman.

1989 Production: 5000 cases.

Principal Wines: Semillon, Late Harvest Semillon, Chardonnay, Syrah (Shiraz) and Cabernet Sauvignon.

Distribution: Principally mailing list and cellar door sales 10 a.m. to 4.30 p.m. 7 days. Select retail distribution in Qld, WA, Vic, and NSW. UK imports through Haughton Fine Wines, Cheshire and Victon Ross, Middlesex.

Prices: $10 to $20 cellar door.

Vintage Rating 1986–89: White: '89, '86, '88, '87. Red: '89, '86, '87, '88.

Tasting Notes:

1989 CHARDONNAY [CS[Colour: light straw-yellow. *Bouquet:* light to medium, with smooth vanillan oak, presumably American; somewhat one dimensional. *Palate:* good fruit weight and intensity, but still to build structure and complexity; at a very rough guess, somewhere around 75.

1988 SEMILLON [65] Colour: medium to full yellow-green. *Bouquet:* somewhat pungent and oily, yet with green fruit characters also evident. *Palate:* as with the bouquet, at once rather broad and slightly oily yet showing some green, herbaceous fruit; and it may be that I am being somewhat unkind. Drink '90–'92.

1989 CABERNET SAUVIGNON [CS] Colour: very good purple-red. *Bouquet:* well made, with light, fresh red berry fruits. *Palate:* lovely berry flavours and superb spicy oak; no doubt a single cask sample, but if the least bit representative, will be a quite lovely wine meriting points in the high 80's.

Summary: The wines tasted for this edition were a major disappointment on the day. I have tasted most of the Tamburlaine wines released during 1988 and early 1989, and have been consistently impressed.

🍇 TERRACE VALE

Location: Deasey's Lane, Pokolbin, 2321; 13 km north-west of Cessnock. (049) 98 7517.

Winemaker: Alain le Prince.

Principal Wines: Varietal white and red table wines (and a vintage port) released under a combination varietal/bin number system. Semillon Bin 1, Semillon Bin 1A, Chardonnay Bin 2, Gewurztraminer Bin 3, Semillon Chardonnay Bin 12, Hermitage Bins 6 and 6A,

Cabernet/Hermitage Bin 76, Pinot Noir and Vintage Port.

Distribution: Principally cellar door sales and mailing list. Cellar door sales 10 a.m. to 4 p.m. 7 days; mailing list as above. Limited Sydney distribution through Trimex Pty Ltd, and Brisbane through Vat & Spirit Pty Ltd.

Tasting Notes:

1989 SEMILLON [CS] Colour: medium yellow-green. *Bouquet:* very good, intense varietal fruit with honeyed/citric characters. *Palate:* a youthful, well made wine with good weight and varietal definition show in slightly herbaceous fruit; some fermentation characters subsisting, but the wine is well on its way to 80 points or more, and was a very considerable distance in front of the '89 Chardonnay at the same stage.

1987 ELIZABETH SAUVIGNON BLANC [74] Colour: very good yellow-green. *Bouquet:* most unusual honeyed/banana aromas evidently coming from the interaction of botrytis and sauvignon blanc. *Palate:* again, a striking and unusual wine which will either be loved or hated; the points are something of a compromise between the two extremes. Certainly it has lusciousness and very good acid. Drink '90–'93.

Summary: As on many prior occasions, the wines of Terrace Vale appeared tremendously variable in quality. There is no question that I am more sensitive than most to sulphide/mercaptan problems, but with the best will in the world I could not find complimentary things to say about the red wines from 1988.

🍇 THALGARA ESTATE

Location: DeBeyers Road, Pokolbin, 2321; 9 km north-west of Cessnock. (049) 98 7717.

Winemakers: Steve Lamb and Phillipa Treadwell.

1989 Production: 1000 cases.

Principal Wines: Chardonnay, Semillon Chardonnay, Shiraz and Shiraz Cabernet.

Distribution: Principally through cellar door sales and mailing list; cellar door sales 10 a.m. to 5 p.m. 7 days. Also sold through selected local restaurants.

Prices: $12.50 to $16 cellar door.

Tasting Notes:

1988 HERMITAGE [68] Colour: light purple-red. *Bouquet:* clean with light vanillan oak; slightly simple and lacking fruit depth. *Palate:* clean and soft, but sweet vanillan oak is just a little too heavy for the fairly light fruit. Drink '91–'94.

1987 HERMITAGE [70] Colour: medium purple-red. *Bouquet:* again, lemony oak, but a very slightly leathery edge tends to flatten the fruit aromas. *Palate:* much better balance, with attractive cherry/red berry fruit showing through, although again there is a very slight flattening influence from what may have been second-class oak. Drink '91–'93.

Summary: A new face on the scene, producing clean, full flavoured if rather oaky reds. No white wines were tasted, but the winemaking team of owner Steve Lamb and consultant Phillipa Treadwell seem to know in which direction they are headed.

❦ *TULLOCH*

Location: De Beyers Road, Pokolbin, 2321; 10 km north-west of Cessnock. (049) 98 7503; Fax (049) 98 7608.

Winemakers: J. Y. (Jay) Tulloch and Patrick Auld.

1989 Production: Not for publication.

Principal Wines: Traditional Hunter Valley red and white wines are released in two grades: Selected Vintage varietals (Chardonnay, Verdelho, Hermitage, Semillon Chardonnay and Vintage Brut Champagne) released in limited quantities, and wines for commercial release: Hunter River Hermitage, Hunter River White Burgundy (produced mainly from semillon with small percentages of chardonnay and verdelho), J.Y. Chablis (produced from semillon) available continuously through retail outlets. Hunter Valley Port and Muscat available at cellar door only.

Distribution: National retail through the Penfolds Group. Cellar door sales 9 a.m. to 4.45 p.m. Monday to Thursday, 9 a.m. to 4.15 p.m. Friday, and 9 a.m. to 5 p.m. Saturday. Mail order enquiries welcome.

Prices: $7.99 to $14.99 retail (approximate discount levels).

Vintage Rating 1986–89: White: '86, '87, '89, '88. Red: '86, '87, '89, '88.

Outstanding Prior Vintages: White: '74, '76, '83. Red: '65, '75, '83.

Tasting Notes:

1989 VERDELHO [69] Colour: light straw-green. *Bouquet:* clean and quite fragrant, with pleasant fruit of some intensity, which will no doubt build further. *Palate:* a very well made, commercial wine with pleasant fruit weight. I find the residual sugar needless, but it is no doubt intentional. Drink '90.

1988 WHITE BURGUNDY [63] Colour: light green-yellow. *Bouquet:* neutral, slightly heavy and fractionally coarse. *Palate:* soft, clean, smooth flavours without any distinctive varietal fruit character, and quite pronounced sweetness. Once again, a deliberately judged commercial style. Drink '90.

1988 CHARDONNAY [84] Colour: medium green-yellow. *Bouquet:* clean; pronounced lemony oak and fruit of light to medium intensity. *Palate:* a firm, clean wine with nice lemony oak and a long, clean and gloriously dry (rather than sweet) finish. Drink '91–'93.

1987 CHARDONNAY [90] Colour: excellent green-yellow, brilliantly clear. *Bouquet:* rich, complex tangy barrel ferment flavours with critic/melon fruit. *Palate:* very tangy, stylish and intense wine showing exemplary oak handling and some outstanding fruit; finishes long and clean, again without excessive sweetness. Drink '90–'93.

1985 SELECTED VINTAGE HERMITAGE [60] Colour: medium red-purple. *Bouquet:* rather light, thin and leafy, lacking fruit richness. *Palate:* soft, aged, extreme Hunter style with leathery flavours and lacking fruit richness. Drink '90–'91.

Summary: The Tulloch chardonnays are in a class of their own; the other wines released under the label are unashamedly commercial and significantly cheaper. However, the quality of the Chardonnay makes it an outstanding buy.

TYRRELL'S WINES

Vintage 1988 - Vat 47

TYRRELL'S WINES
HUNTER RIVER
PINOT CHARDONNAY
PRODUCE OF AUSTRALIA
750 ml

Location: Broke Road, Pokolbin, 2321; 12 km north-west of Cessnock.
(049) 98 7509.

Winemakers: Murray Tyrrell (principal), Mike de Garis.

1989 Production: 350,000 cases.

Principal Wines: A very large range, headed by the "Vat" wines: whites comprise Semillon Vats 1 and 15; Chardonnay Vat 47 and Chardonnay Semillon Vat 63. Red Vats 5, 7, 8, 9, 10 and 11, together with Pinot Noir and Shiraz Merlot. Then follow top commercial varietal white and red releases under Old Winery Label, HVD Label and Belford, and finally the traditional range, including Long Flat White and Long Flat Red. Also top-quality *méthode champenoise* wines from pinot noir, chardonnay and semillon. UK imports through G. Bellonie & Co.

Distribution: Vat wines sold only cellar door and by excellent mailing list with very well-presented brochures (two major mailings each year). Old Winery and traditional releases through national distribution plus substantial exports. Cellar door sales 9 a.m. to 5 p.m. Monday to Saturday.

Prices: $5.50 to $25 cellar door.

Vintage Rating 1986–89: White: '86, '89, '87, '88. Red: '87, '89, '88, '86.

Outstanding Prior Vintages: White: '68, '70, '72, '76, '79, '83. Red: '65, '73, '75, '79, '83, '85.

Tasting Notes:

1988 LONG FLAT WHITE [63] Colour: light to medium yellow-green. *Bouquet:* clean, neutral, slightly green fruit aromas. *Palate:* clean, neutral, well made commercial white relying neither on sugar nor oak for its flavour. Drink '90.

1987 BELFORD SEMILLON [65] Colour: glowing yellow-green. *Bouquet:* soft, bottle-developed camphor characters. *Palate:* a very rich, forceful old style Hunter Semillon which reminds me ever so strongly of a 1967 Drayton Semillon (blended for Draytons by Len Evans) at the same age. Tyrrell has quite deliberately turned the clock back to fashion this wine; I respect his intention, but cannot greatly enjoy the wine. Drink '90–'95.

Summary: Other wines were tasted, but I do not think do justice to Tyrrells. All manner of problems beset the winery in 1988, and at least some of these have had a marked impact on wine quality and consistency. The longer term reputation of Tyrrells as one of the finest producers of semillon (Vat 1) and chardonnay (Vat 47) was not won overnight and should not be lost overnight.

WYNDHAM ESTATE

WYNDHAM ESTATE
HUNTER VALLEY
CHARDONNAY
BIN 222
VINTAGE 1988

Location: Dalwood via Branxton, 2335; 6 km east of town.
(049) 38 1311.

Winemakers: Brian McGuigan (senior winemaker), Jon Reynolds.

1989 Production: 500,000 cases.

Principal Wines: A substantial range of red and white table wines available in three distinct price categories. Benchmark Accredited wines, Bin 888 Cabernet Merlot, Hunter Chardonnay and recently released Verdelho and Chardonnay Cuvee are the flagship wines. These are followed by Oak Cask Chardonnay, Bin 444 Cabernet Sauvignon, Limited Release Semillon, Pinot Noir and Bin 222 Chardonnay Semillon. There is a wide range of more popular styles available, including Chablis Superior, Bin 777 Graves Exceptional, Bin 555 Hermitage, TR2 Traminer and Riesling, GT Bin 6 Gewurztraminer and White Burgundy.

Distribution: Extensive Australian and export sales, with all States distributed by Wyndham except SA, which is distributed by Richard Mackay.

Prices: $6.75 to $16.20 retail.

Vintage Rating 1986–89: '89, '88, '87, '86.

Outstanding Prior Vintages: White: '85. Red: '83.

Tasting Notes:

1989 BIN TR2 TRAMINER RIESLING [67] *Colour:* light yellow-green. *Bouquet:* clean, spicy and fragrant fruit which is not phenolic, although it is fairly light. *Palate:* a purpose-built commercial style, with some fruit flavour, but really driven by strong residual sugar. Drink '90.

1989 HUNTER CHARDONNAY [CS] *Colour:* medium yellow-green. *Bouquet:* clean, with attractive fruit showing good varietal definition in the light, peachy/melon spectrum. *Palate:* tangy and flavoursome, with pronounced peach/melon fruit; if finished off with a touch of oak could be a real surprise packet, but should not rate less than 80 whatever happens to it from this point.

1988 CABERNET MERLOT BIN 888 [89] *Colour:* medium red-purple. *Bouquet:* solid and smooth, with clean, red berry fruit aromas of good weight. *Palate:* rich and full bodied, with sweet cassis/berry fruit; perfectly judged tannins and acid give the wine great structure. Drink '91–'95.

1987 MERLOT [75] *Colour:* medium red-purple. *Bouquet:* light, fragrant leafy/tobacco fruit showing exemplary varietal character. *Palate:* light, fragrant leafy tobacco flavours precisely tracking the bouquet; while the varietal character is very good, the wine could do with just a little more richness. Drink '90–'92.

1987 CABERNET SAUVIGNON BIN 444 [68] *Colour:* purple-red, with a very slightly blackish aspect. *Bouquet:* slightly soft soapy fruit with ripe berry characters. *Palate:* ripe, chocolatey plummy/berry flavours; slightly squashy, reminiscent of over-cropped Coonawarra fruit. Drink '90–'92.

Summary: Wyndham Estate succeeds because it deserves to. Neither its winemaking nor its wine marketing efforts will please the purists, and, indeed, Wyndham has long since decided to by-pass that audience. Its tremendous success in both local and overseas markets comes from an acute perception of what the general public wants and what it is prepared to pay.

Upper Hunter Valley

1988 VINTAGE

The growing season commenced in perfect conditions with good late winter rains and a burst of warm (but not hot) weather encouraging an early but vigorous budburst. Spring continued with sufficient rainfall and warmth to promote continued vigorous growth, and flowering and fruit set took place in ideal, mild conditions. There were no reports of late frosts.

The season continued with mild weather, interspersed with periods of rain which were not either heavy enough nor frequent enough to cause problems. In any event, almost all of the plantings are irrigated, so vine stress is uncommon whatever the conditions.

Despite large crops, vintage began slightly earlier than usual, spurred on by the threat of the rain which was falling in the Hunter Valley but which, by and large, did not upset the Upper Hunter vintage.

As always, there was some variation of quality, with one or two vineyards suffering from the combined effects of fairly dense canopies, exceptionally high yields and some rot in the grapes. Other vineyards had a very good vintage, with semillon especially showing excellent varietal character and soft, though not particularly intense, fruit. The red wines are typically subtle and light bodied, naturally occurring characteristics accentuated by the mild season.

1989 VINTAGE

Once again, budburst was early, thanks to a combination of warm weather and adequate soil moisture. In October the weather turned hot and windy, but the effect of flowering was nowhere near as dramatic as it was in the Lower Hunter. Yields were reduced marginally, but at least some growers felt that this had a beneficial effect on quality by preventing the over-cropping apparent in 1988.

From mid-November until early March the weather remained as perfect as one could reasonably expect. There were many days in which the temperature exceeded 25° C, but only one day when it exceeded 30° C. What is more, the rain which fell throughout January in the Lower Hunter stopped in early January, and the grapes ripened quickly but evenly.

Vintage started two weeks earlier than usual in mid-January, and by early March was all but complete. That early start undoubtedly saved the vintage, for the weather then turned extremely hot, followed by heavy rain which continued right through autumn and winter.

Not surprisingly, all fruit was harvested in very good condition, with no botrytis or other forms of rot. Semillon and sauvignon blanc were outstanding, with good chardonnay. The shiraz was also outstanding, the best since 1984.

THE CHANGES

The Upper Hunter continues to fulfil its role as a major grape and bulk wine supplier to other parts of Australia, and in particular to the Lower Hunter. However, there have been a surprising number of changes among the relatively few wineries which operate within its boundaries.

Arrowfield has been acquired by a group of investors headed by former Sydney retailer Andrew Simon and merchant banker Nicholas Whitlam. It was no coincidence that for many years Arrowfield had made (on a contract basis) the Simon Whitlam wines (which are dealt with in the Lower Hunter chapter). Arrowfield has been renamed Mountarrow, although there is presently a transition phase as existing stocks are marketed and final decisions made on brand and positioning. For this reason the two names are used conjointly in the entry.

Richmond Grove has been moved to the Lower Hunter; a new winery has been erected there for the production of premium wine. No doubt much of the fruit will, however, continue to be grown on the extensive Richmond Grove vineyards in the Upper Hunter. The loss of Richmond Grove is compensated for by the arrival of Serenella and the acquisition of Denman Estate by Rothbury and the subsequent revival in the fortunes of the Denman Estate label (and more importantly, wine quality).

Serenella has had its wines made under contract by Arrowfield, but under the energetic and skilled direction of Letitia (Tish) Cecchini. Houghton Wybong Estate continues its energetic promotion activities, with special functions and special newsletter offerings for its top 500 membership.

But, as ever, the scene is inevitably dominated by Rosemount, which continues to make a broad range of wines (in terms of price) of admirable consistency, and even more admirable quality. Rosemount has been one of the most important players in the export market, and has done as much as any of the largest Australian companies in establishing Australia's reputation in the United States as a maker of fine wine. It is indeed curious that much of its flagship, Roxburgh Chardonnay, is exported, although exports of the bottom-of-the-range Diamond Label are also very large.

❦ARROWFIELD/ MOUNT ARROW

Location: Highway 213, Jerry's Plains, 2330;
20 km south-east of Denman.
(065) 76 4041.

Winemaker: Simon Gilbert.

Principal Wines: The range is currently undergoing rationalisation, and full details are not known at this time. However, a premium series will come out under the name of Simon Gilbert; next will be the Reserve Range, and finally standard releases either under the Arrowfield or Mountarrow label. As with all Upper Hunter wineries the accent is on semillon and chardonnay; in the past Arrowfield has purchased grapes or wine from other parts of Australia, including Cowra, McLaren Vale and Coonawarra, and has even spread its net to New Zealand. It seems probable that this practice will continue.

Distribution: National retail distribution through Concorde Liquor Distributors. Cellar door sales 10 a.m. to 4 p.m. 7 days.

Prices: $9.20 to $25 retail.

Vintage Rating 1986–89: '89, '88, '87, '86.

Tasting Notes:

1988 RESERVE SEMILLON [74] Colour: medium yellow-green. *Bouquet:* quite complex and, equally, quite oaky, with a slightly raw edge to that oak. *Palate:* fruit flavour and intensity is of light to medium weight, with another powerful statement by the lemony/vanillan oak which is again slightly raw. A wine which will quite certainly improve with bottle age, and can then merit higher points. Drink '90–'93.

1988 RESERVE CHARDONNAY [80] Colour: medium yellow-green. *Bouquet:* smooth, soft honeyed/buttery fruit with well-handled oak. *Palate:* very complex with rich, pronounced oak; some will see the wine as altogether too oaky, others will relish the flavour and complexity of that oak. Equally, opinion will polarise as to whether the wine will benefit from bottle age. So, you pay your money and you take your choice. Drink '90–'93.

1988 HAWKES BAY NZ SAUVIGNON BLANC [69] Colour: medium green-yellow. *Bouquet:* of medium weight with typically decadent New Zealand fruit aromas, which are utterly unlike those of Australia. *Palate:* strong herbal/green flavours; there are far better New Zealand sauvignon blanc wines on the market. Drink '90.

1988 PINOT NOIR [69] Colour: light red-purple. *Bouquet:* very clean, but strong lemony oak obliterates whatever varietal character is present. *Palate:* once again, a wine dominated by lemony/vanillan oak; the fruit is merely a vehicle, and the varietal character has had no opportunity to express itself. Nonetheless, will appeal to those who like oaky reds. Drink '90.

1988 HERMITAGE [71] Colour: light to medium red-purple. *Bouquet:* soft, clean cherry fruit with soft vanillan oak. *Palate:* very pronounced vanilla bean oak overwhelms the fruit; the wine is at least spotlessly clean, and once again will appeal to some more than it does to me. Drink '90–'92.

1988 CABERNET SAUVIGNON [CS] Colour: medium to full purple-red. *Bouquet:* potent, powerful, strong, rather extractive and slightly sulphidic aromas. *Palate:* A huge wine with very strong, highly extracted flavour, some vanillan oak, but also a touch of bitterness; still settling down and was tasted immediately prior to bottling. If last-minute adjustments are made, could be very good, for it certainly has far more character and fruit weight than the other Arrowfield reds.

Summary: The future will tell where Arrowfield/Mountarrow heads. As I hardly need say, I would prefer to see reduced expenditure on American oak and more on either better fruit or some good French oak. However, winemaker Simon Gilbert (who is a junior partner in the syndicate) does know how to make clean wines, which is a great start, and has had conspicuous success with the big, rich buttery/oaky semillons and chardonnays in the past.

❦CALLATOOTA ESTATE

Location: Wybong Road, Wybong, 2333;
15 km north-east of Denman and 25 km north-west of Muswellbrook.
(065) 47 8149.

Winemakers: John and Andrew Cruickshank.

1989 Production: Approximately 2000 cases.

Principal Wines: Exclusively cabernet sauvignon vineyard and production. Wines produced are Rose, Cabernet Sauvignon Vat 1 and Cabernet Sauvignon Vat 2.

Distribution: Principally cellar door and mailing list. Cellar door sales 9 a.m. to 5 p.m. winter, 9 a.m. to 6 p.m. summer, 7 days. Mailing list enquiries to 504 Pacific Highway, St. Leonards, NSW, 2065. Limited retail distribution Sydney and Canberra.

Tasting Notes:

1985 CABERNET SAUVIGNON [69] Colour: medium red, with just a touch of purple remaining. *Bouquet:* complex, light, bottle-developed leafy/cigar box/tobacco characters with a distinct regional farmyard overlay. *Palate:* very strong, regional tarry/leathery flavours have come together in a certain fashion in the bottle; a wine which will appeal to those who like extreme Hunter style. Drink '90–'92.

Summary: Callatoota has always remained in the ownership of the Cruickshank family; the assertion to the contrary in the 1988 edition of this book was a typographical gremlin as two lines were misplaced from the Chateau Douglas entry. The other constant factor is the style of the wines, the majority of which are overwhelmed by what some will accept as district character and what I, regrettably, can only see as rampant sulphide.

🍇 CHATEAU DOUGLAS

Location: Muswellbrook, 2333; 20 km north-east of town (vineyard only).
(065) 43 7274.

Principal Wines: Limited range of white and red varietal table wines.

Distribution: Exclusively mail order, but believed to be relatively inactive.

Summary: Wines under the Segenhoe and Chateau Douglas labels still intermittently appear, but the vineyard has for some time now been leased to Tyrrell's, and the wines available on mailing list are produced strictly on a clean-skin basis, and do not necessarily contain Chateau Douglas fruit. The winery was purchased by Tyrrells in December 1987.

🍇 DENMAN ESTATE WINES

Location: Denman Road, Muswellbrook, 2333; 12 km south-west of town.
(065) 47 2473.

Winemaker: David Lowe.

Principal Wines: Semillon, Chardonnay, Sauvignon Blanc, Botrytis Semillon, Pinot Noir, Shiraz and Cabernet Sauvignon.

Distribution: Exclusively by mail order through the Rothbury Estate.

Prices: $8 to $10.

Tasting Notes:

1989 SAUVIGNON BLANC [74] Colour: light green-yellow. *Bouquet:* spotlessly clean, fragrant passionfruit characters, probably yeast-derived with some sauvignon blanc flavour underneath. *Palate:* clean, most attractive fruit salad flavours with a touch of residual sugar; a cunningly made commercial wine with simple but immediate appeal. Drink '90.

1989 CLASSIC HUNTER SEMILLON [59] Colour: light straw, with just a faint onionskin tinge. *Bouquet:* light weight, neutral and plain. *Palate:* clean, but very light and yet to develop any character; in the manner of semillon will improve in bottle, but will never shine. Drink '90–'91.

1986 BOTRYTIS (SEMILLON SAUVIGNON BLANC) [83] Colour: orange-yellow. *Bouquet:* intense botrytis with richness and style, and no excess volatility. *Palate:* very rich and complex mandarin/apricot flavours; once again, a wine of style and quite astonishing quality. Drink '90–'91.

Summary: Rothbury purchased all of the Denman Estate grapes in 1987 and 1988, and followed up by acquiring the vineyard in June 1988. Some pleasant, budget priced wines are being made (although I did not like the 1988 Chardonnay) and there is that exceptional bargain in the form of the 1986 Botrytis.

❦ *HOLLYDENE ESTATE*

Location: Merriwa Road, Hollydene via Denman, 2333; 7 km north-west of Denman. (065) 47 2316

Principal Wines: Bin 001 Tokay, Bin 002 Sauvignon Blanc, Bin 003 Chardonnay, Bin 005 Pinot Noir and Bin 006 Cabernet Franc.

Distribution: Limited retail distribution through Vintex Wines & Spirits and through Ballande Imports.

Prices: $8.80 to $9.95 retail.

Summary: Hollydene has always seemed to me to be the least attractive face of the Wyndham Group. Its wines are frequently bizarre, and I have always had difficulty in reconciling the wine in the bottle with the name on the labels. This apart, quality is seldom inspiring.

❦ *HORDERNS WYBONG ESTATE*

Location: Yarraman Road, Wybong, Muswellbrook, 2333. (065) 47 8127.

Winemaker: Garry Wall.

Principal Wines: Chablis, Semillon, Chardonnay, Spatlese Rhine Riesling, Potters Shiraz, Shiraz and Cabernet Sauvignon.

Distribution: Chiefly through the "Top 500" mailing list, a club concept offering a range of benefits including the opportunity to stay over the weekend at the winery and to participate in exclusive dinners and tastings organised in Sydney and Brisbane. Membership fees are the purchase of two cases of wine per year. Cellar door sales 9 a.m. to 5 p.m. 7 days.

Prices: $8.50 to $12.50 mailing list, less approximately 15% when purchased by the case.

Tasting Notes:

1988 CHARDONNAY [70] Colour: medium to full yellow. *Bouquet:* clean and smooth; although of medium to full intensity, rather one dimensional, and varietal characters not assertive. *Palate:* the light fruit struggles to express itself through strong and somewhat mediocre oak. Should develop in bottle, however, into a pleasant Hunter white burgundy style. Drink '90–'92.

1988 SEMILLON WINEMAKERS SELECTION [69] Colour: light to medium yellow-green. *Bouquet:* strong spicy/nutmeg oak over light fruit. *Palate:* light, crisp fruit again set against potent spicy/nutmeg oak; the oak characters are attractive, and the wine should improve in bottle. Drink '90–'92.

1988 TRAMINER [60] Colour: light yellow-green. *Bouquet:* fresh, but very light fruit and varietal aroma. *Palate:* clean and light, with faint lychee flavours, but the fruit intensity is lacking, and compensated for by a touch of residual sugar. Adequate commercial style. Drink '90.

Summary: If Horderns fails to inspire, it is not for the want of effort on the part of all involved, not the least owners Bob and Theo Smith. The marketing is good, and professional winemaking and consultancy services have been retained. Previous problems in the winery have been largely overcome; I suspect the vineyard is the limiting factor at the moment.

❦ *HORSESHOE VINEYARD*

Location: Horseshoe Road, Horseshoe Valley via Denman, 2328; 17 km south of Denman. (065) 47 3528.

Winemaker: John Hordern.

Principal Wines: Shiraz Mouveau, Chardonnay and Semillon.

Distribution: By mailing list and limited fine wine retail distribution serviced direct ex-winery. Cellar door sales by appointment only.

Prices: $11 to $16 mailing list.

Vintage Rating 1986–89: '88, '87, '89, '86.

Tasting Notes:

1989 SEMILLON [CS] Colour: light to medium yellow-green. *Bouquet:* clean, with rather strong and as yet somewhat integrated oak, but there is good underlying fruit. *Palate:* very strong lemony/spicy oak, but there is a vibrant fruit core; on the evidence of prior years, the fruit/oak balance will be very good by the time the wine is back-blended and bottled; should be headed in excess of 75 points.

1989 CHARDONNAY [CS] Colour: light to medium yellow-green. Bouquet: tangy and clean, with a nice touch of grapefruit and some barrel ferment; medium intensity. Palate: crisp, clean and tangy, showing excellent barrel ferment handling; has lots of potential and is certainly destined for 80 plus.

1988 SEMILLON [80] Colour: light to medium yellow-green. Bouquet: rich, full and complex, with very good balance and weight. Palate: lighter than the bouquet suggests, but once again excellent fruit/oak balance; happily, the wine is dry and has a clean, crisp finish. Drink '90–'93.

1988 CHARDONNAY [70] Colour: medium yellow-green. Bouquet: smooth and quite weighty, but lacks the flair of either the glorious '87 Chardonnay or the promising '89. Palate: of medium intensity; dry, but there are very slightly mouldy/green flavours suggesting there may have been some problems in the vineyard. Drink '90–'91.

1988 SHIRAZ NOUVEAU [73] Colour: medium red-purple. Bouquet: strong carbonic maceration/spicy/pie and peas characters in unmistakable style. Palate: soft berry fruits, quite sweet and complex fruit, with a hint of spice. If you like carbonic maceration wines, this is for you. Drink '90.

Summary: The exceptional 1987 Chardonnay reviewed in the 1988 edition has fulfilled all of its promise, and is still drinking beautifully. As the notes attest, John Hordern (who spent many years at Horderns Wybong) has learnt his trade supremely well, and his handling of oak is exceptionally good.

ROSEMOUNT ESTATE

Location: Rosemount Road, Denman, 2328; 8 km west of town.
(065) 47 2410.

Winemaker: Philip Shaw.

1989 Production: Over 400,000 cases

Principal Wines: A wide range of sparkling white and red table wines variously identified by area (Hunter Valley or Coonawarra), vineyard (e.g. Roxburgh), variety (with special emphasis on Oak Matured Chardonnay) and headed in terms of quality by Roxburgh and Show Reserve wines. The principal commercial release is the Diamond Label range comprising Chablis, Chardonnay, Semillon, Fumé Blanc, Rhine Riesling, Traminer Riesling, White Burgundy, Beaujolais, Pinot Noir, Shiraz and Cabernet Sauvignon. Giants Creek is another individual vineyard name to shortly appear in a mid-price range while Cloud Valley Semillon shows that Ray King of Mildara is not the only marketer able to borrow the good ideas of others.

Distribution: Nationally distributed by own sales force.

Prices: $9.50 to $40 retail.

Vintage Rating 1986–89: '87, '86, '89, '88.

Tasting Notes:

1988 DIAMOND LABEL SEMILLON CHARDONNAY [76] Colour: medium to full yellow. Bouquet: soft, clean honeyed and already quite rich, showing bottle development. Palate: clean and smooth slightly honeyed fruit on a mid-palate of light to medium weight; ever so slightly green finish. Drink '90–'91.

1988 SHOW RESERVE CHARDONNAY [85] Colour: medium to full yellow green. Bouquet: quite scented and fragrant, with peachy/grapefruit aromas and good oak integration. Palate: fresh, full ripe and rich peachy/tangy fruit; there are ever so slightly oily/cosmetic characters, possibly from fruit, possibly from oak, which prevent the wine from gaining even higher points. Drink '90–'93.

1987 ROXBURGH CHARDONNAY [90] Colour: glowing yellow green. Bouquet: enormously potent and aromatic, showing strong barrel ferment/charred oak characters, but with abundant fruit to carry that oak. Palate: an extra dimension of fruit intensity and a quite spectacular oak handling; a huge wine in every respect, with 13.5 % alcohol. When it will be at its best is an intensely subjective judgment. Drink '90–'95.

1985 GRANTS GULLY BOTRYTISED SEMILLON [85] Colour: glowing gold. Bouquet: intense, soft, rich butterscotch/honey fruit and light oak. Palate: intense, complex citric/butterscotch/apricot fruit flavours; very good acid; a wine with both length and complexity. Drink '90–'92.

1988 DIAMOND LABEL SHIRAZ [75] Colour: medium purple-red. *Bouquet:* clean, with attractive berry aromas and a faint hint of spicy oak. *Palate:* soft, clean, complex leafy/gamey/berry fruit flavours with soft tannins, and again a faint hint of spice. Drink '90–'92.

1988 DIAMOND LABEL CABERNET SAUVIGNON [74] Colour: medium purple-red. *Bouquet:* clean, full and very ripe berry fruit. *Palate:* again, very ripe fruit flavours are the dominant force; very lush and complex, but I found the wine a fraction too ripe. Drink '91–'94.

Summary: The ability of the Diamond Label series to win gold medals almost at will at national shows is but one indicator of the quality and consistency of all of the wines under the Rosemount label. As one goes up the range, complexity, weight and richness all increase, reaching a veritable crescendo with Roxburgh Chardonnay. As with all tall poppies in Australia, there are inevitably critics and cynics ready to snipe away, but I do not doubt for one moment the integrity or skill of Philip Shaw and the rest of the team.

🍇 *SERENELLA ESTATE*

Location: Mudgee Road, Baerami via Denman, 2333. (065) 47 5126 or (02) 489 7740 Fax (02) 489 7739.

Winemaker: Letitia (Tish) Cecchini.

1989 Production: 6000 cases, increasing to 150,000 cases by 1992.

Principal Wines: Chardonnay, Semillon, Chablis, White Burgundy, Shiraz and Cabernet Sauvignon.

Distribution: Cellar door sales through tasting room, scheduled to open November/December 1989. Limited fine wine retail outlets and mailing list.

Prices: $5.50 to $9.50 cellar door.

Vintage Rating 1986–89: White: '88, '89, '87 ('86 not made). Red: '87, '88, '86. ('89 not yet rated).

Tasting Notes:

1989 SEMILLON [81] Colour: light green-yellow. *Bouquet:* clean and fine herbaceous fruit well balanced by slightly lemony oak. *Palate:* most attractive, with lemony/tangy almost sauvignon blanc-like flavours; has length and bite, yet is not aggressive. Drink '90–'93.

1989 CHARDONNAY [CS] Colour: light straw-green. *Bouquet:* tangy, with some barrel fermentation/other fermentation characters subsisting, but already shows good style. *Palate:* very strong barrel ferment oak characters, and quite high acid; still coming together; if the oak balance is correctly handled, headed for high points.

1988 CHABLIS [70] Colour: medium to full yellow-green. *Bouquet:* clean, soft and toasty, of medium intensity. *Palate:* clean, soft, round vanillan flavours, not at all in chablis style, but a nice wine nonetheless. Drink '90.

1988 CHARDONNAY [79] Colour: medium yellow-green. *Bouquet:* soft, oaky and rather advanced, with just a suspicion of volatility. *Palate:* very advanced and accessible with soft, peachy fruit surrounded by soft oak; the wine is dry on the palate and finishes with good acid. Drink '90.

1988 HERMITAGE [79] Colour: medium red-purple. *Bouquet:* clean, with strong vanilla bean oak. *Palate:* Once again, very pronounced American oak, but there is substantial fruit to carry the oak, and the wine is well structured. Drink '91–'94.

1987 HERMITAGE [74] Colour: medium red-purple. *Bouquet:* sweet berry fruit of medium to full intensity with a slight medicinal/burnt aroma. *Palate:* very ripe red berry fruit, although once again that slightly burnt character is evident. Drink '90–'93.

Summary: Serenella makes a most auspicious debut. It is not surprising that it has already enjoyed substantial show success and also in the 1989 Australian Smallmakers Top 100 Competition. The consistency and quality of the wines can only enhance the overall reputation of the Upper Hunter.

VERONA VINEYARD

Location: New England Highway, Muswellbrook, 2333; on northern outskirts of town. (065) 43 1055. And at McDonalds Road, Pokolbin, 2321. (049) 98 7668.

Winemaker: Keith Yore.

1989 Production: Limited.

Principal Wines: Four white varietal releases: Chardonnay, Traminer, Semillon, Rhine Riesling; top releases under Estate Grown Premium label.

Distribution: Principally cellar door and mailing list. Cellar door sales 10 a.m. to 5 p.m. Monday to Saturday, noon to 5 p.m. Sunday. Mailing list, PO Box 217, Muswellbrook, 2333. Limited distribution through Hunter Valley Wine Society and Australian Wine Club, and limited Melbourne distribution.

Tasting Notes:

1989 TRAMINER [60] Colour: a slight pink tinge is not an auspicious introduction. *Bouquet:* light, lychee spice varietal character, with slight cosmetic overtones. *Palate:* light, quite fresh varietal flavours balanced by pleasant acid. Drink '90.

1988 SHIRAZ [CS] Colour: medium purple-red. *Bouquet:* quite full fruit, but showing slightly roasted fermentation characters. *Palate:* once again, there is ample sweet fruit flavour but those burnt/roasted flavours of the bouquet once again intrude. Tasted before bottling, and it is possible the wine will be cleaned up.

Summary: The operations of Verona continue at a surprisingly low level given the size and location of the Lower Hunter winery, much of which is used as a storage facility by other wineries in the district. Most of the grape production from both Upper and Lower Hunter is likewise sold.

Hilltops Region

1988 VINTAGE

A wet and mild winter and spring (for the second year in a row) set the vines off on a good start. Spring frosts, sometimes a hazard in the district, were all but absent. The summer was very warm, and one of the earliest harvests on record resulted. Flavours overall were good, with the main four varieties (semillon, chardonnay, pinot noir and cabernet sauvignon) all having good varietal character, and the reds the usual great depth of flavour.

1989 VINTAGE

Another good vintage, with a favourable start to the growing season and no frosts to threaten budburst or flowering. The summer rains which caused near-havoc on the coast did not reach inland over the Great Dividing Range, and all grapes were harvested in very good condition.

Semillon was outstanding while the red wines have their customary colour and flavour.

THE CHANGES

The most significant change has been the acquisition of the senior vineyard and winery in the district, Peter Robertson's Barwang, by McWilliams. It is an obvious vote of confidence in the quality and potential of the district, and McWilliams have already embarked on a major planting programme. It would seem that McWilliams' faith was fully justified: two Semillons made from Barwang fruit, one early picked, the other picked at normal maturity, won a silver and gold medal respectively at their first showing at the 1989 Royal Brisbane Show.

There are two new entries to compensate for the loss of Barwang: Jill Lindsay's Woodonga Hill and Paul and Gail Jurrissen's Hopevale Estate. Woodonga Hill is fairly and squarely in the Hilltops region, while the Hopevale Estate winery and home vineyard is (like The College Winery) situated at Wagga Wagga. Like The College, Hopevale also buys grapes from the Hilltops region to supplement its own plantings of chardonnay, cabernet sauvignon, merlot, frontignan and zinfandel. Unlike The College, where Paul Jurrissen works in the wine school, the Hopevale wines are made using a century-old basket grape press recovered from the nearby Brucedale winery which went out of production around the turn of the century.

CARTOBE VINEYARD

Location: Young Road, Boorowa, 2586; 5 km west of township and 3 km from main Cowra Road. (063) 85 3128.

Winemaker: Geoff Carter.

Principal Wines: Hilltops Rhine Riesling, from dry to auslese style, a Hilltops and a Cowra Chardonnay, a Wooded-Semillon, a Cowra Traminer and a Hilltops Cabernet Sauvignon.

Distribution: Principally cellar door and mailing list. Cellar door sales 9 a.m. to 5 p.m. Friday to Monday inclusive, school holidays and public holidays (other days by appointment); mailing list as above. South-east NSW distribution through J. O'Malley & Co. and Queensland through Classic Wine Distributors, plus some district restaurant listings.

Summary: Cartobe is the other senior citizen of the Hilltops region, having been established in 1979. Some very useful wines have been released over the last few years, although quality does seem to be extremely variable. No information or samples available for this edition.

THE COLLEGE

Location: Boorooma Street, North Wagga Wagga, 2650; 9 km north of town via the Olympic Way. (069) 23 2435.

Winemaker: Andrew Birks.

Principal Wines: A wide range of varietal white and red table wines from an equally diverse number of areas, all of which vary from year to year. Labels clearly identify both.

Distribution: Mixture of cellar door, mail order and retail sales; Sydney wholesale distribution through The Incredible Wine Co. Cellar door sales 9 a.m. to 4 p.m. Monday to Friday, Saturday 11 a.m. to 4 p.m. Mailing list, PO Box 588, Wagga Wagga, 2650.

Tasting Notes:

1988 BOORANGA VINEYARD CHARDONNAY [72] Colour: medium full yellow-green. *Bouquet:* clean and quite complex, with vanillan/peachy/pineapple fruit. *Palate:* good strong flavour, albeit a little less complex than the bouquet; particularly generous on the mid-palate, and a touch of lemony/vanillan oak adds further character. Drink '90–'91.

1988 HILLTOPS BOTRYTIS SEMILLON [77] Colour: medium yellow-green. *Bouquet:* pronounced volatility within the confines of the style; rich citric aromas. *Palate:* intense botrytis influence with vanillan/peach/lime flavours and a long finish. Drink '90–'92.

1988 BOORANGA CABERNET SAUVIGNON [CS] Colour: excellent youthful purple-red. *Bouquet:* clean and attractive, spicy nutmeg oak with clean red berry fruit. *Palate:* most attractive, spicy nutmeg oak with crisp red berry fruit; the wine has lovely balance; by far the best College wine for many years and headed towards 85 points or more if safely bottled.

1987 BOORANGA CABERNET SAUVIGNON CABERNET FRANC [70] Colour: medium red. *Bouquet:* lightly sawdusty/leathery oak with pleasant fruit. *Palate:* much better than the bouquet, with fresh fruit showing good berry flavours; the tannins are soft and the acid in good balance. Drink '90–'93.

OLD CASK HALL MUSCAT [75] Colour: light to medium tawny-red. *Bouquet:* fresh and grapy, with very good muscat aroma. *Palate:* generously flavoured; the material is basically young, but shows good varietal character, and is well balanced.

Summary: The College has produced far too many faulty wines in the past, but is aware of the shortcomings and problems. Certainly, there were enough good wines in this tasting to show that things are improving, and future organisational changes should accelerate the rate of change, as well as enhancing consistency.

HERCYNIA

Location: RMB 97 Prunevale Road, Kingsvale, 2587; 13 km south of Young. (063) 84 4243.

Winemaker: Laurie Doldissen.

Principal Wines: Rhine Riesling, Chardonnay, Sauvignon Blanc and Pinot Noir.

Distribution: Exclusively cellar door and mailing list. Mailing list enquiries to RMB 97 Prunevale Road, Kingsvale, 2587.

Summary: Hercynia has some way to go yet before its wines attract more than a local audience; it is clear that white-wine fermentation equipment is rudimentary, and sweetness is no substitute for fruit flavour. Most of the grapes from 1989 were sold to Brindabella Hills, a winery in the Canberra district.

🍇 *HOPEVALE ESTATE WINERY*

Location: RMB 222 Olympic Way, Wagga Wagga, 2650; 8 km north of Wagga Wagga.
(069) 21 2249.

Winemaker: Paul Jurrissen.

1989 Production: 650 cases.

Principal Wines: Chardonnay and Shiraz (sourced from local growers); Pinot Noir, Sauvignon Blanc and Chardonnay (sourced from Hilltops region); and Chardonnay (sourced from Oakvale Estate Vineyards).

Distribution: Cellar door sales only, initially 9 a.m. to 5 p.m. weekends, other times by appointment.

Prices: $7 to $13 cellar door.

Summary: Hopevale Estate had no wines available for tasting, having sold out of its first releases.

🍇 *NIOKA RIDGE*

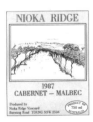

Location: Barwang Road, Young, 2594; 21 km south-east of Young.
(063) 82 2903.

Winemaker: Phil Price.

1989 Production: Not stated.

Principal Wines: Chardonnay, Rhine Riesling, Late Harvest Rhine Riesling, Cabernet Malbec, Cabernet Sauvignon and Vintage Port.

Distribution: Principally cellar door sales 9 a.m. to 5 p.m. 7 days. Limited retail distribution through La Copita, Canberra; mail order through Nioka Ridge Wines, PO Box 813, Young, 2594.

Prices: $7 to $12.50 cellar door; 10% less by the case.

Vintage Rating 1986–89: '87, '86, '89, '88.

Tasting Notes:

1987 CABERNET MERLOT [66] Colour: very good purple-red. *Bouquet:* quite solid, with dark cherry fruits. *Palate:* youthful, yet rather hard and unformed, suggesting it was bottled too early; a faintly leathery finish adds to the hardness. Certainly had potential in the base material, and may yet grow and improve markedly in bottle. Drink '92–'95.

Summary: Phil Price did not go ahead with his sale plans for Nioka Ridge, and continues to produce some of the better wines to come from the district, underlining the quality of the base material.

🍇 *WOODONGA HILL*

Location: Cowra Road, Young, 2594; 10 km north of Young.
(063) 82 2972.

Winemaker: Jill Lindsay.

1989 Production: 600 cases.

Principal Wines: Rhine Riesling, Chardonnay, Soft Shiraz and Cabernet Sauvignon.

Distribution: Almost exclusively cellar door sales 9 a.m. to 5 p.m. 7 days.

Prices: $8 to $14 cellar door.

Vintage Rating 1986–89: '87, '89, '86, '88.

Summary: Unfortunately the three wines tasted from Woodonga Hill were flawed by sulphide. As the vines are gaining maturity, it is to be hoped that this fairly simple winemaking fault can be eliminated, as one can only assume that the potential is there to make good quality wines.

Mudgee

1988 VINTAGE

The early part of the growing season was marked by severe frosts in October which caused much damage to the early varieties in some vineyards. Mudgee is a large area with diverse topography, and some sites are much better protected against frost than others. Initial reaction was one of horror, but very good growing conditions and, in particular, good rains throughout the season did much to restore crop levels. This type of situation occurs quite frequently in France and is one reason why vignerons are always reluctant to assess the ultimate effects of frost damage early in the growing year.

Vintage commenced on schedule in good conditions and some excellent white wines were harvested. Chardonnay, in particular, stood out. The reds are lighter than usual, but do have good balance.

1989 VINTAGE

The season started off in fine style, with ample winter spring rains promoting good budburst and flowering. The frosts which caused damage to the 1988 vintage did not reappear, and conditions remained very favourable until the end of the year.

From this point on the weather turned hot and dry, with extreme heat in mid-January leading to severe leaf burn and defoliation in some vineyards. Rain fell on the first day of vintage, and again on the last (and then continued right through autumn and winter). Those vineyards with supplementary irrigation did not suffer, but the dry land vineyards did inevitably stress quite badly.

Despite the dry conditions, yields overall were above average. On balance, it was a white wine rather than a red wine vintage, with fleshy, full-flavoured semillon and chardonnay. The red wines are soft, with shiraz the pick of the crop.

THE CHANGES

By far the most important change has been the acquisition of the Montrose/Craigmoor/Amberton group of wineries by Wyndham Estate. The logic of the purchase is plain for all to see: Wyndham had long been a major purchaser of grapes in the district, and both through its viticultural trusts and otherwise has embarked on a structured programme of diversifying its fruit sources. In the wake of the acquisition, long-term winemaker and wonderful district identities Carlo and Francesca Corino have departed to their native Italy (or, to be more precise, to Sicily, where Carlo becomes production manager of a very large winery). Wyndham will, however, keep the brands very much alive, consistent with its overall marketing policy.

The new entries are Lowe Family, Seldom Seen, Settlers Creek and Paul Tuminello. The origins of Settlers Creek go back to 1971, when a syndicate of eight, headed by Sydney radiologist Dr Ray Healey, commenced planting a large vineyard. Since that time Settlers Creek has basically been a grape-growing operation, with wines being intermittently made under contract (basically when grape prices were too low) and sold in bulk.

The syndicate has changed substantially over the intervening 17 years, now comprising Ray Healey, Graham Stanford, Max Farr-Jones and Graeme Herring. Stanford and Herring are leading chartered accountants, while Max Farr-Jones' best claim to fame is as father of the captain of the Australian Rugby Union team, Nick Farr-Jones. In 1982 the syndicate purchased one of the Augustine vineyard blocks, and in 1988 acquired the remaining land, including the winery and restaurant complex. In the outcome, modest quantities of both Augustine and Settlers Creek wines will now be sold, chiefly through the Augustine cellar door.

The Lowe Family label is the result of a joint venture between Rothbury winemaker David Lowe and his parents, who are graziers in the district, and who planted chardonnay on their property in the early 1980s. Production started with the '87 vintage. Seldom Seen, while a new label, is a vineyard which has been in existence for a considerable time. When workers were sent to attend the vineyard, they were seldom seen, as it is tucked away behind a line of hills. There is a cellar door operation only at this time; the wines are made by Barry Platt under contract.

Paul Tuminello has been consulting and making wine in the district for well over a decade, having taken a lead role in the early development of Burnbrae. He still has a peripatetic life, the wines being sold not by Paul Tuminello but by Erudgere and through Oddbins Wine Retailers in Sydney.

The other changes are the disappearance of Bramhall and Hill of Gold, both of which have ceased operations. The Hill of Gold vineyards continue in existence, but the winery and label have been closed down following the sale foreshadowed in the 1988 edition of this book.

Overall wine quality is nowhere near as good as it should be. The small wineries in particular have great difficulty in producing white wines which I would class as commercially acceptable. The red wines are very much better: first, the climate of the district is best suited to such wines; and second, reds are far easier to handle in a small winery context.

Needless to say, there are exceptions: Mirramar has produced some excellent chardonnay and good semillon over the years, as has Dave Robertson at Thistle Hill. But overall, the Amberton/ Craigmoor/Montrose triumvirate has had a mortgage on white wine quality, and continued to do so in the district tasting for this edition.

There is much more competition with the red wines: here Huntington Estate takes the lead, benefiting from the very large stocks of older vintage wines it has on offer at any one time. Good though the district's red wines are overall, they could and should be better still.

🍇 AMBERTON

Location: Lowe's Peak Vineyard, Henry Lawson Drive, Mudgee, 2850; 8 km north of township (2 km past Lawson memorial). (063) 73 3910.

Winemaker: Robert Paul.

1989 Production: 20,000 cases.

Principal Wines: Varietal white and red table wines; labels include Semillon, Sauvignon Blanc, Traminer, Chardonnay, Shiraz and Cabernet Sauvignon.

Distribution: Exclusively through American Express Cellarmasters and cellar door.

Prices: $13.50 to $16.50 cellar door.

Vintage Rating 1986–89: '89, '88, '87, '86.

Outstanding Prior Vintages: '82.

Tasting Notes:

1986 SEMILLON [71] Colour: full yellow. *Bouquet:* clean, developed toasty fruit, but starting to drop in intensity. *Palate:* attractive, honeyed/butter fruit at the point of entry to the mouth, but the mid- and back-palate are tending to dip in flavour. A wine which has seen better days. Drink '90.

1986 CABERNET SAUVIGNON [68] Colour: light to medium purple-red, holding its hue well. *Bouquet:* light, rubber raincoat nuances over sweet berry fruit. *Palate:* very pleasant, sweet berry fruit spoilt by that rubber raincoat character, which undoubtedly derives from mercaptan. When first tasted several years ago, I thought the bitterness could have been oak derived, but it is not. Drink '90–'92.

Summary: Wyndham has completely revised and upgraded the Amberton packaging with extremely stylish labels. The wines themselves are those inherited, and it remains to be seen if there will be style changes in the future.

🍇 AUGUSTINE

Location: Airport Road, Mudgee, 2850; 7 km north-east of township. (063) 72 3880.

Winemaker: Various contract makers, all situated outside the Mudgee region.

1989 Production: 1500 cases.

Principal Wines: Chablis, Trebbiano Semillon, Moselle, Chardonnay, Pinot Noir, Cabernet Shiraz and Cabernet Port.

Distribution: Exclusively cellar door sales and mailing list. Cellar door sales 10 a.m. to 4 p.m. 7 days.

Prices: $5 to $10 cellar door.

Tasting Notes:

1989 TRAMINER [65] Colour: medium yellow-green. *Bouquet:* light, spicy varietal character with fairly high free SO_2 evident mid-1989, but which should dissipate by 1990. *Palate:* soft, commercial spicy fruit salad flavours, with considerable residual sugar; a bland, cellar door special. Drink '90.

1989 CHARDONNAY [CS] Colour: medium to full yellow-green. *Bouquet:* very good melon/peach fruit of considerable weight and varietal style. *Palate:* soft, peachy/honey/melon fruit, quite tangy, and with very good oak handling; dry and well balanced. Should rate at least 85. (The notes are an amalgam of the tasting of two bottles, one barrel fermented, the other tank fermented. Both samples were of excellent character.)

1988 CHARDONNAY [70] Colour: medium yellow. *Bouquet:* clean fruit of light to medium intensity, and pronounced bottle-developed toasty oak characters. *Palate:* spicy/clove oak has tended to break-up somewhat prematurely; the fruit, too, is soft, and one wonders whether the wine suffered a minor misfortune during bottling. Drink '90.

Summary: The restaurant at Augustine is strongly recommended, being run by ex-Anders Ousbach employee Peter O'Kelly. With totally professional contract winemaking now in place for Augustine, and with very mature vineyards to draw on, not to mention the vast experience of fine-wine lover Ray Healey, the future looks good.

BOTOBOLAR

Location: Botobolar Lane, Mudgee, 2850; 16 km
    north-east of town.
    (063) 73 3840.

Winemaker: Gil Wahlquist.

1989 Production: 4000 cases.

Principal Wines: A diverse range of labels and
    styles, including Crouchen, Marsanne, Budgee
    Budgee, Chardonnay, Shiraz, St Gilbert,
    Cabernet Sauvignon and Cooyal Port.

Distribution: Almost exclusively cellar door and
    mailing list. (Isolated retail distribution
    including Oak Barrel, Sydney.) The mailing
    newsletter, *Botobolar Bugle,* is an excellent
    publication. UK imports through Vintage
    Roots, Reading, Berkshire.

Prices: $4.50 to $9.90 cellar door.

Vintage Rating 1986–89: '86, '88, '87, '89.

Outstanding Prior Vintages: '76, '80.

Tasting Notes:

1989 CHARDONNAY [55] Colour: light pinkish/
    brown. *Bouquet:* light and plain, slightly oxidised
    fruit with rather cosmetic oak. *Palate:* plain, oily
    and cosmetic with quite pronounced vanilla
    bean American oak, which is simply not suited to
    chardonnay at the best of times. Drink '90.

1988 BUDGEE BUDGEE [59] Colour: light straw-
    yellow. *Bouquet:* extraordinarily muted, given
    the aromatic qualities of the base wine. *Palate:*
    full, soft, sweet fruit salad cellar door style; the
    quite luscious fruit flavours only make the
    absence of bouquet more surprising. Drink '90.

1988 NEW SHIRAZ [60] Colour: very light red.
    Bouquet: extremely light, leafy/cherry fruit, not
    totally clean. *Palate:* light to the point of rose
    weight, with fresh fruit on the fore-palate, but a
    faintly bitter finish. Drink '90.

1986 SHIRAZ [80] Colour: medium red. *Bouquet:*
    soft, clean and gently velvety showing very good

bottle development. *Palate:* attractive, soft, clean
fruity shiraz flavours with negligible oak impact;
light bodied, but has really lovely flavour. Drink
'90–'93.

1986 CABERNET SAUVIGNON [74] Colour: red-
brown. *Bouquet:* soft, aged, velvety and shiraz-
like. *Palate:* soft, roasted/velvety/dark chocolate
flavours, again shiraz-like, but a nice, gentle, old-
fashioned wine which has acquired some grace
with age. Drink '90.

Summary: Gil Wahlquist's love of Mudgee shines
through in everything he does, but in many
ways his velvety reds are the district's best
advertisement.

BURNBRAE

Location: The Hargraves Road, Erudgere via
    Mudgee, 2850; 10 km south-west of Mudgee.
    (063) 73 3504.

Winemakers: Robert B. Mace and Ian MacRae
    (chardonnay).

1989 Production: 2000 cases.

Principal Wines: Semillon Chardonnay,
    Chardonnay, Semillon, Grenache Rosé,
    Cabernet Sauvignon, Shiraz, Shiraz Cabernet
    Sauvignon Malbec, Pinot Noir, Vintage Port
    and Liqueur Muscat.

Distribution: Virtually exclusively cellar door sales
    and mailing list. Cellar door sales 9.30 a.m. to
    5 p.m. 7 days.

Prices: $7 to $12.50 cellar door.

Vintage Rating 1986–89: White: '88, '89 ('86 and
    '87 not rated). Red: '89, '87, '88, '86.

Outstanding Prior Vintages: White: '84. Red: '79,
    '82, '84, '85.

Tasting Notes:

1988 SEMILLON [62] Colour: medium yellow-
    green. *Bouquet:* slightly burnt/medicinal

nuances with fair fruit underneath. *Palate:* soft; light to medium weight honeyed fruit, again showing some burnt caramel flavours. Drink '90.

1989 SHIRAZ CABERNET MALBEC [CS] Colour: medium purple-red. *Bouquet:* soft and complex with sweet, clean berry fruit with a hint of cassis and already complex. *Palate:* full and quite remarkably developed wine already showing style and balance; so precocious it is difficult to know where it is headed.

1988 SHIRAZ [71] Colour: medium to full red-purple. *Bouquet:* clean fruit of light to medium intensity, with soft, lemony oak. *Palate:* pronounced lemony/melon oak, bordering on the aggressive and tends to sit on top of fruit; the wine is at least clean and does have some style. Drink '90–'92.

1987 SHIRAZ CABERNET MALBEC [75] Colour: medium purple-red. *Bouquet:* spotlessly clean, high-toned red berry/plum fruit with light oak. *Palate:* rich, sweet dark berry/dark chocolate flavours on the fore- and mid-palate; does tail away slightly with a fractionally bitter finish. Drink '91–'94.

1987/88 VINTAGE PORT [75] Colour: developed medium red. *Bouquet:* soft, spicy fruit and oak; a wine moving through ruby to tawny port style. *Palate:* quite intense, wood-aged sweet red with plenty of body and flavour; neither fish nor fowl, but if left in oak could develop as an outstanding tawny port. As it is in bottle, a wine to puzzle the purists and please the public. Drink '90–'93.

Summary: The wines of Burnbrae are like the curate's egg: very good in parts. Owners Robert and Pamela Mace are a charming couple, and will always welcome you at the cellar door. A visit is strongly recommended on the basis that you taste before you buy.

CALOOLA

Location: Henry Lawson Drive, Mudgee, 2850; 11 km north of town.
(063) 73 3954.

Winemakers: Hilton, Phillip and Noel Cross.

Principal Wines: Semillon, Burgundy (Shiraz), Claret (Cabernet Shiraz), Tawny Port, Gordo Muscat, Rummy Port and Liqueur Muscat.

Distribution: Exclusively cellar door sales and mailing list. Cellar door sales Saturday 10 a.m. to 5 p.m. and Sunday 11 a.m. to 4 p.m.; Monday, public holidays 10 a.m. to 5 p.m. Mailing list enquiries to Caloola Wines, 29 Burrundulla Avenue, Mudgee, 2850.

Summary: A very small and as yet rather primitive winery specialising in fortified wines of overall modest quality.

CRAIGMOOR

Location: Craigmoor Road, Mudgee, 2850; 5 km north of town.
(063) 72 2208.

Winemaker: Robert Paul.

1989 Production: 15,000 cases.

Principal Wines: Chablis, Semillon Chardonnay, Chardonnay, Semillon, Spatlese Rhine Riesling, Late-Picked Semillon, Shiraz, Cabernet Shiraz, Cabernet Sauvignon, Liqueur Muscat and Port.

Distribution: National wholesale distribution exclusively through Australian Vintners.

Prices: $7.75 to $9.90 retail.

Vintage Rating 1986–89: '89, '87, '88, '86.

Outstanding Prior Vintages: '83.

Tasting Notes:

1989 CHARDONNAY [CS] Colour: light to medium green-yellow. *Bouquet:* initially rather dull and light, but evolved in the glass to show clean, melon peach fruit. *Palate:* attractive medium-weight melon/citric fruit flavours with well handled and balanced oak; showing promise of points in the high 70's.

1988 SEMILLON CHARDONNAY [63] Colour: bright yellow-green of medium depth. *Bouquet:* clean, smooth honey/butter fruit aromas, light and unoaked. *Palate:* clean, but very light indeed, with neutral fruit; may develop slightly more weight and style, as it certainly has freshness on its side. Drink '90.

1988 CHARDONNAY [81] Colour: medium yellow-green. *Bouquet:* very clean and smooth, with melon/grapefruit aromas of medium intensity. *Palate:* clean and very well made; there is good fruit/oak balance and integration, and pleasant slightly citric fruit flavours; a fractionally hard finish will soften with a little more bottle age. Drink '90–'91.

1987 CABERNET SAUVIGNON [70] Colour: medium to full red. *Bouquet:* soft, clean and slightly simple sweet cherry/berry fruit, with light oak. *Palate:* clean, light squashy berry fruit in a style reminiscent of Coonawarra; low tannin. Drink '90–'92.

Summary: The most historic winery in Mudgee, and one of Australia's oldest. All of the wines reviewed were in fact made by Carlo Corino prior to his departure, but there is no reason to suppose that the technical excellence will not continue.

ERUDGERE VINEYARDS

Location: Hargraves/Hill End Road, Erudgere via Mudgee, 2850; 9 km north-west of Mudgee. (063) 72 1118.

Winemakers: Ian MacRae and David Robertson (white wines); Paul Tuminello (red wines).

1989 Production: Approximately 250 cases Rhine Riesling; remainder of grapes sold.

Principal Wines: Two white wines currently on sale, 1989 Varietal Blend, 1989 Rhine Riesling, together with three red wines, covering a span of vintages and being made variously from shiraz, cabernet sauvignon and a blend of cabernet and shiraz.

Distribution: Exclusively cellar door sales and mailing list. Cellar door sales 2 p.m. to 5.30 p.m. weekdays and 10 a.m. to 5 p.m. weekends and public holidays. Mailing list enquiries to 3 Meroo Crescent, Mudgee, 2850.

Prices: $8 to $13 cellar door single bottle, discount for dozens.

Outstanding Prior Vintages: White: '82, '84. Red: '80, '82, '83, '84.

Tasting Notes:

1986 SHIRAZ [80] Colour: medium red-purple, retaining hue well. *Bouquet:* clean, with a touch of mint, and good fruit/oak integration; medium to full intensity. *Palate:* pleasant, sweet red berry fruit flavours and light tannin; the balance and flavour are very good, and the wine is aging well. Drink '90–'93.

1986 CABERNET SAUVIGNON [76] Colour: medium purple-red. *Bouquet:* clean, with quite firm red berry fruit and very slightly dusty oak. *Palate:* firm, clean dark berry fruit, again showing a touch of dusty oak; the wine dips slightly on the back-palate before finishing with soft tannins. Drink '90–'94.

1984 SHIRAZ CABERNET [78] Colour: light to medium red. *Bouquet:* fragrant developed earthy, gently leathery aromas, like a fine old Hunter. *Palate:* similar fragrant earth/velvety fruit flavours in a traditional style but one which makes for easy drinking. Drink '90.

Summary: Erudgere is a very low key operation, but one which benefits from some of the finest vineyards in the region. My high regard for the red wines should be obvious, and the value for money which they constitute no less so. Well worth the effort.

HUNTINGTON ESTATE

Location: Cassilis Road, Mudgee, 2850; 10 km north-east of town. (063) 73 3825.

Winemaker: Bob Roberts.

1989 Production: 12,000 cases.

Principal Wines: White table wine labels include Semillon, Chardonnay, Sweet White Blend. Light reds include Pinot Noir, Dry Rosé and Rosé Medium Dry. Red table wines labelled by variety and progressively changing Bin Number with FB (full-bodied) or MB (medium-bodied) prefix; they include Shiraz, Shiraz Cabernet Sauvignon, Cabernet Sauvignon and Cabernet Merlot.

Distribution: Largely by cellar door sales and regular mailing list. Cellar door sales 9 a.m. to 5 p.m. Monday to Saturday, Sunday 10 a.m. to 5 p.m. Mailing list, PO Box 188, Mudgee, 2850.

Prices: $7.50 to $10 per bottle cellar door, less a case discount of around 15%.

Vintage Rating 1986–89: Red: '86, '88, '87, '89.

Outstanding Prior Vintages: White: '79, '82, '85. Red: '74, '79, '81, '84, '83.

Tasting Notes:

1989 SEMILLON [TS] Colour: excellent light green-yellow. *Bouquet:* light, crisp herbaceous varietal character with a few fermentation characters still lingering. *Palate:* light to medium weight; clean, pleasant accented slightly herbaceous semillon varietal character; may not challenge the wonderful '79 Semillon, but does appear to be the best for a number of years. Will probably rate in the mid-70's, possibly higher.

1989 PINOT NOIR DRY ROSE [70] Colour: light pink. *Bouquet:* light, clean, very pleasant cherry fruit. *Palate:* crisp, clean, dry rosé, very well made; an intelligent use of the variety which, conventionally handled, makes very ordinary wine in the district. Drink '90.

1986 SHIRAZ BIN FB 10 [79] Colour: medium full red-purple. *Bouquet:* full, soft and clean with dark berry fruits with a hint of dark chocolate. *Palate:* full; quite high-toned dark berry fruit flavours, with soft, gentle tannins and a lingering finish. Drink '90–'95.

1986 CABERNET SAUVIGNON BIN FB 11 [72] Colour: medium to full red, with a touch of purple remaining. *Bouquet:* quite complex, with strong gamey characters intruding on fruit. *Palate:* a complex wine with masses of flavour; soft, ripe berry fruit touched by distinct characters of the farmyard. Drink '90–'93.

1983 CABERNET SAUVIGNON (RESERVE) [83] Colour: medium red. *Bouquet:* smooth, cedary and elegant; of light to medium intensity, showing pronounced regional character, but

graceful. *Palate:* just as the bouquet promises, a very graceful wine with soft leathery/velvety feel and flavour; the tannins are quite persistent, but are well controlled. Drink '90–'96.

1981 CABERNET SAUVIGNON (RESERVE) [90] Colour: dark brick-red. *Bouquet:* ripe, rich and firm complex red berry fruits with a touch of mint. *Palate:* a deeply flavoured and structured wine with flavours of mint and red berry; strong tannins. An enormously long lived style. Drink '90–'97.

Summary: Huntington Estate wins the Most Successful Exhibitor Trophy at the Mudgee Show with monotonous regularity, reflecting not only the consistently high quality but the amazing range of wines held in stock, with the red wines on offer in the second part of 1989 coming principally from the '85 and '86 vintages. The wines' prices are as modest as their quality is high.

LOWE FAMILY

Location: Ashbourne Vineyard, Tinja Lane, Mudgee, 2850; (vineyard only).

Winemaker: David Lowe.

1989 Production: 500 cases.

Principal Wines: One wine only made, Chardonnay.

Distribution: Exclusively through Pokolbin Estate in the Lower Hunter Valley and through Pokolbin Estate's wholesale arm, Efficiency Displays Marketing.

Prices: $12.50 recommended retail.

Tasting Notes:

1987 CHARDONNAY [75] Colour: full yellow. *Bouquet:* strong, bottle-developed secondary characters with a distinct Burgundian/cabbagey edge. *Palate:* very full, round and complex flavour with fairly high alcohol evident; does not hold out the promise of improving in bottle. Drink '90.

Summary: David Lowe, the Rothbury winemaker, has vast experience in handling chardonnay, and one can only assume the quality of future wines will be good. The '88 did seem to suffer from bottle variation, with some mouldy/corky bottles. That, however, is something which is almost entirely outside the control of even the most skilled winemaker.

MANSFIELD WINES

Location: Eurunderee Lane, Mudgee, 2850; 7 km north of town.
(063) 73 3871.

Winemaker: Peter Mansfield.

1989 Production: Limited output from Mudgee fruit; balance purchased from other makers in other areas.

Principal Wines: A limited range of table wines comprising Riesling, Gold Gully (Traminer Riesling), Sparkling Muscat, Moselle and Our Entertainer; only the Riesling claims Mudgee on the label.

Distribution: Exclusively cellar door sales 9 a.m. to 6 p.m. Monday to Saturday, 11 a.m. to 6 p.m. Sunday.

Summary: A commercial enterprise which makes relatively little of the wine sold at cellar door, most being purchased elsewhere.

MIRAMAR

Location: Henry Lawson Drive, Mudgee, 2850; 12 km north of town.
(063) 73 3874.

Winemaker: Ian MacRae.

1989 Production: 9000 cases.

Principal Wines: Selected range of white and red table wines and an occasional vintage port. Labels include Semillon, Semillon Chardonnay, Chardonnay, Sauvignon Blanc, Fumé Blanc, Doux Blanc, Traminer Rhine Riesling, Rhine Riesling, Rosé, Pinot Noir, Shiraz, Cabernet Sauvignon and Vintage Port.

Distribution: Principally cellar door and mailing list. Cellar door sales 9 a.m. to 5 p.m. 7 days. Mailing list as above. Limited NSW retail and restaurant distribution.

Prices: $7 to $15 cellar door.

Vintage Rating 1986–89: White: '88, '87, '86, '89. Red: '86, '88, '89, '87.

Outstanding Prior Vintages: White: '79, '84. Red: '78, '84, '85.

Tasting Notes:

1989 FUME BLANC [CS] Colour: light yellow-green. *Bouquet:* light, fruit salad/ gooseberry fruit aromas with some fermentation characters lingering. *Palate:* tropical fruit salad flavours, with a totally inappropriate amount of residual sugar, a feature which marked almost all of the 1989 nominally dry Miramar white wines.

1989 DOUX BLANC [74] Colour: some onionskin tinges. *Bouquet:* intense, perfumed fruit salad/pineapple fruit. *Palate:* quite attractive, full blown dessert sweet wine with tinned tropical/ fruit salad/passionfruit flavours. Striking if unusual. Drink '90–'91.

1988 CHARDONNAY [70] Colour: medium yellow-green. *Bouquet:* typically high-toned, lifted tangy style which has always been Miramar's forte. *Palate:* again, high-toned, barrel ferment citric/fruit pastille flavours; possibly still showing some yeast influence, and varietal fruit may express itself better in a year or so. Drink '90–'92.

1989 ROSE [73] Colour: very good light crimson. *Bouquet:* clean, firm pleasant, slightly herbaceous fruit. *Palate:* quite intense cherry fruit flavours which are light in body despite the intensity of flavour; good rosé. Drink '90.

1988 ROSE [70] Colour: light pink. *Bouquet:* clean, light and smooth, with light fresh fruit which is not particularly aromatic. *Palate:* light, soft and clean, vaguely in the Tavel style; a hint of sweetness; well made commercial rosé. Drink '90.

1988 SHIRAZ [75] Colour: medium purple-red. *Bouquet:* clean, fresh red berry fruit and light oak. *Palate:* again, spotlessly clean with fresh red berry fruit of light to medium weight; a thoroughly modern wine, not at all in traditional district style. Drink '90–'93.

Summary: Ian MacRae is a winemaker of enormous ingenuity who makes substantial quantities of wine both for himself and as a consultant for other wineries in the district, all in a winery which might charitably be described as cramped; the ingenuity (and a great deal of experience) produces white and red wines which are seldom less than good and which can be quite outstanding.

🍇 MONTROSE

Location: Henry Lawson Drive, Mudgee, 2850; 8 km north of town.
(063) 73 3853.

Winemaker: Robert Paul.

1989 Production: 50,000 cases.

Principal Wines: Sparkling styles, white and red varietal table wines including Semillon, Chardonnay, Auslese Rhine Riesling, Sauvignon Blanc, Sauternes, Shiraz, Cabernet Sauvignon and Pinot Noir.

Distribution: Extensive retail distribution by Wyndham Estate in all States except Vic. (Alexander & Patterson) and SA (Richard Mackay). UK imports through Derek Hale.

Prices: $6.75 to $18 retail.

Vintage Rating 1986–89: '89, '86, '88, '87.

Outstanding Prior Vintages: '80.

Tasting Notes:

1988 CHARDONNAY *[75]* *Colour:* bright, light green-yellow. *Bouquet:* pleasant, clean and soft peachy/melon fruit of light to medium intensity, with light oak in support. *Palate:* very light but pleasant soft peachy fruit and perfectly judged oak. Drink '90–'91.

1988 BOTRYTIS SEMILLON [87] *Colour:* medium-full yellow. *Bouquet:* clean, very complex lemony fruit, with little or no oak evident. *Palate:* most attractive, tangy/lemony/citric flavours, crisp and lingering; an unusual but seductive wine. Drink '90–'92.

1987 SHIRAZ [75] *Colour:* medium red-purple. *Bouquet:* one of those wines in which it is difficult to tell whether the aroma is showing spicy characters or is slightly sulphidic; the palate demonstrates that it is in fact simply varietal spice. *Palate:* lively, spicy fruit showing good varietal character and freshness; pleasant soft tannins on the finish. Drink '92–'95.

1987 CABERNET MERLOT [70] *Colour:* youthful, light purple-red. *Bouquet:* again, a somewhat schizophrenic bouquet, initially rather leathery and dull, but then opening up to show red berry fruit. *Palate:* attractive red berry fruits of light to medium weight, showing none of the bitterness the bouquet suggests may be there; the main problem with the wine is that it is excessively callow and really needed more work before it was put in bottle. Drink '90–'94.

1985 CABERNET SAUVIGNON [74] *Colour:* excellent purple-red, holding hue and depth remarkably well. *Bouquet:* solid, dark berries with a hint of dark chocolate and fairly plain oak. *Palate:* rich, deep dark red berry fruit; yet again there is a faint echo of bitterness which seems to toughen up what was so nearly an outstanding wine. Drink '90–'93.

Summary: Montrose is by far the largest winery in the district, effectively making the wine not only for its own label but also for that of Amberton and Craigmoor. Logic says that the integrity of the labels should be preserved, and I have every confidence that logic will prevail.

🍇 MOUNT ILFORD

Location: Mount Vincent Road, Ilford, 2850; off Mudgee Road (signposted).
(063) 58 8544.

Winemaker: Don Cumming.

Principal Wines: Rhine Riesling, Traminer, Sylvaner, Chardonnay, Pinot Noir, Shiraz, Cabernet Sauvignon and Port.

Distribution: Exclusively cellar door and mailing list; mailing list enquiries as above. Cellar door sales 10 a.m. to 4 p.m. 7 days.

Prices: $6 to $10.

Summary: Off the beaten track and nothing known about the quality of its wines.

MOUNT VINCENT MEADERY

Location: Common Road, Mudgee, 2850; 4 km west of town.
(063) 72 3184.

Winemaker/Mead maker: Jane Nevell.

1989 Production: 1500 cases.

Principal Wines: A range of meads and metheglin are the principal attractions, although limited quantities of wine are made, including Rhine Riesling, Cabernet Sauvignon and Muscat.

Distribution: Exclusively cellar door sales and mailing list. Cellar door sales Monday to Friday 10 a.m. to 5 p.m., Sunday and holidays 10 a.m. to 4 p.m.

Prices: $9.90 to $25.80.

Tasting Notes:

YELLOW BOX MEAD [65] *Colour:* medium yellow-green. *Bouquet:* strong, clearly articulated honeycomb aroma. *Palate:* pleasant, tangy honeycomb flavours, slightly sweet; a lingering aftertaste brings an echo of pure honey which is quite fascinating.

Summary: The Mount Vincent Meads are of very high quality (much more so than the fairly ordinary wines on offer) and the beautifully situated meadery is very much worth the visit.

MUDGEE WINES

Location: Henry Lawson Drive, Mudgee, 2850; 5 km north of town.
(063) 72 2258.

Winemaker: Jennifer Meek.

1989 Production: Approximately 560 cases.

Principal Wines: Premium varietal releases headed by Pinot Noir, Chardonnay and Cabernet Sauvignon; also Trebbiano, Traminer, Rhine Riesling and Muscat.

Distribution: Cellar door sales 9 a.m. to 5 p.m. Monday to Saturday, noon to 4 p.m. Sunday.

Prices: $6 to $11 cellar door.

Vintage Rating 1987-89: White: '89, '88 ('87 not rated). Red: '87, '89, '88.

Summary: Mudgee Wines, like Botobolar, is an organic vineyard employing no pesticides but relying on the balance of nature. Winemaking is appropriately rustic, using a 100-year-old press and a lot of help from Jennifer Meek's friends.

PAUL TUMINELLO

Location: Care Erudgere Vineyards, Hargraves/Hill End Road, Erudgere via Mudgee, 2850; 9 km west-south-west of Mudgee.

Winemaker: Paul Tuminello.

Principal Wines: A red wine specialist using grapes grown partly on the Erudgere Vineyard and partly on the original Jack Roth Vineyard. Wines offered include Shiraz, Cabernet Shiraz, Cabernet Sauvignon and Vintage Port.

Distribution: Through Erudgere and retail through Oddbins, Sydney.

Prices: $10 to $12.

Tasting Notes:

1986 SHIRAZ [65] *Colour:* medium red. *Bouquet:* soft rather light fruit with slightly gamey/leathery characters. *Palate:* a little plain, with soft, slightly squashy/ gamey fruit, but given some validity and charm by bottle age. Drink '90.

1986 CABERNET SAUVIGNON [78] *Colour:* medium purple-red. *Bouquet:* pleasant, fairly ripe red berry fruit which could have been exhilarating with a touch of new oak. *Palate:* smooth, clean dark cherry/dark berry fruit, with good weight and developing a velvety texture in bottle. Very high quality material which could have been brilliant with better oak. Drink '90–'94.

1986 SHIRAZ PORT [65] *Colour:* dense purple-red. *Bouquet:* tending to over-extraction with dense, dark chocolate fruit aromas and soft spirit. *Palate:* an immense, very sweet, chocolatey port in old-fashioned Australian style. Drink '90–'94.

Summary: Supremely honest and flavoursome reds which are traditional both by the standards of Mudgee and by Australia as a whole.

 PIETER VAN GENT

Location: Black Springs Road, Mudgee, 2850; 9 km north-east of town.
(063) 73 3807.

Winemaker: Pieter Van Gent.

Principal Wines: Limited range with special interest in chardonnay and fortified wines. Labels offer Chardonnay, Dry Frontignan, Shiraz, Angelic White, Pipeclay Port, Pipeclay Muscat and Pipeclay Vermouth.

Distribution: Virtually exclusively cellar door and mailing list; some exports. Cellar door sales 10 a.m. to 5 p.m. Monday to Saturday, noon to 4 p.m. Sunday. Mailing list enquiries Box 222, Mudgee, 2850.

Summary: Pieter Van Gent prefers neither to exhibit his wines nor to answer impertinent questions from authors and journalists.

PLATT'S

Location: Mudgee Road, Gulgong, 2852; 5 km from Gulgong, 20 km from Mudgee.
(063) 74 1700.

Winemaker: Barry Platt.

1989 Production: 4000 cases.

Principal Wines: Will eventually concentrate on Chardonnay and Sauvignon Blanc. Current releases offer '88 Mudgee Chardonnay, '89

Mudgee Semillon and '87 Mudgee Cabernet Sauvignon.

Distribution: Present limited production sold exclusively by cellar door sales, mailing list and some Sydney retail outlets. Cellar door sales 9 a.m. to 5 p.m. 7 days. Mailing list enquiries to Box 200, Gulgong, 2852.

Prices: $10 to $12 cellar door.

Tasting Notes:

1988 CHARDONNAY [61] Colour: medium straw-yellow. *Bouquet:* fairly hard with some rather ordinary vanillan oak and a hint of volatility. *Palate:* again, suffers from ordinary vanillan/dusty American oak which does not give the fairly light fruit much of a chance to express itself. Drink '90–'91.

1987 CABERNET SAUVIGNON [54] Colour: medium red-purple. *Bouquet:* quite clean, with some leafy/berry fruit and a distinct rough-sawn oak edge with a touch of volatility. *Palate:* almost impossible to assess, with some aldehydic characters and rather fizzy/jumpy finish; gave all the indications that it had only recently been bottled and could conceivably settle down. Drink '91–'92.

Summary: The vineyard and winery are somewhat isolated from the main centre of activity, but worth a visit. Barry Platt has great experience and has strong technical qualifications, having graduated from Geisenhein in Germany. Wine quality has been very disappointing; as on previous occasions, it seems to me that poor oak is at the heart of the trouble.

 SELDOM SEEN VINEYARD

Location: Craigmoor Road, Mudgee, 2850.
(063) 72 4482; Fax (063) 72 1055.

Winemaker: Barry Platt (contract).

1989 Production: 1050 cases.

Principal Wines: Semillon, Chardonnay Semillon, Chardonnay and Cabernet Shiraz.

Distribution: Exclusively cellar door; cellar door sales 9 a.m. to 5 pm. 7 days.

Prices: $8 to $12.

Tasting Notes:

1987 CHARDONNAY [67] Colour: medium straw-yellow. *Bouquet:* light to medium intensity, with quite pronounced oak and some bottle development. *Palate:* pleasant, soft honeyed flavours with some lemony oak, and a touch of sweetness. Drink '90 .

1987 CHARDONNAY [72] Colour: medium yellow-green. *Bouquet:* clean, attractive lemony oak, well integrated; has style. *Palate:* pleasant, soft developed wine of light to medium weight; the same touch of lemony oak evident in the bouquet, with a soft finish fleshed out by a touch of residual sugar. Drink '90.

1987 CABERNET SHIRAZ [73] Colour: medium red-purple, holding hue well. *Bouquet:* pronounced lemony oak over light to medium fruit, with just a touch of astringency. *Palate:* relatively light but clean and quite firm, with lemony/vanillan oak in what is clearly the style of the winery this year. Drink '90–'92.

Summary: The amusingly-named Seldom Seen has come on to the scene with an initial release of remarkably consistent quality.

SETTLERS CREEK

Location: Care of Augustine, Airport Road, Mudgee, 2850; 7 km north-east of township. (063) 72 3880.

Winemaker: Various contract makers.

1989 Production: 1000 cases.

Principal Wines: Chardonnay, Pinot Noir and Aleatico (the latter made in a lightly fortified style).

Distribution: Exclusively cellar door sales and mailing list; cellar door sales 10 a.m. to 4 p.m. 7 days.

Prices: $8 to $15 cellar door.

Tasting Notes:

1989 CHARDONNAY [CS] Colour: medium to full straw-yellow. *Bouquet:* surprisingly forward and developed, with full, soft and quite fleshy buttery/peachy fruit. *Palate:* soft, forward slightly squashy peachy fruit with little oak impact so far evident. Nonetheless, has abundant flavour and will certainly rate in the 70's if it makes its expected progression to bottle.

Summary: Skilled contract winemaker (by wineries in the Lower and Upper Hunter) and a mature vineyard base should assure quality.

STEIN'S WINES

Location: Sandal Park Estate, Pipeclay Lane, Mudgee, 2850; 11 km north-west of town. (063) 73 3991.

Winemaker: Robert S. Stein.

Principal Wines: Semillon Riesling, Chardonnay, Shiraz, Quarry Port, Rum Cask Port and Liqueur Muscat.

Distribution: Chiefly cellar door sales and mailing list. Cellar door sales 10 a.m. to 4 p.m.

Prices: $7 to $10 cellar door.

Vintage Rating 1986–89: White: '86, '89, '87, '88. Red: '88, '89, '87, '86.

Tasting Notes:

1988 SEMILLON RIESLING [59] Colour: light to medium yellow-green. *Bouquet:* clean, neutral and soft, with faint aromatic fruit deriving from the riesling component. *Palate:* a soft, very sweet cellar door style, with the sweetness out of balance with the underlying fruit. Drink '90.

1989 SHIRAZ [CS] Colour: youthful, light to medium purple-red. *Bouquet:* clean, light, fresh red berry fruit, with a slightly herbaceous tang. *Palate:* light and fresh; not over-extracted and made in the modern fashion; promising start.

1988 QUARRY PORT [70] Colour: medium purple-red. *Bouquet:* clean, fresh earthy spirit with nice fruit; medium to full weight, and has some style. *Palate:* solid, dark red fruits; much sweeter than the bouquet suggests, and needs a little more cut to balance that sweetness. Drink '90–'93.

1987 SHIRAZ [64] Colour: light to medium red, with just a touch of purple. *Bouquet:* clean, light lemony oak with light fruit, and a whisper of bitter sulphide. *Palate:* light, lemony/leafy fruit marred by a corresponding trace of sulphidic bitterness. Drink '90–'92.

Summary: Robert Stein is a new arrival on the Mudgee wine scene, but is determined to make this substantial retirement vineyard and winery a successful one. The winery is well equipped and the extensive vineyard should produce fruit of high quality; the vista is superb and the operation well worth a visit.

TALLARA

Location: 'Tallara', Cassilis Road, Mudgee, 2850; 7 km north-east of town (vineyard only).

Winemakers: Barry Platt (contract) and Rick Turner.

1989 Production: Of miniscule proportions.

Principal Wines: One wine only made, Chardonnay; the balance of the production from the 10-hectare vineyard is sold to other winemakers in the district.

Distribution: Principally by mailing list; enquiries to Tinobah Pty Ltd, 15 Upper Spit Road, Mosman, 2088. Limited local restaurant distribution, and occasional weekend cellar door sales.

Tasting Notes:

1987 CHARDONNAY [87] Colour: light to medium yellow-green. *Bouquet:* smooth and clean with sweet peachy fruit and just a hint of barrel ferment. *Palate:* a lovely wine with outstanding spicy peachy fruit, a touch of oak and a long, lingering finish. Drink '90–'92. (Tasting note from last year's edition as no new wine available for tasting).

Summary: Most of the grapes are sold, but a token quantity of chardonnay is made each year under contract by Barry Platt; the '87 is quite outstanding, but earlier vintages were not as impressive.

THISTLE HILL

Location: McDonalds Road, Mudgee, 2850; 10 km west of Mudgee.
(063) 73 3546.

Winemaker: David Robertson.

1989 Production: 2500 cases.

Principal Wines: Chardonnay, Rhine Riesling, Pinot Noir, Cabernet Sauvignon, Port and Liqueur Muscat.

Distribution: Principally mailing list and cellar door sales. Limited distribution through Mudgee and Sydney restaurants and liquor stores. Cellar door sales 10 a.m. to 4 p.m. Monday to Friday and 9 a.m. to 5 p.m. weekends and holidays.

Prices: $9 to $13 cellar door.

Vintage Rating 1986–89: White: '86, '89, '88, '87. Red: '86, '88, '89, '87.

Tasting Notes:

1988 CHARDONNAY [79] Colour: light to medium green-yellow. *Bouquet:* very strong fruit and bottle development, with a distinct touch of volatility. *Palate:* high-toned peachy/honey fruit, again lifted by quite pronounced volatility; given the benefit of the doubt on volatility, as it was in the top 100 Smallmakers Competition in 1989, but some judges would not be so lenient. Drink '90.

1988 PINOT NOIR [65] Colour: a slightly blackish aspect to the red-purple, suggesting fairly high pH. *Bouquet:* solid, plain fruit showing little or any varietal character. *Palate:* vague aspirations to style and varietal definition, with faint tobacco/stemmy characters; overall a pleasant, light and clean red which just happens to be made from pinot noir, however hard the maker tried to produce something better. Drink '90.

1987 CABERNET SAUVIGNON [90] Colour: medium purple-red. *Bouquet:* very clean and smooth, with well structured, deep dark berry fruits and good oak. *Palate:* a lovely, smooth harmonious wine with tastes of dark chocolate set against sweet oak; the structure is good, as is the fruit/oak balance. Drink '91–'95.

1986 CABERNET SAUVIGNON **[90]** *Colour:* medium red-purple. *Bouquet:* soft, sweet berry fruit; clean but quite ripe, with soft oak. *Palate:* spotlessly clean, and smooth, with rich, dark berries and a hint of chocolate; remarkably fresh, and has outstanding mouth-feel. Drink '90–'94.

1985 CABERNET SAUVIGNON **[77]** *Colour:* full purple-red. *Bouquet:* rich, complex briary/ berry undergrowth aromas, but there are ripe fruit aromas there with nice oak. *Palate:* a complex, structured wine with plenty of concentration, but marginally toughened by just a little leathery sulphide, and quite high tannins. Drink '90–'93.

1985 VINTAGE PORT **[74]** *Colour:* full purple-red. *Bouquet:* big, rich concentrated dark berry fruit with strong spirit. *Palate:* very sweet indeed, almost icecream topping, but no doubt rushes out the cellar door. Drink '90–'93.

Summary: David Robertson is a totally dedicated vigneron who has learnt a great deal about winemaking in the past few years and who is totally committed to making wine of quality; Thistle Hill will always be small but is a must on any visit to Mudgee. The cabernets reviewed for this edition were, obviously enough, quite outstanding.

Murrumbidgee Irrigation Area

1988 VINTAGE

The climate of the Murrumbidgee Irrigation Area seldom poses challenges or problems until late in the season. The dry and warm spring and summer, coupled with the universal use of irrigation, virtually guarantee a trouble-free start. It is for this reason that the Murrumbidgee Irrigation Area can produce maximum yields of grapes at relatively low cost, and it is no accident that it produces almost one-fifth of Australia's wine.

However, after a near perfect vintage in 1987, 1988 produced its fair share of problems. An extremely hot prolonged spell of weather in January had two effects: an uncontrolled flood of early ripening varietals coming into over-stretched wineries, and severe stress on the later ripening varieties, causing damage to the vines' metabolic system. Accordingly, notwithstanding the warm conditions, some of the red varieties failed to fully mature and ripen.

In the outcome, quality was no more than average. Semillon, chardonnay and sauvignon blanc probably did best in the white wines, while cabernet sauvignon and shiraz performed to expectations among the reds. The one high spot was the development of botrytis in the late harvested semillon, with some superb wines of this style once again being made.

1989 VINTAGE

If 1988 provided some headaches, 1989 was a year designed to test winemakers and wineries to the utmost. The good news, as it were, is a record crush of 100,749 tonnes (compared with 90,858 tonnes in 1988). There were accordingly no complaints with yields.

However, once again very hot weather, this time in February, caused an avalanche of white varieties to come into over-stressed wineries. Only McWilliams, which had fortuitously planned on reducing its intake and leaving surplus capacity, was really able to cope.

Just when the pressure was starting to slacken off, and winemakers were looking forward to a more leisurely harvest of the reds, the rains came from the north and continued right through the vintage. Some lovely early-harvested shiraz was made, but cabernet sauvignon was badly affected both in terms of quality and quantity–this variety was down 7 per cent compared to 1988.

Finally, the rains put an abrupt end to most of the botrytised material: only those who harvested early and accepted lower than desirable sugar levels made any wine of this style.

THE CHANGES

San Bernadino has gone into receivership for the second time, and at the time of writing it seemed unlikely it would be able to trade out of its difficulties as it did on the prior occasion. On the other hand, the district overall is going through a period of unprecedented (and one would suspect) unsustainable prosperity. The Wine Grapes Marketing Board of Griffith says that average prices increased by around $120 per tonne, producing what it somewhat coyly admits are "excellent grower returns". As in all riverland areas, prices vary irrationally from one variety to the next: irrationally, because the variation reflects not differing production costs (which are basically the same) but distortions in supply and demand. Thus $1400 per tonne was widely paid for chardonnay, with semillon bringing as little as $400 per tonne. At the very high district yields, even the latter price brings a handsome return to the grower,

so one can imagine the profit being made from the more eagerly sought-after varieties.

McWilliams continues to dominate the district both in terms of its volume of production and the quality of its wines. Nor is it letting the grass grow under its feet: it has embarked on an aggressive programme of buying both vineyards in and grapes from premium areas. Its grape purchases include rhine riesling from the Eden Valley and cabernet sauvignon from Coonawarra, while it has acquired the substantial Barwang Vineyard and property in the nearby Hilltops region.

🍇CASELLA

Location: Farm 1471, Yenda, 2681.
(069) 68 1346.

Winemaker: John Casella.

Principal Wines: Trebbiano, Semillon, Pedro Ximinez, Shiraz, Grenache and Cabernet Sauvignon, mostly sold in bulk to private customers for home bottling. Spumante is the only labelled product.

Summary: A small, family-owned and run operation established a little over 20 years ago and dealing exclusively with local clientele.

🍇DE BORTOLI WINES

Location: De Bortoli Road, Bilbul, 2680; 9 km east of Griffith.
(069) 63 5344 and (069) 63 5253.

Winemakers: Darren Bortoli and Nick Guy.

1989 Production: 15,000,000 litres.

Principal Wines: A large range of varietal table wines, both dry and sweet; sparkling wines and fortified wines sold in every type and size of container. More than 60 different wines are on sale at the winery. Since 1982 De Bortoli has produced some of Australia's greatest botrytised sweet table wines from semillon, recently extending to traminer.

Distribution: Extensive retail distribution through own wholesale distribution network. Cellar door sales 8 a.m. to 5.30 p.m. 7 days.

Prices: $4 to $22 (for 1985 Botrytis Semillon Sauternes 375 ml) retail.

Vintage Rating 1986–89: White: '89, '87, '86, '88. Red: '89, '86, '87, '88. Botrytis whites: '87, '88, '86 ('89 not yet rated and may not be made).

Outstanding Prior Vintages: White: '82, '85.

Tasting Notes:

1989 SAUVIGNON BLANC [TS] _Colour:_ very light straw-green. _Bouquet:_ estery grassy aromas, still showing considerable fermentation effects. _Palate:_ very similar estery grassy flavours, slightly spiky, and still to settle down in bottle; does appear to have the requisite aroma and varietal character.

1987 RIVERINA CHARDONNAY [66] _Colour:_ medium yellow-green. _Bouquet:_ strong but relatively unattractive camphor oak. _Palate:_ strong lemony/camphor oak, presumably derived from chips; some slightly green characters also evident, and fairly light fruit. Certainly acceptable, but equally certainly, not great. Drink '90.

1985 RARE DRY BOTRYTIS SEMILLON [61] _Colour:_ full yellow. _Bouquet:_ very developed, with drying camphor characters. _Palate:_ strong apricot/camphor characters and, as the label suggests, allowed to ferment dry; the finish is slightly bitter, and all one can say is that it is a brave experiment which did not really succeed. Drink '90.

1985 SAUTERNES BOTRYTIS SEMILLON [90] _Colour:_ golden bronze. _Bouquet:_ almost searing intensity; extreme botrytis influence with very pronounced volatility to the complex orange peel fruit. _Palate:_ botrytis apricot/orange peel flavours, and once again that volatile lift which is, I hasten to emphasise, an integral and acceptable part of the style. Drink '90–'92.

10 YEAR OLD LIQUEUR MUSCAT [77] _Colour:_ strong tawny, with no red hues showing. _Bouquet:_ intense raisined/luscious fruit, rich and complex. _Palate:_ very rich, textured structure, with very sweet muscat fruit. What it lacks in subtlety it makes up in flavour.

Summary: De Bortoli continues to lead Australia in one wine style: its Botrytis Semillon Sauternes. The currently available wine has won gold medals at every Australian national show of any significance, and continues a line of immense distinction which commenced in 1982. Its other wines remain somewhat pedestrian, although it has obviously accumulated a very useful reserve of fortified muscat.

🍇FRANCO'S WINES

Location: Farm 161, Irrigation Way, Hanwood, 2680; 5 km south of Griffith.
(069) 62 1675.

Winemaker: Salvatore Francis.

Principal Wines: A wide range of generic table and fortified wines.

Distribution: Exclusively cellar door sales 8 a.m. to 6 p.m. Monday to Saturday.

Summary: Another family-owned and run enterprise offering traditional Riverland styles to a local clientele.

🍇 LILLYPILLY ESTATE

Location: Lillypilly Road, off Leeton-Yanco Road, Leeton, 2705; 2 km south-east of Leeton. (069) 53 4069; Fax (069) 53 4980.

Winemaker: Robert Fiumara.

1989 Production: Not stated.

Principal Wines: Tramillon (a blend of semillon and traminer), Fumé Blanc, Chardonnay, Rhine Riesling, Novello, Spatlese Lexia, Noble Rhine Riesling, Noble Muscat of Alexandria, Hermitage, Cabernet Sauvignon, Vintage Port and Red Velvet.

Distribution: Principally cellar door sales and mailing list. Cellar door sales 9 a.m. to 5 p.m. Monday to Saturday. Mailing list enquiries to Lillypilly Estate, PO Box 839, Leeton, 2705. Limited retail distribution direct from winery at Leeton.

Prices: $6.55 to $10.90 cellar door.

Tasting Notes:

1989 CHARDONNAY [TS] Colour: medium to full yellow-green. *Bouquet:* surprisingly full and weighty, with some phenolics which may be taken out of the wine prior to bottling. *Palate:* once again, a very big, high-flavoured wine with strong phenols, and a suspicion of some volatility. If toned down prior to bottling, could be a surprise packet. The wine is not given any oak treatment.

1988 TRAMINER [75] Colour: light yellow-green.

Bouquet: very clean and aromatic, with spicy lychee varietal character. *Palate:* soft flavour and structure, again with some lychee characters; falls away ever so slightly on the finish, and would have benefited from a touch more acid. Nonetheless, an impressive effort. Drink '90.

1988 SPATLESE LEXIA [69] Colour: light to medium yellow-green. *Bouquet:* light and clean, with that unmistakable grapy aroma of frontignac. *Palate:* high flavoured, uncompromisingly sweet, uncompromisingly cellardoor style which people cannot resist buying. Drink '90.

1986 NOBLE RHINE RIESLING [75] Colour: deep yellow-gold. *Bouquet:* intense raisined apricot aromas, lusciously sweet. *Palate:* super raisined, extreme apricot flavours almost beyond grapes; obviously heavily botrytised. Drink '90.

1987 NOBLE MUSCAT OF ALEXANDRIA [78] Colour: medium yellow-green. *Bouquet:* ultra-intense, hyper-grapy, spicy/essency aromas. *Palate:* similar extremely concentrated grapy flavours, almost as if it had been lightly fortified; in fact the effect is simply that of botrytis on Muscat of Alexandria grapes. Quite unique and highly commendable style for those with a sweet tooth. Drink '90–'91.

1989 CABERNET SAUVIGNON [CS] Colour: vivid purple-red. *Bouquet:* clean, youthful berry cassis aromas. *Palate:* young spicy cassis berry fruit; an early tank sample; if taken successfully to bottle could be very good.

1988 RED VELVET [60] Colour: light to medium red-purple. *Bouquet:* clean, soft cherry berry aromas. *Palate:* potent fruit flavours, with marked residual sugar in a lambrusco style. Those who enjoy sweet reds would point this wine much higher, and it certainly is an alternative for sweet white wine drinkers. As winemaker Robert Fiumara emphasises, it should be served chilled. Drink '90.

Summary: Winemaker Robert Fiumara has never been afraid to experiment, and has profited from his lateral thinking. Having registered the brand name Tramillon (and done exceptionally well with the traminer-semillon blend which makes this delicate dry wine) he has experimented with a range of wines, most successfully with the botrytised rieslings and muscats. Here one finds some wines of real quality.

McWILLIAMS

Location: Hanwood Winery, Winery Road,
Hanwood, 2680; 1.5 km south of Hanwood.
(069) 62 1333.
Yenda Winery, Winery Road, Yenda, 2681; on
eastern outskirts of town.
(069) 68 1001.
Beelbangera Winery, Winery Road,
Beelbangera, 2680; on eastern side of main
Griffith-Yenda Road.
(069) 63 5227.

Winemakers: Chief winemaker: J. F. Brayne;
Yenda: G. P. McWilliam and G. Quarisa;
Beelbangera: J.A. Martin and L. W.
McWilliam; Robinvale: Max McWilliam;
Hanwood: B. K. McWilliam and S. Crook.

1989 Production: Not for publication.

Principal Wines: An immense range of wines
made, both table and fortified. Principal
brands are McWilliam's, Hanwood, Max
Markview, Bodega, and Inheritance Hanwood
white and red table wines, and Hanwood
Tawny Port are the most important premium
wines in the 750 ml bottle range. The
Inheritance Collection was introduced in late
1989, providing bottled generic wines; the
quality is above flagon or cask wine. Two-litre
flagons and varietal casks are also made and
sold in vast quantities. Recently introduced
Show Series fortified wines and brandy are of
the highest quality.

Distribution: National retail at all levels, distributed
by McWilliam's own sales force.

Prices: $4.99 to $33 retail.

Tasting Notes:

1989 2 L HILLSIDE CASK RHINE RIESLING [83]
Colour: light to medium yellow-green. *Bouquet:*
strong lime toast fruit, with both depth and the
promise of structure in the palate. *Palate:* has
the structure, length and balance promised by
the bouquet; lime toast fruit; of extraordinary
quality for a cask. Drink '90.

*1989 HANWOOD SEMILLON CHARDONNAY
[74]* Colour: light green-yellow. *Bouquet:*
fragrant and clean, with slightly herbaceous
fruit. *Palate:* attractive, crisp herbaceous fruit
with good mouth-feel and pleasant acid
balance. Technically faultless winemaking.
Drink '90.

*1989 2 L HILLSIDE CASK TRAMINER RHINE
RIESLING [75]* Colour: light straw-yellow.
Bouquet: clean, attractive passionfruit aromas
with some sweetness. *Palate:* very clean, fresh
and attractive light to medium passionfruit
flavours; once again, perfectly balanced and,
once again, outstanding quality in a 2 litre cask.
Drink '90.

*1989 INHERITANCE AUSTRALIAN BEAUJOLAIS
[76]* Colour: vivid light to medium purple-red.
Bouquet: clean fruit, with a touch of slightly
chippy oak. *Palate:* fresh, clean and youthful,
again with a slightly tangy/chippy oak which
nonetheless works well in the wine; good acid
rounds off a lively modern style. I prefer the
wine in the glass to the name on the label,
however. Drink '90.

SHOW SERIES AMONTILLADO SHERRY [90]
Colour: glowing golden. *Bouquet:* intense and
aged, with strong rancio; very powerful yet very
fine. *Palate:* a firm, dry style with a wonderfully
complex back-palate and dry finish. More
Spanish than Australian in style.

SHOW SERIES OROLOSO [93] Colour: yellow-gold.
Bouquet: beautifully smooth and harmonious,
and not the least bit sweet. *Palate:* again, a
wonderfully harmonious wine, more like a
slightly over-sized amontillado; beautifully
balanced with a long finish. I could drink this
sort of Oroloso by the tumblerful every night.

Summary: McWilliams is producing an impressive
array of young, budget priced varietal table
wines and such magnificent old fortified wines
that it was exceedingly difficult to select six
wines from the dozen or so which really
deserved review. There was a time not long ago
when one felt depressed about the future of
McWilliams: if the winemaking and production
team has anything to do with it, it will now be
an exhilarating one.

❦MIRANDA WINES

Location: 57 Jondaryan Avenue, Griffith, 2680; on south-eastern outskirts of town.
(069) 62 4033; Fax (069) 62 6944.

Winemakers: Lou Miranda (production director), plus two qualified winemakers.

1989 Production: Over 1 million cases.

Principal Wines: The usual immense range of wines in every style, shape and size from white varietal table wines in 750 ml bottles to Golden Gate Spumante (for many years in Australia's 12 largest brand sellers), Marsala, Rum Port and others too numerous to mention. The Flagship range white and red table wines are the newly released Wyangan Estate range, including the highly decorated '87 Semillon Sauterne.

Distribution: Cellar door sales 9 a.m. to 6 p.m. Monday to Friday, 9 a.m. to 6 p.m. Saturday and public holidays, 10 a.m. to 6 p.m. Sunday. Wholesale and retail sales throughout Australia.

Prices: $1.99 to $28 retail.

Tasting Notes:

1989 WYANGAN ESTATE SEMILLON [67] Colour: water white. *Bouquet:* light, clean and rather neutral fruit with light, spicy nutmeg oak. *Palate:* very light and crisp, with well balanced light smoky oak; tasted immediately after bottling, and should develop nicely over the next six months prior to its release January/February 1990. Drink '90–'91.

NV MOSELLE [59] Colour: slight straw-pink. *Bouquet:* spicy, slightly oily muscat aromas with plenty of fruit. *Palate:* a highly commercial, very sweet muscat which is perfectly designed for the market it is aimed at. Drink '90.

1987 WYANGAN ESTATE SEMILLON SAUTERNES [87] Colour: full golden yellow. *Bouquet:* super-intense botrytised aromas, with apricot and the expected touch of volatility. *Palate:* very strong apricot botrytis flavours evident; a sweet mid-palate gives way to a quite dry finish, and one would not expect the wine to go on improving. Drink '90.

1989 WYANGAN ESTATE HERMITAGE [CS] Colour: dense purple-black. *Bouquet:* attractive spicy/briary/berry aromas. *Palate:* well handled, rich spicy/berry/briary fruit, very attractive. If this wine makes it safely to the bottle, it will rate close to 80 points.

1987 VINTAGE PORT [79] Colour: medium purple-red. *Bouquet:* complex fruit, with most attractive brandy spirit used in fortification. *Palate:* complex strong red berry fruit lifted by the impact of brandy spirit; attractive dry finish. Drink '90–'94.

Summary: Miranda is a very substantial operation. As the notes indicate, some of the wines are very creditable, with the botrytised semillon and vintage port clearly the best. However, a number of other wines tasted were either indifferent or downright faulty, including some in bottle, and care should be taken in buying. Certainly, the price is right for the best wines.

❦RIVERINA WINES

Location: Farm 1, 305 Hillston Road, Tharbogang via Griffith, 2680; 6 km west of Griffith.
(069) 624 1222.

Winemaker: John Casella.

Principal Wines: The full range of table wine, sparkling wine and fortified wine found throughout the district, chiefly marketed in bulk, with limited quantities marketed under the Riverina Wines and Ballingal Estates brands.

Distribution: Chiefly cellar door sales 9 a.m. to 6 p.m. Monday to Saturday and public holidays, 10 a.m. to 3 p.m. Sunday.

Summary: Riverina Wines is another conventional (within the Riverland terms of reference) winery relying almost entirely on local custom.

ROSSETTO'S WINES

Location: Farm 576, Beelbangera, 2686; 2 km south-east of Beelbangera.
(069) 63 5214; Fax (069) 63 5542.

Winemaker: Ralph Graham.

1989 Production: 80,000 cases.

Principal Wines: Premium white varietals marketed under Mount Bingar label, comprising French Colombard Chablis, Oak Matured Semillon, Sauvignon Blanc, Chardonnay, Traminer, Traminer Riesling, Rhine Riesling, Semillon Moselle, Hermitage and Cabernet Sauvignon; premium fortified white wines comprise Mount Bingar Port, Anniversary Sweet Sherry and Liqueur Muscat; other white and red varietal table wines released under Beelgara brand, with substantial Mount Bingar sales through four-litre cask. Wine-based cream liqueurs and other liqueurs also sold. Finally, substantial sales of bulk wines.

Distribution: Through cellar door, mail orders and retail through own direct sales force. Cellar door sales 8.30 am. to 5.30 p.m. Monday to Saturday.

Prices: $3.99 to $20 retail.

Vintage Rating 1986–89: '87, '89, '88, '86.

Outstanding Prior Vintages: 1980.

Tasting Notes:

1988 MOUNT BINGAR SEMILLON BIN J R 37 [66] Colour: light to medium yellow-green. *Bouquet:* attractive, rich buttery semillon with strong lemony oak. *Palate:* unfortunately, the oak tends to overtake the fruit; a slightly less heavy hand could have made a very good wine indeed. As it is, green oak flavours dominate somewhat. Drink '90–'91.

1988 MOUNT BINGAR CHARDONNAY SEMILLON [79] Colour: medium yellow-green. *Bouquet:* complex, rich buttery biscuity oak; sophisticated and successful oak handling. *Palate:* exceedingly complex oak handling which has succeeded brilliantly; the wine would be in gold medal points if the fruit was just a little stronger. Nonetheless, a very good food wine as it stands. Drink '90–'91.

1987 MOUNT BINGAR HERMITAGE BIN G 31 [72] Colour: medium red-purple. *Bouquet:* clean, soft and light cherry/berry fruit, with a pleasant touch of oak. *Palate:* light, fresh cherry fruit, well balanced with just a hint of oak in the background. Has developed nicely but should not be kept too long. Drink '90–'91.

Summary: Not for the first time, Rossetto's runs counter to the main thrust of the region, doing best with its wooded white and red table wines. Once again, it must be said that these notes do represent the pick of the crop, as it were, and some rather less attractive wines were tasted.

SAN BERNADINO

Location: Farm 644, Leeton Road, Griffith, 2680; on south-eastern outskirts of town.
(069) 62 4944.

Winemaker: Walter Santesso.

Principal Wines: Perhaps the widest and, at times, most imaginative range of wine styles and labels in the entire MIA. The range of table, sparkling, flavoured, non-alcoholic and fortified wine is marketed under three main brand names: Woodridge for the premium varietal table wines; San Bernadino for the remainder of the table and fortified wines; and Castella for the non-alcoholic sparkling and still range.

Distribution: Mainly through supermarkets and liquor chains, with limited fine wine retail distribution; sales both through own repre-sentatives and through distributors or agents in each State. Cellar door sales 9 a.m. to 5.30 p.m. Monday to Saturday.

Summary: The future of San Bernadino is under a black cloud, with no details available for this edition following the return of the company to receivership.

🍇 WEST END WINES

Location: Farm 1283, Brayne Road, Griffith, 2680; 2 km west of township. (069) 62 2868.

Winemaker: William Calabria.

1989 Production: 35,000 cases.

Principal Wines: Principally, Traminer Riesling, Rhine Riesling, Moselle, Chablis, Chardonnay, Hermitage and Cabernet Sauvignon. A range of fortified wines including Bettina Port, Goldminers Port, Brown Muscat and a number of sherries both sweet and dry.

Distribution: Exclusively cellar door sales and mail order. Cellar door sales 8.30 a.m. to 5.30 p.m. Monday to Saturday, noon to 5 p.m. Sunday.

Prices: $3 to $8.90 cellar door.

Summary: West End Wines produces a range of both table and fortified wines at the modest prices typical of the district.

Other Districts

1988 VINTAGE

Any detailed discussion of an area which literally spans the whole of the central and eastern half of New South Wales is beyond the scope of a brief introduction such as this. The summary given for both 1988 and 1989 is necessarily very generalised. The growing season commenced with a wet, mild spring in most areas, with one or two inland regions suffering from frost. All the inland, indeed, experienced a cold October which delayed flowering. Thereafter the weather turned very warm, and in both inland and coastal areas, the grapes ripened quickly leading to an early start to vintage which commenced in hot, dry conditions. The early start proved a boon for coastal districts which were able to partially escape the heavy rainfall which fell in February.

1989 VINTAGE

The year was in many respects similar to 1988, except that inland frosts played no part. A warm, basically hot and dry growing season (October was as hot in this season as it was cold the previous year) led to another early vintage which was then hit by rain later in the harvest.

The Cowra district was a little different, having two excellent vintages largely free of rain, producing abundant yields of high quality grapes, and especially that all-important varietal – chardonnay.

THE CHANGES

There are two new entries: Sandhills Estate and Trentham Estate, while Bridgefarm Wines has changed its name to Camden Estate.

Trentham Estate is the new winery and restaurant complex of former Mildara winemaker Tony Murphy. Beautifully situated on the banks of the Murray River, not far from Mildura, it has produced a most impressive array of first-up wines. In fact, the vineyard has been in existence for some time, and the winemaking facilities likewise, but the wines are only now finding their way onto the retail market. Only a small proportion of total production (the pick of the crop, as it were) is labelled Trentham Estate. The rest is sold to other winemakers.

Sandhills Vineyard has been in existence since 1920, relying on tourist trade passing through Forbes. Operations had to all intents and purposes ground to a halt when it was purchased by John Saleh in January 1989. John Saleh is studying viticulture at the Charles Sturt University, and he has already commenced upgrading the vineyard with new plantings of pinot noir, chardonnay, shiraz and cabernet sauvignon. The tiny production of 1989 Burgundy suggested that there was still a lot of work to be done in the winery.

Camden Estate has likewise been in existence for some time: the vineyards were established by Roseworthy-trained Norman Hanckel in 1974. Until 1988 virtually all the production was sold to other makers, with occasional small parcels being released under various names including Bridgefarm.

Having retired from his other activities, Norman Hanckel has now decided to fully commercialise the wines, and has renamed the property Camden Estate. The vineyard, incidentally, is established on the banks of the Nepean River directly opposite one of the earliest and most important vineyards established in New South Wales, that of William Macarthur.

Finally, in future editions we shall probably find entries for Joadga Vineyard and Eling Forest. The latter, in particular, is an ambitious development 10 km south of Berrima. Both Joadga and Eling Forest are under the direction of Kim and Frances Moginie; Kim Moginie spent some time at Roseworthy and also gained practical viticultural and winemaking knowledge with Arrowfield and Rosemount.

CAMDEN ESTATE

Location: Lot 32, Macarthur Road, Camden, 2570; adjacent to the long Macarthur Bridge. (046) 58 8337

Winemaker: Norman Hanckel (supervising contract makers, notably Vicary's).

1989 Production: 9600 cases.

Principal Wines: Chardonnay has been and will be the single most important release; also Chablis and Traminer blends. A Cabernet Sauvignon was released late in 1989.

Distribution: Cellar door at Camden-Gledswood Homestead (Telephone (02) 606511 to arrange tasting and vineyard inspections). The full range are available for purchase by the bottle, or tasting by the glass at "Tastings at the Rocks", 45 Argyle Street, The Rocks, Sydney. Telephone (02) 241 3239 or Fax (02) 251 7821. Direct distribution from the winery and stocked at leading retail outlets throughout NSW and Australia.

Prices: $8 to $20.

Tasting Notes:

1989 CHARDONNAY [CS] Colour: light to medium yellow-green. *Bouquet:* very full buttery/ butterscotch aromas, exceptionally precocious. *Palate:* rich, full, very forward, round, peachy/ buttery fruit with soft vanillan oak. Will score well and be highly commercial, but looks as if it will develop with great rapidity.

1988 CHARDONNAY [85] Colour: medium yellow-green. *Bouquet:* very clean, with spicy oak married into rich peachy fruit. *Palate:* attractive peachy fruit with pronounced spicy oak which has been very well handled, and it is in good balance (by conventional standards) with the fruit. Drink '90–'92.

1988 CHABLIS [63] Colour: light to medium yellow-green. *Bouquet:* light, slightly green fruit with the faintest hint of spice, possibly from a touch of oak. *Palate:* very light, with green fruit flavours and some characters reminiscent of

lesser quality German wines. Drink '90.

1988 CLASSIC WHITE TR BLEND [69] Colour: light to medium yellow-green. *Bouquet:* highly spiced floral traminer aromas. *Palate:* full flavoured with spicy traminer fruit; it comes as a surprise, and something of a relief, to find it dry. Drink '90.

Summary: Camden Estate once again demonstrates the amiability of chardonnay, which will happily grow in almost any climatic region and produce stylish, full-flavoured wines. The other releases are of adequate, unexciting commercial quality.

CASSEGRAIN

Location: Hastings Valley Winery, Pacific Highway, Port Macquarie, 2444; 7 km west of township. (065) 83 7777; Fax (065) 84 0354.

Winemaker: John Cassegrain.

1989 Production: Not for publication.

Principal Wines: The wines are increasingly made from Hastings Valley grown grapes, the principal wines being Chardonnay, Pinot Noir, Chambourcin, Cabernet Merlot and Cabernet Sauvignon; the other principal wines come from Hunter Valley-grown material.

Distribution: Cellar door sales and mailing list; national retail through Tallerman & Co., Qld; I. H. Baker, NSW; and SA through Regional Liquor Agencies.

Prices: $7 to $20.

Vintage Rating 1986–89: White: '86, '88, '89, '87. Red: '88, '86, '87, '89. (both ratings for Hastings Valley fruit).

Outstanding Prior Vintages: '85.

Tasting Notes:

1989 HASTINGS NOUVEAU [74] Colour: medium purple-red. *Bouquet:* quite firm, with pronounced leafy/tobacco merlot characters, clean and lively *Palate:* pleasant, clean fruity wine of some weight and style; indeed, is almost a little too full-bodied for a true nouveau, but that is something of a carping criticism. Drink '90.

1989 POKOLBIN SEMILLON [CS] Colour: light green-yellow. *Bouquet:* light, clean and crisp herbaceous fruit with good varietal character. *Palate:* crisp, gently herbaceous fruit; has intensity and should develop well, with potential for points in the high 70's, low 89's.

1988 CHARDONNAY FROMENTEAU VINEYARD [80] Colour: medium to full yellow-green. *Bouquet:* of medium intensity with soft , faintly honeyed fruit and attractive spicy oak. *Palate:* spicy clove oak threatens to dominate, but at the end of the day is sufficiently well handled to allow tangy grapefruit varietal character to make its statement. Drink '90–'92.

1987 POKOLBIN CABERNET SAUVIGNON [60] Colour: medium red, with a touch of purple. *Bouquet:* leathery astringent characters pull down the fruit. *Palate:* very good fruit has been spoilt by leathery/bitter sulphide characters. Drink '90–'91.

Summary: The so-called TCA oak-mould problems which have caused problems throughout various sectors of the wine industry in 1988 certainly affected Cassegrain. Two of the wines submitted (notably 1988 Vintage Selection Hastings Valley Chardonnay) were fairly grossly contaminated. The mouldy bitter characters which result in no way reflect the real winemaking skills of John Cassegrain nor the quality of the fruit. The problem has now been identified and should not re-occur in the future.

COGNO BROTHERS

Location: Cobbitty Road, Cobbitty, 2570.
(046) 51 2281.

Winemaker: Giovanni Cogno.

Principal Wines: A diverse range of Italian-accented wines including Frontignan Spatlese, Cobbitty Barbera, Lambrusco, Whisky Port, Liqueur Muscat and Mama Port.

Distribution: Principally cellar door; limited retail and restaurant distribution. Cellar door sales

8 a.m. to 6 p.m. Monday to Saturday, noon to 6 p.m. Sunday.

Summary: Virtually all of the wines sold cellar door to local trade, drawing upon the strong Italian community in the district.

COOPERS TABLETOP ESTATE

Location: Tabletop Road, Tabletop via Albury, 2640; 15 km north of Albury, on Hume Highway.
(060) 26 2366, (060) 26 2210.

Winemakers: Lindsay Cooper and Barry Morey.

Principal Wines: A full variety of wines and wine styles offered, including varietal table wines, sparkling wines, port and sherry.

Distribution: Exclusively cellar door sales: 9 a.m. to 5 p.m. Monday to Saturday and 9 a.m. to 4 p.m. Sunday.

Summary: Another operation marketing virtually exclusively to local trade, but with some excellent wines available from time to time.

COWRA WINES

Location: Boorowa Road, Cowra, 2794; 5 km south of township.
(063) 42 3650, (063) 42 1136.

Winemaker: Simon Gilbert (Mountarrow Winery) (contract).

1989 Production: Approximately 6000 cases.

Principal Wines: Chardonnay, Sauvignon Blanc, Pinot Noir and Cabernet Sauvignon.

Distribution: Cellar door sales, mailing list and limited retail distribution; substantial exports to Japan. Cellar door sales 10 a.m. to 4 p.m. 7 days from Quarry Cellars and the Quarry Restaurant. Mailing list enquiries to PO Box 92, Cowra, 2794.

Prices: $12.60 to $15.50 retail.

Vintage Rating 1986–89: '89, '86, '88, '87.

Summary: The upcoming releases of Cowra Wines were unfortunately not available for tasting for this edition, but releases reviewed over the 12 months prior to writing were all of good commercial quality, the chardonnays particularly impressive.

GILGAI

Location: Tingha Road, Gilgai, 2360; 2 km south of Inverell.
(067) 23 1304.

Winemaker: Dr Keith Whish.

Principal Wines: Limited range of table and fortified wines. Varietal table wines released under Gilgai White or Gilgai Red labels, with variety (Cabernet Shiraz, Malbec, Semillon and Rhine Riesling) usually also specified.

Distribution: Exclusively cellar door and mailing list. Cellar door sales 10 a.m. to 6 p.m. Monday to Friday, noon to 6 p.m. Saturday. Mailing list, PO Box 462, Inverell, 2360.

Summary: A strictly local operation which has threatened to cease production altogether for some years now. Its present status is not known.

GLENFINLASS

Location: Elysian Farm, Parkes Road, Wellington, 2820.
(068) 45 2011.

Winemaker: Brian Holmes.

Principal Wines: Tiny output of limited range: Shiraz, Cabernet Sauvignon and Sauvignon Blanc (the latter first released in 1985).

Distribution: Cellar door only; sales 10 a.m. to 5 p.m. Saturday or by appointment.

Summary: The weekend operation of local solicitor Brian Holmes, output is tiny and profile is low. However, the few wines tasted in prior years have always been of more than acceptable quality given the size and location of the winery.

GREVILLEA ESTATE

Location: Buckajo Road, Bega, 2550; 2 km west of Bega.
(064) 23 006.

Winemaker: Beth Worthy.

Principal Wines: Wines offered for sale come from both estate-grown grapes and, until the vineyards come into full bearing, from the Hilltops region. Wines include Traminer, Rhine Riesling, Chardonnay, Semillon, Spatlese Semillon, Shiraz and Cabernet Sauvignon. Two kiwi-fruit wines are also available.

Distribution: Principally cellar door sales 9 a.m. to 5 p.m. 7 days. Also available mail order (enquiries to PO Box 207, Bega, 2550) and through local restaurants.

Summary: Winemaker Beth Worthy (eldest daughter of owners Jim and Moira Collins) has a degree in biochemistry under her belt. Wine quality is certainly more than adequate for the tourist-oriented cellar door sales nature of the business.

JASPER VALLEY WINES

Location: RMB 880 Croziers Road, Berry, 2535; 5 km south-east of town.
(044) 64 1596.

Winemaker: Michael Kerr.

Principal Wines: A wide range of wines including roadside-stall types. Labels offer White Burgundy, Riesling, Rhine Riesling, Traminer, Traminer Riesling, Moselle, Lambrusco, Summer Red, Cabernet Shiraz, Cabernet Sauvignon, Spumante, Passion Wine, Strawberry Wine and a full range of fortified wines.

Distribution: Principally cellar door and mailing list, with South Coast and local retail distribution. Cellar door sales Monday to Saturday 9.30 a.m. to 5.30 p.m., Sunday 10 a.m. to 5.30 p.m. Mailing list as above.

Summary: Jasper Valley Wines was established as long ago as 1970; while it has changed hands since then, it has always enjoyed good patronage from local trade and from passing tourists.

MARKEITA CELLARS

Location: Mitchell Highway, Neurea, NSW, 2820. (068) 46 7277

Winemaker: Keith F. C. Reinhard.

Principal Wines: Shiraz and Cabernet Sauvignon - Frontignac.

Distribution: Principally cellar door sales and mailing list. Mail order enquiries to above address. Cellar door sales 9 a.m. to 6 p.m. 7 days.

Summary: Nothing is known of wine quality or the level of production.

SANDHILLS VINEYARD

Location: Sandhills Road, Forbes, NSW, 2871. (068) 52 1437

Winemaker: J. Saleh.

1989 Production: 100 cases.

Principal Wines: Rhine Riesling, Shiraz and Mataro.

Distribution: Mainly cellar door sales and mailing list ; enquiries to PO Box 132, Forbes, 2871; cellar door sales 9 a.m. to 6 p.m. Monday to Saturday and noon to 6 p.m.Sunday; closed Tuesday and Wednesday.

Prices: $6.50.

Summary: John Saleh has begun the work of reconstruction; a 1989 Burgundy was simply not of acceptable commercial quality, but hopefully better things are in store.

THE SILOS

Location: 180 Princes Highway, Jaspers Brush, 2535; 10 km north of Nowra. (044) 48 6082.

Winemaker: Alan Bamfield.

1989 Production: Approximately 450 cases

Principal Wines: Shiraz, Cabernet Shiraz, Cabernet Sauvignon, Chardonnay, Rhine Riesling, Sauvignon Blanc, Semillon and Chablis.

Distribution: Exclusively cellar door sales (including sales through licensed restaurant operating on the premises, open for lunch from Wednesday to Sunday and for dinner from Thursday to Sunday); cellar door sales 9 a.m. to 5 p.m. 7 days.

Prices: $6 to $12.50 cellar door.

Summary: A very small cellar door only operation producing wines of modest quality.

TILBA VALLEY

Location: Glen Eden Vineyard, Corunna Lake, via Tilba, 2546; on Old Princes Highway, 1 km north-west of junction with Princes Highway. (044) 73 7308.

Winemaker: Barry Field.

Principal Wines: A variety of wines is offered, some made from estate-grown grapes, others using wine purchased from other regions, notably the MIA. The labels clearly differentiate the varied sources of the material. Estate-produced wines include Semillon Chardonnay, Traminer Riesling and Semillon, while blended wines produced from other regions include Cabernet Sauvignon and Tilba Tawny Port. A honey mead wine is also produced on the estate.

Distribution: Principally cellar door sales, with limited local restaurant distribution, but with mailing list enquiries welcome– addressed as above. Cellar door sales 10 a.m. to 5 p.m. Monday to Saturday, 11 a.m. to 5 p.m. Sunday.

Tasting Notes:

1989 SEMILLON CHARDONNAY OAK FERMENTED [**CS**] *Colour:* some pinking evident. *Bouquet:* very light, herbal tobacco aromas suggesting early picked fruit. *Palate:* light, grassy herbal tobacco fruit; no real problems, and should come together quite nicely by the time it is bottled and offered for sale.

1988 DROMEDARY DEW SEMILLON [**59**] *Colour:* medium straw-yellow. *Bouquet:* rather heavy, with some evidence of uncontrolled fermentation temperatures. *Palate:* full blown, rather blousy fruit with some oily oak; while the description may sound critical, the wine is a lot better than many offered from what might loosely be called tourist wineries. Drink '90–'91.

Summary: Not for the first time, Tilba Valley has submitted wines which the general tourist will find quite pleasant.

TIZZANA

Location: Tizzana Road, Ebenezer, 2756; 18 km north of Windsor. (045) 79 1150.

Winemaker: Peter Auld.

1989 Production: Less than 300 cases.

Principal Wines: Only red varieties planted to date (5 acres), all unirrigated. Recent releases include 1987 Cabernet Sauvignon and 1987 Shiraz wines produced from estate-grown grapes; others offered for sale comprise an exclusive selection (under their own labels) of smaller winery wines, together with a number of 'Tizzana Selection' wines purchased in bottle but labelled by Tizzana.

Distribution: Available from cellar door and selected local (Windsor and Richmond)

restaurants. Enquiries welcome at the above address for addition to mailing list. Cellar door sales noon to 6 p.m. weekends and public holidays; other times by appointment.

Prices: $11.50 to $16.50 for estate wines.

Summary: The strikingly packaged Tizzana red wines were, I have to confess, a major disappointment. A combination of very poor oak, mercaptan and extremely high pH disqualified the wines from review. The building itself has been most beautifully restored, and has an immensely rich history.

TRENTHAM ESTATE

Location: Sturt Highway, Trentham Cliffs, 2738; 10 km upstream of Mildura. (050) 24 8747.

Winemaker: Tony Murphy.

1989 Production: 3800 cases.

Principal Wines: *Méthode Champenoise* Chardonnay, Chardonnay, Sauvignon Blanc, Colombard Chablis, Traminer Riesling, Late Harvest Taminga, Pinot Nouveau, Merlot, Cabernet Merlot and Tawny Port.

Distribution: Substantial cellar door sales, 10 a.m. to 5 p.m. 7 days; also mail order. Mail order to PO Box 242, Gol Gol, 2738. Retail distribution through Carol-Ann Martin Classic Wines, Sydney.

Prices: $6 to $14.

Vintage Rating 1986–89: White: '89, '87, '86, '88. Red: '88, '87, '86 ('89 not yet rated).

Tasting Notes:

1989 FAMILY RESERVE CHARDONNAY [**CS**] *Colour:* strong green-yellow. *Bouquet:* very rich, concentrated and textured, almost to the point of aggression; smoky charred oak married with deep fruit. *Palate:* complex, rich barrel ferment characters with strong grapefruit flavours and tremendous depth and complexity. Utterly precocious, but if it settles down will head towards 90.

1989 PINOT NOIR [**CS**] *Colour:* medium red-purple. *Bouquet:* clean, rather one dimensional simple strawberry aromas, which do show some varietal character. *Palate:* has some real style, with light, clean sappy/strawberry fruit and sensitively handled oak; an extraordinary performance for a pinot noir from such an hospitable part of the world, and will rate 75 if it shows this form in bottle.

1988 COLOMBARD CHABLIS [71] Colour: very good light green-yellow. *Bouquet:* youthful, light and fresh with a hint of fruit spice. *Palate:* pleasant, lively and crisp green fruit flavours with good acid; very much in style. Drink '90.

1988 SAUVIGNON BLANC FUME STYLE [68] Colour: medium to full yellow-green. *Bouquet:* strong, lemony oak is the major contributor to aroma. *Palate:* very oaky, with fruit largely irrelevant; constructed in a manner reminiscent of some of the Mitchelton wines, and really needs a little more fruit flesh. Drink '90.

1988 LATE HARVEST TAMINGA [75] Colour: very good green-yellow. *Bouquet:* clean, tangy, citric/lime fruit aromas, very well made. *Palate:* intense, canned pineapple/lime flavours, very rich and very sweet; made from a CSIRO developed hybrid. Drink '90.

1987 FAMILY RESERVE CHARDONNAY [75] Colour: medium to full yellow-green. *Bouquet:* clean, with solid lemony oak and fruit of medium intensity; a fraction one dimensional. *Palate:* a pleasant smooth wine with nice lemony oak, good flavour and balance; a more dramatic contrast with the '89 could hardly be imagined, but the wine is nonetheless of very good quality. Drink '90–'91.

1985 CHARDONNAY BRUT MC [81] Colour: medium to full yellow-green. *Bouquet:* full, clean, complex and rich bottle-developed aromas with some yeast autolysis. *Palate:* soft, rich and clean with creamy/yeasty flavours and texture; if all this were not enough, also shows some elegance. Drink '90.

Summary: The family estate produced 700 tonnes of grapes in 1989, crushed 250 tonnes, and kept the best 50 tonnes for its own label use. It is a small wonder that it is producing good wines.

❦VICARY'S

Location: Northern Road, Luddenham, 2750; 20 km south of Penrith. (047) 73 4161.

Winemaker: Chris Niccol.

1989 Production: 140 tonnes.

Principal Wines: A full range of wines available cellar door, including fortified and flavoured wines no doubt made elsewhere. Varietal table wines include Semillon, Chablis, Fumé Blanc, Chardonnay, Traminer Riesling, Gewurztraminer, Cabernet Sauvignon, Shiraz, plus excellent Vintage Ports. Generic wines also available in both bottle and flagon. Premium table wines made at the winery from grapes grown in other regions, typically the Hunter Valley, Mudgee and Camden (local).

Distribution: Exclusively cellar door sales and mailing list. Cellar door sales Tuesday to Friday 9 a.m. to 6 p.m., weekends noon to 6 p.m. Mailing list as above.

Prices: $7 to $15 cellar door.

Vintage Rating 1986–89: White: '86, '88, '87, '89. Red: '87, '86, '89 ('88 not rated).

Outstanding Prior Vintages: Red: '85.

Summary: Vicary's is producing some excellent wines, both white and red, from Hunter Valley and Mudgee grapes transported to the winery and made there by the obviously talented winemaker Chris Niccol. The remaining wines on the list are designed to meet the tastes of the local clientele. I am far from clear who buys the first-rate table wines.

❦WOODROW WINES

Location: 'Woodrow', Olympic Way, Junee, 2593; on outskirts of town. (069) 24 1516.

Winemaker: Brian Edwards.

Principal Wines: Very limited and largely experimental batches of Traminer, Chardonnay, Rhine Riesling and Sauvignon Blanc made from 2-hectare plantings.

Distribution: Exclusively cellar door (until sold out). Cellar door sales 10 a.m. to 4 p.m. Saturday and Sunday.

Summary: A tiny operation but one approached with great purpose and seriousness by winemaker/owner Brian Edwards.

Victoria

Bendigo and District

1988 VINTAGE

After more or less normal winter conditions, a relatively cool spring delayed budburst and continuing cool and windy weather caused some flowering and fruit set problems. From that point on, it was a trouble-free vintage with a warm and dry summer virtually eliminating disease from the vineyard and allowing the grapes to ripen in perfect condition. The very warm and dry weather did cause isolated problems with defoliation, and also led a very early start to vintage after a string of cool, late harvests.

Overall, yields were good and quality was high. The white wines are generally full flavoured, but of course this is primarily a red wine district, with shiraz and cabernet sauvignon to the fore. These show all of the richness and body for which the district is renowned.

1989 VINTAGE

Good winter/spring rains and a frost-free budburst and early growing season were followed by near perfect weather at flowering, resulting in a uniform set right across the board. A very cool, cloudy but relatively dry summer followed, and halfway through February there was real concern that the grapes might not fully ripen. This concern apart, it had been an ideal season, and expectations of quality were correspondingly high.

The extreme heat of the second half of February and first week of March common to south-east Australia altered perceptions radically, with the white varieties ripening rapidly and coming into the winery in very good condition. From this point on things went rapidly downhill, with the vines reacting to the extreme stress of the hot period and failing to properly support the red grapes still remaining to be harvested. This was exacerbated by the prolonged period of cold rainy weather that followed, and in a number of vineyards shiraz was badly affected by grey and black mould. Cabernet sauvignon was less affected, but by and large failed to reach desirable sugar levels.

As always, conditions varied across this extensive district and some properties (such as Balgownie) were luckier than others, and are more than happy with the resultant wine quality. Nonetheless, the wines will be light in both flavour and body.

THE CHANGES

Mount Alexander makes its first appearance; owner Keith Walkden has established a large vineyard planted to all the classic varieties. The site is regarded by the local vignerons as excellent, so the potential is there.

Brief mention is made of Chateau Dore, a property that has been in the ownership of the Grose family since 1866. As foreshadowed in the 1988 edition of this book, Harcourt Valley vineyards has been sold; the purchaser was Macedon vigneron (and architect) Philip Honeyman. Mount Ida has been purchased by

Tisdal Wines from its previous owners Leonard French and Dr James Munroe, formally cementing an already close relationship as the Mount Ida wines have been made by Tisdal for many years.

Peter and Robyn Turley have opened a most attractive tasting room at McIvor Creek Winery; Romany Rye (now Eppalock Ridge) has undergone a substantial up-grade, although the promised details did not arrive prior to going to print; Passing Clouds now offers a range of white wines in addition to its district reds; there has been a change of winemaker at Water Wheel Vineyards; and Dominique and Anna Landragin have added a range of beautifully made and packaged still table wines to their sparkling wines.

On the debit side, as it were, Glen Bruce Estate is apparently not going to develop as quickly as owner Bruce Myers had hoped, and Wild Duck Creek Estate has likewise yet to obtain a licence. Overall, the Bendigo region is flourishing, with a large number of small growers adding their weight to one of Australia's top red wine producing regions. It has to be said, however, that some of the wine making practices of the smaller wineries fail to fully capitalise on the quality of the raw material with which they are presented. There were far too many wines in the district tasting that were simply not of commercial standard.

BALGOWNIE ESTATE

Location: Hermitage Road, Maiden Gully, 3551; 8 km west of Bendigo, off Calder Highway. (054) 49 6222.

Winemakers: Stuart Anderson and Lindsay Ross.

1989 Production: 7000 cases.

Principal Wines: Chardonnay, Cabernet Sauvignon, Pinot Noir and Hermitage under Balgownie Estate label made from 100% Balgownie grapes. Premier Cuvee range blended wines from other regions and includes Petit Blanc, Chardonnay and Cabernet Hermitage.

Distribution: Balgownie Estate wines principally mailing list and cellar door sales, with limited retail distribution through fine wine merchants in capital cities. The acquisition of Balgownie by Mildara has resulted in greater availability, but only of Premier Cuvee range. Cellar door sales 10 a.m. to 5 p.m. Monday to Saturday; mailing list enquiries to PO Maiden Gully, 3551.

Prices: $11.50 to $17.50 cellar door.

Vintage Rating: White: '87, '89, '86, '88. Red: '88, '87, '89, '86.

Outstanding Prior Vintages: '73, '76, '80.

Tasting Notes:

1989 CHARDONNAY [CS] Colour: medium to full yellow-green. *Bouquet:* rich honey textured butterscotch aromas. *Palate:* rich honeyed/ butterscotch flavours, showing the complexity of malolactic fermentation, yet (happily) still retaining luscious fruit. Tasted under difficult conditions, but could be quite outstanding, and a long way in front of what seemed to be a fairly disappointing '88.

1989 PINOT NOIR [CS] Colour: medium purple-red. *Bouquet:* of light to medium weight, with smooth red strawberry aromas of unmistakable varietal character. *Palate:* attractive sweet strawberry fruit, quite intense and then finishing with stalky green tannins; as with the Chardonnay, has great potential.

1989 HERMITAGE [CS] Colour: full purple-red. *Bouquet:* complex, rich dark berry fruits with a few fermentation characters persisting. *Palate:* attractive red berry cassis flavours, almost cabernet like, and tannin in perfect balance. The best '89 red tasted from the district.

1988 CABERNET SAUVIGNON [91] Colour: full purple-red. *Bouquet:* clean, concentrated and rich, although still closed in on itself. *Palate:* a big, rich and concentrated wine, spotlessly clean and very well balanced, though still to open up its full fruit complexities; a classic cabernet in the Bordeaux mould. Drink '94–2004.

1988 HERMITAGE [69] Colour: strong and dense purple red. *Bouquet:* complex, with strong meaty/gamey characters on top of concentrated fruit. *Palate:* very complex spicy/gamey/meaty flavours all intermingling, and somewhat jagged acid. A wine needing to come to terms with itself. Drink '93–'97.

Summary: Stuart Anderson appears to have found a more than capable custodian of the Balgownie Estate tradition in Lindsay Ross, a New Zealander who stopped in Australia for two weeks in 1979 on his way back home from Europe and never quite made it. As I have said before, Mildara really is leaving Balgownie Estate alone, and Stuart Anderson (who continues to have a substantial day to day involvement) and Lindsay Ross have produced some superb wines in the last two vintages.

BLANCHE BARKLY WINES

Location: Rheola Road, Kingower, 3517; on western outskirts of Kingower. (054) 43 3664 and (054) 38 8223.

Winemaker: David Reimers.

Principal Wines: Only red wines made, with emphasis on Cabernet Sauvignon.

Distribution: Almost exclusively cellar door sales and mailing list. Cellar door sales 9 a.m. to

5 p.m. Saturday, other times by appointment. Mailing list RMB 348, Kingower, 3517.

Tasting Notes:

1988 CABERNET SAUVIGNON [59] Colour: dense purple-red. *Bouquet:* strong, concentrated fruit with a heavy bitter/leathery sulphidic overlay. *Palate:* some very good cabernet base material once again toughened and made bitter by pronounced sulphides. It is extremely unlikely that cellaring will do anything except accentuate the bitterness. Drink '90–'91.

Summary: It really is distressing to see such an easily corrected fault allowed to so disfigure potentially excellent wine.

CHATEAU DORE

Location: Mandurang, 3551; 8 km south from Bendigo Fountain via Mitchell Street. (054) 39 5278.

Winemaker: Ivan Grose.

1989 Production: Not stated.

Principal Wines: Rhine Riesling, Chardonnay, Shiraz and Cabernet Sauvignon.

Distribution: Exclusively cellar door sales and mail order. Cellar door sales 10.30 a.m. to 5 p.m. Wednesday, Thursday and Saturday; Tuesday 12.30 p.m. to 5 p.m.; Sunday 1 p.m. to 5 p.m.; closed Monday and Friday but open Good Friday.

Summary: Chateau Dore does not exhibit wines in shows nor seek a high profile. Local vignerons are circumspect in their comments, and you should make your own judgment about wine style and quality.

CHATEAU LE AMON

Location: 140 km post, Calder Highway, Bendigo, 3550; 10 km south-west of town. (054) 47 7995.

Winemaker: Philip Leamon.

1989 Production: Not stated, but normally around 2500 cases.

Principal Wines: Semillon/Rhine Riesling, Rhine Riesling, Chardonnay, Shiraz and Cabernet Sauvignon.

Distribution: Substantial cellar door sales and mail order, but also significant retail distribution throughout capital cities. Cellar door sales 10 a.m. to 5 p.m. weekdays (but closed Tuesdays except during school holidays), 10 a.m. to 6 p.m. Saturday and noon to 6 p.m. Sundays. Mailing list enquiries to PO Box 487, Bendigo, 3550.

Prices: $12 to $13.50 cellar door.

Tasting Notes:

1987 CABERNET SAUVIGNON [78] Colour: medium purple-red. *Bouquet:* clean, with attractive relatively soft fruit and lifted lemony oak. *Palate:* a most attractively modulated, gently astringent cabernet, firm and clean, set against attractive lemony oak. Drink '91–'94.

1987 SHIRAZ [72] Colour: medium to full red-purple. *Bouquet:* firm and quite concentrated, with a slightly bitter sulphide-derived leathery edge. *Palate:* strong red berry fruit, complex and structured, and still with richness, yet with a slightly bitter finish. A wine that might have been outstanding. Drink '92–'96.

Summary: Chateau Le Amon seems destined to change hands; the purchaser will acquire a winery and vineyard that, since its establishment in 1973, has produced some of Bendigo's finest red wines.

EPPALOCK RIDGE
(formerly Romany Rye)

Location: Metcalfe Pool Road, Redesdale, 3444; 9 km north of town. (054) 25 3135.

Winemaker: Rod Hourigan.

Principal Wines: Dry White (semillon/chardonnay), Shiraz and Cabernet Sauvignon.

Distribution: Principally cellar door and mailing list. Cellar door sales 10 a.m. to 6 p.m. Monday to Saturday, Sunday noon to 6 p.m. Mailing list enquiries to RSD Redesdale, 3444.

Summary: Changes are in the wind, but it did not blow hard enough to reach me prior to this book going to print.

❦ HARCOURT VALLEY VINEYARDS

Location: 118 km post, Calder Highway, Harcourt, 3453.
(054) 74 2223.

Winemaker: Philip Honeyman.

Principal Wines: Rhine Riesling, Cabernet Sauvignon and Shiraz.

Distribution: Principally cellar door sales and mailing list, with limited retail distribution in Melbourne, Sydney, Canberra, Adelaide and Victorian country towns. Cellar door sales 10 a.m. to 6 p.m. Monday and Thursday to Saturday, noon to 6 p.m. Sunday. Closed Tuesday and Wednesday except public holidays.

Summary: Again, up-to-date details were not forthcoming. It is uncertain whether the Harcourt Valley label will continue, or be merged with Honeyman's Macedon label.

❦ THE HEATHCOTE WINERY

Location: 183-185 High Street, Heathcote, 3523.
(054) 33 2595.

Winemaker: Stephen Reed.

1989 Production: Not stated, but usually in the vicinity of 5000 cases.

Principal Wines: Chardonnay, Chenin blanc, Traminer, Shiraz, Pinot Noir, Cabernet Shiraz, Cabernet Sauvignon and Viognier.

Distribution: Principally cellar door sales and mailing list; limited capital city fine wine retail distribution. Cellar door sales 10 a.m. to 6 p.m. 7 days.

Prices: $8 to $19.50 cellar door.

Vintage Rating 1986-89: White: '87, '88, '86, '89. Red: '86, '87, '89, '88.

Tasting Notes:

1989 GEWURZTRAMINER [78] Colour: excellent, bright, light to medium green-yellow. _Bouquet:_ clean, attractive lychee spice fruit aromas; beautifully made. _Palate:_ attractive light and crisp spicy/lychee fruit; again, very good wine-making evident. Drink '90.

1988 CHARDONNAY [87] Colour: light to medium green-yellow. _Bouquet:_ complex tangy fruit with well-handled spicy oak, and a touch of Burgundian sulphide. _Palate:_ very complex rich and tangy grapefruit characters; an intense wine again showing distinct Burgundian characters. Drink '90–'92.

1987 PINOT NOIR [68] Colour: light to medium red, with just a touch of purple remaining. _Bouquet:_ light, slightly lemony fruit and oak, tending to neutrality and with little varietal character evident. _Palate:_ some light strawberry pinot flavours discernible, but the wine lacks richness and structure. Drink '90.

1986 CABERNET SHIRAZ [73] Colour: medium purple-red. _Bouquet:_ strong lemony oak tends to dominate clean but fairly light fruit. _Palate:_ clean, with rather hard lemony oak dominant; the tannins are soft, but the wine needs more flesh to balance the oak. Drink '90–'93.

Summary: Heathcote consistently produces some of the district's finest white wines, an ironical twist given that its own vineyards are planted exclusively to red grapes. All of the wines are clean (in other words, devoid of sulphide/mercaptan taints) which simply goes to show what careful winemaking and an awareness of the problem can achieve.

❦ HUNTLEIGH

Location: Tunnecliffes Lane, Heathcote, 3523;
8 km north-west of Heathcote. Off Northern
Highway.
(054) 33 2795.

Winemaker: Leigh Hunt.

1989 Production: 340 cases.

Principal Wines: Huntleigh makes and offers two
separately sourced and separately labelled
brands. Under the Huntleigh label, Traminer
and Cabernet Sauvignon; and under the
Leckie's She-Oak Hill Vineyard label, Shiraz.

Distribution: Principally mailing list and cellar
door sales. Mailing list enquiries to PO Box 43,
Heathcote, 3523. Cellar door sales 10 a.m. to
5 p.m. weekends and public holidays or by
appointment.

Prices: $8.50 to $11 cellar door.

Tasting Notes:

1988 LECKIE'S SHIRAZ [69] Colour: medium to
full purple-red. *Bouquet:* strong coconut/
vanillan oak, with solid fruit dulled by just a
whisper of sulphide. *Palate:* big, red berry fruit
and some supporting sweet oak; once again the
wine is needlessly toughened up by a trace of
sulphide. Drink '92–'95.

*1988 HUNTLEIGH CABERNET SAUVIGNON [64]
Colour:* medium red-purple. *Bouquet:* solid,
fairly ripe fruit with a touch of caramel oak and
a trace of leathery bitterness. *Palate:* sweet fruit
with some unusual caramel flavours, almost
certainly deriving from oak. Drink '92–'95.

Summary: A small, basically weekend operation
for former Melbourne stock broker Leigh
Hunt. The tiny production always sells out
fairly rapidly.

❦ JASPER HILL

Location: Drummonds Lane, Heathcote, 3523;
6 km north of Heathcote.
(054) 33 2528.

Winemaker: Ron Laughton.

1989 Production: 2500 cases.

Principal Wines: Georgia's Paddock Riesling,
Georgia's Paddock Shiraz and Emily's Paddock
Shiraz/Cabernet Franc. Beautiful and
innovative packaging a feature of the wines.
1987 Bushfire damage to Georgia's Paddock
caused two year gap in continuity of both
Georgia's Paddock wines. Replaced by
"Friends" Shiraz in 1987 and by "Georgia and
Friends" Shiraz in 1988. Return to 100% estate
grown wine 1989 vintage.

Distribution: Principally cellar door sales and mailing
list; limited fine wine retail Sydney, Melbourne
and Adelaide. Cellar door sales 10 a.m. to 6 p.m.
weekends, when wine available, weekdays by
appointment. Being a small producer, it may be
wise to ring first. Mailing list enquiries to PO Box
110, Heathcote, 3523.

Prices: $13 to $20 cellar door.

Vintage Rating 1986-89: Made irrelevant by effect
of bushfires.

Tasting Notes:

1988 GEORGIA & FRIENDS SHIRAZ [88] Colour:
full red-purple. *Bouquet:* clean and elegant
fruit set against fine, lemony oak. *Palate:* very
complex, with full, strong red berry fruit and
marked, persistent tannins; a cellaring special.
Drink '94–2000.

*1988 EMILY'S PADDOCK SHIRAZ/CABERNET
FRANC [76] Colour:* full red-purple. *Bouquet:*
the lifted characters evident in Georgia's are
even more pronounced in this wine, leading to
a touch of sharpness. *Palate:* very big wine with
strong cassis flavours and pronounced tannins;
the volatility evident on the bouquet will not
worry most consumers but could distract the
technically minded. Drink '93–'97.

Summary: Ron Laughton has learnt a great deal about winemaking in a relatively short career, quite apart from the trauma of the January 1987 bushfires. His red wines thoroughly deserve their reputation and the undoubted loyalty of the Jasper Hill clientele.

🍇 *LANDRAGIN*

Location: 102 Fisken Road, Mount Helen, 3350; 10 km from Ballarat towards Geelong. (053) 41 3941.

Winemaker: Dominique Landragin.

1989 Production: 10,000 cases.

Principal Wines: Méthode champenoise comprising Reserve, Blanc de Noirs and Rosé. Table wines comprising Rhine Riesling, Chardonnay, Shiraz, Cabernet Sauvignon and Cabernets.

Distribution: Virtually exclusively through retail outlets; National Distributors Elders IXL Wines & Spirits. For mailing list enquiries write to Landragin Australia, PO Box 15, Buninyong, 3357.

Prices: Méthode Champenoise : $17.95 to $22.95; Table wines: $11.99 to $18.99.

Tasting Notes:

LANDRAGIN RESERVE NV [70] Colour: light straw yellow, with good mousse. *Bouquet:* full and clean, but tending to fruit-softness. *Palate:* a high flavoured wine, with some spicy notes from the pinot noir component, but lacking the tightness of the very best Australian sparkling wines. Certainly very commercial and easy to drink. Drink '90.

1988 RHINE RIESLING [74] Colour: medium yellow-green. *Bouquet:* developed, soft lime flavours, not particularly aromatic and very slightly broad. *Palate:* a big, full flavoured wine with distinct sweetness in an eminently satisfactory commercial style. Drink '90–'91.

1987 CHARDONNAY [80] Colour: bright light to medium green-yellow. *Bouquet:* smooth, with very well balanced and integrated fruit and oak. *Palate:* the oak is a little more obtrusive than in the bouquet, with smooth melon peach fruit flavours; again, a cunningly wrought wine to satisfy the most discriminating. Drink '90–'91.

1986 CABERNETS [81] Colour: medium red-purple. *Bouquet:* stylish and fragrant, with the softening and aromatic influence of cabernet franc quite evident; the oak is just a little dominant for perfection. *Palate:* uncompromisingly oaky, but does have lovely red berry fruit flavours and gentle balancing tannins; good after taste. Drink '90–'93.

1986 CABERNET SAUVIGNON [87] Colour: medium purple-red. *Bouquet:* clean and firm with well balanced fruit and oak. *Palate:* most attractive, complex, bottle-developed red berry and cedary oak flavours; wine really comes alive on the finish and with the after-taste, having exceptional balance and mouth-feel. Drink '90–'95.

Summary: It is remarkable how the all-important blending skills of the sparkling winemaker have produced such a stylish range of table wines. The sheer quality of the wines is such that the brilliant packaging is probably no more than an added extra, but the combination should certainly ensure ready acceptance in the market place.

🍇 *McIVOR CREEK*

Location: Costerfield Road, Heathcote, 3523; 4 km south of Heathcote (1 km off Northern Highway). (054) 33 2711.

Winemaker: Peter Turley.

1989 Production: 4500 cases.

Principal Wines: Red wine specialist with Shiraz

and Cabernet Sauvignon produced from estate vineyards and from local contract growers at Nagambie, Graytown and Nathalia.

Distribution: Principally through mailing list and cellar door sales. Melbourne retail and restaurant distribution through Alexander and Paterson. Mailing list bulletins twice yearly; address as above. Cellar door sales 10 a.m. to 5.30 p.m. 7 days. BBQ facilities provided and picnic lunches encouraged.

Prices: $7.10 to $11 cellar door.

Tasting Notes:

1988 SHIRAZ [69] Colour: medium purple-red. _Bouquet:_ firm berry fruit with a touch of cabernet-like herbaceousness. _Palate:_ the firm and clean bouquet gives way to a wine which shows all the signs of having just been bottled; some caramel oak and then rather disjointed flavours culminating in a slightly furry finish. Was very possibly seen at its worst moment and may improve markedly once it settles down. Drink '93–'97.

1988 CABERNET SHIRAZ [78] Colour: medium red-purple. _Bouquet:_ light to medium, clean minty fruit and low oak. _Palate:_ strong spicy/minty fruit typical of the district; has much more flavour than the bouquet would suggest; firm structure and good tannin. A touch of new oak would have lifted this wine into the highest class. Drink '93–'99.

Summary: The picturesque hilltop McIvor Creek Winery and tasting facility is well worth a visit. Red wine quality appears promising.

🍇 _MOUNT ALEXANDER VINEYARD_

Location: Calder Highway, North Harcourt, 3453; 2 kms north of Harcourt. (054) 74 2262.

Winemaker: Keith Walkden.

1989 Production: 2500 cases.

Principal Wines: Chardonnay, Rhine Riesling, Sauvignon Blanc, Semillon, Cabernet Sauvignon Merlot, Cabernet Franc Merlot, Shiraz and Pinot Noir.

Distribution: Principally cellar door sales and mailing list; limited retail distribution serviced direct ex-winery. Cellar door sales 9 a.m. to 5.30 p.m. Tuesday to Saturday; open 7 days during holidays and each day through long weekend.

Prices: $10 to $15 cellar door.

Tasting Notes:

1988 RHINE RIESLING/MULLER THURGAU [69] Colour: light straw green. _Bouquet:_ clean, with light pastille fruit aromas and a touch of spice. _Palate:_ very light bodied with light spicy/pastille fruit flavours; cloys fractionally on the finish, but by no means is a bad wine, and by far the best of the four or five Mount Alexander whites tasted. Drink '90.

1989 CABERNET FRANC [CS] Colour: medium purple-red. _Bouquet:_ fresh and clean with herbal/tobacco aromas. _Palate:_ tangy light herbal tobacco flavours which are quite promising.

1988 CABERNET SAUVIGNON CABERNET FRANC MERLOT [75] Colour: dense purple red. _Bouquet:_ quite full and solid, with some minty overtones. _Palate:_ strong minty fruit flavours; the wine dips structurally in the mid-palate, but should fill out with more bottle age. Drink '93–'96.

Summary: Mount Alexander has quite an extensive vineyard established on a prime site, and the potential for quality wine is certainly there. At the moment that quality is extremely variable, particularly with the white wines, and careful selection is recommended. Those reviewed were by far the best of a large range tasted.

🍇 _MOUNT IDA_

Location: Northern Highway, Heathcote (vineyard only).

Winemaker: Jeff Clarke (Tisdall).

1989 Production: 1000 cases.

Principal Wines: Shiraz and Cabernet Shiraz.

Distribution: Limited fine wine retail sales in Melbourne.

Prices: $13 to $18 retail.

Vintage Rating 1986–89: White: '86, '89 ('87 and '88 destroyed by bushfire).

Outstanding Prior Vintages: '82, '84, '85.

Tasting Notes:

1985 SHIRAZ CABERNET [90} _Colour:_ dense purple-red, holding hue extraordinarily well. _Bouquet:_ very youthful and spotlessly clean; warm and rich sweet minty fruit set against warm vanillan oak. _Palate:_ incredibly concentrated rich, minty fruit with soft vanillan/charred oak; is developing exceptionally slowly and will clearly be long lived, although it is already accessible. Drink '90–2000.

Summary: The change in ownership of Mount Ida should not result in any change in wine style, although it is inevitable that in future the price of the wine will more accurately reflect its great quality. Once again, the contrast between skilled and amateur winemaking is painfully obvious.

Mailing list as above. Limited fine wine retail distribution and some interstate merchants.

Prices: $16.50 to $18.50 cellar door.

Tasting Notes:

1987 CABERNET SAUVIGNON [90] _Colour:_ medium to full red-purple. _Bouquet:_ attractive full sweet berry fruit and strong vanillan/coconut oak. _Palate:_ full red berry/plum flavours complexed by stylish spicy oak treatment; beautifully weighted tannins; full, clean, complex and stylish. Drink '94–'99.

1987 BLEND [65] _Colour:_ medium red-purple. _Bouquet:_ attractive red berry fruit marred by bitter sulphide. _Palate:_ lovely berry fruit with a touch of mint, and then that dreaded bitterness on the finish. A disappointment after the superb cabernet of the same year, but you cannot win them all. Drink '90–'93.

Summary: The delightfully eccentric Graeme Leith has once again produced an outstanding red, albeit in tiny quantities: the wine was limited to mailing list customers with a maximum purchase of one case per customer, and is–alas–long gone. It is a mailing list well worth belonging to.

🍇 _PASSING CLOUDS_

Location: Kurting Road, Kingower, 3517; in township.
(054) 38 8257.

Winemaker: Graeme Leith.

1989 Production: 2500 cases approximately.

Principal Wines: Red table wines only estate-produced; Pinot Noir, Shiraz Cabernet and Cabernet Sauvignon. Some white wines made under contract by others.

Distribution: Principally cellar door sales and mailing list; cellar door sales 10 a.m. to 6 p.m. most days, but telephone first for appointment.

🍇 _WATER WHEEL VINEYARDS_

Location: Bridgewater-on-Loddon, 1 km north of Bridgewater, 3516.
(054) 37 3213.

Winemaker: Bruce Trevaskis.

1989 Production: 5500 cases.

Principal Wines: Rhine Riesling, Chardonnay, Chablis, Hermitage, Cabernet Sauvignon, Liqueur Port and Vintage Port.

Distribution: Cellar door sales, mailing list and limited Victorian and retail distribution. Distributed direct in Victoria, and through The Incredible Wine Company in NSW. Cellar door sales 9 a.m. to 5 p.m. Monday to Friday. Saturday 10 a.m. to noon and 1 p.m. to 5 p.m., Sunday noon to 5 p.m.

Prices: $5 to $17 cellar door.

Vintage Rating 1986-89: White: '89, '88, '86, '87. Red: '89, '88, '86, '87.

Tasting Notes:

1989 CHARDONNAY [CS] Colour: bright and clear light to medium green-yellow. *Bouquet:* beautifully handled complex charred oak with good supporting fruit. *Palate:* finely structured wine with complex charred barrel-ferment oak; an absolute revolution in style and quality for this winery, and bursting with promise. Headed towards 90 points.

1988 CABERNET SAUVIGNON [79] Colour: full purple-red. *Bouquet:* big, ripe and full concentrated cabernet. *Palate:* again concentrated ripe and high flavoured, although there is just a faint edge of rough/meaty character which will hopefully settle down with age. Drink '93–'97.

LIQUEUR PORT [79] Colour: dense purple-red. *Bouquet:* spicy/chocolatey/ earthy fruit with clean spirit. *Palate:* soft, clean textured dark chocolate flavours; a real liqueur port made in the sweet Australian mould, but flavoursome and well put together. Drink '90–'95.

Summary: The arrival of Bill Trevaskis has seemingly had an immediate and dramatic impact on the style and quality at Water Wheel. The vineyards are now fully mature, and it would seem great things are in store.

WILD DUCK CREEK ESTATE

Location: Cnr Spring Flat Road and Carboons Lane, Heathcote, 3606; 3.5 km west of Heathcote. (03) 781 2939.

Winemakers: David and Diana Anderson.

Principal Wines: Shiraz only release so far (made from grapes purchased in central Victoria); a Bordeaux-blend will be made from the estate plantings of cabernet sauvignon, cabernet franc, merlot, malbec and petit verdot.

Distribution: Will be cellar door sales (weekends only) and mailing list when licence is granted.

Tasting Notes:

1989 BORDEAUX BLEND [CS] Colour: dense, youthful purple-red. *Bouquet:* full red berry fruits and strong charred oak/barrel-ferment characters. *Palate:* extremely youthful, jumpy high-octane red berry fruits with outstanding potential. Needs much work but could be a great wine.

Summary: The Wild Duck Creek vineyard has proved its worth. A winery is now under construction on-site, and if the wines are kept clean, with adequate SO$_2$ protection, some exciting releases are in store.

YELLOWGLEN

Location: White's Road, Smythesdale, 3551; off Glenelg Highway, south-west of Ballarat. (054) 42 8617.

Winemaker: Jeffrey Wilkinson.

1989 Production: Very large, as befits the market leader in its price bracket.

Principal Wines: Méthode champenoise specialist, offering NV Brut, Brut Cremant, Brut Rosé and Cuvee Victoria (the last a vintage wine).

Distribution: National retail through all types of outlets.

Prices: $12 to $19 retail.

Vintage Rating 1986–89: '87, '86, '88, '89.

Outstanding Prior Vintages: '80.

Tasting Notes:

1987 CUVEE VICTORIA [79] Colour: light yellow-green with good mousse. *Bouquet:* clean with light and lively fruit, and none of the slightly coarse characters evident in earlier vintages. *Palate:* clean, gently fruity, with slightly grassy/green fruit flavours; clean and fresh; just a touch of yeast autolysis to add complexity. Drink '90.

BRUT NV [74] Colour: light green-yellow. *Bouquet:* crisp, clean, slightly green fruit aroma with no evident yeast impact. *Palate:* light, fresh and somewhat green fruit, yet not hard; cleverly made and balanced commercial sparkling wine. Drink '90.

BRUT CREMANT [78] Colour: bright, medium green-yellow. *Bouquet:* clean, smooth and fruity; not complex but very commercial. *Palate:* once again fruit driven; the balance is good and flavourful; an extremely commercial young wine in a distinctively Australian approach to style. Drink '90.

Summary: I have been critical of the inherent quality of the Yellowglen wines for some time now, and I suspect Mildara (Yellowglen's owner) has itself been aware of the problems. However that may be, the wines tasted in July 1989 for this edition were far better than any previously encountered under the Yellowglen label.

clean red berry fruit with lemony oak which is slightly hard on the back palate; soft tannins. Drink '91–'94.

Summary: The Zuber Estate wines are made by Lew Knight at Granite Hills; half the production is marketed by Knights and the other by Zuber, but each wine is in fact identical. The '85 Shiraz was very successful in shows and exhibitions, but on the several occasions I tasted it, I was less enthusiastic. Nonetheless, some good wines at very low cellar door prices can be found at Zuber.

ZUBER ESTATE

Location: Northern Highway, Heathcote, 3523; 1 km north of town.
(054) 33 2142.

Winemakers: Ilbno Zuber and Lew Knight.

1989 Production: Not stated.

Principal Wines: Shiraz, released under vineyard names including House Block and Pink Cliffs.

Distribution: Cellar door sales and mailing list. Cellar door sales 9 a.m. to 5 p.m. Monday to Saturday and Sunday noon to 6 p.m.

Prices: $6 to $10 cellar door.

Tasting Notes:

1986 PINK CLIFFS SHIRAZ [74] Colour: medium purple-red. *Bouquet:* clean berry fruit set against lemony, slightly sawdusty oak. *Palate:*

Central Goulburn Valley

1988 VINTAGE

Once again, the variable winter rainfall across Central Victoria was evident: in contrast to Great Western, winter rainfall was plentiful. However, in common with all of the Southern and Central Victorian regions, cold winds interrupted flowering, particularly in the Mount Helen Vineyard in the Strathbogie Ranges. The late flowering varieties were especially affected, with cabernet sauvignon and rhine riesling ultimately producing much reduced crops.

A warm to hot and very dry summer followed.

The Nagambie region received only 72 mm of rainfall in the five-month period from January to May. Here again the pattern was similar to other Victorian districts: almost no disease, but problems with vine stress and defoliation where supplementary water was not available.

Quality overall was very good. The white wines have abundant flavour, good varietal character and should age well. Some of the red wines are outstanding, with intense colour and body.

1989 VINTAGE

Excellent winter, spring and follow-up rains running through to January ensured the season got away to a flying start, with good set and the promise of above average quantities of high quality grapes. However, once the weather turned warmer in January, downy and powdery mildew required constant vigilance and spraying.

The hot weather at the end of February/ early March arrested disease, and led to the rapid ripening of the white varieties. Those who picked before the rain commenced in mid-March received some superb fruit, with semillon, chardonnay and marsanne all in top condition. Chateau Tahbilk, for one, expects some out-standing white wines from the year.

The pattern then changed dramatically: cold weather and rain prevented shiraz and rhine riesling from ripening before mould became rampant. Chateau Tahbilk left between 60 and 80 tonnes of shiraz unpicked, while at Mitchelton 70 tonnes of rhine riesling was lost as a potential 85-tonne crop became a 15-tonne crop of botrytised late-harvest style.

As always, the tight-skinned, loosely bunched cabernet sauvignon stood up to the rain, and some reasonably elegant cabernet can be expected. It is the year that might have been: a potentially great vintage spoilt by rain.

THE CHANGES

The principal change is the disappearance of Seymour Vineyards. The property was in effect sold in two parcels: some of the vineyards went to two Melbourne solicitors (a husband and wife team) while the winery, cellar door sales and remaining vineyards (but no stock) went to

different ownership and has now been re-named Somerset Crossing (after briefly being called River View Wines).

Osicka's Vineyard, which lies more or less halfway between Central Goulburn district and the Bendigo district and is sometimes included in the latter group, has undergone a minor name change and label facelift. To celebrate this, some very good red wines have been released.

Mount Helen has been listed in its own right for the first time; previously the wines were described under the separate Tisdall entry in the North Goulburn River chapter.

BELVEDERE CELLARS

Location: 399 High Street, Nagambie, 3608; on north-western outskirts of town. (057) 94 2514.

Winemaker: David Traeger.

1989 Production: 1500 cases.

Principal Wines: Cabernet Sauvignon, Shiraz and Cabernet Dolce; also released cellar door only Cabernet Shiraz Merlot, Late Harvest Riesling, Spatlese Lexia and Old Tawny Port.

Distribution: Principally cellar door and mailing list, with wholesale distribution through Vinicol Liquor Distributors, 27 Colebrook Street, Brunswick, 3056. Cellar door sales 10 a.m. to 5 p.m. 7 days. Mailing list enquiries as above.

Prices: Cellar door range $5 to $9; others to $12.80.

Vintage Rating 1986-89: White: '88, '89. Red: '86, '88, '87, '89.

Tasting Notes:

1987 CABERNET SAUVIGNON [80] Colour: medium purple-red. *Bouquet:* clean, with a pleasant blend of red berry and slightly firmer herbaceous cabernet aromas and a touch of lemony oak. *Palate:* very pleasant red berry/dark berry fruit set against lemony oak; soft, lingering tannins; light to medium weight wine with some real pretensions to style. Drink '92–'96.

Summary: Belvedere is moving cautiously; as the notes indicate, the 1987 Cabernet is a lovely wine, but the shiraz of the same vintage was not reviewable due to a high level of volatility.

CHATEAU TAHBILK

Location: Tabilk, 3607; off western side of Goulburn Valley Highway, 8 km south-west of Nagambie. (057) 94 2555.

Winemaker: Alister Purbrick.

1989 Production: 58,000 cases.

Principal Wines: White varietal wines comprise Rhine Riesling, Semillon, Chardonnay, Marsanne and Chardonnay Marsanne (blend). Red wines are Cabernet Sauvignon and Shiraz, together with a yearly release of Private Bin red (usually though not invariably Cabernet Sauvignon) and usually eight years old.

Distribution: National retail distribution through Rhine Castle Wines Pty Ltd (all States). Cellar door sales in one of Australia's most beautiful wineries, 9 a.m. to 5 p.m. Monday to Saturday, noon to 5 p.m. Sunday and all public holidays except Christmas Day and Good Friday. Mailing list also available, address as above.

Prices: $9.60 to $26.95 recommended retail.

Vintage Rating 1986-89: White: '89, '88, '87, '86. Red: '86, '88, '87, '89.

Outstanding Prior Vintages: White: '80, '82. Red: '68, '71, '76, '79, '81.

Tasting Notes:

1989 RHINE RIESLING [77] Colour: light straw-green. *Bouquet:* quite complex, with slight toasty aromas already building. *Palate:* generously flavoured, with strong toasty characters and just a suspicion of phenolics; would appear to be an early drinking style. Drink '90–'91.

1989 SEMILLON [CS] Colour: bright, light green-yellow. *Bouquet:* shows exemplary winemaking; weighty, with a touch of herbaceous varietal character, and a few fermentation characters lingering. *Palate:* potent fruit, very clean; excellent mid-palate weight and richness;

appears to be headed for 85 points or above.

1988 CHARDONNAY [81] Colour: medium straw yellow. *Bouquet:* elegant, light yet complex fruit and oak with some tangy grapefruit aromas. *Palate:* light but stylish; harmonious oak and fruit balance and integration; some tangy grapefruit flavours appear on a clean, crisp finish. Drink '90–'93.

1988 MARSANNE [75] Colour: light straw green. *Bouquet:* classic varietal character, with clean soft honeysuckle fruit and no oak influence. *Palate:* soft and clean, with some honeysuckle flavours again evident; good acid balance in a light and not terribly complex wine. Drink '90–'92.

1987 SHIRAZ [70] Colour: medium red-purple. *Bouquet:* some spicy fruit evident dulled by a whisper of meaty sulphide. *Palate:* again a touch of spice is evident; pleasant and quite complex red berry fruit with good structure; would have rated higher points were it not for the bouquet. Drink '92–'97.

1987 CABERNET SAUVIGNON [81] Colour: medium to full purple-red. *Bouquet:* by the standards of Chateau Tahbilk, very accessible, with some soft plum/berry fruit aromas, and just a touch of astringency. *Palate:* strong plum/cassis/berry fruits, which are then overtaken by typical astringent tannins; the balance does appear to be there and the wine will (as always with Tahbilk) benefit from prolonged cellaring. Drink '94–2000.

Summary: As stated on a previous occasion, Chateau Tahbilk is a rock of ages. There is incredible continuity and style from year to year, subject only to the subtle variations that each vintage necessarily produces. If you like the style, you will never be disappointed when you pull the cork on a bottle of Chateau Tahbilk.

GLENMOUR ESTATE

Location: Johnsons Lane, Northwood, 3660; 10 km north of Seymour.
(057) 92 1229.

Winemaker: Alister Purbrick (contract).

Principal Wines: Dry White (a trebbiano/crouchen blend), Bin 121 (a light dry red made from mataro), Malbec and Spatlese Riesling.

Distribution: Presently exclusively cellar door sales and mailing list. Mailing list enquiries to PO Box 355, Seymour, 3660. Cellar door sales 9 a.m. to 5 p.m. Saturday and public holidays, noon to 5 p.m. Sunday.

Tasting Notes:

1987 BIN 121 MATARO [74] Colour: medium red-purple. *Bouquet:* solid, sweet fruit with a faint touch of spice and clean, lemony oak. *Palate:* again a clean wine, with fractionally nondescript fruit although it is nicely balanced by lemony oak, and rounded off by soft tannin. Drink '91–'94.

1986 MALBEC [79] Colour: dense purple-red. *Bouquet:* rich, sweet berry aromas, almost jammy; quintessential varietal aroma. *Palate:* extreme manifestation of malbec varietal character with strong berry/jammy flavours; has really come on over the last 18 months since it was tasted for the previous edition of this book, and will seemingly go on forever. Drink '90–'95.

Summary: A somewhat esoteric range of wines, with distinct variation in quality; the best are well made.

HAYWARD'S OF WHITEHEADS CREEK

Location: Lot 18A, Hall Lane, Seymour, 3660; 10 km east of Seymour off Kobyboyn Road. RMB 4270.
(057) 92 3050 (Residence).

Winemaker: Sid Hayward.

1989 Production: 4000 litres only.

Principal Wines: Rhine Riesling, Dry Red and Shiraz Port.

Distribution: Exclusively cellar door sales 9 a.m. to 5 p.m. 7 days (excluding Christmas Day and Good Friday).

Prices: $3.50 to $10 cellar door; mostly $6.50.

Vintage Rating 1986–89: White: '87, '88, '89. Red: '87, '86, '88, '89.

Tasting Notes:

1988 DRY RED [67] Colour: youthful medium to full purple-red. *Bouquet:* quite rich fruit with some slightly meaty/gamey characters. *Palate:* youthful fruit; slightly empty structure on the mid-palate, and a trace of bitterness on the finish deriving from those meaty/gamey sulphides. It is to be hoped that these characters do not grow with age. Drink '90–'93.

Summary: The wines of Hayward's are as rustic as the proud proclamation on the label "From bare earth to bottle" suggests they may be. Not all come up to commercially acceptable standards.

HENKE

Location: Lot 30A, Henke Lane, Yarck, 3719; off Mansfield Road, 2 km north of Cathkin and 4 km south of Yarck. (057) 97 6277.

Winemaker: Tim Miller.

1989 Production: 330 cases.

Principal Wines: Shiraz, Shiraz Cabernet and Cabernet Sauvignon.

Distribution: Principally cellar door; limited retail distribution in Melbourne through various specialist retailers.

Prices: $8 to $14.50 retail (depending on vintage).

Summary: Some retailers still stock the '82 vintage

wines of Henke, while the "current" release is 1985. However, no wines were submitted for assessment for this edition.

LONGLEAT

Location: Old Weir Road, Murchison, 3610; 2 km south of town. (058) 25 2294.

Winemakers: Alister Purbrick (consultant) and Peter Schulz.

1989 Production: 3000 cases.

Principal Wines: Under Longleat (estate-grown) label, wines comprise Shiraz, Cabernet Sauvignon, Spatlese Rhine Riesling and Rhine Riesling. Under Murchison label, wines made from other regions comprise Champagne, Muscat and Vintage Port; also soon to be released are the King Valley Chardonnay and Sauvignon Blanc.

Distribution: Principally cellar door sales and mailing list. Cellar door sales 9 a.m. to 6 p.m. Monday to Saturday and 10 a.m. to 6 p.m. Sunday. Open most public holidays. All enquiries to Murchison Vineyard Company Pty. Ltd., Box 25, Murchison, 3610.

Prices: $7.95 to $13.50 cellar door.

Vintage Rating 1986-89: White: '89, '88, '87, '86. Red: '86, '87, '89, '88.

Tasting Notes:

1989 RHINE RIESLING [CS] Colour: very good green-yellow. *Bouquet:* a rather sharp/hard edge takes away from the varietal fruit; it may have been due to free SO_2 and, if so, this should present no problem with bottle age. *Palate:* once again, good fruit depth and varietal character is hardened off somewhat; the wine was tasted when very young and may prove to be far better than the tasting notes would indicate.

1987 LONGLEAT SHIRAZ [77] Colour: medium red-purple. *Bouquet:* strong red berry fruit with a slightly astringent leathery edge. *Bouquet:* very strong red berry fruit bordering on being jammy, but nonetheless full of flavour. Once again, tannin under control. Drink '93–'97.

1986 SHIRAZ [78] Colour: medium purple-red. *Bouquet:* complex sweet berry fruit with a touch of accompanying farmyard aromas. *Palate:* most attractive velvety sweet berry flavours and low tannin; would have rated higher points were it not for the slightly errant bouquet. Drink '92–'95.

Summary: The up-coming releases of Longleat Shiraz show far better balance than prior vintages, which were extremely tannic. Fruit flavours are generous, and the wines should develop well.

MITCHELTON

Mitchelton
Classic Release
MARSANNE

Location: Mitchellstown via Nagambie, 3608; due west of Tabilk, off Goulburn Valley Highway. (057) 94 2710.

Winemaker: Don Lewis.

1989 Production: 1.8 million litres.

Principal Wines: The substantial range of white and red wines comes under three principal releases. At the top end are the Classic Release wines, being re-releases of aged Show Reserve stocks. The premium current release wines comprise the Print Label Cabernet Sauvignon and the Mitchelton series made from grapes grown either at Mitchelton and the Central Goulburn Valley or in other quality areas of Australia (particularly Coonawarra but also Mount Barker in Western Australia), including Rhine Riesling, Botrytis-Affected Rhine Riesling and Cabernet Sauvignon. The Mitchelton label wines include Rhine Riesling, Marsanne (wood matured), Chardonnay

(wood matured), Semillon (wood matured) and Cabernet Sauvignon. Nattier, a sparkling wine, is the most recent addition to the range. The Thomas Mitchell range is dealt with under a separate entry.

Distribution: Extensive eastern State retail distribution through affiliated distribution networks. Cellar door sales from a spectacular modern winery with a host of other attractions too numerous to list exhaustively but including walk-through aviary, 55-m high observation tower and Riverbank Grill open Sundays and public Holidays. Cellar door sales 9 a.m. to 5 p.m. Monday to Saturday and 10 a.m. to 5 p.m Sunday. Very active mailing list with highly informative, regular brochures; address as above.

Prices: $5.60 to $16.20 retail.

Vintage Rating 1986-89: White: '86, '88, '87, '89. Red: '86, '88, '87, '89.

Outstanding Prior Vintages: '78, '80, '81, '84.

Tasting Notes:

NATTIER NV [71] Colour: medium yellow-green. *Bouquet:* quite complex and rich; unusual fruit/varietal character base, but attractive nonetheless. *Palate:* full bodied, rich fruity/creamy style, short on elegance but long on flavour; made from a blend of chardonnay and marsanne. Drink '90–'91.

1989 RHINE RIESLING [85] Colour: light straw green. *Bouquet:* clean, soft lime with very good fruit aromas, exceptionally well made. *Palate:* abundant lime/pineapple fruit flavours, rich and yet not cloying; made from grapes sourced elsewhere than the home vineyard, and a triumph for the vintage. Drink '90–'94.

1988 WOOD MATURED MARSANNE [81] Colour: bright yellow-green of medium depth. *Bouquet:* strong lemony oak in archetypal Mitchelton style partly obscures honeysuckle fruit, but is nonetheless well handled. *Palate:* big, rich, spicy, lemony wine with strong oak influence, although once again supporting fruit is there; good acid should sustain the wine. Drink '90–'95.

1988 WOOD MATURED CHARDONNAY [76] Colour: medium straw, with just a touch of yellow. *Bouquet:* quite complex and weighty, with strong oatmeal oak aromas the dominant feature. *Palate:* rather dusty oatmeal oak, but some quite complex and attractive secondary bottle-developed flavours emerging from the fruit. Drink '90–'92.

1987 SHIRAZ [77] Colour: medium red, with just a touch of purple. *Bouquet:* very clean and stylish with tangy/spicy lemony oak nicely balanced and integrated. *Palate:* the oak is rather more obtrusive than it is on the bouquet, although well handled in that very distinctive Mitchelton style. Some lemony spicy flavours linger in the after-taste. Drink '90–'93.

1985 PRINT LABEL CABERNET MERLOT [76] Colour: medium red. *Bouquet:* attractive, sweet leafy/tobacco aromas showing strong bottle development. *Palate:* soft, very slightly soapy leafy/tobacco flavours, again showing attractive bottle-developed characters. Drink '90–'92.

Summary: In a masked (or blind) tasting of almost 80 district wines, those of Mitchelton stood out as they always do with their ultra-distinctive oak treatment. In this they make a total and fascinating contrast with Chateau Tahbilk, where oak is all but shunned. At the end of the day, the choice between the two styles is a purely personal one.

MOUNT HELEN

Location: Strathbogie Ranges (vineyard only); not open to the public. Wines made and tasting facilities at Tisdall Wines (see separate entry under North Goulburn River). (054) 82 1911.

Winemaker: Jeff Clarke.

1989 Production: Not for publication.

Principal Wines: Rhine Riesling, Chardonnay, Gewurztraminer Late Harvest, Fumé Blanc, Pinot Noir, Cabernet Merlot, Merlot and limited quantities of Chardonnay and Pinot Noir *Méthode Champenoise.*

Distribution: National retail through distributors

in all states; also available cellar door via Tisdall.

Prices: $12.80 to $12.81 retail.

Vintage Rating 1986–89: White: '86, '89, '88, '87. Red: '88, '86, '87, '89.

Outstanding Prior Vintages: '80, '82, '84.

Tasting Notes:

1989 FUME BLANC [CS] Colour: light straw green. *Bouquet:* clean with light, crisp fruit and strong spicy/lemony oak. *Palate:* strong lemony/spicy oak tending to dominate the wine early in its life; the fruit is light but it does appear to have the potential to develop.

1988 RHINE RIESLING [77] Colour: medium yellow-green. *Bouquet:* soft and developed with lime/toast/slightly cheesy aromas. *Palate:* big, soft and full with plenty of lime flavour; fractionally cloying but an easy style to drink. Drink '90–'91.

1988 CHARDONNAY [77] Colour: light straw yellow. *Bouquet:* honeyed/buttery/ butterscotch/peach fruit. *Palate:* soft butterscotch/peach fruit very similar to the bouquet; oak in decided restraint, has good overall flavour and mouthfeel. Drink '90–'92.

Summary; The Mount Helen wines are of course the flagships of Tisdall; for some reason, the potent, full-bodied reds that also grace Mount Helen were not submitted for this tasting. Nonetheless they, like the white wines, are frequently very distinguished.

PAUL OSICKA

Location: Graytown, 3608; off Heathcote-Nagambie Road, 24km west of Nagambie. (057) 94 9235.

Winemaker: Paul Osicka.

1989 Production: Not for publication.

Principal Wines: Limited quantities of white wines made, principal wines are Chardonnay, Hermitage, Cabernet Sauvignon and Vintage Port.

Distribution: Principally cellar door sales and by mail order. Limited retail distribution through Specialist Wine Co., Sydney, and Flinders Wholesale, Melbourne. Cellar door sales 10 a.m. to 5.30 p.m. Monday to Saturday.

Prices: $11 to $16.

Vintage Rating 1986–89: '89, '87, '88, '86.

Tasting Notes:

1987 HERMITAGE [83] Colour: medium purple-red. *Bouquet:* spotlessly clean, with intense pepper spice varietal character. *Palate:* fragrant and lively, with intense pepper spice fruit and a nice touch of supporting oak; has flesh to go with that spicy fruit, and nice rounding tannins. Drink '91–'95.

1986 HERMITAGE [74] Colour: medium red-purple. *Bouquet:* strong spicy/peppery shiraz, ageing remarkably slowly. *Palate:* a pleasant, spicy wine showing rather more development than the bouquet suggests, and lacking the structure and richness of the '87; nonetheless, a pleasant wine. Drink '90–'93.

Summary: Paul Osicka has quietly produced some very good reds over the last decade, and continues that tradition with the wines tasted for this edition.

SOMERSET CROSSING
(formerly River View Wines)

Location: Old Hume Highway (1 Emily Street) Seymour, 3660.
(057) 92 2445.

Consultant/Winemaker: David Traeger.

1989 Production: 4000 cases.

Principal Wines: Shiraz, Cabernet Merlot, Sauvignon Blanc, Rhine Riesling, Le Rouge Nouveau and Chardonnay.

Distribution: Chiefly cellar door and mailing list. Cellar door sales 10 a.m. to 6 p.m. 7 days (except Christmas Day). Limited retail distribution in Victoria through Victorian Wine Consultants, 34 Milton Street, West Melbourne.

Prices: $8 to $12 cellar door.

Tasting Notes:

1989 CHARDONNAY [CS] Colour: light to medium green-yellow, bright and clear. *Bouquet:* clean light and soft, with a hint of peach. *Palate:* light and soft melon/peach fruit; tasted before it had gone to oak, and if well handled at this point should be a good wine.

1988 SHIRAZ [CS] Colour: medium purple-red. *Bouquet:* strong lemony/vanillan American oak. *Palate:* very oaky, but pleasant fruit and certainly free from any fault; the final blended wine will presumably show less wood influence.

1988 CABERNET MERLOT [CS] Colour: medium purple-red. *Bouquet:* clean firm, lemony oak dominates pleasant berry fruit. *Palate:* clean, fresh wine driven by lemony oak; a tangy, crisp low tannin finish. Again drawn from oak shortly prior to bottling; will rate in excess of 75.

Summary: The 1988 and 1989 wines from Somerset Crossing reflect competent winemaking, and augur a new lease of life for the distinctive cellar door sales area on the side of the Old Hume Highway.

THOMAS MITCHELL

Location: Mitchelton Winery, Mitchellstown via Nagambie, 3608; due west of Tabilk on Goulburn Valley Highway.
(057) 94 2388.

Winemaker: Don Lewis.

Principal Wines: Thomas Mitchell is in fact another brand of Mitchelton, but is being actively promoted in its own right and without any front-label reference to Mitchelton.

Distribution: As for Mitchelton.

Prices: $6.95 to $9.50 retail.

Vintage Rating 1986–89: Not relevant due to varied fruit sources for each wine in range.

Tasting Notes:

1989 RHINE RIESLING [89] Colour: light green-yellow. *Bouquet:* extremely well made; elegant and very clean, with medium to full lime/passionfruit aromas. *Palate:* strong passionfruit flavour, possibly due to some yeast influence; very clean; excellent balance and with flavour. Outstanding for a commercial riesling. Drink '90–'92.

1989 FUME BLANC [74] Colour: medium yellow-green. *Bouquet:* soft, quite complex and with some weight and varietal character in a soft, ripe style. *Palate:* a highly commercial wine with soft, mouthfilling fruit, and appreciable residual sugar; cunningly wrought. Drink '90.

1989 CHARDONNAY [79] Colour: medium yellow-green. *Bouquet:* light but smooth gently honeyed/buttery aromas. *Palate:* rather more fruit weight than is evident in the bouquet; smooth melon/grapefruit flavours with a soft, clean finish. Once again, an outstanding wine for the price. Drink ' 90–'91.

1988 PINOT NOIR [68] Colour: medium red-purple. *Bouquet:* clean but slightly cooked fruit with little or no pinot varietal character evident. *Palate:* sweet, slightly cooked fruit; well enough made, but there simply isn't any recognisable pinot flavour. Drink '90–'91.

1988 CABERNET SHIRAZ MERLOT [85] Colour: light to medium purple-red. *Bouquet:* very clean, attractive light, sweet cherry/berry fruit with a hint of spice; little or no oak. *Palate:* spotlessly clean, light and fragrant red berry/cherry fruit flavours, again with a touch of spice evident. A lovely wine that should be enjoyed while all of the fresh fruit is there. Drink '90–'92.

Summary: The current releases of Thomas Mitchell are exceptionally good in a light, fresh and fruity easy drinking style that is ideally suited to today's market.

WALKERSHIRE WINES

Location: Rushworth Road, Bailieston, 3608; 14 km north-west of Nagambie. (057) 94 2726.

Winemaker: John Walker.

Principal Wines: Shiraz, Cabernet Shiraz and Cabernet Sauvignon.

Distribution: Principally cellar door sales and mailing list. Cellar door sales 9 a.m. to 6 p.m. Monday to Saturday, 10 a.m. to 6 p.m. Sunday. Mailing list enquiries to PO Box 74, Nagambie, 3608.

Summary: John Walker is one of the great characters of the district, enthusiastic and individualistic. His wines are, quite simply, massive. However, despite the best of intentions on Walker's part, neither information nor samples were available for this editon.

Gippsland

1988 VINTAGE

The drought pattern that was established over 1986 and 1987 continued. Winter rains were scarce, and dams were left largely empty. Fortunately, there was enough spring rainfall to get the vines away to a reasonable start, and the season then continued cool and dry.

As the summer ended, the weather became unseasonably warm, and all varieties reached very good sugar levels. Some superb chardonnay was made, even though yields overall were very low due to the continuing stress on the vines.

1989 VINTAGE

By far the most significant event was the mid-November deluge, which deposited 350 mm on the region in little more than two days, finally ending a three-year drought and filling all the dams with precious water. Up until this time the spring had been very dry, and continued largely dry through summer and autumn; in the outcome, annual rainfall was roughly equal to the long-term average.

The late February/early March heat wave common to so much of south-east Australia resulted in the earliest harvest date on record for pinot noir; it is also generally regarded as being easily the best ever produced in the region. When the heat wave was over, the weather turned cool and cloudy, with occasional rain leading to some botrytis in the slowly ripening chardonnay and a high level of botrytis in semillon, with some high-class botrytis wine resulting. The rain then ceased, the weather remained cool and the cabernet family grapes–what there were of them– ripened very slowly. There was virtually no merlot picked because of poor weather during flowering, and the cabernet crop when it was finally harvested at less than satisfactory sugar levels was 20% to 30% down in volume. All in all, a very difficult vintage, which is likely to be redeemed only by the pinot noir and botrytised semillon.

THE CHANGES

The most obvious change is the deletion of the word "East" from the area name. The Gippsland region is a very large one, and in truth there are two distinct districts within its boundaries: East Gippsland and West and South Gippsland. This distinction has been recognised in the report commissioned by the Victorian Wine Industry Association, and is obviously a matter of considerable sensitivity to the local vignerons. There are in fact six vineyards in West and South Gippsland and seven in East Gippsland, and by no means all of them support wineries. The boundary between the two districts falls more or less across McAlister Vineyards which, just to be different, classes itself as South-east Gippsland. One new entry this year, Mair's Wines, falls in West and South Gippsland; the other wineries all fall in East Gippsland.

BRIAGOLONG ESTATE

Location: Valencia-Briagolong Road, Briagolong, 3860; 30 km north of Sale.
(051) 47 2322.

Winemaker: Dr Gordon McIntosh.

1989 Production: 200 cases.

Principal Wines: Chardonnay and Pinot Noir. Wines have been made since 1979, released as "standard" (Freestone Creek), or "premium" (Briagolong Estate) according to the winemaker's assessments.

Distribution: Mailing list only; enquiries to 118 Boisdale Street, Maffra, 3860.

Prices: Freestone Creek $120 per case; Briagolong Estate $200 per case.

Vintage Rating 1986–89: Red: '86, '89, '87 (no '88 to be released).

Outstanding Prior Vintages: '83, '84, '85.

Tasting Notes:

1989 CHARDONNAY [CS] Two samples were submitted, one barrel fermented, the other not. Both showed tremendous depth of fruit, but were difficult to assess because of inadequate SO_2 protection. If the wines are protected in the winery and are bottled without problems, quality could be exceptional. If not, oxidation will destroy the fruit.

1989 PINOT NOIR [CS] Almost identical comments apply; there appeared to be very rich, strong varietal fruit under fairly extreme aldehyde owing to inadequate sulphur protection for the samples submitted.

1987 FREESTONE CREEK PINOT NOIR [59] Colour: light red, showing some browning. Bouquet: light, minty leafy aromas indicating only partially ripened pinot. Palate: light, mintycamphor flavours, again an almost certain indication of partial ripening. Drink '90.

Summary: Dr Gordon McIntosh remains fanatically devoted to the production of chardonnay and pinot noir. He has finally conceded that the task of successfully bottling his wines requires specialist attention and, having written off the 1988 vintage, will employ contract bottling services in the future. This is a very large step in the right direction, as there have been real signs over the years of some exceptional material from the now fully mature vines.

GOLVINDA

Location: RMB 4635, Lindenow Road, Lindenow South via Bairnsdale, 3865; 20 km west of Bairnsdale.
(051) 57 1480.

Winemaker: Robert Guy.

Principal Wines: Rhine Riesling, Semillon, Chenin Blanc, Cabernet Sauvignon and Shiraz.

Distribution: Almost exclusively cellar door sales and mail order. Cellar door sales Monday to Saturday 9 a.m. to 6 p.m.; Sundays by appointment. Closed Anzac Day and Good Friday.

Summary: Robert Guy was one of the first vignerons in East Gippsland, but seems to have lost his early enthusiasm. Not all of the wines offered are made from grapes grown in the district.

McALISTER VINEYARDS

Location: Golden Beach Road, Longford, 3851; 9 km from Longford; South-east Gippsland.
(051) 49 7229.

Winemaker: Peter Edwards.

1989 Production: 550 cases.

Principal Wines: The McAlister: a single red wine made from a classic Bordeaux blend of cabernet sauvignon, cabernet franc, petit verdot and merlot in the proportion of 75% cabernet variants and 25% merlot.

Distribution: Cellar door sales–prior phone call appreciated. Also available at The Riversleigh Country Hotel, Bairnsdale; Gatehouse Cellars is an exclusive Melbourne outlet; selected restaurants; The Oak Barrel, Sydney.

Prices: $18 cellar door.

Vintage Rating 1986–89: '87, '88, '86, '89.

Tasting Notes:

1988 THE McALISTER [CS] Colour: dense purple-red. *Bouquet:* strong, rich fruit, with a touch of mould from the laboratory cork used for the sample. *Palate:* marvellously rich and strong with superb fruit and structure; a wine of enormous potential if safely bottled.

Summary: Mould infected corks have destroyed many of the '87 vintage wines, which Peter Edwards had regarded as his best. I believe he became aware of the problem before commercially bottling and corking the '88's; if so, another very good wine will be saved.

MAIR'S WINES

Location: Coalville Vineyard, Moe South Road, Moe South, 3825.
(051) 27 4229; Fax (051) 27 2148.

Winemakers: Stewart Mair; Mavis Mair (viticulturist).

1989 Production: Approximately 175 cases.

Principal Wines: Only one wine made, a Cabernet Sauvignon called Mair's Coalville Red.

Distribution: Almost entirely through mailing list; enuqiries to PO Box 330, Moe, 3825. Cellar door sales by arrangement.

Prices: $240 per case.

Tasting Notes:

1987 COALVILLE RED [85] Colour: medium red-purple. *Bouquet:* clean, fresh, firm leafy/berry fruit with hints of mint and a light touch of oak, all still coming together. *Palate:* light, crisp, clean and tangy red berry flavours with finely grained tannins running throughout, and a very clean, long finish. A wine of remarkable intensity and elegance. Drink '91–'95.

Summary: A tiny operation, run by yet another medical practitioner, but well worth the effort.

NICHOLSON RIVER WINERY

Location: Liddell's Road, Nicholson, 3882; 14 km from Bairnsdale; off Prince's Highway. (051) 56 8241.

Winemaker: Ken Eckersley.

1989 Production: 700 cases.

Principal Wines: Chardonnay, Semillon, Cabernets, Rhine Riesling, Pinot Noir and Shiraz; second label is "Mountview".

Distribution: Exclusively cellar door sales, mailing list and restaurants. Cellar door sales by appointment only; mailing list enquiries to PO Box 73, Nicholson, 3882. Cellar door tasting fee $2 per head, refundable against any purchase made.

Prices: Mountview label $9 to $15 cellar door; Nicholson River label $15 to $28 cellar door.

Tasting Notes:

1988 CHARDONNAY [96] Colour: deep yellow. *Bouquet:* immensely complex fruit and charred oak; exceptionally concentrated, nutty and extraordinarily French in character. *Palate:* magnificently complex and intense wine, which is irresistibly reminiscent of a great Corton Charlemagne or Batard Montrachet; this is really something. Drink '90–'95.

1988 CABERNETS [77] Colour: light to medium purple-red. *Bouquet:* light, minty PK aromas, suggesting partially ripened fruit. *Palate:* redeems the wine with very clean and fresh fruit flavours, still showing pronounced minty fruit, but there is some riper, red berry taste; finishes with low tannin. Drink '91–'94.

Summary: Ken Eckersley has worked hard to improve the quality of the Nicholson River wines, and the current releases have handsomely repaid those efforts.

🍇 *WYANGA PARK VINEYARDS*

Location: Baades Road, Lakes Entrance, 3909; 10 km north of Lakes Entrance. (051) 55 1508.

Winemaker: Andrew Smith.

1989 Production: Approximately 4000 cases.

Principal Wines: Semillon, Crouchen, Rhine Riesling, Sauvignon Blanc, Shiraz and Cabernet Sauvignon.

Distribution: Principally cellar door sales and mailing list. Mailing list enquiries to PO Box 247, Lakes Entrance, 3909. Cellar door sales 9 a.m. to 5 p.m. 7 days.

Prices: $8.50 to $13 cellar door.

Summary: Andrew Smith is slowly lifting the output and profile of Wyanga Park, but it will be some time yet before production starts finding its way onto retail shelves. No new wines were available for this edition.

Geelong

1988 VINTAGE

Spring was wet, windy and cold–conditions frequently encountered in this part of the world. Wind protection was always a major factor in determining flowering and set, particularly given the very strong winds that blew through much of October and November. Somehow or other most vineyards escaped reasonably well, and the ensuing favourable growing season compensated for the minor problems encountered with flowering and fruit set.

A dry February was followed by some rain in March before the commencement of vintage, which started two to three weeks earlier than normal. Almost from the first day of vintage the rain ceased and the weather turned warm, dry and calm. Not surprisingly, there were no fungal or rot diseases, and the chemical composition of the grapes was excellent. For most it was an outstanding year for white wines, and an exceedingly good one for reds.

1989 VINTAGE

A dry winter and early spring was accompanied by abnormally strong winds, which blew from the north right through October and well into November. The rainfall expected in October commenced mid-November and sporadically continued through December and January. In mid-February the heat wave arrived, causing great stress and damage to the vines, albeit hastening the ripening of chardonnay and pinot noir. These two varieties came in in good condition, even if they were not up to the outstanding '88's. When the weather cooled down after the three-week burst of heat, the vines failed to respond to the rain that then fell, and the later ripening varieties–shiraz in particular–suffered very badly. As in so much of Australia, the good wines to appear from the vintage will have been made in the winery rather than the vineyard.

THE CHANGES

Ballanclea has gone; so far as I can determine, Fred Meeker gave up the unequal struggle. Mount Anakie has changed its name to Zambelli Estate in the wake of its acquisition by the Zambelli family, while Clyde Park (which in the last edition was exclusively exporting its wines) has come back on to the local market.

Through the agency of Bannockburn and Hickinbotham Winemakers, the reputation of the district for outstanding pinot noir continues to grow, and will play a key role in establishing an international reputation for Australian pinots.

BANNOCKBURN

Location: Midland Highway, Bannockburn, 3331.
(052) 81 1363.

Winemaker: Gary Farr.

1989 Production: Approximately 5000 cases.

Principal Wines: Chardonnay, Sauvignon Blanc,
Pinot Noir, Cabernet Sauvignon and Shiraz.

Distribution: Principally retail through wholesale
distributors W. J. Seabrook, Melbourne; Fesq &
Co., Sydney; Tucker Caon, Adelaide and Perth.
No cellar-door sales. Mailing list enquiries to
Bannockburn Vineyards, PO Bannockburn,
3331. UK imports through Negociants
International.

Prices: $15 to $30 retail.

Vintage Rating 1986–89: White: '88, '89, '87, '86.
Red: '88, '89, '87, '86.

Outstanding Prior Vintages: '80, '85.

Tasting Notes:

1988 CHARDONNAY [76] Colour: light to medium
green-yellow. *Bouquet:* clean, but very closed;
smooth melon fruit, with oak well integrated
and unobtrusive. *Palate:* a solid wine, with a
hint of spice from the oak and some evidence of
solids fermentation techniques borrowed from
the French; fairly hot alcohol finish. A wine that
demands time in bottle. Drink '92–'95.

1988 PINOT NOIR [90] Colour: medium red, with
a touch of purple. *Bouquet:* rich, complex
plummy fruit with just the right degree of
sappiness. *Palate:* the wine really comes into its
own, with strong plum flavours cut by a touch of
sappiness; tremendous weight and complexity,
and exceptional length. Drink '92 –'94.

1986 SHIRAZ [75] Colour: deep purple-red.
Bouquet: strong, complex carbonic maceration
influence evident. *Palate:* almost riotous dark
berry flavours together with complex pie and
peas maceration influence; low tannin. I do not

enjoy this style with this variety, but others may
do so. Drink '90–'93.

1986 CABERNET SAUVIGNON [87] Colour:
medium to full red-purple. *Bouquet:* quite rich,
dark berry fruit, very ripe and concentrated.
Palate: complex dark berry fruits with very well-
integrated charred oak; rich and mouthfilling,
with soft tannins running throughout. Drink
'91–'97.

Summary: Winemaker Gary Farr is strongly
influenced by his Burgundian winemaking
experience over three vintages. He has
wonderful raw material to work with from the
mixture of fully mature and newer, close
planted vineyards, and is producing wines of
exceptional complexity and style. The only
pity is that there are not more of them.

CLYDE PARK

Location: Midland Highway, Bannockburn, 3331;
(vineyard only).
(052) 81 7274.

Winemaker: Gary Farr.

1989 Production: Approximately 1000 cases.

Principal Wines: Chardonnay and Cabernet
Sauvignon.

Distribution: Exclusively retail through Seabrook
Tucker, Victoria; Caon Tucker, SA; Fesq & Co.,
NSW.

Prices: $16 to $25.

Vintage Rating 1986–89: White: '88, '89, '87, '86.
Red: '86, '88, '87, '89.

Tasting Notes:

1988 CHARDONNAY [78] Colour: light green-
yellow. *Bouquet:* smooth and clean, but rather
closed; good oak integration and, not
surprisingly, a wine similar in style to the
Bannockburn. *Palate:* of medium intensity;
smooth and clean with unobtrusive oak; shows
slightly more fruit and is slightly more

accessible than the Bannockburn of the same year. Drink '90–'92.

1986 CABERNET SAUVIGNON [68] *Colour:* medium red-purple. *Bouquet:* curious mulled berry aromas with carbonic maceration technique dominant. *Palate:* evidently made using carbonic maceration, which I simply cannot cope with in cabernet sauvignon. Drink '90–'91.

Summary: Clyde Park is once again available on local markets following the slow-down in exports. Clyde Park, incidentally, is the vineyard owned by Gary Farr; the wines are, of course, made by Farr at Bannockburn.

IDYLL VINEYARD

Location: 265 Ballan Road, Moorabool, 3221; 7 km north-west of Geelong; 75 km south-west of Melbourne, 80 km south-east of Ballarat. Melway Ref. 223 A5. (052) 76 1280; Fax (052) 76 1537.

Winemaker: Daryl Sefton.

Principal Wines: Classic Dry Gewurztraminer, Gewurztraminer Oak Aged, Chardonnay, Idyll Blush, Idyll Blush, Idyll Glow, Bone Idyll and Cabernet Sauvignon/Shiraz.

Distribution: Cellar door sales, mailing list; wine retail distribution Melbourne through Wayne Leicht Wines Pty Ltd; in Sydney and NSW through Appellation Wines & Spirits Pty Ltd; Canberra La Copita. Significant exports to Europe (Belgium, Holland, Germany, Denmark, Austria, Switzerland) and UK (London, Midlands, Edinburgh and Dublin). Cellar door sales open Tuesday to Sunday 10 a.m. to 5 p.m. Mailing list enquiries as above.

Prices: $10 to $15 retail.

Tasting Notes:

1987 CLASSIC DRY GEWURZTRAMINER [74]

Colour: deep yellow. *Bouquet:* strong, bottle-developed lychee/spice aromas, noticeably softening. *Palate:* soft, developed lychee flavours with a touch of Alsace; could have benefited from a little more acid. Drink '90–'91.

1988 BLUSH [60] *Colour:* light pink-brown. *Bouquet:* slightly oxidised, vaguely Tavel-like. *Palate:* rather nondescript with soft, sweet vaguely European flavours. Drink '90.

1988 BONE IDYLL [78] *Colour:* medium red-purple. *Bouquet:* initially opened rather dull and slightly smelly, but red berry fruits came up as it stood in the glass. *Palate:* much better than the bouquet, with complex spicy/gamey flavours and a lovely fresh feel in the mouth. Very attractive light red style. Drink '90.

1986 CABERNET SAUVIGNON SHIRAZ [76] *Colour:* medium red. *Bouquet:* clean, with very obvious bottle developed tobacco leaf/cigar box characters. *Palate:* complex, leafy berry fruit with a hint of spice, and a long, elegant finish. Against the probabilities, has overtones of a nicely aged Bordeaux. Drink '90–'92.

Summary: The Seftons are indefatigable marketers, and fierce supporters of their idiosyncratic wine styles. You may not always like those wines, but you will never be bored by them.

MOUNT DUNEED WINES

Location: Feehan's Road, Mt Duneed, 3216; off west side of Torquay Road, 10 km past Geelong. (052) 64 1281.

Winemakers: Ken Campbell and Peter Caldwell.

1989 Production: 1000 cases.

Principal Wines: Dry White (semillon/sauvignon blend), Dry Red Blend (cabernet sauvignon/malbec/merlot/shiraz), Malbec, Cabernet Sauvignon and Botrytised Blend (semillon/muscadelle).

Distribution: Principally cellar door sales 10 a.m. to 5 p.m. Saturday, public holidays and school holidays; noon to 5 p.m. Sunday. Retail and restaurant distribution in the Geelong, Bellarine Peninsula and West Coast area.

Prices: $12 to $20 cellar door.

Vintage Rating 1986–89: White: '89, '87, '88, '86. Red: '89, '88, '87 ('86 not rated).

Tasting Notes:

1986 DRY WHITE (SEMILLON/SAUVIGNON) [75]
Colour: medium yellow-green. *Bouquet:* broad, bottle-developed with a hint of matchbox and relatively little fruit. *Palate:* an altogether surprising wine after the very dull bouquet and complex flavours in a distinctly French style and good length. Drink '90–'93.

1986 NOBLE ROT SEMILLON [84] Colour: medium to full yellow. *Bouquet:* extremely complex, intense apricot/lime fruit with some volatility. *Palate:* intense, high-toned and extremely concentrated flavours; the only chink in the armour is a slightly hard finish. Drink '90–'92.

Summary: Bottle age has done wonderful things for the two wines, although this is not the first excellent botrytis white to come out under the Mount Duneed label. Two very full-flavoured but extremely erratic red wines from 1988 (a malbec and a cabernet sauvignon) were also tasted. If they were already bottled by mid-1988, I could not recommend them. If they were still in cask and are cleaned up prior to bottling, the malbec in particular could be very good.

❦PRINCE ALBERT

Location: Lemins Road, Waurn Ponds, 3221; 10 km south-west of Geelong. (052) 43 5091.

Winemakers: Bruce Hyett and Neil Everist.

1989 Production: 800 cases.

Principal Wines: Only one wine made: Pinot Noir.

Distribution: Principally cellar door sales and mailing list, together with restaurants Australia-wide. Sydney retail distribution through Carol Anne Martin Classic Wines; Melbourne, Crittendens, Victorian Wine Centre and Sutherland Cellars. Cellar door sales 9 a.m. to 5 p.m. while wine available (usually only through October).

Prices: Around $14 cellar door.

Vintage Rating 1986–89: '87, '89, '88, '86.

Tasting Notes:

1988 PINOT NOIR [65] Colour: very light red. *Bouquet:* simple, light cherry fruit with rather one-dimensional, slight cordial characters. *Palate:* clean but very light and very simple strawberry flavours, lacking structure and intensity. Drink '90.

Summary: I suspect that Prince Albert has been standing still while the rest of the pinot noir world rushes towards the 21st century. The time was when these were outstanding pinots; alas, they are no longer so, simply because of the likes of Mount Mary, Diamond Valley and (closer to home) Bannockburn.

❦TARCOOLA

Location: Maude Road, Lethbridge, 3332; 5 km north-east of Lethbridge on the Moorabool River. (052) 81 9245.

Winemaker: Alastair Scott.

Principal Wines: Rhine Riesling, Muller Thurgau, Shiraz and Cabernet Sauvignon. All wines, both white and red, offered with substantial bottle age.

Distribution: Principally cellar door sales and mailing list; very limited Melbourne retail distribution.

Summary: Tarcoola has had intermittent problems with frost, and the level of activity is now very low.

❦ZAMBELLI ESTATE
(formerly Mount Anakie)

Location: Staughton Vale Road, Anakie, 3221; (052) 84 1256 or (03) 862 2303.

Winemaker: Paul Chambers.

1989 Production: Approximately 4000 cases.

Principal Wines: The principal releases comprise Rhine Riesling, Semillon, Chardonnay, Shiraz, Biancone and Cabernet Sauvignon.

Distribution: Principally cellar door sales and export; cellar door sales 10.30 a.m. to 5 p.m. Tuesday to Saturday and public holidays; noon to 5 p.m. Sunday. Limited retail distribution through Gipps St Cellars and restaurants.

Tasting Notes:

1989 CHARDONNAY [CS] Colour: very light straw, with a touch of green. *Bouquet:* curious spicy/pepper aromas, possibly from oak, although I am quite frankly not certain; light fruit, still showing the after-effects of fermentation. *Palate:* still fairly light; once again hot, spice characters that were no less easy to diagnose; fermentation characters linger. A 1989 riesling also submitted had echoes of the same spice.

1988 SHIRAZ [81] Colour: dense purple-red. *Bouquet:* huge, concentrated peppery fruit with very slight medicinal/burnt nuances. *Palate:* similarly concentrated dense, pepper/plum fruit, almost viscous richness; soft tannins. Drink '93–'98.

1987 CABERNET SAUVIGNON [85] Colour: slightly opaque purple-red. *Bouquet:* very fragrant with complex leafy/cedary fruit and oak, intertwined with some red berry aromas. *Palate:* quite amazingly flavoured with a cocktail of every berry flavour imaginable; finishes clean and spicy, with low tannin. A wine that could have been given any points between 75 and 95. Drink '92–'96.

Summary: Owner Igor Zambelli and winemaker Paul Chambers continue to produce challenging wines after the departure of the Hickinbotham family. There is no doubting the ability of the vineyard to produce superb fruit, and it is in a way wholly appropriate that wines of somewhat unusual style are being seen(given the past occupancy by the Hickinbothams).

Great Western and District

1988 VINTAGE

In a district in which water for summer irrigation is always scarce, the winter rains are particularly important to replenish dams. The winter rains were in fact well below average, the dams failed to fill, and the season got off to an inauspicious start. However, conditions throughout late August and September delayed budburst (not completed until October for cabernet) and there was accordingly no frost damage.

The early ripening varieties set well, with bunch numbers well up. However, a wet spell in early December affected the set of some of the later ripening varieties such as cabernet. Alternating cool and hot weather in spring and early summer gave way to a very dry and hot summer, broken only by heavy rain in late December and early January and finally another heavy period of rain on 31 March.

Because of the hot, dry conditions, pests and mildew diseases were almost totally absent, and where supplementary water was available the vines flourished. In some vineyards, however, the hot, dry conditions led to defoliation and consequent lack of ripeness. Yields overall were high for chardonnay and shiraz; rhine riesling and cabernet sauvignon (both affected by set problems) were average to slightly above average, as was pinot noir.

Wine quality was excellent, with some outstanding chardonnay showing excellent varietal character and depth; all of the red wines had above average colour, fruit intensity and good varietal definition.

1989 VINTAGE

Unlike other parts of Victoria, the winter rains were good, restoring storage levels in the dams and resulting in strong bud burst. However, persistently strong winds during early spring followed by some rain had an adverse effect on the set of most varieties, although the loss was not severe.

A dry spring turned to a relatively wet and humid summer, necessitating constant spraying against both powdery and downy mildew. The moist conditions were accompanied by very cool weather, and in mid-February there was real concern about the grapes ripening. The three weeks of hot weather that affected the whole of south-east Australia initially did much to advance maturities, and led to intense congestion in the wineries as the white varieties came flooding in. Thanks to the warm weather, most of these were harvested before the rain came in mid-March, and quality overall was good. The rain caused real problems from this point on: baumes levelled off, and in some instances actually dropped as the agonising cat and mouse game between the weather and the wineries continued. In the end, there was substantial losses due to rot in shiraz, and what was harvested was of relatively poor quality. The thick-skinned cabernet did much better, and some elegant though not rich wines can be expected.

A difficult vintage, but not as difficult as in some regions.

THE CHANGES

Ben Nevis Estate will make its appearance next year, but appears to have considerable work in front of it to lift its wines to commercial quality. Garden Gully, last year's new entry, now has its very pleasant and aesthetically pleasing cellar door sales outlet up and running, an unmistakable landmark on the Western Highway as you approach Great Western from Ararat. Donoview has been renamed Donovan, and is to have a label and image revamp.

Overall quality in the district tasting was very good, with a strong performance by Seppelt, and Best's leading the way. Montara once again produced a superlative Pinot Noir (from 1987) with a promising 1989 yet to come. One or two wineries need to either obtain expert consultancy advice or employ a qualified winemaker if they are to provide wines capable of effectively competing in today's market place.

❦ BEST'S

Location: Great Western, 3377; 2 km off Western Highway at 210 km post, just north of Great Western.
(053) 56 2250.

Winemaker: Viv Thomson and Simon Clayfield.

1989 Production: Approximately 14,000 cases.

Principal Wines: Chardonnay, Rhine Riesling, Gewurztraminer, Pinot Meunier, Hermitage Bin No. 0, Pinot Noir, Cabernet Sauvignon and Concongella Brut.

Distribution: Cellar door sales, and capital city fine wine retail distribution. Wholesale distributors, Flinders Wholesale, Melbourne, Vic.; Roger Brown, Sydney, NSW; Seabrook & Seabrook, SA; Websters, Tas.; and Tallerman & Co., Qld. Cellar door sales 9 a.m. to 5 p.m. Monday to Friday and 9 a.m. to 4 p.m. Saturday and public holidays. Closed Sundays, except on public holidays and long weekends when open 12 p.m. to 4 p.m. Closed Christmas Day and Good Friday.

Prices: $11.40 to $19 recomended retail.

Vintage Rating 1986–89: White: '88, '87, '86, '89. Red: '88, '87, '86, '89.

Outstanding Prior Vintages: White: '79, '85. Red: '64, '67, '70, '76, '89, '84.

Tasting Notes:

1989 CHARDONNAY [CS] *Colour:* medium yellow-green. *Bouquet:* complex lemony/toasty fruit with a touch of fermentation character lingering. *Palate:* extraordinarily rich fruit, very smooth with outstanding length and mouth-feel; tangy grapefruit flavours throughout. Gold medal winner 1989 Ballarat Show and promises to be every bit as good as the 1988 Chardonnay reviewed below.

1989 RHINE RIESLING [83] *Colour:* light to medium yellow-green. *Bouquet:* clean, firm and quite aromatic with classic slightly toasty aromas, exhibiting scrupulous winemaking throughout. *Palate:* high quality classic toasty riesling, relatively reserved, and will almost certainly improve further from these already high points. Drink '90–'93.

1988 CHARDONNAY [90] *Colour:* bright yellow-green of medium depth. *Bouquet:* complex charred oak and aromatic lemony/citric overtones to fruit. *Palate:* strongly accented oak set against smooth but very tangy grapefruit chardonnay; lively, long finish. Drink '90–'92.

1988 CHABLIS [75] *Colour:* medium green-yellow. *Bouquet:* pronounced passionfruit/pineapple aromas, rich and striking. *Palate:* high-toned luscious fruit flavours; nothing whatsoever to do with chablis but a quite remarkable wine at the price. Drink '90–'91.

1988 CABERNET SAUVIGNON [90] *Colour:* full purple-red. *Bouquet:* fresh, fragrant red berry/cassis/plum fruit with well balanced and integrated oak. *Palate:* beautifully ripened and structured cabernet fruit flavours in the red berry/cassis spectrum; soft but persistent tannins, and once again oak judged to perfection. Drink '92–2000.

1987 HERMITAGE [89] *Colour:* very good purple-red. *Bouquet:* smooth, clean berry/plum aromas with a touch of sweet vanillan oak. *Palate:* most attractive sweet cherry/plum/berry neatly set against sweet vanillan oak; finishes with soft tannin. Drink '93–'97.

Summary: Best's fully exploits the enormous potential of the Great Western region, producing an exhilarating range of wines across the complete style spectrum. Some of these wines, which will not be available until mid to late 1990, are not only the finest wines to come out under the Best's label, but among the finest ever from the district.

❦ BOROKA

Location: Pomonal Road, Halls Gap, 3381; 5 km from Halls Gap towards Ararat.
(053) 56 4252.

Winemaker: Bernie Breen.

1989 Production: Not stated, but small.

Principal Wines: Sauvignon Blanc, Boroka

Provencale (a light, dry red made from a blend of shiraz, trebbiano and ondenc), Shiraz and Vintage Port.

Distribution: Melbourne retail distribution through J. Harvey Long; however, principally cellar door sales and mailing list. Cellar door sales 9 a.m. to 5 p.m. Monday to Saturday and Sunday 1 p.m. to 5 p.m. Mailing list enquiries to RMB 2072 via Stawell, 3380.

Tasting Notes:

1989 PROVENCALE [63] Colour: bright, clear pink-red. *Bouquet:* soft red cherry fruit, slightly furry, but by no means unpleasant. *Palate:* a light, crisp rosé style with obvious commercial appeal and no significant winemaking fault. Drink '90.

1986 VINTAGE PORT BIN VP 2 [69] Colour: dense purple-red. *Bouquet:* huge chocolatey fruit with slightly hard spirit showing through. *Palate:* spicy/chocolatey fruit, again with some roughness and toughness evident in the spirit; made quite dry, and a thoroughly creditable wine. Drink '90–'95.

Summary: The quality of the Boroka wines is, quite frankly, very variable, but presumably adequate for cellar door trade purposes. The two wines reviewed are certainly the best of those presently available.

 CATHCART RIDGE

Location: Byron Road, Cathcart via Ararat, 3377; 5 km from Ararat along Moyston Road. (053) 52 4082.

Winemaker: Dr Graeme Bertuch.

1989 Production: Approximately 1600 cases.

Principal Wines: Chardonnay, Shiraz and Cabernet Merlot.

Distribution: Retail distribution through Fesq & Co., Melbourne and Sydney, The Wine Merchant, Adelaide, and Lionel Samson & Son, WA.

Prices: $11.50 to $14 retail.

Vintage Rating 1986–89: Chardonnay: '89, '87, '88. Shiraz: '86, '88, '87. Cabernets: '88, '89, '87, '86.

Tasting Notes:

1989 CHARDONNAY [CS] Colour: medium to full yellow. *Bouquet:* big and broad with fairly oily American oak. *Palate:* plenty of oily/coconut American oak evident at an early stage, with fruit still to develop. Moderate potential, but I have reservations about the oak used if it is representative of the final blend.

1988 CHARDONNAY [70] Colour: light to medium yellow-green. *Bouquet:* smooth, gently tangy/honeysuckle/citric fruit aromas. *Palate:* smooth, honeyed fruit, a little one-dimensional but with good flavour. Drink '90–'91.

1988 CABERNET MERLOT [89] Colour: medium to full purple-red. *Bouquet:* very complex, lively leafy/berry fruit set against spicy, lifted oak. *Palate:* absolutely crammed with flavour, with ripe cassis/dark berry fruit and slightly strident oak; the oak lends a touch of bitterness to the finish, which may be fined out before the wine is finally bottled. (Tasted as a complete blend but shortly prior to bottling.) Drink '93–'98.

1987 CATHCART RIDGE SHIRAZ [74] Colour: light to medium red. *Bouquet:* fresh, red berry aromas of light to medium depth and a touch of carbonic maceration character. *Palate:* fresh, light spicy/cherry flavours with a slightly distracting meaty edge. Not in the class of the great '86 Cathcart Ridge Shiraz. Drink '91–'93.

Summary: Dr Bertuch came perilously close to selling Cathcart Ridge a year ago; the district and wine lovers generally should be grateful he did not, for Cathcart Ridge reds are of high quality.

 DONOVAN

Location: Pomonal Road, Stawell, 3380; 5 km south-west of Stawell. (053) 58 2727.

Consultant/Winemaker: Chris Peters.

1989 Production: 2000 cases.

Principal Wines: Couchen, Rhine Riesling, Traminer and Shiraz.

Distribution: Principally cellar door sales and mailing list; wholesale distribution through Victorian Wine Consultants and selected restaurants. Cellar door sales 10 a.m. to 4 p.m. Monday to Saturday and Sunday. Mailing list enquiries to RMB 2017, Stawell, 3380.

Prices: $10 to $12 cellar door.

Vintage Rating 1986–89: '88, '87, '89, '86.

Tasting Notes:

1985 SHIRAZ [83] Colour: bright red-purple. *Bouquet:* clean, medium weight vibrant pepper/spice aromas. *Palate:* a light to medium weight and very elegant wine with pronounced pepper/spice flavours fleshed out by a little tannin. Drink '90–'94.

Summary: As the currently available '85 Shiraz shows, the recently renamed Donovan (formerly Donoview) can produce most attractive red wines. Show and regional tastings of the younger wines were very worrying, but hopefully the wines in question will be cleaned up before they are put in bottle.

🍇 GARDEN GULLY

Location: Western Highway, Great Western, 3377; 15 km west of Ararat.

Winemaker: Warren Randall.

Principal Wines: The initial Garden Gully releases are a mixture of estate-grown, Great Western-grown and selected blended wines covering a range of Rhine Riesling, Traminer, Chardonnay, Shiraz, Cabernet Sauvignon and *Méthode Champenoise* releases.

Distribution: Cellar door sales and mailing list for table wines; exclusive retail distribution of sparkling wine Noble Sauvage through Nicks Wine Merchants, Melbourne. Cellar door sales 10 a.m. to 6 p.m. all days except Tuesday, Wednesday and Christmas Day.

Tasting Notes:

1989 CHARDONNAY [CS] Colour: light to medium yellow-green. *Bouquet:* sophisticated spicy oatmeal oak dominates the fruit. *Palate:* good grapefruit varietal character just discernible under very pronounced oak. A single cask sample, and the blended and finished wine could be very good indeed as the fruit appears to be there.

1988 RHINE RIESLING [87] Colour: bright, light green-yellow. *Bouquet:* fine, firm classic and reserved toasty aromas. *Palate:* beautifully made, fine and light toasty flavours, with just a touch of lime; perhaps lacking just that last touch of fruit richness, although this may build with time. Drink '90–'92.

1987 GEWURZTRAMINER [75] Colour: medium yellow, with a touch of green. *Bouquet:* very clean with strong lychee/spice aromas. *Palate:* light, spicy lychee flavours with exemplary varietal character, needing only greater depth of flavour to take it into gold medal class. Drink '90.

1984 CHARDONNAY PINOT NOIR BRUT [71] Colour: medium to full yellow. *Bouquet:* smooth, broad fruit with slight butterscotch overtones. *Palate:* soft, broad, buttery developed flavours suggestive of chardonnay; pleasant commercial sparkling wine. Drink '90.

1987 SHIRAZ [82] Colour: light to medium red. *Bouquet:* spotlessly clean, fragrant and leafy red berry fruit with light oak. *Palate:* a lively wine of light to medium weight; leafy/minty berry flavours with a faint hint of spice; appropriately low tannin. Drink '90–'93.

Summary: Highly professional winemaking (chiefly contract at Seppelt) shows through in the invariably good wines under this label.

🍇 LANDRAGIN

Location: 102 Fisken Road, Mount Helen, 3350; 10 km from Ballarat towards Geelong. (053) 41 3941.

Winemaker: Dominique Landragin.

1989 Production: 10,000 cases.

Principal Wines: Méthode champenoise; comprising Reserve, Blanc de Noirs and Rosé. Table wines; comprising Rhine Riesling, Chardonnay, Shiraz, Cabernet Sauvignon and Cabernets.

Distribution: Virtually exclusively through retail outlets; National Distributors Elders IXL Wines and Spirits. For mailing list enquiries write to Landragin Australia, PO Box 15, Buninyong, 3357.

Prices: *Méthode champenoise:* $17.95 to $22.95; Table wines: $11.99 to $18.99.

Tasting Notes:

LANDRAGIN RESERVE NV [70] *Colour:* light straw yellow, with good mousse. *Bouquet:* full and clean, but tending to fruit-softness. *Palate:* a high flavoured wine, with some spicy notes from the pinot noir component, but lacking the tightness of the very best Australian sparkling wines. Certainly very commercial and easy to drink. Drink '90.

1988 RHINE RIESLING [74] *Colour:* medium yellow-green. *Bouquet:* developed, soft lime flavours, not particularly aromatic and very slightly broad. *Palate:* a big, full flavoured wine with distinct sweetness in an eminently satisfactory commercial style. Drink '90–'91.

1987 CHARDONNAY [80] *Colour:* bright, light to medium green-yellow. *Bouquet:* smooth, with very well balanced and integrated fruit and oak. *Palate:* the oak is a little more obtrusive than in the bouquet, with smooth melon peach fruit flavours; again, a cunningly wrought wine to satisfy the most discriminating. Drink '90–'91.

1986 CABERNETS [81] *Colour:* medium red-purple. *Bouquet:* stylish and fragrant, with the softening and aromatic influence of cabernet franc quite evident; the oak is just a little dominant for perfection. *Palate:* uncom-promisingly oaky, but does have lovely red berry fruit flavours and gentle balancing tannins; good after taste. Drink '90–'93.

1986 CABERNET SAUVIGNON [87] *Colour:* medium purple-red. *Bouquet:* clean and firm with well balanced fruit and oak. *Palate:* most attractive complex bottle-developed red berry and cedary oak flavours; wine really comes alive on the finish and with the after taste, having exceptional balance and mouth-feel. Drink '90–'95.

Summary: It is remarkable how the all important blending skills of the sparkling wine maker have produced such a stylish range of table wines. The sheer quality of the wines is such that the brilliant

packaging is probably no more than an added extra, but the combination should certainly ensure ready acceptance in the marketplace.

MONTARA

Location: Chalambar Road, Ararat, 3377; 3 km from Ararat on Hamilton Road. (053) 52 3868.

Winemaker: Michael McRae.

1989 Production: Not stated.

Principal Wines: Chardonnay, Ondenc, Chasselas, Rhine Riesling, Pinot Noir, Shiraz, Cabernet Sauvignon and Vintage Port.

Distribution: Principally cellar door and mailing list; limited retail distribution Sydney, through Appellation Wines and Spirits; and Melbourne, Emerald Wines Pty Ltd. Cellar door sales 9.30 a.m. to 5 p.m. Monday to Saturday, 12 noon to 4 p.m. Sunday (during holiday periods). Mailing list enquiries as above.

Prices: $9 to $15 cellar door.

Vintage Rating 1986–89: White: '88, '89, '86, '87. Red: '86, '88, '89, '87.

Outstanding Prior Vintages: 1984.

Tasting Notes:

1988 ONDENC [70] *Colour:* light to medium straw yellow. *Bouquet:* buttery coconut American oak dominates slightly herbal but quite complex fruit. *Palate:* as with the bouquet, the fruit is very light relative to the strong vanillan/coconut oak; will no doubt strongly appeal to those who accept high oak levels. Drink '90–'91.

1988 CHASSELAS [67] *Colour:* medium yellow, with just a touch of green. *Bouquet:* soft slightly buttery/tropical/honeysuckle fruit with an edge of hardness, perhaps from a touch of sulphide.

Palate: soft, pastille/buttery fruit flavours; a simple and uncomplicated commercial wine. Drink '90.

1989 PINOT NOIR [CS] *Colour:* medium purple-red. *Bouquet:* pronounced varietal aroma with youthful sappy/stalky characters. *Palate:* marked cherry/strawberry varietal flavour with a tangy/sappy edge; appears to have great potential and to be a far better style than the over-ripe '88.

1987 PINOT NOIR [93] *Colour:* medium red-purple. *Bouquet:* outstanding, stylish plummy/sappy aromas with considerable depth. *Palate:* outstanding plummy/sappy varietal fruit flavour; perfectly handled oak; a pinot of rare weight and balance with a long yet not bitter finish. Drink '90–'92.

1987 SHIRAZ [88] *Colour:* medium to full purple-red. *Bouquet:* intense peppery fruit, very clean and with oak playing a mere support role. *Palate:* extremely potent, rich peppery/spice flavours with great concentration; good tannins on the mid- to back-palate. Drink '92–'98.

1987 CABERNET SAUVIGNON [91] *Colour:* medium red. *Bouquet:* fresh, fragrant and stylish red berry aromas with just a touch of leafy varietal character. *Palate:* a lovely and elegant red wine with stylish oak handling and beautifully balanced tannin; has developed very quickly and is already at its impressive peak. Drink '90–'92.

Summary: Michael McRae has rated his '87 vintage reds least of the four years; as the notes indicate, I think they are superb. The other noteworthy feature is the quality of the '87 and '89 (though not '88) pinot noirs, adding to the already formidable reputation of Montara for this variety.

 MOUNT CHALAMBER

Location: Off Tatyoon Road, Ararat, 3377; 3 km from town (vineyard only). (053) 52 3768.

Winemaker: Trevor Mast.

1989 Production: 1800 cases.

Principal Wines: Rhine Riesling, Chardonnay, Pinot Noir and *Méthode Champenoise* Chardonnay.

Distribution: By mailing list and wholesale through I. H. Baker & Co. (to retailers and restaurants). No cellar door sales. Mailing list enquiries to Box 301, Ararat, 3377.

Prices: $11.80 to $24.50 retail.

Vintage Rating 1986-89: '88, '89, '87, '86.

Tasting Notes:

1988 RHINE RIESLING [73] *Colour:* medium yellow green. *Bouquet:* rich and clean with full, soft lime and a hint of volatility. *Palate:* full flavoured soft lime fruit on the mid-palate, but finishing a fraction hard, perhaps reflecting that touch of volatility evident in the bouquet. Drink '90–'91.

1988 CHARDONNAY [62] *Colour:* medium to full straw yellow. *Bouquet:* varietal fruit is partially hidden by quite distinct volatility. *Palate:* a tangy, lively wine with that volatility again evident and only just within commercial bounds. Drink '90.

Summary: It seems that an errant yeast affected the 1988 whites from Mount Chalambar; this is something outside the control of the winemaker, and I do not regard these wines as representative of either the skills of winemaker/owner Trevor Mast or the Mount Chalambar label.

MOUNT LANGI GHIRAN

Location: Vine Road, off Buangor-Warrak Road, Buangor, 3375; 6 kms off Western Highway, east of Ararat. (053) 54 3207

Winemaker: Trevor Mast.

1989 Production: 9800 cases.

Principal Wines: Rhine Riesling, Chardonnay,

Shiraz and Cabernet Sauvignon/Cabernet Franc/Merlot.

Distribution: Cellar door sales, mailing list and through I. H. Baker & Co. to selected retailers and restaurants.

Prices: $11.50 to $16.80 cellar door.

Vintage Rating 1986-89: White: '87, '88, '89, '86. Red: '86, '89, '88, '87.

Tasting Notes:

1988 RHINE RIESLING [74] Colour: medium yellow-green. *Bouquet:* soft full fruit, not particularly aromatic. *Palate:* very full soft fruit, slightly blousy but with nice flavour. Drink '90–'91.

1988 PINOT NOIR [69] Colour: dark red-purple. *Bouquet:* strong lemony/American oak masks the fruit and is inappropriate to the style. *Palate:* rich and full flavoured, with a fleshy mid-palate and again strong American oak evident; if varietal character is there, I cannot see it. Drink '90–'93.

1986 SHIRAZ [77] Colour: medium to full red. *Bouquet:* some vanillan oak, but the fruit and varietal character are strangely muffled. *Palate:* full flavoured, big bodied, richly structured wine with lots of weight and considerable tannin; the strong peppery spice that one associates with Mount Langi Ghiran is all but absent from this vintage. Drink '90–'96.

1986 CABERNET SAUVIGNON [59] Colour: medium to full red. *Bouquet:* hard, leathery sulphide characters obscure the underlying fruit. *Palate:* rather better than the bouquet suggests, but again mercaptan evident with some meaty/gamey characters; strong tannin on the finish. Could conceivably improve with time, but I really wonder. Drink '93–'96.

Summary: I have been a consistently outspoken supporter of the Mount Langi Ghiran reds over the years; I can only think that the '86 wines are something of an aberration that should be ignored.

❦ SEPPELT GREAT WESTERN

Location: Moyston Road, Great Western, 3377; off Western Highway, 16 km north-west of Ararat. (053) 56 2202; Fax (053) 56 2300.

Winemakers: Ian McKenzie (chief), Michael Kluczko (sparkling), Tony Royal (white wine).

1989 Production: Not for publication.

Principal Wines: The most important wines from Seppelt viewpoint are the *méhode champenoise* wines; though the majority of these come from a variety of fruit sources all are fermented, tiraged and matured at Great Western. The most important quality labels are Salinger, Great Western Vintage Brut and Fleur de Lys, with occasional releases of single area varietal wines such as Great Western Chardonnay Brut and Drumborg Chardonnay Brut. The Great Western table wines comprise Rhine Riesling, Chardonnay, Hermitage and Cabernet Sauvignon, which are produced in strictly limited quantities.

Distribution: National retail through all types of wine outlets.

Prices: Recommended retail prices subject to intermittent discounting; most wines sell in the $5 to $25 range.

Vintage Rating 1986–89: White: '86, '88, '87, '89. Red: '88, '86, '87, '89.

Outstanding Prior Vintages: '71, '80, '84.

Tasting Notes:

1987 GREAT WESTERN CHARDONNAY BRUT [87] Colour: medium-green yellow with persistent, fine mousse. *Bouquet:* light to medium weight with soft, clean buttery chardonnay varietal aroma very obvious. *Palate:* fine, delicate and creamy blanc de blanc style with lovely balance. Drink '90–'91.

1986 SALINGER [88] Colour: strong, deep onionskin. *Bouquet:* very complex with real champagne overtones, but also very developed. *Palate:* rich, complex forward style with strong fleshy/bready flavours; an idiosyncratic wine that is certainly not classic and which is best appreciated with food. Drink '90.

1986 VINTAGE BRUT [90] *Colour:* medium to full yellow with typical strong and fine mousse. *Bouquet:* complex and strong bready/yeasty aromas showing extended time on lees. *Palate:* very rich biscuity/ bready mid-palate, with almost unctuous sweet fruit. Drink '90–'91.

1988 GREAT WESTERN RHINE RIESLING [88] *Colour:* good green-yellow. *Bouquet:* clean and firm with pronounced floral/lime aromas. *Palate:* full limy fruit of medium to full weight; clean, soft acid finish. Drink '90–'92.

1986 GREAT WESTERN CHARDONNAY [82] *Colour:* medium yellow. *Bouquet:* striking, opulent charred oak is immediately apparent; the fruit is there but the balance is on the cusp. *Palate:* exceptional complex charred oak, rich and striking; once again the fruit struggles in a very stylish but oak-driven wine. Drink '90–'92.

1985 GREAT WESTERN HERMITAGE [89] *Colour:* medium to full red-purple. *Bouquet:* rich, velvety and typical gamey/meaty shiraz, complex and satisfying. *Palate:* very rich, round and velvety texture with a touch of dark chocolate and some gamey characters once again evident; soft persistent tannins. Drink '90–'95.

Summary: Seppelt Great Western is the home of Australia's finest large company sparkling wines but, as the notes indicate, also produces some outstanding still table wines. Such wines tend to stand out like beacons in regional tastings, emphasising the gap that often exists between the exotic but rustic on the one hand and the perfectly shaped and balanced wines of the skilled, professional winemaker on the other.

Macedon

1988 VINTAGE

As I said in last year's edition, Macedon throws into sharp relief the problems of arriving at sensible viticultural regions in Victoria. There can be very substantial geographical, topographical and climatological differences in a relatively small area, yet to recognise each discrete area could result in almost as many regions as there are wineries—more than 130 in Victoria. So, for the time being at least, there have to be subdistricts that fit rather uneasily into the broader regional framework.

Thus in Macedon there are three subdistricts that have only the most tenous links from a viticultural viewpoint; these are the Sunbury region, the Macedon Ranges and Kyneton. Sunbury is without question the warmest of the three subdistricts, but shares with the other two wind problems, particularly at flowering and fruit-set. The other two share a high altitude and a climate that can be forbiddingly cool. All three have a mere smattering of wineries, and are (as I say) married by convenience.

Particularly in the high country, Macedon must necessarily face the type of vintage variation that Europeans are well used to, but Australians are not. And it would be hard to imagine two vintages that would provide more vivid proof of this than in 1988 and 1989. 1988 got away to the usual very late start, with budburst in October and flowering in December (a full four to six weeks later than, say, the relatively nearby Yarra Valley).

The weather remained very cool until mid-March, when a prolonged Indian summer arrived with well over a month of warmer than usual and very dry weather. The grapes not only ripened with far greater rapidity than usual, but attained excellent sugar levels. The red wines, in particular, were outstanding, for most vignerons the best in living memory, exceeding the quality even of the 1986 wines.

1989 VINTAGE

As I say, the contrast was total. There was more or less consistent rain through December and January, which certainly helped canopy growth and potential grape yields, and there was then a burst of warm weather from mid-February until early March which held out the promise of another 1988. However, at this point of time the rain came, temperatures plummeted and the grapes began a long battle towards ripeness that they eventually lost.

The year was saved for those with pinot noir and chardonnay dedicated to sparkling wine making; some fine material for this purpose was harvested. For the table winemakers, and in particular for those attempting to make red wines, it was a year the high country vignerons would prefer to forget. Underlining the diversity of the region, the Sunbury vignerons (and in particular Craiglee and Goonawarra) were able to make some remarkably attractive and well-flavoured dry reds.

THE CHANGES

Macedon may have had a hard time of it in 1989, but it is nonetheless a flourishing region. The new entries are Wildwood, Rochford, Lancefield and Fearn Hyll, the latter a some-what debatable inclusion that more happily fits into the Ballarat subdistrict–except there is no Ballarat region yet accommodated in this book.

Lancefield has the highest profile, with morning and afternoon teas on Saturday and Sunday and a spit roast lunch with live music on Sundays–served outdoors in summer and indoors in winter. It also offers a large range of wines, some from locally grown grapes, and others (at lower prices) made from grapes purchased from other regions of Victoria.

Nearby Rochford is the part-time retreat of Bruce Dowding, who amongst other things is a director of the Grollo Group working in the city three days of the week, but living on the property. He has picked up his winemaking skills in such diverse places as Burgundy and Chateau Tahbilk.

Wildwood has been established by Dr Wayne Stott at Bulla, a mere two kilometres past Tullamarine Airport and just south-east of Sunbury. Wayne Stott studied oenology and viticulture at the Riverina College, and is making wines both from estate-grown grapes and from grapes purchased from other regions –including rhine riesling from the Mornington Peninsula. Finally, David Farnhill is growing rhine riesling, shiraz, pinot noir and cabernet sauvignon near Daylesford, with his first commercial vintage in 1987 and producing a substantial 2000 cases in 1989.

CRAIGLEE VINEYARD

Location: Sunbury Road, Sunbury, 3429;
on southern outskirts of Sunbury town, 35
minutes, drive from Melbourne GPO.
(03) 744 1160 or (03) 744 4489.

Winemaker: Pat Carmody.

1989 Production: Less than 2000 cases.

Principal Wines: Chardonnay, Shiraz, Pinot Noir
and Cabernet Sauvignon.

Distribution: Principally cellar door sales and
mailing list; also fine wine retail distribution in
Melbourne and Sydney. Cellar door sales
10 a.m. to 5 p.m. Monday to Saturday and
noon to 5 p.m. Sunday. Closed Tuesday.

Prices: $12.50 to $18 recommended retail; less
cellar door and mailing list.

Vintage Rating 1986–89: White: '86, '88, '87, '89.
Red: '88, '86, '87, '89.

Tasting Notes:

1989 PINOT NOIR [CS] Colour: light purple-red.
Bouquet: light, clean strawberry/plum varietal fruit.
Palate: clean, light strawberry plum fruit almost
identical to the bouquet; lacks structure early in its
life, but does have exemplary varietal flavour and is
an excellent wine for a difficult vintage. With
proper handling, aspiring to 80 points.

1987 SHIRAZ [90] Colour: medium purple-red.
Bouquet: strong, clean peppery/spicy shiraz fruit
with light oak. *Palate:* pristine varietal flavour,
with enormously rich spicy shiraz flavours and
the requisite fruit weight to carry the spice.
Interestingly, I had no hesitation in giving it a
gold medal in the full bodied dry red class at the
1989 Ballarat Show, although my fellow judges
were not quite so enthusiastic and it ended up
with a high silver medal. Drink '92–'98.

1986 SHIRAZ [85] Colour: medium purple-red.
Bouquet: strong, clean vibrant spicy varietal
shiraz. *Palate:* strong, clean, fresh spicy shiraz
showing beautiful varietal character, and once
again with the requisite fruit weight. Ageing
with verve. Drink '90–'94.

Summary: Craiglee is established on the site of one
of Victoria's more historic wineries, a few
minutes' drive past Tullamarine Airport.
Viticulture is not always easy in this windswept
part of Victoria, but the quality of the wines is
beyond dispute. The shiraz is a particular
favourite of mine, having the fruit weight to
carry the spice and also to age for a decade or
more.

FEARN HYLL ESTATE

Location: Hogan's Road, Daylesford.
(053) 48 6539.

Winemaker: David Farnhill.

1989 Production: Approximately 2000 cases.

Principal Wines: Rhine Riesling, Pinot Noir, Shiraz
and Cabernet Sauvignon.

Distribution: Chiefly cellar door sales, 10 a.m. to
5 p.m. 7 days; mailing list enquiries as above.
Limited Melbourne retail distribution through
Premium Wines, Melbourne.

Prices: $10.50 to $18.50.

Tasting Notes:

1988 WHITE BURGUNDY [77] Colour: light straw-
green. *Bouquet:* smooth, clean, light spicy oak
and fragrant melon fruit. *Palate:* light melon
fruit with quite pronounced citric overtones;
unusual fruit flavours, but really quite delicious.
Drink '90–'92.

1988 LATE PICKED RHINE RIESLING [63] Colour:
developed yellow-orange. *Bouquet:* strong,
slightly blousy/pastille fruit aromas. *Palate:* soft,
sweet camphor/citric/herbaceous flavours, not
altogether harmonious but not unpleasant.
Drink '90.

Summary: Fearn Hyll makes an auspicious debut,
the white burgundy in particular being most
attractive and showing competent winemaking
and oak handling.

❦*FLYNN AND WILLIAMS*

Location: Flynns Lane, Kyneton, on outskirts of town.
(054) 22 2427.

Winemakers: John Flynn and Laurie Williams.

Principal Wines: Cabernet Sauvignon and, in future years, Sauvignon Blanc. Until 1984 wines principally made from vineyard owned by partners at Heathcote. No 1983 wine was produced, and Heathcote vineyard was sold in that year; 1984 and subsequent production coming from two new vineyards established in Kyneton region.

Distribution: Principally direct sales from vineyard to fine wine retailers (including Gatehouse Cellars, Melbourne) and restaurants. Cellar door sales at any time by appointment; no mailing list.

Summary: Output is tiny, and most of the wines are immediately purchased on release by a loyal cellar door clientele. Quality is usually high.

❦*GOONAWARRA*

Location: Sunbury Road, Sunbury, 3429; on southern outskirts of town. Melway ref. Map 113 F10.
(03) 744 7211.

Winemaker: John Barnier/John Ellis.

1989 Production: 10 tonnes.

Principal Wines: Cabernet Franc, Chardonnay and Semillon.

Distribution: Available Goonawarra Vineyard Restaurant plus cellar door sales. Open 10 a.m. to 6 p.m. Wednesday to Friday, weekends and public holidays. Restaurant also open for dinner Wednesday to Saturday plus fixed price Sunday lunch.

Prices: Approximately $14 cellar door.

Vintage Rating 1986–89: White: '86, '88, '89, '87.
Red: '86, '88, '89, '87.

Tasting Notes:

1989 CABERNET FRANC [CS] Colour: dense purple-red. *Bouquet:* somewhat closed in on itself, dense and powerful, still to develop the fragrance expected of cabernet franc. *Palate:* excellent fruit weight and depth; altogether a very good wine for a somewhat difficult vintage, and may well surprise.

1988 CABERNET FRANC [75] Colour: medium red-purple. *Bouquet:* rich and full, but the oak does tend to dominate and varietal fragrance still to come up. *Palate:* dominant oak is the immediate impression; behind this there is the almost silky feel and flavour of cabernet franc. A well-balanced wine that will undoubtedly develop handsomely in bottle. Drink '93–'96.

Summary: Goonawarra's bold experiment in concentrating on cabernet franc rather than cabernet sauvignon seems to be paying dividends. But in truth Goonawarra has far more to offer than a single wine style; the cellar door sales and restaurant complex constitute one of the most enjoyable (and most easily reached) wine venues near Melbourne, and the equally historic Craiglee is but a step away.

❦*HANGING ROCK*

Location: The Jim Jim, Jim Road, Newham, 3442; via Woodend, 8 km north of Woodend.
(054) 27 0542.

Winemaker: John Ellis and Gary Duke.

1989 Production: 10,000 cases.

Principal Wines: The winemaking follows a philosophy of producing, where possible, individual vineyard wines, marketed with a regional identification, e.g. Faraday Chardonnay and Heathcote Shiraz. Others have a more general Victorian origin, including the Cabernet Sauvignon and Merlot blend and Wood Matured Semillon. A range of "Reserve" wines are made from small parcels of outstanding grapes from individual vineyards. Quantities may be as low as 20 dozen for each label, and they are available only from cellar door. The estate vineyard at "The Jim Jim" near Hanging Rock is principally planted for sparkling wine production, with the first release due late in 1990. Small quantities of estate-grown Semillon and Sauvignon Blanc are also produced and available now.

Distribution: Nationally by S. Smith & Son, concentrating on fine wine retail outlets and restaurants. Mailing list commenced September 1989. Cellar door by appointment only.

Prices: $13.50 to $21 retail.

Tasting Notes:

1988 FARADAY CHARDONNAY [75] Colour: medium yellow-green. *Bouquet:* smooth and meaty, not showing particularly strong varietal character nor any great aromatics. *Palate:* plenty of solid flavour with well-balanced fruit and oak; the finish is a little hard thanks to somewhat hot alcohol. Drink '90–'92.

1988 JIM JIM ESTATE SEMILLON [74] Colour: light to medium yellow-green. *Bouquet:* clean, very light, faintly herbaceous fruit with a touch of vanillan oak. *Palate:* extremely acidic and herbaceous, softened by a touch of oak; very much the product of a cool climate, and will probably be long lived, however the acid will be too much for some. Drink '90–'93.

1988 WOOD MATURED SEMILLON [68] Colour: light to medium yellow. *Bouquet:* clean with some pleasant varietal fruit and pronounced oily/lemony oak with a hint of spice. *Palate:* oily/cosmetic German oak flavours submerge the fruit on the mid-palate; the finish is slightly better. Drink '90–'91.

1988 RESERVE MALMSBURY SHIRAZ [75] Colour: dense purple-red. *Bouquet:* rich, deep chocolatey/dark berry fruit and sweet vanillan oak. *Palate:* potent, youthful and underworked, with dark berry fruits that dip slightly on the back-palate. A wine of enormous potential but which seems to have been bottled too early. Drink '93–'97.

1988 HEATHCOTE VICTORIA SHIRAZ [74] Colour: medium purple-red. *Bouquet:* initially strong, deep and peppery, but underneath lurks a touch of pasty/gamey character. *Palate:* complex gamey/minty fruit with quite pronounced acid; the oak is in restraint, and again one has the impression of an underworked wine. Drink '93–'96.

Summary: There can be no doubting the ability of Hanging Rock to produce a wide range of very interesting Victorian wines in the years to come; John Ellis is an immensely experienced and competent winemaker, and a well-equipped winery will allow careful handling of small parcels of interesting grapes.

♣HONEYMAN

Location: Old Post Office Road, Metcalfe, 3448; 2 km south of Metcalfe (vineyard only).

Winemaker: Philip Honeyman.

Principal Wines: Cabernet Merlot and Pinot Noir.

Distribution: Principally by word-of-mouth sales to friends on informal mailing list; limited retail distribution through Gatehouse Cellars, Melbourne. Mailing list enquiries to 71 Brougham Road, Mount Macedon.

Summary: The 4-hectare Honeyman vineyard is situated in no man's land, falling outside the commonly accepted confines of Macedon and likewise outside the Bendigo region (although it shares a style affinity with the wines of that district). However, owners Philip and Julie Honeyman are members of the Macedon Vignerons' Association, and on the basis of this somewhat tenuous link it is treated as being part of the Macedon region. The Bendigo link has been strengthened by the Honeyman acquisition of Harcourt Valley.

KNIGHT GRANITE HILLS

Location: On Lancefield-Mia Mia Road, 25 km east of Kyneton.
(054) 23 7264 or (054) 23 7288.

Winemaker: Lew Knight.

1989 Production: 5000 cases.

Principal Wines: Estate-grown wines comprise Rhine Riesling, Chardonnay, Shiraz and Cabernet Sauvignon; small parcels of Shiraz are also being processed from Heathcote.

Distribution: Retail distribution through Flinders Wholesale, Vic.; Monteclair Wine Agencies, NSW; Tallerman & Co., Qld; B. H. MacLachlan Pty Ltd, SA. Cellar door sales 10 a.m. to 6 p.m. Monday to Saturday, noon to 6 p.m. Sundays. Mailing list address Baynton, RSD 391, Kyneton, 3444.

Prices: $10 to $22 retail.

Vintage Rating 1986–89: White: '86, '88, '87, '89. Red: '88, '86, '87, '89.

Outstanding Prior Vintages: '77, '81.

Tasting Notes:

1988 RHINE RIESLING [90] Colour: light to medium yellow-green. *Bouquet:* intense, perfumed and fragrant lime/passionfruit/toasty aromas. *Palate:* follows logically on from the bouquet, although it is by no means heavy; intense but relatively light lime/toast flavours, and the obvious potential for development in bottle. Drink '90–'93.

1986 SHIRAZ [64] Colour: dull, slightly blackish-purple. *Bouquet:* light fragrant and spicy. *Palate:* very light fruit with pronounced spice; incredibly, tasted as a tank sample immediately prior to bottling at more than three years of age; should have been bottled long ago. Drink '90–'92.

1986 CABERNET SAUVIGNON [63] Colour: medium red-purple. *Bouquet:* light, slightly soapy minty/stemmy fruit with light oak. *Palate:* quite strong flavour, but with a curious chemical edge; once again a wine that has suffered by being left in tank for far too long. Drink '90–'92.

Summary: Knight Granite Hills was the first winery in Australia to produce cool-climate peppery shiraz. Other makers have now followed suit, and some seem to be able to go one step further, gaining greater richness than is possible in the high and very cool hills on which the beautiful but remote Knight vineyard is planted. Earlier bottling of the red wines would give them a greater chance to realise their true potential.

LANCEFIELD WINERY

Location: Woodend Road, Lancefield, 3435; 5 km south-west of Lancefield.
(054) 29 1217.

Winemaker: John Ellis and Andrew Pattison.

1989 Production: 500 cases.

Principal Wines: Macedon, which is a sparkling chardonnay/pinot noir, Gewurztraminer, Chardonnay, Pinot Noir and Cabernets.

Distribution: Cellar door sales 10 a.m. to 6 p.m. weekends; other times by appointment. Mailing list enquiries as above. Limited retail distribution through Flinders Wholesale.

Prices: $10 to $19.50 recommended retail.

Tasting Notes:

1988 VICTORIAN COLOMBARD [69] Colour: light to medium green-yellow. *Bouquet:* curious vanillan/condensed milk edge to aroma. *Palate:* ample fruit salad flavours, again with a touch of condensed milk, but the wine finishes clean. Drink '90–'91.

1988 GEWURZTRAMINER [74] Colour: light to medium yellow-green. *Bouquet:* quite firm, with some herbaceous notes and overtones of lime; more riesling than traminer in style. *Palate:* very crisp, light and delicate, once again closer to riesling than traminer, and for many that will be no bad thing; pleasant, fresh finish. Drink '90–'91.

Summary: The professional skills of contract winemaker John Ellis are very obvious, as is the delicacy of the Gewurztraminer, attesting perhaps partly to young vines, but–more importantly–to the very cool climate of the Lancefield region.

ROCHFORD WINERY

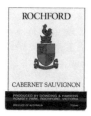

Location: Woodend Road, Romsey Park, Rochford, 3422; 6 km south-west of Lancefield. (054) 29 1428.

Winemaker: Bruce Dowding.

1989 Production: Approximately 1000 cases.

Principal Wines: Presently Rhine Riesling and a cabernet family (Cabernet Sauvignon, Cabernet Franc, Merlot and Malbec) blend which is however labelled Cabernet Sauvignon. Pinot Noir planned for the future.

Distribution: Presently through mailing list only; not open for cellar door sales.

Prices: $9.50 to $14.65 recommended retail.

Vintage Rating 1986-89: '87, '88, '87, '89.

Summary: Rochford is headed towards the 2000 case production, but owner Bruce Dowding is determined not to go beyond that level. His winemaking is intended to be a pleasure, not a pain.

ROMSEY VINEYARDS
(formerly Cope-Williams)

Location: North end of Glenfern Road, Romsey, 3434; 3 km north-west of township. (054) 29 5428; Fax (054) 29 5655.

Winemakers: Gordon and Michael Cope-Williams.

1989 Production: 3000 cases.

Principal Wines: Chardonnay, Pinot Noir and *Méthode Champenoise* backed by red and white blends of estate-grown and contract-grown fruit.

Distribution: Limited fine wine retail distribution: Van Cooth & Co., Vic.; Hayes Fine Wines, NSW, liquor shops and restaurants. Mailing list enquiries to PO Box 18, Romsey, 3434. Cellar door sales weekends and public holidays by appointment during the week.

Prices: $12.50 to $25 (less at cellar door).

Vintage Rating 1986–89: White: '87, '88, '86, '89. Red: '88, '87, '86, '89.

Summary: Romsey Vineyards is situated in one of the coolest parts of the Macedon region, and viticultural progress has been fraught with difficulty and frustration. Gordon Cope-Williams is slowly getting the problems sorted out, and is being rewarded with very high fruit quality even if yields are pitifully low. Some superb *méthode champenoise* wines have also been made in very limited quantity, good enough to defeat Seppelt's entries at the 1987 Ballarat Show.

VIRGIN HILLS

Location: Salisbury Road, Lauriston West via Kyneton, 3444; 24 km west of Kyneton. (054) 23 9169.

Winemaker: Mark Sheppard.

1989 Production: 35 tonnes.

Principal Wines: Only one wine so far commercially released, simply called Virgin Hills. No other description, varietal or generic, is provided on the label. It is in fact a cabernet-dominated blend, with the cabernet content increasing substantially from 1982 and now accounting for approximately 75% of the blend, with the remainder made up by shiraz and a little malbec and merlot.

Distribution: All sold ex-vineyard by mailing list and direct sale to fine wine retailers in Sydney, Melbourne, Brisbane, Perth and Hobart. Mailing list enquiries to PO Kyneton, 3444.

Prices: $168 mailing list.

Vintage Rating 1986–89: '88, '86, '87, '89.

Outstanding Prior Vintages: '74, '75, '76, '85.

Tasting Notes:

1987 VIRGIN HILLS [77] Colour: medium purple-red, with some gas evident both in bottle and in glass. *Bouquet:* clean, of light to medium intensity with complex leafy/mulberry aromas vaguely reminiscent of Coonawarra. *Palate:* vibrant but light-bodied spicy/mulberry/leafy fruit flavours; a well-made, fresh, low alcohol wine. Drink '91–'94.

Summary: The very low-yielding vineyards of Virgin Hills have always produced wines for heroes that demand extended cellaring. The wines have some affinity with Grange Hermitage, and may find themselves under similarly increasing attack as being old fashioned– but never by me. The '87 is something of an exception to the style, reflecting the cool year. I suspect something similar is in store for 1989.

Distribution: Cellar door sales weekends (preferably phone first) and by mailing list; enquiries as above.

Prices: $12.50 to $16.50 cellar door.

Vintage Rating 1988–89: White: '89, '88. Red: '88, '89.

Tasting Notes:

1989 CHARDONNAY [CS] Colour: medium to full yellow-bronze. *Bouquet:* very strong charred/toffee oak. *Palate:* oak dominates the fruit, but if back-blended and balanced with less woody wine, could be good. A unanimous bronze medal at the 1989 Ballarat Show.

1989 SHIRAZ [CS] Colour: strong, youthful purple-red. *Bouquet:* strong red berry/plum/cassis fruit with slightly pencilly oak. *Palate:* high-toned, intense berry fruit; rather hard acid on the finish needs to soften. Obvious potential, perhaps to 80.

Summary: Some very full flavoured and quick striking wines have been produced by Wayne Stott, although a potentially excellent 1988 Cabernet was spoilt by sulphide (if indeed it was a finished wine that I tasted). Wildwood re-emphasises the potential of the Sunbury subdistrict for strongly structured, long-lived reds.

WILDWOOD WINERY

Location: St John's Lane, Wildwood, Bulla, 3428. (03) 307 1118.

Winemaker: Dr Wayne G. Stott.

1989 Production: 300 cases.

Principal Wines: Chardonnay, Cabernet Sauvignon, Cabernet Franc, Merlot and Pinot Noir.

Mornington Peninsula

1988 VINTAGE

Good late winter and early spring rain set the vines off to a good start. The only significant problem in the entire growing season came in mid-November, when gale force winds affected the flowering of early-ripening varieties.

By the end of November, warm and settled conditions arrived which continued through to the end of December, allowing the later varieties to flower and set well.

Unusually fine and warm weather prevailing right from December through to mid-March resulted in a vintage commencing two weeks earlier than average. More importantly, it allowed the grapes to reach unprecedented sugar and flavour levels, easily the best since 1980.

Right across the board, the character and quality of the wines is outstanding, from intensely flavoured yet delicate rhine rieslings through to opulent chardonnays and on to deeply coloured and opulent red wines with excellent varietal character.

1989 VINTAGE

Winter and spring rains were lower than normal, and the weather remained very dry and extremely windy up until mid-November, once again affecting the flowering of early varieties, particularly in those vineyards without adequate wind-break protection. Later varieties, however, set well notwithstanding the advent of rain, which then continued on and off right through the growing season.

Constant spraying against mildew was required, and botrytis was an ever-present threat from the moment of fruit set onwards. The three-week burst of extreme heat to the end of February and March temporarily dried out the mildew and rot problems, and led to a sharply accelerated commencement of picking. Chardonnay and pinot by and large came into the wineries in good conditions, although berry shrivel and collapse was seen in pinot and some sunburn/rot problems with chardonnay. From mid-March onwards it was a test of viticultural skill: the best vineyards ultimately harvested cabernet sauvignon in prime condition, the least well-maintained produced grapes in relatively poor condition. There may well prove to be considerable variation in final wine quality, with winery skills also playing a part. Not an easy vintage, but probably marginally less difficult than in the Yarra Valley, as botrytis did not take much of a hold.

THE CHANGES

There are more new entries for the Mornington Peninsula than any other single chapter in the book. This is partly due to the rapidly expanding operations of the Hickinbotham family, which is establishing its winery and vineyard in the district and is making and marketing varietal wines giving full credit to the grower vineyard. Hence, a number of vineyards are included that have sold their wine to the Hickinbothams but whose wines are nonetheless identifiable.

The Hickinbotham satellites include Allens Vineyards, a 0.5 hectare vineyard at Red Hill established by Bill and Pam Allen in 1983 with plantings of cabernet sauvignon and chardonnay. Cotton Springs Vineyard, at Flinders, was started way back in 1973 by Bill and Gwen Ulbrick. Finally, St Neot's Estate was established in 1980 by Philip and Elvala Ayton, and now comprises 1.8 hectares of semillon, chardonnay, riesling, cabernet sauvignon, pinot noir and merlot.

Craig Avon is a slightly larger vineyard with 2.2 hectares that commenced in 1986; Ken and Helen Lang are doing it on their own, being one of the relatively few vineyard and winery operations not to have their wines either contract made or made with the help of technical consultants. Hoffert Balnarring Estate Vineyard (one of the two non-irrigated vineyards) is in the same category; Bud Hoffert and son Patrick should have wines available by the time this edition is published. Ron and Carol Jones at Erinacea are on a similar time schedule, with a Bordeaux-style blend of cabernet sauvignon, cabernet franc and merlot, made from their 0.8 hectare vineyard planted in 1985, expected on the market in 1990.

Kings Creek Vineyard, although appearing for the first time in this edition, has quietly been making wines for several years now and is into its second release. 2.4 hectares were planted in 1982 to pinot noir, chardonnay and cabernet sauvignon by a syndicate comprising the Glover, Bell and Scarborough families. Bill and Sarah Glover are the main movers and managers, and the wines have been made by various contract makers over the years including Bruce Hyatt (of Prince Albert), Tod Dexter and—more recently–Kathleen Quealy.

Massoni Main Creek Vineyard is very much the hobby of Leon and Vivienne Massoni; situated 300 metres above sea level, it commands the most magnificent view of the Peninsula. For licensing reasons the wines will only be available through very few selected outlets, made under contract by Peter Cumming of Hickinbotham. Paringa Estate is one of the stars of the newcomers; school teacher Lindsay McCall commenced plantings in 1985 with shiraz and cabernet sauvignon; further plantings of chardonnay and pinot noir have since lifted the vineyard to 2.2 hectares. Tod Dexter helped Lindsay McCall make the quite outstanding '88 reds, which are reviewed in this edition.

Shoreham Vale is owned by David and Jill Heathershaw, who established their Red Hill South vineyard in 1985, planted to chardonnay and cabernet sauvignon. Subsequent plantings of rhine riesling and shiraz have extended the vineyard to 2 hectares; Bob Hollick is the consultant viticulturist and will no doubt cast an interested eye over the non-irrigated vines.

Red Hill Estate has disappeared; Bob Hollick, former chief viticulturist in the Mildara empire, has acquired the vineyard from Dr Roger Buckle, and the 1989 fruit was sold to Mildara. It has been made by Mildara on an experimental basis, and no decision has been taken as to whether it will be released as a separate wine. Finally, Tuerong Estate vineyard and restaurant makes its appearance. Gennaro Mazzella and Gwen Riggs acquired the existing vineyards in 1984, and have recently extended the plantings to 2.8 hectares with additional chardonnay, cabernet sauvignon merlot and malbec. The wines are currently made by Peter Cumming and the tiny quantities available will be sold only through the marvellous Italian restaurant established by Mazzella. He comes to the Mornington Peninsula with great experience in wine and food.

For the statistically minded, there are 45 grower members of the Mornington Peninsula Viticultural Association, and there is more than 100 hectares of vineyards. Chardonnay, cabernet sauvignon and pinot noir have the lion's share of those plantings. For those less interested in statistics and more in the quality of the wine in the bottle, the Mornington Peninsula continues to show the way to all other new wine regions with the technical excellence and consistency of its wines.

ALLENS VINEYARDS

Location: Redhill-Shoreham Road, Red Hill, 3937.
Melway Map 193 J12.
(059) 89 2044.

Winemaker: Hickinbotham Winemakers.

Principal Wines: Chardonnay and Cabernet
Sauvignon.

Distribution: Solely through Hickinbotham
Winemakers, under Hickinbotham
Winemakers label but showing the vineyard
name.

Tasting Notes: See under Hickinbotham
Winemakers.

Summary: This 0.5 hectare vineyard was
established in 1983 and is now producing some
very high quality, mature fruit.

BALNARRING VINEYARD

Location: Bittern-Dromana Road, Balnarring,
3926; Melway Map 163 C11.
(059) 89 5258.

Winemaker: David Wollan (contract).

1989 Production: Not stated.

Principal Wines: Chardonnay, Rhine Riesling,
Traminer, Pinot Noir and Cabernet Merlot.

Distribution: Chiefly cellar door sales and mailing
list. Cellar door sales every day. Limited retail
distribution on the Mornington Peninsula,
chiefly through Ritchies Stores.

Prices: $10 to $15 cellar door.

Vintage Rating 1986–89: White: '88, '87, '89, '86.
Red: '87, '88, '86, '89.

Tasting Notes:

1988 RHINE RIESLING [85] Colour: light yellow-
green. *Bouquet:* very concentrated and potent
with strong lime aromas. *Palate:* intense lime

fruit flavours, much more concentrated than
one usually finds on the Mornington Peninsula,
although by no means unusual for Balnarring.
Drink '90–'91.

1988 GEWURZTRAMINER [74] Colour: very light
straw-green. *Bouquet:* clean, but very light fruit
with a faint touch of lychee/spice. *Palate:*
ultra-commerical in style with some sweetness
boosting the overall flavour, although it does
show pleasant varietal character. Drink '90.

1987 CABERNET MERLOT [78] Colour: full
purple-red. *Bouquet:* intense, fragrant berry
fruit with just a slight suspicion of a gravelly
overlay. *Palate:* intense, firm, concentrated
cherry/red berry flavours with obvious merlot
influence; soft tannins throughout the structure;
again, a big wine by the standards of the
Mornington Peninsula, although not by the
standards of Coonawarra or Clare. Drink
'91–'94.

Summary: The red wines produced at Stan Paull's
Balnarring vineyard over the past few years
have been absolutely enormous in terms of
weight, colour and extract. They underline the
subregional differences that exist in the
Mornington Peninsula, and are at the far
extreme to, say, Main Ridge. David Wollan, as
contract winemaker, seems to be coming to
terms with the power of the fruit.

COTTON SPRINGS VINEYARD

Location: 9B Musk Creek Road, Flinders, 3929.
Melway Map 197 G1.
(059) 89 6193.

Winemaker: Hickinbotham Winemakers.

Principal Wines: Sauvignon Blanc, Chardonnay,
Malbec and Cabernet Sauvignon, all made and
marketed by Hickinbotham Winemakers, but
with the Cotton Springs Vineyard shown
prominently on the label.

Tasting Notes: See under Hickinbotham
Winemakers.

Summary: This is one of the oldest vineyards in
the Mornington Peninsula area, and the
quality of the wines is exemplary.

♥ CRAIG AVON VINEYARD

Location: Craig Avon Lane, Merricks North, 3926.
Melway Map 161 J11.
(059) 89 7465.

Winemaker: Ken Lang.

1989 Production: Approximately 30 cases.

Principal Wines: Chardonnay, Pinot Noir and
Cabernet Blend.

Distribution: Purely by mailing list at this juncture;
enquiries welcome.

Summary: This 2.2 hectare vineyard will produce
its first fully commercial crop in 1990; the tiny
quantities of the 1989 vintage wines made
(Chardonnay and Cabernet Sauvignon) were
not available for tasting at the time of writing.

♥ DROMANA ESTATE

Location: Cnr Harrisons Road and Bittern-
Dromana Road, Dromana, 3936; 3 km inland
from Dromana. Melway Map 160 J6.
(059) 87 3275.

Winemaker: Garry Crittenden.

1989 Production: 2000 cases, Dromana Estate; 3000
cases, Schinus Molle.

Principal Wines: The principal label is Dromana
Estate, which is exclusively reserved for estate-
grown and made Chardonnay, Pinot Noir and
Cabernet Merlot. Winemaker/proprietor
Garry Crittenden has also developed a second
label, Schinus Molle, the wines of which are
not necessarily Mornington Peninsula-sourced.
These comprise Sauvignon Blanc, Chardonnay
and Cabernet.

Distribution: East coast fine wine retail distribution
through Dorado Wine Company; SA and WA,
The National Wine Broker; Tas., David
Johnstone & Assoc. Substantial mailing list
sales; enquiries to PO Box 332, Mornington,
3931. Winery visits/cellar door sales strictly by

appointment. UK imports through Haughton
Fine Wines, Chorley, Cheshire.

Prices: $15 to $19 mail order; $16 to $21 retail.

Vintage Rating 1986–89: White: '88, '89, '87, '86.
Red: '89, '88, '87, '86.

Tasting Notes:

1989 DROMANA ESTATE PINOT NOIR [CS]
Colour: medium purple-red. *Bouquet:* intensely
fragrant plum/dark cherry aromas with lovely
spicy oak. *Palate:* similar plum/dark cherry
flavours, again with excellent oak handling;
almost certainly headed to more than 90 points.

1989 SCHINUS MOLLE CHARDONNAY [CS]
Colour: light yellow-green. *Bouquet:* ripe, crisp
melon fruit with nicely balanced and integrated
oak; some fermentation characters. *Palate:*
tangy fresh grapefruit/melon fruit; good weight
and length; a cool style, notwithstanding its
predominantly McLaren Vale origin. Around
85 points.

1989 SCHINUS MOLLE GEMBROOK SAUVIGNON
BLANC [TS] Colour: light straw-green.
Bouquet: of light to medium weight, with classic
gooseberry/herbaceous fruit with a faint touch
of smoky tobacco. *Palate:* light, crisp and clean;
beautifully made and already showing real style.
Varietal character is exemplary. 85 to 90 points.

1988 DROMANA ESTATE CHARDONNAY [90]
Colour: medium yellow-green. *Bouquet:*
beautifully balanced and modulated with cool
melon fruit; neither barrel ferment characters
nor oak are assertive. *Palate:* very attractive
varietal melon fruit flavours, with a long clean
finish; has the structure and weight to age with
grace. Drink '90–'92.

1988 CABERNET MERLOT [90] Colour: medium
to full purple red, brilliantly clear. *Bouquet:*
clean and intense ripe berry aromas with
a touch of mulberry; oak perfectly balanced.
Palate: complex sweet red berry fruits with
quite pronounced vanillan oak; soft, lingering
tannins; more structure than any previous
Dromana Cabernet Merlot, but nonetheless
amazingly accessible now. Drink '90–'95.

1988 SCHINUS MOLLE CABERNET [84] Colour:
medium full purple-red. *Bouquet:* complex berry
aromas with a strong Coonawarra influence
evident in some meaty/leafy characters. *Palate:*
supple, rich, complex berry fruit with that

Coonawarra character again evident; low tannin but good length. Drink '90–'93.

Summary: The wines of Dromana Estate (and for that matter, the second label, Schinus Molle) go from strength to strength. Garry Crittenden is a master viticulturist and a most fastidious winemaker; as always, attention to detail is its own reward.

ELGEE PARK

Location: Wallaces Road, Merricks North, 3926. Melway Map 161 G3. (059) 89 7338; Fax (059) 89 7424.

Winemaker: Daniel Green with Gary Baldwin (consultant).

1989 Production: 2000 cases approximately.

Principal Wines: Rhine Riesling, Chardonnay and Cabernet Merlot (the latter with cabernet franc in the blend). Experimental quantities of Viognier.

Distribution: Through mailing list (to Junction Road, Merricks North, 3926), and limited number of high-quality bottle shops, hotels and restaurants on the Mornington Peninsula, Sydney and Melbourne.

Prices: $12 to $18 mailing list.

Vintage Rating 1986–89: White: '88, '87, '86 ('89 not rated). Red: '87 ('86, '88 and '89 not rated).

Outstanding Prior Vintages: '80.

Summary: Elgee Park, owned by Mr and Mrs Baillieu Myer, is the best-equipped winery on the Mornington Peninsula and has some of the longest-established vineyards. It has proved most important in leading the way for the district, not only with its own invariably good wines, but also by acting as a contract maker for a number of small vineyards during their infancy.

ERINACEA

Location: Devonport Drive, Rye, 3941. Melway Map 169 A11. (059) 88 6336.

Winemaker: Ron Jones.

Principal Wines: A single Bordeaux blend of Cabernet Sauvignon, Cabernet Franc and Merlot.

Summary: The first release from this 0.8 hectare winery is expected some time in 1990.

HICKINBOTHAM

Location: Cnr Wallaces Road and Nepean Highway, Dromana, 3936. Melway Map 160 J3. (059) 81 0355 or (03) 397 1872.

Winemakers: The Hickinbotham family and Peter Cummings.

1989 Production: An absolutely astonishing number of different parcels of wine, all made in small quantities, but adding up to a very substantial amount in total.

Principal Wines: Hickinbotham Winemakers' specialty is taking small parcels of grapes (perhaps as little as one tonne at a time) and turning these into distinct lots of wine (in quantities as small as 50 dozen) identified by variety and by the vineyard name. These are then made available either by mailing list or, if through a retailer or restaurant, often on a single outlet exclusive basis. A number of the individual wines come from the Mornington Peninsula, but others do not: the Hickinbotham net extends to the Bellarine Peninsula, Geelong, Gippsland and the Yarra Valley to name a few districts.

Distribution: The principal method of access at the present time is through the Hickinbotham mailing list; enquiries to 2 Ferguson Street,

Williamstown, Vic., 3016. The on-site winery will open in 1990, and no doubt a cellar door sales facility will then be established.

Prices: Very substantial from wine to wine, but the median price is $264 per dozen.

Tasting Notes:

1988 ALLEN CHARDONNAY [90] Colour: medium yellow-green. *Bouquet:* clean, rich and smooth with exceptionally concentrated and deep fruit. *Palate:* uncommonly rich and concentrated honeyed fruit flavours with a supremely rich texture; an altogether unusual style for the Peninsula, but absolutely delicious. Drink '90–'92.

1988 ALLEN CABERNET SAUVIGNON [84] Colour: very good purple-red. *Bouquet:* clean, complex mulberry/berry fruit with light oak. *Palate:* high flavoured slightly gamey/spicy characters; a fruit, rather than oak, driven wine. Drink '92–'96.

1988 COTTON SPRINGS CABERNET SAUVIGNON [87] Colour: full purple-red. *Bouquet:* firm, classic, even austere cabernet sauvignon, spotlessly clean. *Palate:* strong, berry/briary/cassis ripe fruit with considerable concentration; the tannins are low and the wine is accordingly accessible. Drink '91–'94.

1988 ST NEOTS CABERNET SAUVIGNON [79] Colour: full purple-red. *Bouquet:* clean and firm briary/berry cabernet sauvignon with light oak in support. *Palate:* light and soft plum flavours intermingling with dark berries; the structure is relatively light, and the wine falls away ever so slightly on the finish. Drink '90–'93.

Summary: The Hickinbotham family has strong genes: all of the members have seemed to have inherited enquiring minds with a bent to lateral thinking, whether it comes to viticulture, winemaking or wine marketing. The lateral approach is bound to stir controversy, but any questions must surely be answered by the outstanding quality of the wines in the glass.

❦ HOFFERT BALNARRING ESTATE VINEYARD

Location: 87 Bittern-Dromana Road, Balnarring, 3926. Melway Map 163 B11. (059) 89 5330.

Winemaker: Bud and Patrick Hoffert.

Principal Wines: Sylvaner, Traminer, Chardonnay and Cabernet Sauvignon.

Distribution: Limited local retail and restaurant distribution; cellar door sales planned late 1989/early 1990; mail order enquiries to above address.

Summary: Nothing is known of the very small production from one of the few non-irrigated vineyards in the region.

❦ KARINA VINEYARD

Location: Harrisons Road, Dromana, 3936. Melway Map 160 J6. (059) 81 0137.

Winemaker: Graeme Pinney.

1989 Production: Approximately 700 cases.

Principal Wines: Rhine Riesling, Sauvignon Blanc and Cabernet Merlot.

Distribution: Principally by mailing list; enquiries to above address. Limited local restaurant and retail distribution.

Prices: $13 to $18 cellar door.

Vintage Rating 1986–89: White: '88, '89, '87 (no '86). Red: '88, '89 (no '86, '87).

Tasting Notes:

1988 RHINE RIESLING [83] Colour: light green-yellow. *Bouquet:* fragrant, clean, marked passionfruit/peach aromas. *Palate:* very good balance and flavour with some light toasty characters starting to emerge from bottle development; a quite long, dry finish. Drink '90–'91.

1988 SAUVIGNON BLANC [87] Colour: light green-yellow. *Bouquet:* pronounced sweet gooseberry fruit aromas showing excellent fruit weight, depth and varietal character. *Palate:* again, exemplary sauvignon blanc varietal character, though not quite as rich as the bouquet would suggest; the wine has a tangy finish with good length. Drink '90.

Summary: Karina has produced some lovely white wines in 1988, although the single red wine tasted was not in the same class. A cask sample prior to bottling, it was presumably not indicative of quality.

KINGS CREEK

Location: 237 Myers Road, Bittern, 3918. Melway Map 163 F8.
(059) 83 2102.

Winemakers: Kathleen Quealy and Brian Fletcher.

1989 Production: Approximately 660 cases.

Principal Wines: Chardonnay, Pinot Noir and Cabernet Sauvignon.

Distribution: Chiefly cellar door sales and mailing list; cellar door sales 10 a.m. to 4 p.m. first Sunday each month. Mailing list enquiries as above. Selected retailers and restaurants in Melbourne and the Mornington Peninsula.

Prices: $20 to $22 cellar door.

Vintage Rating 1986-89: White: '86, '87 ('88 and '89 not rated). Red: '87 ('88 and '89 not rated).

Tasting Notes:

1987 CHARDONNAY [75] Colour: medium yellow-green. *Bouquet:* light, clean peach/melon fruit aromas with light oak. *Palate:* slightly raw and slightly unintegrated oak; the fruit is light and developing very slowly. Drink '90–'91.

1987 PINOT NOIR [67] Colour: light red, with a touch of purple. *Bouquet:* fragrant, sappy pinot noir varietal aroma of light to medium weight. *Palate:* fails to live up to the attractive bouquet with stemmy/sappy/coffee/leafy flavours with insufficient core. Drink '90.

1988 CABERNET SAUVIGNON [77] Colour: light to medium red-purple. *Bouquet:* fragrant, sweet

and clean mulberry fruit with good oak. *Palate:* soft; of light to medium weight with gentle berry/mulberry fruit and light supporting oak; soft tannins. Drink '90–'91.

Summary: Kings Creek is the creation of the Glover, Bell and Scarborough families, and is noteworthy for offering some of the few bottle matured wines available on the Peninsula.

MAIN RIDGE ESTATE

Location: Lot 48, William Road, Red Hill, 3937; Melway Map 190 C4.
(059) 89 2686.

Winemaker: Nat White.

1989 Production: 1000 cases.

Principal Wines: An eclectic, if not esoteric, range of varietal table wines including Pinot Meunier (in tiny quantities), Chardonnay, Pinot Noir, Cabernet Sauvignon and Cabernet Franc.

Distribution: Cellar door sales by appointment; mailing list enquiries to PO Box 40, Red Hill South, 3937. Limited restaurant and fine wine retail distribution, chiefly in Melbourne.

Prices: $20 to $22 recommended retail.

Vintage Rating 1986–89: White: '86, '89, '88, '87. Red: '86, '88, '89, '87.

Outstanding Prior Vintages: '80.

Tasting Notes:

1988 CHARDONNAY [83] Colour: light green-yellow. *Bouquet:* elegant, fragrant and stylish; aromas of white peaches and some barrel-ferment characters. *Palate:* intense, long peachy fruit, with the oak in restraint; has all the style to develop beautifully in bottle. Drink '90–'92.

1988 PINOT NOIR [86] Colour: strong purple-red. *Bouquet:* complex with strong leafy/herbaceous overtones and a touch of the spice one associates with Main Ridge; also strawberry nuances. *Palate:* a good, positively flavoured pinot noir with strawberry fruit complexed by some sappy characters; to be enjoyed while that strawberry fruit is still there. Drink '90.

1988 CABERNET SAUVIGNON [80] Colour: medium purple-red. *Bouquet:* quite assertive cabernet fruit with a touch of gravel astringency. *Palate:* fresh red berry/cherry fruit flavours of light to medium weight, and finishing with soft tannins; a typical light and elegant Mornington cabernet. Drink '91–'94.

Summary: The Main Ridge style continues to be quite distinctive in Mornington Peninsula terms; the vineyard is very cool, and this shows in the fruit characters. The wines are always immaculately made with the maximum of tender loving care from proprietor/winemaker Nat White.

❦ MASSONI MAIN CREEK VINEYARD

Location: Mornington-Flinders Road, Red Hill, 3937. Melway Map 194 D6. Enquiries (059) 89 2060.

Winemaker: Peter Cummings (contract).

Principal Wines: Only one wine made: Chardonnay.

Distribution: By wholesale only to selected liquor outlets.

Summary: Leading Melbourne restaurateur Leon Massoni and his wife Vivienne are determined that their vineyard will remain a hobby and not a millstone around their neck. Accordingly, output will always be limited and restricted to a few retail outlets.

❦ MERRICKS ESTATE

Location: Thompsons Lane, Merricks, 3916 (near Balnarring). Melway Map 192 B9. (059) 89 8352.

Winemakers: George Kefford and family and Selma Lowther. Chardonnay made by Alex White.

1989 Production: 1200 cases.

Principal Wines: Given tiny production, a wide

range including Chardonnay, Pinot Noir, Shiraz and Cabernet Sauvignon.

Distribution: Principally mailing list. Limited restaurant distribution and selected retail outlets.

Prices: $21.95 retail.

Vintage Rating 1986–89: White: '88, '87, '86 ('89 not rated). Red: '86, '88, '87 ('89 not rated).

Tasting Notes:

1988 CHARDONNAY [75] Colour: medium to full yellow-green. *Bouquet:* clean, with fairly neutral oak; some grapefruit characters, but not particularly aromatic. *Palate:* clean, light and fresh, with the delicacy of flavour and structure that often comes from young vines; really needs more structure and intensity to rate top points. Drink '90.

1988 SHIRAZ [79] Colour: full red-purple. *Bouquet:* quite fully gamey characters with a faint pepper spice overlay. *Palate:* the pepper literally explodes in the mouth, almost overwhelming the gamey varietal shiraz underneath; a somewhat schizophrenic style, and I am not absolutely certain which way it will develop. Drink '91–'94.

1988 CABERNET SAUVIGNON [84] Colour: medium red-purple. *Bouquet:* clean and of medium weight; minty aromas predominate. *Palate:* almost identical smooth, clean, minty flavours in radically different style to the shiraz; the wine does have flesh, and the overall flavour and structure is most attractive; nice supporting oak and low tannin. Drink '92–'96.

Summary: Melbourne solicitor George Kefford has established a vineyard that produces outstanding shiraz and cabernet sauvignon, the former very sparingly planted in the region. It certainly suggests that micro-climate and soil have a major impact in the region, and that subregions may ultimately develop.

MOOROODUC ESTATE

Location: Derril Road, Moorooduc, Mornington Peninsula, 3936. Melway Map 152 H2. (059) 78 8585 or (03) 696 4130.

Winemaker: Dr Richard McIntyre (consultant Nat White).

1989 Production: 600 cases (reduced by wind damage).

Principal Wines: Chardonnay, Pinot Noir and Cabernet Sauvignon.

Distribution: Principally by mailing list; enquiries to PO Box 239, Albert Park, 3206. Limited retail and restaurant distribution.

Prices: $19 retail.

Vintage Rating 1986–89: White: '88, '89, '87, '86. Red: '88, '89, '86, '87.

Tasting Notes:

1988 CHARDONNAY [90] Colour: medium yellow-green. *Bouquet:* complex rich and stylish grapefruit/peach fruit perfectly balanced and integrated with good oak. *Palate:* very rich and complex; high classed toasty oak flavours perfectly balanced with peach/melon fruit. Drink '90–'93.

1988 PINOT NOIR [74] Colour: light red-purple. *Bouquet:* rather woody-stemmy aromas lacking intense varietal fruit. *Palate:* acceptable light plummy pinot flavours but lacks intensity and structure in the mid-palate; somewhat surprisingly, does have some length to the finish. Drink '90.

1988 CABERNET [79] Colour: medium purple-red. *Bouquet:* light, lifted and fragrant light berry aromas. *Palate:* as the bouquet promises, fragrant, with ripe leafy/berry flavours allied with a touch of mint; light tannin; fresh early drinking style with a suggestion of slightly under-ripe fruit. Drink '90–'92.

Summary: Medical practitioner Dr Richard McIntyre is producing some lovely wines, doing most of the work himself and simply relying on some consultancy advice. In these circumstances, the chardonnay is quite outstanding.

PARINGA ESTATE

Location: 44 Paringa Road, Red Hill South, 3937. Melway Map 191 D9. (059) 89 2669.

Winemaker: Lindsay McCall (consultant Tod Dexter).

1989 Production: Approximately 550 cases.

Principal Wines: Chardonnay, Shiraz and Cabernet Sauvignon the only wines presently made; however, subsequent plantings of merlot, cabernet franc and pinot noir will extend the range.

Distribution: Exclusively cellar door sales and mail order; cellar door sales by appointment only. Mailing list enquiries to address above. Limited Peninsula retail outlets.

Prices: $14 to $17 cellar door.

Tasting Notes:

1988 SHIRAZ [85] Colour: full red-purple. *Bouquet:* very complex and rich, with clean red berry fruit and marked spice/pepper. *Palate:* vibrantly clean, riotous pepper/spice flavours; there is adequate fruit weight to carry these characters; a clean, well-made and well-balanced wine of great style. Drink '93–'96.

1988 CABERNET SAUVIGNON [87] Colour: medium to full purple-red. *Bouquet:* clean and deep, but not particularly fragrant when tasted July 1989. *Palate:* very good fruit with deep cassis/dark berry flavours and excellent oak integration and balance; the sweet vanillan oak harmonises well with the very strong fruit. A wine of both power and length. Drink '94–'98.

Summary: Lindsay and Margaret McCall could not have got Paringa Estate off to a better start. Provided there is no bottling mishap (the wines were tasted immediately prior to going into bottle) they and consultant winemaker Tod Dexter can feel very pleased with themselves.

🍇 *SHOREHAM VALE*

Location: Red Hill - Shoreham Road, Red Hill South, 3937. Melway Map 196 B4.

Winemakers: Gordon and Michael Cope-Williams (Romsey Vineyards contract).

Principal Wines: Will eventually comprise Rhine Riesling, Chardonnay, Shiraz and Cabernet Sauvignon. Chardonnay and Cabernet Sauvignon will be marketed first.

Summary: Yet another new operation with wine quality yet to be tested in the commercial market, but with Bob Hollick as viticultural consultant and the Cope-Williams's to make the wines, all should be well.

🍇 *ST NEOT'S ESTATE*

Location: 63 Red Hill-Shoreham Road, Red Hill South, 3937. Melway Map 290 K11. (059) 89 2023.

Winemaker: Hickinbotham Winemakers (contract).

Principal Wines: As with Allens and Cotton Springs, the wines are made and marketed by Hickinbotham Winemakers under the Hickinbotham label but with St Neot's shown as the vineyard source. The principal wines will be made from Semillon, Chadonnay, Riesling, Cabernet Sauvignon, Pinot Noir, Cabernet Sauvignon and Merlot.

Distribution: Listed through Fanny's Restaurant and by mail order through Hickinbotham Winemakers.

Tasting Notes: See Hickinbotham entry.

Summary: The vineyard was established in 1980, and some first-class fruit is now being produced; skilful winemaking by the Hickinbothams does the rest.

🍇 *STONIER'S MERRICKS*

Location: 62 Thompsons Lane, Merricks, 3916 (near Balnarring). Melway Map 192 B9. (059) 89 8352.

Winemaker: 1982-86 vintages: the late Stephen Hickinbotham. From 1987: Tod Dexter at Elgee Park Winery with private consultancy.

1989 Production: 850 cases.

Principal Wines: Chardonnay, Cabernet Sauvignon and Pinot Noir.

Distribution: Principally by mailing list; enquiries as above. Limited retail distribution through Gatehouse Cellars, Melbourne; and Hayes Fine Wines at Len Evans, Sydney.

Prices: $22.50 retail.

Vintage Rating 1986–89: White: '88, '86, '87, '89. Red: '86, '87, '88, '89.

Tasting Notes:

1988 CHARDONNAY [80] Colour: light to medium yellow-green. *Bouquet:* light melon grapefruit flavours with a touch of barrel ferment; elegant. *Palate:* excellent cool-climate melon fruit with a touch of barrel ferment character again evident; crisp and clean in the mouth. Drink '90–'91.

1989 PINOT NOIR [CS] Colour: a very good medium red-purple. *Bouquet:* smooth, clean cherry/strawberry fruit together with a light touch of spicy oak. *Palate:* a fresh, fine wine; the spicy oak makes a greater statement than on the bouquet, but combines beautifully with delicate strawberry pinot flavour. Headed to 85 plus points.

1988 CABERNET SAUVIGNON [90] Colour: medium purple-red. *Bouquet:* very clean, fragrant classic cabernet fruit with aromas of dark berry/mulberry and just a touch of leafy astringency. *Palate:* beautifully modulated fruit flavours showing perfectly ripened cabernet with all of its facets; oak is sensitively handled in what is a supremely elegant wine with great length to the finish. Drink '92–'97.

Summary: Stonier's Merricks has produced some
marvellous wines over the past few years. Brian
Stonier is one of the great characters of the
Peninsula, with a sense of humour that might
best be described as disconcerting. However,
there is nothing flippant about his wines.

TUERONG ESTATE VINEYARD

Location: Mornington-Flinders Road, Red Hill,
3937. Melway Map 190 D8.
(059) 89 2129.

Winemaker: Peter Cumming (contract).

1989 Production: 45 cases.

Principal Wines: Only one wine made: Chardonnay.

Distribution: Will be available exclusively through
Tuerong Estate restaurant.

Prices: Around $34 to $40 on the restaurant wine list.

Summary: Gennaro Mazzella runs a traditional
neopolitan restaurant at Tuerong Estate. In
Gennaro's words: "There are no red checked
tablecloths here or candles in empty chianti
bottles. At Tuerong the watch word is
'authenticity'." The menu is fixed, as is the
starting time of both lunch and dinner. It is an
experience worth having.

Murray River

1988 VINTAGE

A normal start to the growing season was soon followed by a period of unusually hot weather coinciding with flowering. The hot, windy days resulted in very uneven fruit set. However, there was then a distinct turn for the better: ideal weather prevailed right through the ripening period and continued through to the end of vintage. The absence of rain, and warm but not excessively hot weather, produced disease-free grapes with excellent chemical composition. The problems lay with yield: there was very substantial variation from one vineyard to the next but overall crop levels were sharply down, with all red varieties suffering, cabernet sauvignon the most.

The quality of the wines produced was good, with the reduced quantity of red wines being particularly good, showing deep colour, good varietal flavour and good acid/tannin balance. The whites also had good flavour but were low in acid.

1989 VINTAGE

A vintage that escaped the worst of the problems that affected much of south-east Australia, but which could not be described as great. The opening and early part of the year were propitious enough, but humid and rainy conditions from mid-February onwards caused particular problems with the lesser, high yielding varieties of dense canopies. There was some very poor sultana and mediocre gordo, both important grapes for the task and bulk wine market. Machine-pruned chardonnay, on the other hand, performed much better, with the bunches handing on the outside of the canopy and avoiding the mould and rot problems that affected other varieties and other trellis systems.

THE CHANGES

The reports of the demise of Lindemans' Matthew Lang range carried in the 1988 edition were premature: even if Matthew Lang is long since dead, his name and label live on. Indeed, the quality of the wines under this label (produced from all parts of Australia, including Coonawarra, but also from Karadoc fruit) continued to impress. Overall, the Murray River (both in Victoria and South Australia) continues to provide the base of the Australian wine pyramid. Whether the grape prices attracted in 1988 and, even more, in 1989 will allow it to continue this role remains to be seen; the price of cask wine simply cannot sustain prices of $800 per tonne, let alone the $1400 to $1500 per tonne paid for chardonnay in 1989.

♥ *ALAMBIE WINES*

Location: Nangiloc Road, Nangiloc, 3494.
(050) 29 1546.

Winemaker: David Martin.

1989 Production: Approximately 1.5 million litres.

Principal Wines: All wines, exclusively made from estate-grown grapes, are sold in bulk to other winemakers, packagers and re-users.

Summary: A number of Alambie wines were entered in the 1989 Ballarat Wine Show. Because they will not appear in any identifiable form on the commercial market, I have not provided tasting notes, but they were of exceptionally high standard.

♥ *BEST'S—LAKE BOGA*

Location: St Andrew's Vineyard, Lake Boga, 3584.
(050) 37 2154.

Winemakers: Viv Thomson and Simon Clayfield.

1989 Production: Approximately 25,000 cases.

Principal Wines: A number of table wines, both white and red, are produced; not all are released under the Best's label. By far the most important estate release is Best's Victorian Cabernet Sauvignon. Other regular releases are Victorian Shiraz, Victorian Rhine Riesling and Victorian Chenin Blanc. The wines that appear under the Best's Victorian label are entirely or predominantly from Lake Boga, e.g. the Victorian Shiraz and Chenin Blanc are 100% from Lake Boga. The Victorian Rhine Riesling and Cabernet Sauvignon may contain up to 25% Great Western.

Distribution: Retail distribution as for Best's Great Western. Cellar door sales 9 a.m. to 5 p.m. Monday to Friday and 9 a.m. to 4 p.m. Saturday and public holidays. Closed Sundays except on public holidays and long weekends, when open 12 noon to 4 p.m. Closed Christmas Day, Good Friday and Anzac Day.

Prices: $7.60 to $11.70 recommended retail.

Vintage Rating 1986–89: White: '89, '88, '87, '86. Red: '87, '89, '86, '88.

Tasting Notes:

1989 VICTORIAN CHENIN BLANC [81] Colour: light yellow-green. *Bouquet:* pungent, aromatic fruit of considerable depth, still showing some fermentation characters mid-1989 that will be gone long before the end of the year. *Palate:* beautifully made young, crisp wine with soft fruit salad flavours in true varietal style. Drink '90–'91.

1989 VICTORIAN RHINE RIESLING [83] Colour: light to medium yellow-green. *Bouquet:* clean, firm aromatic/toasty fruit; classic and showing very careful winemaking. *Palate:* high quality, classic reserved rhine riesling in the very best style; no yeast overlay or extravagant fruit characters. Drink '90–'92.

1988 CHABLIS [75] Colour: medium green-yellow. *Bouquet:* distinct passionfruit/pineapple aromas, almost into fruit essence. *Palate:* high-toned, high flavoured essency fruit; a bit extreme for chablis, but has masses of character. Drink '90.

1987 VICTORIAN CABERNET SAUVIGNON [65] Colour: medium purple-red. *Bouquet:* fractionally light and dull, lacking fruit intensity. *Palate:* soft and clean, with quite attractive cherry/berry fruit flavours, albeit a little one-dimensional. Adequate commercial red, but not up to the occasionally great vintages under this label. Drink '90–'91.

Summary: The St Andrews vineyard of Best's situated at Lake Boga has for a long time provided fresh but soft, early-maturing commercial wines that have above-average fruit flavour.

♥ *BULLERS BEVERFORD*

Location: Murray Valley Highway, Beverford, 3590; 14 km north of Swan Hill.
(050) 37 6305.

Winemaker: Richard Buller Junior.

1989 Production: About 1300 tonnes of grapes crushed; a little over 50% is for distillation to make fortifying spirit.

Principal Wines: A full range of generic and varietal table wines, principally white but also red, offered in bottle and in 10-litre and 20-litre soft-pack cases. Likewise, a range of fortified wines including sherries of all styles. Most of the tawny and vintage ports are made at Rutherglen. White table wines include Rhine Riesling, Spatlese Muscat Blanc, Colombard, Chenin Blanc, Chablis, Sylvaner, Spatlese Lexia, White Burgundy, Riesling and

Moselle; red wines include Rutherglen Shiraz, Cabernet Merlot, Cabernet Sauvignon, Liqueur Muscat, Tokay and Frontignac.

Distribution: Substantial cellar door and mailing list sales, with cellar door sales both at Rutherglen and Beverford. Cellar door sales 9 a.m. to 5 p.m. Monday to Saturday, 10 a.m. to 6 p.m. Sunday. Mailing-list enquiries to PO Box 28, Rutherglen, 3685. Victorian distribution through Melbourne office (telephone (03) 570 1717).

Prices: Table wines $5 to $10 retail

Tasting Notes:

1988 CHENIN BLANC [74] Colour: light yellow-green. *Bouquet:* clean, soft fruit salad/tutti-frutti characters. *Palate:* again, a touch of fruit salad flavour on a particularly good mid-palate; finishes crisp and clean. Drink '90.

1987 WOODED SEMILLON [73] Colour: light straw-yellow-green. *Bouquet:* clean and quite fragrant lemony fruit and oak. *Palate:* pleasant, lightly wooded, light lemony fruit, with crisp, clean acid on the finish. Drink '90–'91.

1986 CABERNET MERLOT [74] Colour: medium red-purple. *Bouquet:* clean, minty fruit with sweet oak. *Palate:* clean, fruity minty flavours with soft tannin. Drink '90–'93.

Summary: An old family company with dual residence, at Rutherglen and here at Beverford. The Riverland produces the light table wines, with particular emphasis on the whites; Rutherglen produces the great fortifieds and big reds. Quality is reliable and the prices are very modest.

CAPOGRECO WINES

Location: Riverside Avenue, Mildura, 3500; between 17th and 18th Streets. (050) 23 3060.

Winemaker: Bruno Capogreco.

Principal Wines: A range of table, fortified, dessert and flavoured wines (including vermouths), all made in the Italian style and without the addition of preservatives, marketed in 750 ml bottles and in 2-litre flagons. Premium table wines include Rhine Riesling, Moselle, Cabernet Sauvignon, Barbera, Shiraz Mataro, Claret and Rose Light Red. Herb-infused

dessert wine Rosso Dolce particularly good.

Distribution: Exclusively cellar door sales and mail order; no bulk sales. Cellar door sales 10 a.m. to 6 p.m. Monday to Saturday and most public holidays. Mailing list enquiries to PO Box 7, Cabarita via Merbein, 3505.

Summary: A small cellar door operation making some interesting fortified and flavoured wines, with Rosso Dolce an understandably great favourite with the local clientele.

LINDEMANS' KARADOC

Location: Nangiloc Road, Karadoc, on Calder Highway; 27 km east of Mildura. (050) 24 0303.

Winemakers: Wayne Falkenburg, Paul Gordon, Alyson Samuel and Sheryl Henriks directed by company oenologist, Phillip John.

1989 Production: Not for publication.

Principal Wines: Lindemans Premier Selection Chardonnay, Bin 65 Export Chardonnay, Bin 95 Export Sauvignon Blanc and Bin 45 Export Cabernet Sauvignon all basically made from locally grown fruit. Matthew Lang range is also nominally housed here, although the base material comes both from the Murray River and from elsewhere.

Distribution: Very heavily directed to export, but the Matthew Lang range and Premier Selection range are nationally distributed through Lindemans' own distribution network. UK imports through IDV Gilbey House.

Prices: $2.99 to $7.75 retail.

Tasting Notes:

1989 MATTHEW LANG TRAMINER RIESLING [79] Colour: light yellow-green. *Bouquet:* very clean, fresh and crisp spicy traminer, with obvious spice. *Palate:* again, the traminer component dominates the blend, but the riesling provides some crispness and helps the acid structure; the residual sugar is beautifully controlled. Gold medal winner Brisbane Show 1989. Drink '90.

1988 PREMIER SELECTION RHINE RIESLING [85] Colour: light green-yellow. *Bouquet:* perfectly made and spotlessly clean, highly aromatic lime/toasty aromas. *Palate:* has considerable weight, depth and intensity; once again, flavours of lime and toast, and a crisp, firm but dry finish. Drink '90.

Summary: Lindemans' Karadoc Winery is now the blending, storage and packaging centre for all wines produced for the Lindeman Group, and most of the company's senior oenologists are stationed there. As is the case with all of the big companies, Lindemans is incapable of making poor wines. As the tasting notes indicate, it can indeed produce some exceptionally good wines at prices that give no clue to their quality. The Premier Selection Rhine Riesling had in fact won three gold medals at national wine shows by the time this edition went to print.

MILDARA

Location: Wentworth Road, Merbein, 3505; 11 km west of Mildura.
(050) 25 2303.

Winemakers: Alan Harris (senior winemaker), Andrew Fleming, Andrew Peace and David Teirney.

Principal Wines: Church Hill Range comprises Chardonnay, Fumé Blanc, Chablis, Cabernet Merlot, Rhine Riesling. Fortifieds comprise Cavendish Port, Benjamin Port, George Fino Sherry, Chestnut Teal, Supreme Dry, Stratford Port and the Rio Vista range. Brandy includes Morgon Brown Pot Still, Supreme and Special.

Distribution: National retail through all types of outlets.

Prices: $5 to $11; Brandy to $20.

Tasting Notes:

1989 CHURCH HILL RHINE RIESLING [74] Colour: very good green-yellow. *Bouquet:* strong and full lime fruit, though slightly broad. *Palate:* firm, tangy wine with weight and length; lime flavours are already acquiring a touch of old-style kerosene, but the wine has character. Drink '90.

1989 FUME BLANC [54] Colour: light straw-green. *Bouquet:* rather neutral, with slightly oily/hard characters, possibly deriving from oak chips. *Palate:* rather hard and oily chippy oak with very light fruit. Drink '90.

1989 CHURCH HILL CHARDONNAY [64] Colour: light yellow-green. *Bouquet:* somewhat oily, with reasonable fruit but some slightly bitter characters. *Palate:* again, ripe fruit with reasonable length and acid, but the faint bitter characters evident in the bouquet once again make their presence felt. Drink '90.

CAVENDISH PORT [82] Colour; light, clear tawny. *Bouquet:* of light to medium intensity, stylish and fragrant, with good rancio and lovely freshness. *Palate:* clean, stylish tawny with very good rancio flavour and definition, and obvious age; cleansing dry finish.

BENJAMIN PORT [73] Colour: medium tawny. *Bouquet:* rich and complex with some fortified sweet white characters. *Palate:* luscious, sweet light/tokay-like; lots of flavour, although the style is commercial rather than classic.

GEORGE FINO SHERRY [72] Colour: very pale, almost watery. *Bouquet:* fine, with nice flor character. *Palate:* crisp, clean, very dry, light-weight flor style that needs a little more heart, but which does come again on the finish.

Summary: The Church Hill range is unpretentious and inexpensive; you basically get what you pay for. The Mildara operation at Merbein in terms of quality centres around the fortified range. Here, again, it was very interesting to correlate the points given in a blind tasting with retail prices: once more, it was a case of getting what you paid for.

🍇 MILDURA VINEYARD
(Formerly Fitzpatrick Estate)

Location: Campbell Avenue, Irymple, 3498; 10 km from Mildura.
(050) 24 5843.

Owners: Murrayland Fruit Juice Group. Operations Manager: Mr Bruce Holm.

Winemaker: Neville Hudson. Phillip Rentree (product manager).

Principal Wines: By far the greatest part of the production is sold either as clarified grape juice or as wine in bulk to other winemakers and re-packagers. A small percentage is estate bottled and released under a series of labels. Premium-quality table wines are released comprising Chardonnay, Rhine Riesling, Chablis, Traminer, Vintage Port, Ruby Cabernet and Cabernet Sauvignon, while Spumante, Passion Wine and Strawberry Wine are released under the Mildura Vineyards label. Non-alcoholic wines are also made and released under the Sparkling Golden Lexia label. (Highly commended.) There is, in addition, the usual range of fortified wines in bottles and bulk wines sold in 15-litre casks.

Distribution: Principally cellar door and mailing list; cellar door sales 10 a.m. to 4.30 p.m. Monday to Saturday; Sundays 1 p.m. to 4.30 p.m. and most public holidays. Mailing list enquiries to PO Box 695, Irymple, 3498.

Prices: $2.99 to $7 recommended retail.

Summary: A recent change of ownership meant that no wines were available for tasting.

🍇 MURRAY VALLEY WINES

Location: 15th Street, Mildura, 3500; within precincts of town.
(050) 23 1500.

Winemaker: George Kalamastrakis.

Principal Wines: A range of Greek-influenced wines, some made in traditional Greek style, including Riesling Hock, Moselle, Retsina, Claret and Kokinella. Specialist in various fortified and flavoured wines.

Distribution: Cellar door, mailing list and substantial bulk trade with Melbourne Greek community.

Summary: A cellar door operation catering exclusively for local clientele with a strong ethnic bias.

🍇 ROBINVALE WINES

Location: Sea Lake Road, Robinvale, 3549; 5 km south of Robinvale.
(050) 26 3955.

Winemaker: William Caracatsanoudis.

Principal Wines: A wide range of table wines, sparkling wines, fortified wines, flavoured wines, fruit-based wines and non-alcoholic wines is made.

Distribution: Chiefly cellar door sales and mail order; cellar door sales 9 a.m. to 6 p.m. Monday to Saturday, 1 p.m. to 6 p.m. Sunday. Melbourne distribution through Flinders Trading.

Summary: A small operation with a limited geographic market, but making some red and fortified wines of commendable quality.

North-East Victoria

1988 VINTAGE

The region encompassed by North-east Victoria is becoming increasingly diverse, as both vineyards and wineries start to penetrate the foothills and valleys of the Australian Alps. Any vintage overview necessarily carries with it the limitations of any generalisation. But none-theless, the 1988 vintage was as close to perfection as one is likely to find. Spring was mild, and the late frosts, which can be devastating, were entirely absent. Soaking rain on New Year's gave unirrigated vineyards a perfectly timed boost, and the crops ripened in fine and mild conditions, there being only a few hot days in the entire season. The vineyards were completely unstressed, and all of the grapes were harvested in prime condition without any sign of disease.

Vintage started between two and three weeks earlier than 1987, with good yields of shiraz, rhine riesling, chenin blanc and sauvignon blanc, although cabernet sauvignon yields (as in so much of Victoria) were reduced. Chardonnay was also somewhat down on normal.

The chemical composition of the grapes was as good as one could hope for, and overall quality ranged from good to great. Chardonnay and rhine riesling were significantly better than in 1986 or 1987, while the shiraz was quite out-standing, with a greater depth of colour, flavour and spicy varietal character than had been seen for many years.

Finally, and most importantly, the great fortifieds of the district flourished: muscat grapes were harvested up to 27 baume, making it a true vintage year for muscat and tokay.

1989 VINTAGE

The season started comfortably enough, with good spring rains and cool and moist growing conditions promoting vigorous growth, but requiring constant spraying against mildew. Some wet weather towards the end of February, coupled with high humidity, exacerbated the problem, but as at mid-March all of the signs were there for an abundant vintage of good quality grapes.

Indeed, the white varieties harvested up to mid-March produced good wines, some very good. But in the second half of March the rain started, driven down from the north, and simply did not let up. All of the red wines were affected to a lesser or greater degree; the thin-skinned shiraz suffered particularly, but even cabernet sauvignon and merlot were struck by mould and by water dilution.

At one stage the rain was so heavy and persistent that it was impossible to gain access to the vineyards to pick the grapes, and the longer the vintage went the worse the problems became. Those who picked their reds early in the rainy period did best, and some pleasant light wines (pinot noir, early picked shiraz, tarrango and so on) were made. However, it will not be a year for cabernet sauvignon, and it was a complete write-off for the fortified wines.

Brown Brothers' Whitlands vineyard, which had benefited from the warm conditions in 1988, came good once again in 1989: its exposure to wind meant that mould was far less of a problem (helped also by the thin vertical trellis training in the vineyard), and the free draining soil permitted access at all times.

Nonetheless, if 1988 is a year to remember, 1989 is a year most vignerons would prefer to forget.

THE CHANGES

The major change in the district has been the sale of the historic All Saints winery to a South Australian syndicate headed (most visibly) by Michael Fallon, formerly marketing director of Wolf Blass Wines. The new team is determined to inject new life into All Saints, and will no doubt handsomely succeed. It has tremendous assets in terms of All Saints history, vineyards and wine stocks; its best Muscat and Tokay may yet challenge the supremacy of the big four producers.

There has been another change of ownership at Mount Prior following a disastrous foray into the export market. This will result in the wines from the 1990 vintage (to be made at Mount Prior) coming back on to the Australian market, although the refurbishment of the winery and the appointment of a new winemaker was still pending at the time of writing. Gayfers has gone, but in its place there is a new entry: Ron and Joan Mullett have opened Rosewhite Vineyard in the Happy Valley district near Myrtleford. The vineyard was first planted in 1984 at an altitude of 300 metres on the road to Mount Beauty; the initial plantings are of chardonnay, gewurztraminer, pinot noir and cabernet sauvignon, with shiraz planned for the future.

Wine quality at an extensive district tasting for the book was consistently good, with very few faulty wines—and most of those were 1989 wines, which will almost certainly be corrected prior to bottling. Brown Brothers continues to push the pace with its table wines. The new (and officially so-named) Kindergarten Winery (a winery-within-a-winery) provides a wonderful opportunity for the Brown Brothers winemakers to make small parcels of quality wine, while also operating as a self-funding research and development facility. Yet with all the skill and consistency of the Brown Brothers wines, the very greatest wines of the region are, of course, the muscats and tokays. The tasting of these for this book was one of the highlights of the year.

ALL SAINTS

Location: All Saints Road, Wahgunyah, 3687; 4 km north-east of Wahgunyah.
(060) 33 1922; Fax (060) 33 3515.

Winemakers: Andrew Sutherland Smith and Max Cofield.

1989 Production: Approximately 800 tonnes.

Principal Wines: The wines of All Saints have recently received a major facelift. There are three principal ranges. The least expensive is the Elm Tree Drive range, comprising Fumé Blanc (classic dry white), Hermitage, Fine Old Tawny Port and Muscat. The next most expensive is the Swan Crest range, comprising Marsanne, Chardonnay/Semillon, Rhine Riesling, Chenin Blanc, Shiraz, Cabernet Shiraz, Reserve Tawny Port, Liqueur Muscat and Liqueur Tokay. Finally comes the premium Lyrebird range of Chardonnay, Cabernet Merlot, Museum Release Tawny Port, Liqueur Muscat and Liqueur Tokay.

Distribution: Wholesale distribution through Concorde Liquor Pty Ltd, Vic., NSW and Qld; S. & V. Wine Merchants, SA; N.Z.A. Marketing, WA; and Capricorn Wines Pty Ltd, ACT. Cellar door sales through historic and imposing winery 9 a.m. to 5 p.m. Monday to Saturday and 11 a.m. to 5 p.m. Sunday. Mail orders welcomed to All Saints Wines Estate, Wahgunyah, 3687.

Prices: $7.50 to $15 recommended retail; old fortified wines more expensive.

Vintage Rating 1986–89: White: '89, '88, '87, '86. Red: '89, '86, '88, '87.

Tasting Notes:

1989 SWAN CREST RHINE RIESLING **[67]** *Colour:* light yellow-green. *Bouquet:* youthful, lifted aromatics with slight fermentation characters persisting, and a suspicion of volatility. *Palate:* again, very youthful with some lift, and fractionally oily fruit. Has flavour, and the wine may well improve dramatically with a few months in bottle prior to release. Drink '90.

1989 SWAN CREST CHARDONNAY/SEMILLON **[75]** *Colour:* very light yellow-straw. *Bouquet:* clean, fresh, estery fruit, as yet rather light, but well made and has obvious development potential. *Palate:* light/smoky fermentation characters lingering; a well-balanced wine with good acid and excellent fruit which should come on nicely in bottle. Drink '90–'91.

1989 SWAN CREST CHENIN BLANC **[75]** *Colour:* light straw-yellow-green. *Bouquet:* fresh, youthful and fruity; well made, although some fermentation characters still linger. July 1989. *Palate:* fresh, clean and crisp; light fruit salad flavours; good balancing acid. Drink '90.

1989 SWAN CREST MARSANNE **[CS]** *Colour:* medium yellow with a touch of green. *Bouquet:* very strong spicy oak with good underlying fruit. *Palate:* strong lemony/spicy oak carries through to the finish, where a slight hot clove/ spice character intrudes; the fruit has been well handled, but the oak needs to be restrained in the final blend. If it is, the wine will be headed to 80 points or more; if it is not, it will be headed to 74 or less.

LYREBIRD LIQUEUR TAWNY PORT **[90]** *Colour:* dark tawny with an olive rim. *Bouquet:* extremely rich, luscious raisined tea leaf; classic tokay. *Palate:* magnificent old luscious/raisined wine, immensely complex and concentrated, with tea leaf/fish oil flavours.

LYREBIRD LIQUEUR MUSCAT **[91]** *Colour:* deep tawny, with an olive rim. *Bouquet:* extremely concentrated, and very old, complex aromas, with clean spirit. *Palate:* extremely complex and concentrated; strong luscious grapy mid-palate moving to a dry, textured finish; of the highest possible quality.

Summary: There is no question that the new ownership and management at All Saints has brought immediate changes for the better. The 1989 whites and reds look full of promise, and particularly so given the difficulties of the vintage. The Lyrebird Show Series Tokays and Muscats are now consistently winning gold medals and major trophies at the wine shows, and it is not hard to see why. They outpointed all but the top Chambers Rosewood wines and the top Morris Muscat in the tasting for this edition.

AVALON

Location: RMB 9556, Whitfield Road, Wangaratta, 3678; 46 km south of Wangaratta. (057) 29 3629.

Winemaker: Doug Groom.

1989 Production: Approximately 1000 cases.

Principal Wines: Semillon, Chardonnay, Pinot Noir and Cabernet Sauvignon.

Distribution: Through local retailers in Wangaratta; cellar door sales by appointment; through Richard Farmer, Canberra; and by mailing list, with enquiries as above.

Prices: $9 to $11 cellar door.

Vintage Rating 1986–89: White: '89, '87, '88 ('86 not rated). Red: '88, '89, '87 ('86 not rated).

Tasting Notes:

1989 SEMILLON [CS] Colour: medium yellow-green. *Bouquet:* most attractive barrel ferment characters with a touch of charred oak, and good underlying fruit. *Palate:* beautiful fruit and oak handling; an elegant wine with balance, flavour and already showing some structural richness. Headed towards 85 points or more if it safely makes the transition to bottle.

1989 CHARDONNAY [CS] Colour: light green-yellow, still slightly cloudy. *Bouquet:* light fruit with slightly raw, sawdusty oak. *Palate:* of light to medium weight, with fresh grapefruit flavours; good balance and once again a wine with considerable potential if the oak settles down (which it usually does).

Summary: The 1989 Avalon white wines are, quite simply, a vast improvement on earlier releases. Obviously, Doug Groom has been able to install some refrigeration, and thereby control white wine fermentation temperatures. His undoubted experience and qualifications are now bearing fruit.

BAILEYS

Location: Cnr Taminick Gap Road and Upper Taminick Road, Glenrowan, 3675; 6 km north-west of Glenrowan. (057) 66 2392.

Winemaker: Steve Goodwin.

1989 Production: 3800 cases.

Principal Wines: One of the three greatest fortified wine producers in the north-east, also producing a range of table wines including Chablis, Chardonnay, Colombard, Rhine Riesling, Auslese Aucerot, Auslese Rhine Riesling, Classic Hermitage, Winemakers Selection Hermitage, Cabernet Sauvignon and Cabernet Sauvignon Hermitage. Incomparable fortified Muscat and Tokay released under three labels: Warby Range, Founder and Winemakers Selection (the last formerly HJT).

Distribution: Substantial cellar door and mailing list sales; also extensive wholesale distribution through Emerald Wines, Melbourne; Caon Tucker & Co., Adelaide; Caon Tucker & Co., Perth; Fesq & Co., Sydney; Tallerman & Co., Brisbane; elsewhere through own distribution network. Cellar door sales 9 a.m. to 5 p.m. Monday to Friday, 10 a.m. to 5 p.m. Saturday, Sunday and public holidays. Mailing list enquiries to RMB 4160, Glenrowan, 3675.

Prices: Table wines $6.95 to $15.95 recommended retail; fortified wines $7.50 to $48 recommended retail.

Vintage Rating 1986–89: White: '89, '87, '88, '86. Red: '88, '89, '87, '86.

Outstanding Prior Vintages: '83, '85.

Tasting Notes:

1989 COLOMBARD [67] Colour: strong, bright green-yellow. *Bouquet:* very fragrant fruity/ tropical/toasty aromas, possibly yeast influenced. *Palate:* unexpectedly, and incongruously for the variety, of spatlese sweetness; it may be commercial, but I really cannot see the logic. Drink '90.

1986 CLASSIC HERMITAGE [80] Colour: full red, still retaining some purple hues. *Bouquet:* firm, strong dark berry aromas with slight astringency. *Palate:* big, richly structured and tannic wine with abundant dark chocolate/dark berry flavours and lemony vanillan oak. Drink '92–'98.

1986 CLASSIC HERMITAGE [85] Colour: full red-purple. *Bouquet:* clean and deep dark fruits/dark chocolate aromas. *Palate:* a complex, richly structured wine with deep, dark berry fruit and persistent tannins. A cellaring classic. Drink '94–2000.

1987 CABERNET SAUVIGNON [83] Colour: medium to full purple-red. *Bouquet:* firm red berry fruits and strong charred oak, which can momentarily be mistaken for sulphide. *Palate:* strong, complex ripe fruit flavours in a red berry/cassis spectrum; good charred oak handling, and a lingering finish. Drink '92–'99.

WARBY RANGE TOKAY [88] Colour: medium red-tawny. *Bouquet:* fine, fragrant tea-leaf varietal character with excellent fresh fruit and clean spirit. *Palate:* very smooth, medium to full palate with perfectly delineated varietal character; a long, lingering fine, dry finish. Absolutely outstanding at the price.

WINEMAKERS SELECTION OLD LIQUEUR MUSCAT [87] Colour: medium to full tawny, with a slightly olive rim. *Bouquet:* intense, sweet, strong muscat varietal aroma, with pronounced raisined fruit and clean spirit. *Palate:* extremely rich and luscious; raisined/weighty palate with tremendous depth to the flavour, and balanced by a long, basically dry, finish.

Summary: The Baileys style of muscat and tokay is immediately recognisable, with that extra raisined lusciousness. Some prefer the extreme elegance of Chambers, others the balance and complexity of Morris. But no one would quarrel with the exceptional value-for-money offered by the full range of Baileys' fortifieds, with the Warby range material almost ludicrously cheap. The dry reds, too, are very much on the ascendant.

BOOTHS' TAMINICK

Location: Taminick via Glenrowan, 3675; 7 km north-east of Glenrowan. (057) 66 2282.

Winemaker: Cliff Booth.

Principal Wines: Trebbiano, Shiraz and Cabernet Sauvignon.

Distribution: All wine sold cellar door and by specialised mail order, particularly to corporate and public service wine clubs. Cellar door sales Monday to Saturday 9 a.m. to 5 p.m.

Summary: Cliff Booth is one of the most traditional and conservative in this region of traditional and conservative winemakers, seeing no need to answer impertinent questions or in any way publicise his full-bodied, traditional north-eastern reds.

BROWN BROTHERS

Location: Milawa, 3678; off main Glenrowan-Myrtleford Road, 16 km south-east of Wangaratta. (057) 27 3400.

Winemaker: John G. Brown.

1989 Production: Not for publication, but very substantial.

Principal Wines: An extremely wide range of varietal table wines, released in several series. Firstly, there is the traditional Milawa range (comprising 6 different white and red varietals and 2 red blends); then follows the Limited Production series (13 or 14 different varietals); then come the King Valley wines including Koombahla, Meadow Creek and Whitlands; the Family Reserve wines, being the best Riesling, Chardonnay and Cabernet or Cabernet blend of each vintage; and finally the Classic Vintage releases, principally of red wines, but also including Noble Riesling, released after 5 years or more, and the red wines often up to 10 or more years.

Distribution: Extensive cellar door facilities, regular mailing list brochures and bulletins among the best in the country; very extensive retail distribution through its own distribution network in Melbourne, Sydney, Adelaide and Brisbane with agents in Perth and Tasmania. Also significant export sales. Agents: USA, Banfi; UK, Michael Druitt Wines. Cellar door sales 9 a.m. to 5 p.m. Monday to Saturday, 10 a.m. to 6 p.m. Sunday (not open Christmas Day, Boxing Day, New Year's Day, Anzac Day a.m. or Good Friday). First-class and constantly patronised tasting facilities. Mailing list enquiries to Brown Brothers Milawa Vineyard Pty Ltd, Milawa, 3678.

Prices: $7 to $20 retail; mature vintage releases and fortified wines higher.

Vintage Rating 1986–89: White: '87, '86, '88, '89. Red: '86, '88, '87, '89.

Outstanding Prior Vintages: '66, '70,' 72, '78, '82.

Tasting Notes:

1989 KING VALLEY RHINE RIESLING [80] Colour: light to medium yellow-green. *Bouquet:* highly aromatic, floral pineapple/fruit salad aromas. *Palate:* clean; quite intense lime/toast fruit flavours with plenty of fruit weight; crisp, dry finish. Drink '90–'91.

1989 VICTORIAN CHENIN BLANC [74] Colour: light to medium green-yellow. *Bouquet:* strong, rich fruit, surprisingly forward and with good depth. *Palate:* not quite as much fruit flavour or depth as the bouquet promises, a lack compensated for by a degree of residual sugar; pleasant acid rounds off a thoroughly commercial and pleasant wine. Drink '90.

1983 NOBLE RIESLING [84] Colour: deep, glowing golden brown. *Bouquet:* complex, intense raisined apricot/orange peel aromas in unmistakable Noble Riesling style. *Palate:* a classic, old style (if there is such a thing) botrytised riesling; complex raisiny fruit; through a combination of bottle age and botrytis, varietal character has been lost, but other things have come in its place. I really wonder, however, whether the wine should have been released when it was somewhat younger. Drink '90–'92.

1989 TARRANGO [75] Colour: vivid, light red-purple. *Bouquet:* spotlessly clean, with fresh, light cherry aromas and a slightly leafy tang. *Palate:* fresh, light leafy cherry fruit; dry, with good acid balance; a lovely, light, modern wine. Drink '90.

1987 KOOMBAHLA CABERNET SAUVIGNON

[77] Colour: medium red. *Bouquet:* clean, fragrant, lifted minty/leafy aromas, light and fresh. *Palate:* very pleasant clean leafy/minty fruit flavours; while light-bodied, has some intensity and a long finish. Drink '90–'93.

1987 SHIRAZ MONDEUSE CABERNET [75] Colour: medium purple-red. *Bouquet:* clean, light and fresh, with a slight touch of fresh earth. *Palate:* light to medium weight; fresh, clean and lively with a distinct touch of pepper/spice; again, a wine in the modern idiom. Drink '90–'93.

Summary: Brown Brothers manages to produce an immense array of wines covering every variety and style known and, for good measure, coming from a number of vineyard and area sources, although virtually all fall within Victoria. The image is very much the family winemaking concern (which it is), but that should not disguise either the fact of its size (very substantial) nor the quality and reliability of its competitively priced wines.

BULLERS CALLIOPE

Location: Three Chain Road, Rutherglen, 3685; off Murray Valley Highway, 5 km west of Rutherglen. (060) 32 9660.

Winemakers: The Buller Family; Richard senior and Andrew.

1989 Production: Approximately 2000 cases.

Principal Wines: Principally red table and fortified wines from the Calliope vineyard at Rutherglen (cheaper generic table wines, white varietal table wines and Cabernet Sauvignon come from Beverford Vineyard on the Murray River). Vineyard speciality is Calliope Vintage Port; also very good Liqueur Muscat and Liqueur Frontignac in a somewhat lighter style than those of Bailey and Morris. ·

Distribution: Principally cellar door and mailing list; cellar door sales 9 a.m. to 5 p.m. Monday to Saturday, 10 a.m. to 5 p.m. Sunday. Victorian distribution through Melbourne office (telephone number (03) 570 1717).

Prices: Table wines $6 to $8; fortified wines $5 to $22 cellar door.

Tasting Notes:

LIQUEUR TOKAY _[79] Colour:_ medium tawny, with a touch of olive on the rim. _Bouquet:_ rich and full, with strong tea leaf varietal aroma. _Palate:_ rich, concentrated tea-leaf/caramel flavours with surprising richness; remarkable value at the price (around $10).

LIQUEUR MUSCAT _[75] Colour:_ medium red-tawny. _Bouquet:_ sweet, clean grapy muscat aromas. _Palate:_ soft and sweet grapy/muscaty flavours; quite sweet, and obviously has a relatively high component of young material, but that material is of well above average quality. Once again, great value (also $10).

Summary: The Buller family take a somewhat low-key and certainly no-nonsense approach to both winemaking and wine marketing, although the development of their new Indigo Valley vineyard may see some change in attitude. Until that time occurs, some great bargains are to be had at the cellar door.

🍇 CAMPBELLS

Location: Murray Valley Highway, Rutherglen, 3685; 3 km west of Rutherglen. (060) 32 9458.

Winemaker: Colin Campbell.

1989 Production: 35,000 cases.

Principal Wines: The emphasis is on distinctive regional styles in both table and fortified wines. Principal white varietals are Rhine Riesling and Chardonnay, while the reds feature Bobbie Burns Shiraz, Rutherglen Shiraz, Malbec and Durif. These are supplemented by older vintage wines and special cellar releases. The fortified wines comprise Vintage Port, Old

Rutherglen Port, Old Rutherglen Tokay, Old Rutherglen Muscat and Merchant Prince Muscat.

Distribution: Cellar door sales, mailing list and retail and restaurant distribution all significant. Wholesale distribution through Caldbecks in all States. UK distribution through Walter S. Siegel Ltd. Cellar door sales from 9 a.m. to 5 p.m. Monday to Saturday and 10 a.m. to 5 p.m. Sunday. Mailing list enquiries to PO Box 44, Rutherglen, 3685.

Prices: Table wines $7.70 to $12.50 retail; fortified wines $12.60 to $40 retail.

Vintage Rating 1986–89: White: '88, '89, '86, '87. Red: '86, '87, '88, '89. Fortified: '86, '88, '89, '87.

Tasting Notes:

1986 CLASSIC REGIONAL RHINE RIESLING [76] _Colour:_ light to medium yellow-green. _Bouquet:_ clean and remarkably youthful, with light toasty/lime aromas. _Palate:_ impressively clean, crisp and fresh light toasty/passionfruit flavours; the wine is bone dry, and finishes with good acid. Drink '90–'92.

1987 MALBEC [68] Colour: medium red, with just a touch of purple remaining. _Bouquet:_ clean, but some volatility evident together with light, lemony oak. _Palate:_ conforms to the bouquet, with lifted lemony fruit and oak flavours and low tannin. Drink '90–'92.

1986 SHIRAZ [76] Colour: medium to full red-purple. _Bouquet:_ firm and full, with just a slight roasted edge. _Palate:_ very soft, full and fruity with sweet cherry/berry fruit, soft tannin and light oak; despite its high pH, maturing slowly and with considerable style. Drink '92–'96.

OLD RUTHERGLEN TOKAY [76] Colour: light golden-tawny. _Bouquet:_ youthful and fresh; light to medium weight tea leaf varietal character. _Palate:_ smooth, clean and fresh flavours, again with pronounced varietal character; made in a deliberate style, and represents a valid alternative to the more luscious complexity of the older tokays from other wineries.

OLD RUTHERGLEN MUSCAT [74] Colour: light to medium red-tawny. _Bouquet:_ clean, youthful and fresh grapy aromas, slightly sweet and simple, but showing good muscat varietal character. _Palate:_ very young, clean and simple style with sweet fruit and fair muscat delineation; once again, deliberately fashioned in an alternative style with the accent on youth.

MERCHANT PRINCE BROWN MUSCAT [80]
Colour: tawny-red of medium depth. _Bouquet:_ clean, sweet raisiny/muscaty fruit. _Palate:_ clean, sweet grapy/raisiny muscat, made in a fruit-driven style; although the oldest of the Campbell range, and by far the most expensive, lacks the final structural complexity of the greatest muscats of the region.

Summary: Campbells is one of the most progressive of the district wineries (except, of course, for Brown Brothers) and has done much in recent years both to diversify table wine production and to develop a distinctive muscat and tokay range of wines. Colin Campbell is a highly intelligent winemaker who thinks hard about the market niches he wishes to occupy. His efforts have, in my view, succeeded.

🍇 CHAMBERS ROSEWOOD

Location: Off Corowa-Rutherglen Road, Rutherglen, 3685; 2 km north-west of Rutherglen.
(060) 32 9641.

Winemaker: Bill Chambers.

1989 Production: Approximately 10,000 cases plus bulk wine.

Principal Wines: An unusual array of table wines and some great fortified wines. Table wines include Rhine Riesling, Moselle-style Trebbiano, Riesling Gouais, Spatlese Rhine Riesling, Cabernet Shiraz, Cabernet/Blue Imperial/Alicante Bouchet and Lakeside Cabernet Sauvignon. Fortified wines include a range of old sherries including ports, an excellent Flor Fino and an even better Amontillado; Liqueur Muscat and Liqueur Tokay, Special Liqueur Muscat; and intermittent releases of very old Tokay and Muscat of the highest possible quality.

Distribution: Principally cellar door sales and mail order. Cellar door sales 9 a.m. to 5 p.m. Monday to Saturday. Mail orders to W. H. Chambers and Son, PO Box 8, Rutherglen, 3685. Some retail distribution through Emerald Wines, Melbourne.

Prices: $4.50 to $60 (for Old Liqueur Muscat).

Tasting Notes:

OLD LIQUEUR TOKAY [96] Colour: brown, with a pale green-olive rim. _Bouquet:_ the ultimate in both style and varietal character; intense tea leaf, yet almost ethereally delicate. _Palate:_ again, an absolutely remarkable combination of elegance, concentration and complexity; despite its intensity, neither heavy nor sweet, and has a wonderfully clean, drying finish.

OLD LIQUEUR MUSCAT [96] Colour: mahogany, with no reds whatsoever, yet no greens either. _Bouquet:_ incredibly fragrant, intense raisined fruit, yet none of the heaviness of Baileys (in particular), nor even Morris. _Palate:_ the ultimate in intensity; some caramel sweetness on the fore-palate leading on to an explosive finish that lingers and lingers almost indefinitely; mere words cannot describe the extraordinary combination of delicacy and power. An absolutely unique Australian fortified wine.

Summary: The Old Liqueur Tokay and Old Liqueur Muscat of Chambers are in a class and style all of their own, unlike those of either Morris or Baileys; while far older than the top releases of either of those two makers, the wines somehow or other retain greater delicacy and freshness. Each time someone buys a bottle, Bill Chambers simply puts the price up.

🍇 FAIRFIELD VINEYARD

Location: Murray Valley Highway, Browns Plains, via Rutherglen, 3685; 13 km east of Rutherglen.
(060) 32 9381.

Winemaker: Steve Morris.

Principal Wines: White Hermitage, Light Red, Rosé, Durif, Cabernet Sauvignon, Dry Sherry, White Port, Ruby Port and Vintage Port, all made using 19th-century winemaking equipment from the estate and using traditional winemaking techniques.

Distribution: Exclusively cellar door sales 9 a.m. to 5 p.m. Monday to Saturday and 12 p.m. to 5 p.m. Sunday (occasionally closed Sunday, look for sign).

Summary: Fairfield is one of the most historic mansions in the entire north-east, and has been lovingly restored by Melba Morris

Slamen, granddaughter of G. F. Morris. The house is open to guided tours on Saturdays, public holidays and school holidays from 11 a.m. to 3 p.m.

GEHRIG BROTHERS

Location: Cnr Murray Valley Highway and Howlong Road, Barnawartha, 3688; 6 km north of town.
(060) 26 7296.

Winemaker: Brian Gehrig.

1989 Production: 5000 cases.

Principal Wines: Chenin Blanc, Rhine Riesling, Sauterne, Pinot Noir, Shiraz, Cabernet Sauvignon; also a range of 7 different ports, 5 sherries and brown muscat.

Distribution: Principally cellar door sales 9 a.m. to 5 p.m. Monday to Saturday and 10 a.m. to 5 p.m. Sunday. Victorian distribution through Flinders Wine Company (03) 584 5233.

Prices: $5 to $10 cellar door.

Vintage Rating 1986–89: White: '89, '88, '86, '87. Red: '86, '88, '87, '89.

Tasting Notes:

1988 RHINE RIESLING [59] Colour: very light yellow-green. *Bouquet:* relatively broad fruit, with a somewhat hard and volatile edge. *Palate:* again, some volatility evident which makes the wine rather hard and partially obscures varietal fruit. Drink '90.

1987 SHIRAZ [74] Colour: light to medium purple-red. *Bouquet:* light, peppery shiraz, with a touch of lemony oak. *Palate:* attractive light fruit with strong pepper/spice varietal flavour; fractionally one dimensional due in part to some old oak flavours. Drink '90–'93.

1985 VINTAGE PORT [79] Colour: medium to full red-purple. *Bouquet:* clean spirit, with that hallmark touch of fresh earth; clean red berry

fruit. *Palate:* most attractive sweet berry/cassis/dark chocolate fruit flavours with firm, clean spirit; well balanced and well made.

OLD TAWNY PORT [73] Colour: medium tawny-red. *Bouquet:* lively, complex and stylish with quite pronounced sweet fruit and a nice touch of rancio. *Palate:* quite young, but has some style, with a sweet mid-palate balanced by a crisp, drying finish.

Summary: The Gehrig family is slowly modernising the ancient and inadequate winemaking equipment formerly in use, and wine quality is improving in consequence. The best wines are clearly the tawny and fortified ports.

HJT VINEYARDS

Location: Keenan Road, Glenrowan, 3675; 5 km north-west of Glenrowan on the shores of Lake Mokoan.
(057) 66 2252.

Winemakers: Harry and Catherine Tinson.

1989 Production: 1000 cases.

Principal Wines: Rhine Riesling, Chardonnay, Pinot Noir and Cabernet Sauvignon.

Distribution: Principally cellar door sales, mailing list and retail distribution in Melbourne, Sydney retail distribution through the Specialist Wine Company; Victorian country distribution service direct ex-winery. Mailing list enquiries to PO Box 620, Wangaratta, 3677. Cellar door sales 10 a.m. to 5 p.m. Friday, Saturday, public holidays and long weekends.

Prices: $8.50 to $11.90 cellar door.

Vintage Rating 1986–89: White: '87, '86, '88 ('89 not yet rated). Red: '86, '87, '88 ('89 not yet rated).

Tasting Notes:

1987 CABERNET SAUVIGNON [65] Colour: medium red. *Bouquet:* fairly complex, but marred by strong gamey/meaty sulphide-derived characters.

Palate: quite developed, with leafy/gamey flavours; the impression is of a fairly high pH wine. Drink '91–'93.

Summary: It was disappointing not to taste any of the younger chardonnays for which HJT has become justly famous. Those of 1984 and 1985, in particular, were (and are) quite superb.

🍇 _JOHN GEHRIG WINES_

Location: Oxley, 3678; on Oxley to Milawa Road ("Snow Road"), 13 km south-east of Wangaratta.
(057) 27 3395.

Winemaker: John Gehrig.

1989 Production: 10,000 cases.

Principal Wines: Rhine Riesling, Rhine Riesling-Kabinett, Chenin Blanc, Chardonnay, _Méthode Champenoise_ Brut Reserve Blanc de Noir, Pinot Noir, Merlot, Cabernet-Merlot, Vintage Port and Tawny Port.

Distribution: Principally cellar door sales and mailing list; cellar door sales 9 a.m. to 5 p.m. Monday to Saturday and 10 a.m. to 6 p.m. Sunday. Distribution through Ron Westwood Agencies, Vic.; Monteclair Agencies, NSW.

Prices: $6.50 to $18.90 retail.

Vintage Rating 1986–89: White: '87, '88, '89, '86. Red: '88, '87, '89, '86.

Tasting Notes:

1988 CHARDONNAY [79] Colour: very good green-yellow. _Bouquet:_ strong, slightly raw lemony oak, but showing real style and some barrel ferment characters. _Palate:_ complex, stylish barrel ferment treatment; the oak is a fraction strong, but the base material has been very well handled and should grow in bottle. Drink '90–'92.

1988 PINOT NOIR [57] Colour: medium red. _Bouquet:_ light herbal/tobacco aromas, with a slight volatile lift. _Palate:_ extremely light, slightly herbal flavours lacking fruit richness or structure. Drink '90.

1988 CABERNET MERLOT [78] Colour: medium red-purple. _Bouquet:_ very smooth and clean, with minty/lemony fruit and oak nicely balanced and integrated. _Palate:_ crisp, with attractive sweet berry/cherry flavours and light tannins; an extremely well-made, light, modern early drinking style. Drink '90–'92.

1988 MERLOT [78] Colour: medium red-purple. _Bouquet:_ clean leafy/berry fruit with a faint touch of fresh earth. _Palate:_ very clean, with pleasant leafy/berry fruit showing good varietal character and nice supporting lemony oak; low tannin finish to another extremely well-made drinking style. Drink '90–'92.

Summary: John Gehrig has not had an easy time of it recently, but you would not guess that from the majority of his 1988 wines, which are of excellent quality in a consistent, fresh, early drinking style.

🍇 _JOLIMONT_

Location: Cnr Murray Valley Highway and Corowa Road, Rutherglen, 3685.
(060) 32 9922.

Winemaker: Howard Anderson.

1989 Production: 9000 cases.

Principal Wines: Wines produced principally from Rutherglen grown fruit, comprising table wines, _méthode champenoise_ and traditional Rutherglen fortified styles. Rougenfant, a soft, early drinking, dry red style is produced from Cabernet Sauvignon grown at Cowl Cowl Station on the Lachlan River near Hillston in central New South Wales.

Distribution: Principally cellar door sales, mailing list and selected retail. Cellar door sales 10 a.m. to 5 p.m. 7 days. Mailing list enquiries to Drummond Street, Rutherglen, 3685.

Prices: $8.20 to $21.

Vintage Rating 1986–89: White: '86, '89, '88, '87. Red: '89, '88, '87, '86.

Tasting Notes:

1989 RHINE RIESLING [74] Colour: light to medium yellow-green. *Bouquet:* full and rather broad, with plenty of depth and already showing development. *Palate:* full-bodied lime/pineapple flavours with appreciable residual sugar, which is however quite well balanced; a very commercial cellar door style. Drink '90.

1989 HERMITAGE BLANC [CS] Colour: yellow-green. *Bouquet:* big, rich and soft with a touch of honey/lychee. *Palate:* very sweet, with strong honey/peach flavours; a fascinating semi-sweet style made from botrytised hermitage, and a brilliant attempt to make a silk purse out of a sow's ear.

1989 SAUVIGNON BLANC SEMILLON [72] Colour: very good light to medium green-yellow. *Bouquet:* light smoky/gooseberry aromas, ever so typical of very young sauvignon blanc. *Palate:* clean; of light to medium weight with quite good gooseberry varietal fruit flavours; happily, made dry. Drink '90–'91.

1986 CABERNET SAUVIGNON METHODE CHAMPENOISE [66] Colour: strong red. *Bouquet:* potent and full, somewhere in the fashion of the older Seppelt Sparkling Burgundies (except for the varietal base). *Palate:* strong cherry fruit with a touch of varietal astringency; the finish, too, is a little heavy. Nonetheless, an interesting wine which could conceivably improve with further bottle age. Drink '90–'93.

1986 SHIRAZ [75] Colour: medium red, with just a touch of purple. *Bouquet:* clean and quite solid fruit, but very slightly dulled by what appears to be some old oak. *Palate:* much better than the bouquet would suggest; a solid wine with depth and length to red berry/cherry fruit flavour. Drink '91–'95.

1986 CABERNET SAUVIGNON [73] Colour: medium red. *Bouquet:* sweet berry fruit and slightly dusty/common oak. *Palate:* clean, fresh red berry fruit with soft tannin; a little simple in structure, and would have benefited from some new oak. Drink '91–'94.

LIQUEUR TOKAY [75] Colour: tawny-walnut. *Bouquet:* light, youthful tea leaf aromas, showing good varietal character, allied with some complexity. *Palate:* rich, sweet tea leaf fruit;

tending to simplicity, and needs a little more acid lift.

Summary: Jolimont is housed in one of the most striking buildings in Rutherglen, with the brand new extensions of the Tuileries Restaurant providing a focal point for dining in the region. Tourists are catered for at every turn, and whether your interest lies in history, wine or food (or a little of each), Jolimont is a compulsory visiting point.

JONES WINERY

Location: Chiltern Road, Rutherglen, 3685; 2 km east of town. (060) 32 94 96.

Winemaker: Les Jones.

Principal Wines: White Hermitage, Rutherglen Pedro and Shiraz.

Distribution: Exclusively cellar door sales 9.30 a.m. to 5 p.m. Monday to Friday and 9 a.m. to noon Sunday.

Summary: The psychedelic labels of Jones Winery are entirely at odds with the otherwise extreme conservatism of the operation. Les Jones "does not have time" for impertinent authors asking impertinent questions about his wines.

MARKWOOD ESTATE

Location: Morris Lane, Markwood via Milawa, 3678; 6 km east of Milawa. (057) 27 0361.

Winemaker: F. J. (Rick) Morris.

1989 Production: Approximately 1000 cases.

Principal Wines: Chardonnay, Shiraz and Cabernet Sauvignon, Flor Sherry and a range of ports.

Distribution: Exclusively cellar door sales and mailing list. Cellar door sales 9 a.m. to 5 p.m. Monday to Saturday. Mailing list enquiries to RMB 84, Markwood via Milawa, 3678.

Summary: A tiny operation with all wine sold cellar door. Rick Morris does not believe in comparative wine-tastings.

❦ *MORRIS*

Location: Mia Mia Vineyard, Rutherglen, 3685;
   15 km east of Rutherglen, 1.5 km off Murray
   Valley Highway.
   (060) 26 7303.

Winemaker: Mick Morris.

1989 Production: Not for publication.

Principal Wines: In addition to producing some of
   north-eastern Victoria's greatest fortified wines
   (principally Muscat and Tokay), Morris also
   offers a full range of cask wines and premium
   varietal table wines including Rhine Riesling,
   Sauvignon Blanc, Chardonnay, Durif, Cabernet
   Sauvignon, Pinot Noir, Shiraz and Blue
   Imperial. The full range of fortified wines is
   headed by Liqueur Muscat and Liqueur Tokay,
   and at the top of the range are Old Premium
   Liqueur Muscat and Old Premium Liqueur
   Tokay.

Distribution: National retail through Orlando
   distribution network. Cellar door sales and
   mailing list also available; cellar door sales 9
   a.m. to 5 p.m. Monday to Saturday, 10 a.m. to
   5 p.m. Sunday. Mailing list enquiries to
   Morris Wines Pty Ltd, Mia Mia Vineyard,
   Rutherglen, 3685.

Prices: Table wines $8.50 to $14.50 recommended
   retail; fortified wines $8.95 to $38.50.

Tasting Notes:

1988 SAUVIGNON BLANC [64] Colour: very good
   green-yellow. *Bouquet:* complex tropical/lantana
   aromas, striking but non-varietal. *Palate:* very
   peculiar lantana/decomposed vegetation
   characters, at once sweet and sour. An odd wine
   that may appeal to others more than it did to
   me. Drink '90.

1988 CHARDONNAY [77] Colour: medium-full
   yellow, with just a touch of green. *Bouquet:* quite
   complex and strong, with pronounced lemony
   oak; a fraction heavy and one dimensional.
   Palate: strong lemony oak set around a core of
full-flavoured fruit; once again, heaviness in
   the flavour and structure tends to make it a
   little one dimensional; on the other hand, one
   should never really complain about too much
   flavour. Drink '90–'91.

1988 BOTRYTIS SEMILLON [79] Colour: glowing
   yellow-green. *Bouquet:* very strong botrytis
   influence with apricot/raisin aromas and high
   volatility. *Palate:* super-intense raisined butter-
   scotch/botrytis flavours; once again, the volatility
   is very obvious. A wine that will have enormous
   appeal to some and none at all to others; the
   points given are something of a compromise
   between the two views. Drink '90–'91.

1987 DURIF [78] Colour: full red, with just a touch
   of purple. *Bouquet:* immense, concentrated
   and rich aromas of plums and dark chocolate.
   Palate: a huge and striking wine with flavours of
   dark chocolate and plum giving way to pervasive
   tannins, and lifted by a touch of volatility that
   may well be quite deliberate; again, a wine to
   polarise opinion. Drink '93–2000.

MORRIS LIQUEUR TOKAY [73] Colour: pale
   golden. *Bouquet:* rather light and slightly
   dusty, with some tea leaf varietal character.
   Palate: light, slightly common oily characters,
   possibly deriving from fortifying spirit which
   was not up to the mark; although a bottom of
   the range product, slightly disappointing.

OLD PREMIUM LIQUEUR MUSCAT [90] Colour:
   dark tawny-olive. *Bouquet:* extremely rich, concentrated, luscious and raisiny; an aged wine that
   proclaims its class. *Palate:* magnificent aged and
   concentrated wine, with a luscious, textured mid-
   palate, and a marvellously dry, long-lasting
   finish.

Summary: Mick Morris's mastery of the fortified
   wines of north-eastern Victoria is unchallenged.
   Orlando, who own Morris, have enough sense
   to allow him to continue to make red wines
   from the varieties and in the manner he has
   always made them. They offer an altogether
   different perspective in a wine world that
   otherwise has become boringly similar.

❦ *MOUNT PRIOR*

Location: Cnr River Road and Popes Lane, Rutherglen,
   3685; 12 km south-west of Rutherglen.
   (060) 26 5591.

Summary: Following a further change of ownership, Mount Prior will again be making wine for the Australian market, but no details were available at the time of writing.

 *PFEIFFER*

Location: Distillery Road, Wahgunyah, 3687; midway between Corowa and Rutherglen, off Three Chain Road.
(060) 33 2805.

Winemaker: Chris Pfeiffer.

1989 Production: 6000 cases.

Principal Wines: Rhine Riesling, Chardonnay, Spatlese Frontignac, Auslese Tokay, Shiraz Cabernet, Pinot Noir, Gamay and Cabernet Sauvignon; Liqueur Muscat and Liqueur Tokay, Tawny Port, Vintage Port.

Distribution: Almost exclusively cellar door sales and mailing list. Cellar door sales 9 a.m. to 5 p.m. Monday to Saturday, Sunday 11 a.m. to 4 p.m. Mailing list enquiries to PO Box 35, Wahgunyah, 3687.

Prices: $7.20 to $12 (table wines); $11 to $15 (fortified wines) cellar door.

Vintage Rating 1986–89: Table wine: '88, '87, '86, '89. Fortified wine: '88, '86, '87, '89.

Tasting Notes:

1989 RHINE RIESLING [73] Colour: light green-yellow. *Bouquet:* clean and full fruit, but slightly oily/blousy. *Palate:* a full-flavoured and weighty wine, with solid fruit-flavour; just misses that touch of refinement, possibly due to the inclusion of some pressings material, but possibly due to problems in the vineyard. Nonetheless, one of a series of radically improved wines. Drink '90–'91.

1988 PINOT NOIR [67] Colour: medium full red. *Bouquet:* firm, with a slightly herbaceous edge to cherry fruit; fairly complex and, apart from a faint suspicion of aldehyde, very well made. *Palate:* quite strong, herbal fruit flavours, clean and well balanced; once again, the ghost of a slightly aldehydic character comes to haunt on the finish. Drink '90.

1988 CHARDONNAY [77] Colour: light to medium yellow-green. *Bouquet:* potent and quite complex, with evidently high alcohol and a not unattractive whisper of sulphide. *Palate:* quite rich and smooth, with subtle oak; well made with plenty of character and style. Drink '90–'91.

OLD DISTILLERY TOKAY [78] Colour: medium tawny. *Bouquet:* of medium weight; soft, tea-leaf aromas with some "feel"; good spirit and rancio. *Palate:* a complex wine, powerful though young; good spirit; a wine with verve and cut.

OLD DISTILLERY MUSCAT [71] Colour: light to medium red, with some tawny hues. *Bouquet:* clean fruit, with fair varietal character, but slightly woody. *Palate:* again slightly woody, with fractionally simple fruit; has abundant flavour, and future bottlings should improve markedly as the solera settles down and the wood impact diminishes.

Summary: Chris Pfeiffer's main love in life, and his main winemaking experience, has centred around fortified wines. The initial releases of tokay and muscat show the promise one would expect, and no doubt even better things are in store as his base of wine matures. Table wine quality has been disconcertingly variable in the past, but it too seems to be settling down, and as the notes indicate he made a very attractive chardonnay in 1988 which, it must be said, will have sold out even by the time this book is released.

 *READS*

Location: Pound Road, Oxley, 3678; on King River, 0.5 km from Oxley.
(057) 27 3386.

Winemaker: Kenneth Read.

1989 Production: Not stated.

Principal Wines: Chardonnay, Crouchen, Rhine Riesling, Sauvignon Blanc, Cabernet Shiraz, Cabernet Sauvignon and Vintage Port.

Distribution: Limited Melbourne distribution; principally cellar door sales, and mailing list. Cellar door sales 9 a.m. to 6 p.m. Monday to Saturday, 10 a.m to 6 p.m. Sunday.

Prices: $7.50 to $14 cellar door.

Summary: The single '89 wine (Sauvignon Blanc) tasted was not in condition for review. However, Reads continues to grow slowly, and seems to be a permanent part of the Milawa/Oxley winescape.

ROSEWHITE

Location: Happy Valley Road, Happy Valley; 8 km north-west of Myrtleford, 3737 and 4 km off the Ovens Valley Highway.
(057) 52 1077.

Winemaker: Ron Mullett.

1989 Production: Approximately 700 cases.

Principal Wines: Chardonnay, Pinot Noir and Cabernet Sauvignon.

Distribution: Presently exclusively through cellar door sales 10 a.m. to 9 p.m. Friday, 10 a.m. to 5 p.m. Saturday to Monday. Other times by appointment.

Prices: $11.95 to $14.95 cellar door.

Tasting Notes:

1988 PINOT NOIR BIN 2 [74] Colour: light purple-black, indicating high pH. *Bouquet:* good spice/nutmeg/sappy pinot aroma, although high pH again evident. *Palate:* has real aspirations to style; the varietal character is a real (and pleasant) surprise. The high pH does mean the wine will mature and tire quickly, however. Drink '90.

Summary: The other two Rosewhite wines tasted suffered from oak-handling problems. The 1988 Bin 2 Pinot Noir, however, holds out real promise; it would seem the soil and climate are well suited to the variety.

ST LEONARDS

Location: Wahgunyah, 3687; 12 km north-west of Rutherglen.
(060) 33 1004.

Winemakers: Roland Kaval and Eddie Price.

1989 Production: 12,000 cases.

Principal Wines: A diverse and always interesting range of table wines, invariably described by variety only, and all estate grown. These include Chardonnay, Semillon, Gewurztraminer, Orange Muscat, Chenin Blanc, Sauvignon Blanc, Shiraz, Cabernet Sauvignon, Cabernet Franc/Merlot and Malbec. Also limited range of fortified wines. A $2 rebatable tasting fee is charged.

Distribution: Cellar door sales 7 days, 9 a.m. to 5 p.m. Monday to Saturday, 11 a.m. to 5 p.m. Sunday.

Prices: $7.50 to $15 cellar door.

Vintage Rating 1986–89: White: '87, '88/'89, '86. Red: '86, '87/'88, '89.

Tasting Notes:

1988 CHENIN BLANC [85] Colour: bright yellow-green. *Bouquet:* perhaps a fraction broad, but with very pronounced fruit salad aromas and just a touch of free SO_2. *Palate:* an extremely rich wine, full of character; there is lovely weight and mouth-feel on the mid- and back-palate, together with that typical tutti-frutti chenin blanc flavour; one of the best examples of this variety I have seen. Drink '90–'91.

1988 CHARDONNAY [76] Colour: medium yellow-green. *Bouquet:* firm, complex lemony oak tending to dominate somewhat at this stage; the fruit is there, but needs time to come up. *Palate:* has life and considerable elegance; a firm, crisp style, needing to build fatness on the mid-palate; the track record of these wines suggests it will do just that, and if it does it will merit substantially higher points. Drink '91–'94.

1987 SHIRAZ [77] Colour: medium red-purple. *Bouquet:* clean; light to medium spicy peppery fruit. *Palate:* clean, fresh, light to medium spicy/peppery wine in the modern style; light oak and low tannin; an extraordinary turn-around in style from some of the giants of the past from St Leonards, but attractive for all that. Drink '91–'93.

Summary: St Leonards has long been a favourite of mine, producing an extraordinary range of white and red varietal wines that seldom disappoint and that usually have great flavour, character and style. Recent extensions and renovations to the tasting and sales facility add another dimension to one of the most beautifully situated wineries in the whole of the north-east. The $2 tasting fee is a small price to pay.

STANTON AND KILLEEN

Location: Murray Valley Highway, Rutherglen, 3685; 3 km west of town.
(060) 32 9457.

Winemaker: Chris Killeen.

1989 Production: Around 10,000 cases.

Principal Wines: Red table and fortified wine specialist; top-quality table wines released under the Moodemere label, including Cabernet Shiraz and Durif; fortified wines include Special Old Liqueur Muscat, Liqueur Muscat, Liqueur Tokay, Vintage Port, Liqueur

Port and Old Tawny Port. A range of cheaper sherries is also produced.

Distribution: Chiefly cellar door sales and mailing list. Cellar door sales 9 a.m. to 5 p.m. Monday to Saturday and 11 a.m. to 4 p.m. Sunday. Mailing list enquiries to PO Box 15, Rutherglen, 3685. Limited Sydney and Melbourne wholesale distribution through W. J. Seabrook & Co., Melbourne and The Oak Barrel, Sydney.

Prices: Table wines $7 to $13 cellar door; fortified wines $5 to $25 cellar door.

Vintage Rating 1986–89: Table wines: '87, '86, '89, '88. Fortified wines: '86, '87, '88, '89.

Outstanding Prior Vintages: '72, '75, '76, '80, '83.

Tasting Notes:

1988 MOODEMERE CABERNET SAUVIGNON [61] Colour: medium red, with a touch of purple. *Bouquet:* strong jammy/berry aromas, slightly cooked and with some hay/straw aromas suggestive of fruit oxidation. *Palate:* very sweet jammy fruit, all suggestive of fruit left too long on the vine. Drink '91–'93.

1986 MOODEMERE DURIF [74] Colour: dark blackish-red. *Bouquet:* concentrated strong dark berry/plum fruits with a slightly extractive overtone. *Palate:* pronounced rich dark chocolate/red berry varietal character with typical lingering tannins; a huge wine very much in the style one should expect from this variety. Drink '93–'98.

1985 VINTAGE PORT [73] Colour: medium red-purple. *Bouquet:* clean and fresh earthy spirit with strong sweet fruit; some new oak nuances seem inappropriate. *Palate:* complex herbal/spice/aniseed flavours, again showing good use of fortifying spirit; a solid port with improvement in front of it.

Summary: Stanton and Killeen has refused to make white wine, and more power to it for doing so. Instead, it concentrates on the smooth reds and no less smooth fortified wines that it makes so well. These are not the heavyweights of the district, but do have a legitimate place in the scheme of things nonetheless. The vintage ports can occasionally be quite outstanding.

North Goulburn River

1988 VINTAGE

A trouble-free growing season was the hallmark of the year. Cool and moist conditions in winter and spring gave way to a warm, dry summer, almost totally free of disease. With irrigation almost universal, growers were able to avoid the stress problems that affected other parts of Victoria, and yields were up to 30% in excess of average.

Not surprisingly, the wines are clean but relatively light bodied, the red wines particularly so.

1989 VINTAGE

The season started well enough, with a relatively moist and cool start followed by a prolonged period of dry, warm weather that—as events turned out—fortunately led to an earlier start than usual. However, the rain came in mid-March; long before picking was completed, and prematurely terminated the vintage for many vineyards. The ground became so wet that it was impossible to use machine harvesters, and the conditions were such that hand-picking was neither feasible or economic.

Against all the odds, some very pleasant wines have been made, with Monichino and Tisdall both showing just what sophisticated winemaking can achieve.

THE CHANGES

Broken River Wines makes its debut. It is a syndicate of local growers, with Frank Dawson as viticulturist and a number of contract grape-growers including David Traeger, Jeff Clarke and a specialist sparkling wine producer. For the time being the grapes are all provided by a vineyard at Lemnos, but in future years will be supplemented by additional fruit from a new vineyard in the Strathbogie Ranges.

Overall wine quality is led in fine style by Monichino and Tisdall; the others have to work hard to match the standard of the leaders.

❦ *BROKEN RIVER WINES*

Location: Cosgrove Road, Lemnos, 3631; 8 km east of Shepparton.
(058) 29 9293 or (058) 29 9486.

Winemakers: Contract makers including David Traeger and Jeff Clarke.

1989 Production: Not stated.

Principal Wines: Chenin Blanc Vino Verde, Chenin Blanc Chardonnay, Cabernet Franc Carbonic Maceration and Cabernet Franc; a sparkling Chenin Blanc to be released in the future.

Distribution: Initially principally through cellar door sales; until opening hours firmly established telephone for an appointment.

Tasting Notes:

1989 CHENIN BLANC VINO VERDE [CS]
Colour: light straw-yellow. *Bouquet:* potent, rough and slightly hard fruit aromas. *Palate:* a rather green, hard wine made from early picked chenin blanc grapes, and deserving its vino verde name. Should settle down, however, and provide an interesting seafood style.

1989 CABERNET FRANC CARBONIC MACERATION [CS] *Colour:* bright light purple-red. *Bouquet:* extreme carbonic maceration pie and peas style. *Palate:* similarly extreme maceration style; it is not what I personally like, but others do accept it.

Summary: These are early days yet at Broken River, but with the viticultural experience of Frank Dawson and competent contract winemaking, there is no reason why its aims and aspirations should not be realised.

❦ *MONICHINO*

Location: Berrys Road, Katunga, 3640; 8 km north of Numurkah.
(058) 64 6452.

Winemaker: Carlo Monichino.

1989 Production: Reduced from the normal 9000 cases by adverse vintage conditions.

Principal Wines: Premium varietal releases comprise Rhine Riesling, Sauvignon Blanc, Semillon, Chardonnay, Spatlese Frontignac, Orange Muscat, Malbec, Cabernet Sauvignon, Vintage Muscat and Liqueur Raisin. Also a limited range of generic fortified wines sold in bottle, flagon and bulk containers.

Distribution: Substantial cellar door and mailing list sales; cellar door sales 9 a.m. to 6 p.m. Monday to Saturday, and 10 a.m. to 6 p.m. Sunday and all public holidays. Mailing list enquiries to PO Katunga, 3640. Limited Melbourne retail distribution through Flinders Wholesalers.

Prices: Table wines $7 to $9.50 cellar door; fortified wines $9 to $16 cellar door.

Vintage Rating 1986–89: White: '87, '86, '88, '89. Red: '86, '88, '87, '89.

Outstanding Prior Vintages: '80, '82, '84, '85.

Tasting Notes:

1989 SEMILLON [CS] *Colour:* bright light green-yellow. *Bouquet:* clean, fresh and highly protected, with some herbaceous varietal character. *Palate:* light, crisp and clean; an extremely well made wine that has balance and good potential for 80 or more points.

1989 SAUVIGNON BLANC [CS] *Colour:* light green-yellow. *Bouquet:* light to medium weight smoky/gooseberry varietal character; well made, with a few fermentation "armpit" aromas lingering. *Palate:* light but very clearly defined varietal character; crisp smoky/armpit/gooseberry fruit; nice clean finish. Once again, should rate 80 or more points.

1989 CHARDONNAY [CS] *Colour:* light straw-yellow. *Bouquet:* lemony oak dominates light fruit. *Palate:* strong lemony oak makes varietal character irrelevant; a single cask sample and the blended and finished wine may be far better balanced.

1989 AUTUMN ROSE [75] *Colour:* light pink. *Bouquet:* very clean, fresh sweet strawberry fruit. *Palate:* a perfectly made light rosé; slightly sweet, and highly commercial. Drink '90.

1988 MALBEC MERLOT [76] *Colour:* medium purple-red. *Bouquet:* firm fruit, minimal oak and just the faintest whisper of bitterness. *Palate:*

firm and quite rich red berry fruit; not particularly complex but well made apart from that suggestion of bitterness. Drink '90–'92.

LIQUEUR MUSCAT NV **[75]** _Colour:_ light tawny with a tinge of pink. _Bouquet:_ pronounced muscat/grapy varietal aroma, youthful rich and clean. _Palate:_ literally, grapes in a bottle; clean light spirit; entirely fruit driven and not the least bit complex, but absolutely delicious. Drink '90.

Summary: Carlo Monichino is an unsung hero of the district, applying scrupulous winemaking techniques (including field crushing) and jealously guarding (through careful handling and cool fermentation temperatures) every scrap of fruit flavour his vineyard gives him. His '89 white wines are a triumph of winemaking in a very difficult vintage.

🍇_PHILLIPS' GOULBURN VALLEY WINERY_

Location: 52 Vaughan Street, Shepparton, 3630; within commercial precincts of town. (058) 21 2051.

Winemakers: Contract: Don and Paul Phillips.

Principal Wines: Shiraz and Cabernet Sauvignon.

Distribution: Principally cellar door sales 9 a.m. to 6 p.m. Monday to Saturday. Mailing list enquiries as above.

Prices: $9 cellar door.

Summary: A very small and low profile operation with expertise provided by wine retailer Don Phillips.

🍇_TISDALL_

Location: Cornelia Creek Road, Echuca, 3564; within township. (054) 82 1911.

Winemaker: Jeff Clarke.

1989 Production: Not for publication.

Principal Wines: Wines are made from a number of different sources and released in a number of different ranges. Premium table wines under the Mount Helen label are from the Mount Helen vineyard situated in the Strathbogie Ranges in central Victoria (see separate entry in Central Goulburn); then there is the Tisdall label, coming from the Rosbercon vineyard at Echuca. In addition, there is a limited range of wine under the Selection Series label made from grapes purchased from other Victorian regions. Hopwood Estate range was first introduced in 1986 at the bottom end of the price range, and Winemakers Reserve at the top end. Tisdall Rosbercon wines comprise Chardonnay, Rhine Riesling, Chablis, Chenin Blanc, Fumé Blanc, Sauvignon Blanc Semillon, Shiraz, Cabernet, Cabernet Merlot and Cabernet Sauvignon. Selection Series and Hopwood Estate wines available cellar door only.

Distribution: National retail through distributors in all states; also significant cellar door and mailing list sales. Cellar door sales 10 a.m. to 5 p.m. Monday to Saturday and noon to 5 p.m. Sunday. Toll-free phone orders on (008) 03 4235 or order through PO Box 615, Echuca, 3564.

Prices: Hopwood Estate $6.50 cellar door; Tisdall $9.50 to $12.50 retail.

Vintage Rating 1986–89: White: '86, '89, '88, '87. Red: '88, '86, '87, '89.

Outstanding Prior Vintages: '80, '82, '84.

Tasting Notes:

1989 TISDALL CHENIN BLANC **[71]** _Colour:_ light straw-yellow. _Bouquet:_ soft, clean, light to medium weight; light tropical fruit. _Palate:_ light fruit salad flavours with clean, crisp acid finish. Drink '90.

1989 TISDALL SAUVIGNON BLANC SEMILLON **[75]** _Colour:_ bright, light to medium green-yellow. _Bouquet:_ crisp, toasty, lemony aromas to a well-made wine. _Palate:_ soft, lime/toasty/herbaceous fruit with good flavour; a suspicion of volatility that will, however, be irrelevant to most consumers. Drink '90.

*1988 TISDALL SAUVIGNON BLANC SEMILLON
[72] Colour:* light to medium green-yellow.
Bouquet: soft and clean tropical/passionfruit
aromas. *Palate:* slightly blousy tropical fruit
flavours, and the wine has a fractionally hard finish.
Drink '90.

1988 TISDALL CHARDONNAY [78] Colour: light
straw-yellow. *Bouquet:* stylish and smooth
honeyed/peach aromas. *Palate:* clean and smooth
honeyed peach mouthfilling fruit; simple one-
dimensional oak, probably from oak chips, but a
very attractive wine at the price. Drink '90–'91.

1988 TISDALL CABERNET MERLOT [79] Colour:
medium to full red-purple. *Bouquet:* very clean;
attractive red berry fruit; light oak. *Palate:* smooth
and clean fresh red berry/cherry fruit, and soft
but persistent tannins; in the mainstream of this
ever-reliable wine style from Tisdall. Drink
'90–'93.

Summary: The Tisdall wines are back on form
after a brief period of uncertainty, representing
very good value for money in a mid-priced
range.

Pyrenees

1988 VINTAGE

A dry winter left water reserves low, but near perfect conditions in spring, with calm, relatively warm conditions, resulted in a perfect bud-burst, no frost damage and excellent fruit set. The weather continued cool until the end of December, but hot and dry conditions then prevailed through until the end of March. Diseases and mildews were absent, and the grapes ripened in perfect condition.

Increased bird activity resulted in minor damage to crops, but good yields of high-quality grapes of all varieties were harvested in a season that was one of the earliest on record, commencing between two and four weeks earlier than normal for each variety.

Quality was uniformly high. All of the white wines have good varietal flavour and above average weight, while the reds are deep coloured, well balanced and rich.

1989 VINTAGE

The early season conditions were almost a mirror reverse of those of 1988. Excellent winter rains replenished surface water storage and dams, but very windy conditions during flowering affected fruit set with all varieties, in particular merlot and to a lesser degree cabernet sauvignon.

The dry and windy conditions of spring gave way to a cool and quite wet summer, with outbreaks of powdery mildew in some vineyards. The mildew was arrested by the period of hot weather at the end of February, and another relatively early vintage started at the end of February for sparkling wine and in early March for the first white table varieties. The wet, cool conditions that prevailed over Victoria from the middle of March spoilt what might have been an outstanding vintage; the red wines are light and lacking in fruit richness.

THE CHANGES

There are no new entries, but the level of activity in the region continues to increase. Chateau Remy has spent in excess of $1 million expanding its sparkling winemaking facility, while Luigi Bazzani has opened a superb restaurant and accommodation complex at Warrenmang. Dalwhinnie, too, has established its own winery and cellar door sales facility designed by owner-architect Ewan Jones. The first vintage will be made at Dalwhinnie in 1990.

With some consulting advice and assistance from state government oenologist Drew Noon, Ian Summerfield has burst upon the scene with some outstanding 1988 reds which swept all before them at the 1989 Ballarat Wine Show. Finally, the range of wines released by Chateau Remy has also increased with two white wines sourced from the Clare Valley. Now that Quelltaler has been sold by the Remy group, I am not certain whether these white wines will continue.

The district tasting was, I must confess, somewhat disappointing, notwithstanding the excitement of the Summerfield wines. Al-together too many red wines showed sulphide faults, ranging from bitter leathery characters through to gamey, rotten meat aromas and tastes.

CHATEAU REMY

Location: Vinoca Road, Avoca, 3467;
7 km west of Avoca.
(054) 65 3202.

Winemaker: Vincent Gere.

1989 Production: Sparkling wine 30,000 cases;
table wines 10,000 cases.

Principal Wines: Méthode champenoise under
Chateau Remy labels, Cuvee Speciale, Royal
Vintage and Rosé Premier; red wine under
Blue Pyrenees Estate label; white wines Clos St
Charles and "S" Semillon.

Distribution: National retail through own
distribution network.

Prices: Sparkling $12 to $20 retail; table $14 to $19
retail.

Tasting Notes:

*1984 ROYAL VINTAGE METHODE CHAMPENOISE
[61] Colour:* light to medium straw-=yellow.
Bouquet: hard and rather stripped, lacking fruit
and varietally nondescript. *Palate:* hard green
fruit characters are evident in a common base
wine; extended bottle maturation has not covered
up the inherent deficiencies. Drink '90.

ROSE PREMIER NV [55] Colour: pink, with some
onionskin tones. *Bouquet:* rather hard and
green, with a slightly smelly edge. *Palate:* similar
hard, green flavours and a bitter finish. Drink
'90.

1987 "S" SEMILLON [50] Colour: straw-yellow.
Bouquet: stripped hot solids fermentation characters,
and also some oxidation. *Palate:* oily, hard and
devoid of fruit flavour; again some oxidation
seemingly at work. Drink '90.

1986 BLUE PYRENEES [59] Colour: medium red
with just a touch of purple. *Bouquet:* soft with
slight meaty/gravelly mercaptan-derived aromas
over soft fruit. *Palate:* dull, and once again flawed
by stale mercaptan flavours. Drink '90.

Summary: It gives me no pleasure to be so critical
about the Chateau Remy wines, but the truth is
that however committed the ownership may
be, the wines are simply not up to commercial
quality, and certainly do not support the obvious
effort put into their packaging and marketing.

DALWHINNIE

Location: Taltarni Road, Moonambel, 3478;
winery operating 1990.
(054) 67 2388 or (054) 67 2292.

Winemaker: Rodney Morrish, Mt Avoca (contract).

1989 Production: 3,000 cases.

Principal Wines: Chardonnay, Shiraz and Cabernet
Merlot.

Distribution: Retail distribution through Van Cooth
& Co., Melbourne; Carol-Ann Martin Classic
Wines, Sydney; and Gullin & Co. exports. Also
extensive mailing list; enquiries to Dalwhinnie
Wines, RMB 4378 Moonambel, 3478. Cellar
door sales 10 a.m. to 5 p.m. Monday to Saturday
and noon to 5 p.m. Sunday.

Prices: $15 to $22 cellar door.

Vintage Rating 1986–89: White: '88, '87, '86 ('89
not rated yet). Red: '86, '88, '87, '89.

Outstanding Prior Vintages: '80, '82, '84.

Tasting Notes:

1989 CHARDONNAY [CS] Colour: white straw-
yellow. *Bouquet:* light and relatively soft fruit with
some coconut/vanillan characters, presumably
from oak. *Palate:* pleasant peachy/buttery fruit
of medium weight; clearly has potential.

1988 CHARDONNAY [80] Colour: medium yellow-
green. *Bouquet:* complex with charred oak/
barrel ferment characters and lifted honey/
peach fruit. *Palate:* again complex flavours of
melon/peach/ grapefruit chardonnay with tangy,
ever so slightly hessiany oak; has style. Drink
'90–'92.

1987 SHIRAZ [69] Colour: medium red-purple. *Bouquet:* strong gamey/meaty characters, possibly deriving from carbonic maceration but equally possibly from mercaptan. *Palate:* strong minty/red berry fruit surrounded by meaty/gamey farmyard flavours and a suspicion of spritzy acid on the finish. A wine with an uncertain future. Drink '91–'93.

1987 CABERNET SAUVIGNON [67] Colour: medium red-purple with gas evident. *Bouquet:* rather light and slightly thin, lacking fruit richness; some gamey/meaty aromas. *Palate:* again, lacks fruit richness and again shows some of those fizzy/gassy characters in the shiraz. Drink '91–'93.

Summary: The '87 reds of Dalwhinnie are puzzling; tasted in July 1989 they were presumably bottled rather than tank samples and have some upsetting flavours and characteristics. However, some outstanding '88 reds are to follow in due course.

MOUNT AVOCA

Location: Moates Lane, Avoca, 3467; 6 km west of town.
(054) 65 3282.

Winemakers: John Barry and Rodney Morrish.

1989 Production: 10,000 cases.

Principal Wines: Cabernet Sauvignon, Shiraz, Trebbiano, Chardonnay, Semillon, Sauvignon Blanc. All reds are kept in cask for one to two years before bottling.

Distribution: Substantial cellar door and mailing list sales; wholesale distribution through De Bortoli Wines Pty Ltd. Cellar door sales 9 a.m. to 5 p.m. Monday to Friday, 10 a.m. to 5 p.m. Saturday, noon to 5 p.m. Sunday. Mailing list enquiries to PO Box 60, Avoca, 3467 (or telephone (03) 419 8586).

Prices: $9 to $15.

Vintage Rating 1986–89: White: '89, '87, '88, '86. Red: '89, '86, '88, '87.

Tasting Notes:

1989 SAUVIGNON BLANC [TS] Colour: very good green-yellow. *Bouquet:* smoky grassy/gooseberry aromas with distinct fermentation characters still lingering. *Palate:* excellent grassy tobacco variety character of light to medium weight, with a crisp acid finish. Should live up to the promise of the earlier brilliant sauvignon blanc releases from Mount Avoca.

1988 SEMILLON [68] Colour: bright green-yellow of medium depth. *Bouquet:* slightly smelly, old socks aromas, apparently deriving from re-used oak barrels. *Palate:* very much better than the bouquet, firm, with a touch of herbaceous varietal fruit; may well develop in bottle and throw off the uncertain bouquet. If it does it will merit much higher points. Drink '91–'93.

1988 CHARDONNAY [75] Colour: medium to full yellow-green. *Bouquet:* full tangy grapefruit and tangy French oak with distinct lift. *Palate:* high toned, lifted tangy fruit flavours bordering on the aggressive; may well settle down given time. Drink '90–'92.

1986 SHIRAZ [66] Colour: light to medium red-purple. *Bouquet:* rather closed and slightly dull, with some leathery bitter aromas. *Palate:* of light to medium weight with red berry fruit tinged by bitterness and finishing hard. A wine flawed by mercaptan. Drink '90–'92.

Summary: The white wines of Mount Avoca continue to impress, but the 1986 red wines are extremely disappointing. The cabernet sauvignon of that year is grossly flawed by mercaptan.

REDBANK

Location: Sunraysia Highway, Redbank, 3467; 3 km south of Redbank, opposite 200 km post.
(054) 67 7255; Fax (054) 67 7255.

Winemaker: Neill Robb.

1989 Production: 4000 cases.

Principal Wines: Sally's Paddock is the principal estate-grown red wine followed by Redbank Cabernet. A number of other red wines, identified both by variety and by vineyard or subdistrict, are also made each year from grapes purchased in and around the Pyrenees region. A few years ago the first white wine (Alexandra Kingsley Chardonnay) made its appearance under the Redbank label.

Distribution: Largely cellar door and mailing list; wholesale distribution through W. J. Seabrook & Son, Melbourne; The Specialist Wine Co., Sydney; B. H. MacLachlan, Adelaide; and Vat Wine & Spirit, Brisbane. Significant exports to USA, UK and Germany. Cellar door sales 9 a.m. to 5 p.m. Monday to Saturday, 10 a.m. to 5 p.m. Sunday.

Prices: $5.90 to $25.50 cellar door.

Summary: Wines were supplied for the regional tasting conducted with this edition, but a variety of vicissitudes befell them. The two 1987 reds (Sally's Paddock and Cabernet Sauvignon) were corked, which is hardly the winemaker's fault but one cannot help but worry that both wines were so affected. The 1988 Alexandra Kingsley Chardonnay was not reviewable on conventional terms. Redbank has a fine reputation, and the tasting was surely not representative.

🍇 *SUMMERFIELD*

Location: Moonambel, 3478; on the western outskirts of town on Moonambel-Stawell Road. (054) 67 2264.

Winemaker: Ian L. Summerfield.

1989 Production: 2400 cases.

Principal Wines: Champagne *Méthode champenoise* (made from trebbiano), Hermitage and Cabernet Sauvignon.

Distribution: Principally cellar door sales and mailing list. Cellar door sales 9 a.m. to 6 p.m. Monday to Saturday and 10 a.m. to 6 p.m. Sunday. Mailing list enquiries to Summerfield Vineyards, Moonambel, 3478.

Prices: $8 to $14 cellar door.

Vintage Rating 1986-89: '88, '87, '89, '86.

Outstanding Prior Vintages: '79, '80, '83, '84.

Tasting Notes:

1988 SHIRAZ [91] Colour: full red-purple. *Bouquet:* very rich, full and clean with pungent sweet American oak matching opulent red berry fruit aromas. *Palate:* commensurately rich and full, with nearly identical sweet vanillan oak perfectly harmonising with abundant soft red berry fruit flavours and beautifully balanced tannins. Drink '94–2002.

1988 CABERNET SAUVIGNON [90] Colour: dense purple-red. *Bouquet:* strong, rich and concentrated cassis fruit supported by rich, vanillan American oak. *Palate:* lusciously rich and concentrated ripe cabernet fruit married with sweet vanillan oak; soft, lingering tannins on the finish. In two separate tastings the fruit was the first impression on both bouquet and palate. Drink '94–2002.

1987 SHIRAZ [75] Colour: medium purple-red. *Bouquet:* very complex, with gamey overtones to rich berry fruit. *Palate:* a lively wine with striking spicy/meaty flavours and rather jumpy acid; has potential, and was in fact tasted from tank immediately prior to bottling. If cleaned up could be even better. Drink '93–'96.

Summary: To say that Summerfield has hit a purple patch with its 1988 reds is an understatement. They stood out both at the Ballarat Show and at a subsequent regional tasting, and if they make their way safely to bottle should be outstanding when released towards the end of 1990.

🍇 *TALTARNI*

Location: Taltarni Road, Moonambel, 3478; 5 km north-west of Moonambel.
(054) 67 2218; Fax (054) 67 2306.

Winemakers: Dominique Portet and Greg Gallagher.

1989 Production: 60,000 cases.

Principal Wines: Taltarni Cuvee Brut, Brut Tache and Royale and Blanc de Blanc (chardonnay) (four *Méthode champenoise* sparkling wines), Blanc Des Pyrenees (chablis style), Fumé Blanc, Rhine Riesling, Rosé des Pyrenees, French Syrah (the Taltarni adopted name for shiraz), Cabernet Sauvignon, Reserve Des Pyrenees (cabernet malbec blend) and Merlot (100%).

Distribution: Extensive fine wine retail sales through all states and capital cities. Cellar door sales 10 a.m. to 4.15 p.m. Monday to Saturday. Mailing list available; enquiries to Taltarni Vineyards, Moonambel, 3478.

Prices: $8.50 to $17 Victorian retail.

Vintage Rating 1986–89: White: '86, '89, '88, '87. Red: '86, '88, '89, '87.

Outstanding Prior Vintages: '79, '82, '84.

Tasting Notes:

1989 FUME BLANC [91] Colour: light straw-yellow. *Bouquet:* superb crisp/gooseberry varietal character, intense and perfectly modulated. *Palate:* outstanding sauvignon blanc flavours with crisp, clean and tingling fruit leading on to a long, clean finish. The best Taltarni Fumé so far. Drink '90–'91.

1989 RHINE RIESLING [78] Colour: very light straw-green. *Bouquet:* light and crisp, with highly protected fruit showing careful wine-making. *Palate:* crisp and toasty fruit with considerable elegance; should develop well over the next 12 months or so, gaining additional mid-palate weight. Drink '90–'91.

1986 FRENCH SYRAH [81] Colour: dense purple-red. *Bouquet:* deep, concentrated and firm fruit with some astringency evident. *Palate:* a wine absolutely loaded with flavour; as the English would have it, chunky fruit with typical lingering tannins that commence on the mid-palate and carry through to the finish. Drink '95–2004.

1986 CABERNET SAUVIGNON [88] Colour: dense purple-red. *Bouquet:* strong, dark black currant/cassis fruit; good oak in support. *Palate:* enormously concentrated and dense wine with strong tannins running throughout; certainly not for the faint-hearted and to be approached with caution for the next five years at least. Drink '95–2010.

Summary: The 1986 vintage was Dominique Portet's tenth, and he celebrated that fact in fine style. I have tasted the 1986 reds on a number of occasions; the richness is always there, but once or twice I did worry fractionally about the tannins. On other occasions I felt the fruit, for once, was there to carry the tannins. It will certainly be interesting to see how they develop in the long term. In the short term, there is the quite lovely Fumé Blanc.

🍇 *WARRENMANG*

Location: Mountain Creek Road, Moonambel, 3478; 2 km east of town.
(054) 67 2233.

Winemaker: Christopher Sim.

1989 Production: 4000 cases.

Principal Wines: Chardonnay, Shiraz, and Grand Pyrenees.

Distribution: Principally mailing list and cellar door sales; wholesale distribution to fine wine retailers through Emerald Wines, Vic., (03) 3501111, cellar door sales 9 a.m. to 5 p.m. Monday to Saturday and 10 a.m. to 5 p.m. Sunday. Mailing list enquiries to Warrenmang Vineyard, Moonambel, 3478.

Prices: $10 to $15 cellar door.

Vintage Rating 1986–89: Red: '87, '89, '86, '88.

Tasting Notes:

1986 GRAND PYRENEES [65] Colour: medium purple-red. *Bouquet:* quite attractive, elegant leafy fruit with just a faint leathery edge. *Palate:* tangy, leafy herbaceous fruit with light, lemony oak in support. Drink '90–'94.

Summary: Of the four vintages of Grand Pyrenees from 1985 to 1988, the '86 is by far the best. The other wines are, quite frankly, a cause for some concern, although the '88 was tasted from cask and will hopefully be cleaned up prior to bottling.

Southern and Central Victoria

1988 VINTAGE

The grouping of wineries under this chapter is strictly a marriage of convenience. There is no geographic, climatic or viticultural rationale underlying the group, so the discussion of vintage thus becomes difficult to say the least. However, the more important entries do fall into two basic areas: in the western districts, centred around Drumborg and Portland, fall Cherritta, Crawford River, Kingsley, Seppelt Drumborg and–at its furthest or most western extremity–St Gregory's Vineyard. These five do constitute a reasonably coherent climatic sub-district. Then, across in the central highlands of Victoria are Delatite, Flowerdale, Giaconda and Murrindindi.

For the western districts, 1988 was generally regarded as a very good year. Indeed, Crawford River and Kingsley rated as their best in the last four years. Overall, white wines faired better than reds, but in an area in which viticulture can be marginal (witness the disastrous 1987 vintage), none of the vignerons had any complaints.

In the central highlands the pattern was similar: the warm, Indian summer autumn allowed the grapes to reach full maturity, something that cannot be taken for granted at Flowerdale, Murrindindi or Delatite.

1989 VINTAGE

Given the marginal climate of the western districts the already discussed and long history of vintage failures, 1989 was a veritable miracle. The season was basically warm and dry, with slightly below average rainfall; flowering and fruit set took place without hindrance from wind or rain, and the grapes all reached very good maturity. Seppelt says it was the best vintage both in terms of quality and quantity that it has ever encountered in the area.

For the highlands, it was a year in which the white varieties and pinot noir did well, and in which the late varieties (cabernet and cabernet family) struggled hard but failed at the end to reach acceptable sugar and flavour levels.

THE CHANGES

There are two departures and one arrival, which has at least had the benefit of slightly tidying up the illogical grouping of previous years. The departures are Hickinbotham Winemakers (now with a home in the Mornington Peninsula, where the entry will be found) and Wantirna Estate (which has been formally welcomed into the bosom of the Yarra Valley where its entry will likewise be found). The arrival is St Gregory's Vineyard, which proves that Australians are prepared to try any-thing. It is situated just off the Wimmera Highway, 70 km west of Horsham or 40 km west of Naracoorte. It is planted to 2 hectares of cabernet sauvignon and shiraz, with just a token smattering of durif and touriga yet to come into bearing. The initial planting was made in 1977 as a retirement project for

Gregory Flynn, and the touriga planting gives a clue as to his intentions: the making of port. This is the only style made, and having regard to the climate it is not surprising that he is aiming at a dryer style.

🍇 CHERRITTA WINES

Location: Port Road, Branxholme, 3302; off Hamilton-Portland Road at Wallacedale North sign.
(055) 78 6251.

Winemaker: John Sobey.

Principal Wines: Rhine Riesling, Chardonnay, Shiraz and Cabernet Sauvignon, with Moselle-style Rhine Riesling the principal wine, but all wines made in very limited quantities.

Distribution: By mailing list; cellar door sales by appointment only. Retail distribution through Victorian Wine Centre.

Summary: A small winery that has been established for a number of years now, but operating with a low profile.

🍇 CRAWFORD RIVER

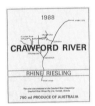

Location: Crawford via Condah, 3303; turn off Henty Highway.
(055) 78 2267.

Winemaker: John Thomson.

1989 Production: 2200 cases.

Principal Wines: Rhine Riesling, Beerenauslese Rhine Riesling, Semillon/Sauvignon Blanc and Cabernet Sauvignon.

Distribution: Cellar door sales by appointment. Limited distribution through Melbourne retailers, principally The Liquor Cabinet, Richmond Hill Cellars, Sutherland Cellars and Victorian Wine Centre and through Specialist Wine Co., Sydney. Wines also available at better Melbourne restaurants.

Prices: $10 to $15 per bottle and $15 (per half-bottle of Beerenauslese) mailing list.

Vintage Rating 1986–89: White: '88, '89, '86, '87. Red: '88, '86, '89, '87.

Tasting Notes:

1988 SEMILLON/SAUVIGNON BLANC [62]
Colour: light green-yellow. *Bouquet:* clean but very light fruit with pronounced lemony oak. *Palate:* light bodied and crisp, but rather warm pencil-shavings oak does not flatter the wine. Drink '90–'91.

1988 RHINE RIESLING [65] Colour: light to medium yellow-green. *Bouquet:* light, crisp fruit with a touch of matchbox aroma. *Palate:* light, herbaceous/citric fruit in typical cool climate style; firm and somewhat bitter; however, these wines often blossom with age and I may be doing the wine a grave injustice. Drink '90–'93.

1986 CABERNET SAUVIGNON [67] Colour: medium red-purple. *Bouquet:* soft bottle-developed aromas with tobacco leaf and cedar and a whisper of oxidation. *Palate:* of medium weight, with pleasant fruit showing some sweet berry fruit, but pulled back by rather plain, old oak. Drink '90–'93.

Summary: Western Districts grazier John Thomson, with almost no outside technical assistance but with the benefit of study at Riverina College under his belt, has produced some quite marvellous wines over the years. It is a cold and windswept place, and you will never find luscious up-front wines from here: patience is the key word, with a steely elegance the principal reward.

🍇 DELATITE

Location: Stoney's Road, Mansfield, 3722; approximately 10 km south-east of town.
(057) 75 2922; Fax (057) 75 1528.

Winemaker: Rosalind Ritchie.

1989 Production: Approximately 11,500 cases.

Principal Wines: A limited range of fine varietal table wines comprising Riesling, Dead Man's Hill Gewurztraminer, Chardonnay, Late-picked

Riesling, New Shiraz, Pinot Noir, Cabernet Sauvignon Merlot, Malbec, Shiraz and a Cabernet blend Devil's River. "Ritchie" label releases for selected varietals from other regions.

Distribution: Equally divided between cellar door sales, mail order and fine wine merchants and restaurant distribution. Cellar door sales 9 a.m. to 6 p.m. 7 days; mailing list enquiries to PO Box 246, Mansfield, 3722. Wholesale distribution through Fesq & Co., Sydney; Van Cooth & Co., Melbourne; and John Cook, National Wine Broker, Adelaide. UK imports through Anthony Byrne Fine Wines, Cambridgeshire.

Prices: $158 to $260. Cellar door sales $150 to $252 per case 750 ml.

Vintage Rating 1986–89: White: '87, '86, '89, '88. Cabernet styles: '88, '86, '87, '89. Pinot Noir: '89, '88, '87, '86.

Tasting Notes:

1988 RIESLING [65] Colour: extremely pale, almost water white. *Bouquet:* somewhat stripped and lacking fruit. *Palate:* again very light and lacking fruit, although it does have quite good structure and sugar/acid balance; a wine that suffered greatly at bottling, and never quite threw off the problems. Drink '90.

1988 CHARDONNAY [69] Colour: attractive, light spicy/nutmeg oak with faint citric/lemon fruit. *Palate:* once again very light, with the oak lacking the spicy tang it exhibited in the bouquet, tending to the one-dimensional; showing the after-effects of bottling problems. Drink '90–'91.

1988 PINOT NOIR [74] Colour: very good purple-red of medium depth. *Bouquet:* clean, strong and fresh eucalypt mint aromas, wholly regional and equally totally non-varietal. *Palate:* pristine, clean, firm minty flavours; a beautifully made wine within the straitjacket of the district. Drink '90–'92.

1988 DEVIL'S RIVER [76] Colour: medium to full red-purple. *Bouquet:* full, clean and soft minty/berry fruit; oak not evident. *Palate:* full flavoured, with pronounced minty/eucalypt characters and soft tannins; in the mainstream of the Delatite style. Drink '93–'97.

1987 CABERNET MERLOT [81] Colour: medium to full purple-red. *Bouquet:* dense, briary and concentrated, somewhat closed in on itself. *Palate:* richly concentrated and structured ripe fruit with strong berry and very good tannins; the oak plays merely a support role. Drink '92–'95.

1987 DEVIL'S RIVER [77] Colour: medium purple-red. *Bouquet:* clean with full, soft minty/berry fruit. *Palate:* full, soft minty/red berry fruits with considerable richness; the structure and balance is also good. Drink '91–'93.

Summary: The wines of this high-altitude, cool-climate vineyard are always distinctive. The aromatic white wines are very European in style and, not surprisingly, have a strong following in the United Kingdom. The red wines by and large share a common core of minty/eucalypt character; this seems to transcend variety, and while many good judges find it appealing, I have the feeling that it should be a background component rather than aroma and flavour. However, this is something forced on Delatite: winemaking skills are not in question.

🍇 *FLOWERDALE*

Location: Yea Road, Flowerdale, 3717; 2 km north of Flowerdale Hotel on the main Flowerdale-Yea Road.
(057) 80 1432.

Winemaker: Rosalind Ritchie (contract).

Principal Wines: Chenin Blanc, Chardonnay, Traminer and Pinot Noir.

Distribution: Exclusively cellar door sales and mailing list; cellar door sales noon to 5 p.m. Sunday and 10 a.m. to 5 p.m. Saturday. Mailing list enquiries to RMB 6513, Yea Road, Flowerdale, 3717.

Summary: The Flowerdale vineyard is in an undeniably cold part of Victoria, and obviously full fruit ripeness is going to be a struggle. If it is achieved the results could be spectacular, particularly given that winemaking is now in such competent hands.

GIACONDA

Location: Cnr Wangaratta and McClay Roads, Beechworth, 3747; 9 km south-west of Beechworth.
(057) 27 0246.

Winemaker: Rick Kinzbrunner.

1989 Production: 700 cases.

Principal Wines: Chardonnay, Pinot Noir and a Cabernet Sauvignon Cabernet Franc Merlot blend.

Distribution: Principally retail through wholesale distributors W. J. Seabrook & Son; cellar door by appointment only with no tastings. Mailing list enquiries to RMB 6481; Eldorado, 3746. UK imports through Yapp Bros, Wiltshire.

Prices: $17.50 to $22.50 retail.

Vintage Rating 1986–89: White: '89, '88, '86, '87. Pinot Noir: '89, '88, '87, '86. Cabernet: '86, '87, '88 ('89 not rated).

Tasting Notes:

1989 CHARDONNAY [CS] Colour: green-yellow, still slightly cloudy from yeast lees. _Bouquet:_ quite complex; of medium weight, with strong yeast lees influence. _Palate:_ fresh, firm peachy/grapefruit flavours, with the finish still to soften and oak still to make its statement. To my taste, one of the most promising Giaconda Chardonnays yet made.

1989 PINOT NOIR [CS] Colour: light purple-red. _Bouquet:_ complex, sweet cherry fruit with a hint of Burgundian plumminess. _Palate:_ does not live up to the very promising bouquet, with rather leafy/tobacco flavours; it is very difficult to tell whether the bouquet or the palate will ultimately tell the tale.

Summary: Giaconda is a brightly blazing new star in the firmament; Rick Kinzbrunner has managed to seize the imagination and attention of the wine-growing public in a very short period of time. His future progress will be watched with considerable interest.

KINGSLEY

Location: 50 Bancroft Street, Portland, 3305; cellar door sales outlet within precincts of town.
(055) 23 1864.

Winemaker: B. Seppelt & Sons Ltd, Great Western (contract).

1989 Production: 350 cases.

Principal Wines: Rhine Riesling and Traminer only releases to date; Cabernet Sauvignon in the future.

Distribution: Virtually exclusively mailing list and cellar door sales. Mailing list enquiries as above; cellar door sales 1 p.m. to 4 p.m. 7 days. Restaurant distribution through Edward Henty restaurant, Portland.

Prices: $8 to $12 cellar door.

Vintage Rating 1986–89: '88, '89, '87 ('86 not rated).

Tasting Notes:

1988 RHINE RIESLING [69] Colour: medium yellow-green. _Bouquet:_ soft, decadent, lychee/tropical aromas, obviously botrytis influenced. _Palate:_ full but most unusual tropical/tutti frutti flavours, again showing obvious botrytis influence; left with some residual sugar, which suits the style. An interesting wine that was tasted twice in totally different circumstances, with identical terminology used to describe it on each occasion. Drink '90–'91.

Summary: Tom Beauglehole has done all the rights things in establishing Kingsley; however, one suspects that remoteness from mainstream marketing may prove as difficult as the somewhat erratic western districts climate.

MURRINDINDI VINEYARDS

Location: RMB 6070, Cummins Lane, Murrindindi, 3717.

Winemaker: Hugh Cuthbertson.

1989 Production: 800 cases.

Principal Wines: Chardonnay and Cabernet Blend (cabernet sauvignon, merlot and cabernet franc).

Distribution: Principally mail order and through limited retail outlets.

Prices: $16 cellar door.

Vintage Rating 1986–89: '88, '86, '87, '89.

Tasting Notes:

1988 CABERNET MERLOT [CS] Colour: strong purple-red. _Bouquet:_ soft, with pleasant minty/berry fruit aromas and a touch of leathery astringency. _Palate:_ attractive red berry flavours with a touch of mint; has good concentration and weight; if that touch of astringency (sulphide) is removed prior to bottling, will be excellent.

1987 CABERNET MERLOT [76] Colour: strong purple-red. _Bouquet:_ quite complex, with good concentration but marred by a trace of astringency. _Palate:_ a strongly flavoured and structured wine, with red berry/cassis fruit and soft tannins running throughout; a cool climate style, but certainly not thin, and the best Murrindindi red yet made. Drink '91–'96.

Summary: Murrindindi is the family vineyard of Melbourne wine identity Hugh Cuthbertson, who has had a varied career, at one stage owning Talavera but now working in the fine wine section of Mildara.

SAINT GREGORY'S VINEYARD

Location: Bringalbert South Road, Bringalbert South, via Apsley, 3319; 40 km east of Naracoorte.
(055) 86 5225 or (03) 772 2196.

Winemaker: Gregory Flynn.

1989 Production: 150 cases.

Principal Wines: Exclusively Port.

Distribution: Mailing list; address as above.

Prices: $10.

Summary: Two barrel samples of 1989 vintage port in differing varietal proportions were tasted, showing strong, deep sweet fruit. The older vintages have been marred by indifferent old oak, a problem that Gregory Flynn is aware of and is addressing. In any event, St Gregory's must certainly be able to claim the title of Australia's most unique port.

SEPPELT DRUMBORG

Location: Drumborg, Victoria, 3304; 31 km north of Portland (vineyard only).
(055) 27 9257.

Winemaker: Ian McKenzie (chief winemaker) and Mike Toomey (vineyard manager).

Principal Wines: After an extensive replanting and grafting, the 46 hectares now established are chardonnay, cabernet sauvignon, pinot noir, pinot meunier and rhine riesling. Current Drumborg table wine releases are of Traminer, Rhine Riesling and Cabernet Sauvignon; the Traminer will be phased out after the 1985 vintage, and a 100% Drumborg Chardonnay Brut will occasionally be made.

Distribution: Fine wine retailers.

Prices: $13 to $24.

Vintage Rating 1986–89: White: '89, '88, '86, '87. Red: '89, '86, '88 (no '87 made).

Outstanding Prior Vintages: '78, '80, '82.

Summary: The Seppelt Drumborg vineyard has been a most wayward child, promising much but constantly spoiling things through the worst imaginable behaviour. Seppelt had got to the point of giving it three more years before making a decision to close down the operation. The good '88 and outstanding '89 vintages have now assured its future. Unfortunately, through some oversight none of the upcoming releases were tasted, but quality is always good.

Yarra Valley

1988 VINTAGE

A warm and dry spring led to early budburst and to expectations of a return to a more normal start to vintage after the four cool and late vintages from 1984 to 1987. However, cold, windy and often wet conditions prevailing from October through to December both slowed things down and caused problems with fruit set; chardonnay was particularly affected in some vineyards, cabernet sauvignon in others.

With the arrival of the new year, there was a dramatic change in the weather, which became hot and dry right through January and February. The initial expectations of an early start to vintage materialised with pinot noir, much of which was harvested in hot, warm weather in early March. A four-day spell of rain, the last to be seen until the end of vintage, then slowed proceedings dramatically, with all other varieties being harvested at a leisurely pace through to mid-April.

The grapes were all picked in absolutely prime condition, and for most vignerons it was a very good to outstanding vintage. Some great pinot noirs were made, and some rich, full-bodied chardonnays and cabernets. The aromatic varieties, headed by rhine riesling, also did well.

1989 VINTAGE

It was a year in which it was dry when it should have been wet, hot when it should have been cool, and windy when it should have been calm. Right from the outset there were problems: October and early November, normally very wet months, saw barely a drop of rain as strong northerly winds blew at times with gale force, causing damage to young growing tips. Just as the vines commenced to flower the rain came, upsetting the usually imperturbable pinot noir, and also significantly interrupting the flowering and set of chardonnay.

The weather then continued changeable from the second half of December through to mid-February, with more or less constant rain causing widespread outbreaks of mildew in vineyards with a less-than-perfect spray programme. In mid-February, the heat wave arrived and persisted for three weeks, causing pinot noir to ripen at an astonishing rate and chardonnay to suffer from sunburn. Some vineyards reported the earliest start ever as pinot noir was hurriedly picked to prevent the continuation of the already evident collapse in the berries.

At the end of the three-week heat wave the rain came and the weather turned cool. Some vineyards by this time had commenced to defoliate, but even those that kept the full canopy seemed unable to ripen semillon or cabernet sauvignon. For a full three weeks there was virtually no activity, and most of the later ripening varieties were not picked until late April or early May, which meant that for one or two wineries it was not only the earliest start on record, but the latest finish.

Some good wines will be made, but they will be exceptions rather than the rule. Bailey Caroddus, veteran of the district with 17 vintages under his belt, declared the worst vintage he had ever known.

THE CHANGES

There are numerous new entries (ten in all) and one or two departures. Without doubt, the most important of the new arrivals is Domaine Chandon, the multi-million dollar wholly owned development of Moet et Chandon. The winery is now fully built and the cellar door sales and tastings facility will be open from the middle of 1990. Its substantial vineyards will come into production progressively from 1990 onwards, although it will always be the policy of Domaine Chandon to produce a multi-regional blend. It is by far the largest winery and vine-yard development in the Yarra Valley to date, and by far the most significant

However, the acquisition of St Huberts, mentioned in last year's edition, has led to substantial changes (and growth) in that direction. A large vineyard development known as Eyton-on-Yarra has commenced under the aegis of St Huberts; a substantial restaurant facility is planned, and it has also given rise to a separate brand of Andrew Rowan. Because the price structure, not to mention the grape sources, of the Andrew Rowan range is different, it is separately treated in this book. Tunnel Hill is in the same category: it is a separate brand being developed by Tarrawarra, again with a lower price and (by inference) being of lesser quality, although I am not certain that the tastings of either Andrew Rowan or Tunnel Hill necessarily suggest this is always so.

Lovegrove of Cottles Bridge and Shantell are two fully fledged wineries, each with their own substantial and relatively mature vineyards in support. Lovegrove of Cottles Bridge is across in the St Andrew's region, not so far from Diamond Valley; consultancy advice from Gary Baldwin of Oenotec has paid dividends, with the initial releases all being very good quality. Shantell has moved from being a grape producer (selling much of its crop to Coldstream Hills for a number of years) to winemaker; Shan and Turid Shanmugan devote an enormous amount of time to the operation, Turid having given up her post as a university lecturer to become a full-time viticulturist, and Shan taking time off

from his medical practice to assist both in vineyard and in winery. Kathleen Quealy is consultant, and once again her technical input has been invaluable: Shantell has produced some quite lovely wines.

Lirralirra should have been in the last edition; somehow or other the gremlins got to it. It does have a somewhat low profile, being part grape grower and part winemaker. The original intention was to produce a single Sauternes-style botrytised semillon sauvignon blanc, but the weather and other factors have encouraged the production of dry white wines instead.

Yarra Vale, owned by long-term Yarra Valley residents the Norris family, and Boolarong, owned by Dr Ian Hanson, are both very much in their infancy. Boolarong has two vineyard sources: one and a half hectares of cabernet sauvignon and cabernet franc established at Lower Plenty in 1983, and a little under 4 hectares on a separate property on the Old Healesville Road, Yarra Glen, planted to cabernet sauvignon, cabernet franc, merlot, pinot noir, shiraz, sauvignon blanc and a few experimental rows of Italian varieties in 1988. All of the wines made to date have been experimental only. The Norris's Maddens Lane Winery is in fact the site of what was previously Prigorje: most of the Prigorje vineyard was sold to Yarra Yering (that vineyard now being called Underhill), but there are 2 hectares of semillon, chardonnay and pinot noir surrounding the winery that have passed to Geoffrey and Felicity Norris. Winemaking to date has been carried out under contract at Yarra Burn.

Chateau Yarrinya has changed its name to Yarrinya Estate, while Wantirna Estate is now officially part of the Yarra Valley, following adoption and ratification by the Yarra Valley Vignerons of boundaries for the district proposed by the Victorian Wine Industry Association.

Finally, there have been two behind-the-scenes changes: both Diamond Valley and Lillydale Vineyards now have their own immaculately equipped on-site wineries.

❦ *ANDREW ROWAN*

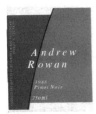

Location: Cnr St Huberts Road and Maroondah Highway, Coldstream, 3770; 6 km north-east of Coldstream.
(03) 739 1421; Fax (03) 739 1015.

Winemaker: Brian Fletcher.

Principal Wines: A series of wines made variously from 100% Yarra Valley fruit or blended with Barossa Valley material, basically sourced from sister operation Kies Estate. The wines include Dry White, Chardonnay, Shiraz, Pinot Noir and Cabernet Sauvignon.

Distribution: Extensive retail distribution through I. H. Baker Wines & Spirits, NSW, Vic., Qld and WA; Seabrook and Seabrook, SA; and Rutherglen Wine Co., Tas. Cellar door sales and mailing list also available; cellar door sales 9 a.m. to 5 p.m. Monday to Friday, 10.30 a.m. to 5.30 p.m. weekends and 10 a.m. to 5.30 p.m. public holidays. Mailing list enquiries to above address.

Prices: $7.50 to $11.10 cellar door.

Vintage Rating 1986-89: Not relevant owing to varied fruit sources.

Tasting Notes:

1988 DRY WHITE [61] Colour: light green-yellow. *Bouquet:* clean, light and fragrant grapy aromas, suggestive of some frontignac or muscat in the blend. *Palate:* clean and light, with pleasant balance and again a grapy frontignac influence; a commercial style, made fairly dry. A blend of Yarra Valley and Barossa material. Drink '90.

1987 CHARDONNAY [70] Colour: medium yellow-green. *Bouquet:* attractive, light to medium peachy/fig fruit aromas; clean, with well-integrated oak. *Palate:* does not deliver quite as much as the bouquet promises; a lighter and more simple wine, rather one dimensional and lacking style; fractionally hard acid on the finish. Nonetheless, a good wine at the price. Drink '90.

1986 SHIRAZ [58] Colour: medium purple-red. *Bouquet:* soft; some biscuity/lemony oak, and fruit of light to medium intensity. *Palate:* rather sharp biscuity/lemony oak with definite signs of either bacterial or oxidation problems on the palate. Once again a wine that falls away a little after a reasonable start. Drink '90.

1986 CABERNET SAUVIGNON [73] Colour: medium purple-red. *Bouquet:* light, rather leafy cabernet aroma with fair varietal character; the oak is rather dull. *Palate:* once again, there are leafy cabernet flavours that are quite pleasant, but which are held back by rather dull, old oak. May well appeal to those who do not enjoy positive oak flavours in wine. Drink '90–'92.

Summary: It is no great secret that the new owners of St Huberts found some wines in the cellar that simply did not measure up to the high standards expected of the Yarra Valley and of St Huberts in particular. Thus the Andrew Rowan range can be regarded as a sheer case of expediency. I would like to think that it is more than this: that in the future we will see wines planned from the outset to be blends, as there is obvious synergy available in some years. What is important is full disclosure, and the back labels of the Andrew Rowan range provide just that.

❦ *BIANCHET*

Location: Lot 3, Victoria Road, Lilydale, 3140; 5 km north of town.
(03) 739 1779 or (03) 739 1776.

Winemaker: Lou Bianchet.

1989 Production: 2000 cases.

Principal Wines: Chardonnay, Gewurztraminer, Verduzzo, Semillon, Pinot Noir, Shiraz, Cabernet Sauvignon and Merlot.

Distribution: Substantial cellar door sales and

mailing list; cellar door sales 10 a.m. to 6 p.m. weekends, public holidays and every day in January. Fine wine retail sales and restaurants serviced either direct from winery or through Roger Brown, Sydney.

Prices: $9 to $16 cellar door.

Vintage Rating 1986–89: '88, '86, '87, '89.

Tasting Notes:

1987 GEWURZTRAMINER **[74]** *Colour:* medium yellow, with a touch of green. *Bouquet:* soft and clean, with pleasant, bottle-developed fruit and some varietal lychee/spice. *Palate:* very good varietal flavour, with rich lychee spice characters similar to the bouquet; fractionally phenolic and hard on the finish, something very difficult to avoid with this variety when it is invested with middle palate flavour. Drink '90.

1987 SEMILLON **[66]** *Colour:* medium yellow-green. *Bouquet:* strong burgundian/sulphidic overtones, complex and non-Australian. *Palate:* high flavoured, with a distinct burgundian cabbage tang and grip; a very distinctive wine that might have great appeal to those more concerned with style than technical perfection. Drink '90–'93.

1987 CHARDONNAY **[71]** *Colour:* medium to full yellow-green. *Bouquet:* soft, butterscotch aromas with a hint of burgundian bottle-developed complexity. *Palate:* again showing bottle-developed flavours; if there had been a little more richness than the fruit core, would have merited very high points. Once again, a wine with individuality. Drink '90–'91.

1987 PINOT NOIR **[59]** *Colour:* medium red. *Bouquet:* developed, sappy/tobacco flavours with a slight farmyard background. *Palate:* really falls away, the fruit is dying and the absence of any new oak does not help. A better wine a year ago. Drink '90.

1986 SHIRAZ **[68]** *Colour:* medium red-purple, slightly dull. *Bouquet:* light but pleasant leafy/minty fruit with just a hint of spice; oak is not evident. *Palate:* light, leafy/spicy flavours suggesting a degree of shading of the fruit and relatively high pH levels. Drink '90–'91.

1988 MERLOT **[72]** *Colour:* bright purple-red of medium depth. *Bouquet:* youthful, clean, light and fresh minty aromas, but little of the character one hopes for from merlot. *Palate:*

clean, attractive, fruity/minty flavours, fractionally one dimensional and certainly not particularly varietal. However, has the redeeming feature of freshness. Drink '90–'91.

Summary: Lou Bianchet makes full-flavoured and generously proportioned wines that sell at highly competitive prices by the standards of the Yarra Valley. The lack of new oak barrels is a limiting factor on style and, to a degree, quality.

BOOLARONG VINEYARD

Location: Old Healesville Road, Yarra Glen; 3775 (vineyard only); also 49 Cleveland Avenue, Lower Plenty, 3093.
(03) 439 7425.

Winemaker: Ian Hanson.

1989 Production: Approximately 100 cases.

Principal Wines: Only one wine so far made, a blend of Cabernet Franc and Cabernet Sauvignon.

Distribution: Not yet released.

Summary: Ian Hanson is still to move beyond the stage of experimental winemaking to commercial production; the four vintages tasted (from '86 to '89) showed widely differing style, with the influence of vintage very marked. It is Ian Hanson's intention to gradually reduce the time devoted to his dentistry practice and increase his involvement in viticulture and winemaking.

COLDSTREAM HILLS

Location: Lot 6, Maddens Lane, Coldstream, 3770; 15 km north-east of Lilydale.
(059) 64 9388; Fax (059) 64 9389.

Winemaker: James Halliday.

1989 Production: Approximately 11,000 cases.

Principal Wines: Chardonnay, Semillon, Sauvignon Blanc, Pinot Noir, Cabernet Merlot and Cabernet Sauvignon (the latter a Bordeaux blend of approximately 80% cabernet sauvignon and equal quantities of merlot and cabernet franc). Particularly with Pinot Noir and Chardonnay, there are often two releases each year, with different vineyard origins shown on the label: Coldstream Hills now has fifteen hectares of its own vineyards (not all in bearing) but also has long-term contract purchase arrangements with other Yarra Valley growers.

Distribution: National retail through Tucker/Seabrook/Caon Group and by mailing list; mailing list enquiries as above. Substantial exports; UK through H. Sichel & Sons Ltd., USA and NZ exports Negociants International.

Prices: $22 to $26 retail.

Vintage Rating 1986-89: '88, '86, '87, '89.

Summary: Tasting notes are not provided because Coldstream Hills is the author's own winery. However, in the 12 months prior to writing this book, Coldstream Hills enjoyed the highest cumulative success rate of any exhibitor at the shows it entered, amassing 13 trophies, 26 gold medals, 16 silver medals and 14 bronze medals from 63 entries. It should be added that Coldstream Hills does not enter in wine shows at which James Halliday judges.

DIAMOND VALLEY VINEYARDS

Location: Kinglake Road, St Andrews, 3761. (03) 710 1484.

Winemaker: Dr David Lance.

1989 Production: 4500 cases.

Principal Wines: Estate-grown Rhine Riesling, Pinot Noir and Cabernets (a blend of cabernet sauvignon, merlot, cabernet franc and malbec). A range of Blue Label wines has also been developed, produced from fruit grown in neighbouring vineyards.

Distribution: Principally by mailing list and through restaurant and fine wine retail sales in most states. Retail distribution through Yarra Valley Wine Consultants, Vic.; Haviland Wine Co., NSW; Barrique Fine Wine Agency, Qld; Cuvee Pty Ltd, WA, and Tim Seats Pty Ltd., NT. Mailing list and other enquiries as above.

Prices: $10 to $20 mailing list.

Outstanding Prior Vintages: '81, '82.

Tasting Notes:

1988 CHARDONNAY [57] Colour: medium yellow-straw. *Bouquet:* a range of somewhat strange, somewhat volatile aromas, a touch of camphor and then green oak. *Palate:* poor, green oak dominates the wine, and there is again some evidence of the volatility at work in the bouquet; it may well be that this was not a representative bottle. Drink '90.

1988 PINOT NOIR [82] Colour: red-purple of medium depth. *Bouquet:* very clean and fragrant; of light intensity only, with sappy/tobacco aromas. *Palate:* once again, shows very clear varietal definition, and reminds me greatly of some Oregon pinot noirs; good balance, structure and length; does not have the final richness nor the wonderful oak of the magnificent '87 from Diamond Valley. Drink '90-'91.

1988 CABERNETS [71] Colour: medium red, with just a touch of purple. *Bouquet:* complex, light leafy/minty/squashy berry aromas, Coonawarra-like. *Palate:* clean, light leafy/minty berry flavours, again strongly reminiscent of Coonawarra; needs greater weight and structure for top points. Drink '90-'93.

Summary: Diamond Valley is one of Australia's foremost producers of pinot noir, making magnificent wines in 1986 and 1987. All of its other wines are complex, elegant and relatively light bodied, and do not always show up in large masked tastings, particularly when pitted against brawnier wines from other regions. Now that Diamond Valley has its own winery, the future must hold out even more promise.

❦ *DOMAINE CHANDON*

Location: "Green Point", Maroondah Highway, Coldstream, 3770; 19 km north-east of Lilydale. (03) 739 1110.

Winemakers: Dr Tony Jordan with Wayne Donaldson (with input from Moet et Chandon through Edmond Maudiere and Richard Geoffroy).

1989 Production: 15,000 cases.

Principal Wines: Méthode champenoise wines only produced; the first release in May 1989 (cuvee 86.1) was a Blanc de Blanc (100% chardonnay). The second release (cuvee 87.1) late in 1989 was a blend of chardonnay and pinot noir. The principal release each year will be a blend of pinot noir, chardonnay and pinot meunier. A significant part of the cuvee will come from the Yarra Valley grapes, particularly from Domaine Chandon's own extensive vineyards. Each cuvee will also incorporate contract grown fruit from many parts of south-eastern Australia and Tasmania.

Distribution: Australia, nationally through Swift and Moore Pty Ltd. New Zealand, through Hancocks Fine Wine & Spirit Merchants. Cellar door sales and tastings from mid-1990.

Prices: $21.

Tasting Notes.

DOMAINE CHANDON NV CUVEE 86.1 [90] Colour: outstanding fine bead; the hue light to medium yellow-green. *Bouquet:* complex, bready/creamy/yeast autolysis aromas with remarkable complexity. *Palate:* very complex, rich and textured, belying its 100% chardonnay base and suggesting the inclusion of some pinot noir or pinot meunier; if there is to be criticism, it may be that it is ever so slightly short on the finish. Drink '90.

DOMAINE CHANDON NV CUVEE 87.1 [92] Colour: light to medium yellow-straw, again with very good bead (good mousse). *Bouquet:* very fine and fragrant, with classically reserved fruit aromas, and again significant yeast autolysis effect. *Palate:* superb style and structure, has intensity without heaviness; the pinot noir component is not assertive, but provides backbone and a very long finish. Drink '90–'93.

Summary: I took great care to assess the Domaine Chandon wines in masked tastings so as not be prejudiced by the influence of the label. I for one have no doubt that they are equal to the very best Australian sparkling wines so far produced. In the interest of full disclosure, I should indicate that I am a director of Domaine Chandon, but in a strictly non-executive capacity, playing no part in winemaking.

❦ *FERGUSSON'S*

Location: Wills Road, Yarra Glen, 3775; 4 km north of Yarra Glen. (059) 65 2237.

Winemaker: Kerrie Haydon.

1989 Production: Almost totally destroyed by fire.

Principal Wines: Chenin Blanc, Rhine Riesling, Chardonnay, Shiraz, Cabernet Sauvignon and Cabernet Franc Merlot.

Distribution: Cellar door sales, mailing list and national retail distribution through Victorian Wine Consultants, Melbourne. Cellar door sales 10 a.m. to 5 p.m. Monday to Saturda and, noon to 5 p.m. Sunday. Mailing list enquiries as above.

Prices: $11.75 to $19.50 cellar door.

Outstanding Prior Vintages: '82 (Cabernet Sauvignon), '83 (Shiraz), '86 (Cabernet Sauvignon), '87 (Shiraz) and '88 (Chardonnay).

Tasting Notes:

1988 RHINE RIESLING [73] Colour: light straw-green. *Bouquet:* very fragrant, clean, soft tropical peach/passionfruit aromas. *Palate:* soft, clean and of light to medium fruit weight; fairly sweet and aimed squarely at the cellar door. Drink '90.

1986 SHIRAZ [74] Colour: light red-purple. *Bouquet:* soft, gently sweet, with a touch of chocolate, but no spice. *Palate:* clean, light and soft; a basically featureless wine without any real fault, but no highlights either; low tannin. Drink '90–'91.

Summary: The Fergusson winery/restaurant complex was largely destroyed by fire shortly after the 1989 vintage. A tiny quantity of Chardonnay and Cabernet Sauvignon was salvaged, and some packaged goods were likewise saved. By the time of publication a rebuilt complex should be open, again providing what has always been one of the most popular tourist locations in the Yarra Valley.

 *HALCYON DAZE VINEYARD*

Location: Uplands Road, Chirnside Park, 3116; 5 km north-west of Lilydale. (03) 726 7111.

Winemaker: Richard Rackley.

1989 Production: 750 cases.

Principal Wines: Rhine Riesling, Chardonnay, Cabernet Sauvignon, Cabernet Franc, Merlot blend.

Distribution: Principally by mailing list, enquiries to PO Box 310, Lilydale, 3140. Cellar door sales by appointment. Limited restaurant and fine wine retail distribution.

Prices: $12 to $18 cellar door.

Vintage Rating 1986–89: White: '86, '87, '88 ('89 not rated). Red: '86, '87, '88 ('89 not rated).

Tasting Notes:

1988 KNOX CHARDONNAY [62] Colour: very good green-yellow. *Bouquet:* strong, mead-like honeycomb aromas; non-vinous. *Palate:* similar pronounced honeycomb/mead flavours; presumably

a by-product of oxidation, or possibly partly from oak. I cannot recollect encountering anything quite like it before. Drink '90.

1987 BC RIESLING [65] Colour: bright green-yellow. *Bouquet:* soft, honeyed and sweet, although the botrytis influence is not strong. *Palate:* sweet, rich and soft; against all of the odds, some of the honeycomb flavours of the chardonnay; soft acid and, as with the bouquet, the botrytis influence is not strong. Drink '90.

1987 CABERNET [62] Colour: medium red-purple. *Bouquet:* light, leafy red berry fruit with a distinct gravelly mercaptan edge. *Palate:* pleasant fruit with a slightly bitter, mercaptan-derived finish; good material that has not been finished well. A blend of cabernet sauvignon, merlot and cabernet franc. Drink '90–'91.

Summary: Richard Rackley is still going through a learning curve at Halcyon Daze; he is certainly ambitious, producing difficult-to-make white wine styles in a very small winery context.

 *KELLYBROOK*

Location: Fulford Road, Wonga Park, 3115; approximately 10 km north-west of Lilydale. (03) 722 1304.

Winemaker: Darren Kelly.

1989 Production: 1200 cases.

Principal Wines: Kellybrook produces both table wines and various forms of cider, the latter produced using classic fermentation and maturation techniques and employing specially grown cider apples. Table wines include Chardonnay, Traminer, Rhine Riesling, Pinot Noir, Brut *Méthode champenoise*, Late Picked Rhine Riesling, Shiraz, Cabernet Sauvignon and Vintage Port. Ciders include Vintage Champagne Cider Brut, Farmhouse Cider, Old Gold (Vintage), Liqueur Cider and Potstill Apple Brandy (Calvados).

Distribution: Cellar door sales and mailing list; limited retail trade and restaurant distribution. Cellar door sales 9 a.m. to 6 p.m. Monday to Saturday and Sunday 11 a.m. to 6 p.m. Mailing list enquiries as above.

Prices: $8 to $19 cellar door; Calvados $30.

Vintage Rating 1986–89: White: '89, '88, '87, '86. Red: '88, '89, '87, '86. Cider: '89, '86, '88, '87.

Tasting Notes:

1988 CHAMPAGNE CIDER [69] Colour: medium to full yellow. *Bouquet:* strong, complex high-toned/aromatic apple spice characters. *Palate:* spicy/cinnamon apple flavours, totally distinctive; the wine does have a somewhat hard finish, however. Drink '90.

1988 SHIRAZ [76] Colour: bright purple-red of medium depth. *Bouquet:* clean and fresh, with strong mint, a hint of leather spice and minimal oak. *Palate:* a crisp, minty wine with a pleasant touch of spice; clean and well made, in distinct cool-climate style; light oak influence. Drink '91–'94.

1988 CABERNET SAUVIGNON [90] Colour: medium to full purple-red. *Bouquet:* spotlessly clean, fine, elegant classic berry cabernet aromas of medium intensity, with very good oak integration. *Palate:* classic Bordeaux-like cabernet sauvignon; smooth, clean perfectly ripened berry fruit and soft, persistent tannins on a very long finish. Drink '93–'98.

Summary: The dry table wines of Kellybrook are simply not of commercial quality. The cider based wines, by contrast, are invariably good, while Darren Kelly has produced some outstanding red wines from the 1988 vintage.

 *LILLYDALE VINEYARDS*

Location: Davross Court, Seville, 3139. (03) 642 016.

Winemakers: Alex White and Martin Grinbergs.

1989 Production: 8500 cases.

Principal Wines: Rhine Riesling, Gewurztraminer, Chardonnay, Yarra Dry White, Sauvignon Blanc, Pinot Noir and Cabernet Sauvignon.

Distribution: In Melbourne available in restaurants and fine wine retailers. Distributed in Sydney by Fesq & Co., in Queensland by Tallerman & Co., and in South Australia by Porter & Co. Mailing list enquiries to PO Box 313, Lilydale, 3140. Cellar door sales 10 a.m. to 5 p.m. 7 days.

Prices: $9 to $18.75 retail.

Vintage Rating 1986–89: White: '86, '88, '89, '87. Red: '89, '86, '88, '87.

Outstanding Prior Vintages: '83, '84.

Tasting Notes:

1988 CHARDONNAY [60] Colour: straw-yellow. *Bouquet:* very light and rather thin, with a hint of plasticine, the origin of which I cannot guess. *Palate:* faintly herbaceous, rather light and thin fruit and oak flavours, again with a touch of plasticine. Obviously enough, very disappointing for a fine vineyard. Drink '90.

1986 GEWURZTRAMINER [86] Colour: light green-yellow. *Bouquet:* potent, clean, intense spicy/lychee varietal character, yet not heavy. *Palate:* has lovely light, clearly defined and extraordinarily fresh varietal character; made bone dry and it is not phenolic; tasted entirely blind with no idea of its vintage, and all the more remarkable for a three-year-old. Fully deserved its trophy and gold medal at the 1989 Melbourne Wine Show. Drink '90–'92.

1986 CABERNET SAUVIGNON [65] Colour: youthful light purple-red. *Bouquet:* light berry fruit with odd light biscuity/glue paste aromas. *Palate:* pleasant, sweet berry fruit flavours spoilt by the same glue paste characters as appear in the bouquet; this was a lovely wine when it was young, and I cannot for the life of me work out what has happened to it over the past two years. Drink '90–'91.

Summary: Lillydale Vineyards is now in its own winery, commissioned immediately prior to (or rather during) the 1988 vintage. The low rating of two of the wines reviewed is a major concern, but it is how they came up in the tasting and, as much as one would like to, one cannot play favourites or alter points after the event. Clearly, they do not do justice to the deservedly higher reputation that Lillydale Vineyards has.

🍇 _LIRRALIRRA ESTATE_

Location: Paynes Road, Lilydale, 3140.
Melway Map 172 E10.
(03) 735 0224.

Winemaker: Allan Smith.

1989 Production: Very small, several hundred cases only.

Principal Wines: Semillon, Semillon Sauvignon Blanc and Cabernet Sauvignon (the latter "swapped" with Yarra Burn).

Distribution: By mailing list; address as above. Cellar door sales and tastings by appointment only. Very limited retail and restaurant distribution, chiefly local.

Tasting Notes:

1986 SEMILLON [65] Colour: medium yellow-green. _Bouquet:_ of light to medium intensity and smooth; yet to develop any real character, but this may come with time. _Palate:_ fair fruit weight, marred somewhat by hard phenolics, which may soften with age but which presently lead to a somewhat rough and not totally clean aftertaste. Drink '90–'92.

1988 CABERNET SAUVIGNON [69] Colour: medium to full purple-red. _Bouquet:_ complex Coonawarra pie and peas fruit evidencing grapes picked in a wide spectrum of ripeness. _Palate:_ pronounced minty/leafy pie and peas flavours, again reminiscent of Coonawarra; quite good concentration. Drink '91–'94.

Summary: The 4-hectare vineyard of Lirralirra, planted in 1981, is still to realise its full potential and the original aims of Allan and Jocelyn Smith–to produce a true sauterne-style botrytised white.

🍇 _LONG GULLY_

Location: Long Gully Road, Healesville, 3777; 2 km north-west of town.
(059) 62 3663; Fax (03) 807 2213.

Winemaker: Peter Florence.

1989 Production: Approximately 4800 cases.

Principal Wines: Sauvignon Blanc, Rhine Riesling, Chardonnay, Semillon, Pinot Noir, Cabernet Sauvignon, Merlot, Malbec and Cabernet Franc.

Distribution: Extensive retail distribution through A. H. Distributors, NSW; National Wine Broker all other states. UK imports through Haughtons Fine Wines. Cellar door sales noon to 5 p.m. weekends and public holidays; other times by appointment. Enquiries and mailing list enquiries to head office, PO Box 1073, Windsor, 3181, telephone (03) 807 4246.

Prices: $10 to $15 cellar door.

Vintage Rating 1986–89: White: '86, '87, '89, '88.
Red: '86, '87, '89, '88.

Tasting Notes:

1989 RHINE RIESLING [64] Colour: medium yellow-green. _Bouquet:_ rather stalky and hard fruit with a camphor overtone. _Palate:_ some oily/spicy flavours of the kind one encountered from time to time in the Yarra Valley with this variety; some phenolic bitterness on the finish does not help. In some ways, European in style, and may be more appreciated there. Drink '90–'91.

1989 SEMILLON [68] Colour: very light straw-green. _Bouquet:_ clean, with highly accentuated herbal/grassy aromas reminiscent of New Zealand or the Margaret River. _Palate:_ of light to medium weight, with flavours identical to those of the bouquet; a very creditable effort for what was an appalling vintage for this variety, and those extreme characters do appeal to some consumers. Drink '90–'92.

1988 SAUVIGNON BLANC [67] Colour: light green-yellow. _Bouquet:_ light tobacco/herbal/

grassy aromas, with a touch of PK mint into the bargain. *Palate:* as with the semillon, a carbon copy of the bouquet; herbal/grassy/PK mint characters all present. Drink '90–'91.

1988 CHARDONNAY [63] Colour: medium yellow-green. *Bouquet:* light, non-varietal herbal/grassy fruit aromas. *Palate:* definite unripe herbaceous/tobacco overtones; seems to have been picked too early or, alternatively, was over-cropped. Drink '90–'91.

1989 PINOT NOIR [CS] Colour: light to medium red-purple. *Bouquet:* light and clean, with varietal fruit present but subdued; the oak is somewhat dull. *Palate:* much better than the bouquet suggests, with very good varietal character showing in soft plummy flavours; has length; better oak could have made a great wine. Even with the indifferent oak, headed to the high 70's.

1988 CABERNET SAUVIGNON [90] Colour: impenetrable purple-red. *Bouquet:* extremely concentrated with dense, rich dark berry fruit aromas. *Palate:* an immense, chewy deep wine with strong American oak; juice run-off techniques could have been used. Whatever the technique, a quite excellent full-bodied cabernet. Drink '93–'98.

Summary: Long Gully has produced excellent Cabernet Sauvignon in both 1987 and 1988; the other wines show considerable variation but the potential is there, and the will to succeed likewise.

LOVEGROVE OF COTTLES BRIDGE

Location: Lot 21 Kinglake Road, Cottles Bridge, 3099.
(03) 718 1569.

Winemaker: Ian Leamon.

1989 Production: Approximately 1100 cases

Principal Wines: Chardonnay, Cabernets and Pinot Noir.

Distribution: Principally mailing list, address as above. Selected retail outlets and restaurants.

Prices: $18 to $20.

Tasting Notes:

1988 CHARDONNAY [79] Colour: medium yellow-green. *Bouquet:* some hessiany overlay to quite rich, peachy fruit. *Palate:* very full, sweet, peachy fruit with pronounced hessiany/biscuity oak still to soften and fully integrate; has plenty of flavour and good potential. Drink '90–'91.

1987 CABERNET MERLOT [77] Colour: medium red-purple. *Bouquet:* clean; pronounced minty edge to some sweet fruit; oak in restraint. *Palate:* clean; of light to medium intensity; again, pronounced minty flavours with minimal oak; a fraction one dimensional. Drink '91–'94.

Summary: Lovegrove of Cottles Bridge makes an auspicious debut; consultancy advice, coupled with the experience of winemaker Ian Leamon, should pay dividends for owner Malcolm Lovegrove.

MADDENS LANE WINERY

Location: Maddens Lane, Gruyere, 3139; 15 km north-east of Lilydale. (059) 64 9279.

Winemaker: Yarra Burn (contract).

Principal Wines: Semillon, Chardonnay and Pinot Noir.

Distribution: Almost exclusively mailing list; mailing list enquiries as above. Local restaurant distribution.

Summary: Maddens Lane winery has only very recently been established by the Norris Family, and no wines were available for tasting at the time of writing.

🍇 _MONBULK WINERY_

Location: Macclesfield Road, Monbulk;
   5 km south of Seville.
   (03) 756 6965.

Winemakers: The Jabornik family.

Principal Wines: Kiwi fruit wines are the principal
   product, but increasing quantities of Rhine
   Riesling, Chardonnay, Shiraz, Pinot Noir and
   Cabernet Franc will be made as the vines come
   into production.

Distribution: Almost exclusively cellar door and
   mailing list; mailing list enquiries as above.
   Cellar door sales noon to 6 p.m. weekends and
   public holidays; otherwise by appointment.

Prices: $6.60 to $11.

Summary: The Kiwi fruit wines produced at
   Monbulk are absolutely delicious, and already
   have a strong following.

🍇 _MOUNT MARY_

Location: Coldstream West Road, Lilydale, 3140;
   3 km west of Coldstream.
   (03) 739 1761.

Winemaker: Dr John Middleton.

1989 Production: Dr Middleton has a policy of not
   disclosing production; while limited, new
   plantings should see an increase.

Principal Wines: Two dry whites and two dry reds,
   with a blended wine and a varietal wine in each
   group. White wines are Chardonnay, and a
   sauvignon blanc, semillon, muscadelle blend;
   red wines Pinot Noir, and a cabernet sauvignon
   (50%), cabernet franc (20%), merlot (25%),
   malbec (3%) and petit verdot (2%) blend.
   These percentages are for vines in the vineyard
   and not necessarily for the wine in the bottle.

Distribution: Exclusively mailing list; very small
   quantities find their way into the retail trade
   and into restaurants. No cellar door sales.

Prices: $21 to $24 mailing list.

Vintage Rating 1989–89: Ratings vary in each year
   from wine to wine.

Outstanding Prior Vintages: Again, ratings vary.

Tasting Notes:

1987 PINOT NOIR **[72]** _Colour:_ medium red, with
   some gas still evident from recent bottling.
   Bouquet: light and faintly minty, with just a trace
   of strawberry. _Palate:_ lacks focus with slightly
   boiled/sweet flavours; new oak is conspicuous by
   its absence; for all this, it was tasted shortly after
   bottling, and I have seen previous vintages of
   Mount Mary Pinot improve out of all sight once
   they are settled down. Drink '91–'94.

1987 CABERNETS **[78]** _Colour:_ light to medium
   red-purple, not particularly intense. _Bouquet:_
   some herbaceous notes and a hint of cigar box;
   red berry fruits lurk quietly underneath.
   Palate: light, very elegant Bordeaux style; not
   particularly intense, but once again may well
   build intensity in bottle, and once again, I may
   be doing the wine an injustice as it was tasted
   very shortly after bottling. Drink '93–'98.

Summary: 1987 was not a year noted for its intensity
   or fruit weight. Perhaps the somewhat
   disappointing performance of the wines is a
   reflection of the year of their recent
   remodelling. I must say, however, that I simply
   could not accept the very disappointing 1988
   white wines, which seem to have been
   demolished during bottling.

🍇 _OAKRIDGE ESTATE_

Location: Aitken Road, Seville, 3139; off Wandin
   Creek Road, 3 km from Seville.
   (059) 64 3379.

Winemaker: Michael Zitzlaff.

1989 Production: 2000 cases.

Principal Wines: Specialising in Cabernet

Sauvignon (a Bordeaux blend).

Distribution: Retail distribution through Wayne Leicht Wines, Vic., Oddbins, NSW and Classic Wine Merchants, SA. UK imports through Fine Wines Express. Also extensive mailing list; enquiries to PO Box 13, Seville, 3139. Cellar door sales 10 a.m. to 5 p.m. weekends and public holidays only.

Prices: $20 to $25 cellar door.

Tasting Notes:

1987 CABERNET SAUVIGNON [74] Colour: light red-purple. *Bouquet:* very light, leafy/spicy/ slightly meaty aromas, lacking either the style or fruit intensity and depth of all of the prior releases. *Palate:* very light leafy/tobacco style with high acid; very much the product of a light vintage. Drink '91–'94.

Summary: After a seemingly endless string of magnificently rich, complex and generously proportioned wines, the '87 comes as a disappointment, but perhaps also partially reflecting a medium red wine year. On all reports, Oakridge bounced back to its best form in 1988.

 OLD GIPPSLAND ESTATE

Location: Old Gippsland Road, Seville, 3139; 9 km north of Seville.
(03) 735 1729.

Winemaker: Garry Evans.

Principal Wines: A wide variety of grapes planted included sauvignon blanc, sylvaner, chardonnay pinot noir, merlot and cabernet sauvignon.

Distribution: No licence yet held; will be offered cellar door and by mailing list.

ST HUBERTS

Location: Cnr St Huberts Road and Maroondah Highway, Coldstream, 3770; 6 km north-east of Coldstream.
(03) 739 1421; Fax (03) 739 1015.

Winemaker: Brian Fletcher.

1989 Production: 250 tonnes.

Principal Wines: Rhine Riesling, Chardonnay, Shiraz, Pinot Noir and Cabernet Sauvignon. Second label is Andrew Rowan (see separate entry).

Distribution: National retail distribution through I. H. Baker Wines & Spirits, NSW, Vic., Qld and WA; Seabrook & Seabrook, SA; and Rutherglen Wine Co., Tas. Cellar door and mailing list sales. Cellar door sales 9 a.m. to 5 p.m. Monday to Friday, 10.30 a.m. to 5.30 p.m. weekends, 10 a.m. to 5.30 p.m. public holidays. Mailing list enquiries as above.

Prices: $9.20 to $19.90 cellar door.

Vintage Rating 1986–89: '88, '86, '87, '89.

Tasting Notes:

1988 ST HUBERTS RESERVE CHARDONNAY [90] Colour: light to medium green-yellow. *Bouquet:* complex, stylish spicy oak and wonderfully clean, rich fruit. *Palate:* a high quality wine in every respect; fragrant; spicy oak never threatens to overwhelm lovely, fine grapefruit/melon/fig fruit; complex, and with a long finish. Drink '90–'93.

1987 SHIRAZ [87] Colour: light to medium purple-red, holding its hue well. *Bouquet:* clean and fresh sweet cherry; no spice, but equally, no vegetal characters. *Palate:* clean red berry/ cherry fruit flavours of light to medium weight, with a faint echo of spice on the finish; a lovely fresh wine to be enjoyed while the fruit is there. Drink '90–'92.

Summary: Brian Fletcher, the very experienced St

Huberts winemaker, has been working hard both in the vineyard and winery to ensure the full potential of St Huberts is realised. As the tasting notes indicate, his efforts are bearing fruit.

SEVILLE ESTATE

Location: Linwood Road, Seville, 3139. (059) 64 4556.

Winemaker: Dr Peter McMahon.

1989 Production: 1735 cases.

Principal Wines: Chardonnay, Riesling and Beerenauslese, Shiraz, Pinot Noir and Cabernet Sauvignon. UK imports through Fine Wine Review, Blackheath, London. Occasional Rhine Riesling Trockenbeerenauslese also made when vintage conditions permit.

Distribution: Largely by mailing list; limited fine wine retail distribution in capital cities and selected restaurants. No cellar door sales. Mailing list enquiries to Linwood Road, Seville, 3139.

Prices: $10.50 to $20 mailing list.

Tasting Notes:

1989 RHINE RIESLING [83] Colour: very light straw-green. *Bouquet:* light, with strong herbaceous overtones, almost sauvignon blanc-like. *Palate:* crisp and youthful, with passionfruit overlain by some herbaceous characters; lingering acid on a long, clean finish. Drink '90-'93.

1988 CHARDONNAY [75] Colour: light straw-yellow. *Bouquet:* tending to neutrality, and rather closed, but without fault. *Palate:* clean, smooth peach/melon fruit of light to medium weight; a restrained, if not austere, style which should age gracefully if not spectacularly. Drink '90-'92.

1987 RIESLING BEERENAUSLESE [90] Colour: glowing yellow-green. *Bouquet:* intense, extremely complex honeyed/lime botrytis aromas. *Palate:* a very complex and stylish botrytised style, with flavours of lime/pineapple and an extremely luscious mid-palate, followed by a classically cleansing acid finish. Beautifully made and beautifully balanced. Drink '90-'96.

1987 PINOT NOIR [59] Colour: light to medium red, with just a touch of purple. *Bouquet:* very light, and rather dull, with minimal fruit and minimal varietal character. *Palate:* dull, thin and leathery, lacking fruit. Drink '90.

1987 CABERNET SAUVIGNON [63] Colour: medium red-purple. *Bouquet:* slightly soapy/shaded fruit characters with lemony/spicy oak. *Palate:* a melange of lemony, slightly spicy, leafy flavours, all suggesting shaded fruit; funnily enough, the wine has its attraction in a non-classic fashion. Drink '90-'92.

1986 SHIRAZ [80] Colour: clear, light purple-red. *Bouquet:* clean, spicy/leafy aromas of light to medium intensity, and little oak influence. *Palate:* clean, fresh spicy/berry flavours; oak makes a more positive statement than it does on the bouquet; all in all, a very attractive modern style of shiraz. Drink '90-'94.

Summary: I found the 1987 reds from Seville Estate disappointing, but all of the other releases to be of the usual very high quality, with the Rhine Riesling Beerenauslese absolutely outstanding. Seville Estate remains not only one of the oldest, but one of the best Yarra Valley wineries.

SHANTELL VINEYARD

Location: Off Melba Highway at 60 km sign post, Dixons Creek, 3775. (059) 65 2264 or (03) 819 4563 b/h.

Winemakers: Shan and Turid Shanmugam, Kathleen Quealy (Consultant).

1989 Production: 1400 cases.

Principal Wines: Chardonnay, Semillon, Pinot Noir and Cabernet Sauvignon.

Distribution: Cellar door sales weekends and public holidays 10 a.m. to 5 p.m. Mailing list enquiries welcome; address above.

Prices: $10 to $18.

Tasting Notes:

1989 CHARDONNAY [CS] *Colour:* excellent light green-yellow. *Bouquet:* high-class aromatic spicy barrel-ferment oak characters together with strong citric/melon grapefruit. *Palate:* superbly rich and weighty wine full of mouthfilling melon/grapefruit flavour; beautiful oak handling; outstanding with a long finish. If this barrel sample is even remotely representative of the wine in the bottle, will easily score 90 points.

1988 CHARDONNAY [75] *Colour:* medium yellow-green. *Bouquet:* strong, complex fruit showing good depth and varietal character; slightly hessiany oak. *Palate:* plenty of flavour, again showing slightly malty/hessiany oak in a style that I know others accept, but which I always find somewhat distracting. A more than useful wine, nonetheless. Drink '90–'92.

1988 PINOT NOIR [70] *Colour:* good red-purple. *Bouquet:* carbonic maceration characters dominate varietal character, giving slightly cooked/jammy aromas. *Palate:* once again, the carbonic maceration characters overwhelm varietal fruit and structure; others obviously accept this style far more readily than I do, as the wine has won a gold and a silver medal. Experience suggests that with time the maceration influence will decrease and the varietal character may have a better chance of expressing itself. Drink '90–'93.

1988 CABERNET SAUVIGNON [85] *Colour:* strong purple-red. *Bouquet:* clean, firm and discrete fruit with underlying power and very good oak handling. *Palate:* strong, textured vanillan oak flavours with full, youthful berry fruit flavours. A lovely young cabernet at the start of its life. Drink '93–'98.

Summary: Shantell has made what might, without exaggeration, be described as a dream debut. The most startling wine is the '89 Chardonnay, which, given the vintage, is astonishingly good.

❦ *TARRAWARRA*

Location: Healesville Road, Yarra Glen, 3775; 9 km east of Yarra Glen.
(059) 62 3311; Fax (059) 62 3887.

Winemaker: David Wollan.

1989 Production: Not for publication.

Principal Wines: Initial releases Chardonnay only. First Pinot–1988 vintage.

Distribution: National wholesale through Tucker/Seabrook/Caon. No cellar door sales. Mailing list enquiries to above address. UK imports through Cellarworld Ltd, London.

Prices: $25 to $27 retail.

Vintage Rating 1986–89: Chardonnay: '87, '88, '89, '86. Pinot Noir: '89, '88 (first vintage).

Tasting Notes:

1988 PINOT NOIR [CS] *Colour:* medium red-purple. *Bouquet:* clean strawberry fruit showing nice varietal character, but lacking structural complexity. *Palate:* clean, light strawberry fruit, with crisp, slightly raw oak; again, a fraction one dimensional.

1988 CHARDONNAY [79] *Colour:* distinct onion-skin hue. *Bouquet:* very attractive spicy oak, and rather more fruit than the very disappointing colour would promise. *Palate:* again, much better than the oxidation indicated by the colour (and which presumably occurred at bottling) would suggest; smooth, honeyed gently peachy fruit with some well-balanced spicy oak. An exceedingly difficult wine to point; in terms of making and handling it is much the best of the Tarrawarra wine made to date but, equally, was hit at bottling. By the time of its release in 1990 it may have improved out of all recognition. Drink '91–'94.

Summary: David Wollan is a highly intelligent winemaker and would be the first to agree that the Tarrawarra style will progressively evolve as information is gained from each succeeding vintage and as the vineyard gains maturity. The evolution of that style may well go down its own particular path, but one can say with confidence that if you buy a bottle of Tarrawarra, it will not be just another chardonnay.

TUNNEL HILL

Location: Tarrawarra Winery, Healesville Road, Yarra Glen, 3775; 9 km east of Yarra Glen. (059) 62 3311.

Winemaker: David Wollan.

1989 Production: Not for publication.

Principal Wines: Chardonnay and Pinot Noir.

Distribution: Limited trade distribution only through The Wine Company. Mailing list and other trade enquiries to address above.

Prices: $15 to $16.

Tasting Notes:

1988 CHARDONNAY **[78]** *Colour:* light green-yellow. *Bouquet:* clean, light to medium peachy/melon fruit with very smooth, beautifully balanced and integrated oak. *Palate:* fresh and vibrant peachy fruit of light to medium weight; there is a slight hole in the fore-palate, which should fill out with time. Drink '90–'92.

1988 PINOT NOIR **[73]** *Colour:* medium red-purple. *Bouquet:* clean with pleasant strawberry/plum fruit varietal character, but rather simple. *Palate:* light, clean simple strawberry fruit; a faint touch of plum; simply lacks structural complexity, but at least some of this may come with time in bottle. Drink '90–'92.

Summary: Whether it is the intention or not, Tunnel Hill will inevitably be seen as the second label of Tarrawarra, despite the fact that it is separately distributed and despite the fact that Tarrawarra has gone and will continue to go to some lengths to sharply distinguish the two brands. The Tarrawarra and Tunnel Hill wines were tasted in the same large masked tasting and, however indirectly, were compared with each other by that process. All one can say is that the price differential between the two ranges is very substantial, while the quality differential is somewhat less.

WANTIRNA ESTATE

Location: Bushy Park Lane, Wantirna South, 3152; 25 km due east of Melbourne. (03) 801 2367.

Winemaker: Reg Egan, assistant Maryann Egan.

1989 Production: 950 cases.

Principal Wines: Chardonnay, Pinot Noir and Cabernet Merlot.

Distribution: Principally mailing list; enquiries to PO Box 231, Glen Waverley, 3150. No cellar door sales. Limited fine wine retail distribution through selected wine merchants and restaurants.

Prices: From $19 to $24 recommended retail; less on mailing list.

Vintage Rating 1986–89: White: '88, '89, '87, '86. Red: '87, '88, '89, '86.

Outstanding Prior Vintages: '69, '70, '74, '77, '78, '82 ('81 Pinot), '84.

Tasting Notes:

1988 CHARDONNAY **[70]** *Colour:* light straw-green. *Bouquet:* an edge of volatility seems to thin out the fruit character and aroma. *Palate:* a very austere entry to the mouth with rather herbaceous fruit, but then progressively expands, with a nice touch of oak and a surprisingly long and elegant finish. Drink '90–'92.

1986 PINOT NOIR **[65]** *Colour:* light red. *Bouquet:* rather old dusty/varnishy oak sits on top of lighter fruit. *Palate:* aged, bottle-developed sappy/tobacco flavours like a fine old burgundy that has passed its best; should have been released (and drunk) two years ago. Drink '90.

Summary: Wantirna has always given its wine substantial bottle age prior to release. Usually this works, particularly with the cabernet family blends (not available for tasting for this edition), but I have grave reservations about holding back pinot noir for so long. I also have the uneasy feeling that overall Wantirna's wines are remaining static in an environment that grows more competitive as each day passes.

WARRAMATE

WARRAMATE
Rhine Riesling
1988

This wine is made from Rhine Riesling grapes grown on the lower slopes of the Warramate Hills overlooking the Yarra Valley of Victoria.

Bottled by the Makers:
J. R. & J. M. CHURCH,
GRUYERE, VICTORIA.
Produce of Australia   12.0% ALC./VOL.   750 mls.
PRESERVATIVE (220) ADDED.

Location: 4 Maddens Lane, Gruyere, 3770; 11 km north-east of Lilydale.
(059) 64 9219.

Winemaker: Jack Church.

Principal Wines: Rhine Riesling, Shiraz and Cabernet Sauvignon.

Distribution: Principally cellar door sales and mailing list; limited fine wine retail distribution. Cellar door sales 9 a.m. to 6 p.m. Saturday, 10 a.m. to 6 p.m. Sunday. Weekdays by appointment. Mailing list enquiries as above.

Prices: $10.50 to $15.50.

Vintage Rating 1986–89: White: '88, '89, '87, '86. Red: '88, '86, '89, '87.

Tasting Notes:

1989 RHINE RIESLING [65] Colour: light medium yellow-green. *Bouquet:* highly aromatic and floral, and although the fruit intensity is lacking, some citric aromas. *Palate:* rather common and plain, lacking fruit richness, and in a style that is frequently encountered in the Yarra Valley. If one accepts Clare Valley or Eden Valley as providing role models, then Yarra Valley fails with the variety. Drink '90–'92.

1988 SHIRAZ [87] Colour: very good purple-red. *Bouquet:* solid, full fruit with a nice touch of spice. *Palate:* rich, red berry fruit with some spicy undertones; a wine with great structure, and a gently powerful, long-lasting finish, with perfect acid balance. Drink '93 - '98.

1988 CABERNET SAUVIGNON [78] Colour: dense red-purple. *Bouquet:* solid, dense berry fruit with slight gamey overtones. *Palate:* rich, ripe

and chewy berry/gamey flavours, with strong vanillan oak. Drink '93–'99.

Summary: Warramate has a superb vineyard site with a fully mature vineyard established way back in 1969. Fruit quality has never been in doubt, and some glorious reds were made in 1988.

YARRA BURN

Yarra Burn
Sauvignon Blanc/Semillon
1989
Produce of YARRA VALLEY, Australia.
Made by D. & C. Fyffe, Settlement Road, Yarra Junction 3797
11.3% ALC/VOL   Preservative 220 added   750 ml

Location: Settlement Road, Yarra Junction, 3797; 2 km Warburton side of Yarra Junction.
(059) 67 1428.

Winemaker: David Fyffe.

1989 Production: 7000 cases.

Principal Wines: Pinot Noir, Chardonnay, Sauvignon Blanc/Semillon, Cabernet Sauvignon, Pinot Noir *Méthode champenoise* and Light Shiraz.

Distribution: Fine wine retail distribution through Haviland Wine Co., NSW; Vance Palmer, Qld; Wayne Leicht Wines, Vic.; Lionel Sampson & Son, WA; Chace Agencies, SA. UK imports through I.F.P Pty Ltd, Melbourne. Also substantial cellar door and mailing list sales; cellar door sales 10 a.m. to 5 p.m. Monday to Saturday, noon to 5 p.m. Sunday. Mailing list enquiries as above.

Prices: $12 to $21 cellar door.

Tasting Notes:

1989 SAUVIGNON BLANC SEMILLON [67] Colour: light yellow-green. *Bouquet:* ultra-herbal/tobacco/grassy aromas, lacking fruit richness. *Palate:* a carbon copy of the bouquet; very crisp and very dry, but inevitably lacking mouthfeel and fruit richness. Drink '90–'91.

1988 CHARDONNAY [71] Colour: light green-yellow. *Bouquet:* fragrant, but with unusual peppermint/herbal overtones to the fruit. *Palate:* strong, cool climate peppermint flavours with a tangy finish, all strongly suggestive of imperfectly ripened fruit. Better oak might have helped lift the wine. Drink '90–'91.

1988 PINOT NOIR [65] Colour: blackish purple-red. *Bouquet:* very pronounced maceration aromas with a gamey/meaty edge. *Palate:* strong, high flavoured gamey/meaty characters with a touch of bitterness; made in a style that really is not attractive and which does not enhance the fruit. Drink '90.

1987 CABERNET SAUVIGNON [65] Colour: medium red, with a touch of purple. *Bouquet:* gamey meaty aromas, suggestive of carbonic maceration, but I wonder whether they are not sulphide-derived. *Palate:* quite complex, but once again with those strong gamey/meaty characters of the bouquet that I am afraid are simply mercaptans. Drink '90–92.

Summary: Yarra Burn has made many brilliant wines over the years; I hardly need say that I found the current releases disappointing, but I should sound a note of caution: others may have less difficulty with the style than I do, and wonder what on earth the fuss is all about. Yarra Burn itself remains one of the most attractive winery/restaurant complexes in the Yarra Valley, and a visit is surely recommended.

❦ *YARRA RIDGE*

Location: Glenview Road, Yarra Glen, 3755; 1.5 km north-east of town.
(03) 730 1613.

Winemakers: Louis Bialkower and Peter Steer.

1989 Production: 6000 cases.

Principal Wines: Chardonnay, Sauvignon Blanc, Pinot Noir and Cabernet Sauvignon.

Distribution: National retail through Dorado Wine Company. Also mailing list; enquiries to Yarra Ridge Vineyard, PO Box 275, Yarra Glen, 3775. No cellar door sales.

Prices: $15.25 to $18 retail.

Vintage Rating 1986–89: '89, '88, '86, '87.

Tasting Notes:

1989 SAUVIGNON BLANC [88] Colour: light green-yellow. *Bouquet:* very clean with pronounced herbal/tobacco aromas, and some goose-berry fruit as well; of light to medium intensity. *Palate:* similar, highly accented varietal herbal/gooseberry flavours; does have back-palate weight and plenty of style. Drink '90–'92.

1989 CHARDONNAY [CS] Colour: light green-yellow. *Bouquet:* exceptionally fragrant, with spicy/tangy clove oak. *Palate:* again, an enormous contribution from clove/spice American oak, almost Portuguese in the intensity of its extraction; there are lovely citric/grapefruit flavours in the fruit to back up the oak; the balance will have to be watched before the wine goes to bottle to prevent the oak from becoming too assertive. Trophy winner as Best 1989 Victorian White at the Royal Melbourne Show and certainly headed towards 90 points if that balance is preserved.

1988 CHARDONNAY [86] Colour: very good green-yellow. *Bouquet:* smooth and clean, with typical Yarra Valley melon/grapefruit aromas and beautifully integrated oak. *Palate:* harmonious, balanced and smooth peach/melon fruit with subtle oak; developing well in bottle and will live on. Drink '90–'93.

1988 BOTRYTIS SEMILLON [79] Colour: deep yellow. *Bouquet:* tropical butterscotch fruit with distinct volatility and relatively light oak. *Palate:* intensely sweet and rich apricot/tinned peach flavours, marginally cut back by volatility; almost too much of a good thing. It seems a pity that the non-Yarra Valley origin of the grapes is nowhere mentioned on front or back label. Drink '90–'92.

1989 PINOT NOIR [CS] Colour: excellent purple-red. *Bouquet:* clean, attractive plum/strawberry fruit with just a touch of mint; good oak handling and integration. *Palate:* excellent weight, richness and intensity; lovely strong plum flavours and good length; an absolutely outstanding wine for the year, and if it lives up to its potential, should rate 90.

1988 CABERNET SAUVIGNON [74] Colour: purple-red, ever so slightly dull. *Bouquet:* clean; of medium intensity, with slightly leafy/herbal overtones. *Palate:* clean, but one dimensional, with that classic doughnut hole in the back-palate; low tannins. May well improve with further time in bottle. Drink '92–'96.

Summary: I will be most surprised if, in the fullness of time, the 1989 wines from Yarra Ridge do not emerge as the best made in the Yarra Valley that year. It was on the strength of these wines that Yarra Ridge won the trophy as the Most Successful Exhibitor in the Victorian wine classes at the 1989 Royal Melbourne Show.

YARRA VALE

Location: Lot 7, Maroondah Highway, Coldstream, 3770.
(059) 62 5266.

Winemaker: Domenic Bucci.

1989 Production: 3600 cases (approximately).

Principal Wines: Chadonnay, Sauvignon Blanc, Pinot Noir and Cabernet Family Blend.

Distribution: Cellar door sales and mail order; cellar door sales 10 a.m. to 5 p.m. 7 days. Mailing list enquiries as above.

Prices: $12 to $16 (approximately).

Vintage Rating 1987–89: White: '88, '87, '89. Red: '88, '87, '89.

Tasting Notes:

1988 CHARDONNAY [55] Colour: light straw-green. *Bouquet:* inappropriate and rather poor oily/ coconut oak entirely dominates the fruit. *Palate:* a replica of the bouquet, with hard, oily coconut oak the only discernible flavour. Drink '90.

1988 PINOT NOIR [55] Colour: very light red. *Bouquet:* clean, but light to the point of non-existence. *Palate:* very light, faint strawberry/ cough medicine flavours. Drink '90.

1987 CABERNET [60] Colour: light to medium red-purple. *Bouquet:* light and fairly neutral fruit with a slight glue paste aroma. *Palate:* very light, faint red berry flavours with rather undistinguished old oak. Lacks intensity. Drink '90.

Summary: The Yarra Vale wines reviewed were made under contract from young vines; it now

has its own very well designed and equipped winery which came into operation in 1989, and the vines are of course gaining maturity. Whether the 1989 vintage gave any respite is doubtful. From 1990, however, we will no doubt see a radical change in the style and quality of the Yarra Vale wines.

YARRA YERING

Location: Briarty Road, Coldstream, 3770; off Maddens Lane, 15 km north-east of South Lilydale.
(059) 64 9267.

Winemaker: Dr Bailey Carrodus.

1989 Production: 3000 cases.

Principal Wines: Dry White No. 1 (semillon and sauvignon blanc), Chardonnay, Pinot Noir, Dry Red No. 1 (a blend of cabernet sauvignon, malbec and merlot) and Dry Red No. 2 (85% shiraz plus various other Rhone varieties). UK imports through Nicks Wine Merchants International.

Distribution: Cellar door sales and mailing list; retail through Nicks Wine Merchants, Melbourne and The Oak Barrel, Sydney; other national distribution through The Wine Broker. Cellar door sales 10 a.m. to 5 p.m. Saturday, noon to 5 p.m. Sunday and public holidays while stocks last.

Prices: $17 to $35 cellar door.

Tasting Notes:

1987 PINOT NOIR [83] Colour: medium red-purple. *Bouquet:* full, soft cherry/ plum fruit with very good varietal definition, and medium intensity. *Palate:* rich and full plummy fruit with good weight and ripeness; has looked better, and seems to be going through a slightly closed stage of its evolution when tasted. Drink '90–'93.

1987 PINOT NOIR NEW VINES [80] Colour: strong red-purple. *Bouquet:* concentrated and quite ripe plummy fruit, but varietal character is somewhat muted. *Palate:* a ripe wine with quite strong plum flavour yet somehow or other closed; the oak, too, is not quite in the harmony with the fruit. Once again, a wine that may improve with another 12 months. Drink '90–'91.

1987 DRY RED NO. 1 [90] Colour: medium full purple-red. *Bouquet:* rich, full and concentrated briary/berry aromas of great complexity. *Palate:* full, rich dark berry/soft plum flavours with soft tannins running throughout; a wine with unusual weight, balance and style. Drink '92–2000.

1987 DRY RED NO. 2. [92] Colour: very good purple-red. *Bouquet:* full, sweet red berry fruit with a lovely hint of spice; oak in restraint. *Palate:* fractionally more spice than is evident in the bouquet, yet it never overwhelms the sweet fruit; soft tannins to a superbly structured wine with exceptional flesh and mouthfeel. Drink '91–2000.

Summary: The 1987 reds of Yarra Yering make a triumphant return to form after Dr Bailey Carrodus appeared to miss a beat in 1986, when a touch of the old foe (volatility) allied with a few other strange characters took away from the richness and complexity that is the hallmark of Yarra Yering.

🍇 *YARRINYA ESTATE*

Location: Pinnacle Lane, Dixon's Creek, 3775; 8 km north of Yarra Glen. (059) 65 2271.

Winemakers: Stephen Webber/David Ellis.

Principal Wines: Riesling, Gewurztraminer, Chardonnay, Pinot Noir, Shiraz and Cabernet Sauvignon.

Distribution: Retail distribution through De Bortoli Wines' own distribution system; also cellar door sales and mailing list; cellar door sales 9 a.m. to 5 p.m. Monday to Friday, 10 a.m. to 5.30 p.m. Saturday and Sunday. Mailing list enquiries to De Bortoli Yarrinya Estate, address as above.

Prices: $14 to $28 retail.

Tasting Notes:

1989 CHARDONNAY [CS] Colour: light green-yellow. *Bouquet:* clean, gentle fig/grapefruit with well-integrated light oak; of light to medium intensity. *Palate:* a very smooth, beautifully made and understated wine with exceptional oak balance and integration; fig/melon/peach fruit flavours of very elegant style. Seems certain to rate in the high 80's.

1987 CHARDONNAY [89] Colour: medium yellow-green. *Bouquet:* strong, rich and forceful complex fruit and oak, with very slightly bitter cabbage burgundian characters. *Palate:* rich, complex and full bodied with obvious barrel-ferment character; excellent structural complexity and weight; a little overwhelming at the moment, despite its age, and will benefit from further time in bottle. Drink '90–'93.

1989 PINOT NOIR [CS] Colour: medium red-purple. *Bouquet:* very strong leafy/tobacco aromas, lacking fruit richness. *Palate:* strong, exaggerated leafy/tobacco flavours that will grow rather than diminish with age; certainly shows varietal character, and is similar to other pinot noirs from the Yarra Valley I have tasted from the 1989 vintage. Much will depend on the evolution of the wine over the next 12 months or so; should rate somewhere in the 75 to 80 range.

1986 PINOT NOIR [65] Colour: medium red. *Bouquet:* bottle-developed burgundian farmyard aromas, with the fruit starting to fade. *Palate:* aged, soft tobacco/leather tastes, with slightly overripe fruit starting to break up somewhat. Should have been sold and drunk before now. Drink '90.

1985 SHIRAZ [68] Colour: medium red, with a touch of purple. *Bouquet:* complex, soft gamey/farmyard characters. *Palate:* soft, complex farmyard/gamey fruit with some vanillan oak, and showing obvious bottle development. Drink '90–'91.

1986 CABERNET SAUVIGNON [70] Colour:

medium purple-red. *Bouquet:* of light to medium intensity, with the fruit hidden by rather raw, lemony oak. *Palate:* clean, but very rough sawn, green oak edges out pleasant red berry flavours; may soften and come together with further time, as the lingering tannins are good. Drink '90–'94.

Summary: Yarrinya Estate has grown rapidly in the ownership of the De Bortoli family; a new restaurant/cellar door sales area was due to open in October 1989, while the vineyards have been greatly extended. More importantly still, wine quality has greatly improved.

❦ YERINGBERG

Location: Maroondah Highway, Coldstream, 3770; 18 km north-east of Lilydale.
(03) 739 1453.

Winemaker: Guill de Pury.

1989 Production: 1000 cases.

Principal Wines: Marsanne, Chardonnay, Pinot Noir and "Yeringberg" (the last a blend of cabernet sauvignon, merlot and malbec).

Distribution: Almost exclusively mailing list; small quantities available in Victorian Wine Centre, Nicks of Doncaster, Melbourne Airport Fine Wines, Sutherland Cellars, Melbourne, and The Oak Barrel, Sydney. UK imports through Nicks Wine Merchants International. Mailing list enquiries as above.

Prices: $14 to $20 mailing list.

Vintage Rating 1986–89: White: '88, '87, '89, '86. Red: '86, '87, '88, '89.

Outstanding Prior Vintages: '77, '79, '80, '81, '85, '86.

Tasting Notes:

1987 PINOT NOIR [82] Colour: light red-purple. *Bouquet:* quite stylish and intense sappy/plum varietal aroma. *Palate:* fragrant, although light, sappy/tobacco fruit flavours with some red fruits still present; all of the indications of a pinot to be drunk early before the sappy tobacco characters take complete hold. Drink '90.

1988 CHARDONNAY [88] Colour: light green-yellow. *Bouquet:* soft, quite rich melon/fig/grapefruit, with light oak. *Palate:* melon/fig fruit of considerable weight and intensity; oak in restraint in a wine with a long finish. Multiple trophy medal winner at the 1988 Lilydale Show. Drink '90–'92.

1987 YERINGBERG [80] Colour: medium purple-red. *Bouquet:* fragrant, complex, leafy/cedary notes with some red berries. *Palate:* soft, complex red berry/cigar box/cedar flavours; rather less intense and weighty than most Yeringbergs, with low tannin; a product of the vintage. (Yeringberg is a blend of the Cabernet family grapes and is simply named that). Drink '91–'95.

Summary: If Yarra Yering has a challenger in producing wines of enormous depth of flavour and longevity, that challenge must come from Yeringberg. Both vineyards produce low yields from now fully mature vines, and the concentration of the fruit is utterly distinctive. The wines that Guill de Pury now makes are surely in a similar style to those made by his grandfather a century ago.

South Australia

Adelaide Hills

1988 VINTAGE

Good winter and spring rains ensured an even budburst, which took place between early- and mid-October. However, barely had the season started when a severe hail storm swept through the northern end of the Barossa ranges, particularly affecting areas around Eden Valley. A few vineyards were affected so badly that no crop was harvested; overall, those hit by the hail had their yield reduced by half. In some instances a second crop formed, which was ultimately to redeem an otherwise disastrous situation. In the southern part of the ranges, around Piccadilly Valley, set was once again disappointing owing to wet and moist conditions at flowering.

From this point on things improved. A warmer than usual summer, which nonetheless never reached levels sufficient to induce stress, produced beautifully ripened grapes with levels of around 13°, even among the second crop vineyards. Overall, quality was good to outstanding, with the red wines falling firmly into the latter category and many of the chardonnays likewise. Rhine riesling was very good, with high aromatics and quite intense flavour. A great vintage year in quality terms, even if not in quantity.

1989 VINTAGE

Budburst occurred normally and evenly, but a week of hot weather at the end of October and early November brought flowering forward, particularly in the southern parts of the ranges, and a prolonged period of wet and at times windy conditions caused havoc in flowering and set. In the south, yields were reduced by up to 50%, bad enough in itself but having further repercussions when a 10-day heatwave arrived on 4 March.

Because of the low crop levels, the grapes ripened even more rapidly than normal. Those trying to harvest grapes for sparkling wine had literally one week in which to harvest, an impossible task. Petaluma calculates it harvested only one quarter of what it might have reasonably expected, owing to the combined effects of the set problems and the subsequent heat. The good news, as it were, came with the white and red table wines, where once again excellent maturities were received with high alcohol and high acid. Some see it as an outstanding red wine year, others as an outstanding white wine year; apart from yield problems, and apart from the sparkling wine problems, some very good wines will be made in this high altitude neck of the woods.

THE CHANGES

An absolute plethora of new entries: Ashton Hills, Basket Hill Range, Glenara, Grove Hill, Malcolm Creek, Piccadilly Fields, Robert Hamilton and Wilsons. Ashton Hills has finally come of age with significant commercial production of riesling, chardonnay, cabernet sauvignon and pinot noir. Previously the tiny quantities were twinned with Stephen George's other (though quite separate) Galah Wines, for which there is now a separate entry. The 3.5-hectare vineyard was planted in 1982/83, 4 km north-east of Mount Lofty. It is somewhat unusual in the Piccadilly Valley in that all of its grapes are used for dry table wine, whereas most of the others are dedicated either totally or partially to sparkling winemaking. The vineyard is in fact owned and managed by Stephen George's father-in-law, Peter van Rood; George helps work the vineyard and buys all the grapes.

Basket Hill Range is still very much in its infancy, even though it has a fairly long history. Phillip Broderick planted his first vines (400 cabernet sauvignon and malbec) way back in 1980; these were doubled in 1984 with plantings of cabernet franc and merlot; extended again in 1986, 1987 and finally 1988, but all in small steps, for the total area under vine is still less than 2 hectares. Broderick hopes to purchase an additional piece of land nearby which would enable him to lift the vineyard area to a little over 3 hectares, still with the aim of producing a Bordeaux blend of cabernet sauvignon, cabernet franc merlot and malbec similar to that which he presently produces. All of the wines, incidentally, have been made under contract, in the first few years by Stephen George and in 1988 and 1989 by Petaluma.

Glenara has an unexpectedly long history: this former fruit orchard was first planted to shiraz and cabernet sauvignon way back in 1971, followed by rhine riesling in 1972, chardonnay 1984, merlot in 1987, cabernet franc in 1988 and pinot noir in 1989. In the initial years Leigh and Jan Verall, who own and run Glenara, sold all of their grapes. However, since 1983 they have had small parcels made under contract by Trevor Jones in some (but not all) years. These were put aside and now form the basis of the cellar door sales operation that was opened at the end of September 1988. The plans are now to turn all of the vineyard's production into Glenara wines, which will see sharp increases in availability through 1990 and 1991, ultimately reaching between 6000 and 7000 cases per year.

Grove Hill, like Basket Hill Range, is still in its infancy, producing only 50 cases in 1989 made under contract by Petaluma. However, by 1990 8 hectares of vineyard will have been established, and when this comes into bearing Grove Hill will be a significant producer. Malcolm Creek is the family operation of Reg Tolley of Tolley's Pedare. It is and always will be a small operation, thereby avoiding any problems of conflict of interest that might otherwise exist. Piccadilly Fields is the newest of all; it is run by Sam Virgara and Robert Johnson; apart from the fact that Sam Virgara worked for a while at Petaluma, I have only scanty details of the operation, although its 1989 Chardonnay ensured the inclusion of Piccadilly Fields in this edition. Robert Hamilton & Son own and run Springton Wine Estate, with a history stretching back to the 1850s. It passed into the ownership of the Hamilton family in 1944, and was part of the assets acquired by Mildara in 1979. In June 1981 Robert and Mark Hamilton purchased the winery back from Mildara along with 18 hectares of nearby land. In 1975 a comprehensive planting programme was commenced, and then extended in 1984. Varieties propagated now include rhine riesling, chenin blanc, white frontignac, semillon, shiraz, cabernet sauvignon, cabernet franc and malbec, while chardonnay was planted in 1989.

Finally there is Wilsons, the sparkling wine venture of former Krondorf-partner Ian Wilson, the clever and aggressive advertising campaign of which will have caught the eye of most wine drinkers (in case you don't remember, it has the punch line "Ian Wilson has the Frogs on the Hop", graphically illustrated). For the time being the grapes are in fact being sourced in McLaren Vale, although as from 1989 an increasing percentage will come from the Adelaide Hills, grown partly on vineyards, partly by the Wilson interests and partly by contract growers. Petaluma is, and for the foreseeable future will remain, contract winemaker. Ian Wilson is a man of energy and ambition, and Wilsons is destined to grow quickly into a significant premium sparkling wine venture.

Craneford and Holmes Estate have effectively been merged into a single operation: Colin Forbes has purchased the Holmes Estate winery in Springton, which conducts a combined cellar door and restaurant operation, the latter through Cafe C.

How far and how quickly the Adelaide Hills viticultural and winemaking scene will grow depends not on the enthusiasm or the operators nor the quality of the grapes or wine. At least in the Piccadilly Valley region, environment-sensitivity arising out of its water catchment status may well prove a limiting factor. As one moves further north, this will not be an inhibitor. The other unresolved issue in the south is climate at flower and fruit set: long-term records indicate the pattern of the last four years to have been aberrational, but one has to wonder at what point one has to accept that aberrational is no longer that, but normality. Nowhere is quality in dispute, and there were very few poor wines in what turned out to be a surprisingly large district tasting.

ASHTON HILLS

Location: Box 231, Ashton 5137 (no cellar door sales). (08) 390 1243.

Winemaker: Stephen George.

1989 Production: 1280 cases.

Principal Wines: Rhine Riesling (current vintage '87), Chardonnay (first commercial vintage 1988 available from September 1989), Pinot Noir (current vintage 1988) and Cabernet (first commercial vintage 1988 available early 1990).

Distribution: Principally mailing list; postal address as above. Limited distribution Adelaide retail and restaurants.

Prices: $10 to $14.50 mailing list.

Tasting Notes:

1989 RHINE RIESLING [80] Colour: light green-yellow-straw. *Bouquet:* clean but light, with slight lemony/herbaceous characters. *Palate:* clean and fresh, with distinct lemony fruit flavours; crisp, but finished a fraction short. Drink '90–'92.

1989 PINOT NOIR [CS] Colour: medium red, with a touch of purple. *Bouquet:* clean, relatively light cherry fruit with a touch of mint. *Palate:* lively minty cherry flavours, with a touch of sappiness; still building complexity and obviously needing more time in oak; the varietal and fruit aromas and flavours are correct. A little difficult to assess, but headed somewhere above 75.

1988 CABERNET SAUVIGNON [71] Colour: very good purple-red. *Bouquet:* light leafy/minty fruit aromas, with a hint of bitter astringency. *Palate:* light leafy/minty flavours with some length, though no great depth; there is a distinct touch of astringency on the finish which is particularly obvious in what is essentially a light-bodied wine. Drink '91–'94.

Summary: The Ashton Hills Vineyard will give of its best reluctantly, but when it does give its best the wines will be superb. It is to be hoped that Stephen George can realise his ambition of building a small winery on-site, allowing him to make hand-crafted wines in the real sense of that term.

BASKET RANGE WINES

Location: Blockers Road, Basket Range, 5138. (08) 390 1515 (vineyard only).

Winemaker: Petaluma (contract).

1989 Production: 75 cases.

Principal Wines: Cabernet Sauvignon/Franc/ Merlot/Malbec.

Distribution: Mail order sales only; address as above.

Prices: $13 mailing list.

Tasting Notes:

1988 CABERNET SAUVIGNON BLEND [CS] Colour: strong and bright purple-red. *Bouquet:* firm, with obvious charred oak/barrel ferment characters. *Palate:* clean, but aggressive oak; needs softening by work and (if it were possible) back blending. The flavours are correct and clean, and my only concern lies over the level of oak. With even a little bit of luck and management, will be headed over 90 points.

Summary: A venture in its infancy, but the vineyard mix is an interesting one, particularly the potential contribution from a higher than usual proportion of malbec.

BRIDGEWATER MILL

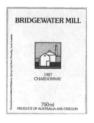

Location: Mount Barker Road, Bridgewater, 5155; at the heart of the township of Bridgewater. (08) 339 3422.

Winemaker: Brian Croser.

Principal Wines: Chardonnay, Sauvignon Blanc, (from the Clare and Coonawarra) Cabernet

Malbec, Rhine Riesling (from Clare), Bridgewater Brut (McLaren Vale Pinot Noir and Chardonnay from Clare).

Distribution: Through cellar door sales at Bridgewater Mill, 11 am. to 5 p.m. 7 days, and national retail through I. H. Baker Wines & Spirits.

Prices: $8 to $15 retail.

Vintage Rating 1986–89: Chardonnay: '88, '87, '89, '86. Sauvignon Blanc: '89, '88, '87, '86. Cabernet Malbec: '88, '87, '89 ('86 not rated). Rhine Riesling: '87, '88, '89, '86. Bridgewater Brut: '87, '89, '88, '86.

Tasting Notes:

1989 SAUVIGNON BLANC [90] Colour: bright yellow-green. *Bouquet:* intense and vibrant gooseberry, with the faintest touch of passionfruit. *Palate:* intense yet not heavy, with perfectly ripened sauvignon blanc flavours, primarily gooseberry but with the appropriate touch of tart, herbaceous flavour in the background. One of the very best Australian sauvignon blancs I have ever tasted. Drink '90–'91.

1988 RHINE RIESLING [78] Colour: light to medium yellow-green. *Bouquet:* deep, with pronounced lime aromas, but uncharacteristic broadness. *Palate:* again, a somewhat surprising style from Bridgewater Mill, with abundant flavour in the lime spectrum, but bordering on being heavy and suggesting some pressings material (in fact, highly unlikely, but that is the impression one gains). Drink '90–'93.

1988 CHARDONNAY [83] Colour: medium yellow-green. *Bouquet:* very complex, with deep fruit and a touch of charred oak; fractionally hard. *Palate:* rich, full and complex honeyed/peachy fruit, with masses of flavour although, like the Riesling, seemingly a little short on finesse. Drink '90–'93.

1987 CABERNET MALBEC [79] Colour: very good purple-red. *Bouquet:* spotlessly clean, with very strong minty/PK fruit aromas. *Palate:* mirrors the bouquet with very pronounced minty fruit and excellent oak integration and balance; I simply find the minty characters a little too extreme for my taste. Drink '91–'95.

Summary: The Bridgewater Mill releases are, not surprisingly, invariably good, some being totally exceptional. In retrospect, it may be that I found certain of the wines a little heavy because they were tasted in the Adelaide Hills regional tasting, in which one finds extremely delicate and fine flavour and structure, whereas the Bridgewater Mill wines themselves come from a variety of other districts.

CRANEFORD

Location: Main Street, Springton, 5235; in centre of town.
(085) 68 2220

Winemaker: Colin Forbes.

1989 Production: 2200 cases.

Principal Wines: Rhine Riesling, Chardonnay, Cabernet Sauvignon, Shiraz and Sparkling Burgundy.

Distribution: Mailing list and through selected retailers serviced from agents in SA, Vic., NSW and Qld. Cellar door sales 11 am. to 5 p.m.

Prices: $9 to $15 cellar door.

Vintage Rating 1986–89: White: '88, '89, '87, '86. Red: '87, '88, '89 ('86 not rated).

Tasting Notes:

1987 RHINE RIESLING [62] Colour: light to medium yellow-green. *Bouquet:* rather hard and stripped, suggesting fermentation at higher than normal temperatures. *Palate:* shows similar characteristics, although the wine does have greater richness and weight than the bouquet would suggest; cloys somewhat on the finish. Drink '90.

1987 CABERNET SAUVIGNON [65] Colour: medium purple-red. *Bouquet:* soft, with some dark chocolate dark berry aromas and a touch of aldehyde. *Palate:* high-flavoured, fully ripened fruit, but again faintly aldehydic. Drink '90–'92.

Summary: The Caneford wines submitted for this tasting were disappointing. I can only assume that Colin Forbes, who is a very experienced winemaker, has had some transitional settling-in problems to contend with.

EDEN SPRINGS WINES ESTATE

Location: Boehm Springs Road, Springton, 5253; 7 km from Springton and signposted. (085) 64 1056.

Winemaker: Rob Dundon (contract).

1989 Production: Approximately 3500 cases.

Principal Wines: Fumé Blanc, Rhine Riesling, Shiraz Cabernet and Tawny Port.

Distribution: Virtually exclusively cellar door sales 10 am. to 5 p.m. 7 days.

Prices: $10 to $12 cellar door.

Tasting Notes:

1989 RHINE RIESLING [87] Colour: medium yellow-green. *Bouquet:* clean with masses of generous lime/toast aroma, yet not overblown. *Palate:* good, rich lime/toast fruit flavours with ample weight and a long finish. Drink '90–'93.

Summary: The sole Eden Springs wine submitted to this tasting was of outstanding quality, particularly given that final acid adjustment and fining had not been carried out. I was nonetheless happy to judge the wine as a finished wine because of its great flavour and character. Theoretically it can only get better. Once again, the advantages of skilled contract winemaking are obvious.

GALAH WINE

Location: Box 231 Ashton, 5137. (08) 390 1243.

Winemaker: Stephen George.

1989 Production: 1000 cases.

Principal Wines: Galah Wine is an unusual, if not unique, operation offering wines, some of which are made by Stephen George, some are purchased in bulk and perhaps blended, still others are purchased already bottled. Whatever the source of grapes or wine, only small quantities of each wine are offered (120 dozen or less). (See also separate Ashton Hills entry in this chapter.)

Distribution: Exclusively mailing list; postal address as above.

Prices: $5.50 to $9.

Vintage Rating 1986-89: Not relevant because of varied district and vineyard sources of the Galah wines.

Tasting Notes:

1987 CHARDONNAY [80] Colour: light to medium yellow-green. *Bouquet:* smooth and clean, of medium to full intensity, with honeyed fruit and discrete oak. *Palate:* clean, fine and harmonious wine with light to medium melon/fig fruit, again very reserved. Unusually long-lived style. Drink '90–'93.

1986 SAUVIGNON BLANC [75] Colour: very good, full yellow-green. *Bouquet:* developed, with a nice touch of oak, but lacking distinctive varietal character. *Palate:* soft, clean mouth-filling bottle-developed flavours; once again, varietal character is not marked, but the wine has good fruit-weight and balance. Drink '90–'91.

Summary: I greatly enjoyed the mature bottle-developed white wines of Galah, which also happen to offer exceptional value for money. However, I found distressing sulphides in the two reds ('87 Shiraz and '87 Cabernet Sauvignon) submitted.

GLENARA WINES PTY LTD

Location: 126 Range Road, North Upper Hermitage, SA, 5131. (08) 380 5056.

Winemaker: Andrew Garrett (contract).

1989 Production: 1400 cases.

Principal Wines: Chardonnay, Rhine Riesling, Cabernet Sauvignon and Shiraz.

Distribution: Cellar door sales 10 a.m. to 5 p.m. 7 days, mail order; enquiries to address above; some fine restaurants.

Prices: $11.70 to $13.80.

Tasting Notes:

1989 RHINE RIESLING [80] Colour: bright green-yellow. *Bouquet:* abundant, classic and full toasty/lime fruit. *Palate:* soft, with pronounced toasty flavours, and a little less fruit richness and sweetness than the bouquet would suggest, finishing a little short. Superb on the bouquet, less so on the palate, but this may lengthen with time in the bottle. Drink '90–'92.

1989 CHARDONNAY [CS] Colour: medium to full yellow-green. *Bouquet:* solid fruit with quite pronounced lemony oak, but as yet a fraction one dimensional. *Palate:* a very big, rich wine with lemony French (possible Vosges) oak; in terms of flavour and structure, very forward. Will rate high 70's/low 80's.

Summary: The Glenara decision to move from grape growing to winemaking seems fully justified.

GROVE HILL WINES

Location: 120 Old Norton Summit Road, Norton Summit, 5136.
(08) 390 1437.

Winemakers: Various contract (chiefly Petaluma).

1989 Production: 50 cases.

Principal Wines: Chardonnay, *Méthode champenoise* and Pinot Noir.

Distribution: By appointment and mailing list only. No cellar door sales.

Prices: $15 to $20 mailing list.

Tasting Notes:

1986 CHARDONNAY [69] Colour: medium yellow-green. *Bouquet:* intense, potent lifted bouquet showing some volatility. *Palate:* the volatility evident on the bouquet slightly thins out the palate, but there are pleasant bottle-developed flavours and the wine has good fruit and oak balance. Drink '90.

Summary: The '87 Grove Hill Chardonnay submitted for the tasting was made in tiny quantities, and it is not the least bit surprising that it should have a minor technical fault. The quality promises well for the future once production reaches truly commercial levels.

HEGGIES VINEYARD

Location: Cnr Heggies Range Road and Tanunda Creek Road, Adelaide Hills (vineyard only). (085) 64 2423.

Winemaker: Alan Hoey and Simon Adams.

1989 Production: 14,000 cases.

Principal Wines: Chardonnay, Rhine Riesling, Botrytis Affected Late Harvest Rhine Riesling and Cabernet/Merlot.

Distribution: National through Samuel Smith & Son Pty Ltd, offices in each state.

Prices: $11 to $18 retail.

Vintage Rating 1986–89: White: '87, '89, '86, '88. Red: '88, '89, '87, '86.

Outstanding Prior Vintages: White: '82, '84.

Tasting Notes:

1988 RHINE RIESLING [80] Colour: medium yellow-green. *Bouquet:* abundant soft, fruity pineapple/lime aromas, clean and showing pleasant bottle development. *Palate:* abundant soft and rich pineapple/lime fruit, again showing a most pleasant touch of bottle development. A relatively forward style for this vineyard, and not at all typical. Drink '90–'91.

1988 CHARDONNAY [87] Colour: medium to full yellow, with just a touch of green. *Bouquet:* big, rich buttery/peachy fruit and well-handled charred oak. *Palate:* soft, rich peachy/butter fruit with a nice touch of spicy oak; the restraint in the oak handling is very welcome. Drink '90–'93.

1988 LATE HARVEST BOTRYTIS RHINE RIESLING [88] Colour: medium to full yellow. *Bouquet:* intense lime/fruit with a hint of apricot; excellent varietal character shining through the botrytis influence. *Palate:* full, soft and rich with fruit showing flavours of lime, apricot and peach, and has rather more botrytis modification of varietal flavour than does the bouquet; soft balancing acid rounds off an excellent, late harvest style. Drink '90–'92.

1987 CHARDONNAY [82] Colour: full yellow, with a touch of green. *Bouquet:* very complex, rich, honeyed/peachy "Dolly Parton" style. *Palate:* full, soft, honeyed buttery flavours with peachy fruit; a touch more acid on the finish would have merited higher points. Drink '90–'91.

1985 CHARDONNAY [88] Colour: medium to full yellow-green. *Bouquet:* complex charred oak with distinct burgundian cabbagey characters, possibly deriving from bottle development. *Palate:* a very complex wine, with superb oak handling; the fruit is only of light to medium weight and intensity, though still surprisingly crisp. A wine to be drunk now before any of that fruit fades. Drink '90.

1987 CABERNETS [65] Colour: medium red. *Bouquet:* lemony oak is out of balance with rather thin, leafy and slightly dull fruit. *Palate:* strong lemony oak is once again the driving force; the fruit appears prematurely tired and really needs more richness. Drink '90–'91.

Summary: The full range of Heggies Vineyard white wines, from dry riesling through chardonnay to late harvest botrytised rhine riesling are truly excellent. Each vintage of chardonnay seems to be getting better, indeed. However, the red wines (pinot noir and cabernets) fall a long way behind in quality, being thin and light.

HENSCHKE

Location: Moculta Road, Keyneton, 5353; 5 km north of Keyneton.
(085) 64 8223.

Winemaker: Stephen Henschke.

1989 Production: Approximately 40,000 cases.

Principal Wines: Hill of Grace, Cyril Henschke Cabernet Sauvignon, Mount Edelstone, Keyneton Estate, Malbec, White Burgundy, Semillon, Chardonnay, Sauvignon Blanc, Rhine Riesling, Dry White Frontignac, Rhine Riesling Spatlese and Rhine Riesling Auslese. Tilley's Vineyard White Burgundy is a new addition to the range.

Distribution: Substantial fine wine retail distribution in all states, with wholesale agents in each state (notably I. H. Baker). Also cellar door sales 9 a.m. to 4.30 p.m. Monday to Friday and 9 a.m. to noon Saturday. Mailing list enquiries to C. A. Henschke & Co., PO Box 100, Keyneton, 5353.

Prices: $11.20 to $17.70 retail.

Tasting Notes:

1989 RHINE RIESLING [87] Colour: brilliant green-yellow. *Bouquet:* intense lemony/citric fruit with a light touch of toast in the background; strong and clean. *Palate:* excellent intensity, with lime/citric/passionfruit flavours. Very good length and style. Drink '90–'93.

1988 SEMILLON [90] Colour: medium green-yellow. *Bouquet:* spotlessly clean; superb oak and fruit balance and integration; strong varietal semillon to carry the oak. *Palate:* similarly exemplary oak handling which perfectly complements the fruit; spicy oak flavours are set against honeyed semillon. An outstanding wine. Drink '90–'94.

1988 CHARDONNAY [92] Colour: medium to full yellow. *Bouquet:* voluptuous, rich and ripe in a full burgundian style; complexity has been achieved without sacrificing clean fruit. *Palate:* unctuous and rich fruit and oak of wonderful depth; again burgundian in weight and feel, even Montrachet. Drink '90–'93.

1987 MOUNT EDELSTONE SHIRAZ [76] Colour: medium purple-red. *Bouquet:* clean, full soft vanillan oak and rich berry fruit. *Palate:* fragrant, soft cherry berry fruit with light oak; rather less weighty and complex than the bouquet suggests. Drink '91–'94.

1987 CYRIL HENSCHKE CABERNET SAUVIGNON [87] Colour: medium red-purple. *Bouquet:* very clean; spicy, sophisticated oak with attractive red berry fruit. *Palate:* complex ripe berry/cassis fruit with excellent oak balance and integration; the wine is not heavy in the palate, but has length. Drink '91–'97.

1987 KEYNETON [68] Colour: medium purple-red. *Bouquet:* quite weighty fruit, but with some medicinal/burnt characters. *Palate:* high-flavoured wine with dark berry fruits, but once again those roast/burnt medicinal characters are evident. Drink '90–'93.

Summary: Stephen Henschke produces a

bewildering array of outstanding white and red wines, interspersed with the increasingly rare wine of lesser quality. His ability to judge the correct amount of oak, and type of oak, to go with the often outstanding fruit at his disposal is second to none. In my opinion, one of the top small-to-medium wineries in Australia.

HILL-SMITH ESTATE

Location: Flaxman Valley Road, Adelaide Hills (vineyard only).
(085) 64 2423.

Winemakers: Robert Hill-Smith; Alan Hoey (consultant).

1989 Production: 7500 cases.

Principal Wines: Fumé Blanc, Semillon, Chardonnay, Shiraz and Late Harvest Semillon.

Distribution: National distribution through Tucker/Seabrook/Caon Group.

Prices: $11 to $14 retail.

Vintage Rating 1986–89: White: '88, '89, '87, '86. Red: '88, '89, '87, '86.

Outstanding Prior Vintages: White: '84.

Tasting Notes:

1989 FUME BLANC [70] Colour: light to medium green-yellow. _Bouquet:_ still building intensity; slightly smoky overtones typical of young sauvignon blanc. _Palate:_ light, crisp, herbaceous fruit with smoky overtones, in perfect fumé style. Will build richness in bottle by 1990. Drink '90–'91.

1988 SEMILLON [75] Colour: medium to full yellow. _Bouquet:_ strong toasty/ lemony oak sits on top of fruit. _Palate:_ almost identical to the bouquet, although some sweet honeyed fruit does appear at the end of the palate; a good food style. Drink '90–'92.

1988 CHARDONNAY [76] Colour: full yellow.

Bouquet: clean and smooth, with quite full bottle-developed honeyed fruit. _Palate:_ ample, soft honeyed/buttery developed light burgundy style with some oak; varietal character is muted in both bouquet and palate. Drink '90–'91.

1987 SHIRAZ [83] Colour: strong and clear purple-red. _Bouquet:_ very smooth and clean, with dark berries of medium to full intensity. _Palate:_ clean and fresh, with attractive red berry fruits; the oak is well restrained, and the tannins are of light to medium weight; a lovely modern red wine style, to be enjoyed for its fruity, fresh flavours. Drink '90–'92.

1987 CABERNET SAUVIGNON [65] Colour: medium red-purple. _Bouquet:_ slightly common/mawkish red berry fruit. _Palate:_ rather better than the bouquet promises with sweet berry fruit flavours; however, the wine lacks intensity of flavour and is rather simple. Drink '90–'91.

Summary: A reliable range of wines at competitive prices; the over-dependence on oak of earlier releases is no longer a worry.

KARL SEPPELT GRAND CRU ESTATE

Location: Ross Dewell's Road, Springton, 5235; 4 km south-west of Springton.
(085) 68 2378.

Winemaker: Presently made by contract at various wineries, including Petaluma, Yalumba.

1989 Production: 2800 cases.

Principal Wines: Rhine Riesling, Chardonnay, Shiraz and Cabernet Sauvignon.

Distribution: Partially by mailing list; enquiries to Grand Cru, PO Box 153, Mount Pleasant, 5253. Cellar door sales, credit cards accepted. Increasing retail distribution through Vintage Cellars, Adelaide; Crittendens, Melbourne and Sydney; Lionel Samson, Perth; and Queensland Liquor Supplies, Brisbane.

Prices: Approximately $7 to 9 mailing list.

Tasting Notes:

1989 EDEN VALLEY RHINE RIESLING [80] Colour: light to medium yellow-green. *Bouquet:* clean, with toasty rather than fruity/lime aromas dominating; of medium intensity. *Palate:* unexpectedly, is the reverse of the bouquet, with clean, fruity, slightly tropical flavours dominant; there is a touch of fruit sweetness, rather than residual sugar and the wine has good length. Drink '90–'92.

1988 CHARDONNAY [87] Colour: light to medium green-yellow. *Bouquet:* strong, complex fruit and oak, with distinct burgundian (cabbagey/vegetal) overtones. *Palate:* very elegant with complex grapefruit flavours of light to medium intensity; again a touch of burgundy is there in the style; not a heavy wine, but is very long in the mouth. Not surprisingly, a gold medal winner on the national show circuit. Drink '90–'92.

1987 EDEN VALLEY RHINE RIESLING [80] Colour: medium yellow-green. *Bouquet:* clean; of medium intensity, with lime/tropical fruits. *Palate:* very rich, full fruit salad/lime/tropical flavours, mouth-filling and soft. Drink '90–'91.

1986 CHARDONNAY [79] Colour: medium to full yellow. *Bouquet:* full, quite complex, tangy grapefruit aroma leading to some burgundian characters. *Palate:* complex, soft, honeyed/buttery, bottle-developed flavours; smooth but less intense and stylish than the bouquet would suggest. Drink '90–'91.

1987 CABERNET SAUVIGNON [74] Colour: medium red, with a touch of purple. *Bouquet:* clean, relatively light leafy/tobacco/red berry melange. *Palate:* clean but relatively light-bodied leafy/minty/berry flavours, with a low oak profile; no fault, but lacks complexity. Drink '91–'94.

1986 CABERNET SAUVIGNON (SPECIAL CUVEE) [81] Colour: full purple-red. *Bouquet:* full, deep and dense dark chocolate and ripe, sweet berry aromas intermingle. *Palate:* ripe and deep chewy/dark chocolate flavours with persistent, although soft, tannins running right through the wine. An extended maceration wine made at Holmes Estate on an experimental basis. Drink '93–'99.

Summary: The label, while visually almost identical, will slowly change from Grand Cru to Karl

Seppelt as existing stocks run down. Many would think the change of name is a very appropriate one, although that is in no way to suggest that the wines are not very good: they are. The experimental cabernet, by the way, is available ex-mailing list, but only on special request.

MALCOLM CREEK

Location: Kersbrook SA, Adelaide Hills Wine region (vineyard only).
30 Barracks Road, Hope Valley, SA, 5090 (production).
(08) 264 2255.

Winemaker: Reg Tolley.

1989 Production: 500 cases.

Principal Wines: Chardonnay and Cabernet Sauvignon.

Distribution: Available through some selected South Australian restaurants and liquor stores. Small export to New Zealand, also direct contact R. L. & E. M. Tolley, 30 Barracks Road, Hope Valley, SA, 5090, telephone (08) 264 2255.

Prices: $13.50 to $16.

Vintage Rating 1986–89: White: '88, '86, '89, '87. Red: '86, '89, '87, '88.

Tasting Notes:

1986 CHARDONNAY [74] Colour: medium to full yellow. *Bouquet:* complex, rich and toasty oak with tangy fruit; has zip and style. *Palate:* similarly, complex and punchy wine, but after such a promising start, is slightly flawed by a hard, phenolic finish. Might well transform itself with food when those phenolics would not be so obvious. Drink '90–'92.

1986 CABERNET SAUVIGNON [82] Colour: medium to full red-purple. *Bouquet:* clean, rich and full with vanillan oak together with sweet berry/minty fruit. *Palate:* very clean and full minty/berry fruit flavours with fairly high tannin levels throughout, which linger on the finish. Drink '92–'97.

Summary: If a major winemaker is to have his own weekend hobby (which seems to be very much like a bushman's holiday), quality needs to be good. I do not think that Reg Tolley has any reason to regret establishing Malcolm Creek.

❦ MOUNTADAM

Location: High Eden Road, High Eden Ridge; 5 km west of Eden Valley township; 5235. (085) 64 1101.

Winemaker: Adam Wynn.

1989 Production: 7000 cases.

Principal Wines: Riesling, Chardonnay, Pinot Noir, Cabernet Sauvignon and Chardonnay Pinot Noir Sparkling.

Distribution: Fine wine retail distribution through wholesale in all states. Mail orders to Mountadam Vineyard, High Eden Ridge, Eden Valley, 5235. Tastings and winery tours by appointment; cellar door sales 9 a.m. to 3 p.m. Monday to Friday. UK imports through Haughton Fine Wines and Hicks and Don.

Prices: $12 to $19 cellar door; $27 sparkling wine.

Vintage Rating 1986–89: '87, '88, '86 ('89 not yet rated).

Tasting Notes:

1988 RHINE RIESLING [64] Colour: distinct straw tones. _Bouquet:_ very light, clean, discrete and reserved, with a slightly powdery edge. _Palate:_ rather hard, slightly oily flavours lacking fruit intensity; I am at a loss to understand whether this is a vineyard characteristic, or is a result of winemaking decisions. The wine was tasted in a large, masked line-up, and performed identically to the fashion of earlier vintages. Perhaps I am missing the point. Drink '90.

1988 CHARDONNAY [55] Colour: straw yellow, with some brown aspects. _Bouquet:_ oily and hard with hot ferment characters and what I imagine is some malolactic fermentation influence. _Palate:_ the fruit has been entirely subjugated to making techniques designed to invest the wine with complexity. My reaction to the style, and the points awarded, concerns me greatly, but I cannot change facts. One favourable thing I can find to say is that this is unquestionably a style that will develop and improve in bottle. Drink '92–'95.

1988 PINOT NOIR [85] Colour: medium purple-red. _Bouquet:_ clean and quite complex; an attractive combination of plummy and leathery aromas of medium intensity. _Palate:_ most attractive soft fruit floods the fore-palate, leading on to strong plum flavours on the mid-palate; the wine has texture and structure, with admirable pinot varietal character. Drink '91–'93.

1988 CABERNET SAUVIGNON [62] Colour: medium red-purple. _Bouquet:_ full, somewhat burnt/biscuity characters with a touch of sulphide. _Palate:_ extractive, ripe fruit with meaty/sulphide characters again evident. Drink '93–'96.

Summary: It appalls me to review the Mountadam wines (with the honourable exception of the Pinot Noir) in this fashion. Wine lovers will simply have to decide for themselves whether they agree with Robert Parker (who gives the wines tremendously high points) or myself. I wish that I could say that it is purely a question of style; while certainly style (and thereby personal opinion) enters into it, my notes would suggest it goes a little deeper still.

❦ ORLANDO STEINGARTEN

Location: (Vineyard only) Eastern Barossa Ranges, due east of Rowland Flat, north of Trial Hills Road (off Sturt Highway).

Winemaker: Robin Day (chief winemaker).

1989 Production: Limited quantity made.

Principal Wines: Only one wine produced: Orlando Steingarten Riesling, normally as a dry white wine but Spatlesen were made in 1976 and 1979.

Distribution: Very restricted output. Selectively available through leading fine wine stockists in capital cities.

Prices: $17.85.

Tasting Notes:

1988 RHINE RIESLING [78] Colour: light yellow-green. *Bouquet:* discrete and closed; there is latent power, with almost oily lime fruit lurking underneath. *Palate:* similarly concentrated and flavoured; that hint of traminer oiliness from high altitude/cool climate viticulture; a powerful, long-lived style. Drink '90–'94.

Summary: Steingarten is one of the great romantic follies, a venture that one would expect of an eccentric weekend winemaker but not one of the major wine companies. Despite all of the difficulties, Orlando perseveres, and deserves all the more credit for doing so. The quality of the wine is more often than not some reward, even though production remains pitifully small and uncertain.

PETALUMA

Location: Spring Gully Road, Piccadilly, 5151. (08) 339 4011.

Winemaker: Brian Croser.

Principal Wines: The principal Adelaide Hills release is the *Méthode champenoise*, simply named Croser. Adelaide Hills Chardonnay has been a component of Petaluma Chardonnay from 1985 in increasing proportion. The first Pinot Noir table wine was made in 1989. For other Petaluma entries see the Clare Valley and Coonawarra sections of this book.

Distribution: National fine wine retail distribution through wholesale agents in each state. Cellar door sales at Bridgewater Mill. No mailing list.

Prices: Croser $25 to $26.50; Chardonnay $27 to $28.50.

Vintage Rating 1986–89: Croser: '88, '89, '87, '86. Chardonnay: '89, '88, '87, '86.

Outstanding Prior Vintages: Chardonnay: '78, '89, '82, '84.

Tasting Notes:

1987 CROSER [90] Colour: light to medium yellow-green, with very good mousse. *Bouquet:* discrete but noticeably bready, with fine fruit underneath. *Palate:* of the highest possible quality with fine, classic delicate fruit; slight lemony notes, with superb acid balance; an exceptionally long finish. Drink '90–'91.

1987 CHARDONNAY [90] Colour: light to medium yellow-green. *Bouquet:* smooth, melon fig fruit of medium intensity, with subtle and beautifully integrated oak. *Palate:* more oak impact evident than in the bouquet, with some spicy characters, but nonetheless subservient to fruit; a marvellously harmonious and balanced wine, again noteworthy for the length of its finish. Drink '90–'94.

Summary: Croser wine is a tall poppy, and knockers must inevitably have their say. However, I have consistently given the wine very high marks in masked tastings, and believe it stands with the very finest of the new generation of Australia's sparkling wines. The chardonnay is a welcome return to form after (to me) one or two slightly disappointing releases.

PEWSEY VALE

Location: Browne's Road, Pewsey Vale, Adelaide Hills (vineyard only). (085) 64 2423.

Winemaker: Alan Hoey.

1989 Production: 22,000 cases.

Principal Wines: Rhine Riesling, Botrytis Rhine Riesling and Cabernet Sauvignon.

Distribution: National through Samuel Smith & Son Pty Ltd offices in each state.

Prices: $8 to $11 retail.

Vintage Rating 1986–89: White: '89, '88, '86, '87. Red: '88, '87, '86, '89.

Outstanding Prior Vintages: White: '84, '73, '69. Red: '84, '75, '76.

Tasting Notes:

1989 RHINE RIESLING [84] Colour: light to medium yellow-green. *Bouquet:* clean, firm floral passionfruit/lime fruit. *Palate:* clean passionfruit lime flavours replicating the bouquet; of light to medium intensity, but the balance and flavour are good and the finish, while crisp, is quite fruity and long. Drink '90–'92.

1987 CABERNET SAUVIGNON [75] Colour: medium red-purple. *Bouquet:* herbal leafy/tobacco aromas of light to medium intensity. *Palate:* more weight than is evident on the bouquet, with quite rich, complex herbal/leafy/berry flavours; proclaims its cool climate origins, perhaps a little stridently so. Drink '91–'94.

Summary: Pewsey Vale has for a long time produced some of Australia's outstanding rhine riesling, which does consistently well in the show ring. The cabernet sauvignon, by contrast, tends to be a little light and lean in style.

🍇 *PICCADILLY FIELDS*

Location: Udy's Road, Piccadilly, 5151.

Winemakers: Sam Virgara and Robert Johnson.

Principal Wines: Believed to be only Chardonnay.

Distribution: Initially only by mail order enquiry to above address.

Tasting Notes:

1989 CHARDONNAY [CS] Colour: light yellow-green, with a touch of straw. *Bouquet:* excellent fragrant, barrel-ferment aromas with good lemony/spicy oak set against crisp melon/grapefruit fruit. *Palate:* crisp, clean, light and flavoursome with excellent potential to grow in the bottle. If it is safely bottled, will rate above 80.

Summary: Piccadilly Fields is in its infancy; details are skimpy, but it is a name worth watching out for.

🍇 *ROBERT HAMILTON & SON*

Location: Hamilton's Road, Springton, 5235. (085) 68 2264 or (08) 267 5385.

Winemaker: Robert Hamilton (and consultants).

1989 Production: 4000 cases.

Principal Wines: Rhine Riesling, Semillon, Chardonnay, Shiraz, Cabernet Sauvignon and Cabernet Shiraz.

Distribution: Cellar door and wholesale in all states; cellar door sales 10 a.m. to 4 p.m. 7 days.

Prices: $7.14 to $13.38.

Outstanding Prior Vintages: White: '82. Red: '85.

Tasting Notes:

1985 CABERNET SAUVIGNON SHIRAZ [85] Colour: medium red-purple. *Bouquet:* clean, full, soft dark chocolate fruit, still remarkably fresh. *Palate:* full, soft red berry/dark chocolate flavours; an altogether attractive wine which is fruit, rather than oak, driven. Drink '90–'93.

Summary: If all of the Robert Hamilton & Son wines are as good as the single wine tasted for this edition, it is a label I shall watch for in the future. The northern end of the Adelaide Hills does provide wines of quite different style to the southern end, but even this is at the fleshier and weightier end of the spectrum.

🍇 *SEPPELT PARTALUNGA*

Location: Adelaide Hills (vineyard only). (085) 68 2470.

Winemakers: Ian McKenzie (chief winemaker) and Tony Royal (white wines), vineyard manager Kym Ludvigsen.

1989 Production: Very limited.

Principal Wines: Partalunga Rhine Riesling and a Cabernet Sauvignon scheduled for future release.

Distribution: National fine wine retail, mainly premium wine stockists; quantities available still very restricted.

Prices: $13.

Vintage Rating 1986–89: White: '87, '88, '89 ('86 not rated). Red: '88, '89, '87 ('86 not rated).

Tasting Notes:

1988 RHINE RIESLING [81] Colour: light yellow-green. _Bouquet:_ fine, discrete lime/passionfruit aromatics in very good style. _Palate:_ beautifully made wine with light fruit flavours again showing flavours of lime and passionfruit; has real delicacy, and the winemaker has obviously avoided the temptation to prop the wine up either with residual sugar or a few extra phenolics. Drink '90–'91.

Summary: This vineyard, in which plantings commenced in 1982 at a height of 500 metres, will eventually produce chardonnay, sauvignon blanc, rhine riesling and cabernet sauvignon. The chardonnay is currently used in premium and sparkling wine blends, and the cabernet sauvignon is the next release due. I believe Seppelt's high expectations of the vineyard are justified.

 STAFFORD RIDGE

Location: (vineyard only) Stafford Ridge, Lenswood, 5240. (08) 272 2105.

Winemaker: Geoffrey Weaver.

1989 Production: 3500 cases.

Principal Wines: Rhine Riesling, Chardonnay and Cabernet Merlot.

Distribution: Principally mailing list; enquiries to 2 Gilpin Lane, Mitcham, 5062. Limited restaurant and fine wine retail distribution through Peter Connolly Victorian Wine Consultants, Melbourne (03) 328 3033.

Prices: $12 to $18 cellar door.

Vintage Rating 1986–89: '88, '89, '87.

Tasting Notes:

1988 RHINE RIESLING [82] Colour: brilliant yellow-green. _Bouquet:_ full, rich tropical lime/passionfruit aromas. _Palate:_ masses of rich, soft passionfruit/fruit salad/tropical fruit; a luscious, mouth-filling style that is not, however, sugar sweet. Drink '90–'92.

1987 CABERNET SAUVIGNON MERLOT [74] Colour: medium red-purple. _Bouquet:_ light, sappy, lemony fruit and oak, fractionally simple. _Palate:_ very light, leafy/herbaceous style suggesting shaded or partially unripe fruit; reminiscent of a light year Bordeaux. Drink '90–'92.

Summary: Geoff Weaver is of course the highly talented Thomas Hardy white winemaker who has been given limited right of private practice, as it were. All future releases will come exclusively from Stafford Ridge; Weaver expects the weight of his red wines to increase as the years go by, and there is much to look forward to.

WILSONS

Location: No winery established or planned at present; wines made by contract at Petaluma under Ian Wilson's direction. (08) 231 9555.

Winemaker: Ian Wilson.

1989 Production: 12,000 cases.

Principal Wines: One wine: Wilson's, a premium non-vintage sparkling wine presently utilising McLaren Vale chardonnay and pinot noir, but in the near future moving to predominantly Adelaide Hills grown material.

Distribution: To restaurants and fine wine retailers through Van Cooth & Co., Vic.; Caldbecks

NSW and Qld; Classic Wine Merchants, SA and
Fine Wine Wholesalers, Perth; trade enquiries
to Woods Hill Vineyards Pty Ltd, 389 King
William Street, Adelaide (Fax (08) 231 9256).

Prices: $20 retail.

Tasting Notes:

WILSONS NV [75] Colour: light to medium yellow-
green, with good mousse. *Bouquet:* quite
complex, with tangy/citric/apple aromas and
just a touch of matchbox. *Palate:* strong fruity
flavours, perhaps a little assertive, but certainly
in blanc de blanc style; a touch of sweetness
produces a thoroughly commercial result.
Drink '90.

Summary: Every now and then you see a new
brand come on to the market that you know
will succeed. Wilsons is one of those; it will
succeed because of the knowledge and skill of
all of those involved in producing and
marketing the product, and not because of the
inherent quality of the early releases, which will
inevitably be workmanlike but no more.

Adelaide Metropolitan Area/ Adelaide Plains/Others

1988 VINTAGE

Even by the standards of this very warm and dry viticultural region, the 1988 growing season was exceptional. Only 1 mm of rain fell between 1 January and the end of harvest and, not surprisingly, the vintage had one of the earliest starts and earliest finishes on record. As I have commented in previous editions, the growing conditions are in many ways identical to those of the Riverland, with supplementary irrigation absolutely essential. The corollary is fruit that is almost invariably harvested free from any disease, and a very low spray requirement (particularly fungicides) in the vineyards.

In no small part due to the hot, windy and dry conditions, yields for most varieties were down, with cabernet sauvignon, chardonnay, sauvignon blanc and rhine riesling giving as little as 2.5 tonnes per hectare. Shiraz, colombard, chenin blanc and semillon did rather better.

For the third year running, vignerons were very pleased with wine quality, the low yields no doubt adding to both flavour and colour (the latter in the reds).

1989 VINTAGE

Somewhat milder conditions, broken only by a week of very hot weather at the end of October and early November, led to expectations of an extremely good vintage. As ever, disease in the vineyard played absolutely no part in shaping the destiny of the year, and yields were generally higher than in 1988.

Vintage commenced early as usual, and the varieties that came in before the middle of February should produce excellent wine. From this point on the situation deteriorated rapidly, with quality declining day by day as the heatwave continued. As in other regions, winemakers gave preference to the premium varieties, and these should be good. The lesser varieties will make exceedingly ordinary wines.

THE CHANGES

The most noticeable change is a subtle addition to the chapter heading: the word "others". This is designed to accommodate two new entries: Boston Bay Wines and Delacolline Estate, which mark the start of yet another viticultural region in South Australia on the Eyre Peninsula near Port Lincoln. Boston Bay is by far the larger venture of the two, with the 1989 vintage producing around 2000 cases. The grapes are picked into plastic-lined containers, which are packed into refrigerated pantechnicons for transport to the Barossa Valley where the wines are contract made at Basedow by Doug Lehmann.

Delacolline Estate is in its infancy; what partner Tony Bassett engagingly describes as "a motley collection of enthusiasts, comprising a lawyer, a pharmacist, a farmer, a surgeon and a shipyard proprietor" have planted a little over 3 hectares, principally to rhine riesling and cabernet sauvignon, with smaller plantings of shiraz, merlot, semillon, sauvignon blanc and chardonnay. Here Tim Knappstein is contract winemaker, and I (or rather Tony Basset, the lawyer in the motley collection) have more to say of the wines in the summary to the entry.

The climate is entirely unlike that of the Adelaide Plains. The vineyards face the cool water of the Spencer Gulf to the east, and are sheltered from the prevailing westerlies that blow in from the Great Australian Bight to the west. This maritime atmosphere, with its moderate humidity and stable, cool temperatures, combines with quick draining limey soil to produce grapes that are quite evidently of good quality.

The other modest addition is Patritti Wines, a long-established operation on the south-west outskirts of Adelaide, producing wines from an extensive vineyard in the Blewitt Springs Area. Wine quality is modest.

Finally there is a cosmetic change: Woodley Wines is now listed under Queen Adelaide, the latter being the Woodley brand which is one of Australia's leaders.

ANGLESEY

Location: Heaslip Road, Angle Vale, 5117; 0.7 km south of Angle Vale, and 10 km south of Gawler.
(085) 24 3157; Fax (085) 24 3517.

Winemaker: Lindsay Stanley.

1989 Production: 10,000 cases.

Principal Wines: Whites–four varietals: Semillon, Chardonnay, Sauvignon Blanc, Chenin Blanc plus a Chablis style. Reds–Cabernet/Malbec, Shiraz/Cabernet, Cabernet/Merlot, Q.V.S. Red (Cabernet/Shiraz/Malbec).

Distribution: National retail through wholesalers in each state except Tasmania and Northern Territory. Cellar door sales 10 a.m. to 5 p.m. Monday to Friday; weekends by appointment.

Prices: $7 to $11 retail.

Vintage Rating 1986–89: '89, '88, '86, '87.

Outstanding Prior Vintages: '84.

Tasting Notes:

1989 CHENIN BLANC [70] Colour: light to medium green-yellow. _Bouquet:_ pleasant fruit salad characters under some lingering after-effects of fermentation, which will have disappeared by 1990. _Palate:_ once again, quite good varietal character showing in the fruit salad/ tropical spectrum of flavours. Soft clean finish. Drink '90.

1989 SAUVIGNON BLANC [CS] Colour: light to medium yellow-green. _Bouquet:_ very clean, with strong, spicy nutmeg oak. _Palate:_ beautifully handled spicy/nutmeg oak; it seems to me almost certain that the wine will be back-blended with steel-fermented wine and, if so, could be very good indeed, rating in the high 70's.

1988 SEMILLON [61] Colour: medium to full yellow-green. _Bouquet:_ rather plain, slightly oily oak competes with quite full herbaceous fruit. _Palate:_ a rather heavy, oily wine with lots of flavour; it really hangs around in the mouth, cloying the finish. Drink '90.

1986 SHIRAZ CABERNET [59] Colour: medium red. _Bouquet:_ of light to medium intensity and rather plain, with dull, old oak and somewhat tired fruit. _Palate:_ an old-fashioned style, high in alcohol and with old oak very evident. Drink '90–'91.

Summary: Anglesey tries enormously hard to market and promote its wines, and has recently undertaken a major philosophical change in direction in moving away from the complex white and red blends favoured by former consultant Max Schubert to a more conventional varietal approach. Whether the vineyards will give the varietal definition necessary for the new tack to succeed still remains to be seen.

BOSTON BAY WINES

Location: Lincoln Highway, Port Lincoln, 5606; 6 km north of Port Lincoln.
(086) 84 3600 or (086) 84 3521/(086) 82 5605 (A/H).

Winemakers: Doug Lehmann and Roger Harboard (Basedow Wines).

1989 Production: 2000 cases.

Principal Wines: Rhine Riesling, Riesling Spatlese, and Cabernet Sauvignon and Merlot (as from vintage 1989).

Distribution: Cellar door sales and selected bottle shops. Mailing list enquiries to PO Box 364, Port Lincoln, 5606.

Prices: $9.90 to $11.90 recommended retail.

Tasting Notes:

1989 RHINE RIESLING [77] Colour: medium yellow-green. _Bouquet:_ clean and crisp; of light to medium intensity, with quite pronounced herbaceous characters. _Palate:_ fresh, clean and crisp; light to medium herbaceous/lime flavours; a silver medal winner in the open vintage rhine riesling class at Brisbane 1989. Drink '90–'91.

1989 SPATLESE RIESLING [62] Colour: light green-yellow. *Bouquet:* very light, and lacking varietal fruit of any description. *Palate:* a light, commercial cellar door style with some acid crispness, but lacking fruit intensity. Drink '90.

1988 RHINE RIESLING [71] Colour: medium yellow-green. *Bouquet:* clean, with tropical/lime fruit aromas of fair weight. *Palate:* plenty of flavour and fruit, although slightly heavy on the tongue, either from a touch of pressings or from a little residual sugar; highly commercial style. Drink '90.

Summary: The dry rhine riesling of Boston Bay underlines the promise of the Eyre Peninsula viticultural region. Competent contract winemaking does the rest.

DELACOLLINE ESTATE

Location: Whillas Road, Port Lincoln, 5606. (086) 82 5277 (Tony Bassett).

Winemaker: Tim Knappstein (contract).

1989 Production: 200 cases.

Principal Wines: Rhine Riesling (100 cases) and Cabernet Sauvignon (100 cases).

Distribution: Will initially be mail order.

Prices: Not yet determined.

Summary: I was not able to taste the wines, but could not resist giving you Tony Bassett's overview of them: "The Rhine Riesling has been made at Clare by Tim Knappstein. It will include about 5% of Clare Valley material in 1989 as it was picked a little green. The red wine has been produced at our vineyard with a little remote guidance from Knappstein. It has been produced by committee. So far it shows no signs of suffering the same fate as the horse which finished up as a camel."

GORDON SUNTER

Location: Care of St Hallett (see Barossa Valley entry).

Winemaker: Stuart Blackwell.

Principal Wines: Chablis, Rhine Riesling, Cabernet Sauvignon and Tawny Port.

Distribution: Presently principally mail order and through isolated retailers serviced direct from administration office. All enquiries to PO Box 12, Tanunda, 5352. When cellar door established, cellar door sales will be 9 a.m. to 5 p.m. Friday to Sunday inclusive.

Summary: The Gordon Sunter label is presently having a rest while Stuart Blackwell comes to grips with the rapidly escalating St Hallett crush. However, it has not been abandoned: future releases are on the drawing board.

LAURISTON & BAROSSA VALLEY ESTATES

Location: Heaslip Road, Angle Vale, 5117; 8 km south-east of Gawler. (085) 24 3100.

Winemaker: Colin Glaetzer.

1989 Production: The equivalent of 110,000 cases.

Principal Wines: There are now two principal releases from Lauriston: the Barossa Valley Estates range comprising Sauvignon Blanc, Rhine Riesling, Semillon, Chardonnay, Late Picked Frontignac, Hermitage and Cabernet Sauvignon; and the Lauriston range comprising Chardonnay, Sauvignon Blanc, Cabernet Shiraz and *Méthode champenoise* Vintage Brut, which may be made at Lauriston or alternatively purchased from other makers either within the Berri Renmano Group or outside it.

Distribution: National retail through Berri Renmano Wines (sales). Cellar door sales

9 a.m. to 5 p.m. Monday to Friday, 11 a.m. to 5 p.m. Saturday and 1 p.m. to 5 p.m. Sunday.

Prices: $8.99 to $10.99.

Tasting Notes:

1988 LAURISTON CHARDONNAY [84] Colour: deep yellow. _Bouquet:_ ultra buttery/ butterscotch/honeyed style. _Palate:_ huge, luscious peachy/buttery wine; the ultimate one-glass style unless you are fighting highly spiced Asian food. Gold medal winner 1989 Sydney Show. Drink '90.

1988 BAROSSA VALLEY ESTATES CHARDONNAY [74] Colour: medium to full yellow. _Bouquet:_ smooth, solid fruit with a slightly burnt/medicinal edge. _Palate:_ very strong flavour; however, there is a touch of mould in the wine I tasted, either deriving from cork taint or from some barrel taint from a chlorine-derived compound; in any event, there was a touch of bitterness on the finish of an otherwise full-flavoured wine. Drink '90.

1988 LAURISTON CABERNET SAUVIGNON [CS] Colour: medium purple-red. _Bouquet:_ clean, with scented/spicy oak still to integrate with attractive red berry fruit. _Palate:_ high-toned spicy American oak with rich, red berry fruit; a cunningly made wine with real potential, tasted not long before bottling. Should rate in the mid 80's.

1987 BAROSSA VALLEY ESTATES HERMITAGE [65] Colour: light red-purple. _Bouquet:_ clean, light and rather leafy fruit dominated by lemony oak; lacks the richness of earlier vintages. _Palate:_ almost identical to the bouquet; light lemony oak dominates, and the wine is not rich. Drink '90–'91.

1987 BAROSSA VALLEY ESTATES CABERNET SAUVIGNON [62] Colour: light red, with just a touch of purple. _Bouquet:_ clean but very light leafy fruit and soft vanillan oak. _Palate:_ clean, light and very developed leafy fruit; low in concentration and tannin, and will not develop in bottle. Drink '90.

1987 LAURISTON CABERNET SAUVIGNON SHIRAZ [61] Colour: medium red-purple. _Bouquet:_ strong, scented oily/lemony German oak with light fruit. _Palate:_ pronounced cosmetic lemon drops/oily oak completely obscures fruit; a concocted wine, but others may like it more than I did. Drink '90–'91.

Summary: After a succession of excellent, full-flavoured and rich wines released under the Barossa Valley Estates labels, the current releases seem to have faltered somewhat. Given the fierce competition for top-quality fruit, and given the price at which these wines are sold, this hardly comes as a surprise. At least for the wines reviewed for this edition, Lauriston carries the winery flag with pride.

🍇 PATRITTI WINES

Location: 13-23 Clacton Road, Dover Gardens, 5048; 5 km south-west of Adelaide. (08) 296 8261

Winemaker: Geoffrey A. Patritti.

1989 Production: Approximately 500 tonnes crushed.

Principal Wines: A limited range of traditionally labelled table wines including Claret and Burgundy; also semi-dry red wines; full range of fortified, sparkling and flavoured wine, and also grape juice. Wines sold under various labels including Blewitt Springs Estate and Patritti Wines.

Distribution: Principally mail order and cellar door sales, with substantial bulk sales. Cellar door sales 9 a.m. to 6 p.m. Monday to Saturday.

Summary: A traditional business now threatened by the ever-increasing pressures of urban sprawl and by changed wine-buying habits and tastes.

🍇 PRIMO ESTATE

Location: Old Port Wakefield Road, Virginia, 5120; 2 km north of Virginia township. (08) 380 9442.

Winemaker: Joe Grilli.

1989 Production: 9000 cases.

Principal Wines: Riesling, Sauvignon Blanc, Colombard, Chardonnay, Auslese,

Beerenauslese, Shiraz, Cabernet Sauvignon, "Joseph" Double Pruned Cabernet Sauvignon and "Joseph" Cabernet Merlot Moda Amarone.

Distribution: Significant national fine wine distribution through wholesale distributors in each state. Also cellar door sales and mailing list. Cellar door sales 9 a.m. to 5 p.m. Monday to Friday, Saturday 10 a.m. to 4.30 p.m., closed Sunday. Mailing list enquiries to PO Box 77, Virginia, 5120.

Prices: $9 to $20 recommended retail.

Vintage Rating 1986–89: White: '88, '87, '89, '86. Red: '87, '88, '86, '89.

Tasting Notes:

1989 COLOMBARD [74] Colour: light green-yellow. *Bouquet:* threw off the after-effects of fermentation as it sat in the glass to produce strong citric/grassy fruit aromas of good style. *Palate:* a well-made wine, with good fruit intensity; green fruit flavours are offset by a perfectly judged touch of residual sugar. Drink '90.

1989 RIESLING [70] Colour: light yellow-green. *Bouquet:* well made but rather light and lacking fruit intensity. *Palate:* clean but light, if not a little hollow, tropical/lime riesling flavours; may well fill out dramatically by 1990 and merit higher points. Certainly, there is no fault in the winemaking. Drink '90.

1989 SAUVIGNON BLANC [CS] Colour: light green-yellow. *Bouquet:* clean, very light, faintly herbal aromas and a suggestion of a touch of oak. *Palate:* light, crisp herbal/gooseberry varietal character; well made, although the fruit was still to build mid-1989.

1989 CHARDONNAY [CS] Colour: light yellow-green, with a touch of straw. *Bouquet:* youthful, smoky/grapefruit/herbaceous aromas, showing careful winemaking. *Palate:* again, very youthful, with highly protected smoky/ grapefruit flavours; in its infancy, but has obvious potential.

1986 BOTRYTIS RIESLING AUSLESE [79] Colour: light to medium green-yellow. *Bouquet:* light, fragrant and floral aromas with a strong Germanic lime character. *Palate:* amazingly youthful, and again strongly reminiscent of a good German spatlese, with riesling fruit flavour largely unmodified by the effect of botrytis. Strongly recommended to those who do not like super intense sweet white wines. Drink '90–'92.

1988 JOSEPH CABERNET MERLOT MODA AMARODE [90] Colour: medium to full purple-red. *Bouquet:* clean, elegant and smooth red berry aromas with beautifully balanced oak; good depth to ripe but not over-ripe fruit. *Palate:* most attractive, clean, strong fruit with very good oak balance and integration; soft persistent tannins add to the structure, and to the future, of a beautifully crafted wine. Drink '91–'96.

Summary: Joe Grilli is a highly intelligent and talented winemaker who sees no reason to apologise for the limitations imposed on him by the Adelaide Plains, and in fact sees a challenge in taking the Primo wines beyond simple varietal character and excellence. His lateral thinking has produced a range of highly distinctive and innovative wines of genuine style and quality.

🍇 QUEEN ADELAIDE

Location: Seppeltsfield via Tanunda, 5352; 7 km north-east of Tanunda. (085) 62 8028.

Winemaker: Ian McKenzie (chief).

1989 Production: Very substantial, but not for publication.

Principal Wines: Queen Adelaide Riesling, Queen Adelaide Chardonnay, Queen Adelaide Spatlese Lexia, Queen Adelaide White Burgundy, Queen Adelaide Chablis, Queen Adelaide Claret, Queen Adelaide Vintage Brut Champagne, Three Roses Sherry, Lord Melbourne Port principal brands, with Queen Adelaide Riesling one of the largest brand sellers in Australia. Also very limited occasional releases of small parcels of high-quality Cabernet Sauvignon from Coonawarra such as the Queen Adelaide Classic Hermitage 1985.

Distribution: National retail distribution at all levels.

Prices: $5.99 to $7.99.

Vintage Rating 1986–89: White: '89, '88, '87, '86. Red: '87, '88, '89, '86.

Tasting Notes:

1989 CHARDONNAY [78] Colour: light to medium straw-green. _Bouquet:_ soft, rich, smoky/ peachy fruit with plenty of weight and varietal character. _Palate:_ soft, clean fruit untrammelled by oak; has plenty of flavour, and finishes with crisp acid; there is none of the sweetness of the '88 and prior vintages; surely the best value chardonnay on the Australian market. Drink '90.

Summary: Queen Adelaide Chardonnay is the largest selling chardonnay in Australia, representing 10% of all sales through hotels and liquor stores. The quality of the wine under the Queen Adelaide label has been transformed since its acquisition by Seppelt, and all of the wines in the series can be purchased with confidence.

TOLLEY'S PEDARE

Location: 30 Barracks Road, Hope Valley, 5090; 15 km from Adelaide GPO.
(08) 264 2255; Fax (08) 263 7485.

Winemakers: Chris Tolley (chief) and Robert Scapin.

1989 Production: 2.2 million litres.

Principal Wines: Rhine Riesling, Gewurztraminer, Chardonnay, Chablis, Colombard/ Semillon, Sauvignon Blanc, Spatlese Frontignac, Pinot Noir, Shiraz Cabernet and Cabernet Sauvignon: also a limited range of fortified wines and a Chardonnay/Pinot Noir Bottle-fermented Vintage Brut.

Distribution: National retail through wholesalers in each State. Significant fine wine retail distribution through wholesale agents in all States. Also cellar door sales at Barossa Valley winery 10 a.m. to 5 p.m. Friday and Saturday, and at Hope Valley winery 7.30 a.m. to 5 p.m. Monday to Friday and 9 a.m. to 5 p.m. Saturday. Mailing list enquiries to PO Box 313, St. Agnes, 5097.

Prices: Cellar Reserve around $6 retail and Selected Harvest between $8.50 to $15 retail.

Vintage Rating 1986-89: White: '87, '88, '86, '89. Red: '86, '87, '89, '88.

Tasting Notes:

1989 RHINE RIESLING [85] Colour: very good green-yellow. _Bouquet:_ soft, clean toasty lime aromas showing exemplary varietal character, and with good style. _Palate:_ attractive lime/toast flavours to a perfectly structured riesling, with a long, soft finish. A remarkably good wine for the year. Drink '90–'92.

1989 GEWURZTRAMINER [80] Colour: medium to full yellow-green. _Bouquet:_ intense, essency and pungent oily traminer character; the ultimate in Parisian boudoire style. _Palate:_ a tour de force of essency varietal character; in some ways a bit too much, although one cannot help admire the fruit and winemaking; it would demand spicy Asian cuisine to tame it down. Drink '90–'91.

1988 CHARDONNAY [82] Colour: very good green-yellow. _Bouquet:_ strong barrel ferment characters with lovely charred/spicy oak set against tangy grapefruit. _Palate:_ a lively wine, again showing sophisticated spicy oak, but with good supporting fruit; has length on a pleasantly acid finish. Drink '90–'92.

1987 SEMILLON [79] Colour: light green-yellow. _Bouquet:_ extremely sophisticated spicy/nutmeg oak, but there is some fruit in support. _Palate:_ light and crisp; sophisticated spicy/nutmeg oak is again the main flavour contributor; the wine may develop more flesh with age; clever handling of an oaky style that will greatly appeal to some. Drink '90–'93.

1986 CABERNET SAUVIGNON [77] Colour: medium red-purple. _Bouquet:_ clean and quite complex, with red berry fruit surrounded by lemony oak. _Palate:_ lemony oak threatens to dominate gently astringent cabernet fruit, but the wine is redeemed by a clean, fresh finish. Drink '90–'94.

Summary: Tolley's Pedare has always offered competitively priced, well-made wines. The current releases are especially commendable, particularly if you enjoy the complexities offered by clever oak handling.

Barossa Valley

1988 VINTAGE

Good winter and spring rains, the latter falling in October, got the growing season off to a very good start. However, the joy was short-lived for some growers: severe hail storms towards the end of October decimated significant areas of vineyard in the southern parts of the valley. Conditions then turned significantly warmer than 1987, and a severe hot spell in early December had an adverse effect in flowering, reducing yields or some varieties by up to 20%.

January and early February were cool, but the weather then became hot, leading to an early vintage after a succession of late and cool years.

Vintage got under way in early March in fine hot weather, tempered by cold nights and early morning fogs.

Despite the hail and set problems, yields overall were better than in other parts of southern Australia, suggesting that some vineyards produced very high yields. Overall the quality was good, but not up to the outstanding '86 and '87 vintages. White and red quality were largely indistinguishable, with the vast majority of wineries placing the years either second or third out of the four vintages 1986 to 1989 inclusive.

1989 VINTAGE

Once again, good winter/spring rains promoted healthy and regular budburst. Unlike 1988, flowering and set took place in good conditions, with all varieties performing well. The early- and mid-summer was cool, and not very different to the mild conditions encountered from 1984 through to 1987. In the run-up to Christmas there were no more than three or four hot days, and by early February everything promised a good vintage with a well above average yield.

In mid-February the heatwave arrived, and for the next three weeks temperatures were seldom below 35°, often reaching 40°. It was a year in which many of the varieties had soft and thin skins, and there was an immediate adverse reaction to the heat. As the days went by the panic increased, and for virtually three weeks machine harvesters worked on 24-hour shifts (normally they only harvest at night), filling wineries to capacity and placing enormous loads on refrigeration plants.

When the heatwave passed the vines were able to partially adjust moisture balance within the system, leading to a drop in sugar levels. As in other parts of Australia, the photo-synthetic mechanisms of the vines were apparently damaged beyond repair, for sugar levels by and large only partially recovered. It seems that the vines simply shut down their systems, deciding they would wait for 1990.

Quality and style are likely to be extremely irregular: part will depend on the capacity of wineries to handle the influx of fruit; part on picking dates; part on the vineyard situation and, in particular, soil quality (with those vineyards on light soil suffering most); and finally on the degree of ruthlessness exercised by the wineries in wine selection for given quality levels. Overall, it was a better year for white wine than for red, particularly with the early picked white varieties and those given preference in congested winery conditions. Three wineries obviously had great success with their reds, but for most it was a very poor year: colours are good, but the wines lack mid-palate flesh and will all have to rely on heavily corrected acid.

THE CHANGES

Probably the most significant event has been the return of the prodigal son: Grant Burge has set himself up in splendid style in the Moorooroo Cellars established by William Jacob in 1871. William Jacob had built his house nearby almost 30 years earlier, and gave his name to Jacobs Creek. The property passed into the ownership of the Gramp family (and hence Orlando) during the First World War and in 1972 was converted to the Wine Keller Restaurant by Colin Gramp.

Happily, the conversion has not affected the character and style of the original building, which has been restored without regard to cost and now serves as the corporate headquarters and cellar door tasting facility for Grant Burge Wines. The wines themselves are made at Ryecroft in the McLaren Vale, but almost all come from Grant Burge's own vineyards; he is by far the largest vineyard owner in the Central Barossa Valley.

Other new entries are Bourchier Wines and The Willows. Rod Bourchier was a senior winemaker at Yalumba for many years, before a brief stint at Baileys in north-eastern Victoria. He has now returned to the Valley to set up his own business, but also acts as a consultant—most interestingly to a joint venture in Russia between Australian and Russian interests. Bourchier's operating base is presently in transit; until mid-1989 it was on the Barossa Valley Highway at Nuriootpa, but new and more suitable premises were being sought.

The Willows Vineyard has been set up by Peter and Michael Scholz; the Scholz family has been growing grapes in the Valley for generations, and Peter Scholz is one of the winemakers at Peter Lehmann Wines. While most of the family's grapes are still sold, a small quantity is being made and sold solely through the cellar door and mailing list.

Chateau Yaldara also continues to revise its wine range under the energetic direction of Jim Irvine, with Acacia Hill a new brand recently introduced to the market. In the same vein Karlsburg is now known as Charles Cimicky Wines, while Chatterton has finally quietly faded away.

There have also been two ownership changes, one minor, the other major. Rovalley has changed hands, and the new owners seem interested in upgrading its quality and its image.

The other highly significant development was the sell-down by the Orlando management buy-out team of slightly over 50% of the capital of Orlando to the French spirits group, Pernod Ricard. As always the industry is full of rumours, with all sorts of extravagant tales, all completely inconsistent with each other. Time alone will show just what impact it has on the local management, which does retain a board majority.

The Barossa Valley is a prime example of the synergy that exists between big and small, young and old makers in a major and long-established wine district. Through the simple effect of peer pressure and no doubt through the activities of the Local Vignerons Association, badly made wines are a rarity. As I have said in previous editions, there is also a growing awareness of and determination to protect the priceless inheritance of more than a century of grape growing and winemaking on a major scale. In this, tourism and winemaking are inextricably linked, and even if the wines of the Barossa Valley are seen in some quarters as being very reliable but not brilliantly exciting, the Barossa has no shortage of wonderful characters among its winemakers. The combination of this human resource with the history and buildings of the Valley is a potent one.

BAROSSA SETTLERS

Location: Trial Hill Road, Lyndoch, 5351; 3 km south-east of Lyndoch.
(085) 24 4017.

Winemakers: Howard Haese with Douglas Lehmann (contract).

1989 Production: Approximately 2100 cases.

Principal Wines: Rhine Riesling, Late Harvest Rhine Riesling, Auslese Rhine Riesling, Shiraz Claret, Cabernet Sauvignon, Sweet Sherry and Vintage Port.

Distribution: Exclusively cellar door: 10 a.m. to 4 p.m. Monday to Saturday, 1 p.m. to 4 p.m. Sunday.

Prices: $6.50 to $10.50 table wines; $11 to $15 fortified.

Tasting Notes:

1989 RHINE RIESLING [65] Colour: medium yellow-green. _Bouquet:_ slightly toasty and oily, with fruit aroma diminished. _Palate:_ a slightly hard wine that lacked fruit flavour early in its life; will undoubtedly build some additional character with further time in bottle. Drink '90–'91.

1987 RHINE RIESLING [85] Colour: light to medium yellow-green. _Bouquet:_ very youthful, crisp and clean with light passionfruit aromas; abundant style. _Palate:_ crisp, fresh, fine and clean, again showing youthful, elegant passionfruit flavours; a quite lovely wine still at the start of its life. Drink '90–'93.

1985 CABERNET SAUVIGNON [85] Colour: medium red. _Bouquet:_ clean, soft, sweet vanillan oak and berry fruit of medium to full intensity. _Palate:_ harmonious, smooth and stylish wine now at its peak; soft cedar/vanillan oak married with a touch of herbaceous cabernet varietal character and well-balanced tannins. Drink '90–'92.

1986 COMMEMORATIVE VINTAGE PORT [89] Colour: dense red-purple. _Bouquet:_ complex, fragrant brandy spirit with rich fruit. _Palate:_ rich, full and complex, with high-toned spirit and vibrant berry fruit. Has improved markedly over the last 18 months, and obviously has a long future in front of it. Drink '90–'97.

Summary: An old horse stable built in 1860 now houses the Barossa Settlers cellar door sales area, attesting to the length of time that the Haese family has owned this most beautiful vineyard. The wines reviewed for this edition do represent the pick of the bunch, and the very high points hardly need further comment. Some of the other wines under the label are less exciting, but always workmanlike.

BASEDOWS

Location: 161-165 Murray Street, Tanunda, 5352; on northern outskirts of township.
(085) 63 2060; Fax (085) 63 3597.

Winemaker: Douglas Lehmann.

1989 Production: The equivalent of 24,000 cases.

Principal Wines: A full range of table and fortified wines, with some very old reserves of base fortified wines to draw on. Table wines include white Burgundy, Chardonnay, Rhine Riesling, Spatlese White, Frontignac, Hermitage, Cabernet Sauvignon, special release reds, and Old Tawny Port.

Distribution: Substantial cellar door sales; mailing list sales; wholesale distribution through Classic Wine Marketers, SA; Caldbecks, Vic. and Qld; I. H. Baker, WA; Carol Anne Martin Classic Wines, NSW. Cellar door sales 10 a.m. to 5 p.m. 7 days. Mailing list enquiries to PO Box 32, Tanunda, 5353.

Prices: Table wines $9.50 to $13 retail, fortified wines $11 to $14 retail.

Vintage Rating 1986–89: White: '86, '88, '89, '87. Red: '86, '88, '89, '87.

Outstanding Prior Vintages: White: '83, '84. Red: '80, '82, '84.

Tasting Notes:

1988 RHINE RIESLING **[90]** *Colour:* medium full yellow. *Bouquet:* clean, rich and intense fruit with some developed toasty characters. *Palate:* a wonderfully full-flavoured and stylish wine; fine yet positive riesling flavour, toasty with a touch of lime; exceptional overall flavour and balance. Drink '90–'91.

1988 WHITE BURGUNDY **[93]** *Colour:* medium yellow-green. *Bouquet:* a tour de force of oak and fruit handling and balance; honeyed and smooth, intense yet not heavy or aggressive. *Palate:* lives up to the promise of the bouquet; the harmony and balance is so perfect it is impossible to tell where oak starts and fruit finishes (or vice versa); made from 100% semillon, and will develop over the years with exceptional grace. Drink '90–'94.

1988 CHARDONNAY **[90]** *Colour:* medium full yellow-green. *Bouquet:* rich, clean, full pineapple/honey fruit, again showing absolutely perfect oak handing. *Palate:* the oak is skilfully woven into soft honeyed/peachy/pineapple flavours; a ripe, full style in classic Australian mould. Drink '90–'91.

1986 WINEMAKERS SELECTION HERMITAGE **[78]** *Colour:* very good medium red. *Bouquet:* clean, with a touch of cedar/cigar box secondary aromas developing; clean but fractionally closed fruit. *Palate:* an elegant style showing attractive bottle development, again with those cedary/cigar box flavours and fruit of light to medium weight. Drink '90–'93.

1985 WINEMAKERS SELECTION CABERNET SAUVIGNON **[70]** *Colour:* medium red with a touch of purple. *Bouquet:* clean, civilised and harmonious, with tobacco/leafy bottle-developed aromas. *Palate:* starting to show its age; of light to medium weight, with slightly leathery characters and lacking fruit richness. Drink '90.

OLD TAWNY PORT **[78]** *Colour:* light to medium red-tawny. *Bouquet:* light, fresh and clean; a fraction simple. *Palate:* clean, fresh fruit with smooth and well-chosen fortifying spirit; simply needs more age in cask. Drink '90.

Summary: The quality of the Basedow whites (with the Semillon White Burgundy as its spearhead) is remarkable. Indeed, if I had to nominate a single winery as producing the best value for money white wines in Australia in the mid-priced range, Basedow would be the choice.

The Dinner at Eight Trophy awarded to the White Burgundy at the 1989 Brisbane Wine Show for Best One Year Old White of Show was no more than justice.

BERNKASTEL

Location: Cnr Para and Langmeil Roads, Tanunda, 5352; on north-western outskirts of township. (085) 63 2597.

Winemaker: Ray Ward.

Principal Wines: A limited range of traditional Barossa Valley styles, centred on Rhine Riesling, White Burgundy, Cabernet Sauvignon and various ports.

Distribution: Principally cellar door sales 10 a.m. to 5 p.m. 7 days. Limited eastern states retail distribution through Regal & Ross Distributors.

Summary: Only one sample (an unreviewable tank sample of '86 Cabernet Sauvignon, which should have been in bottle anyway) was submitted for this edition. The '85 Cabernet Sauvignon was a lovely wine, but the white wines in prior years have tended to be distinctly ordinary. Generally, a very low-key operation dependent on cellar door sales and a low price strategy.

BETHANY WINES

Location: Bethany Road, Bethany via Tanunda, 5352; 3 km east of Tanunda township, situated in an old quarry overlooking the Bethany Village, near corner of Light Pass and Bethany Roads.
(085) 63 2086.

Winemakers: Robert Schrapel and Geoff Schrapel.

1989 Production: 5000 cases.

Principal Wines: Chardonnay, Fumé Blanc,

Bethany Reserve Rhine Riesling, Steinbruch Spatlese Rhine Riesling, Auslese Rhine Riesling, Schlenke's Gully Shiraz, Cabernet Sauvignon, "Old Quarry" Vintage Port and Frontignac White Port.

Distribution: Largely cellar door sales and mailing list; mailing list enquiries to PO Box 245, Tanunda, 5352. Cellar door sales 10 a.m. to 5 p.m. Monday to Saturday and 1 p.m. to 5 p.m. Sunday. Limited retail distribution through S. & V. Wine Merchants, 17 The Parade, Norwood, S.A.

Prices: $7.50 to $11.50 cellar door.

Vintage Rating 1986–89: White: '87, '89, '88, '86. Red: '87, '88, '89, '86.

Tasting Notes:

1989 RHINE RIESLING [76] Colour: medium yellow-green. *Bouquet:* pleasant lime/pineapple fruit of moderate intensity and with some toasty characters. *Palate:* soft lime/pineapple flavours, with a touch of toast; medium weight, and should develop very well in bottle. Drink '90–'93.

1989 CHARDONNAY [CS] Colour: light yellow-straw. *Bouquet:* light to medium fruit with some barrel-ferment-type characters, and quite pronounced lemony oak. *Palate:* pronounced spicy/lemony oak with a few slightly cosmetic nuances. The wine has been well handled, but fruit richness is still developing. Should rate in the 70's.

1988 RESERVE RHINE RIESLING [83] Colour: a light to medium yellow-green. *Bouquet:* crisp, clean and elegant classic lime/toast aromas. *Palate:* light, clean, crisp and fine style with very good balance and length; a fraction more mid-palate weight would have taken it into the highest class. Drink '90–'92.

1986 AUSLESE RHINE RIESLING [75] Colour: medium full yellow-green. *Bouquet:* quite intense, with lime fruit and some bottle-developed camphor characters emerging. *Palate:* attractive, soft lime/apricot flavours with a soft finish; has developed well over the last 18 months, but now at its peak. Drink '90.

1987 CABERNET SAUVIGNON [62] Colour: medium red, with the purples fading fast. *Bouquet:* somewhat soapy, high pH aromas, lacking varietal fruit intensity. *Palate:* rather soapy/spongy flavours again suggestive of a high pH base wine; soft, and not unpleasant to drink now. Drink '90.

Summary: A small family owned and run winery producing wines from the family's vineyards of honest quality, with the white wines especially good.

❦BOURCHIER WINES

Location: 26 Washington Street, Angaston, 5353; in precincts of township (office and administration only).
(085) 64 2607; Fax (085) 62 3034.

Winemaker: Rod Bourchier.

1989 Production : The equivalent of 16,000 cases, though most of it sold in bulk.

Principal Wines: Bourchier Wines operates principally on a wine consultancy/contract winemaking basis (through the company name Vinovation Pty Ltd) servicing the interwinery trade. It both makes in bulk and selects wines made by others for private or restaurant labelling. Small quantities of wines made by Bourchier will be sold by mail order and through cellar door once a permanent cellar-door sales outlet has been established. Fruit sources are diverse.

Distribution: Presently through mail or phone order only; enquiries to phone or fax as above.

Tasting Notes:

1988 LATE PICKED MUSCAT OF ALEXANDRIA [63] Colour: medium yellow-green. *Bouquet:* grapy but rather broad and a little coarse. *Palate:* clean, pronounced pastille grapy flavours; certainly has flavour and varietal character, but lacks that edge of finesse that the best wines of this type occasionally achieve. Drink '90.

1985 CHARDONNAY [77] Colour: glowing yellow-green of medium to full depth. *Bouquet:* smooth, honeyed/toasty bottle-developed characters; Australian white burgundy style rather than varietal. *Palate:* pleasant, smooth, light to medium weight bottle-developed white burgundy with soft, vanillan oak. Drink '90.

1987 SHIRAZ [67] Colour: medium purple-red. *Bouquet:* youthful fresh berry fruit with strong spicy/clove oak. *Palate:* hot clove oak obliterates fruit; should have been used in a back-blend situation; the oak is said to be French, but has a Portuguese-type taste. It is possible that time will benefit the wine. Drink '92–'95.

Summary: The Bourchier Wines, one suspects, have been selected by Rod Bourchier in the course of his wine consultancy business. Many of them seem far too oaky, the non-reviewed '85 Coonawarra Cabernet Sauvignon in particular suffering from prolonged exposure in indifferent oak. Style and quality may well settle down as a more permanent base is found for the operation.

🍇 *BURGE FAMILY WINEMAKERS–WILSFORD*

Location: Gomersal Road, Lyndoch, 5351; on north-eastern outskirts of township. (085) 244 644.

Winemakers: Noel and Rick Burge.

1989 Production: 2900 cases.

Principal Wines: For many years a strong reliance on fortified wines and in particular ports for which they have quite a reputation. In recent years, however, greater emphasis is being placed on quality table wines following a restructuring within the company coupled with a consequent upgrading of vineyards, production and marketing. The varietal dry whites on offer include Chardonnay, Riesling and White Frontignac together with "Trinity", an oak-matured blend of Semillon, Muscadelle and Sauvignon Blanc. In certain years a dry, aperitif style *Méthode champenoise*, labelled Draycott Brut, is also produced. Dry reds include an early drinking style "Clochemerle", a Cabernet/Merlot/Malbec Blend and a traditionally hearty Barossa-style Hermitage. (Recent plantings of Merlot and Cabernet Franc are expected to yield commercial quantities for the 1990 vintage). Further

plantings in Spring 1989 will include Semillon, Sauvignon Blanc, Merlot, Cabernet Franc and Touriga (for ports). Company grown grapes account for approximately 95% of the total crush and now, in accordance with company policy, all grapes crushed originate from the Lyndoch Valley region only.

Distribution: Almost exclusively cellar door and mail order. Cellar door sales 10 a.m. to 5 p.m. Monday to Saturday, 11 a.m. to 4 p.m. Sunday. Newsletter, mailing list and mail order enquiries to: Freepost 3, Burge Family Winemakers, PO Box 330, Lyndoch, SA, 5351.

Prices: $8 to $15 (some older fortifieds are more) cellar door.

Tasting Notes:

1988 RHINE RIESLING [69] Colour: medium yellow-straw. *Bouquet:* big, broad, bottle-developed style with slightly subdued fruit aroma. *Palate:* broad and toasty, with some pressings characters; plenty of flavour, though a little short on finesse. Drink '90.

1987 DRAYCOTT HERMITAGE [75] Colour: medium purple. *Bouquet:* solid fruit, though not particularly aromatic; pleasant vanillan/American oak. *Palate:* clean, solid, ripe and chewy fruit with gentle tannins. A well-made, traditional style with plenty of flavour. Drink '91–'95.

PRIVATE RESERVE VERY OLD PORT [74] Colour: medium tawny. *Bouquet:* aromas of biscuit and fresh cut bread, an unusual introduction. *Palate:* infinitely better and more stylish than the bouquet; rich, but has real tawny port style, with good length and cut to the finish.

Summary: Much work is being done at Burge Family–Wilsford, but it seems there is still a fair way to go. The wood-matured white wines are simply not acceptable; one suspects that there is insufficient refrigeration capacity in the winery. However, Rick Burge has vast experience, and must know what has to be done.

CHARLES CIMICKY WINES
(formerly Karlsburg)

CHARLES CIMICKY
SAUVIGNON BLANC
1989
WOOD MATURED

PREMIUM AUSTRALIAN WINE 750ML

Location: Gomersal Road, Lyndoch, 5351;
4 km north-west of town.
(085) 24 4025.

Winemaker: Charles Cimicky.

1989 Production: 2000 cases.

Principal Wines: Limited quantities of premium
bottled wine produced from vines surrounding
the winery. Varieties grown are cabernet
sauvignon, merlot, shiraz, sauvignon blanc and
rhine riesling.

Distribution: Selected restaurants and premium
wine retailers together with cellar door sales
and mailing list; cellar door sales 10 a.m. to
4 p.m. 7 days. Mailing list enquiries to PO Box
69, Lyndoch, 5351.

Prices: $9.20 to $18.

Vintage Rating 1986–89: White: '88, '86, '87, '89.
Red: '88, '89, '87, '86.

Tasting Notes:

1989 SAUVIGNON BLANC [75] Colour: light to
medium yellow-green. *Bouquet:* quite
pronounced herbal/tobacco varietal character
achieved at the expense of more weight and
richness. *Palate:* pleasant, well-balanced wine
of light to medium weight, with slightly smoky
herbal/tobacco fruit flavours; in the modern
mould, although I would personally like to see
more richness. Drink '90–'91.

1987 CABERNET MERLOT [79] Colour: very
good light to medium red-purple. *Bouquet:*
extraordinarily fresh red berry fruits of light to
medium intensity and light, new French oak;
an "unmade" wine yet to soften or integrate.
Palate: attractive spicy oak handling, very clean,
with red berry fruits and just a hint of dark
chocolate; again, very fresh and still needing
the softening effects of bottle age, although

equally it will not be a long-lived wine; low
tannin. Drink '92–'94.

Summary: It is not the first time that the wines of
Charles Cimicky (or Karlsburg as it once was)
have surprised and impressed me. They
deserve a wider audience in the eastern states.

CHARLES MELTON WINES

Location: Krondorf Road, Tanunda, 5352;
3 km south of Tanunda.
(085) 63 3606.

Winemaker: Graeme Melton.

1989 Production: 1000 cases.

Principal Wines: An esoteric, small range of red
wines including Rosé, Hermitage Pinot Noir,
Nine Popes (a grenache shiraz blend) and
Sparkling Burgundy.

Distribution: Almost exclusively cellar door sales
9 a.m. to 5 p.m. 7 days. Mail order welcome.
Very limited Sydney and Adelaide fine wine
and restaurant distribution.

Prices: $8 to $13 cellar door.

Tasting Notes:

1988 NINE POPES [72] Colour: medium purple-
red. *Bouquet:* soft, velvety red berry fruits with
classic shiraz gamey/leathery overtones.
Palate: complex, velvety gamey berry fruit
flavours of light to medium weight; soft, clean
finish. Drink '90–'92.

1987 PINOT HERMITAGE [73] Colour: light to
medium purple-red. *Bouquet:* very complex
with strong gamey/animal farmyard aromas
which are, however, vaguely burgundian and
not unattractive. *Palate:* quite complex
gamey/velvety flavours and texture; no
semblance of pinot varietal character, but that
is beside the point; finishes with soft tannins.
Drink '90–'91.

Summary: Graeme (Charlie) Melton is still a
young man, but has already established himself
as one of the great eccentrics of the Barossa
Valley. His neat little wooden winery is very
definitely worth a visit; any hour of the day, any
day of the week, you will find Charlie or his
wife in attendance.

🍇 CHATEAU DORRIEN

Location: Cnr Sturt Highway and Seppeltsfield Road, Dorrien, 5352; 3 km north of Tanunda. (085) 62 2850.

Winemaker: Fernando Martin.

Principal Wines: Rhine Riesling, Chablis, Chenin Blanc, Semillon Sauternes, Cabernet Shiraz, Pinot Cabernet, Cabernet Sauvignon and a range of ports.

Distribution: Cellar door sales only 10 a.m. to 5 p.m. 7 days. Restaurant at winery serves traditional German-based Barossa food.

Prices: $6.90 to 14.50 cellar door.

Vintage Rating 1986–89: '87, '88, '86, '89.

Tasting Notes:

1988 PINOT CABERNET [55] Colour: dark red-purple. *Bouquet:* slightly burnt and heavy fruit with a touch of lemony oak, and appreciable volatility. *Palate:* the blend of pinot noir and cabernet sauvignon is a strange one at the best of times, and does not work in this wine; volatility also intrudes. Drink '90.

Summary: Chateau Dorrien is an imaginatively restored and highly decorative tourist facility first and foremost; winemaking (and mead-making) is carried out on a limited scale. A feature of Chateau Dorrien is the wonderful murals painted on 10 large concrete wine vats (left over from the old days of Chateau Dorrien) by South Australian artist Una Leybourne. A very useful place to take the family.

🍇 CHATEAU YALDARA

Location: Gomersal Road, Lyndoch, 5351; 4 km north-west of township. (085) 24 4200.

Winemakers: Hermann Thumm (Chateau Yaldara), and Jim Irvine (Lakewood).

1989 Production: The equivalent of almost 40,000 cases.

Principal Wines: A wide range of products from white and red table wines, sparkling wines and fortified wines. Recently the range has been extended to include varietal table wines under the Lakewood and Acacia Hill labels. The Lakewood includes a Semillon Sauvignon Blanc, Chardonnay Chenin Blanc, *Méthode champenoise* Brut, Rhine Riesling, Chablis and Cabernet Merlot. The newly released Acacia Hill label comprises a Chablis and a Hermitage. Other releases under the Chateau Yaldara label are Riesling Spatlese and Lyndoch Valley Riesling and Moselle. Red wines include Cabernet Shiraz, Cabernet Sauvignon, Beaujolais and Claret. The Sparkling wine range includes Champagne, Gold Label Brut and Sparkling Burgundy.

Distribution: Chateau Yaldara maintains its own wholesale distribution system through Australia. Substantial cellar door sales through strikingly ornate and beautifully maintained winery and hospitality complex, including garden bistro open daily serving coffee, cake and light meals. Cellar door sales 9 a.m. to 5 p.m. daily. Tours conducted daily.

Prices: Lakewood range $6.90 to $11.90 retail; Acacia Hill $5.90.

Tasting Notes:

1989 LAKEWOOD CHABLIS [62] Colour: medium yellow-green. *Bouquet:* neutral, with slightly oily overtones and understandably neither varietal nor particularly fruity. *Palate:* quite full, but showing an utterly inappropriate touch of residual sugar; a very peculiar definition of chablis. Drink '90.

1989 ACACIA HILL CHABLIS [63] Colour: light to medium straw-yellow. *Bouquet:* very light and neutral, lacking any definition, but without fault. *Palate:* light, neutral and clean without significant fruit; again, a touch of inappropriate residual sugar provides the main flavour base. Drink '90.

1989 CHARDONNAY [71] Colour: medium to full yellow-green. *Bouquet:* quite complex and rich fruit, surprisingly forward and complete. *Palate:* falls away slightly after the very promising bouquet; soft, honeyed flavours, not particularly varietal, and there is a suspicion of yeast-derived volatility. Nonetheless, a very creditable wine at its price. Drink '90.

1987 LAKEWOOD SAUTERNES [84] Colour: medium yellow-orange. *Bouquet:* quite intense and rich, with raisined/apricot aromas. *Palate:* luscious and intense apricot/peach flavours; a very high-flavoured wine, with volatility (inevitably part of such styles) well under control. Drink '90–'91.

1989 CHATEAU YALDARA BEAUJOLAIS [67] Colour: bright light red. *Bouquet:* clean, simple cherry aromas. *Palate:* similar light, soft and simple cherry fruit, which cloys fractionally on the finish; lacks that sparkle this style requires. Drink '90.

1989 LAKEWOOD SOFT RED [68] Colour: light, bright pink-red. *Bouquet:* clean, light and fresh, with a hint of cherry. *Palate:* light, fresh and clean cherry flavours; lacks fruit intensity/ sparkle, but certainly more than adequate for its purpose. Drink '90.

1986 LAKEWOOD CABERNET MERLOT [77] Colour: youthful purple-red of medium depth. *Bouquet:* rich, spicy oak yet to integrate with attractive berry fruit. *Palate:* consistent with the colour and bouquet, amazingly youthful and callow; shows all of the signs of prolonged storage in tank before being whisked through wood; was in the disabilities that that regime imposes, well handled, and one has to give credit to the base wine quality. Drink '91–'94.

1965 RICH OLD PORT [80] Colour: shows extreme age with a deep olive rim. *Bouquet:* extremely aged rich liquor style, which needs the re-freshing influence of some younger material. *Palate:* an amazing old wine, way into liquor style and almost beyond even that; certainly nothing to do with a conventional tawny port.

Summary: The stable wines were spread through a very large district tasting which was, of course, conducted blind. On reading those notes with the label identities revealed, I must confess to some suspicion that some of the wines have almost identical ancestry.

☙ELDERTON

Location: 3 Tanunda Road, Nuriootpa, 5355; 200 metres south of Nuriootpa Post Office. (085) 62 1058 or (008) 88 8500; Fax (085) 62 2844.

Winemakers: Neil Ashmead and James Irvine (contract winemaker).

Principal Wines: Rhine Riesling, Chablis style, Hermitage, Domain Nouveau (light red), Pinot Noir, Cabernet Merlot and *Méthode champenoise.*

Distribution: Wholesale distribution through Australian Vintners Pty Ltd, NSW, Qld and ACT; Van Cooth & Co., Vic.; Lionel Samson Pty Ltd, WA; Caldbecks, SA; Tasmanian Fine Wines, Tas.; and Northern Australia Liquor Wholesalers, Northern Territory. UK imports through Nicks Wine Merchants International. Cellar door sales 10 a.m. to 5 p.m. Monday to Saturday, 1 p.m. to 5 p.m. Sunday. Mailing list, PO Box 394, Nuriootpa, 5355.

Prices: $8.89 to $19.50 recommended retail.

Tasting Notes:

1989 RHINE RIESLING [73] Colour: medium to full yellow-green. *Bouquet:* soft, rich pineapple lime aromas with some slightly burnt medicinal yeast effects still lingering, but which will probably dissipate with time. *Palate:* a big, high-flavoured broad wine with pineapple fruit and a soft, highly commercial finish. Forward style. Drink '90.

1988 PINOT PRESSINGS [59] Colour: impenetrable purple-black. *Bouquet:* huge vanillan oak, with very strong ripe fruit and not the faintest resemblance of varietal character. *Palate:* a quite extraordinary wine with huge pressings character, even if made from low yielding, old vine shiraz; I have seen pinot noir pressings from the Hunter Valley and from cooler parts of the world, but never once seen anything like this. In any event, it is simply too big for anything other than a winter's night barbecue, although it will no doubt live for ever. Drink '95–2005.

1986 HERMITAGE [80] Colour: medium red-purple. *Bouquet:* very clean, smooth attractive bottle development, with lemony/vanillan American oak balanced by softly ripe fruit. *Palate:* smooth and clean, with very well-integrated and balanced lemony/vanillan oak; simply lacks the structural complexity of the greatest Barossa shiraz wines. Drink '91–'94.

1984 COMMAND HERMITAGE [75] Colour: very good purple-red. *Bouquet:* complex gamey/leafy/farmyard aromas showing significant bottle development. *Palate:* complex, soft, gamey/leafy/berry flavours, with a markedly soft and slightly soapy finish. Now at its best. Drink '90–'91.

Summary: Neil Ashmead is a tireless and highly skilled marketer who has turned Elderton into a national brand from a standing start in 1983. Wine quality is consistent (although that pressings pinot noir still has my tongue tied) and I am delighted to report that the beaujolais name is being removed from Domain Nouveau.

🍇 GNADENFREI ESTATE

Location: Seppeltsville Road, Marananga; 6 km north-east of Tanunda, 5352. (085) 62 2522.

Winemaker: Malcolm Seppelt.

Distribution: Cellar door sales only and through restaurant at winery. Cellar door sales 9 a.m. to 5.30 p.m. 7 days.

Summary: Malcolm Seppelt is a member of the Seppelt family, but parted company with Seppelt many years ago and has kept a relatively low profile since he established Gnadenfrei, preferring neither to talk to the press nor to exhibit wines in shows.

🍇 GRANT BURGE

Location: Sturt Highway, Jacobs Creek via Tanunda, 5352; 2 km south of town. (085) 63 3700; Fax (085) 63 2807.

Winemaker: Grant Burge.

1989 Production: The equivalent of just under 20,000 cases.

Principal Wines: Eden Valley Rhine Riesling, Semillon, Chardonnay, Sauvignon Blanc, Barossa Frontignac, Non Vintage Sparkling Wine, Merlot, Very Old Liqueur Frontignac and Very Old Tawny Port. All of these wines are made from Grant Burge's nine different vineyards, which stretch from the Barossa Ranges at Eden Valley to the southern end of the Barossa Valley at Lyndoch.

Distribution: National retail through a wide range of liquor outlets. UK imports through S. Wines Ltd, 21 Burnaby Street, Chelsea.

Prices: $9.20 to $16.20 retail.

Tasting Notes:

1989 BAROSSA FRONTIGNAC [69] Colour: light to medium yellow-green. *Bouquet:* soft and floral slightly spicy/grapy fruit, lacking intensity. *Palate:* pleasant grapy flavours, quite sweet, but offset by good acid balance; simply lacks intensity, although may grow somewhat with six or so months in the bottle. Drink '90.

1988 EDEN VALLEY RHINE RIESLING [76] Colour: medium yellow-green. *Bouquet:* solid, clean and full, with strong regional lime aromas. *Palate:* a big, very high-flavoured commercial style, again showing typical Eden Valley lime characters; mouth-filling food wine. Drink '90–'91.

1988 CHARDONNAY [72] Colour: medium to full yellow, suggesting some skin contact. *Bouquet:* solid and rather oaky, lacking fruit richness. *Palate:* again, an oak-driven wine with solid fruit flavours which lack distinctive varietal character; headed towards an Australian white burgundy style. Drink '90.

1988 MERLOT [CS] Colour: medium to full red. *Bouquet:* very clean, with pronounced leafy/tobacco/violets aroma showing excellent varietal definition. *Palate:* fine and fragrant fruit, once again with surprisingly accurate varietal flavour; will hopefully go to bottle quickly and should then be drunk while young. Will merit points well into the 80's.

VERY OLD TAWNY PORT [67] Colour: medium to full tawny-red. *Bouquet:* some vanillan oak evident, with clean and fresh fruit. *Palate:* very young material with some new oak showing;

needs time in cask to gain rancio and tawny style.

VERY OLD LIQUEUR FRONTIGNAC [64] *Colour:* medium golden, with pink tinges. *Bouquet:* scented, grapy, aromatic and youthful. *Palate:* fresh, clean light and grapy fruit; very commercial but most certainly not very old——very young, more like it.

Summary: No one should doubt Grant Burge's commitment to the Barossa Valley, nor his determination to make a commercial success on a national scale of his new label. One suspects he will not rest until he passes Krondorf in sales.

HERITAGE WINES

Location: Seppeltsfield Road, Marananga, via Tanunda, 5352; 6 km north-east of Tanunda. (085) 62 2880.

Winemaker: Stephen Hoff.

1989 Production: 3200 cases.

Principal Wines: Semillon, Chardonnay, Rhine Riesling, Shiraz, Cabernet Sauvignon and Cabernet Franc.

Distribution: Principally cellar door 9 a.m. to 5 p.m 7 days. Also limited retail distribution through Adelaide, Melbourne and Sydney. For mailing list write to PO Box 129, Angaston, SA 5353.

Prices: $8.25 to $12.50 recommended retail.

Vintage Rating 1986–89: '86, '87, '88, '89.

Tasting Notes:

1987 CLARE VALLEY RHINE RIESLING [92] *Colour:* medium to full yellow-green. *Bouquet:* clean, with strong, classic bottle-developed toasty characters. *Palate:* gloriously intense and stylish lime/toasty fruit, with a wonderfully long, crisp and intense finish, aided by perfect acid balance. Glorious now but should live for years. Drink '90–'95.

1988 CABERNET FRANC [67] *Colour:* youthful purple-red. *Bouquet:* rather simple, fairly light and slightly soapy fruit aromas. *Palate:* shows rather more, but still rather callow/simple; simply one can see the softness that cabernet franc is meant to possess, but that is why it is so often blended with cabernet sauvignon. Drink '90–'91.

Summary: Stephen Hoff seems to bob up with an outstanding wine every vintage (I still remember a lovely 1986 Chardonnay), but to also produce some very ordinary wines; thus alongside the victorious '87 Rhine Riesling stood unreviewable '87 Semillon and '87 Chardonnay. A winery that is very well worth the short detour off the main highway, but taste before you buy.

HIGH WYCOMBE WINES

Location: Bethany; 3 km east of Tanunda, 5352. (085) 63 2776.

Winemaker: Colin Davis.

Principal Wines: Rhine Riesling, Hock, Colombard, Riesling, Frontignac, Bethany Red, Claret, Cabernet Shiraz and Bethany Port.

Distribution: Exclusively cellar door 9 a.m. to 5 p.m. 7 days.

Summary: Small output of unpretentious wines made in a traditional manner from traditional varieties.

HOFFMANNS

Location: Para Road, North Para via Tanunda, 5352. (085) 63 2983.

Winemakers: Peter Lehmann and team (contract).

Principal Wines: Now concentrating on producing

high quality fortified wines, featuring Bulk Port and Sweet Sherry (bring your own container or alternatively these can be purchased), Special Reserve Tawny Port, Oak Heritage Tawny Port, Oak Tawny Port and Liqueur Muscat. These last two wines contain some very old material and have an average age of 18 years.

Distribution: Retail distribution handled direct from winery. Cellar door sales and regular mailing list available. Cellar door sales (incorporating Peter Lehmann cellar door sales) 9 a.m. to 5 p.m. Monday to Friday, 11 a.m. to 4 p.m. Saturday, Sunday and public holidays. Excellent picnic grounds available by the banks of the Para River. Mailing list enquiries to PO Box 315, Tanunda, 5352.

Prices: $6.50 to $18 cellar door.

Tasting Notes:

OAK HERITAGE PORT [77] Colour: aged, deep olive rim. *Bouquet:* obvious age with earthy spirit and a not unexpected lift of volatility. *Palate:* lots of sweet fruit in an aged, concentrated liqueur style; once again, the volatility is present, but is perfectly acceptable in a wine of this style and age.

HOFFMANNS SPECIAL RESERVE PORT [75] Colour: medium tawny. *Bouquet:* some rancio evident; a touch of volatility; good style and grip. *Palate:* rather younger and fresher than the bouquet would suggest; of medium intensity with clean spirit.

LIMITED BOTTLING OLD TAWNY [85] Colour: medium to full tawny, with just a touch of red. *Bouquet:* very good style and weight, with clean spirit and a pungent but not aggressive rancio lift. *Palate:* a rich, structured, full-blown Australian tawny style with abundant character and flavour.

Summary: Hoffmanns is, as the notes indicate, concentrating on its fortified wine styles, of which it has excellent stocks.

KAISER STUHL

Location: Tanunda Road, Nuriootpa, 5355; 2 km south of township.
(085) 62 0389.

Winemakers: John Duval (chief winemaker) and Rod Chapman (production manager).

Principal Wines: Table wines centre on the Ribbon range, comprising Green Ribbon Rhine Riesling, Red Ribbon Shiraz. Brands also include a Black Forest range in three styles: Soft Light Red, Crisp Dry White and Moselle style. The Kaiser Stuhl Rosé also fits into this group. Next come Bin 22 Beaujolais, Bin 33 claret, Bin 44 Riesling, Bin 55 Moselle, Bin 66 White Burgundy and Bin 77 Chablis. Summer Wine is one of the largest selling sparkling wines (non-bottle fermented) in Australia. Special Reserve and Brut champagnes are also sold. A full range of casks and flagons is also marketed. There is the usual range of ports and sherries in 750 ml bottles. Pottery Port in a gift pack is also included in the Port range.

Distribution: National through retail outlets at all levels. Cellar door sales Monday to Friday 9 a.m. to 5.30 p.m., public holidays and Saturday 10 a.m. to 5 p.m. and Sunday 1 p.m. to 5 p.m. Cellar door sales in the Penfolds complex.

Prices: $3.99 to $9.99 cellar door.

Vintage Rating 1986–89: White: '87, '88, '89, '86. Red: '86, '87, '88, '89.

Tasting Notes:

1989 GREEN RIBBON RHINE RIESLING [84] Colour: medium yellow-green. *Bouquet:* reserved, toasty but very good varietal aroma of light to medium intensity; will clearly build in bottle. *Palate:* excellent style, with elegant intense lime fruit and a hint of toast; does not rely on residual sugar for its flavour or mouth-feel and is beautifully balanced. Outstanding commercial white white. Drink '90–'94.

1987 RED RIBBON SHIRAZ [69] Colour: medium

purple-red. *Bouquet:* rather muted fruit with slightly dusty/sawdusty oak aromas. *Palate:* light, fresh red berry fruit with slightly dusty/chippy oak; a light-bodied wine still in compartments, yet without a long future. Drink '90–'91.

NV BLACK FOREST SOFT LIGHT RED **[70]** *Colour:* light red, with a touch of purple. *Bouquet:* soft cherry/creaming soda aromas. *Palate:* soft, sweet cherry fruit on the mid-palate, moving to a quite dry finish; an extremely cleverly made, highly commercial wine. Drink '90.

Summary: Once again, Kaiser Stuhl Green Ribbon Rhine Riesling rises above itself. It is one of the unsung heroes of the commercial riesling market—unsung, that is, except when it comes up with trophies at national shows with a few years under its belt. The other wines in the Kaiser Stuhl range are simple commercial wines of the quality one expects in a 2-litre cask but with the convenience of a 750 ml bottle.

KELLERMEISTER WINES

Location: Barossa Valley Highway, Lyndoch, 5351; 1.5 km east of Lyndoch.
(085) 24 4304 or (085) 24 4303.

Winemakers: Ralph and Trevor James.

Principal Wines: Forty different wines are offered on the current list, covering virtually every style and variety; table wines are often identified not only by variety, but also by vineyard and area (all grapes are purchased); a full range of sparkling and fortified wines also available. Each wine is necessarily made in restricted quantities.

Distribution: Almost exclusively cellar door sales and mailing list. Limited local restaurant distribution. Mailing list enquiries to PO Box 195, Lyndoch. Cellar door sales 9 a.m. to 6 p.m. 7 days.

Summary: Kellermeister has no fixed winemaking abode; small quantities of wines are made, finished off or purchased by Kellermeister at or from other wineries in the Barossa Valley. Overall quality is quite good, even if style can vary somewhat.

KIES ESTATE

Location: Hoffnungsthal Road, Lyndoch, 5351; cellar door sales 1 km north of Lyndoch on Barossa Valley Highway.
(085) 24 4511.

Winemaker: Brian Fletcher.

1989 Production: The equivalent of 65,000 cases.

Principal Wines: Chardonnay, Semillon Blanc, Cabernet Sauvignon, Cabernet Franc, Shiraz, Rhine Riesling, Traminer and Muscat of Alexandria.

Distribution: Retail distribution through I. H. Wines & Spirits, NSW, Vic., Qld and WA; Seabrook & Seabrook, SA; and Rutherglen Wine Company, Tas. Cellar door sales 9 a.m. to 5 p.m. Monday to Friday and 10 a.m. to 5 p.m. weekends and public holidays. Mailing list available; enquiries to PO Box 4, Lyndoch, 5351.

Prices: $4 to $14.20 retail.

Vintage Rating 1986–89: '89, '88, '87, '86.

Tasting Notes:

1988 CHARDONNAY **[80]** *Colour:* medium to full yellow. *Bouquet:* voluminous and quite complex, with very pronounced charred/lemony oak. *Palate:* some bottle-developed characters emerging; quite rich fruit, again with strong lemony charred oak the main driving force; a wine that I have tasted on five or six occasions and always had different opinions about. It has, however, topped the Australian Smallmakers Wine competition two years running, so others would point it even more highly than I. Drink '90.

1988 CLASSIC DRY WHITE **[64]** *Colour:* light green-yellow. *Bouquet:* highly scented bath salts/floral frontignan characters. *Palate:* scented, grapy frontignac-like flavours but with a curious extra dimension that cloys on the finish. If you like fruit concoction flavours, the wine will appeal greatly. Drink '90.

VERY OLD PORT (13 YEARS) *[86]* *Colour:* medium tawny with a touch of olive. *Bouquet:* soft, vanillan/dusty aromas with some rancio character. *Palate:* very rich, complex mid-palate with a classically drying back palate and finish; would have rated even higher were it not for the slightly dusty bouquet.

Summary: One suspects that St Huberts (the new owners) and Brian Fletcher (the new winemaker) are still trying to come to terms with some rather curious wines in the Kies cellar. The Classic Dry Red sold during 1989 was anything but that, and was really not of anything remotely approaching commercial quality. However, there are some lovely wines, notably the 1988 Chardonnay. It will be interesting to see what future vintages produce.

❦ KRONDORF

Location: Krondorf Road, Tanunda, 5352; 7 km south-east of town. (085) 63 1245.

Winemaker: Nicholas Walker.

Principal Wines: Top of the range releases are the Show Reserve Burge & Wilson Chardonnay and Burge & Wilson Cabernet Sauvignon. Next follow limited edition Chardonnay, Sauvignon Blanc, Cabernet Sauvignon and Cabernet Franc Cabernet Sauvignon. At the bottom end come the standard releases of Chablis, Shiraz Cabernet, Barossa Valley Rhine Riesling and Coonawarra Hermitage.

Distribution: National retail through all types of liquor outlets.

Prices: Show Reserve $18; limited edition $12; commercial range $7.

Vintage Rating 1986–89: White: '87, '88, '89, '86. Red: '88, '86, '87, '89.

Tasting Notes:

1989 CHABLIS *[70]* *Colour:* light green-yellow. *Bouquet:* some green citric/colombard-like fruit aromas of light to medium intensity. *Palate:* pleasant citric/herbal fruit, again suggesting some colombard; quite good acid and fair chablis style. Drink '90.

1988 BAROSSA VALLEY RHINE RIESLING *[64]* *Colour:* light to medium yellow-green. *Bouquet:* firm, with a slightly herbaceous edge and a touch of camphor, all tending to diminish riesling character. *Palate:* of medium weight, clean and rather plain fruit with some depth; a workmanlike commercial wine. Drink '90.

1988 SHOW RESERVE CHARDONNAY *[85]* *Colour:* medium yellow-green. *Bouquet:* smooth, clean, well-integrated fruit and oak of medium to full intensity; so good is the integration that the bouquet is almost one dimensional. *Palate:* first-class oak handling; while the fruit is not full, the oak does not really throw the wine out of balance and certainly adds to the flavour and feel; pleasant acid on the finish is another plus. Drink '90–'91.

1986 RESERVE EDEN VALLEY RHINE RIESLING *[93]* *Colour:* medium yellow-green. *Bouquet:* glorious toasty/lime aromas, rich, full and complex, yet retaining exceptional life. *Palate:* rich, full and toasty; sweet lime fruit in best area style is still there in abundance; a superbly complex and high flavoured wine. Drink '90–'94.

1987 COONAWARRA HERMITAGE *[72]* *Colour:* medium red-purple. *Bouquet:* rather subdued fruit with a faintly leafy/leathery astringency; light, leafy berry fruit which proclaimed its Coonawarra origin in the Barossa Valley tasting in which the wine was assessed; obviously over-cropped and lacks fruit weight/richness. However, competent winemaking has produced a totally acceptable commercial wine. Drink '90–'91.

1985 SHOW RESERVE CABERNET SAUVIGNON *[77]* *Colour:* medium to full brick-red. *Bouquet:* slightly roasted/old-fashioned style. *Palate:* light, full, slightly roasted dark chocolate fruit flavours; very traditional red in style; a real throw-back. A blend of Coonawarra and McLaren Vale material in which the McLaren Vale has taken control. Drink '90–'92.

Summary: With the Krondorf wines you basically

pay for what you get, with very clearly delineated quality breaks between the price levels.

LEO BURING

Location: Sturt Highway, Tanunda, 5352;
2 km north-east of Township.
(085) 63 2184.

Winemaker: John Vickery (winemaker/manager).

Principal Wines: A very substantial range of table wines, which fall into a number of groupings. The highest quality wines, both white and red, are released under the Reserve Bin labels incorporating a system of bin numbers that change each year. Releases of Show Reserves include some of the greatest rhine rieslings in the country. These are followed by the Leo Buring Varietal Collection of white and red table wines: Chardonnay, Fumé Blanc, Rhine Riesling, Shiraz, Cabernet and Pinot Noir. Next come such popular wines as Leibfrauwine. The range is completed with a prestige 3L Signature Cask including Colombard/Chardonnay, Fumé Blanc and Shiraz Cabernet. All these wines as well as some limited release wines are available at the cellar door of Leo Buring's Chateau Leonay at Tanunda.

Distribution: National retail distribution at all levels. UK imports through Nicks International Wines.

Prices: From $8.50 for 3L casks; $6.50 and $7.50 for Varietals; $12 for Reserve Bins and up to $50 plus for Show Reserve releases.

Vintage Rating 1986–89: White: '89, '86, '88, '87. Red: '89, '86, '88, '87.

Outstanding Prior Vintages: White: '72, '75, '79, '73. Red: '83, '85.

Tasting Notes:

1979 EDEN VALLEY RHINE RIESLING BIN DW 116 [86] Colour: medium yellow-green, still bright and youthful. *Bouquet:* clean, firm, toasty, still surprisingly reserved and relatively non-aromatic. *Palate:* very firm, spotlessly clean, extraordinarily undeveloped Peter Pan style; lovely toasty flavours but without the fruit core of the very greatest show reserves. Drink '90–'94.

1977 WATERVALE RHINE RIESLING BIN DWG 41 [90] Colour: medium to full yellow, with a touch of green. *Bouquet:* clean, rich honeyed toasty aromas; fantastic style, although in blind tastings one can be uncertain whether this is a great old riesling or a great old unwooded semillon. *Palate:* full, rich honeyed fruit, almost sweet, and then a classic dry, long finish. Cannot improve, but is certainly showing no signs of decay. Drink '90–'92.

1973 EDEN VALLEY RHINE RIESLING BIN DWC 17 [95] Colour: medium to full yellow-green. *Bouquet:* superlative bottle-developed toasty/lime aromas, still with some crispness. *Palate:* gloriously smooth, honeyed/toasty/lime flavours; holding both fruit and structure; quite simply, a great wine. Drink '90–'92.

1988 BAROSSA/COONAWARRA CABERNET SAUVIGNON [90] Colour: very good purple-red. *Bouquet:* strong French oak with solid fruit in which the blend has resulted in perfect fruit ripeness balance; concentrated yet elegant. *Palate:* ultra-stylish charred French oak set against strong and perfectly flavoured cabernet; nicely balanced tannins round off what seems certain to be a great wine. While a tank sample, has been pointed because it did seem complete. Drink '93–'98.

1987 BAROSSA/COONAWARRA CABERNET SAUVIGNON [81] Colour: medium purple-red. *Bouquet:* clean, full sweet red berry fruit with a touch of vanillan oak. *Palate:* pleasant, soft, well-balanced cherry/berry fruit perfectly integrated with soft vanillan oak; rounded off by soft tannins.

1986 BAROSSA/COONAWARRA CABERNET SAUVIGNON DR 494 [77] Colour: medium full red-purple. *Bouquet:* ripe cassis/berry fruit, but the oak is slightly dull. *Palate:* strong, red berry fruit held back from top points by a very slight old oak character. Drink '90–'93.

Summary: One of the compensations for the endless and at times agonising tastings for this book came with the marvellous array of old Buring Rhine Rieslings, all of which are or will

be available on the Classic re-release
programme. Certainly they are expensive, but
they fully merit their price. They are great
wines by world standards. However, the three
reds also provided a fascinating exercise,
showing a progressive change in the attitude of
the Lindeman group to the use of oak (and, of
course, expenditure on it). The late Leo
Buring must be well content with the way his
name is being protected and remembered.

🍇 _MOCULTA WINE CO._

Location: Truro Road, Moculta, 5353; 7 km north-
east of Angaston.
(085) 63 9065.

Winemakers: John Doughty and Doug Lehmann
(contract winemaker).

Principal Wines: Rhine Riesling, White Frontignac,
Shiraz/Cabernet Sauvignon, Shiraz, Tawny Port.

Distribution: Principally cellar door sales and
mailing list; cellar door sales 9 a.m. to 5 p.m.
7 days. Mailing list enquiries to PO Box 80,
Moculta, 5353. Also selected restaurant wine
lists.

Summary: Moculta takes its grapes from a variety
of sources including estate-grown grapes, a
leased vineyard on the Moculta-Angaston road,
and from contract-purchased grapes which are
then principally made elsewhere under
contract. The contract-made wines are good;
the estate-made Tawny Port is distinctively less
successful and is not recommended.

🍇 _ORLANDO_

Location: Sturt Highway, Rowland Flat, 5350;
immediately north of township.
(085) 24 4500.

Winemakers: Robin Day, Ivan Limb, Leon Deans,
Bernie Hickin, Tom Van der Hoek, David
Morris and Stephen Obst.

1989 Production: 68,000 tonnes (the equivalent of
4,420,000 cases.

Principal Wines: Orlando takes grapes from all
over South Australia, the principal regions
being Barossa, Eden and Clare Valleys,
Coonawarra, Padthaway, McLaren Vale and the
Riverland. The Eden Valley is the most
important source of high-quality Rhine
Rieslings and traminer; Coonawarra,
Padthaway, McLaren Vale and the Riverland for
Chardonnay; and Coonawarra/Padthaway for
Cabernet Sauvignon. At the top end of the
Premium Wines comes the Jacaranda Ridge
Coonawarra Cabernet Sauvignon and the
legendary Steingarten Rhine Riesling. Also
included in this bracket is Flaxman's Eden
Valley Traminer, arguably the finest traminer in
Australia. After this classic series comes The
Saint Range comprising St Helga Eden Valley
Rhine Riesling, St Hilary Chardonnay and St
Hugo Coonawarra Cabernet Sauvignon. Then
follows the newly released Gramps Five
Generations Range, all vintaged from Barossa
Valley fruit, and comprising a Cabernet Merlot,
Pinot Noir, Chardonnay, Rhine Riesling and
botrytised Semillon. Then follows the RF
series of Chardonnay and Cabernet Sauvignon.
Jacob's Creek Claret is by far the largest-selling
bottled red wine in Australia, outselling its
nearest competitor (Seaview Cabernet
Sauvignon) by 3 to 1. Jacob's Creek Rhine
Riesling is the second-largest-selling rhine
riesling and the recently released Jacob's Creek
Chablis is Australia's number one selling
chablis style with Jacob's Creek Beaujolais
being the biggest selling Australian Beaujolais
style. Orlando is also the dominant force in
the cask market. The Coolabah range of casks
is consistently of better quality than those of
any other company. More recently, Orlando
has entered the two-litre cask market under the
Orlando brand with five vintage varietal styles.
Orlando also has a major presence in the
bottle fermented Sparkling Wine market
achieved since its introduction in 1980 of
Carrington Brut Champagne. Since then, with
the addition of Carrington Brut de Brut and
Carrington Blush, the Carrington range has
become the second biggest brand in this
market. More recently Carrington Cremant, a
non-vintage Chardonnay/Pinot Noir Brut and
Carrington Sparkling Burgundy, a non-vintage
blend of Shiraz and Pinot Noir, have been
released to compete in the premium sparkling
segment.

Distribution: National retail at all levels.

Prices: $6.99 to $19.99 retail.

Vintage Rating 1986–89: White: '86, '87, '88, '89. Red: '86, '87, '88, '89.

Tasting Notes:

1989 GRAMPS RHINE RIESLING [79] Colour: light to medium green-yellow. _Bouquet:_ quite rich and strong spicy/traminer-like overtones which seems to be the hallmark of Orlando's handling of this variety. _Palate:_ very high-flavoured, high-toned, spicy wine, again with traminer overtones; does have definitive flavour and fruit. Time and again Orlando is accused of blending traminer in its top of the range wines, and time and again it denies that accusation. For the consumer it is, in any event, a completely irrelevant discussion. Drink '90–'91.

1989 ST HELGA RHINE RIESLING [83] Colour: light to medium green-yellow. _Bouquet:_ clean, quite soft with fragrant fruit salad aromas. _Palate:_ clean, with very well-balanced fruit and acid; again the flavours are in the fruit salad range, promising a great deal of flavour and relatively early development. Drink '90–'91.

1989 JACOB'S CREEK CHABLIS [72] Colour: light to medium green-yellow. _Bouquet:_ clean and crisp, but with good fruit intensity. _Palate:_ a very clean, well-made wine with quite solid fruit flavours, almost tending more to white burgundy in style than chablis, but none the worse for that. Yet another success under this label. Drink '90.

1988 ST HILARY CHARDONNAY [80] Colour: light straw-green. _Bouquet:_ complex barrel-ferment aromas with smoky/melon fruit and good oak integration and balance. _Palate:_ a lively, tangy wine with melon/grapefruit flavours, and again some evidence of barrel-fermentation. Has style, and should develop nicely. Drink '90–'92.

1986 SHOW SHIRAZ [90] Colour: medium to full red-purple. _Bouquet:_ clean, rich berry fruit with excellent oak balance and integration. _Palate:_ an outstandingly rich and complex wine with exemplary American oak handling; soft, textured and velvety in the manner of all great shiraz. Has a very long future. Drink '92–'97.

1986 ST HUGO CABERNET SAUVIGNON [88] Colour: medium to full red. _Bouquet:_ very complex red berry/cassis/leafy fruit aromas. _Palate:_ once again, a complex, almost riotous assemblage of fruit flavours, running across the amalgam of spicy/berry/leafy characters; finishes with soft tannins. Little wonder the wine has received seven gold medals. Drink '90–'93.

Summary: Orlando is one of Australia's most important makers of high-quality wines. It consistently produces wines of unimpeachable quality that regularly outpoint most others in the same price bracket. Orlando does care about grape quality, and has a dedicated team of very skilled winemakers, so its consistency and quality are guaranteed.

PENFOLDS

Location: Tanunda Road, Nuriootpa, 5355; 2 km south of township.
(085) 62 0389.

Winemakers: The Penfolds winemaking team headed by John Duval.

Principal Wines: Specialist red winemakers of the highest reputation and quality; in descending order of price are Australia's greatest red wine, Grange Hermitage, then Bin 707 Cabernet Sauvignon followed by Magill Estate, then St Henri Claret, Bin 389 Cabernet Shiraz, Bin 28 Kalimna Shiraz and Bin 128 Coonawarra Shiraz. Koonunga Hill Claret has, since 1976, established itself as one of the best value-for-money red wines in the lower half of the market. Over the years some quite magnificent show release wines have appeared under non-repeating bin numbers. For many, 1962 Bin 60A is the greatest red produced in Australia in the last 30 years; others of note are Bin 58 of 1961, Bins 61, 62, 63 and 64 of 1963 and Bin 7 of 1967. In more recent times the Show Bins have made a more than welcome reappearance with a magnificent 1980 Bin 80A and the equally great 1982 Bin 820. The limited range of white wines comprise Chardonnay, Chardonnay Semillon, Fumé Blanc and Bin 202 Traminer Riesling.

Distribution: National through retailers at all
levels. Cellar door sales Monday to Friday 9 a.m.
to 5.30 p.m., public holidays and Saturdays
10 a.m. to 5 p.m., and Sundays (long weekends
only) noon to 4 p.m.

Prices: A wide range from $4.99 to $60 (for
Grange hermitage) but with discounting often
making a nonsense of theoretical retail prices.

Vintage Rating 1986–89: White: '88, '89, '87, '86.
Red: '86, '87, '89, '88.

Outstanding Prior Vintages: White: '82, '80, '78.
Red: '82, '80, '83, '76, '71.

Tasting Notes:

1988 SEMILLON CHARDONNAY [84] Colour:
bright, strong green-yellow. _Bouquet:_ rich, full
spicy/nutmeg oak with plenty of honeyed/
buttery fruit. _Palate:_ a cunningly wrought wine
with lovely spicy oak and very generous honeyed/
buttery/peachy fruit. Drink '90–'92.

1987 MAGILL ESTATE [86] Colour: medium to
full red-purple. _Bouquet:_ full, rich and
complex, with strong lemon/vanillan oak.
Palate: complex vanillan/lemony American
oak with strong red berry fruit underneath; of
medium to full weight, and soft persistent
tannins. In the absolute mainstream of Penfolds
red winemaking style. Drink '91–'96.

1987 ST HENRI [80] Colour: medium to full
purple-red. _Bouquet:_ strong lemony/vanillan
oak with smooth red berry fruits; complex.
Palate: a very rich wine with pronounced
tannins running throughout; the fruit is fully
ripened and perhaps fractionally old fashioned
in style, which is presumably precisely what the
winemakers intended. Drink '93–2000.

1987 CABERNET SHIRAZ BIN 389 [74] Colour:
medium to full purple-red. _Bouquet:_ clean, with
quite ripe berry fruit aromas of medium to full
intensity and pronounced American oak.
Palate: again, very clean with strong lemony/
vanillan American oak dominating the fruit;
soft tannins will provide structural balance, but
the fruit intensity is not quite there. Drink
'91–'94.

1986 CABERNET SAUVIGNON BIN 707 [92] Colour:
dense purple-red. _Bouquet:_ strong vanillan
American oak woven into deep, ripe,
concentrated cassis/berry fruit. _Palate:_ extraordinarily concentrated and rich with coconut/

vanillan oak and unctuous dark berry/
cassis/dark chocolate flavours, finishing with
sweet fruit rather than astringent tannins.
Drink '92–2000.

1984 GRANGE HERMITAGE [90] Colour: dense
red-purple. _Bouquet:_ firm and deep, with
strong toasty/vanillan/barrel-ferment aromas.
Palate: by the standards of most Granges, the
fruit appears almost subdued and vanilla
bean/barrel-ferment oak characters tend to
dominate at this juncture. The tannins are
soft, but there is no question over the long
term future of the wine. After the opulence of
the '82 and '83 vintages, the cool 1984 year has
had its mark on the wine. Drink '92–2010.

Summary: Some of the 1987 Penfolds reds seem a
slight let down after the magnificence of the
'86 reds; however, it is very much a question of
degree. What is more, taken as a whole, the
most recent and up-coming releases of
Penfolds clearly entitle it to be recognised as
Australia's finest red winemaker.

🍇 _PETER LEHMANN_

PETER LEHMANN
BAROSSA VALLEY
CHARDONNAY

Location: Samuel Road off Para Road, Tanunda,
5352; 1.5 km north-west of Tanunda.
(085) 63 2500; Fax (085) 63 3402.

Winemakers: Peter Lehmann, Andrew Wigan,
Peter Scholz and Leonie Bain.

1989 Production: Approximately 10,000 tonnes
(the equivalent of 65,000 cases).

Principal Wines: Specialist winemakers of quality
Barossa Valley table wines and vintage ports
under the Peter Lehmann and Masterson
labels. Wines under the Peter Lehmann label
include Rhine Riesling, Dry Semillon, Chenin
Blanc, Fumé Blanc, Semillon/Chardonnay,
Chardonnay, Bortytis Semillon Sauternes,
Brut Absolu, Cabernet Sauvignon, Pinot Noir,
Shiraz Dry Red, Shiraz/Tokay, Shiraz
Cabernet, Beaujolais and Vintage Port. The
Masterson label is represented by Rhine

Riesling, Dry Chablis and Dry Red.

Distribution: Extensive retail distribution through the Tucker Seabrook Caon Group in all states except WA, where Johnson Harper are the wholesale agents. Masterson is distributed by John Cawsey & Co. Cellar door sales 9 a.m. to 5 p.m. Monday to Friday 11 a.m. to 4 p.m. Saturday, Sunday and public holidays. Attractive picnic grounds by the banks of the Para River. For mailing list write to PO Box 315, Tanunda, SA 5352.

Prices: $8.49 to $12.89 Peter Lehmann label; $3.45 Masterson label.

Vintage Rating 1986–89: White: '87, '86, '88, '89. Red: '88, '89, '87, '86.

Outstanding Prior Vintages: '89, '82.

Tasting Notes:

1988 CHARDONNAY [65] Colour: light to medium green-yellow. *Bouquet:* strong oily/vanillan/chippy oak seems to sit on top of fruit. *Palate:* very similar oily/vanillan/chippy oak flavours dominate; there is some fruit present, and the wine will probably flesh out somewhat over the next few months. Adequate commercial style. Drink '90.

1988 SEMILLON SAUTERNES [81] Colour: light to medium yellow-orange. *Bouquet:* raisined, luscious fruit, a hint of volatility and lemony/charred oak all present. *Palate:* strong sweet fruit is balanced by penetrating acid and quite obvious oak; a very high-toned wine, still coming together; the finish is good and the potential for yet higher points is obvious. Drink '90–'92.

1987 CABERNET SAUVIGNON [77] Colour: medium purple-red. *Bouquet:* very clean with pleasant, red berry aromas and a touch of cassis; the oak is well integrated. *Palate:* fresh, clean, pleasant red berry/cassis flavours and soft tannins; a gentle wine that does not rely on obvious oak, and is already nearing its peak. A worthy successor to the quite outstanding '86 vintage. Drink '93–'97.

1986 SHIRAZ [83] Colour: light to medium red. *Bouquet:* pronounced spicy fruit aromas with some cedar/cigar/old polished wood, bottle-developed characters. *Palate:* spicy fruit and oak intermingle so completely it is difficult to tell from whence the spice comes; an elegant wine with life and lovely flavour; a reversion to the old days with a small percentage of tokay blended in. Drink '90–'94.

1985 VINTAGE PORT BIN AD 2004 [81] Colour: medium to full red, showing some development. *Bouquet:* potent, rich and very complex high-toned brandy spirit aroma. *Palate:* similarly high-toned style, almost identical to the preceding vintages; very spicy fragrant fruit; is one of those wines that entrance some and are disliked by others. Peter Lehmann has suggested on the label when it will reach its peak.

Summary: The Lehmann saga continues. He has given his life's blood to the Barossa Valley and to Peter Lehmann Wines for so many years no one pays much attention, but Peter Lehmann is truly more than a mere Baron of the Barossa.

ROCKFORD

Location: Krondorf Road, Tanunda, 5352; 3 km south of Tanunda.
(085) 63 2720.

Winemaker: Robert O'Callaghan.

Principal Wines: A range of varietal wines made from grapes purchased throughout a number of South Australia's wine regions including the Eden Valley, the Adelaide Plains, the Barossa Valley and the Southern Vales. Wines include Eden Valley Rhine Riesling, Adelaide Plains Sauvignon Blanc, Spatlese White Frontignac, Rhine Riesling Botrytis Cinerea, Alicante Bouchet, Shiraz Cabernet, Cabernet Sauvignon, Muscat of Alexandria, Tawny Port and Shiraz Vintage Port. Future releases will, however, concentrate increasingly on the Barossa Valley, eventually to the exclusion of all other districts.

Distribution: Exclusively cellar door sales and mailing lists; cellar door sales 11 a.m. to 5.30 p.m. 7 days. Mailing list enquiries to PO Box 142, Tanunda, 5352.

Tasting Notes:

1989 EDEN VALLEY RHINE RIESLING [78] Colour: bright, full green-yellow. *Bouquet:* very floral, full lime/pineapple estery fruit. *Palate:* an extremely full, soft and ever so slightly sweet wine with abundant lime/pineapple fruit;

everything in the wine shows the impact of mature, low yielding vines. Drink '90–'93.

1988 EDEN VALLEY RHINE RIESLING [77] Colour: medium yellow-green. *Bouquet:* full, rich, lush tropical/passionfruit/lime aromas. *Palate:* very full, high flavoured tropical/ pineapple lime fruit, with residual sugar even more pronounced that in the '89; a wine custom-built for the cellar door. Drink '90–'91.

1988 VINE VALE RHINE RIESLING [74] Colour: medium yellow-green. *Bouquet:* solid, deep fruit with distinct heaviness and strong lime flavours. *Palate:* a huge wine, almost thick, the rhine riesling drinker's answer to red wine, with enormous extract and flavour. Drink '90–'95.

1989 ALICANTE BOUCHET [73] Colour: light to medium purple-red. *Bouquet:* clean, soft cherry plum fruit. *Palate:* quite complex, despite its softness, with plum/cherry flavours and just a hint of gaminess; again, a cellar door special. Drink '90.

1987 BASKET PRESS SHIRAZ [77] Colour: medium to full red-purple, showing some development. *Bouquet:* deep and still rather closed fruit yet to really open up; some vanillan oak. *Palate:* complex, developed wine with an almost chewy mid-palate; very clean and nicely judged vanillan oak. Drink '91–'95.

Summary: Some quite surprising wines come out under the Rockford labels, full of flavour and character. Given that Rocky O'Callaghan is the winemaker, this is only proper. The quality of the current releases is once again exceptional, but O'Callaghan's attention to correspondence is deplorable. Accordingly, there is a dearth of information on price and other such details.

ROSEWORTHY

Location: Roseworthy Agricultural College, Roseworthy, 5371; 6 km from town and 12 km north-west of Gawler.
(085) 24 8057; Fax (085) 24 8007.

Winemakers: Andrew Markides (winery manager) and Clive Hartnell (winemaker).

1989 Production: 6000 cases.

Principal Wines: Chardonnay, Rhine Riesling, *Méthode champenoise,* Spatlese, Cabernet Sauvignon/Merlot, Angaston Shiraz, Amontillado Sherry, Old Liqueur Tawny Port, Vintage Port and Old Liqueur Brandy.

Distribution: Cellar door sales 10 a.m. to 4.30 p.m. Monday to Friday. Mailing list enquiries to above address. Retail distribution to Vintage Cellars and other selected stores, SA; Emerald Wines, Vic.; Oak Barrel Wines, ACT and NSW.

Prices: $9 to $14.

Vintage Rating 1986–89: White: '89, '87, '88, '86. Red: '88, '89, '87, '86.

Tasting Notes:

NV BRUT RESERVE [79] Colour: light to medium yellow-straw. *Bouquet:* shows good style with some cracked yeast, biscuity aroma. *Palate:* quite high flavour, but an obviously correct base wine has been used (in fact a blend of chardonnay and pinot noir); some slightly green flavours, which are not at all unpleasant; once again yeast autolysis also evident. A considerable surprise, and a very pleasant brut. Drink '90–'91.

1988 ANGASTON SHIRAZ [73] Colour: dense purple-red. *Bouquet:* clean, but dense and high extractive aromas, with a touch of mint. *Palate:* again, very extractive; there are minty fruit flavours before the mid-palate dips into some form of black hole; against all the odds, the tannins are surprisingly under control. To say the least, a challenging wine. Drink '93–'97.

1987 CABERNET MERLOT [74] Colour: light red-purple. *Bouquet:* clean, light leafy fruit with light lemony oak. *Palate:* very light leafy/ minty fruit with strong overtones of Bordeaux-style merlot from an intermediate vintage; hints of tobacco carry on the similarity. Drink '90–'92.

1988 VINTAGE PORT [67] Colour: medium to full purple-red. *Bouquet:* solid, dark berry fruit aromas and fairly plain fortifying spirit. *Palate:* precisely tracks the bouquet, with rather plain dark fruits, not helped by ordinary spirit. Should gain some complexity in bottle, of course. Drink '93–'97.

Summary: An interesting cross-section of wines that are very much better than those of the Riverina College, or as it now is, Charles Sturt University (the other teaching institution). For the sake of completeness I should add that two wooded white wines were not reviewable, suffering from very poor, oily oak.

ROVALLEY

Location: Sturt Highway, Rowland Flat, 5352; 5 km north-east of Lyndoch.
(085) 24 4537; Fax (085) 24 4066.

Winemakers: Karl Lambert (chief executive) and Christopher Schmidt (winemaker).

Principal Wines: A major shake-up is planned for Rovalley following a change of ownership. A premium range will be established of Chardonnay, Sauvignon Blanc, Semillon, Chenin Blanc, Traminer-Riesling, Botrytis Rhine Riesling, Old Liqueur Frontignac and Old Liqueur Port.

Distribution: Cellar door sales 8.30 a.m. to 4.30 p.m. Monday to Friday; 10 a.m. to 4 p.m. weekends and holidays. Wholesale distribution through James Richardson Pty Ltd.

Prices: Premium table wine $7.50 to $12; Fortifieds $3.30 to $25.

Summary: Extensive modifications and rejuvenation of the winery are underway, and one hopes that the somewhat questionable reputation of Rovalley is a thing of the past.

ST HALLETT

Location: St Hallett's Road, Tanunda, 5352; 4 km south of Township.
(085) 63 2319.

Winemaker: Stuart Blackwell.

Principal Wines: A revamped range of white and red table wines and fortified wines, including Colombard Rhine Riesling, Semillon Sauvignon Blanc, Chardonnay, Cabernet Merlot, and Old Block Shiraz (the grapes for which come from a 100-year-old vineyard).

Distribution: Wholesale distribution in SA, Vic. and NSW provide retail distribution. Substantial cellar door sales 9.30 a.m. to 4.45 p.m. Monday to Friday and 10 a.m. to 4 p.m. weekends. Mailing list enquiries to PO Box 120, Tanunda, 5352.

Prices: $12 to $15 retail table wines; $10 to $26 fortified wines.

Tasting Notes:

1989 SEMILLON SAUVIGNON BLANC _[81]_ _Colour:_ light to medium green-yellow. _Bouquet:_ beautifully made, with good fruit weight and quite pronounced gooseberry sauvignon blanc character. _Palate:_ excellent fruit length, balance and style; the varietal blend works to perfection as the semillon adds richness to the underlying tangy/gooseberry sauvignon flavours. Drink '90–'91.

1989 CHARDONNAY _[82]_ _Colour:_ medium green-yellow. _Bouquet:_ intense grapefruit aromas with complementary lemony oak. _Palate:_ complex oak handling with nicely judged and weighted flavours: lemony oak against tangy grapefruit chardonnay; has length. Drink '90–'91.

1986 OLD BLOCK SHIRAZ _[85]_ _Colour:_ medium to full red-purple. _Bouquet:_ clean, dense dark berry/dark chocolate fruit with just a touch of sweet American oak. _Palate:_ a very clean wine, full and rich; a fresh fore-palate with dark berry/chocolate flavours gives way to a textured, deep and rich finish with soft tannins. Comes as no surprise to find that this lovely shiraz is made from very old vines. Drink '92–2000.

1987 CABERNET MERLOT _[68]_ _Colour:_ medium red-purple. _Bouquet:_ plain with some rather dull soapy/leathery aromas. _Palate:_ a jumpy, slightly metallic wine with some dark chocolate flavours; suggestive of a red that has suffered sulphide, has been cleaned up, but is still to come together. Tasted immediately after bottling and may have been at its worst. Drink '91–'94.

Summary: Co-owner Bob McLean has undoubted marketing expertise, and used to know about public relations. However, answering correspondence does not appear to be part of the agenda, and once again, vital details are missing. That is a pity, because winemaker (and junior partner) Stuart Blackwell has certainly done his bit for the cause. On a slightly more serious note, St Hallett is throwing out a strong challenge in a carefully selected sector of the market.

SALTRAM

Location: Angaston Road, Angaston, 5353; 1 km west of township.
(085) 64 2200; Fax (085) 64 2876.

Winemakers: Mark Turnbull (chief) and David Norman (assistant).

1989 Production: Very substantial but not for publication.

Principal Wines: A wide range of bottled wines and fortified wines is marketed under a number of label series. The Saltram flagship is the Mamre Brook range, which includes a Chardonnay and a Cabernet/Shiraz. The highest-quality wines are marketed under the Pinnacle label, comprising Rhine Riesling, Sauvignon Blanc, Pinot Noir, Chardonnay and Cabernet Sauvignon. Then follows a range of varietal whites and reds including Chardonnay, Rhine Riesling, Sauvignon Blanc, Cabernet Sauvignon, Shiraz, as well as generics such as Chablis, White Burgundy, Traminer Riesling and Claret. Saltram also produce and market the long-running Metala Claret. The fortified wines include tawny ports such as Old Lodge, Ludlow's and the prestigious Mr Pickwick's Particular Port.

Distribution: National retail through Continental Seagram Pty Ltd branches. UK imports through The George Morton Company & Oddbins. Cellar door sales 9 a.m. to 5 p.m. Monday to Friday and noon to 5 p.m. weekends. Mailing list/mail orders available; enquiries to PO Box 321, Angaston, 5353.

Prices: Vary widely according to quality and style, cellar-door prices range from around $6 to $16. Fortified wines vary from $7 to $40.

Vintage Rating 1986–89: White: '89,'88, '87, '86. Red: '86, '87, '89, '88.

Outstanding Prior Vintages: '67, '71, '76, '80, '82, '83, '85.

Tasting Notes:

1989 PINNACLE SELECTION SAUVIGNON BLANC [85] Colour: light to medium straw-yellow. *Bouquet:* potent, rich gooseberry/tropical fruit showing astonishingly good varietal character. *Palate:* somewhat firmer and leaner than the bouquet suggests, but will probably grow in bottle; potent, tangy high-toned flavours could indeed lift the wine to 90 points. Drink '90–'92.

1988 PINNACLE SELECTION CHARDONNAY [78] Colour: medium yellow-green. *Bouquet:* strong, complex charred/slightly hessiany oak and rich, full fruit. *Palate:* complex, charred oak is extremely well handled; at this juncture it tends to dominate the fruit, but will probably come into better balance over the next year. Drink '90–'92.

1988 MAMRE BROOK CHARDONNAY [73] Colour: medium yellow-green. *Bouquet:* slightly oily/vanillan/lemon oak with fruit of light to medium intensity; rather one dimensional. *Palate:* strong vanillan oak flavours, which seem to be American-derived, are somewhat inappropriate to the variety, and certainly have a one-dimensional effect. For all that, the wine is not short of flavour. Drink '90–'92.

1984 MAMRE BROOK CABERNET SHIRAZ [75] Colour: dense red. *Bouquet:* concentrated dark chocolate/dark berry fruit characters, yet somehow lacking fragrance. *Palate:* big, strong brawny old style Australian red, long on flavour and short on finesse; will undoubtedly have its followers. Drink '90–'95.

Summary: The wines submitted to the district tasting were all at the top end and, as the notes indicate, performed very well. However, in recent times I have been consistently impressed with the quality of the wines at the bottom end of the range, which have tended to out point wines from other producers with rather higher price tags attached. After a long period of hibernation, the Saltram machine seems to have begun a long march.

Location: Seppeltsfield via Tanunda, 5352;
7 km north-east of Tanunda.
(085) 63 2626.
Chateau Tanunda, Basedow Road,Tanunda,
5352.

Winemakers: James Godfrey and Nigel Dolan.

1989 Production: Very substantial but not for
publication.

Principal Wines: Seppeltsfield Winery produces
Seppelt's famed tawny ports, Para Liqueur
Port, Seppeltsfield Tawny, Seppeltsfield Tawny-
21, Old Trafford and Mount Rufus. Each year
a 100-year-old vintage Para Liqueur Port is
released in tiny quantities, selling for over
$2000 per bottle. DP90 Tawny Port is
legendary for its quality and scarcity, while
Seppelt's equally distinguished range of
sherries (Flor Fino DP117, Amontillado DP116
and Oloroso DP38) are also matured at
Seppeltsfield. Seppelt's Chateau Tanunda
ferments the base wines for sherries, and
ferments and matures all of the South
Australian-based red wine drawn from the
Barossa Valley, Eden Valley, Southern Vales,
Langhorne Creek, River Murray and
Padthaway areas. Chateau Tanunda also
handles the premium cabernet sauvignon
grown on the company's long-established
though small Dorrien Vineyard. Premier
Vineyard Cabernet is made from premium
grapes grown at Seppelt and contract
(Langhorne Creek) vineyards.

Distribution: National retail through a wide range
of liquor outlets.

Prices: Basically within the $7 to $25 range for
table wines; discounting has some impact, but
not to the extent of other major companies.
Fortified wines $10 to $40 retail.

Vintage Rating 1986–89: White: '89, '86, '88, '87.
Red: '89, '86, '88, '87.

Outstanding Prior Vintages: '78, '81, '84.

Tasting Notes:

1988 GOLD LABEL CHARDONNAY **[88]** _Colour:_
medium to full yellow, with just a touch of
green. _Bouquet:_ an almost unbelievably well-
made wine given the quantity in which it is
produced; very complex, with perfect fruit/oak
balance and integration; lovely varietal
melon/grapefruit aromas. _Palate:_ fresh, clean
and vibrant melon/peach fruit; the oak is
perfectly judged in a support role that never
threatens to overwhelm the fruit. By a very
long way, the best volume selling chardonnay
on the market. For the record, a blend of
predominantly Barooga and Barossa material.
Drink '90–'92.

1988 BLACK LABEL CHARDONNAY **[85]** _Colour:_
bright yellow-green. _Bouquet:_ complex but fruit
driven wine, with melon/honey/grapefruit
aromas and every so slightly oily oak. _Palate:_
fine, fresh but relatively understated melon/
grapefruit/fig fruit flavours; the oak is in total
restraint; a wine destined to age with grace in
bottle, not a common characteristic in Australian
chardonnay. A blend of Barooga, Great Western
and Barossa material. Drink '90–'93.

1987 BLACK LABEL HERMITAGE **[77]** _Colour:_
medium purple-red. _Bouquet:_ clean,
pronounced minty/fruit aromas of light to
medium intensity. _Palate:_ strong minty
flavours, almost into toothpaste; very clean,
with light tannin and soft oak; Some judges
greatly admire strong minty characters; I would
rather see them a little more subdued. Drink
'90–'93.

SHOW FINO SHERRY BIN DP 117 **[92]** _Colour:_
light to medium yellow-straw. _Bouquet:_ superb
fine, fresh aromatic flor characters with
absolutely no oak influence, precisely as it
should be. _Palate:_ fine, intense marked nutty
flor flavours on the mid-palate, and a lingering,
dry finish. Not surprisingly, has amassed six
trophies between 1987 and 1989.

SHOW OLOROSO SHERRY BIN DP 38 **[91]**
Colour: deep golden brown with a pale olive
rim. _Bouquet:_ soft and round, with a tweak of
spirit and quite strong rancio. _Palate:_ a big,
rich, sweet middle-palate flavour with complex
rancio characters; superb balancing acid leads
to a dry finish.

SHOW TAWNY PORT BIN DP 90 **[96]** _Colour:_
glowing old tawny with a golden-brown rim.
Bouquet: fine, intense rancio with magnificent

edged spirit. *Palate:* almost unbelievably complex mid-palate with fine, intense lingering finish and perfect acid.

Summary: Seppelt makes the greatest wood-aged fortified wines in Australia; the only problem is that they do not have a wider and more appreciative reception. The standard of its table wines is consistently good; Seppelt simply does not know how to make an indifferent wine.

TARCHALICE

Location: Research Road, Vine Vale via Tanunda, 5352; 4 km north-east of Tanunda. (085) 63 3005.

Winemaker: Christopher M. Schmidt.

1989 Production: 3000 cases.

Principal Wines: Rhine Riesling, Spatlese Rhine Riesling, Botrytised Rhine Riesling, Gewurztraminer, Cabernet Merlot, Shiraz, Cabernet Sauvignon, Cabernet Franc and a range of ports.

Distribution: Principally cellar door sales and mailing list; cellar door sales 10 a.m. to 5 p.m. Monday to Saturday; 11 a.m. to 5 p.m. Sunday. Limited retail distribution Adelaide.

Prices: $6.50 to $16.50 cellar door.

Vintage Rating 1986–89: White: '89, '86, '88, '87. Red: '86, '89, '88, '87.

Summary: The Schmidt family have been growers in the Barossa Valley for many years, and became makers upon the graduation of Christopher Schmidt from Roseworthy Agricultural College several years ago. Wine style and quality are as yet a little uncertain.

TOLLANA

Location: Tanunda Road, off Sturt Highway, Nuriootpa, 5355; 2 km south of township. (085) 62 0389.

Winemakers: John Duval (chief winemaker) and Rod Chapman (production manager).

Principal Wines: A recent reappraisal of wines led to Tollana diversifying grape sources and no longer relying solely on its excellent Woodbury Vineyard in the High Eden Hills. Woodbury continues to supply Eden Valley Rhine Riesling and the great Cabernet Sauvignon Bin TR 222. The range has been rationalised since the Penfolds takeover of Tollana and will now comprise mainly premium 750 ml Cabernet Sauvignon, Shiraz, Chardonnay, Sauvignon Blanc, Riesling and Botrytis Rhine Riesling.

Distribution: National into retail shops at all levels through Penfolds' own distribution network.

Prices: $7.95 to $13.95 retail.

Vintage Rating 1986–89: White: '87, '88, '89, '86. Red: '86, '88, '87, '89.

Outstanding Prior Vintages: White: '78, '82. Red: '82, '80, '76.

Tasting Notes:

1989 EDEN VALLEY RHINE RIESLING [78] *Colour:* medium green-yellow. *Bouquet:* soft, clean, rich and remarkably full lime/tropical aroma. *Palate:* an exceptionally full-flavoured and forward wine early in its life; had the feel of a wine that had been in bottle for at least one year; could develop very well, and very much in the manner of the '88 tasted only one month previously. Drink '90.

1988 EDEN VALLEY RHINE RIESLING [82] *Colour:* full yellow-green; deep and advanced. *Bouquet:* super-rich, intense lime pineapple aromas; quite striking. *Palate:* high-flavoured limy fruit, with a very slightly broad but soft finish; once again, remarkably developed. Drink '90.

1988 CHARDONNAY [90] *Colour:* medium yellow-green. *Bouquet:* very complex, full and stylish grapefruit, with excellent charred oak and barrel-ferment characters. *Palate:* lively, crisp tangy fruit, full of style; very good charred oak/barrel-ferment characters add complexity but do not threaten the fruit in any way. Drink '90–'91.

1988 BOTRYTIS RHINE RIESLING [82] *Colour:* medium to full yellow. *Bouquet:* full, soft tropical/fruit salad/apricot aromas. *Palate:* soft, rich, fleshy tropical/vanillan flavours; very sweet and could perhaps have done with a touch more residual sugar. A very good wine, but not in the olympian class of the '87. Drink '90–'91.

1987 CABERNET SAUVIGNON BIN TR 222 [77] *Colour:* medium red, with just a touch of purple. *Bouquet:* clean; strong lemony oak; an attractive spicy edge to fruit aroma of light to medium intensity. *Palate:* a clean, smooth and relatively light-bodied wine with well-integrated oak; the spicy and lemony flavours come together nicely, and it finishes with low tannin. Drink '90–'93.

Summary: Tollana adds another impressive arm to the Penfolds group octopus. It would be indeed interesting to know when and how the decisions are taken governing the grape and/or wine resources made available for the Tollana label; some of these wines threaten to upstage what I can only guess would be regarded as superior label products within the Penfold group.

VERITAS

Location: 94 Langmeil, Road, Tanunda, 5352; 3 km north of township.
(085) 63 2330.

Winemaker: Rolf Binder.

1989 Production: 6500 cases.

Principal Wines: Semillon Sauvignon Blanc, Rhine Riesling, Tramino, Rhine Riesling White Frontignac Spatlese, Leanyka, Cabernet Franc Merlot, Cabernet Sauvignon, Shiraz Cabernet Sauvignon Malbec, Bikaver Bull's Blood, and a range of ports, sherries, vermouths and even a Oom Pah Pah Port.

Distribution: Exclusively cellar door sales and mailing list. Cellar door sales 9 a.m. to 5 p.m. Monday to Friday and 11 a.m. to 5 p.m. weekends and public holidays. Mailing list enquiries to PO Box 126, Tanunda, 5352. UK imports through Lay and Wheeler Limited, Colchester.

Prices: $6 to $12 cellar door.

Vintage Rating 1986–89: White: '89, '86, '88, '87. Red: '89, '87, '88, '86.

Outstanding Prior Vintages: '84, '80.

Tasting Notes:

1987 SHIRAZ CABERNET MERLOT [74] *Colour:* medium red-purple. *Bouquet:* clean; of light to medium intensity, with very slightly minty/leafy fruit and well-integrated oak. *Palate:* clean and light minty/berry flavours with low tannin; a precisely defined, soft and light early drinking style. Drink '90–'92.

1987 CABERNET FRANC MERLOT [78] *Colour:* medium red, with a touch of purple. *Bouquet:* very clean, with strong vanillan oak, nice red berry fruits and a touch of chocolate. *Palate:* light, fragrant leafy/tobacco flavours showing excellent varietal style for a blend of this nature; low tannin. One might wish for more concentration, but that is not the nature of the varieties used. Drink '90–'92.

1987 CABERNET SAUVIGNON [74] *Colour:* medium red-purple. *Bouquet:* clean, soft very slightly squashy red berry fruit with light oak. *Palate:* soft, flavoursome red berry/plum fruits with some vanillan oak in support; easy, smooth and fairly light-bodied style. Drink '90–'92.

Summary: The 1989 white wines submitted had sampling problems that did not allow them to be meaningfully reviewed; the three red wines, by contrast, were extraordinarily consistent in style and quality. They are all elegant, and this style does not always fare well in large tastings, where bigger, brawnier wines tended to stand out. Certainly, they are ideally crafted for restaurants or those who wish to buy and drink rather than buy and cellar.

🍇 WARD'S GATEWAY CELLARS

Location: Lyndoch, 5351; between Sandy Creek and Lyndoch.
(085) 24 4138.

Winemaker: Ray Ward.

Principal Wines: Rhine Riesling, Colombard, White Burgundy, Chablis, Frontignac, Late Picked Frontignac, Shiraz, Bin 1 Dry Red, Shiraz Cabernet, Cabernet Sauvignon, Hailstone Port, Tawny Port.

Distribution: Exclusively cellar door sales (and mail order). Cellar door sales 9 a.m. to 5.30 p.m. Monday to Saturday.

Summary: The first winery in the Barossa Valley on the way from Adelaide, producing small quantities of traditional wines in unpretentious surroundings and with well-used winemaking equipment.

🍇 THE WILLOWS VINEYARD

THE
WILLOWS
VINEYARD

1987
Shiraz

Location: Light Pass Road, Light Pass, Barossa Valley, 5355.
(085) 62 1080.

Winemakers: Peter and Michael Scholz.

1989 Production: Approximately 2000 cases.

Principal Wines: Rhine Riesling, Semillon, Pinot Noir, Shiraz and Cabernet Sauvignon.

Distribution: Exclusively cellar door sales and mailing list; cellar door sales 10.30 a.m. to 4.30 p.m. 7 days.

Prices: $7 to $15 cellar door.

Summary: Unfortunately, no samples were available, but on all accounts the quality of the wines is good.

🍇 WOLF BLASS

Location: Bilyara Vineyards, Sturt Highway, Nuriootpa, 5355; 4 km north of township.
(085) 62 1955; Fax (085) 62 2156.
Adelaide Office: Level 2, 64 Hindmarsh Square, Adelaide, 5000.
(08) 232 0255; Fax (08) 232 1059.

Winemakers: John Glaetzer, Stephen John, Chris Hatcher and Christa Binder.

1989 Production: In excess of 400,000 cases, probably greatly so.

Principal Wines: The range comprises Classic Dry White, Yellow Label Rhine Riesling, Traminer Riesling, Spatlese Rhine Riesling, Green Label Frontignan Traminer, White Label (Chablis style), South Australian Chardonnay, Yellow Label Cabernet Shiraz, Grey Label Cabernet Sauvignon, Black Label Cabernet Sauvignon Shiraz, Brown Label Hermitage, Red Label Shiraz Cabernet, Presidents Selection Cabernet Sauvignon, Chardonnay Cuvee Champagne and 15-year-old Tawny Port.

Distribution: National retail to virtually all fine wine retailers through Remy Blass in all States other than NT (CUB) and Tas. (Chancellor's). Cellar door sales 9.15 a.m. to 4.30 p.m. Monday to Friday, noon to 4.15 p.m. weekends and public holidays.

Prices: $7.99 to $27.50 retail.

Tasting Notes:

1989 YELLOW LABEL RHINE RIESLING [90] Colour: light green-yellow. *Bouquet:* clean, full and rich lime/tropical/passionfruit aromas. *Palate:* a lovely, high-flavoured lime/tropical style with excellent fruit intensity and equally good balance. Drink '90–'91.

1988 CLASSIC DRY WHITE [77] Colour: medium yellow-green. *Bouquet:* very strong lemony oak and faint citric fruit aroma. *Palate:* strong, spicy/lemony oak is undoubtedly a major contributor to flavour, but the wine has very good feel in the mouth, and is an exceedingly cunningly wrought commercial wine; it came as no surprise to find that it was made by Wolf Blass. Drink '90–'91.

1988 SOUTH AUSTRALIAN CHARDONNAY [74] Colour: medium yellow-green. *Bouquet:* pronounced lemony oak is well handled but does dominate the fruit, which is rather light. *Palate:* pronounced, one-dimensional lemony oak; pleasant, clean fruit underneath, but the wine is structurally weak. Drink '90–'91.

1988 RED LABEL SHIRAZ CABERNET [76] Colour: very good purple-red. *Bouquet:* smooth and full, with solid dark berry fruit complexed by minty/gamey nuances. *Palate:* sweet, red berry fruit; soft, easy commercial style with low tannins; once again no surprise to find the Wolf Blass label on the wine. Drink '90–'91.

1986 BROWN LABEL HERMITAGE [86] Colour: medium red-purple. *Bouquet:* very clean, with complex lemony oak set against ever so slightly leafy fruit. *Palate:* the flavour and the structure of the wine are really excellent; light berry fruit lies at the core, and lovely tannins run through the wine. Drink '90–'93.

1984 BLACK LABEL CABERNET SAUVIGNON SHIRAZ [89] Colour: medium red. *Bouquet:* unusually fragrant, with lemony oak and leafy fruit. *Palate:* very stylish and plenty of flavour despite its age; red berry fruits are set in a cocoon of soft lemony oak, with some lingering barrel ferment characters; soft tannins round the wine off. Drink '90–'94.

Summary: Discipline, consistency, attention to detail in the winery and unremitting efforts in the market place are just a few of the factors that make the Wolf Blass operation such a remarkable one. If most Australian winemakers could take even a small leaf out of Wolf's book, there would be no stopping the Australian industry. Long known as a red wine specialist, Wolf Blass Wines is now the largest maker of rhine riesling in Australia; having assimilated that fact, then consider the quality of the standard Yellow Label Riesling. Little wonder the Wolf Blass domination of the Australian show system continues.

❦ *YALUMBA*

Location: Eden Valley Road, Angaston, 5353; 3 km south of township.
(085) 64 2423; Fax (085) 64 2549.

Winemakers: Described by Yalumba as "the Yalumba Team", headed by Brian Walsh and Geoff Linton.

1989 Production: Approximately 16,500 tonnes.

Principal Wines: The wines of S. Smith & Son Pty Ltd are marketed under four distinct labels. The first is the traditional Yalumba label, covering a range of wines and styles made from grapes not necessarily estate grown. Premium wines include Signature Collection Varietals, "D" *Méthode champenoise*, Brut de Brut Vintage Champagne and Galway Pipe Tawny Port. Next are the Hill Smith Estate wines made from estate-grown grapes on vineyards owned and made by members of the family and including Shiraz, Wood Matured Semillon, Cabernet Sauvignon, Chardonnay and Sauvignon Blanc; the wines are aimed particularly at the export market. Two new series of budget-priced wines under the Country Wines and Gourmet Series have further expanded the range. The remaining two brands are Pewsey Vale vineyard (Rhine Riesling, an occasional Botrytis Affected Rhine Riesling and Cabernet Sauvignon), and Heggies Vineyard, destined to produce Rhine Riesling (both dry and botrytis affected), Chardonnay, Pinot Noir, Cabernet Sauvignon, blended with Cabernet Franc, Viognier and Merlot. (See separate entires for each of Hill Smith Estate, Heggies and Pewsey Vale under Adelaide Hills.)

Distribution: National retail at all levels, principally through own offices in each of the eastern states.

Prices: $4.99 to $28 retail.

Vintage Rating 1986–89: White: '88, '89, '87, '86.
Red: '88, '86, '87, '89.

Outstanding Prior Vintages: White: '82. Red: '84, '77, '76.

Tasting Notes:

1989 COUNTRY WINES CHABLIS [74] Colour: light to medium green-yellow. *Bouquet:* well made, with striking, pungent passionfruit aroma. *Palate:* clean, and surprisingly rich, again showing strong passionfruit flavours; finishes crisp and light as befits a chablis; the strong passionfruit may possibly be yeast influence and may diminish with time. Drink '90.

1988 SIGNATURE COLLECTION CHARDONNAY [76] Colour: glowing, full yellow. *Bouquet:* smooth and rich, already showing some bottle-development and good handling of lemony oak. *Palate:* smooth, full, pleasant bottle-development with a touch of honey and, again, strong lemony oak; soft easy drinking style for immediate consumption. Drink '90.

1987 BRUT DE BRUT CHAMPAGNE [81] Colour: medium to full yellow-green. *Bouquet:* rich and toasty, with almost scented fruit complexity. *Palate:* most attractive, full-flavoured wine with creamy flavours echoing the scent of the bouquet; has real style and body. Drink '90.

1987 GALWAY HERMITAGE [77] Colour: medium red-purple. *Bouquet:* clean, with slightly herbaceous overtones to the fruit and quite pronounced lemony oak. *Palate:* pleasant, clean, oak-driven wine of light to medium weight, with some nice red berry fruit, and finishing with soft tannins. No doubt just what it was intended to be. Drink '90–'92.

1987 COONAWARRA CABERNET SAUVIGNON [80] Colour: medium red, with just a touch of purple. *Bouquet:* quite firm, with lemony/spicy oak to the fore. *Palate:* a wine that came up in the glass, with the intensity and length building; is by no means full bodied, but the combination of faintly spicy/clovy oak and leafy fruit flavours works well. Drink '90–'93.

1986 SIGNATURE COLLECTION CABERNET SHIRAZ [75] Colour: bright red-purple of medium depth. *Bouquet:* clean, and in the inevitable Yalumba style, quite pronounced lemony/vanillan oak. *Palate:* very youthful with pleasant berry fruit still to fully integrate with clean but slightly dusty/lemony oak; while light bodied, should come on nicely over the next year or so. Drink '90–'92.

Summary: A large range of Yalumba wines were tasted for this edition and were all remarkably consistent. It would be nice to see a little more fruit and slightly less reliance on oak, but on the other hand the wines no doubt have strong commercial appeal.

Clare Valley

1988 VINTAGE

The quartet of cool vintages did not become a quintet. A dry and hot summer resulted in an early vintage after a succession of late harvests, and right throughout the growing season the vines were under a lesser or greater degree of stress. Drip irrigation is now widespread in the Valley, but those vineyards without supplementary water suffered badly, with yields down by as much as 30%. The quality of the grapes from these highly stressed vines likewise suffered. The other problem for the season was hail, which, while not as widespread as the hail leading up to the 1987 vintage, did cause crop losses of between 5% and 10% in some parts of the Valley. The one saving grace, as it were, was that there was almost no mould or rot: the Clare Valley is surely one of the most fortunate areas in Australia, with minimal need to use fungicides. It was a better year for white wines than it was for reds: five makers, indeed, rated it best among the last four years, although more placed it last or second last. Much the same pattern is evident with the reds, except that the overall rating is lower, with more than half the producers rating it second or third in the last four vintages.

1989 VINTAGE

Unseasonably heavy rains in November (and running through into December) were a mixed blessing. The relatively warm and dry winter had left soil moisture reserves low, and the rain was badly needed to restore moisture balance. On the other hand, the rain and cold windy weather grossly upset flowering in some varieties, with cabernet the most affected and sauvignon blanc less so. In the final outcome, cabernet yields were down by between 5% and 30%.

The rain cleared in early December, and the growing season continued cool and mild through to early February. There was then the dramatic change with the south-east Australian heatwave, which resulted in 14 consecutive days in which the temperature peaked at between 35° C and 38° C. The extreme stress placed on the vines had unpredictable effects. Those planted on good deep soils stood up relatively well; those planted on marginal soils were devastated. In some vineyards, bunches of grapes that were less than half ripe, still relatively hard and green, collapsed as the vines translocated all of the available moisture out of the berries.

Picking of the white varieties started in earnest around 23 February, two weeks earlier than normal. As in other parts of Australia, picking went on 24 hours per day as winemakers struggled to harvest their premium white varieties before total collapse occurred. Then, in mid-March, the rains came as the red varieties were being picked. Those who picked reds before the rain (notably malbec) may make some very high quality wine, while those who waited until after the rains stopped and the vines' systems had partially dried out will at least have reds with some flavour. However, alcohol levels will be unusually low across most varieties, as the vines never really recovered from the stress effects of the heat. Once again, it was a marginally better year for whites than it was for reds, but there is relatively little in it. Some very pleasant wines have been made (as was the case in 1988), but this will be due to skills in the winery and to a rigorous selection of only the best material.

THE CHANGES

After a year of upheaval in 1987 (notably the acquisition of Quelltaler Estate by Wolf Blass Wines and of Stanley Leasingham by Thomas Hardy), things quietened down in the Valley. Martindale, a second label for the Barry Family, has faded away. Quelltaler Estate is now known as Eaglehawk Estate, while the only change of ownership sees Hutt River Estate within the Andrew Garrett empire.

When travelling around Australia for the 1988 edition of *Australian Wine Guide* the district tasting stood out as by far the best in terms of quality and consistency of quality. There was not quite the same exhilaration this time around, and I think the reason is not hard to find: the 1988 and 1989 vintages basically on show were two very difficult years. By and large, the small winemakers of the Clare Valley nonetheless seem to be doing a better than average job when compared with their fellows in other districts.

❦ THE CLARE ESTATE

Location: Polish Hill River, Sevenhill, 5453;
6 km east of Sevenhill via Clare (vineyard only).

Winemakers: The Penfolds winemaking team headed by John Duval.

1989 Production: Not stated, but very limited under The Clare Estate.

Principal Wines: Two wines only released: Chardonnay and a Merlot/Malbec/Cabernet Sauvignon/Cabernet Franc Blend ("The Clare Estate").

Distribution: National retail through Penfolds' own distribution system.

Prices: $14.75 to $17.85 retail.

Vintage Rating 1986–89: White: '88, '87, '89, '86. Red: '86, '87, '89, '88.

Tasting Notes:

1987 CHARDONNAY [84] Colour: medium to full yellow-green. *Bouquet:* very rich, scented spicy/ nutmeg oak; structurally complex. *Palate:* of medium weight, with clean melon fruit surrounded by strongly accented oak; the wine has a pleasantly dry, lingering finish. Drink '90–'92.

1986 THE CLARE ESTATE [87] Colour: bright purple-red of medium depth. *Bouquet:* clean, soft and smooth, with well-integrated and balanced lemony oak. *Palate:* light to medium fresh berry fruit flavours with beautifully handled French oak; an unusually elegant wine. Drink '90–'94.

Summary: A great deal of the production from Penfolds 100-hectare vineyard in the Polish Hill River is used as a blend-component in various Penfolds premium wines. Clearly, some of the very best material is reserved for these two low-volume, high-quality wines.

❦ DUNCAN ESTATE

Location: Spring Gully Road, Clare, 5453;
3 km south of Clare.
(088) 43 4335 or (088) 42 2447 (A/H).

Winemaker: Blair Duncan.

1989 Production: Approximately 1400 cases.

Principal Wines: Rhine Riesling, Lake Picked Traminer Riesling, Cabernet Sauvignon, Cabernet Shiraz and Shiraz Merlot.

Distribution: Principally cellar door sales and mailing list (PO box 50C, Clare, 5453), and limited sales through local restaurants. Cellar door sales 10 a.m. to 4 p.m. 7 days.

Prices: $6 to $10 cellar door.

Vintage Rating 1986–89: White: '89, '88, '86, '87. Red: '88, '89 ('87 and '86 not rated).

Tasting Notes:

1989 RHINE RIESLING [TS] Colour: very light green-yellow. *Bouquet:* still very much showing the effects of fermentation, with a suspicion of volatility. *Palate:* still evolving; there are some strange flavours and tastes in the wine that are very possibly due to the inclusion of around 10% of sauvignon blanc, an unusual blend if ever there was one. Difficult to know precisely where the wine is headed.

1989 LATE PICKED TRAMINER RIESLING [TS] Colour: light green-yellow. *Bouquet:* some lime/passionfruit flavours with the after-effects of fermentation still lingering. *Palate:* grapy and spicy, with the traminer influence obvious; an above average cellar door style as it does have fruit weight as well as simple sweetness.

1988 SHIRAZ MERLOT [CS] Colour: medium purple-red. *Bouquet:* good fruit, although it is slightly closed, with a faint gravelly edge. *Palate:* shows all of the hallmarks of an unfinished wine, with somewhat jumpy acid.

Summary: Duncan Estate is one of the newer and

smaller wineries in the Clare Valley, and is still feeling its way. Prior vintages have, however, produced one or two excellent wines, even if those submitted for this edition were a little difficult to evaluate.

EAGLEHAWK ESTATE
(formerly Quelltaler Estate)

Location: Main North Road, Watervale, 5452; 1 km north-east of town.
(088) 43 0003.

Winemaker: Stephen John.

Principal Wines: 1989 Fumé Blanc, 1989 Rhine Riesling, 1987 Shiraz Merlot Cabernet, Quelltaler Hock, Granfiesta Flor Sherry, Treloars Tawny Port. Also Premium Wood Aged Semillon and Noble Gold Semillon under Quelltaler brand name.

Distribution: National through Remy Blass & Associates. Cellar door sales 8 a.m. to 5 p.m. Monday to Friday, 11 a.m. to 4 p.m. weekends and public holidays.

Prices: $7.50 to $35 recommended retail.

Tasting Notes:

1989 EAGLEHAWK RHINE RIESLING [90] Colour: light green-yellow. *Bouquet:* clean, relatively light and quite reserved, but with classic toasty/lime characters. *Palate:* the wine really comes into its own, with both length and intensity. Once again, the flavours are in the lime/toast spectrum and the wine is perfectly balanced. Drink '90–'94.

1989 EAGLEHAWK FUME BLANC [CS] Colour: medium yellow-green. *Bouquet:* clean; of light to medium weight with very bland fruit, and equally bland oak. *Palate:* crisp and clean, but rather light and hollow early in its life, with varietal character muted. Needing to build flesh and character to merit much above 70.

1988 QUELLTALER NOBLE GOLD [76] Colour: full yellow. *Bouquet:* soft, luscious tropical fruits with some volatility. *Palate:* high-toned, vigorous, tangy flavours; the volatility teeters on the edge of acceptability. Drink '90–'91.

1987 QUELLTALER WOOD AGED SEMILLON [83] Colour: very good green-yellow. *Bouquet:* complex, sauterne-like slightly cabbagey overtones. *Palate:* complex, rich and honeyed, with some real pretensions to style; bottle-age has greatly helped. Drink '90–'92.

1987 EAGLEHAWK SHIRAZ MERLOT CABERNET [74] Colour: light to medium purple-red. *Bouquet:* clean, with some lemony oak and fruit of light to medium intensity. *Palate:* pleasant, light red berry fruit flavours with gentle, lemony oak and finishing with low tannin; needs more weight and structure for higher points. Drink '91–'93.

Summary: Eaglehawk Estate is now firmly on its way, it would seem, having won quite an extraordinary number of gold medals at the 1989 Brisbane Show, and with the product range selling more or less in accord with the dictates of supremo Wolf Blass.

FAREHAM ESTATE

Location: Main North Road, Watervale, 5452; 3 km north of Auburn.
(088) 49 2098.

Winemakers: Peter Rumball (consultant).

1989 Production: 30,000 cases.

Principal Wines: The table wines have been discontinued, and only sparkling wines are made: Vintage Cuvee Deluxe, Non Vintage Brut and Sparkling Burgundy, all made by the *Méthode champenoise.*

Distribution: Through wholesale agents in each state (NSW, Blue Hills Liquor Distributors), cellar door sales 10 a.m. to 4 p.m. 7 days; mailing list enquiries welcome. UK imports through S. Wines, Chelsea.

Prices: $9.50 to $25.

Tasting Notes:

1985 VINTAGE CUVEE DELUXE [62] *Colour:* onion-skin. *Bouquet:* somewhat dull, with hard, green and slightly smelly characters. *Palate:* once again, very hard and green; the wine is made from a blend of pinot noir and chardonnay, but the grapes must have been picked exceedingly early, for it is very hard to find any fruit or style in the wine. Drink '90.

NV SPARKLING BURGUNDY [76] *Colour:* full red. *Bouquet:* exceedingly rich, sweet red berry fruit. *Palate:* a high-flavoured yet very unusual sparkling burgundy, with spicy fruit and a suggestion that carbonic maceration may have been used in fashioning the base wine; against all of the odds, it comes together very well. Drink '90–'92.

Summary: Fareham Estate is now an entirely separate operation from Peter Rumball Wines, the latter being a brand without any real home at the moment. The marketing is handled quite separately, and Fareham Estate is in fact a division of Southern Beverage Corporation Pty Ltd, an Adelaide-based company specialising in contract bottling.

🍇 *HUTT RIVER ESTATE*

Location: Main North Road, Clare, 5453; 1 km north of Clare. (088) 42 2450.

Winemakers: Andrew Garrett and Warren Randall.

Principal Wines: Rhine Riesling, Shiraz and Port.

Distribution: Principally cellar door sales and mailing list. Very limited retail distribution and local restaurants. Mailing list enquiries to

PO Box 395, Clare, SA, 5453. Cellar door sales 9 a.m. to 5 p.m. 7 days, except Christmas and Good Friday.

Prices: $10.50 all products cellar door; $6 per dozen discount for cash.

Vintage Rating 1986–89: White: '87, '88, '86, '89. Red: '86, '87 ('88 and '89 not made).

Tasting Notes:

1987 RHINE RIESLING [64] *Colour:* light yellow-green. *Bouquet:* light, firm and slightly herbaceous fruit which is extraordinarily youthful and undeveloped. *Palate:* very light, seaweed/herbaceous flavours that essentially lack fruit and in particular varietal character. Drink '90–'91.

1987 SHIRAZ [78] *Colour:* full purple-red. *Bouquet:* rich, ripe red berry/cassis fruit, almost into creaming soda, but attractive for all that. *Palate:* soft, clean and ripe cherry/berry fruit flavours; structurally a little simple, but has attractive flavour. Drink '90–'94.

1986 PORT [65] *Colour:* red with a touch of tawny. *Bouquet:* soft, developed with some evidence of wood age and some complexity. *Palate:* is neither a tawny port, a vintage port nor a ruby port, but a combination of all three. For those unconcerned with the subtleties of style, perfectly adequate.

Summary: Hutt River is still managed by Frank and Barbara Sheppard, who retired to the Clare Valley after selling their very large wine transport business. I have to confess it is a mystery to me why they should have sold the operation to Andrew Garrett, but they did so, and it appears the label will continue.

🍇 *JEFFREY GROSSET*

Location: King Street, Auburn, 5451; 0.5 km east of town. (088) 49 2175.

Winemakers: Cate and Jeffrey Grosset.

1989 Production: 4500 cases.

Principal Wines: White and red table wines including Polish Hill Rhine Riesling, Chardonnay and Cabernet Sauvignon.

Distribution: Wines sold principally through cellar door sales and mailing list. Cellar door sales from early September 10 a.m. to 5 p.m. Wednesday to Sunday while wine available. Telephone to check on availability. Mailing list enquiries as above. Limited retail and restaurant distribution. UK imports through Gullin & Co.

Prices: $11 to $15 cellar door.

Vintage Rating 1986–89: White: '87, '86, '89, '88. Red: '87, '86, '89, '88.

Outstanding Prior Vintages: '82.

Tasting Notes:

1989 WATERVALE RHINE RIESLING [88] Colour: light to medium green-yellow. *Bouquet:* light, and rather reserved, but with toasty lime characters starting to build. *Palate:* crisp, clean and intense, with a markedly long finish; really comes into its own after a somewhat weak bouquet, and will undoubtedly flourish in bottle. Drink '90–'93.

1989 POLISH HILL RHINE RIESLING [71] Colour: light green-yellow. *Bouquet:* firm, with a hint of matchbox and a trace of volatility. *Palate:* once again, some fractionally sharp volatility is evident; there is fruit present, even though it is not particularly rich, and perhaps that volatility will be less evident once the wine settles down. Drink '90–'92.

1987 CHARDONNAY [70] Colour: light to medium yellow-green. *Bouquet:* extraordinarily un-developed and light, with little varietal character showing. *Palate:* light, lemony oak with some lift to the finish; amazingly youthful, and I cannot see it ever developing real style or richness. Drink '90–'93.

1987 CABERNET SAUVIGNON [85] Colour: medium red-purple. *Bouquet:* spotlessly clean, with marked spicy oak and quite intense red berry fruit. *Palate:* once again, a spotlessly clean wine of light to medium weight, low tannin and fresh, elegant fruit flavours. A style that I would prefer to drink young rather than old. Drink '90–'92.

Summary: Cate and Jeffrey Grosset are two of the most talented winemakers in the Clare Valley,

consistently making outstanding wines through meticulous attention to detail and by ruthlessly culling any barrel they do not consider to be up to the high standards they set for themselves.

JIM BARRY WINES

Location: Main North Road, Clare, 5453. (088) 42 2261.

Winemaker: Mark Barry.

1989 Production: 25,000 cases.

Principal Wines: Watervale Rhine Riesling, Chardonnay, Sauvignon Blanc, Lavender Hill Moselle, Armagh Shiraz, Cabernet Sauvignon, Cabernet Merlot, Sentimental Bloke Port and Old Walnut Tawny Port.

Distribution: Substantial cellar door sales 9 a.m. to 5 p.m. Monday to Friday; 10 a.m. to 4 p.m. Saturday and public holidays; 11 a.m. to 2.30 p.m. Sunday. Wholesale distribution SA and Vic., Van Cooth & Co.; NSW and ACT, Oak Barrel Wines; WA, Lionel Samson Pty Ltd; Tas., Boags Liquor Ltd; and Classic Wine Merchants, NT.

Prices: $8 to $40 cellar door.

Vintage Rating 1986–89: '87, '86, '89, '88.

Tasting Notes:

1989 WATERVALE RHINE RIESLING [80] Colour: light green-yellow. *Bouquet:* clean, firm classic toasty/lime aromas. *Palate:* clean and crisp, with a suspicion of hollowness on the back-palate; the aroma and flavour is correct, and the wine may well fill out very nicely by the time of release. Drink '90–'93.

1989 FLORITA VINEYARD RHINE RIESLING [79] Colour: light green-yellow. *Bouquet:* clean, soft, rich lime/passionfruit. *Palate:* clean, with similarly accentuated lime/passionfruit flavours of medium weight; the wine is fractionally blowsy. Drink '90–'92.

1989 SAUVIGNON BLANC [72] Colour: bright, light green-yellow. _Bouquet:_ clean, light, slightly herbaceous varietal fruit with a hint of tobacco. _Palate:_ light, clean and soft; well made, simply lacking final fruit intensity and varietal character. Drink '90–'91.

1988 THE ARMAGH [93] Colour: medium red-purple. _Bouquet:_ glorious, clean spicy oak with lovely berry fruit. _Palate:_ beautifully handled, complex spicy oak with silky, red berry fruit; shows all of the mastery one expects from a maker such as Wolf Blass, and is utterly unexpected coming from this winery. Drink '94–2000.

1988 CABERNET SAUVIGNON [88] Colour: medium purple-red. _Bouquet:_ ultra sophisticated, spicy/charred oak with very good red berry fruit. _Palate:_ fresh, red berry fruits and sophisticated oak still to finally mesh together, but will do so with time; of medium weight and of good length. Drink '94–'99.

1987 CABERNET SAUVIGNON [87] Colour: very good purple red. _Bouquet:_ clean, lively and fresh red berry fruits with light oak; although fruit-driven, has weight and texture. _Palate:_ fresh, clean red berry/cherry/cassis fruit, with just a touch of oak; an elegant wine. Drink '92–'96.

Summary: The red wines of Jim Barry tasted for this edition were, quite frankly, astonishingly good, although an earlier vintage of The Armagh (the strikingly packaged Grange Hermitage pretender) might have been seen as a portent of things to come.

Total production distributed through Caon & Co., Adelaide; Tyrrell's Vineyards Pty Ltd, New South Wales; Falkland Enterprises, Victoria and Queensland; The Oak Barrel Winery Pty Ltd, Canberra; and Associated Liquor Merchants Ltd, Perth.

Prices: $9.95 to $15.99 retail.

Tasting Notes:

1988 CHABLIS [71] Colour: medium yellow-green. _Bouquet:_ highly floral tropical fruit aromas. _Palate:_ clean, soft and gently fruity with a fairly dry finish; medium weight and—appropriately—without oak influence. Drink '90.

1988 RHINE RIESLING [79] Colour: medium yellow-green. _Bouquet:_ some bottled-developed characters starting to add complexity to passionfruit/lime aroma. _Palate:_ soft and clean, with some toasty characters building; has good weight and length. Drink '90–'94.

1987 CABERNET SAUVIGNON [77] Colour: light to medium red-purple. _Bouquet:_ soft, slightly squashy ripe berry fruit characters and a hint of tobacco leaf. _Palate:_ leafy/berry flavours with a nice touch of smoky oak; the tannins are light, and the finish crisp and clean. Not a heavyweight. Drink '90–'92.

Summary: Brian Barry is one of the most experienced winemakers and wine judges in Australia, but curiously has never aspired to make his own Jud's Hill wines, which have been contract-produced at various South Australian wineries under Brian Barry's general direction. The wine quality is good, but one cannot help but feel that it is not as good as it might have been had Brian Barry made it.

❦ _JUD'S HILL_

Location: Farrell Flat Road, 2 km east of Clare, 5343 (vineyard only).
Postal address: PO Box 128, Stepney, SA, 5069.

Winemaker: Brian Barry.

Principal Wines: Four wines are now made: Chablis, Rhine Riesling, Cabernet Sauvignon and Cabernet Sauvignon Merlot.

Distribution: No cellar door sales or mailing list.

❦ _LINDEMANS_

Location: No vineyards retained, only label.

Winemakers: John Vickery and Phillip John.

1989 Production: Nil.

Principal Wines: Current production has now been discontinued, but there are stocks of high quality old vintage wines that will from time to time be included in Lindemans Classic Releases.

Distribution: National retail at all levels.

MINTARO CELLARS

Location: Leasingham Road, Mintaro, 5415; on south-western outskirts of township (well signposted).
(088) 43 9046.

Winemaker: James Pearson.

1989 Production: 2000 cases.

Principal Wines: Rhine Riesling and Cabernet Sauvignon.

Distribution: Virtually exclusively cellar door and mailing list. Cellar door sales dawn to dusk 7 days.

Prices: $8.50 to $14 cellar door.

Vintage Rating 1986–89: White: '87, '89, '88, '86. Red: '88, '87, '86, '89.

Tasting Notes:

1989 RHINE RIESLING [77] Colour: light green-yellow. *Bouquet:* intense, tropical/passionfruit characters, no doubt deriving partly from yeast and which will subside somewhat before the wine is released. *Palate:* a high-toned wine, still showing some after-effects of fermentation; there is also the suspicion that it may be a fraction hollow on the mid to back-palate. Drink '90–'93.

1988 LATE PICKED RHINE RIESLING [73] Colour: light to medium yellow-green. *Bouquet:* clean, of light intensity and still relatively closed and undeveloped. *Palate:* clean, pleasant lime flavours, weighty more than sweet, but does lack structural complexity and lift. Drink '90–'91.

1987 CABERNET SAUVIGNON [66] Colour: medium to full purple-red. *Bouquet:* soft fruit of medium intensity with some gamey overlay, and light oak. *Palate:* gamey/leafy flavours, with pronounced tannins in the basically light fruit; better oak might have helped. Drink '90–'92.

Summary: The township of Mintaro is one of South Australia's outstanding tourist attractions, with its diminutive (excepting the grand Martindale Hall) stone buildings remarkably preserved. In more recent times, Mintaro Cellars has also been bringing fame to the town: its 1985 Rhine Riesling was the top rated Light Bodied White Wine at the 1989 Smallmakers Wine Competition.

MITCHELL

Location: Hughes Park Road (known locally as Skillogalee or Skilly Road), Skillogalee Valley, Sevenhill via Clare, 5453; 3 km south-west of Sevenhill.
(088) 43 4258 or (088) 43 4264.

Winemaker: Andrew Mitchell.

1989 Production: 12,000 cases.

Principal Wines: Watervale Rhine Riesling, Wood Aged Semillon, Chardonnay, Peppertree Vineyard Shiraz and Cabernet Sauvignon.

Distribution: Substantial retail and export sales together with active cellar door sales and mailing list. Retail distribution through Rutherglen Wine Co., Melbourne; The Specialist Wine Co., Sydney; Caon Tucker & Co., Adelaide; Tasmanian Fine Wine Distributors, Hobart and the Premium Wine Co., Perth. Cellar door sales 10 a.m. to 4 p.m. 7 days. Mailing list as above.

Prices: $11 to $16.50 retail.

Vintage Rating 1986–89: White: '87, '88, '89, '86. Red: '87, '86, '88, '89.

Outstanding Prior Vintages: White: '77, '80, '82, '84. Red: '77, '80, '82, '84.

Tasting Notes:

1989 WATERVALE RHINE RIESLING [75] Colour: light straw-green. *Bouquet:* clean and firm, but rather neutral, with reserved, herbaceous notes and a touch of SO_2 *Palate:* clean, but very light and crisp, lacking fruit flesh and somewhat short on the finish. There is absolutely no problem with the winemaking, and the wine may blossom in the next 12 months or so. Drink '90–'92.

1989 SEMILLON [CS] Colour: medium straw-yellow. *Bouquet:* clean, with slightly minty oak characters and pleasant herbaceous varietal fruit. *Palate:* once again, slightly distracting minty/PK flavours are evident, as is relatively high acid; clearly, a wine still in its infancy, but those minty characters do suggest partially ripened fruit.

1989 CHARDONNAY [CS] Colour: light straw-yellow. *Bouquet:* already showing good style with pleasant fruit and oak integration; smooth and clean. *Palate:* as suave as the bouquet would suggest, being very smooth and already well-balanced; however, the fruit is light and still to build distinctive varietal character. Headed somewhere around 75 to 80 points.

1987 PEPPERTREE SHIRAZ [84] Colour: medium red-purple. *Bouquet:* full, fragrant, classic peppery/spice fruit, clean and appealing. *Palate:* classic Rhone pepper/spice to a wine with structure and weight; a scintilla more red berry fruit would have lifted it into olympian class. Drink '92–'96.

1987 CABERNET SAUVIGNON [84] Colour: medium to full red-purple. *Bouquet:* strong vanillan/condensed milk oak aromas threaten the fruit. *Palate:* a transformation; the fruit flavours show perfectly ripened cabernet with ripe berry flavours just tinged with a touch of leafiness; the oak is in perfect harmony and balance, and the wine finishes clean and firm. Drink '93–'97.

Summary: Without question, one of the Clare Valley's—and indeed Australia's—finest small wineries, specialising in riesling and cabernet sauvignon, but with more than useful second strings in wood-aged semillon, chardonnay and shiraz. Andrew and Jane Mitchell work tirelessly and tenaciously promoting their wines, and fully deserve their undoubted success.

MOUNT HORROCKS

Location: Mintaro Road, Leasingham, 5452; 300 metres east of Main North Road. (088) 43 0005.

Winemaker: Jeffrey Grosset (consultant).

1989 Production: 4000 cases.

Principal Wines: White and red table wines, identified by variety and occasionally by district, including Watervale Rhine Riesling, Watervale Semillon, Chardonnay, Cordon Cut Rhine Riesling, and Cabernet Merlot.

Distribution: Principally through cellar door and by mailing list. Cellar door sales 10 a.m. to 5 p.m. 7 days while stock's available from release in September. Mailing list enquiries to PO Box 72, Watervale, 5452. Retail and restaurant distribution through selected outlets in all principal cities. UK imports through Cellar World.

Prices: $10 to $12.50 recommended retail.

Vintage Rating 1986–89: White: '87, '88, '86. Red: '87, '88, '86 ('89 not rated).

Tasting Notes:

1988 CORDON CUT RHINE RIESLING [77] Colour: full yellow. *Bouquet:* very complex, rich, high-toned apricot fruit. *Palate:* soft, round apricot flavours with moderate acid; attractive and full flavoured dessert wine, even if fractionally simple. Drink '90–'92.

1987 CABERNET MERLOT [74] Colour: light red-purple. *Bouquet:* light, leafy tobacco characters with a very pronounced merlot varietal influence. *Palate:* pronounced, leafy tobacco flavours, strongly reminiscent of wines of St Emilion in a moderate vintage. Drink '90–'93.

Summary: I found the three dry white wines (from 1988) of Mount Horrocks to be unacceptably affected by volatility, presumably yeast-derived. This is not the first time I have had such difficulties with Mount Horrocks whites, and I can only assume that it is the particular yeast strain that the winery chooses to employ. For the life of me, I cannot imagine why it persists with it.

PAULETTS

PAULETTS

1988
POLISH HILL RIVER
RHINE RIESLING

PRODUCED BY PAULETT WINES
POLISH HILL, SOUTH AUSTRALIA

Location: Polish Hill Road, Polish Hill River;
4 km east of Sevenhill, 5453.
(088) 43 4328.

Winemaker: Neil Paulett.

Principal Wines: Main release Rhine Riesling and
Shiraz; small quantities of other wines
including Sauvignon Blanc and Cabernet
Merlot also intermittently available.

Distribution: Principally cellar door sales and
mailing list; cellar door sales 10 a.m. to 4.30
p.m. 7 days. Also wholesale through Regional
Liquor Agencies, SA; Yarra Valley Wine
Consultants, Vic.; and Fin Vin Agencies, NSW.

Prices: $8 to $13 cellar door.

Vintage Rating 1986–89: White: '88, '89, '87, '86.
Red: '89, '88, '87, '86.

Tasting Notes:

1989 RHINE RIESLING [68] Colour: light straw-
green. *Bouquet:* full, but quite broad, if not a
fraction coarse. *Palate:* broad and a little hard,
lacking fruit intensity, may improve with time.
Drink '90–'92.

1989 SAUVIGNON BLANC [80] Colour: light
straw-green. *Bouquet:* quite potent, with ample
ripe gooseberry varietal fruit. *Palate:* rather
lighter than the bouquet suggests, although the
flavours are similar, and the wine should
develop very well, possibly meriting even higher
points than those accorded. Drink '90–'93.

1987 POLISH HILL RIVER SHIRAZ [79] Colour:
medium purple-red. *Bouquet:* tangy and zesty
with lifted, lemon-drops oak. *Palate:* attractive
spicy varietal fruit flavours throw off the lemony
oak of the bouquet; fresh and flavoursome, with
a touch of minty also showing, and finishes with
low tannin. Drink '90–'94.

Summary: Neil Paulett took a long time to find
and establish his own vineyard, having started
his career at the Upper Hunter at the old

Penfold's Wybong Winery. In his
undemonstrative fashion, he has set about
showing us all just why the wait was worthwhile.
Even now, production is tiny and on a part-
time basis, as Neil Paulett is also assistant
winemaker at Stanley Leasingham.

PETALUMA

Location: Off Farrell Flat Road, Clare, 5453;
4 km east of township (vineyard only).
(08) 42 2858

Winemaker: Brian Croser.

Principal Wines: Rhine Riesling, wholly from
Petaluma's own vineyard at 500 metres above
sea level. Chardonnay used for Petaluma
Chardonnay between 1984 and 1988.

Distribution: National fine wine retail distribution
through wholesale agents in each state. Cellar
door sales at Bridgewater Mill. No mailing
list.

Prices: $15 to $16.50.

Vintage Rating 1986–89: '87, '86, '89, '88.

Outstanding Prior Vintages: '80, '85, '79, '84.

Tasting Notes:

1988 RHINE RIESLING [86] Colour: light to
medium green-yellow. *Bouquet:* still very
discrete and reserved, with some lime/
passionfruit characters building. *Palate:* showing far more than the bouquet, with crisp
lime/passionfruit flavours, long and intense; a
wine with great balance all the way through to
the finish. Drink '90–'95.

Summary: Petaluma's Rhine Riesling is of the
highest quality, and those lucky enough to have
the '80 vintage in their cellars will attest to the
great cellaring capacity the wine has.

PIKES POLISH HILL RIVER ESTATE

Location: Polish Hill River Road, Sevenhill, 5453;
6 km east of Sevenhill.
(088) 43 4249 (088) 43 4237 (a/h).

Winemaker: Neil Pike.

1989 Production: 6000 cases.

Principal Wines: Rhine Riesling, Chardonnay, Sauvignon Blanc, Cabernet Sauvignon, Cabernet Franc Merlot Blend and Shiraz.

Distribution: Mailing list, cellar door and national retail through Seabrook, Tucker, Caon Group. Cellar door sales 10 a.m. to 5 p.m. most weekends, public holidays and school holidays but advisable to phone first. Mailing list enquiries to PO Box 54, Sevenhill via Clare, 5453. UK imports through S. Wines Ltd, Chelsea, and Haughton Fine Wines, Chorley.

Prices: $10 to $16 retail; $9 to $14 cellar door.

Vintage Rating 1986–89: White: '87, '86, '88, '89. Red: '86, '87, '88, '89.

Tasting Notes:

1989 SAUVIGNON BLANC [75] Colour: very good light green-yellow. *Bouquet:* fairly light, with some gooseberry varietal character and the inevitable hint of armpit fermentation characters, which will dissipate by the time the wine is released. *Palate:* has some length and intensity: the fruit is of moderate weight and shows good although not great varietal flavours; may well build character rapidly in bottle, but will not be long lived. Drink '90–'91.

1988 RHINE RIESLING [70] Colour: medium yellow-green. *Bouquet:* firm, with quite intense lime fruit at the core, but a slightly powdery edge. *Palate:* quite firm, reserved lime fruit, but then tailing away somewhat and finishing rather thin and skinny. Drink '90–'91.

1989 CHARDONNAY [CS] Colour: excellent green-yellow. *Bouquet:* still to build real fruit intensity or varietal character, but clean and well balanced. *Palate:* attractive touch of light spicy/lemony oak, and some structural complexity starting to build; all Clare Valley Chardonnays are notoriously slow starters, and the wine could well rate in the 80's by the time it is bottled and released.

1988 SHIRAZ [75] Colour: good purple-red. *Bouquet:* high-toned minty/leafy characters with light oak. *Palate:* like the bouquet, very clean, but showing marked minty/leafy fruit, which is not really what one would expect from Clare Valley Shiraz; finishes with low tannin. Drink '90–'93.

1988 CABERNET BLEND [78] Colour: medium to full purple-red. *Bouquet:* quite complex with minty/berry/leafy fruit and restrained oak. *Palate:* a wine in modern style with complex red berry/leafy/minty flavours, no doubt partly deriving from the varietal blend used. Drink '92–'96.

Summary: Neil Pike doubles up as assistant winemaker at Mitchell, while partner and brother Andrew Pike is in charge of Penfolds' Clare Vineyard. They make a formidable team, for Pikes is one of the ascendant stars of the Clare Valley, producing excellent wines.

ROSENBERG CELLARS

Location: Main North Road, Watervale, 5452; on southern outskirts of town. (088) 43 0131.

Winemaker: Terry Blanden.

1989 Production: 1500 cases.

Principal Wines: Cottage White Riesling, Chenin Blanc and Rosé.

Distribution: Exclusively cellar door sales; weekdays by appointment. Weekends 10 a.m. to sunset; a sign on the Main North Road clearly indicates whether the winery is open or closed.

Prices: $8 cellar door.

Tasting Notes:

1989 COTTAGE WHITE [67] Colour: medium to full yellow, with just a touch of green. *Bouquet:* soft, full but rather broad. *Palate:* rich, solid pineapple/lime fruit with appreciable sweetness. Useful cellar door style. Drink '90.

1989 ROSE [70] Colour: light pink. *Bouquet:* light with a faint biscuity edge to grenache-type fruit. *Palate:* clean and crisp, with well-balanced acid and residual sugar; well-made, attractive commercial style. Drink '90.

Summary: Owner/winemaker Terry Blanden has acquired one of the most historic houses and wine cellars (the cellars are in fact underneath the house) in the Clare Valley, situated prominently by the Main North Road. Wine styles are quite consciously directed at the tourist trade, which will no doubt find its way to the cellar door.

❦ SEVENHILL

Location: College Road, Sevenhill via Clare, 5453;
1 km north-east of town.
(088) 43 4222.

Winemakers: Brother John May and John Monten.

1989 Production: Approximately 14,500 cases.

Principal Wines: A substantial range of wines offered, ranging from varietal releases through to generics. Wines include White Burgundy, Rhine Riesling, Traminer Frontignac, Dry Tokay, Clare Riesling, Shiraz, Cabernet Sauvignon, Merlot Cabernet Franc and Cabernet Sauvignon Malbec, together with a limited range of fortified wines, including Liqueur Tokay, Verdelho, Touriga Port and Vintage Port. A substantial output of sacramental wines in addition.

Distribution: Principally cellar door and mailing list. Cellar door sales 8.30 a.m. to 4.30 p.m. Monday to Friday, Saturday 9 a.m. to 4 p.m. Limited capital city distribution through fine wine retailers. Mailing list as above.

Prices: $5 to $13.50 cellar door.

Vintage Rating 1986–89: White: '87, '86, '88, '89. Red: '87, '86, '88, '89.

Outstanding Prior Vintages: White: '75, '77, '76, '80. Red: '75, '76, '77, '82.

Tasting Notes:

1989 RHINE RIESLING [82] Colour: medium green-yellow. _Bouquet:_ soft, toasty lime fruit, quite forward and precocious. _Palate:_ rich and full toasty/lime fruit flavours on the mid-palate, which become slightly harder on the finish. Drink '90–'92.

1989 WHITE BURGUNDY [75] Colour: medium yellow-green. _Bouquet:_ clean, with strong, lemony/spicy oak. _Palate:_ attractive, light lemony oak set against light fruit; a good food wine, but lacking richness early in its life. Prior releases have been absolutely outstanding, and

this wine may yet surprise. Drink '90–'92.

1989 COLLEGE WHITE [64] Colour: light to medium green-yellow. _Bouquet:_ opulent and potent fruit, well handled. _Palate:_ fails to live up to the promise of the bouquet, being very sweet, although no doubt the style is intended (for the cellar door). Drink '90.

1988 CABERNET SAUVIGNON MALBEC [85] Colour: deep, dark purple-red. _Bouquet:_ full, dense, complex, ripe red berry fruits. _Palate:_ like the bouquet, very clean, with full, sweet, ripe red berry/plum flavours, ripe yet not over ripe; soft, persistent tannins round off a striking wine. Drink '93–2000.

1988 CABERNET SAUVIGNON [90] Colour: medium to full purple-red. _Bouquet:_ spotlessly clean, with strong minty/red berry fruit and excellent oak integration. _Palate:_ full, smooth and rich; sweet fruit with a touch of mint is perfectly balanced by oak; good tannins will ensure longevity for a most stylish cabernet. Drink '93–2000.

TOURIGA PORT [78] Colour: medium red, with just a touch of tawny. _Bouquet:_ some wood-aged characters, and a suggestion of the back-blending of some very old material. _Palate:_ cunningly constructed wine with a most appealing mix of young and old flavours; there is real style to the finish, even though overall the wine does not fit into any particular port category.

Summary: Sevenhill has produced more rabbits out of the hat over the past few years than most Australian wineries. First there was the wonderful 1988 White Burgundy and some very good rieslings; now the red wines have returned to the majestic power and flavour of earlier years. Part of the reason, of course, lies in the excellent vineyards owned by Sevenhill, but the winemaking skills of Brother John May and John Monten should not be under-estimated. All in all, an unfashionable label that deserves to be very much more fashionable.

❦ SKILLOGALEE

Location: Off Hughes Park Road, Skillogalee Valley, Sevenhill via Clare, 5453; 3 km south-west of Sevenhill.

Winemaker: Andrew Mitchell (contract).

Principal Wines: Rhine Riesling Bin 2, Late Harvest Rhine Riesling, Cabernets, Shiraz, Vintage Port and Gewurztraminer.

Distribution: Principally cellar door and mailing list. Cellar door sales 10 a.m. to 5 p.m. 7 days. Mailing list, PO Box 9, Sevenhill via Clare, 5453. Retail sales Melbourne and Sydney.

Tasting Notes:

1988 BIN 2 RHINE RIESLING [75] Colour: medium to full yellow-green. *Bouquet:* soft and rich, if not voluptuous, lime/pineapple fruit. *Palate:* soft, slightly broad, but ever so flavoursome lime/pineapple riesling, with a soft finish. Drink '90–'92.

1987 CABERNET [66] Colour: dense purple-red. *Bouquet:* strong, deep, concentrated minty/berry fruit, slightly extractive. *Palate:* seemingly overworked, with gamey/minty/berry flavours giving way to a trace of bitterness on the finish. Drink '92–'95.

Summary: Skillogalee changed hands just as I was writing this chapter of the book. I was not able to find out the plans of the new owners, but no doubt the label will continue.

🍇 *STANLEY LEASINGHAM*

Location: 7 Dominic Street, Clare, 5453; on southern outskirts of town. (088) 42 2555.

Winemakers: Chris Proud (chief winemaker) and Neil Paulett.

Principal Wines: The range has been rationalised to include Leasingham and Hutt Creek labels only, comprising Leasingham Rhine Riesling, Chardonnay, Semillon, Cabernet Malbec and Shiraz; and Hutt Creek Claret, Riesling and Chablis.

Distribution: National distribution through the Hardy Wine company in all states. Cellar door sales 9 a.m. to 5 p.m. Monday to Friday, Saturday 10 a.m. to 4 p.m.

Prices: $3.99 to $8.99 recommended retail.

Vintage Rating 1986–89: White: '88, '87, '86, '89. Red: '89, '88, '86, '87.

Outstanding Prior Vintages: White: '89, '78, '73, '77. Red: '80, '71, '75.

Tasting Notes:

1989 RHINE RIESLING [88] Colour: medium straw-green. *Bouquet:* clean, but in typical style of the year, slightly closed; hints of lime and passionfruit are there. *Palate:* a very good wine, with lovely lime/passionfruit flavours which are both persistent and very well balanced; the wine does not dip on finish like so many others of the year. Something of a surprise packet. Drink '90–'93.

1989 SEMILLON [CS] Colour: bright, light green-yellow. *Bouquet:* clean and balanced, with already well-integrated lemony Nevers oak. *Palate:* surprising richness from the fruit, with lemony oak nicely balanced and integrated; still building structural complexity, but should be headed to 80 or thereabouts.

1988 CHARDONNAY [71] Colour: medium to full yellow. *Bouquet:* complex, bottle-developed cabbagey fruit characters with strong vanillan oak. *Palate:* strong, American oak does not suit or flatter the variety; there is some citric varietal fruit. Drink '90–'91.

1988 SHIRAZ [87] Colour: intense purple-red. *Bouquet:* clean, with complex lemony oak balanced by strong, clear fruit. *Palate:* red berry fruit flavours with soft, textured tannins are the first impression, followed by quite pronounced lemony oak. The wine does have the requisite balance and should develop extremely well. Drink '92–'97.

1987 CABERNET MALBEC [74] Colour: slightly dull red-purple. *Bouquet:* strong vanillan/lemon oak with quite full fruit underneath. *Palate:* once again, strong, lemony/vanillan oak tends to be the major flavour contributor; structure comes from persistent tannins. Drink '92–'95.

Summary: Thomas Hardy may well have rationalised the product range, but it has not shown any inclination to disturb the remarkably low prices at which the Leasingham wines sell. Some exceptional bargains are to be found in almost every vintage under the Leasingham label.

⚜ TAYLORS

Location: Mintaro Road, Auburn, 5451;
3 km north-east of town.
(088) 49 2008; Fax (088) 49 2240.

Winemaker: Andrew Tolley.

1989 Production: 170,000 cases.

Principal Wines: Chardonnay, Rhine Riesling, White Burgundy, Chablis, Hermitage, Pinot Noir and Cabernet Sauvignon.

Distribution: National retail sales through most liquor stores, chains and hotels. Cellar door sales 10 a.m. to 5 p.m. Monday to Saturday and public holidays, Sunday 10 a.m. to 4 p.m.

Prices: $7.53 to $12.54 recommended retail in SA.

Vintage Rating 1986–89: White: '87, '89, '88, '86. Red: '89, '88, '87, '86.

Outstanding Prior Vintages: White: '82, '79. Red: '76, '78, '79.

Tasting Notes:

1989 RHINE RIESLING [81] Colour: light green-yellow. *Bouquet:* clean, neutral and rather closed, with a hint of herbaceous fruit. *Palate:* in typical style for this vintage, is much better than the bouquet suggests, with weight, intensity and flesh; a touch of sweetness adds to the back-palate and lengthens the finish. Drink '90–'92.

1989 CHABLIS [69] Colour: light green-yellow. *Bouquet:* light and fractionally thin, with quite pronounced herbaceous/green fruit aromas. *Palate:* light, dry crisp and clean, with similar herbaceous flavours to the bouquet. An authentic chablis style. Drink '90.

1989 CHARDONNAY [CS] Colour: light green-yellow. *Bouquet:* light, clean herbaceous/grapefruit characters with minimal oak influence. *Palate:* pleasant light to medium weight herbaceous/grapefruit flavours; well made, although does lack intensity and complexity. Depending on its evolution, should rate somewhere between 75 and 80.

1988 HERMITAGE [74] Colour: strong purple-red. *Bouquet:* clean, firm and rich with good berry fruit and subdued oak. *Palate:* soft, red berry fruit on the mid-palate is ever so slightly flawed by a touch of bitterness on the finish. Drink '92–'95.

1988 CABERNET SAUVIGNON [74] Colour: medium purple-red. *Bouquet:* clean and smooth, with American oak dominant. *Palate:* strong, vanilla bean American oak sits on top of quite good fruit; those with a taste for oak would no doubt rate the wine higher. Drink '92–'96.

1987 CABERNET SAUVIGNON [86] Colour: medium red, with a touch of purple. *Bouquet:* very fragrant and exceptionally complex cigar box/leafy/tobacco/spicy characters all inter-mingling in quite intense fruit. *Palate:* similar multi-faceted fruit flavours in a leafy/spicy/berry spectrum; has the structural elegance of a fresh, young Bordeaux red from a minor Chateau. Drink '92–'97.

1986 CABERNET SAUVIGNON [74] Colour: strong purple-red. *Bouquet:* pleasant bottle-developed aromas with dusty oak and leafy fruit. *Palate:* pleasant, light leafy cabernet with a touch of cigar box and very light tannins; no fault, simply lacks richness. Drink '90–'94.

Summary: The three Cabernet Sauvignons of Taylors continue a distinguished line. The '86 will be on release through much of 1990, and towards the end of that year the 1987 will become available. If it lives up to its promise, it should be one of the best-value cabernets on the market.

🍇 TIM ADAMS WINES
(formerly Adams & Wray)

Location: Warenda Road, Clare, 5453; 2 km southeast of town (formerly Robertson's wines). (088) 42 2429.

Winemaker: Tim Adams.

1989 Production: 3000 cases.

Principal Wines: Semillon, Rhine Riesling, Tim Adams Shiraz and Tim Adams Aberfeldy Vineyard Shiraz.

Distribution: Largely cellar door sales and mailing list. Cellar door sales 10 a.m. to 5 p.m. 7 days, while stocks last. Wholesale distribution through Chace Agencies, Adelaide & NT; Yarra Valley Wine Consultants, Melbourne; Haviland Wine Co., Sydney. UK imports through Gullin & Co.

Prices: $8 to $10.50 cellar door.

Vintage Rating 1986–89: White: '89, '88, '87 ('86 not rated). Red: '88, '87, '86, '89.

Tasting Notes:

1989 RHINE RIESLING [90] Colour: light to medium green-yellow. _Bouquet:_ clean, firm, discrete toasty/lime aromas. _Palate:_ classic and very intense toasty lime fruit with a long finish; crisp and non-phenolic; outstanding regional style. Drink '90–'93.

1989 SEMILLON [87] Colour: medium to full yellow-green. _Bouquet:_ opulent, sophisticated spicy oak. _Palate:_ identical oak to the bouquet, together with strong, tangy, herbaceous fruit with excellent mouthfeel. Drink '90–'93.

1988 ABERFELDY VINEYARD SHIRAZ [72] Colour: bright purple-red. _Bouquet:_ some gamey overtones to leafy/berry fruit. _Palate:_ high-toned lantana/gamey/leafy fruit; a very unusual wine, with fruit characters out of the ordinary and reminiscent of some of those obtained from time to time from Skillogalee Vineyard. Drink '91–'93.

1988 TIM ADAMS SHIRAZ [90] Colour: medium red-purple. _Bouquet:_ firm, concentrated, dark berry fruit with good oak; cool, almost cabernet-like fruit. _Palate:_ firm, rich and concentrated, with complex, textured fruit; again more like cabernet than shiraz, with lovely dark berry flavours and perfectly balanced oak. Drink '93–'99.

Summary: The current releases from Tim Adams are by and large quite superb, far better than anything we have previously seen from this former Stanley Leasingham winemaker who is now doing his own thing on a small, hand-crafted scale.

🍇 TIM KNAPPSTEIN WINES

Location: 2 Pioneer Avenue, Clare, 5453; at northern end of town. (088) 42 2600; Fax (088) 42 3831.

Winemaker: Tim Knappstein.

1989 Production: 38,000 cases.

Principal Wines: Rhine Riesling, Fumé Blanc, Chardonnay, Gewurztraminer, Cabernet Sauvignon, Cabernet Merlot and Beerenauslese Rhine Riesling.

Distribution: Available through most fine wine retailers in capital cities and in many of the better restaurants. Significant cellar door sales: open 9 a.m. to 5 p.m. Monday to Friday; 10 a.m. to 5 p.m. Saturday and public holidays; 11 a.m. to 4 p.m. Sunday. UK imports through Avery's of Bristol.

Prices: $12 to $18 retail.

Vintage Rating 1986–89: White: '87, '89, '88, '86. Red: '86, '87, '89, '88.

Outstanding Prior Vintages: White: '77, '80, '82, '85, '87. Red: '75, '80, '84, '86, '87.

Tasting Notes:

1989 RHINE RIESLING [87] Colour: light green-yellow. _Bouquet:_ immediately accessible, soft, tropical lime/toast fruit of medium to full intensity. _Palate:_ masses of flavour in a tropical/lime spectrum; very good weight, no excess phenolics. A wine that runs entirely counter to most '89 Clare Valley Rhine Rieslings. Drink '90–'92.

1989 CHARDONNAY [89] Colour: medium yellow-green. *Bouquet:* exceptionally forward, complex and stylish wine with strong nutmeg/spice oak and a trace of volatile lift. *Palate:* exceedingly complex and stylish, with strong grapefruit and very good oak handling; already bottled August 1989, and once again, not at all typical of the normally slow developing Clare Chardonnays. Drink '90–'91.

1989 GEWURZTRAMINER [77] Colour: bright green-yellow. *Bouquet:* clean, with pronounced spicy/lychee fruit of medium to full intensity. *Palate:* strong, spicy varietal character; has length, yet avoids excessive phenolics. Drink '90.

1989 BEERENAUSLESE RHINE RIESLING [80] Colour: medium yellow-green. *Bouquet:* slightly powdery/dusty edge to peach/passionfruit aromas. *Palate:* intense peach flavours with very good acid, and a long, lingering finish. Drink '90–'93.

1988 CABERNET MERLOT [80] Colour: bright and strong purple-red. *Bouquet:* pronounced meaty/gamey carbonic maceration influence with pleasant red berry fruit underneath. *Palate:* complex red berry flavours strongly influenced by maceration; a lively, high-flavoured individual style that does work not withstanding my lack of enthusiasm for the use of this winemaking technique applied to cabernet styles. Drink '91–'95.

1987 CABERNET SAUVIGNON [65] Colour: light to medium red-purple. *Bouquet:* very light leafy fruit with some lemony oak. *Palate:* light, leafy/squashy berry fruit flavours, vaguely reminiscent of Coonawarra; lacks fruit strength. Drink '90–'92.

Summary: The winery is situated in the historic stone buildings of the Enterprise Brewery within a few paces of the centre of the town of Clare. Tim Knappstein is still very much in charge notwithstanding the ceding of majority ownership to Wolf Blass wines, and wine quality remains very good.

WATERVALE CELLARS

Location: North Terrace, Watervale, 5452; off Main North Road in township. (088) 43 0069.

Winemaker: Robert Crabtree.

1989 Production: Approximately 3000 cases.

Principal Wines: Riesling, Semillon, Shiraz Cabernet Sauvignon and Muscat.

Distribution: Principally cellar door and mailing list. Cellar door sales 9 a.m. to 5 p.m. most days. Limited wholesale distribution through Porter & Co., SA; Barrique Fine Wines, NT and Qld; Westwood Wine Agencies, Vic. Small UK imports through Windrush Wines, Cirencester.

Prices: $8 to $12 per bottle cellar door.

Tasting Notes:

1989 RHINE RIESLING [75] Colour: light green-yellow. *Bouquet:* firm, clean and toasty with good fruit in a passionfruit/lime spectrum. *Palate:* clean and potent as it enters the mouth, but falls away on the middle and back-palate, and finishes rather short. Despite that, by far the best riesling to yet come from Watervale Cellars. Drink '90–'92.

1988 SHIRAZ CABERNET SAUVIGNON [CS] Colour: strong purple-red. *Bouquet:* quite complex, with gamey/minty characters, but still needing work. *Palate:* big and fleshy, with complex gamey fruit; needs aeration and handling, something that winemaker Robert Crabtree intended. If it fulfils even a small part of its potential, will rate above 75.

Summary: Robert Crabtree's wine odyssey from his English birthplace to France and thence to Australia has come to a contented and fulfilled finish at Watervale, where he is making some attractive and distinctive red wines.

WENDOUREE

Location: Wendouree Road, Clare, 5453; 2 km south of township.
(088) 42 2896.

Winemaker: Tony Brady.

1989 Production: 3000 cases.

Principal Wines: Virtually exclusively red wines, with the occasional fortified wine, including fortified Rhine Riesling and fortified Muscat of Alexandria; 1984 saw first dry Rhine Riesling. Red wines include Cabernet Sauvignon, Cabernet Malbec, Shiraz and Shiraz Mataro.

Distribution: Principally cellar door and mailing list. Cellar door sales 10 a.m. to 4.30 p.m. Monday to Saturday. Closed Sunday and between Christmas and New Year. Mailing list enquiries to PO Box 27, Clare, 5453. Very limited wholesale distribution to W. J. Seabrook, Melbourne; Jules Guerassimoff, Brisbane; and The Oak Barrel, Sydney.

Prices: $10 to $14 cellar door.

Vintage Rating 1986–89: '86, '87, '88 ('89 not yet rated).

Outstanding Prior Vintages: '75, '78, '80, '83.

Tasting Notes:

1988 MUSCAT OF ALEXANDRIA [75] Colour: medium straw-yellow. *Bouquet:* strong grapefruit and a stab of spirit. *Palate:* well made; the wine has been sufficiently fermented before fortification to gain vinosity and the spirit is well integrated; sweet on the mid-palate, and then finishes dry. Drink '90.

1987 SHIRAZ [85] Colour: dense purple-red. *Bouquet:* hugely concentrated and powerful, pulled inwards into itself. *Palate:* a huge wine closed a knotted fist; tasted blind I wrote "does seem to have the potential to soften and open up"; now, knowing what the wine is, its

bloodlines guarantee that it will do so; the tannins are persistent but under control. Drink '95–2005.

1987 CABERNET MALBEC [81] Colour: full red-purple. *Bouquet:* rich, clean and full with ripe cassis/berry fruit, touched by spice. *Palate:* full, high-toned minty flavours with persistent tannins; still evolving and will gain greatly in complexity as it slowly opens up. Drink '94–2002.

Summary: Tony Brady guards the rich inheritance of A. P. Birk's Wendouree quietly, indeed shyly, but with a deeply felt passion. Here may be found some of Australia's most remarkable red wines.

THE WILSON VINEYARD
(formerly Wilson's Polish Hill River Vineyards)

Location: Polish Hill River; 4 km east of Sevenhill via Clare, 5453.
(088) 43 4310; Fax (088) 43 4381.

Winemaker: John Wilson.

1989 Production: 3200 cases.

Principal Wines: Rhine Riesling, Chardonnay, Cabernet Shiraz/Malbec, Cabernet Sauvignon, Pinot Noir and Zinfandel.

Distribution: Cellar door sales, mailing list and retail distribution. Wholesale distribution through Porter & Co., SA and NT; Fesq and Co., for NSW, Vic.; David Johnson & Associates, Tas.; Tallerman & Co., Qld. Cellar door sales weekends only 10 a.m. to 4.30 p.m.; mailing list with excellent newsletter; enquiries to Box 11, Sevenhill, 5453.

Prices: $7 to $10 cellar door.

Vintage Rating 1986–89: White: '88, '89, '86, '87. Red: '88, '87, '86, '89.

Outstanding Prior Vintages: '81, '84, '85.

Tasting Notes:

1989 RHINE RIESLING [79] *Colour:* light green-yellow. *Bouquet:* pungent lime/citric fruit, clean and full. *Palate:* very full flavoured and slightly broad, with masses of fruit; almost inevitably, slightly phenolic on the finish. Drink '90–'92.

1987 PINOT NOIR [69] *Colour:* light red-purple. *Bouquet:* very developed with light, leathery/sappy varietal fruit. *Palate:* very light and slightly bitter, but John Wilson obviously worked very hard in the making of this wine; better oak could have produced a quite surprising result. Drink '90.

1987 RX CABERNET SHIRAZ MALBEC [71] *Colour:* medium red-purple. *Bouquet:* complex, bottle-developed leafy/gamey characters. *Palate:* light to medium leafy fruit with a strong gamey overlay, possibly from some carbonic maceration; lacks fruit richness. Drink '90–'92.

1987 CABERNET SAUVIGNON [90] *Colour:* medium red-purple. *Bouquet:* complex, textured, classic cabernet sauvignon in a restrained yet deep style. *Palate:* strong, ripe red berry fruit with a lovely touch of cigar box, and a firm, clean finish. Drink '91–'97.

Summary: Dr John Wilson is a tireless worker for wine in general and the Polish Hill region in particular. Hard work and good intentions do not necessarily produce great wine, and it was particularly pleasing to find out just how well his wines had fared in this year's tasting. He deserves his success.

Coonawarra

1988 VINTAGE

1988 will always be remembered as the vintage that might have been. After a propitious start to the season, with an even and vigorous budburst and early shoot formation suggesting a higher crop level than in the previous few years, the disastrous October frosts struck. Although very severe, the effect of the frost was not uniform: it did not affect the later varieties such as cabernet sauvignon, and it did not affect every part of Coonawarra. Some blocks escaped unscathed, whereas others were completely burnt, forcing the dormant secondary buds to shoot.

The frost damage was made more irksome by the extremely favourable growing conditions that then prevailed through the remainder of the vintage. It was one of the warmest for many years, and resulted in the earliest vintage of the '80s. Because of the warm, dry conditions, with very low rainfall, disease and fungal problems were all but non-existent. As the overwhelming percentage of vineyard in Coonawarra is irrigated, all except a few dry-land blocks were protected from the stress that high temperatures in January would otherwise have caused.

All varieties ripened quickly and evenly, and with mechanical harvesters working around the clock, it was one of the shortest vintages ever experienced. Despite the radical turn around in conditions compared to the preceding four years, and despite the widespread belief that cool years result in the best vintages, it was a good year for both whites and reds. There is a near unanimous view that for red wines it was second only to 1986 (one or two placing it in front).

1989 VINTAGE

The season commenced on schedule, and flowering took place in calm and settled conditions, resulting in good set. A single hail storm caused localised damage, and there was no repetition of the frosts of 1987.

The last significant rain fell at the end of September, the growing season then turning very warm and dry. It seems it was these conditions that led to the grapes having abnormally soft skins, something that was to lead to considerable problems as harvest approached. Until February, at least, all seemed well, but then Coonawarra felt part (though not the full force) of the heatwave that gripped south-east Australia. This led to very rapid sugar accumulation, and to an early start to the vintage. It was not long underway before there was a dramatic change in the weather, with persistent cold weather accompanied by misty rain. It was the view of many vignerons that it was these conditions, rather than the preceding heat, that prevented high-cropping vineyards reaching satisfactory sugar levels.

Shiraz was the worst affected variety: it was either picked early (with potential alcohol of less than 10°) or not at all. Most of it fell into the latter category, simply rotting on the vine. Rhine riesling was satisfactory, but one had to be very selective both in picking and in eventual wine selection. Chardonnay was generally quite good, although here, too, alcohol levels are well below normal. Just as in

1988, Cabernet Sauvignon (with its smaller berries and tougher skins) provided the best wines from the region. Heavily cropped vineyards did not do particularly well, but the lighter bearing patches produced excellent wine.

Merlot tended to over crop, but the increasingly common practice of running part of the juice out of the ferment was used to produce good wines from all of the cabernet and merlot family grapes.

THE CHANGES

There were no new winery or cellar door operations started during 1988 or 1989, but the district nonetheless continues to be the focus of attention in Australian premium red wine-making. Plantings have been extended dramatically, with further large vineyards on the drawing board. This is causing enormous concern among the longer-established vineyards and wineries. The concern turns on the red soil/black soil dichotomy. Conventional wisdom has it that quality grapes can only be grown on the red soil, or terra rosa, which is a weathered form of the limestone base that underlies Coonawarra. The richer black soils are water-retentive, and while promoting vine vigour, will (so the argument goes) simply produce high crops of inferior, partially ripened grapes. The establishment views the newcomers on the black soils as simply wishing to trade on the reputation of Coonawarra and fears that in doing so, the markedly inferior wines will destroy that very reputation.

Not surprisingly, there is a concerted move afoot to agree to a Coonawarra Appellation, which would basically limit the region to the fairly clearly defined boundaries of the red soil.

It is a reputation worth protecting. Coonawarra's red wines continue to sweep all before them in both Australian and overseas wine competitions. In 1988 Greg Clayfield of Lindemans was the International Winemaker of the Year; in 1989 it was John Duval of Penfolds, but winning the title largely because of the Coonawarra wines of Wynns and Penfolds itself. The 1989 Jimmy Watson Trophy went, yet again, to a Coonawarra red: the volume-selling, low-cost Jamiesons Run of Mildara.

❦ *BOWEN ESTATE*

Location: Main Penola-Naracoorte Road, Penola, 5277; 4 km north of township. (087) 37 2229.

Winemaker: Doug Bowen.

1989 Production: 7000 cases.

Principal Wines: Rhine Riesling, Chardonnay, Shiraz and Cabernet Sauvignon Merlot.

Distribution: Substantial cellar door and mailing list sales; cellar door 9 a.m. to 5 p.m. Monday to Saturday. Mailing list enquiries to PO Box 4B, Coonawarra, 5263. Fine wine distribution through Tucker Seabrook Caon, Melbourne and Sydney; and Classic Wine Merchants, Adelaide.

Prices: $10.50 to $15.25 recommended retail.

Vintage Rating 1986–89: White: '89, '87, '88 ('86 not rated). Red: '89, '87, '86, '88.

Outstanding Prior Vintages: White: '82, '84, '81. Red: '79, '84, '82, '80.

Tasting Notes:

1988 CABERNET SAUVIGNON MERLOT [CS] Colour: medium red, with a touch of purple. *Bouquet:* complex charred oak with some lemony fruit; quite rich. *Palate:* soft, chewy ripe berry flavours, rich and thick; a wine clearly not finished, and headed somewhere either side of 80 points.

1987 SHIRAZ [78] Colour: medium to full red-purple. *Bouquet:* very complex spicy/gamey fruit, proclaiming its Coonawarra origin. *Palate:* again, exceedingly complex, indeed bordering on the aggressive, with strong spicy/medicinal fruit; something of a departure in style for Bowen Estate. Drink '92–'96.

1987 CABERNET MERLOT [90] Colour: medium to full red, with some purple remaining. *Palate:* ripe, dark berry fruit with gently sweet

vanillan oak. *Palate:* a richly textured wine with lots of body and depth; smooth, dark fruit flavours dominate the palate, with oak nicely in restraint. Drink '92–'99.

Summary: Doug Bowen is not only one of the great characters of Coonawarra, but one of its finest producers of red wines. Bowen Estate has a very strong mailing list clientele, sure in the knowledge that its wines will not only be very good, but very reasonably priced.

❦ *BRANDS LAIRA*

Location: Penola-Naracoorte Highway, Coonawarra, 5263; 11 km north of Penola. (087) 36 3260; Fax (087) 36 3208.

Winemakers: Bill and Jim Brand.

1989 Production: 18,000 cases.

Principal Wines: Chardonnay; Shiraz, Cabernet Sauvignon, Cabernet Merlot; Cabernet Sauvignon Sparkling Burgundy. Limited special releases of Original Vineyard Shiraz and of Family Reserve Wines. Cellar door only individual varietal wines, Merlot, Pinot Noir, Malbec and Rhine Riesling.

Distribution: Fine wine retail distribution through Brands Regional Vintners, NSW; S. & V. Wine Merchants, SA; and Tasman Wine Co., Vic. Cellar door sales 8 a.m. to 5 p.m. 7 days. Mailing list enquiries to PO Box 18, Coonawarra, 5263.

Prices: $11 to $22.50 retail.

Vintage Rating 1986–89: White: '87, '89, '88, '86. Red: '88, '87, '86, '89.

Tasting Notes:

1987 LAIRA SHIRAZ [74] Colour: medium to full purple-red. *Bouquet:* clean, soft plummy fruit with good oak balance and of medium to full intensity. *Palate:* soft, slightly squashy berry flavours in fairly extreme Coonawarra/ machine harvest style, a description that will be meaningless to some but readily understood by others. Drink '91–'95.

1987 CABERNET MERLOT [90] Colour: medium red-purple, showing the first signs of development. *Bouquet:* clean and harmonious, with full, ripe but not over-ripe, berry fruits. *Palate:* rich and full, with the same beautifully ripened sweet berry flavours promised by the bouquet; there are also touches of plum in the background. In every way, a wine of perfect balance. Drink '92–'98.

1987 CABERNET SAUVIGNON [75] Colour: light to medium red-purple. *Bouquet:* a fraction closed, with a faintly squashy character to moderately sweet berry fruit. *Palate:* ripe, sweet fruit tending to being ever so slightly jammy; low tannin. Drink '90–'94.

1986 ORIGINAL VINEYARD SHIRAZ [80] Colour: medium to full red-purple. *Bouquet:* clean, solid and bottle-developed dark chocolate/ dark berry aromas. *Palate:* rich, clean and smooth, with good fruit and oak balance, and good tannins. Drink '91–'96.

Summary: The red wines of Brands have been models of consistency over the past four years or so. I do not think the chardonnay comes up to the same high standard, and there were significant problems with the '88 sample submitted for the tasting. But that is of small moment: it is for the red wines that Brands are, and always will be, best known.

CHATEAU REYNELLA

Location: No vineyards owned; fruit purchased from vineyards owned by Coonawarra Machinery Co.

Winemaker: David O'Leary.

Principal Wine: Cabernet Sauvignon.

Distribution: National retail through The Hardy Wine Co. in all states.

Prices: $11.99 retail.

Vintage Rating 1986–89: '87, '89, '86, '88.

Tasting Notes:

1987 CABERNET SAUVIGNON [72] Colour:

medium red, with a touch of purple. *Bouquet:* clean, but dominated by lemon/vanillan oak. *Palate:* once again, strong lemon/vanillan oak is the major contributor to flavour; clean fruit is present, but is a little plain. Drink '90–'94.

Summary: Chateau Reynella's Coonawarra operations are now little more than a memory of the past, the last rhine riesling having been produced in 1985. Red wine quality is adequate, if unexciting.

HOLLICK WINES

Location: Racecourse Road, Coonawarra, 5263; first winery north of Penola, 2 km from town. (087) 37 2318; Fax (087) 37 2952.

Winemakers: Ian Hollick and Pat Tocaciu.

1989 Production: 15,000 cases.

Principal Wines: Rhine Riesling, Chardonnay, Cabernet Merlot, Pinot Noir and Shiraz.

Distribution: Cellar door sales, mailing list and fine wine retail distribution through wholesale agents in each state. Cellar door sales 9 a.m. to 5 p.m. 7 days. Mailing list enquiries to PO Box 9B, Coonawarra, 5263. UK imports through Haughton Fine Wines, Cheshire.

Prices: $10 to $16 retail.

Vintage Rating 1986–89: White: '88, '89, '86, '87. Red: '88, '87, '89, '86.

Tasting Notes:

1989 RHINE RIESLING [78] Colour: light green-yellow. *Bouquet:* light but clean, with lime/tropical fruit aromas. *Palate:* pleasant lime flavours with more weight than most of the district's rieslings of the year, and seemingly unaffected by botrytis. Drink '90–'92.

1989 CHARDONNAY [TS] Colour: light green-yellow. *Bouquet:* clean and quite aromatic, with aromas of fig and melon; fairly intense. *Palate:* strong lemony/melon/citric fruit with very good potential; a tank sample prior to receiving any oak treatment, and with outstanding potential if the right oak is used.

1988 CHARDONNAY [70] Colour: very developed full yellow. *Bouquet:* broad, full, developed characters, strongly suggesting extensive use of skin contact. *Palate:* likewise, very developed, and with some slightly phenolic flavours. Drink '90.

1988 SHIRAZ [75] Colour: medium to full red-purple, showing some development. *Bouquet:* quite fragrant and attractive herbal characters of medium intensity. *Palate:* developed herbal flavours with soft, lemony oak; an early maturing style. Drink '90–'91.

1988 CABERNET MERLOT [90] Colour: strong, bright purple-red. *Bouquet:* most attractive lifted, fragrant spicy fruit and oak. *Palate:* light, fragrant and fresh red berry/cherry fruit, with superbly handled and sympathetic spicy oak. Once again, a style that I would prefer to drink while it retains its youth. Drink '90–'93.

Summary: The arrival of Pat Tocaciu to partner Ian and Wendy Hollick at Hollick Wines creates a truly formidable team. Pat Tocaciu was for many years senior winemaker at Tollana, and was responsible for the innumerable outstanding wines made by that company. Hollick has already achieved much (amongst other things one of Coonawarra's many Jimmy Watson Trophies), but even more can be confidently expected in the future.

HUNGERFORD HILL

Location: Main Penola-Naracoorte Road, 1 km north of Penola. (087) 37 2613.

Winemaker: Adrian Sheridan.

Principal Wines: Rhine Riesling, Chardonnay, Shiraz, Cabernet Merlot and Cabernet Sauvignon.

Distribution: Cellar door sales and national retail distribution. Significant fine wine retail distribution through wholesale agents in each State. Cellar door sales 9 a.m. to 5 p.m. Monday to Friday, 10 a.m. to 5 p.m. weekends.

Prices: $11.50 to $21 retail.

Vintage Rating 1986–89: White: '88, '86, '87, '89. Red: '86, '88, '87, '89.

Outstanding Prior Vintages: '82, '84.

Tasting Notes:

1987 SHIRAZ [65] Colour: medium red-purple, slightly dull. *Bouquet:* machine-harvested fruit at its least attractive, with porty/stewed aromas. *Palate:* again, a melange of very ripe and under-ripe fruit flavours, and again a slightly soapy edge suggestive of high pH material. Drink '90–'91.

1987 CABERNET MERLOT [70] Colour: medium red-purple. *Bouquet:* light, leafy/tobacco fruit with the merlot influence quite strong. *Palate:* similar leafy/tobacco flavours, coming in part from the merlot; needs greater weight and intensity. Drink '90–'92.

Summary: The current Coonawarra releases from Hungerford Hill are, quite frankly, very disappointing. In years gone by it regularly produced some of the best Coonawarra reds, and I am at a loss to explain why the quality should have slipped so dramatically.

JAMES HASELGROVE

Location: Main Penola-Naracoorte Road, Coonawarra, 5263; 3 km north of Penola. (087) 37 2734.

Winemaker: James Haselgrove (wines made under contract).

Principal Wines: Rhine Riesling, Gewurztraminer, Later Harvest Riesling, Auslese Riesling, Nouveau, Shiraz, Cabernet Sauvignon and Cabernet Shiraz.

Distribution: Substantial cellar door sales in both Coonawarra and McLaren Vale; also mailing list. Cellar door sales 9 a.m. to 5 p.m. 7 days. Mailing list enquiries to PO Box 231, McLaren Vale, 5171, including free membership of "The Inner Wine Circle". Significant fine wine retail distribution through wholesale agents in each state. "Wine Tasters" lunch available with James Haselgrove wines served; call for details.

Prices: $8.90 to $18.90 cellar door.

Vintage Rating 1986–89: White: '86, '87, '89, '88.

Red: '86, '87, '88, '89.

Tasting Notes:

1988 RHINE RIESLING [55] Colour: some pinking evident. *Bouquet:* full, but somewhat phenolic and coarse. *Palate:* better, although the inherent broadness and coarseness of the base material is patched over by some residual sugar. Drink '90.

1987 AUSLESE RIESLING [72] Colour: medium yellow-green. *Bouquet:* firm and hard, lacking the luscious fruit one expects from an auslese. *Palate:* infinitely better than the bouquet, with sweet, intense rhine riesling fruit nicely balanced by crisp acid. A Jekyll and Hyde wine if ever there was one. Drink '90–'91.

1988 NOUVEAU [68] Colour: bright red-purple. *Bouquet:* slightly dull, with typical meaty maceration aromas. *Palate:* clean, with fair fruit of medium intensity, and rather less over-maceration influence than is evident in the bouquet; simply lacks sparkle. Drink '90.

1987 SHIRAZ [74] Colour: medium red-purple. *Bouquet:* full and soft, with some spicy oak and ripe, dark chocolate fruit. *Palate:* much less intense than the bouquet would suggest, with slightly squashy, spicy/berry flavours coming from heavily cropped vines. Drink '90–'92.

1987 CABERNET SHIRAZ [72] Colour: medium to full red-purple. *Bouquet:* bottle-developed leafy/cedary/cigar box characters with quite pronounced lemony oak. *Palate:* a virtual carbon copy of the bouquet, with complex, aged cedary/leafy/minty fruit and lemony oak. Drink '90–'93.

Summary: James Haselgrove also has on offer a larger than usual array of wines covering both style and vintage. As I have said before, quality tends to be variable, and it is best to taste before buying. These ones were my personal choices from a wider range; yours may of course be different.

❦ *KATNOOK ESTATE*

Location: Off main Penola-Naracoorte Road, Coonawarra, 5263; 4 km north of Penola. (087) 37 2394.

Winemakers: Wayne Stehbens and Mike Davies.

Principal Wines: Rhine Riesling, Sauvignon Blanc, Chardonnay and Cabernet Sauvignon.

Distribution: Principal distribution through wholesale agents in each state using fine wine retailers in all capital cities and major towns. Cellar door sales 9 a.m. to 4.30 p.m. Monday to Friday, Saturday 10 a.m. to 4.30 p.m. No mailing list.

Prices: $14.75 to $24.95 retail.

Tasting Notes:

1989 SAUVIGNON BLANC [TS] Colour: light green-yellow. *Bouquet:* clean, with light varietal character, still building weight and complexity. *Palate:* clean fruit with a touch of slightly oily oak; a wine in its infancy, and it will (on all known form) improve radically.

1988 RHINE RIESLING [77] Colour: light green-yellow. *Bouquet:* quite firm, with a slightly herbaceous edge. *Palate:* clean and firm, again showing some slight herbaceous characters; an understated wine that is fresh and crisp, but lacks fruit richness. Drink '90–'92.

1988 CHARDONNAY [80] Colour: medium yellow-green. *Bouquet:* clean, with good fruit and oak balance; still remarkably undeveloped and still a little one dimensional. *Palate:* markedly more complex than the bouquet with herbal/melon fruit and nicely balanced and integrated oak. Drink '90–'93.

1986 CABERNET SAUVIGNON [82] Colour: bright, clear, purple-red. *Bouquet:* showing some bottle development, with classically restrained varietal fruit free of any of the extravagant Coonawarra characters. *Palate:* rich, strong deep fruit, with dark berry/cassis flavours; textured and very complex, finishing with a touch of astringency. Drink '94–2000.

Summary: Katnook is the flagship label of the very substantial Yunghanns family interest in Coonawarra represented by the large vineyard holdings of the Coonawarra Machinery Company. The second label is Riddoch Estate, discussed separately later in this chapter, and not to be confused with Wynns John Riddoch brand. Just how the consumer is meant not to be confused is in fact beyond my comprehension.

🍇 KIDMAN

Location: Glenroy Road Coonawarra, SA, 5263 (vineyard only).

Winemaker: Thomas Hardy (contract).

1989 Production: Approximately 1000 cases.

Principal Wines: Terra Rossa Wines (which produces the Kidman label) is another major independent grape grower, although on a substantially smaller scale than Coonawarra Machinery Company. Only two wines made: Rhine Riesling and a red wine, labelled as Cabernet Sauvignon or, in best Australian tradition, Great Red Wine of Coonawarra. Wines with considerable age still available.

Distribution: Sold exclusively through Dan Murphy's Cellar, Melbourne.

Summary: The Kidman vineyards are now managed and operated by Thomas Hardy, which buys all of the substantial production; a small quantity is turned separately into wine and sold back for release under the Terra Rosa label.

🍇 KOPPAMURRA

Location: Off main Penola-Naracoorte Road, halfway between Penola and Naracoorte, just south of Struan.
(087) 64 7483.

Principal Wines: Cabernet Sauvignon and Cabernet Sauvignon Merlot Cabernet Franc (blend).

Distribution: Limited retail distribution in Sydney and Melbourne direct from vineyard.

Summary: Like Kidman, Koppamurra is in recess.

🍇 LADBROKE GROVE

Location: Millicent Road, Penola, 5277;
1.5 km south of township.
(087) 37 2997 (winery only).

Winemaker: Made under contract at various wineries and matured on estate winery.

Principal Wines: Hermitage and Cabernet Sauvignon.

Distribution: Principally cellar door sales and mailing list. Cellar door sales 10 a.m. to 8 p.m. most days. Mailing list enquiries as above, cellar door sales situated at Bushmans Inn restaurant, Coonawarra Motor Lodge, 114 Church Street, Penola. Phone (087) 37 2364.

Summary: After a promising start, Ladbroke Grove appears to be struggling. No wines were available for tasting for this edition, and the level of activity is said to be low.

🍇 LECONFIELD

Location: Main Penola-Naracoorte Road, Coonawarra, 5263; 3 km north of Penola. (087) 37 2326.

Winemakers: Dr Richard Hamilton and John Innes.

1989 Production: Approximately 11,000 cases.

Principal Wines: Rhine Riesling, Chardonnay, Cabernet Sauvignon, Cabernet Shiraz and Cabernet Merlot.

Distribution: Significant cellar door sales at Coonawarra and McLaren Vale; also mailing list. Cellar door sales 9.30 a.m. to 4.30 p.m. Monday to Friday, 11 a.m. to 4 p.m. weekends and public holidays. Mailing list enquiries to PO Box 162, Penola, 5277. Fine wine retail distribution in Adelaide, Melbourne, Sydney and Canberra through The Wine Broker.

Prices: $9.50 to $14.50 cellar door.

Vintage Rating 1986–89: White: '86, '88, '89, '87. Red: '86, '88, '87, '89.

Outstanding Prior Vintages: White: '86. Red: '80, '78, '82.

Tasting Notes:

1989 RHINE RIESLING [68] Colour: medium straw-yellow. *Bouquet:* somewhat hard, with slightly stripped fruit. *Palate:* clean and firm, but tending to hardness; may fill out in bottle and merit higher points by the time of release. Drink '90–'91.

1989 CHARDONNAY [CS] Colour: medium yellow-green. *Bouquet:* smooth with some weight and faint PK/mint oak characters. *Palate:* again, slightly odd PK mint/herbal flavours are present, which may indeed derive from the fruit rather than the oak. As yet of somewhat indeterminate style and quality.

1987 SHIRAZ [88] Colour: dense purple-red. *Bouquet:* clean, smooth but quite intense fruit with perfectly balanced oak. *Palate:* fragrant spicy/berry flavours, with a touch of plum; again, the balance between fruit and oak, and between fruit and tannins, is as good as one could wish for. Drink ' 92–'98.

1987 CABERNET MERLOT [78] Colour: medium red. *Bouquet:* clean, light red berry fruit with leafy overtones, no doubt from the merlot; soft lemony oak. *Palate:* strong lemony/stalky characters, partly fruit derived and partly oak derived; an austere wine in the style of a lesser Bordeaux. Drink '91–'95.

1987 CABERNET SAUVIGNON [81] Colour: developed red-purple. *Bouquet:* takes a while to come up in the glass, ultimately expressing itself in a cool, herbaceous style. *Palate:* more immediately accessible, showing multi-faceted flavours in inimical Coonawarra fashion; a fruit, rather than oak, driven wine. Drink '91–'95.

Summary: Leconfield has not lived up to the exceptional promise of its '78 and '80 Cabernet Sauvignons; it is not that the current releases are bad (they are in fact an improvement over recent vintages), but rather that other producers have lifted their quality to leave Leconfield a little behind. I have the feeling it could do better still.

LINDEMANS

Location: Main Penola-Naracoorte Road, Coonawarra, 5263; 9 km north of Penola. (087) 36 3205.

Winemakers: Greg Clayfield, with Phillip John, Lindemans' company oenologist.

Principal Wines: Limestone Ridge Shiraz Cabernet, St George Vineyard Cabernet Sauvignon and, in the wake of its 1986 Jimmy Watson Trophy, Pyrus, a blend of Cabernet Sauvignon Cabernet Franc Merlot and Malbec.

Distribution: National retail at all levels. UK imports through I.D.V., Gilbey House, Essex.

Prices: $27 retail.

Vintage Rating 1986–89: '86, '88, '87, '89.

Outstanding Prior Vintages: '76, '78, '80.

Tasting Notes:

1988 LIMESTONE RIDGE SHIRAZ CABERNET [86] Colour: dense purple-red. *Bouquet:* complex, concentrated in pronounced Lindemans style, with strong lemony oak and clean fruit. *Palate:* rich, full and concentrated, with dark fruit flavours and soft but pervasive tannins; pronounced lemony oak. Drink '94–2000.

1988 PYRUS [90] Colour: deep purple-red. *Bouquet:* superbly rich and concentrated, with exceptional fruit and oak balance. *Palate:* structured and layered, with full-blown red berry fruit and a complex web of oak flavours of differing types; to my way of thinking, better than the '85 Pyrus. Drink '94–2002.

1988 ST GEORGE CABERNET SAUVIGNON [CS] Colour: strong purple-red. *Bouquet:* youthful and clean, with fresh, lemony oak not entirely integrated. *Palate:* fresh and spotlessly clean red berry/cherry fruit with very slightly raw, lemony oak; a cask sample still requiring final blending and adjustment, but clearly will be good.

1987 PYRUS [83] Colour: medium red-purple. *Bouquet:* clean, with pronounced lemony oak in unmistakable Lindemans style; smooth fruit. *Palate:* once again, lemony/vanillan oak is dominant, there is sweet fruit there to give balance and support to the oak; in a cellar style, but one that I think is going to change somewhat in the next few years. Drink '92–'96.

1987 ST GEORGE CABERNET SAUVIGNON [82]
Colour: light to medium red-purple. *Bouquet:* clean, but that lemony/vanillan oak of which Lindemans was so fond at the time is dominant. *Palate:* clean and stylish, but standing out in a masked tasting as only possibly coming from one maker—Lindemans; clean but well balanced and with low tannins on the finish. Drink '92–'96.

1986 ST GEORGE CABERNET SAUVIGNON [90]
Colour: full red-purple. *Bouquet:* concentrated, deep fruit with a slightly astringent charred oak edge. *Palate:* rich, strong, deep fruit with dark berry/cassis flavours; strongly textured and given additional complexity by a touch of astringency. Drink '93–2000.

Summary: Lindemans is a major contributor to the reputation of Coonawarra as the producer of Australia's finest red wines; two Jimmy Watson Trophies in six years is but one indicator of quality. The most interesting development is the emergence of distinct styles within the individual vineyards making up the red-wine range. Forget the big company image; these are quality reds of the highest order.

❦ MILDARA

Location: Main Penola-Naracoorte Road, Coonawarra, 5263; 9 km north of Penola. (087) 36 3380; Fax (087) 36 3307.

Winemaker: Gavin Hogg.

Principal Wines: A tightly controlled and selected range of brands falling in distinct price categories. At the bottom end is Coonawarra Rhine Riesling and Coonawarra Hermitage; then comes Jamiesons Run Chardonnay and Jamiesons Run (predominantly Shiraz); next is Coonawarra Cabernet Sauvignon and finally Alexanders (a Bordeax blend).

Distribution: National retail through all types of outlets.

Prices: $6, $11, $15 and $22 respectively for the four group bands.

Vintage Rating 1986–89: White: '88, '86, '87, '89. Red: '86, '88, '87, '89.

Outstanding Prior Vintages: White: '85, '79. Red: '63, '64, '69, '79, '85, '82.

Tasting Notes:

1989 RHINE RIESLING [63] Colour: light straw-yellow. *Bouquet:* diminished fruit and somewhat hard. *Palate:* firm, hard and again lacking fruit, though no significant winemaking fault. Drink '90.

1987 HERMITAGE [75] Colour: medium red-purple. *Bouquet:* clean, light fruit with soft vanillan oak and slightly squashy berry characters. *Palate:* soft, clean vanillan oak tends to dominate, but the wine does have a pleasantly clean finish and is of remarkable quality for its price. Drink '90–'92.

1987 JAMIESONS [74] Colour: medium red with a touch of purple. *Bouquet:* clean fruit of light to medium intensity with lemony oak threatening to dominate. *Palate:* the threat of the bouquet is realised, with dominant lemony oak over clean, light fruit. Drink '90–'92.

1987 CABERNET SAUVIGNON [71] Colour: medium red-purple. *Bouquet:* leafy/stalky/tobacco/berry fruit in exaggerated Coonawarra style. *Palate:* a jumble of spicy/leafy/slightly meaty flavours, all showing the less successful side of Coonawarra viticulture. Drink '90–'92.

1987 ALEXANDERS [59] Colour: excellent red-purple. *Bouquet:* aggressive, raw, pencilly oak over slightly gamey fruit. *Palate:* swamped by most unpleasant raw and unintegrated oak. Drink '93–'96.

Summary: Having won the 1989 Jimmy Watson Trophy at the Royal Melbourne Show with its 1988 Jamiesons (a much richer and fleshier wine than the 1987), and having turned in another year of record profits, Mildara will no doubt be unconcerned about the relatively modest showing of its wine in this edition. I am left to wonder what went wrong with the 1987 Alexanders.

PENFOLDS

Location: Main Penola-Naracoorte Road, Coonawarra, 5263; 12 km north of Penola (vineyard only).

Winemakers: John Duval (senior winemaker) and assistants.

1989 Production: Most of the vineyard resources go to form part of the big-name wines such as Bin 707. Production of Bin 128 not for publication.

Principal Wines: Bin 128 Coonawarra Claret only.

Distribution: national retail at all levels.

Price: Nominally $10 retail, but invariably sells for under $10.

Vintage Rating 1986–89: '86, '88, '87, '89.

Tasting Notes:

1987 BIN 128 [69] Colour: medium red. *Bouquet:* clean, but lemony oak tends to dominate. *Palate:* clean, with pleasant fruit, but lemony oak again tends to sit rather stodgily on top of the fruit. Drink '91–'94.

1986 BIN 128 [80] Colour: dark red-purple. *Bouquet:* clean, rather closed in on itself but with considerable depth to the fruit; light touch of toasty oak. *Palate:* solid, deep ripe varietal shiraz with length and balance; as one would expect, the best Bin 128 for a decade or more. Drink '92–'97.

Summary: Most of the grapes from Penfolds extensive Coonawarra vineyards go into its top region-blended wines, with Bin 128 the only 100% Coonawarra release. For some reason, Penfolds has elected to keep the wine at the bottom end of the price-scale, which has necessarily meant low expenditure on oak, and precluded any selection of the best available material in the first place. However, years such as 1986 make their own statement.

PENOWARRA

Location: Main Penola-Naracoorte Road, Penola, 5277; 3 km north of township.
(087) 37 2458.

Winemakers: Ken Ward and Ray Messenger.

Principal Wines: Rhine Riesling, Shiraz and Cabernet Sauvignon, Vintage Port and Shiraz Port.

Distribution: Exclusively cellar door sales 9 a.m. to 5 p.m. 7 days (occasionally closed during weekdays). Mailing list enquiries to PO Box 229, Penola, 5277.

Prices: $7 to $10.

Summary: Penowarra is only a part-time business for owners Ray and Kay Messenger, and it does not take an active part in district winery activities. No samples were available for tasting.

PETALUMA

Location: Evans Vineyad, Main Penola-Naracoorte Road, Coonawarra, 5263; 13 km north of Penola (vineyard only).
Sharefarmers Vineyard,
11 km north of Evans Vineyard in the Hundred of Joanna (vineyard only).

Winemaker: Brian Croser.

Principal Wines: Cabernet Merlot blend simply entitled Coonawarra and sometimes a Botrytis Affected Rhine Riesling. Some Chardonnay used between 1980 and 1985 for Petaluma Chardonnay.

Distribution: Through fine wine retailers in all capital cities; cellar door sales at Bridgewater Mill. No mailing list.

Prices: $27 to $28.50.

Vintage Rating 1986–89: '88, '87, '86, '89.

Outstanding Prior Vintages: '85, '79, '82.

Tasting Notes:

1986 COONAWARRA [90] Colour: bright and very youthful purple-red. *Bouquet:* spotlessly clean, with red berry/cassis fruit showing no off-characters; soft oak. *Palate:* an exceptionally youthful and clean fruit-driven wine, with lively cassis/berry flavours; the structure is excellent, and although the tannins are light and soft, the finish is very long. Drink '92–'97.

Summary: Good though the '86 Petaluma is, a preview of the '87 suggests even better things are in store. Each year since 1984 seems to have produced wines with increasing structure and fruit weight, and the oak support seems less erratic than it once was.

REDMAN

Location: Main Penola-Naracoorte Road, Coonawarra, 5253; 10 km north of Penola. (087) 36 3331.

Winemaker: Bruce Redman.

1989 Production: 20,000 cases.

Principal Wines: Only two wines made: Claret and Cabernet Sauvignon (latter in bottles, magnums and imperials).

Distribution: National and UK through Thomas Hardy to retailers at all levels. Cellar door sales 9 a.m. to 5 p.m. Monday to Saturday. No mailing list.

Prices: $9.50 to $14.50.

Vintage Rating 1986-89: '87, '88, '89, '86.

Outstanding Prior Vintages: '69, '70, '76, '84.

Tasting Notes:

1987 CLARET [65] Colour: medium red, with just a touch of purple. *Bouquet:* slightly dull fruit, with some biscuity/medicinal characters showing. *Palate:* distinct burnt/medicinal edge to fruit of light to medium weight; slight old oak characters do not help. Drink '90–'93.

1987 CABERNET SAUVIGNON [63] Colour: medium red-purple. *Bouquet:* some biscuity/leathery sulphides, and very light fruit. *Palate:* of light to medium weight with unusual medicinal/ant/crushed beetle characters;

altogether an odd wine. Drink '90–'91.

Summary: Redman seems content to carry on much as it has always done; it really should take a look at what is going on in the district before it is left too far behind.

RIDDOCH

Location: c/- Katnook Estate, of which Riddoch is the second label.

Winemakers: Wayne Stehbens and Mike Davies.

1989 Production: Substantial but not for publication; all except the Chardonnay are from 100% Coonawarra material.

Principal Wines: Rhine Riesling, Fumé Blanc, Chardonnay and Cabernet Sauvignon.

Distribution: National retail, limited cellar door sales through Katnook Estate.

Prices: $9.50 to $12.35 retail.

Tasting Notes:

1989 RHINE RIESLING [75] Colour: light green-yellow. *Bouquet:* clean, aromatic fruit with an intriguing herbal/spice edge. *Plate:* clean and fine, with slightly green fruit flavours, but good acid; well made, although it is just a fraction hollow. Drink '90–'91.

1989 FUME BLANC [73] Colour: light green-yellow. *Bouquet:* clean but light, with a faint varietal tobacco/herbal edge. *Palate:* light, clean and quite crisp, but the fruit is a little thin on the ground. Drink '90–'91.

1986 CABERNET SHIRAZ [80] Colour: medium red. *Bouquet:* clean and smooth, with pleasant bottle-developed characters, although not particularly aromatic or fruity. *Palate:* rich, firm dark berry fruit with well-balanced and integrated oak; the wine has good structure and length. Drink '91–'95.

Summary: The 1986 Cabernet Shiraz was, of course, the Jimmy Watson Trophy winner at the Royal Melbourne Show of 1987. It is a good wine, although at this distance could hardly claim to be the best among the many great reds of 1986. Put into the context of their price, the Riddoch Wines assume an altogether different cast, offering excellent value for money.

❦ THE RIDGE WINES

Location: Naracoorte Road, Coonawarra, 5263; 10 km north of Coonawarra, 5263. (087) 36 5071.

Winemaker: Sid Kidman.

1989 Production: 1250 cases.

Principal Wines: Rhine Riesling, Shiraz and Cabernet Sauvignon.

Distribution: Exclusively cellar door sales and mail order; cellar door sales 9 a.m. to 5 p.m. 7 days.

Prices: $8.60 to $11.50 cellar door.

Vintage Rating 1986–89: White: '87, '88, '89, '86. Red: '87, '88, '89, '86.

Tasting Notes:

1988 RHINE RIESLING [78] Colour: medium yellow-green. *Bouquet:* clean, firm lime aromas in good fruit style. *Palate:* fresh and clean, with light to medium lime flavours, followed by a firm but balanced finish. Drink '90–'92.

1986 CABERNET SAUVIGNON [54] Colour: medium to full red-purple. *Bouquet:* rather leathery fruit with bilgy old oak. *Palate:* again, light fruit has been dulled and obscured by rather poor, old oak. Drink '90.

Summary: A cellar door sales operation still finding its way, but at least pointing in the right direction with a good rhine riesling.

❦ ROSEMOUNT ESTATE

Location: Main Penola-Naracoorte Road, Penola, 5270; on northern outskirts of town (vineyard only). (065) 47 2467.

Winemaker: Phillip Shaw.

Principal Wines: Cabernet Sauvignon only current release.

Distribution: National retail through fine wine merchants; extensive restaurant representation. No cellar door sales nor mailing list.

Prices: $20.75 retail.

Vintage Rating 1986–89: '86, '88, '87, '89.

Tasting Notes:

1987 RESERVE CABERNET SAUVIGNON [85] Colour: medium to full red-purple. *Bouquet:* clean and potent leafy/berry fruit with above-average richness. *Palate:* similarly potent leafy/berry/dark fruits with a touch of tobacco; skilled oak handling adds complexity, and the wine has good acid on the finish. Drink '92–'98.

Summary: Rosemount is still coming to grips with its own Coonawarra vineyard. It has not been afraid to experiment with trellising and pruning techniques, and the difficult 1988 and 1989 vintages have not made life any easier. It may be a few years yet before the full potential of the vineyard is reflected in an expanded product range.

❦ ROUGE HOMME

Location: C/- Lindemans, Main Penola-Naracoorte Road, Coonawarra, 5263; 9 km north of Penola.

Winemakers: Greg Clayfield, with Phillip John, Lindemans' company oenologist.

Principal Wines: Chardonnay, Export Estate Dry White, Pinot Noir, Claret and Cabernet Sauvignon. Old vintages of Cabernet Sauvignon and Claret from time to time; currently 1980 Claret Classic Release ($30).

Distribution: National retail at all levels; UK imports through Avery's of Bristol.

Prices: $9 to $15.

Vintage Rating 1986–89: White: '86, '88, '87, '89. Red: '86, '88, '87, '89.

Outstanding Prior Vintages: '76, '78, '80.

Tasting Notes:

1989 CHARDONNAY [CS] Colour: light to medium yellow-straw. *Bouquet:* attractive, smoky/spicy barrel-ferment characters, with fruit of light to medium intensity. *Palate:* very sophisticated, spicy barrel-ferment oak with as-yet fairly light fruit; needs to be back-blended with wine from stainless steel; every potential for points in the mid 80's.

1988 CHARDONNAY [79] Colour: medium yellow-green. *Bouquet:* full and rich, with strong peachy fruit. *Palate:* full, ripe honeyed/ peachy fruit with slightly sawdusty/ hessiany oak. Drink '90–'92.

1989 PINOT NOIR [85] Colour: light red-purple. *Bouquet:* excellent spicy oak handling which perfectly fits the weight and style of the faintly cherry fruit. *Palate:* again, outstanding oak treatment, although there is good underlying fruit, with flavours of cherry and strawberry. A breakthrough in this style for Lindemans. Drink '90–'91.

1987 CLARET [71] Colour: medium red. *Bouquet:* exaggerated Coonawarra gamey/ lemony/leafy characters. *Palate:* ultra-typical leafy/berry/meaty/medicinal flavours all shouting at each other; a vineyard, rather than the winemaker, at work. Drink '90–'92.

1987 CABERNET SAUVIGNON [90] Colour: bright, full purple-red. *Bouquet:* clean, with firm, well ripened berry fruit and pronounced lemony oak which just stays within the bounds. *Palate:* classic rich, firm and beautifully ripened cabernet; there is ample fruit to carry the oak, and the wine has a notably long finish. Drink '92–'98.

1986 CABERNET SAUVIGNON [85] Colour: medium to full red. *Bouquet:* solid, with some bottle-developed characters and primary fruit aroma dropping as other complexities build. *Palate:* very pleasant, clean, sweet dark berry/ cassis fruit; suave rather than voluptuous, and finishes well. Drink '91–'95.

Summary: The Rouge Homme label goes from strength to strength as its attentions become increasingly fixed on red wines, with chardonnay the only white wine available on the local market. It seems, too, that Rouge

Homme might be on the verge of unlocking the secret of handling pinot noir in Coonawarra.

🍇 *WYNNS*

Location: Memorial Drive, Coonawarra, 5263; 2 km west of Coonawarra township. (087) 36 3266.

Winemaker: Peter Douglas.

Principal Wines: Rhine Riesling, Chardonnay, Pinot Noir, Hermitage, Cabernet Hermitage, Cabernet Sauvignon and John Riddoch Cabernet Sauvignon.

Distribution: National retail at all levels.

Prices: $7.60 to $30 retail.

Vintage Rating 1986–89: '86, '88, '87, '89.

Outstanding Prior Vintages: '82, '80, '76, '75, '66, '62, '55.

Tasting Notes:

1989 RHINE RIESLING [75] Colour: medium yellow-green. *Bouquet:* strong and rich lime/ pineapple characters, suggesting some botrytis influence. *Palate:* very soft, rich and high-flavoured wine that is quite at odds with most of the rieslings of the vintage, but should be exceedingly well received at the price. Drink '90.

1989 CHARDONNAY [CS] Colour: medium yellow-green. *Bouquet:* already shows good fruit and oak balance and integration. *Palate:* follows the bouquet closely with well-balanced and integrated French oak and pleasant melon/peach fruit. Yet another of a series of excellent wines under this label is in the making.

1988 PINOT NOIR [74] Colour: full purple-red. *Bouquet:* rather extractive and heavy, with sweet plummy fruit. *Palate:* again, seems to have been somewhat overworked; there are masses of plummy (and quite burgundian) fruit, but the tannins are very high, as is the overall extract. Could be a surprise packet in the long term. Drink '90–'93.

1987 CABERNET HERMITAGE [70] Colour: medium to full red. *Bouquet:* already showing some development, with slightly roasty/gamey edges to the fruit. *Palate:* exaggerated gamey/ leafy fruit characters in that manifestation of Coonawarra that I for one would rather not see—and it was certainly not there in 1986, for example. Drink '92–'95.

1987 CABERNET SAUVIGNON [75] *Colour:* medium to full red-purple. *Bouquet:* very ripe jammy fruit, almost port-like. *Palate:* as the bouquet promises, jammy/cassis/plum fruit; a throwback to some of the cabernets from 1980. Drink '93–'97.

1987 JOHN RIDDOCH CABERNET SAUVIGNON [81] Colour: dense red-purple. *Bouquet:* clean with very concentrated vanilla bean oak and dark chocolate fruit. *Palate:* huge, rich and concentrated dark berry flavours with very high tannin levels; almost impossible to approach yet, and once it has a few more years on its side, could become a formidable wine. Drink '94–2005.

Summary: It was almost inevitable that the 1987 red wines of Wynns would come to something of an anti-climax after the superlative wines of 1986. Perhaps it is nothing more than a salutary reminder that much of the winemaking takes place in the vineyard, and that years like 1986 come along once every 10 years or so. The 1987 red wines, incidentally, are not due for release until April 1990.

Tasting Notes:

1988 SHIRAZ [CS] Colour: deep, opaque purple-red. *Bouquet:* dense, full and clean dark berry fruit aroma. *Palate:* very youthful; full, markedly ripe fruit, with tannins under control; appears to have great potential and should be headed for points well into the 80's.

1988 CABERNET SAUVIGNON [90] Colour: dark deep purple-red. *Bouquet:* very clean, concentrated and rich, with perfect oak and berry fruit balance. *Palate:* an enormous, rich and concentrated wine with high tannins, good oak and abundant fruit. Pointed shortly before bottling, because it did appear to be complete. Drink '94–2003.

Summary: The 1988 Zema Estate reds are unlikely to be released much before the end of 1990 at the earliest. They will, however, be well worth the wait, promising to be by far the best to come out under the Zema label. Intervening vintages have suffered somewhat from the effects of sulphides. The local vignerons all agree that the vineyard is one of the best in Coonawarra, the fruit quality exemplary.

🍇 ZEMA ESTATE

Location: Main Penola-Naracoorte Road, Coonawarra, 5263; 0.5 km south of Coonawarra township. (087) 36 3219.

Winemaker: Ken Ward (consultant).

1989 Production: 3000 cases.

Principal Wines: Rhine Riesling, Late Harvest Rhine Riesling, Shiraz and Cabernet.

Distribution: Cellar door sales and mailing list; cellar door sales 9 a.m. to 5 p.m. 7 days. Mailing list enquiries to PO Box 12, Coonawarra, 5263. Retail distribution through Seabrook & Seabrook, Adelaide; and Westwood Wine Agencies, Melbourne.

Prices: $9 to $12 cellar door.

Outstanding Prior Vintages: '82, '84.

Langhorne Creek

1988 VINTAGE

Budburst occurred on schedule in this normally reliable region, and the vines grew well in the early part of the season. However, very windy and occasionally wet conditions during flowering severely affected fruit set and led to reduced yields in most varieties. Thereafter the weather turned warm, and an early vintage of fruit in very good condition got underway. There was no change in the weather pattern, and an early start led to an early conclusion— hastened by the reduced yields.

1989 VINTAGE

Budburst and flowering passed without incident, and the vines flourished in the relatively cool (and occasionally wet) growing season that followed. Langhorne Creek was not spared the South Australian heatwave, which arrived in mid-February and which led to rapid sugar accumulation in all varieties. However, like neighbouring McLaren Vale, the rains that visited other districts from the middle of March basically stayed away, and the season was decidedly more successful than in many other districts.

THE CHANGES

There are no changes to the players: the real task of Langhorne Creek is to supply very large quantities of grapes to major wine companies such as Wolf Blass, Lindemans and Penfolds. It is an area in which grapes can be grown very economically, and the softness of the wines seems to go very well in regional blends.

BLEASDALE

Location: Wellington Road, Langhorne Creek,
5255; 17 km east of Strathalbyn.
(085) 37 3001.

Winemaker: Michael Potts.

1989 Production: 45,000 cases.

Principal Wines: A substantial range of table,
sparkling and fortified wines released under
both varietal and generic labels. White wines
include Rhine Riesling, Verdelho and
Colombard; red wines include Cabernet
Sauvignon, Shiraz Cabernet, Malbec, Special
Vintage Shiraz and Private Bin Hermitage.
Tiny quantities of very old, high-quality Heysen
Madeira also available at winery (one bottle
per customer limit). Dry red and fortified
wines sold with significant bottle-age.

Distribution: National distribution through Elders-
IXL Ltd. Cellar door sales 9 a.m. to 5 p.m.
Monday to Saturday, 11 a.m. to 5 p.m. Sunday.
Mailing list enquiries to PO Box 1, Langhorne
Creek, 5255.

Prices: $4.50 to $9.50 table wines cellar door; $4 to
$25 fortified wines; retail prices slightly higher.

Vintage Rating 1986–89: '88, '86, '89, '87.

Outstanding Prior Vintages: '78, '80, '82, '84.

Tasting Notes:

1989 WOOD MATURED VERDELHO [78] Colour:
medium yellow-green. *Bouquet:* voluminous
lemony/peachy fruit aromas, strongly
reminiscent of chardonnay; well-integrated,
light oak. *Palate:* disappoints slightly after the
wonderful bouquet; the fruit flavour dips
slightly on the mid-palate, although has
reasonable length, thanks in part to some
sweetness. A well-made, extremely commercial
style. Drink '90–'91.

1985 SHIRAZ CABERNET [74] Colour: excellent
red-purple of medium depth, bright and clear.
Bouquet: pleasant ripe sweet red-berry fruit,

with little or no oak impact. *Palate:* soft and
generous red berry/plum fruit flavours with a
touch of mint, and a nice twist of acid on the
finish. Drink '90–'92. (Most recent red wine
made available taken from 1988 edition.)

Summary: No new red wines were available for
tasting for this edition: the wines are often
kept for considerable periods of time in large
storage before bottling and release. However,
there is a consistency in the style, with a fruit
softness that runs through all the wines. They
demonstrate just why Langhorne Creek has
been a happy hunting-ground for major wine
blenders such as Wolf Blass, Penfolds and
Lindemans.

BREMER WINES

Location: Wellington Road, Langhorne Creek,
5255; in the centre of the township.
(085) 37 3048 or (085) 37 3070.

Winemaker: Bill Davidson.

Principal Wines: Limited range of white and red
varietal table wines comprising Chardonnay,
Rhine Riesling, Cabernet Shiraz and Malbec.

Distribution: Substantial cellar door sales and
mailing list. Significant restaurant distribution
in SA, limited retail distribution in Vic.,
through SPW Distributors Pty Ltd. Cellar door
sales 9 .30 a.m. to 5 p.m. Monday to Saturday
and 11.30 a.m. to 5 p.m. Sunday. Mailing list
enquiries to PO Box 136, Langhorne Creek,
5255.

Summary: No up-to-date information was
available, and I have the suspicion that Bremer
Wines is winding back its activities.

TEMPLE BRUER

Location: Milang Road, Strathalbyn, 5255; 14 km
south of Strathalbyn.
(085) 37 0203.

Winemakers: David Bruer and Barbara Bruer (manager).

1989 Production: 107 tonnes (the equivalent of 6500 cases).

Principal Wines: Cabernet Merlot, Shiraz/Malbec, Botrytis Riesling and Eden Valley Riesling.

Distribution: Cellar door sales and mail order. Cellar door sales and tastings are located in the Wine Vat restaurant building in Langhorne Creek, approximately 7 km east of the vineyard and winery. Distribution through Australian Vineyard Distributors in NSW and Vic.; Queensland Liquor Supplies, Qld; and Southmark Agencies Pty Ltd, WA. Mail order, winery and vineyard visits enquire to Temple Bruer Wines Pty Ltd, RSD 226, Strathalbyn, 5255. UK imports through S. Wines Ltd, Chelsea.

Prices: Cellar door and mail order: red $99 per dozen; Eden Valley Riesling $99; Botrytis Riesling $117 per dozen for 375 ml bottles; $189 per dozen for 750 ml bottles.

Vintage Rating 1986-89: White: '89, '87, '88, '86. Red: '88, '89, '86, '87.

Tasting Notes:

1989 EDEN VALLEY RHINE RIESLING [79] *Colour:* light green-yellow. *Bouquet:* rich, full pungent lime aromas in mainstream district style. *Palate:* soft and rich, flavours of lime and passionfruit; well made and with abundant flavour. Drink '90–'93.

1987 SHIRAZ MALBEC [74] *Colour:* medium red-purple. *Bouquet:* exceedingly complex, and appearing to change in the glass from moment to moment, varying from well-hung meat through to pie and peas maceration characters through to spice. *Palate:* very high-toned, spicy/leafy flavours with light to medium tannin; a very interesting wine that I could not help but liking, even though it is not a style I usually find attractive. Drink '90–'92.

Summary: The Bruers run a substantial vine propagation business, and David Bruer has been a long-time lecturer at Roseworthy Agricultural College. Wine quality is, to put it mildly, variable: there is a vineyard style, but at times it takes on very strange manifestations. I have a sneaking suspicion that a particular form of mercaptan is steadily working away behind the scenes.

Padthaway

1988 VINTAGE

After a promising start, the district was devastated by the October frosts; these dealt an even heavier blow to Padthaway than they did to Coonawarra. Large areas of vineyard were totally burnt off when the temperature fell to minus 3° centigrade; crop losses between 50% and 80% resulted, with an overall loss across all vineyards and all varieties of almost 50%. Chardonnay was the most affected, Cabernet Sauvignon the least.

After four cool years, a very warm growing season followed. Given the very low crops that most the vines then carried, it was hardly surprising that what fruit there was ripened very rapidly, and that vintage was over quickly, starting in early March and finishing in mid-April.

Some astonishing white wines were made from the tiny second harvest crops that resulted. Initially it was thought that these were deficient in flavour, but Lindemans, for example, made remarkable sauvignon blanc and chardonnay.

1989 VINTAGE

The season got off to a superb start, only fair given the disastrous commencement to the 1988 vintage. Budburst, flowering and fruit set all proceeded unimpeded, and were followed by an extremely slow, cool ripening period. The arrival of the February heatwave changed things dramatically: notwithstanding the fact that most of the vines had bumper crops (they had recovered well from the frosts of the previous year), sugar commenced to accumulate at an unprecedented rate. In retrospect, it seemed clear that much of the accumulation was due simply to the effects of dehydration, and that when the heat ended and the balance of the vines returned to normal, there was in some cases a drop in the sugar level. What is more, the pattern experienced in other regions repeated itself: the vines' systems failed to function normally, and ripening occurred at a snail's pace. Those who made a decision to pick probably did better than those who decided to hold on, particularly with the reds. Seppelt was one of the early harvesters, and is more than pleased with the quality of the cabernet sauvignon and shiraz. However, collapse and mould was widespread in areas of dense canopy and high yield, and only a small percentage of the crop reached optimum maturity. As ever, there will be some very good wines out of the district, simply because it is such a fine grape growing region: what is poor for Padthaway is likely to be very good for a less favoured viticultural area.

THE CHANGES

There are no new entries, but there has been considerable ongoing activity behind the scenes. The sole limiting factor on the rapid expansion of viticulture that would otherwise take place is the lack of availability of any new water-drawing rights for irrigation. Thus, only those blocks with existing water rights can be effectively planted to vine, and these are few and far between. Nonetheless, Andrew Garrett Wines has become a major holder in the dis- trict, and the reputation of the district as the producer of superb chardonnay and sauvignon blanc grows day by day.

LINDEMANS PADTHAWAY

Location: Padthaway via Naracoorte, 5271 (vineyard only).

Winemakers: Greg Clayfield, assisted by Phillip John, company oenologist.

1989 Production: Not for publication.

Principal Wines: Chardonnay, Sauvignon Blanc (Fumé Blanc), Verdelho, Rhine Riesling, Pinot Noir and Cabernet Sauvignon.

Distribution: National retail through all types of outlets.

Prices: $9.50 to $18.50 recommended retail; with the quality of these wines now better understood, discounting is on the wane.

Vintage Rating 1986–89: White: '87, '86, '88, '89. Red: '86, '87, '89, '88.

Tasting Notes:

1989 RHINE RIESLING [79] Colour: very good green-yellow. *Bouquet:* fragrant toasty/lime, showing good fruit for the year. *Palate:* quite surprising fruit-weight and richness; sweet fruit on the mid-palate and a pleasant finish. Drink '90–'91.

1989 CHARDONNAY [CS] Colour: light to medium green-yellow. *Bouquet:* clean but fairly light fruit, with faintly oily vanillan oak. *Palate:* the oak is better flavoured and balanced, but the fruit seems a little hollow and one dimensional; tasted in its infancy, and could come together well.

1988 FUME BLANC [85] Colour: medium to full yellow-green. *Bouquet:* strong, classy toasty/charred oak, very complex and stylish; the fruit is slightly irrelevant. *Palate:* glorious spicy/clove oak dominates all else, but has been beautifully handled. Underneath there is some gooseberry sauvignon to be tasted. Drink '90–'93.

1988 CHARDONNAY [86] Colour: medium yellow-green. *Bouquet:* complex, rich and developed, with full although every so slightly biscuity oak.

Palate: fresh and elegant melon/grapefruit flavours more than hold their own with smooth oak; while of light to medium intensity, is a very stylish wine. Drink '90–'94.

1987 FUME BLANC [90] Colour: medium yellow-green. *Bouquet:* complex, full fruit wine with ripe gooseberry aromas. *Palate:* very strong varietal characters; an uncommonly rich, fruit-driven wine with ripe gooseberry/tobacco flavours of unusual complexity. Drink '90–'91.

1987 CHARDONNAY [92] Colour: medium yellow-straw. *Bouquet:* complex, rich and textured, showing lovely bottle-development. *Palate:* wonderfully rich, honeyed and textured; peachy buttery fruit is perfectly balanced against soft, faintly spicy, oak. Drink '90–'93.

Summary: The virtual failure (in terms of quantity) of the 1988 vintage forced Lindemans to prolong (by allocation) the release life of the '87s, and it will move very quickly through to the '89s. Partly for this reason, and partly because the chardonnay and fumé blanc are so clearly the best wines that Lindemans produces from Padthaway, I thought it was interesting to provide current tasting notes of each of the three vintages. In a combined Coonawarra Padthaway tasting for this book, the wines stood out with their sheer class.

PADTHAWAY ESTATE

Location: At Padthaway township, adjacent to highway.
(087) 65 5039.

Winemaker: Leigh Clarnette.

1989 Production: 5500 cases.

Principal Wines: Pinot Chardonnay Brut, Pinot Noir Brut Rosé and two table wines, Chardonnay and Pinot Noir.

Distribution: Cellar door, mailing list, and through the Padthaway Estate Restaurant. Cellar door sales 9 a.m. to 5 p.m. Friday, Saturday and Sunday; other times by appointment. Mailing-list enquiries to Padthaway Estate, Padthaway, 5271.

Prices: $14 to $19 cellar door and mail order.

Vintage Rating 1986–89: White: '86, '89, '88, '87. Red: '89, '86, '87 ('88 not rated).

Tasting Notes:

1986 CHARDONNAY [82] *Colour:* bright, glowing yellow-green. *Bouquet:* generous, smooth honeyed/buttery fruit and oak, aging with considerable grace. *Palate:* very smooth and clean, with surprisingly light peach/melon/honey flavours. Another wine that demonstrates the capacity of Padthaway Chardonnay to benefit from extended cellaring. Drink '90–'93.

1985 BRUT PINOT CHARDONNAY CHAMPAGNE [75] *Colour:* onion-skin/ straw. *Bouquet:* quite complex though rather austere; French rather than fruity Australian. *Palate:* precisely as the bouquet promises, distinctly austere, with some flavours of old socks, yet does have style. Drink '90–'91.

1985 BRUT ROSE [79] *Colour:* light pink. *Bouquet:* light, but somewhat against the odds, cleaner and more fruity than the blend. *Palate:* light, slightly smoky pinot flavours with good mouth-feel and structure; I cannot recollect tasting a better Australian rosé. Drink '90–'92.

Summary: Padthaway Estate offers magnificent accommodation and a high-class restaurant. It also has a substantial vineyard, a small part of the production of which is vinified for the estate by Thomas Hardy. It is the only Padthaway producer to offer wines at the cellar door, and is a more-than-welcome new arrival. The recent appointment of Leigh Clarnette as executive winemaker is the first stage of an ambitious programme to commence on-site winemaking.

Location: Adjacent to Padthaway township, approximately 75 km north of Naracoorte (vineyard only). (087) 65 5047.

Winemakers: Ian McKenzie (chief), plus others.

Principal Wines: Only occasional individual vineyard releases (such as Padthaway Cabernet-Merlot 1987) but Rhine Riesling, Chardonnay, Shiraz and Cabernet Sauvignon play a major role in many of the more important Seppelt wines, such as the Seppelt Black Label and Gold Label ranges and Chardonnay and Pinot Noir in premium sparkling wines.

Distribution: National retail at all levels.

Prices: $10 to $18.50.

Vintage Rating 1986–89: White: '86, '87, '89, '88. Red: '89, '88, '86, '87.

Outstanding Prior Vintages: '81, '84, '78.

Tasting Notes:

1986 SHOW CHARDONNAY [83] *Colour:* full yellow, with just a touch of green remaining. *Bouquet:* extremely rich, complex, charred barrel-ferment oak; a tour de force in oak handling. *Palate:* inevitably, an oak-driven wine, but one showing exemplary skills and which is highly commercial; I would have liked to see just a little more fresh fruit to counter the oak. A blend of Padthaway and Barooga material. Drink '90–'91.

1987 CABERNET MERLOT [75] *Colour:* medium red-purple. *Bouquet:* very light leafy/tobacco/herbal fruit with pronounced merlot influence. *Palate:* light, elegant leafy/red berry/tobacco flavours; very low tannin. Both in terms of structure and flavour, looking very much like a middle rank St Emilion wine from an intermediate year. Drink '90–'92.

Summary: Seppelt seems to regard its Padthaway vineyard as a prime source of material for blending with wines made in other regions, and 100% Padthaway releases are few and far between. Nonetheless, it is somewhat surprising that Seppelt has not developed a 100% Padthaway chardonnay to emulate those of Lindemans and Thomas Hardy. For the time being, at least, the Seppelt Padthaway red wines seem to have an equally important place in the scheme of things.

🍇 THOMAS HARDY

Location: Padthaway, adjacent to main highway (vineyard and crushing facility only). (087) 65 6060.

Winemakers: White—Tom Newton; red—David O'Leary.

1989 Production: Not for publication.

Principal Wines: A wide range of varietal table wines is produced, with the Padthaway vineyard providing by far the greatest part of Hardy's wines. Siegersdorf Rhine Riesling now contains Padthaway material; various varietals under various labels have been released over the years, with the Hardy Collection range introduced mid-1985 and including Chardonnay, Sauvignon Blanc, Fumé Blanc, Chardonnay, Beerenauslese Rhine Riesling, Pinot Noir and Rhine Riesling. Classic Cuvee *Méthode champenoise* first released in 1987.

Distribution: National through The Hardy Wine Company—all states.

Prices: $7.99 to $13.99 retail.

Vintage Rating 1986–89: White: '86, '89, '88, '87. Red: '87, '89, '86, '88.

Outstanding Prior Vintages: White: '80, '82, '85. Red: '78, '79, '82.

Tasting Notes:

1988 COLLECTION PADTHAWAY SAUVIGNON BLANC [77] Colour: light green-yellow. *Bouquet:* attractive herbaceous fruit with light, smoky overtones suggestive of some barrel fermentation. *Palate:* crisp, clean herbaceous fruit with a touch of tobacco leaf; it is almost impossible to tell whether oak has been used or not; finishes fresh and crisp. Drink '90–'91.

1988 COLLECTION PADTHAWAY/CLARE CHARDONNAY [90] Colour: light green-yellow. *Bouquet:* elegant and harmonious, with very good fruit/oak balance; aromas of melon,

fig and grapefruit. *Palate:* a beautifully balanced and constructed wine with flavours of grapefruit/melon /fig, and oak playing a carefully judged support role. Is very much a food wine in a bigger style than one is used to from Thomas Hardy, presumably because of the Clare material. Drink '90–'93.

1987 EILEEN HARDY CHARDONNAY [92] Colour: glowing green-yellow. *Bouquet:* exceedingly complex and lively; tangy grapefruit/melon set against charred oak. *Palate:* again, still amazingly fresh and lively, with tangy grapefruit augmented by superb smoky/charred oak. Drink '90–'94.

Summary: Thomas Hardy disputes with Lindemans the title to premier white wine producer in Padthaway; while perhaps not as consistent as Lindemans, its Reserve Chardonnays and Beerenauslese Rhine Rieslings are supremely great wines.

Riverland

1988 VINTAGE

The season got away to a reasonable start with even budburst. Flowering took place in calm conditions and set was good, but the number of bunches per vine was significantly less than normal, resulting in an immediate decrease in yield of between 20% and 30% throughout the whole region. Those to suffer most were cabernet sauvignon, shiraz and gordo. No sooner had vignerons faced up to this unwelcome news than two severe and widespread hail storms devastated the chardonnay, resulting in crop losses ranging from moderate to total.

Mild growing conditions followed thereafter; indeed, so cool was the weather that vintage started two weeks later than normal, notwithstanding the low crop levels. However, once vintage started, sugar accumulation accelerated, resulting in a very short harvest period. What grapes were picked were of excellent quality, with chardonnay, cabernet sauvignon and shiraz being the best seen for many years.

1989 VINTAGE

Cool and calm conditions during flowering promoted good fruit set, and yields bounced back strongly after the reduced 1988 vintage. Bunch numbers were back to normal, and above average yields resulted.

In some respects the vintage was a repetition of 1988: very cool and mild conditions led to slow ripening up until mid-February, when the heatwave led to frighteningly fast sugar accumulation and to some problems with sunburn.

Mechanical harvesters were forced to work around the clock, but some very good riesling and chardonnay were harvested. While fruit quality overall was not quite as good as 1988, it was certainly more than useful when the substantial yields were taken into account.

THE CHANGES

There are two new entries, Kingston Estate Wines and Wein Valley Estates. Kingston Estate was in fact established in 1979, but has not previously been listed because hitherto almost all of its production has been sold either in bulk or in "cleanskin" bottles for the buyers' own brand market. However, Kingston Estate intends to establish its own labels within the next two years, buoyed by its success at the 1988 Adelaide Wine Show where its Chardonnay of that year won a silver medal.

Wein Valley Estates is another substantial operation that, until recently, has not been much seen in the market place under its own label. It is unusual in that, while it is a private company, it involves its 160 grape growers in all aspects of winemaking through to bottling. Output is large, and much of the wine is still sold in bulk, both on local and export markets.

The importance of the Riverland to

Australian viticulture can be best gauged from the fact that in 1986/87 it produced 31% of all chenin blanc grown in Australia, 27% of all sauvignon blanc, 23% of all shiraz, 11% of all chardonnay, 10% of all pinot noir and 8% of all rhine riesling.

ANGOVE'S

Location: Bookmark Avenue, Renmark, 5341
(head office);
1320 North East Road, Tea Tree Gully, 5091
(principal administration branch).
(085) 85 1311.

Winemaker: Frank Newman.

Principal Wines: A complete range of table and
fortified wines is made. The table wines are
Angove's Varietal releases (8 white wines and a
red wine); Bin Reference Claret Sauvignon/
Shiraz and Shiraz/Malbec; the Reserve Series
Tregrehan Claret, Brightlands Burgundy,
Bookmark Riesling, Nanya Moselle and Golden
Murray Sauterne, Special Riesling, Moselle and
Claret; and the 2-litre flagon and 5-litre cask
range. The range of brandies are St Agnes Old
Brandy, Old Liqueur Brandy and Three Star
Brandy. There is a range of sherries plus
vintage and tawny port. Finally there are the
flavoured fortified wines headed by Marko
Vermouth and Stone's Ginger Wine.

Distribution: National retail at all levels through
the company's own distribution network in all
states except Tas., where independent
wholesale distributors are utilised. Cellar door
sales at Renmark and Tea Tree Gully 9 a.m. to
5 p.m. Monday to Friday.

Prices: Nominally falling between $7.25 and $9.50,
frequently discounted to substantially lower
levels.

Tasting Notes:

1988 CHARDONNAY [76] Colour: medium full
yellow-green. *Bouquet:* very elegant, with well-
integrated oak; against all the odds, akin to a
cool climate chardonnay. *Palate:* fine, elegant
restrained melon/citric fruit with light but well
integrated oak. Drink '90.

1988 RHINE RIESLING [69] Colour: medium
yellow-green. *Bouquet:* clean but very light
with a slight herbaceous edge to the fruit.
Palate: has reasonable length with a hint of

passionfruit, and fleshed out by perceptible but
not excessive residual sugar. Drink '90.

1988 GEWURZTRAMINER [65] Colour: light green-
yellow. *Bouquet:* some herbaceous characters, not
particularly varietal, but clean and fresh. *Palate:*
extremely unusual flavours for a warm-grown
traminer with tangy/herbaceous flavours;
obviously early picked, and retains good acid.
Drink '90.

1986 SHIRAZ MALBEC [74] Colour: medium red-
purple. *Bouquet:* distinct Italian red wine/
chianti-like characters, perhaps partly deriving
from storage in large old oak. *Palate:* the Italian
connection continues, with light, soft, slightly
dusty fruit, with warm, sweet berry flavours
followed by a twist of acid on the finish. An
intriguing and appealing wine. Drink '90–'91.

1986 CABERNET SAUVIGNON [77] Colour:
medium red-purple. *Bouquet:* light but classic
herbaceous/ tobacco aromas; a wine as surprising
in its fashion as the chardonnay. *Palate:* is rather
more conventional, with sweet cassis/berry
flavours and good structure; finishes with faintly
sharp acid that may or may not soften. Drink
'90–'91.

Summary: Year after year Angoves produces
varietal white and red wines that are supremely
honest, almost invariably showing good varietal
definition, and which represent outstanding
value for money.

BERRI ESTATES

Location: Sturt Highway, Glossop, 5344; 3 km
south-east of Berri.
(085) 83 2303.

Winemaker: Reg Wilkinson

1989 Production: 29 million litres (the equivalent
of 3 million cases).

Principal Wines: Specialists in 5-litre wine casks,
fine old fortifieds and bulk sales to other

wineries. A range of 750 ml bottles in low to medium price bracket called Brentwood.

Distribution: National retail in all states direct except in Western Australia and Tasmania where product is sold through agents. Substantial and growing exports to North America, the UK (Hallgarten Wines, Luton), Europe and South-East Asia.

Prices: $4.49 for Brentwood range.

Summary: The major 750 ml table wine sales of the Berri/Renmano Group are channelled through Renmano, Barossa Valley Estates and Lauriston. There are only three bottled wines sold by Berri under the new Brentwood range: Fruity Lexia, Riesling and Claret. They are honest but unambitious wines.

BONNEYVIEW

Location: Sturt Highway, Barmera, 5345; due east of Berri.
(085) 88 2279.

Winemaker: Robert Minns.

Principal Wines: Traminer Riesling, Chardonnay, Frontignan Blanc, Shiraz, Cabernet Merlot, Nookamka Touriga Port, Shiraz Liqueur Port and Currant Liqueur Port.

Distribution: Exclusively by cellar door sales and mail order; cellar door sales 9 a.m. to 5.30 p.m. 7 days. Mail order as above.

Summary: A boutique winery by the standards of the Riverland, producing wines marketed exclusively to local trade; those last tasted were of modest but certainly acceptable quality.

COUNTY HAMLEY

Location: Cnr Bookmark Avenue and Twenty-Eighth Street, Renmark, 5341; off Sturt Highway.
(085) 85 1411.

Winemakers: T. and M. Bodroghy.

Principal Wines: A limited range of table and fortified wines including Vin Fumé, Rhine Riesling, Late Harvest Rhine Riesling, Chardonnay, Cabernet Sauvignon Tete de

Cuvee, Pinot Noir, Bin 53 Port and Regimental Vintage Port.

Distribution: Principally cellar door sales and mailing list; cellar door sales 10 a.m. to 5.30 p.m. 7 days. Mailing list enquiries to PO Box 483, Renmark, 5341.

Summary: Over the years County Hamley has produced some very unusual wines using unconventional fermentation techniques. The quality and style of the present releases are not known.

KINGSTON ESTATE
(formerly Apollo Winery)

Location: Kingston-on-Murray, SA, 5331.
(085) 83 0244.

Winemaker: Bill Moularadellis.

1989 Production: 900,000 litres (the equivalent of 100,000 cases).

Principal Wines: Rhine Riesling, Chardonnay, Sauvignon Blanc, Shiraz, Cabernet Sauvignon and Merlot.

Distribution: Most wine sold either in bulk or under buyers-own-brand particularly for retailers and restaurants. A quality selection is being retained and matured for the Kingston Estate label to be distributed both locally and on export markets within the next two years.

LUBIANA

Location: School Road, Moorook, 5332.
(085) 83 9320.

Winemaker: Steve Lubiana.

Principal Wines: A full range of table and fortified wines; premium wines include Chardonnay, Special Bin Cabernet Malbec Shiraz, Anniversary Port, 1973 Vintage Port, Old Muscat and Old Liqueur Frontignac; then follow 11 whites and 7 red table wines with either varietal or generic labels, and almost 20 fortified wines, including vintage ports of 5 vintages from 1974 to 1978.

Distribution: Principally cellar door sales and

mailing list; limited wholesale distribution direct ex-winery to selected retailers in capital cities. Cellar door sales 9 a.m. to 5 p.m. Monday to Friday. Mailing list enquiries to PO Box 50, Moorook, 5332.

Summary: A substantial operation, with much of the wine sold in bulk or in flagon.

RENMANO

Location: Sturt Highway, Renmark, 5341; on south-western outskirts of town. (085) 86 6771.

Winemaker: Paul Kassebaum.

1989 Production: 13 million litres (the equivalent of 140,000 cases).

Principal Wines: Renmano 2-litre wine casks and 750 ml table wines released under Chairman's Selection range comprising Chardonnay Bin 104, Traminer Riesling Bin 204, Sauvignon Blanc, Rhine Riesling Bin 604, Cabernet Sauvignon Bin 460 and Merlot Bin 540; Rumpole Tawny Port, Cromwell Tawny Port, Paringa Hill Hermitage, Lockley Ridge Colombard Chardonnay and Chabrel VSOP Brandy. Very large sales in bulk also made.

Distribution: National retail in all states direct except in Western Australia and Tasmania where product is sold through agents. Substantial and growing exports to North America, the UK (Hallgarten Wines, Luton), Europe and South-East Asia. Cellar door sales 9 a.m. to 5.30 p.m. Monday to Saturday, and 9 a.m. to noon on Sundays of long weekends. Mailing list enquiries to PO Box 238, Berri, SA, 5343.

Prices: Chairman's Selection range $9 to $14 retail.

Tasting Notes:

1989 CHAIRMAN'S SELECTION RHINE RIESLING BIN 604 [80] Colour: bright yellow-green.

Bouquet: full, fragrant, intense and surprisingly rich lime/pineapple. *Palate:* full and soft toasty/lime/pineapple fruit; has masses of flavour; almost inevitably, does have a slightly hard finish. Drink '90–'92.

1989 CHAIRMAN'S SELECTION SAUVIGNON BLANC [81] Colour: medium yellow-green. *Bouquet:* clean, quite luscious gooseberry fruit with surprising weight. *Palate:* soft, fleshy wine with good varietal character and mouth-feel; no oak influence. Drink '90–'91.

1988 CHAIRMAN'S SELECTION CHARDONNAY BIN 104 [90] Colour: deep, advanced yellow. *Bouquet:* extreme peaches and cream rich fruit with luscious and strong complex oak. *Palate:* a massively rich, bosomy peaches and cream style that appeals directly to the senses rather than to the mind, and literally sweeps one away. Multiple gold and trophy medal winner that should have been drunk before now, but if not, drink '90.

1988 CHAIRMAN'S SELECTION CABERNET SAUVIGNON BIN 460 [74] Colour: medium purple-red. *Bouquet:* clean, with good varietal red berry fruit and quite pronounced oak. *Palate:* light berry fruit is threatened by strong, charred/vanillan oak; the finish lifts again with some herbaceous varietal flavours. Drink '90–'93.

Summary: Renmano is now the indisputable king of the Riverland. It has another outstanding chardonnay in the pipeline to follow the 1988 vintage, the latter winning the Tucker Seabrook Caon Trophy for the champion wine (white or red) to appear in Australian wine shows in the 1988/89 circuit.

WEIN VALLEY ESTATES

Location: Nixon Road, Monash, 5342. (085) 83 5225.

Winemaker: Otto Konig.

1989 Production: 5,775,000 litres (the equivalent of 641,666 cases)

Principal Wines: A wide range of table, sparkling, fortified and flavoured wines together with spirits, liqueurs and Retsina. Sold under various labels including Wein Valley Estates,

Mesoyia Retsina, Champelli, Black Label Premium and Ouzo 21.

Distribution: Wholesale distribution through Incredible Wine Co., NSW; Horvid Nominees Pty Limited, Vic.; and Liquor Mate, SA. Also cellar door sales and mail order. Cellar door sales 9 a.m. to 4 p.m. Monday to Friday and 11 a.m. to 3 p.m. Saturday.

Prices: $3.07 to $5.94 retail.

Summary: An operation that has successfully targeted ethnic groups across Australia as its market.

Southern Vales

1988 VINTAGE

One summary of the 1988 vintage, provided by the local vignerons association to the Australian Wine & Brandy Corporation, put things this way: "Whilst 1988 proved a difficult vintage in many Australian wine growing regions, McLaren Vale once again demonstrated its reliability with respect to both grape quantity and quality. The heat which affected the West Australian vintage, the hail which touched Clare, the Barossa Valley and the Riverland, the frost which decimated grape yields in the south-east, the rain which inundated the Hunter Valley were all kind enough to by-pass McLaren Vale."

And indeed, McLaren Vale enjoyed an excellent growing season, which resulted in crops that equalled or exceeded the high yields of 1986 and 1987. The dry and warm summer kept disease at bay, and the grapes were harvested in prime condition. Chemical composition was good, with correct sugar/acid balance and pH levels, and colour extraction in the reds was immediate.

Yet for all that, it was not a great vintage. This may have been due in part to the high yields, and in part to the warm conditions that prevailed throughout the actual harvest period. Overall, white wine quality is marginally in front of red wine, with six wineries rating it the best over the past four years. The vast majority, however, placed it second or third, with 1987 still highly rated for its fruit intensity.

While the red wines have excellent colour, they too lack the richness and intensity of 1986 and 1987. Only two wineries placed '88 first, the majority rating it third.

1989 VINTAGE

After a normal winter, spring rains petered out by the second week of September, heralding what was to be a cool but very dry spring and summer. The absence of rain meant that flowering and fruit set took place in ideal conditions, and all looked promising for a high quality vintage of above average yield. Sporadic mildew attacks were quickly dealt with, and fruit condition on the vines (most receiving supplementary water these days) looked excellent as vintage approached. The heatwave, which started in mid-February and continued through to the end of the first week of March, caused what was described by one senior winemaker as total panic. Wineries overflowed as the white grapes started to come in two weeks earlier than normal, the red grapes four weeks earlier.

The only viable option was to concentrate on the premium varieties, leaving the second-rate varieties to take their chances. Just when it seemed all was lost, the heatwave ended, and the vintage turned cool and dry. The rains which then caused so many problems in the Clare Valley in Coonawarra and throughout Victoria stayed away, and vintage settled down to normal. Indeed, baumes dropped for a while as the vines returned moisture to the berries, and patience was required.

While it was not a great year, there is no question some good wines will be made. Chardonnay, in particular, looks promising, with opulent flavour and structure. Much depended on the capacity of the winery to handle the influx of grapes, and much, too, on the status of the vineyards. For this reason, opinions are sharply divided: five wineries rated it as their top year in the past four; an equal number rated it last.

If opinions varied on the white wines, the polarisation with red wines was absolutely dramatic. With remarkably few exceptions, the vintage was rated either first or last, with the majority rating it last. While some good merlot was made, both shiraz and cabernet sauvignon will tend to be porty/jammy traditional styles, and very clever winemaking will be needed to fashion them into wines acceptable into today's market.

THE CHANGES

The Southern Vales continues to be one of the most highly populated (in terms of both the number of wineries and the number of independent grape growers) and active wine districts in Australia. Once again, it acted as the pace-setter for grape prices: McLaren Vale chardonnay was in extraordinary demand, and the prices paid had a domino effect across the rest of Australia. In turn, the ever-growing Andrew Garrett empire was regarded by most other makers and growers in the region as playing a lead role, even though Garrett himself is anxious to downplay that role. He is responsible for one of the new entries in this edition, McLaren's on the Lake, which is the name of the extensive winery/convention centre/restaurant/motel complex that is now corporate headquarters. The McLaren's on the Lake wines are sold cellar door and through the American Express Westpac direct mail operations, but performed extraordinarily well in the district tasting.

Another new entry of note is Bosanquet Estate, and once again there is an indirect Garrett connection. One of the partners in the operation behind Bosanquet is Tony McEntegart, who is said to have been the financial wizard behind the Andrew Garrett phenomenon. Together with two other financial investors, he has joined forces with Robert Dundon, and both Bosanquet Estate and Beresford are now housed in the historic Horndale winery which has been entirely re-equipped and upgraded for premium winemaking.

Other inclusions are Donolga, Manning Park, Tinlins and Ross McLaren Estate. All except the last have in fact been operating for some time, albeit on a relatively low key.

The very large district tasting was impressive. It is not hard to see why McLaren Vale grapes can earn such high prices: fruit quality and varietal character are both immediately obvious and very enjoyable. There was a low percentage of faulty wines, although I could not help wonder why so many makers seemed happy to condemn chardonnay worth $2000 per tonne to indifferent oak—either too old or American when French (which is admittedly more expensive) should be used.

Southern Vales has undergone a change of ownership and an even more significant change in winemaking personnel, all of which has led to a marked increase in wine quality. Hugo Estate, too, deserves a mention for providing the top rated full-bodied red wine in the 1989 Australian Smallmakers Wine Exhibition.

ANDREW GARRETT WINES

Location: Kangarilla Road, McLaren Vale, 5171; 1 km east of McLaren Vale township. (08) 323 8853.

Winemakers: Andrew Garrett and Warren Randall.

1989 Production: Not stated; only a relatively small part of the very large crush.

Principal Wines: Limited range of premium-quality table wines including Chardonnay, Fumé Blanc, Rhine Riesling, Pinot Noir, Shiraz, Cabernet Merlot and N.V. Pinot Noir (_Méthode champenoise_). The modestly named "Ultimate" series will be released in the second half of 1990.

Distribution: Principally retail, but also cellar door sales and limited mailing list sales. Cellar door sales 10 a.m. to 5 p.m. 7 days; mailing list enquiries to above address. Fine wine retail distribution through wholesale agents in Sydney, Suntory Aust. Pty Ltd; Melbourne, The Wine Company; Adelaide, Chace Agencies; ACT, Harry Williams & Co.; NT, North Australian Liquor Wholesalers; Perth, National Liquor; Tas., David Johnstone & Associates.

Prices: $12 to $16 recommended retail.

Vintage Rating 1986–89: White: '89, '86, '88, '87. Red: '87, '86, '88, '89.

Tasting Notes:

1988 FUME BLANC [74] Colour: medium yellow-green. _Bouquet:_ very rich spicy/nutmeg/clove oak. _Palate:_ hot, spicy/clove oak dominates and almost burns the palate, so rich is it; a wine that should have been back blended with some non-wooded material. However, for those who like oak (and there are plenty) the wine may have very great appeal. Drink '90–'91.

1988 CHARDONNAY [81] Colour: medium yellow-green. _Bouquet:_ clean and smooth honeyed aromas of medium to full intensity, but a fraction one dimensional. _Palate:_ full, rich and clean peach/honey/butter flavours, with well-integrated oak. Drink '90.

1988 AVERIL GARRETT LATE PICKED RHINE RIESLING [65] Colour: medium to full yellow-green. _Bouquet:_ clean lime/toast aromas showing good varietal character. _Palate:_ a soft, clean easy drinking wine in a thoroughly commercial mould. Drink '90.

1987 CABERNET MERLOT [64] Colour: medium to full red. _Bouquet:_ sweet berry fruit overwhelmed by strong, spicy Portuguese-type oak with clove/spice characters. _Palate:_ very strong clove/spice oak flavours throw the wine out of balance and lead to bitterness on the finish. Once again, a more gentle hand would have produced a far better wine. Drink '90–'94.

1986 CABERNET MERLOT [85] Colour: medium red. _Bouquet:_ clean and fresh with scented red berry aromas. _Palate:_ attractive, fresh elegant red berry flavours and very soft tannins; a stylish wine with the merlot influence obvious. Drink '90–'95.

LIQUEUR TAWNY PORT (18 Y.O.) [80] Colour: very good tawny, with no red hues apparent. _Bouquet:_ shows true tawny port style with marked rancio and lift; again, a rich tawny with lots of flavour; sweet fruit on the mid-palate gives way to a long, cleansing dry finish.

Summary: Whatever else one may say, things are never dull with Andrew Garrett. At times he, his winemaking empire and his wines seem to tremble on the knife's edge; not everything succeeds. While there were some excellent wines reviewed in this edition, some of the wines not reviewed were of a lesser quality.

BERESFORD

Location: Old Heritage Horndale Winery, Lot 1000, Fraser Avenue, Happy Valley, 5067; 5km east of Reynella. (08) 322 2344; Fax (08) 322 2402.

Winemaker: Robert Dundon.

1989 Production: 13,000 cases.

Principal Wines: Four wines only are made:

Sauvignon Blanc, Chardonnay, Pinot Noir and a blend of Cabernet Sauvignon/Cabernet Franc.

Distribution: By mailing list and through distributors in each state: Chace Agencies, SA; The Wine company, Vic.; The Haviland Wine Company, NSW; Vance Palmer, Qld; Standard Distillers, WA and Harry Williams & Co., ACT. UK importers Horseshoe Wines; USA importers Chempro, also exports to NZ and Singapore with Negociants. Mailing list enquiries to PO Box 5, Happy Valley, SA, 5067.

Prices: $11 to $12 retail.

Vintage Rating 1986–89: White: '89, '87, '88, '86. Red: '86, '87, '88 ('89 not yet rated).

Tasting Notes:

1988 SAUVIGNON BLANC [80] Colour: light straw-yellow. *Bouquet:* clean; of medium intensity with good balance and style; soft gooseberry aromas with a hint of honey. *Palate:* clean honeyed/gooseberry flavours; very smooth and quite stylish; oak not evident. Drink '90.

1988 CHARDONNAY [79] Colour: medium yellow-green. *Bouquet:* faintly cabbagey edge to an otherwise full and complex aroma showing some bottle development. *Palate:* a potent, firm and complex wine that is infinitely better than the bouquet promises; long, lingering grapefruit flavours. Drink '90–'91.

1988 PINOT NOIR [69] Colour: medium purple-red. *Bouquet:* very pronounced carbonic maceration pie and peas aromas that obliterate any varietal character. *Palate:* light bodied, and again showing very marked carbonic maceration characters making varietal flavour irrelevant; other good judges like this wine (and this style) much better than I do, so my points should be looked at with a jaundiced eye if you like maceration wines. Drink '90.

1986 CABERNET SAUVIGNON CABERNET FRANC [60] Colour: medium red-purple. *Bouquet:* clean, light and leafy aromas. *Palate:* very light bodied with rather thin, leafy fruit with pronounced lemony oak. A deliberately underplayed wine that I believe has gone too far over the edge. Drink '90–'91.

Summary: Rob Dundon has very definite ideas on wine styles: the whites are generous and full flavoured, the reds light bodied and, according to Rob Dundon, ideal food wines. As the points and notes indicate, I relate to his white wine philosophy, but not that of his red wines. Others will no doubt agree with Robert Dundon, and disagree with me. Such is the pleasure of wine.

BOSANQUET ESTATE

Location: Old Heritage Horndale Winery, Lot 1000, Fraser Avenue, Happy Valley, 5067; 5km east of Reynella.
(08) 322 2344; Fax (08) 322 2402.

Winemaker: Robert Dundon.

1989 Production: 40,000 cases.

Principal Wines: Five wines only are made: Fumé Blanc, Riesling, Semillon Chardonnay, St Helene Cabernet/Shiraz and Sparking wine.

Distribution: Through retailers; South Australia serviced direct from winer; The Wine Company, Vic.; The Haviland Wine Company, NSW; and Standard Distillers, WA. Exports to the UK and USA. Mailing list enquiries to PO Box 5, Happy Valley, SA, 5067.

Prices: $6.99 recommended retail.

Vintage Rating 1986–89: White: '89 (first vintage). Red: '87, '88, '89.

Tasting Notes:

1989 RHINE RIESLING [TS] Colour: full medium green. *Bouquet:* full fruit but smelly, wet dog fermentation characters that will hopefully be cleaned up before the wine goes into bottle. *Palate:* has lots of flavour, but it is difficult to get past the bouquet. May have been an errant sample.

1989 FUME BLANC [74] Colour: light to medium green-yellow. *Bouquet:* quite full, tropical fruit with good weight; clean. *Palate:* plenty of smooth tropical/honeyed flavours, with good weight and balance. Drink '90.

Summary: The strikingly labelled and packaged Bosanquet wines (just what does that label depict?) seem likely to be formidable competitors in their price range. The winery had only just commenced operations at the time of writing, and we shall hear more of it in the future.

🍇 CAMBRAI

Location: Hamiltons Road, McLaren Flat, 5171. (08) 323 0251.

Winemaker: Graham Stevens.

Principal Wines: An unusual offering of varietal table wines including Chablis, Chardonnay, Rhine Riesling, Gewurztraminer, Zinfandel, Pinot Noir, Hermitage, Cabernet Sauvignon, Pinot Hermitage, Pinot Cabernet, Cabernet Malbec Merlot, Vat 52 Show Burgundy and Vintage Port.

Distribution: Principally cellar door and mailing list. Cellar door sales 10 a.m. to 5 p.m. 7 days; mailing list enquiries to PO Box 206, McLaren Vale, 5171. Wines also available through selected restaurants and bottle shops.

Summary: Without doubt, the outstanding wines coming from Cambrai at the present time are the vintage ports, particularly those based on shiraz. Given the success that Reynella and Thomas Hardy have had for so long, it is surprising that McLaren Vale vignerons have not thrown out the challenge before now. Graham Stevens is certainly doing so.

🍇 CHAPEL HILL

Location: Chapel Hill Road, McLaren Vale, 5171. (08) 323 8429.

Winemaker: Bevan Wilson.

1989 Production: Approximately 3000 cases.

Principal Wines: A limited range of traditional McLaren Vale styles including Rhine Riesling, Chardonnay, Sauvignon Blanc, Shiraz, Cabernet Sauvignon and Vintage Port. Fortified wines offered ex-cellars with some bottle-age.

Distribution: Some retailers, cellar door and mailing list. Cellar door sales 11 a.m. to 5 p.m. 7 days. Mailing list enquiries to PO Box 194, McLaren Vale, 5171. Occasional restaurant listing in Adelaide.

Prices: $7.50 to $10 cellar door.

Tasting Notes:

1989 RHINE RIESLING [70] Colour: light green-yellow. *Bouquet:* quite full and soft, with toasty/passionfruit aromas. *Palate:* full flavoured lime/passionfruit, but very sweet—too sweet for a dry rhine riesling, but no doubt highly commercial. Drink '90.

1986 CABERNET SAUVIGNON [78] Colour: medium to full red-purple. *Bouquet:* solid, sweet berry fruit nicely set against sweet vanillan/spicy oak. *Palate:* full, sweet berry fruit with spicy/tangy vanillan oak, with a hint of Portuguese-type oak also present; has length and flavour. Drink '90–'94.

Summary: There have been some changes at Chapel Hill, and if winemaker Bevan Wilson was responsible for both the current releases, he should be well pleased. Chapel Hill is a cellar door specialist, and there is the added attraction of the adjacent Chapel Hill Park.

🍇 CHATEAU REYNELLA

Location: Reynella Road, Reynella, 5161; on southern outskirts of township. Also at Main Road, McLaren Vale, 5171 (Tintara Cellars). (08) 381 2266, cellar door; (08) 381 7397, McLaren Vale and (08) 323 8676.

Winemakers: Fortified—Bill Hardy; red—David O'Leary; white—Tom Newton; sparkling—Tom Newton.

1989 Production: Not stated, but large.

Principal Wines: Wines made from both Coonawarra and Reynella grapes. (See separate entry for Coonawarra.) Southern

Vale wines comprise Vintage Reserve Chablis, Chardonnay, Rosé, Vintage Reserve Claret, Cabernet Sauvignon, Cabernet Malbec Merlot, Vintage Port (one of Australia's two greatest) and an Old Cave Tawny Port (10 years).

Distribution: National retail distribution through The Hardy Wine Company.

Prices: $4.99 to $11.99.

Vintage Rating 1986–89: White: '88, '89, '86, '87. Red: '87, '89, '86, '88.

Outstanding Prior Vintages: White: '80, '81, '85. Red: '78, '80, '82.

Tasting Notes:

1988 VINTAGE RESERVE CHABLIS [74] Colour: light straw-green. *Bouquet:* neutral and clean; gently fruity, with no reliance on oak. *Palate:* light and crisp, with some slightly herbaceous fruit flavours (from sauvignon blanc) together with a touch of fruit salad (from chenin blanc); nice tang to finish and deserves the chablis name. Drink '90.

1987 CHARDONNAY [87] Colour: growing yellow-green. *Bouquet:* intense, perfumed spicy oak and fruit. *Palate:* most attractive wine of light to medium weight with fresh, lively and zesty fruit; spicy oak is perfectly balanced. Drink '90 –'91.

1982 CABERNET MALBEC MERLOT [75] Colour: medium red. *Bouquet:* complex with full dark chocolate aromas; stylish and rich, yet not heavy. *Palate:* a big, firm wine with dark chocolate overtones; much more flesh and weight than one usually finds under this label. Drink '90–'95.

OLD CAVE PORT [77] Colour: light tawny-red. *Bouquet:* high toned with some rancio, and not heavy. *Palate:* good Australian tawny port style with typically sweet and fruity mid-palate, but again shows rancio character, and has an appropriately dry finish.

Summary: Chateau Reynella makes sophisticated table wines that demand nothing of the consumer other than simple enjoyment, and massive vintage ports of great complexity that imperiously commend both attention and respect. The winery, reception areas and gardens are magnificent and ought not to be missed under any circumstances.

☙ COOLAWIN

Location: Chandlers Hill Road, Clarendon, 5157. (08) 383 6138.

Winemakers: Brian Light and Gregory O'Keefe.

1989 Production: 50,000 cases.

Principal Wines: Rhine Riesling, Frontignan Spatlese, White Burgundy, Chablis and Shiraz made from selected grapes grown in the Southern Vales region.

Distribution: National by Concorde Liquor and cellar door sales 10 a.m. to 5 p.m. 7 days.

Prices: $4 to $6 retail.

Tasting Notes:

1989 RIESLING [74] Colour: light to medium yellow-green. *Bouquet:* soft honey-suckle/ tropical fruit of medium weight. *Palate:* potent fruit with lime/herbaceous flavours and again some honeysuckle character; a crisp, slightly green acid finish; more than creditable given the price. Drink '90.

1989 FRONTIGNAN SPATLESE [78] Colour: light green-straw. *Bouquet:* clean, light to medium citric/grapy fruit. *Palate:* beautifully handled commercial wine with intense lime/grapy flavours and very good balancing acid; superb handling of a difficult variety in a difficult vintage. Drink '90.

1988 SHIRAZ [84] Colour: medium purple-red. *Bouquet:* medium weight clean cherry/berry/ spicy/leafy aromas of quite surprising charm and complexity. *Palate:* attractive clean cherry/berry fruit, with hints of spice and soft tannin. Drink '92–'95.

Summary: The Coolawin label is the bottom-of-the-range of Normans Wines. As in previous years, the quality of the wines has been absolutely astonishing given their price. One note of caution, however: I suspect there may be more than one bottling of some of the wines, for I have seen some evidence of variation in quality and style over the last year or so.

CORIOLE

Location: Chaffeys Road, McLaren Vale, 5171; 6 km north of township. (08) 323 8305.

Winemakers: Mark Lloyd and Stephen Hall.

1989 Production: 12,000 cases.

Principal Wines: The principal wines are Shiraz, Cabernet Sauvignon and Chenin Blanc. Also small quantities of Chardonnay and Sangiovese.

Distribution: Substantial cellar door and mailing list sales; cellar door sales 9 a.m. to 5 p.m. Monday to Friday; 11 a.m. to 5 p.m. Saturday and Sunday. Mailing list enquiries to PO Box 9, McLaren Vale, 5171. Fine wine retail distribution through agents. Vic. and NSW, Fesq & Co.; Qld, Bond Liquor; WA, Lionel Samson; SA, Classic Wines; Tas., David Johnstone and Assoc.; and ACT, Jim Murphy. UK imports through Bibendum Wine Ltd.

Prices: $10 to $16.50 retail.

Vintage Rating 1986–89: White: '89, '88, '87, '86. Red: '89, '86, '88, '87.

Outstanding Prior Vintages: White: '84. Red: '74, 76, '80, '84.

Tasting Notes:

1988 CHARDONNAY [90] Colour: medium to full yellow-green. *Bouquet:* exceptionally rich and complex barrel ferment characters utilising superb French oak, reminiscent of that of Francois Freres. *Palate:* a very rich, Dolly Parton style with high fruit flavours and strong, complex charred oak. McLaren Vale at its best, and oak selection and handling at its best. Drink '90–'91.

1988 SANGIOVESE [67] Colour: medium red-purple. *Bouquet:* solid, and not particularly aromatic nor with any distinctive fruit aroma. *Palate:* pleasant and soft with slightly simple cherry fruit flavours. Drink '91–'93.

1988 CABERNET SAUVIGNON [CS] Colour: medium to full red-purple. *Bouquet:* slight biscuit/straw edges to solid, ripe fruit. *Palate:* strong, very ripe berry/cassis fruit; a cask sample that is headed towards 80 points or more if it is given the usual last minute bottling adjustments.

1987 CABERNET SAUVIGNON [71] Colour: medium purple-red. *Bouquet:* solid, with perfectly ripened cabernet allied with a trace of astringency. *Palate:* excellent cabernet fruit that is, however, ever so slightly toughened up by that trace of gravelly astringency. Drink '92–'95.

1986 CABERNET SHIRAZ FRENCH OAK [64] Colour: medium to full red-purple. *Bouquet:* slightly leathery/sulphidic aromas dull the fruit. *Palate:* better, with quite attractive lemony French oak; has some style and good fruit; would have been given much higher points were it not for that errant bouquet. Drink '90–'93.

Summary: Coriole has long been a favourite of mine, even if the red wines made between 1985 and 1987 seemed to have all shown slight sulphide characters. The fruit base is wonderful, and the 1988 Chardonnay and Cabernet Sauvignon suggest a return to top form.

CURRENCY CREEK

Location: Winery Road, Currency Creek, 5214; due south of Strathalbyn. (085) 55 4069 or (008) 08 8127 (Toll Free); Fax (085) 55 4100.

Winemakers: White—Brian Croser/Petaluma (contract); red—Phillip Tonkin, Brian Barry (consultant); cellar door—Phillip Tonkin.

1989 Production: Not stated.

Principal Wines: Limited range of high-quality table wines comprising Semillon, Rhine Riesling, Late Harvest Rhine Riesling, Chardonnay, Sauvignon Blanc, Shiraz, Cabernet Sauvignon, Pinot Noir and Champagne.

Distribution: Significant cellar door and mailing
list sales. Cellar door sales from 10 a.m. to
5 p.m. 7 days. Mailing list enquiries to PO Box
545, Currency Creek 5214. Wholesale
distribution through Specialist Wine Company,
Sydney; Van Cooth Pty Ltd, Melbourne; Moore
Agencies Pty Ltd, Adelaide; and J.D. & F.J.
Davies, Gold Coast, Qld.

Vintage Rating 1986–89: White: '89, '87, '86, '88.
Red: '89, '87, '86, '88.

Tasting Notes:

1989 SAUVIGNON BLANC [85] Colour: light
green-yellow. *Bouquet:* pungent gooseberry
aromas, very rich and potent, with slight armpit
fermentation characters soon to dissipate.
Palate: youthful, potent and rich, with strong
varietal fruit flavours, and some sweetness.
Drink '90–'91.

1989 PINOT NOIR [CS] Colour: strong purple-
red. *Bouquet:* solid and clean with some cherry
fruit. *Palate:* distinct cherry/sarsaparilla fruit
flavours; a pleasant warm area pinot noir with
genuine varietal character. Should rate 75 or
more.

1988 PINOT NOIR [74] Colour: developed
medium red. *Bouquet:* attractive slightly jammy
sweet cherry aromas. *Palate:* very light and,
while slightly sweet, less cooked than the
bouquet suggest. A more than creditable effort.
Drink '90.

1987 CABERNET SAUVIGNON [64] Colour: bright
red-purple. *Bouquet:* attractive cabernet fruit
under sweaty/smelly armpit characters. *Palate:*
again, very good fruit is marred by meaty/
farmyard characters giving a rather bitter finish.
Drink '91–'93.

1986 CABERNET SAUVIGNON [67] Colour: light
to medium red-purple. *Bouquet:* light and
rather thin leathery/leafy aromas. *Palate:* light
leafy/lemony fruit and oak showing quite good
bottle development, albeit lacking richness.
Drink '90–'92.

1986 VINTAGE BRUT [70] Colour: very light
straw. *Bouquet:* quite stylish and clean aromas
that are at once slightly green yet creamy.
Palate: high flavoured, with distinct green fruit
character, and finishes fractionally hard.
Nonetheless, an above average sparkling wine.
Drink '90–'91.

Summary: The Wolly Tonkin/Santa Rosa/
Currency Creek white wines (the names have
been used interchangeably over the years,
although Currency Creek now seems to be the
final choice) have been consistently good.
Recently considerable progress has been made
with pinot noir in a district that is
fundamentally not suited to that style.

D'ARENBERG

Location: Osborn Road, McLaren Vale, 5171;
4 km north of township.
(08) 323 8206 or (08) 323 8315.

Winemakers: F. d'A. Osborn and C. d'A. Osborn.

Principal Wines: Rhine Riesling, White Burgundy,
Noble Riesling, Chardonnay, Gloucester Blanc,
Burgundy, Shiraz, Cabernet Sauvignon, Claret,
Tawny Port, Vintage Port and White Muscat.
All red table wines offered with considerable
bottle-age, and a wide range of vintages usually
available.

Distribution: Substantial retail distribution through
Peter Walker Wines, Vic.; Regional Liquor
Agencies, SA; Halloran Manton, NSW and Qld;
Caldbeck, WA; large parcels also to E.E.C.
Cellar door sales 8.30 a.m. to 5 p.m. Monday to
Friday; 10 a.m. to 5 p.m. Saturday and public
holidays and noon to 4 p.m. Sunday.

Prices: $4 to $13 cellar door.

Vintage Rating 1986–89: White: '87, '89, '88, '86.
Red: '86, '89, '88, '87.

Outstanding Prior Vintages: White: '85. Red: '67,
'73, '76, '82.

Tasting Notes:

1989 GLOUCESTER BLANC [72] Colour: very
light green-yellow. *Bouquet:* clean and soft,
with fragrant fruit salad aromas. *Palate:* light
weight, crisp and clean fruit salad flavours; well-
made, easy drinking commercial style. Drink
'90.

1989 WHITE BURGUNDY [71] Colour: light green-
yellow. *Bouquet:* quite solid with some pressings
characters and a hint of lime. *Palate:* firm
flavour with citric/lime characters again evident,
and likewise some pressings; however, has guts
and is certainly in style. Drink '90–'91.

1989 RHINE RIESLING [74] Colour: medium yellow-green. *Bouquet:* shows exceptional development with rich toasty/lime aromas of good weight and depth. *Palate:* full soft and rich pineapple fruit flavours; again, very advanced. Would have rated higher points were it not for the concern about the rate of its development. Drink '90.

1987 NOBLE RIESLING [90] Colour: golden orange. *Bouquet:* rich, raisined luscious/apricot botrytis aromas, clean and full. *Palate:* intense, rich apricot/peach flavours showing very strong botrytis influence; the acid balance is good and volatile acidity under control. Drink '90–'93.

1984 MUSCAT OF ALEXANDRIA [77] Colour: golden-yellow. *Bouquet:* super rich grapy aromas, clean and full and in the mainstream of this specialized style. *Palate:* a near perfect example of this lightly fortified sweet wine which takes its inspiration from the Rhone Valley's Beaumes de Venise; the spirit is integrated, and the wine has the requisite vinosity. Drink '90–'92.

1987 SHIRAZ [74] Colour: medium purple-red. *Bouquet:* attractive, clean fresh red berry/cherry fruit. *Palate:* fresh cherry fruit flavours tail away on a slightly soapy finish; by no means a bad wine, but fractionally disappointing after the promise of the bouquet and early palate. Drink '90–'93.

TAWNY PORT [71] Colour: medium tawny-red. *Bouquet:* solid, clean and of medium weight, but lacking rancio. *Palate:* much better and more stylish, with good structure and an intense, long, cleansing finish.

Summary: Father d'Arry and son Chester Osborn constitute a formidable team these days. The range of wine style has extended substantially from the base of traditional, soft Burgundy-style reds, and are remarkably consistent in quality given the now diverse range. Prices are modest and value for money exceptionally good.

DENNIS'S DARINGA CELLARS

Location: Kangarilla Road, McLaren Vale, 5171; on northern outskirts of township. (08) 323 8665.

Winemaker: Peter Dennis.

Principal Wines: Limited range of high-quality varietal table wines: Chardonnay, Sauvignon Blanc, Rhine Riesling, Shiraz Cabernet, Cabernet Sauvignon, Vintage Port, Old Tawny Port and Mead.

Distribution: Principally cellar door sales and mailing list. Cellar door sales 10 a.m. to 5 p.m. 7 days; mailing list enquiries to PO Box 30, McLaren Vale, 5171. Limited fine wine retail distribution in Sydney, Oporto Imports; Melbourne, W. J. Seabrook; Adelaide, Porter & Co.

Prices: $11 to $11.50 cellar door.

Vintage Rating 1986–89: White: '87, '86, '88, '89. Red: '87, '86, '88, '89.

Outstanding Prior Vintages: Red: '80, '82, '85.

Tasting Notes:

1988 CHARDONNAY [75] Colour: light to medium green-yellow. *Bouquet:* lemony oak together with grapefruit aromas and a hint of matchbox. *Palate:* very lively/tangy wine with strong grapefruit flavours; may develop extremely well in bottle. Drink '90–'92.

Summary: Over the years some quite wonderful chardonnays have appeared under the Dennis label, often flowering with one or two years in bottle. I suspect the '88 vintage may follow down this track.

DONOLGA WINERY

Location: Main South Road, Aldinga, 5173. (085) 56 3179.

Winemaker: Nick Girolamo.

1989 Production: Approximately 2500 cases.

Principal Wines: Rhine Riesling, Chardonnay, Sauvignon Blanc, Shiraz, Cabernet Shiraz, Cabernet Sauvignon and various fortified wines.

Distribution: Exclusively cellar door sales 10 a.m. to 5 p.m. 7 days.

Prices: $5.75 to $14.90.

Summary: A small, exclusively cellar door operation; the quality of the wines is unknown to me.

GENDERS

Location: Recreational Road, McLaren Vale, 5171; on north-eastern outskirts of township. (08) 323 8689.

Winemaker: Keith Genders.

Principal Wines: Limited range of traditional McLaren Vale table and fortified wines, many offered with substantial bottle-age.

Distribution: Virtually exclusively cellar door.

Summary: Genders is probably the most traditional (and reclusive) of the Southern Vales makers. Production appears to be dwindling rapidly.

GEOFF MERRILL

1987
South Australian
Cabernet Sauvignon

Location: Mount Hurtle Winery, Corner Pimpala and Byards Road, Reynella, 5161. Restoration of old Mount Hurtle Winery (est. 1897) (08) 381 6877.

Winemaker: Geoff Merrill.

1989 Production: 12,000 cases.

Principal Wines: Only two wines made each year, one white, one red: Semillon/Chardonnay blend and a Cabernet/Cabernet Franc blend (labelled Cabernet Sauvignon).

Distribution: Fine wine retail and restaurant distribution through Tucker & Co. (NSW, Qld & Act); Rutherglen Wine Co. (Vic.); Caon Tucker (SA & WA). UK imports through Atkinson Baldwin & Co. Ltd. Also through

mailing list: enquiries to PO Box 386, McLaren Vale, SA, 5171. Cellar door sales 10 a.m. to 4 p.m. Monday to Friday, noon to 4 p.m. weekends.

Prices: $18 to $22 cellar door.

Vintage Rating 1986–89: White: '87, '86, '88, '89. Red: '87, '86, '88, '89.

Outstanding Prior Vintages: White: '81, '84. Red: '80, '83, '84.

Tasting Notes:

1988 SEMILLON CHARDONNAY [CS] Colour: medium yellow-green. *Bouquet:* pronounced though well-handled lemony/spicy oak. *Palate:* of light to medium weight; again, strong spicy/lemony oak is very much in evidence; should settle down by the time of its release mid to late 1990 and will merit points in the mid 70's.

1987 CABERNET SAUVIGNON [79] Colour: light to medium purple-red, very youthful. *Bouquet:* youthful, light, sweet berry fruit oak still to fully integrate. *Palate:* amazingly youthful wine still to come together after relatively (for a 1987 wine) recent bottling; will develop considerable elegance with age. Drink '92–'96.

Summary: The beautifully restored Mount Hurtle Winery (which gives its name to the second wine made by Merrill—see separate entry) is one of the show pieces of the Southern Vales, and is situated within two minutes' drive of the other great show piece—Chateau Reynella. The wines are invariably crafted with care and precision.

HUGO

HUGO

1987 McLAREN FLAT

SHIRAZ

PRODUCT OF AUSTRALIA · 750ml · 12.8% ALC. VOL.

Location: Elliott Road, McLaren Flat, 5171; off Kangarilla Road, approximately 4 km from McLaren Flat. (08) 383 0098; Fax (08) 383 0446.

Winemaker: John Hugo.

1989 Production: 8000 cases.

Principal Wines: Six wines made: Rhine Riesling, Lake Picked Rhine Riesling, Chardonnay, Shiraz, Muscat of Alexandria and Tawny Port. Shiraz offered with substantial age; usually kept in oak for 18 months.

Distribution: Principally cellar door sales and mail order. Cellar door sales 10.30 a.m. to 5 p.m. Monday to Sunday. Limited fine wine distributon through The Wine Company, Vic.; Carol-Ann Martin Classic Wines, Sydney. UK imports through Elite Wines Ltd and Haughton Fine Wines.

Prices: $7 to $13 cellar door.

Vintage Rating 1986–89: White: '86, '87, '88, '89. Red: '86, '89, '87, '88.

Outstanding Prior Vintages: White: '84.

Tasting Notes:

1989 CHARDONNAY [CS] *Colour:* medium full yellow. *Bouquet:* smooth, rich honeyed fruit with toasty oak. *Palate:* very rich honeyed/peachy wine with masses of flavour and weight, suggesting extended skin contact; headed towards 90 points if it makes it safely to bottle, but will certainly be an early drinking style.

1988 CHARDONNAY [82] *Colour:* medium to full yellow-green. *Bouquet:* ripe and full with strong, slightly hessiany oak. *Palate:* a ripe and luscious style with complex flavour and structure; again the oak is just ever so fractionally hessian-like, leading to a slight hole in the back of the palate. These subtleties will escape most tasters. Drink '90.

1988 SHIRAZ [CS] *Colour:* dense purple-red. *Bouquet:* very clean with full, rich berry fruit and high-class charred oak. *Palate:* strong clove/spice Portuguese-type oak, rich and penetrating, but meeting its match in rich cassis/berry fruit. An outstanding wine from the barrel rating in the high 80's.

1987 SHIRAZ [70] *Colour:* medium red-purple. *Bouquet:* rather raw and very pronounced lemony oak still to fully integrate. *Palate:* pleasant, clean shiraz fruit, light to medium weight dominated by lemony oak; while that oak level is too high for my palate, some will accept it. Drink '91–'94.

Summary: Hugo's production has leapt from 1500 to 8000 cases in two years, and the wines have received widespread acclaim. As the tasting notes indicate, I find myself in full agreement with the high rating accorded to the wines.

☙INGOLDBY

Location: Ingoldby Road, McLaren Flat, 5171; 1 km north of township. (08) 383 0005.

Winemaker: Walter Clappis.

1989 Production: 11,000 cases total production; 6000 cases to be released under Ingoldby label.

Principal Wines: Rhine Riesling, Sauvignon Blanc, Cabernet Shiraz, Hermitage, Cabernet Sauvignon and also a Late Picked Frontignac.

Distribution: Significant cellar door sales 9 a.m. to 5 p.m. Monday to Friday; 11 a.m. to 5 p.m. weekends and public holidays. Mailing list enquiries as above. Wholesale distribution through Festival City Wines, Adelaide; Harvey Long Wine Co., Melbourne; Australian Cellar Door Distributors, Brisbane; and De Bono Wine Distributors, Sydney. UK imports through Gullin & Co.

Prices: $9.99 to $16.99 retail.

Vintage Rating 1986–89: White: '88, '86, '89, '87. Red: '87, '86, '88, '89.

Outstanding Prior Vintages: White: '84. Red: '85.

Tasting Notes:

1989 SAUVIGNON BLANC [78] *Colour:* medium yellow-green. *Bouquet:* strong herbal/tobacco varietal aromas. *Palate:* again, intense herbal/tobacco flavours showing good varietal character; a little more fruit flesh would have made an absolutely first class wine. Drink '90–'91.

1988 CHARDONNAY [64] *Colour:* light to medium straw-yellow. *Bouquet:* strong lemony/green oak dominates the fruit. *Palate:* hard lemony/green oak dominant in precisely the same way as the bouquet. Tasted very shortly prior to bottling, and the oak may be cut somewhat at that stage. Drink '91–'93.

1989 FRONTIGNAC SPATLESE [68] *Colour:* very light straw-yellow. *Bouquet:* light, clean faintly grapy varietal aromas. *Palate:* clean, grapy commercial cellar door style with quite good acid. Drink '90.

1987 SHIRAZ [55] Colour: good purple-red, bright and clear. *Bouquet:* leathery/gravelly sulphide-derived aromas obliterate fruit. *Palate:* gravelly/leathery mercaptan destroys what might have been a good wine. Drink '90.

1987 CABERNET SAUVIGNON [90] Colour: medium to full red-purple. *Bouquet:* very complex spicy/lemony/clove oak; clean and of medium intensity. *Palate:* sophisticated spicy/lemony oak with clean, lively cherry/berry flavours, and a long, low tannin finish. A greater contrast to the shiraz could not be imagined. Drink '91–'96.

Summary: Life is never dull when Walter William Wilfred Clappis (commonly known as Bill) is around.

JAMES HASELGROVE

Location: Foggo Road, McLaren Vale, 5171. (08) 323 8706.

Winemaker: James Haselgrove (together with contract winemakers).

Principal Wines: Both Coonawarra and McLaren Vale wines released (for Coonawarra wines see Coonawarra entry). McLaren Vale wines comprise Chablis, Vintage Port and Tawny Port; also a McLaren Vale "Futures" Shiraz.

Distribution: Substantial cellar door and mailing list sales, including the membership of "The Inner Wine Circle". Cellar door sales 9 a.m. to 5 p.m. 7 days; mailing list enquiries to PO Box 231, McLaren Vale, 5171. Retail distribution through fine wine retailers in capital cities. Also "Wine Tasters" available with James Haselgrove wines served.

Prices: $7.90 to $10.90 cellar door.

Vintage Rating 1986–89: White: '89, '87 ('86, '88 not rated). Red: '86, '89, '87, '88.

Tasting Notes:

BRUT VINTAGE 1987 [60] Colour: light to medium yellow-green. *Bouquet:* green citric fruit aromas, with a slight matchbox edge. *Palate:* slightly oily green/citric fruit flavours, which may well have been acceptable a few years ago, but which have now been overtaken by better base material. Drink '90.

1987 McLAREN VALE FUTURES SHIRAZ [66] Colour: medium to full red-purple. *Bouquet:* dense and concentrated, with some faintly gamey sulphides. *Palate:* a full, strong, high-flavoured wine marred by gamey characters which lead to slightly bitterness on the finish. Drink '90–'93.

Summary: Most of the James Haselgrove wines come from the extensive Coonawarra vineyards owned by the family company, and are reviewed in the Coonawarra chapter. Those from McLaren Vale tend to be honest and workmanlike, even if they lack excitement.

KAY BROTHERS AMERY

Location: Kays Road, McLaren Vale, 5171; 5 km north of township. (08) 323 8211.

Winemaker: Colin Kay.

Principal Wines: A full range of table and fortified wines comprising Rhine Riesling, Late Harvest Frontignac, Late Harvest Rhine Riesling, Cabernet Shiraz, Pinot Noir, Blackwood Estate Shiraz, Block 6 Shiraz, Cabernet Sauvignon, Vintage Port, Ruby Port, Tawny Port and Liqueur Muscat. Shiraz and Ruby Port also offered in 10-litre casks and 200-litre drums.

Distribution: Principally cellar door and mailing list sales, with very limited eastern states retail distribution in capital cities. Cellar door sales 8 a.m. to 5 p.m. Monday to Friday; 10 a.m. to 5 p.m. Saturday; Sunday and public holidays noon to 5 p.m. Mailing list enquiries to PO Box 19, McLaren Vale, 5171.

Prices: $7 to $10 cellar door.

Vintage Rating 1986–89: White: '88, '87, '86, '89. Red: '88, '87, '86, '89.

Outstanding Prior Vintages: White: '73, '75, '80. Red: '71, '75, '78, '82.

Tasting Notes:

1986 BLOCK 6 SHIRAZ [77] Colour: medium red-purple. *Bouquet:* stylish spicy fruit with a nice touch of lemony oak showing pleasant bottle development. *Palate:* a wine that has aged nicely in bottle and acquired some elegance; the oak is perhaps just a fraction assertive. Drink '90.

Summary: Kays' Amery vineyards include some of the oldest shiraz in the Barossa Valley. The winery, too, has a long family tradition, and is no less rich in history. As the tasting note indicates some very nice reds are produced; most of the white wines of my acquaintance have, however, suffered from bitter mercaptans.

McLARENS ON THE LAKE

Location: Kangarilla Road, McLaren Vale, 5171; 1 km east of McLaren Vale township. (08) 323 8853.

Winemakers: Andrew Garrett and Warren Randall.

1989 Production: Not stated; part of the large Andrew Garrett corporate crush.

Principal Wines: A range of budget priced varietal wines with the distinctive duck-in-a-bib-label.

Distribution: Through the American Express/ Westpac Wine Club outlets.

Tasting Notes:

1988 SEMILLON SAUVIGNON BLANC [59] Colour: bright green-yellow of medium depth. *Bouquet:* broad and slightly blousy, with a burnt Friars Balsam medicinal edge. *Palate:* rather stalky and hard, with unripe green fruit characters. Drink '90.

1988 SEMILLON [75] Colour: very good medium yellow-green. *Bouquet:* clean; of medium to full intensity, with slightly sweet vanillan oak. *Palate:* clean and smooth, with good fruit and oak balance and integration; of medium weight overall. Skilled use of oak chips. Drink '90–'91.

1988 RHINE RIESLING [77] Colour: light to medium yellow-green. *Bouquet:* light, clean and toasty with a touch of lime. *Palate:* clean and soft with pleasantly balanced slightly sweet passionfruit/lime flavours; wholly commendable. Drink '90–'91.

1988 CLARE VALLEY RHINE RIESLING [89] Colour: bright green-yellow. *Bouquet:* clean, fine and fragrant intense passionfruit/lime fruit aromas. *Palate:* beautifully flavoured and balanced wine; quite firm with classic passionfruit/lime varietal fruit showing perfect modulation. Almost unbelievable at the price. Drink '90–'93.

1988 CHARDONNAY [89] Colour: light to medium yellow-green. *Bouquet:* full, rich, sweet and spicy complex fruit and oak. *Palate:* very rich spicy/nutmeg oak with full, sweet fruit; a high-toned style. Drink '90–'92.

1988 SHIRAZ [90] Colour: very good purple-red of medium depth. *Bouquet:* full, rich traditional dark chocolate/velvet fruit with some spice. *Palate:* rich, full, opulent spicy dark berry/dark chocolate fruit; very good balance and length; Australian shiraz at its best. Drink '91–'96.

Summary: It is true that these were the best of the McLarens on the Lake submitted in the 200-plus wine district tasting, but they are of astonishing quality given their position in the market place. Indeed, I was left wondering why Andrew Garrett should wish to introduce his "Ultimate" label when he seems to already have it in the form of McLarens on the Lake.

MAGLIERI

Location: Douglas Gully Road, McLaren Flat, 5171; 3 km north of township. (08) 383 0177.

Winemaker: John Loxton.

Principal Wines: A range of wine styles sold in bottles and flagons including Semillon, Rhine Riesling, Traminer Riesling, Shiraz, Cabernet Sauvignon, Lambrusco, Spumantes, Vintage Port and Tawny Port. All wines offered with some considerable bottle-age.

Distribution: Principally cellar door sales and mailing list. Cellar door sales 9 a.m. to 4 p.m. Monday to Saturday and 12 p.m. to 4 p.m. Sunday. Mailing list enquiries as above. Wholesale agents—Festival City Wines and Spirits, Adelaide; Gully Wines, Melbourne; and Consolidated Liquor, Brisbane.

Summary: Maglieri describes itself as "The House of Lambrusco" but, at least from a technical viewpoint, its strength lies with fortified wines.

MANNING PARK WINES

Location: Chalk Hill Road, McLaren Vale, 5171. (08) 323 8209.

Winemaker: Allan McLean.

Principal Wines: A limited range of table and fortified wines.

Distribution: Exclusively through cellar door sales and mail order. Mail orders as above. Cellar door sales 10 a.m. to 5 p.m. Monday to Saturday; 11 a.m. to 5 p.m. Sunday.

Summary: A long established, but nonetheless low key, operation of which the local winemakers say little.

MARIENBERG

Location: Black Road, Coromandel Valley, 5051; between Clarendon and Blackwood. (08) 270 2384.

Winemaker: Ursula Pridham.

Principal Wines: White Burgundy, Chablis, Rhine Riesling, Sauvignon Blanc, Rosengarten, Beerenauslese, Pinot Noir, Shiraz, Cabernet Shiraz and Cabernet Sauvignon. Red wines all offered with at least 5 years' bottle-age, white wines mainly 1-3 years' bottle age.

Distribution: Substantial retail distribution through wholesale agents in Vic. (Westwood Wine Agencies), NSW (Australian Vintners), Qld, WA and SA; also some exports to the UK. Cellar door sales 9 a.m. to 5 p.m. Monday to Friday and on weekends of school and public holidays and festivals; 10 a.m. to 5 p.m. Saturday; and noon to 5 p.m. Sunday. Mailing

list enquiries to PO Box 220, Blackwood, 5051.

Prices: $9.95 to $14.50 recommended retail.

Tasting Notes:

1988 SAUVIGNON BLANC [54] Colour: light straw-yellow. _Bouquet:_ neutral fruit and rather hard lemony oak. _Palate:_ neutral fruit flavours and hard, slightly oily oak that does not add either texture or flavour to the wine. Drink '90.

1984 CABERNET SAUVIGNON [82] Colour: medium red. _Bouquet:_ light, slightly leafy fruit; very clean, though developing some attractive secondary cigar box aromas. _Palate:_ attractive minty red berry flavours; a beautifully structured wine with a clean, long finish. Drink '90–'94.

Summary: Marienberg is developing a reputation for its very attractive cabernet sauvignons, usually released when at least five years old, yet retaining unusual youth and freshness. The '81 Cabernet was outstanding; so is the '84.

MASLIN BEACH

Location: Sherriff Road, Maslin Beach, 5170; 9 km south-west of McLaren Vale. (08) 386 1092.

Winemaker: Allan Dyson.

1989 Production: Approximately 2500 cases.

Principal Wines: Six wines, made from estate-grown grapes, and all made and bottled on the estate: Fumé Blanc, Chardonnay, Sauvignon Blanc, Pinot Noir, Vintage _Méthode champenoise_ (extra dry) and Cabernet Sauvignon.

Distribution: Selected retailers in Adelaide and Sydney (Sydney agent, Roger Brown); mailing list PO Box 208, McLaren Vale, 5171; cellar door sales 10 a.m. to 5 p.m. 7 days.

Prices: $8.50 to $15 cellar door.

Vintage Rating 1986–89: White: '88, '89, '87, '86. Red: '86, '88, '87, '89.

Tasting Notes:

1988 SAUVIGNON BLANC [74] Colour: light to medium yellow-green. *Bouquet:* quite elegant, with complex fruit and oak; slightly medicinal characters do make a fleeting appearance. *Palate:* strong fruit and oak, with good use of just a touch of residual sugar; the fruit flavours are long and the balance good; would have been pointed higher were it not for the bouquet. Drink '90–'92.

1988 FUME BLANC [NP] what I assume to be the same base wine totally destroyed by dreadful oak.

1988 PINOT NOIR [64] Colour: medium red-purple. *Bouquet:* lemony oak that is unsuited to the variety obliterates varietal character. *Palate:* once again, strong lemony oak is really the only flavour; quite acceptable as a red wine, particularly for those with an oaky tooth. Drink '90.

1987 CABERNET SAUVIGNON [58] Colour: medium to full red-purple. *Bouquet:* very sweet berry fruit with some gamey overlay. *Palate:* full-flavoured cabernet picked too late and invested with a touch of farmyard character. Does have flavour, and others may like it more. Drink '90–'93.

Summary: Allan Dyson is a vastly experienced viticulturist, and almost invariably produces very rich, full-flavoured wines. In some instances, things seem to have gone wrong in the winery.

❦ MAXWELL

Location: 24 Kangarilla Road, McLaren Vale, 5171; on eastern outskirts of township. (08) 323 8200.

Winemaker: Mark Maxwell; meadmaker Ken Maxwell.

1989 Production: The equivalent of approximately 5000 cases, although some is sold in bulk.

Principal Wines: A limited range of table and fortified wines, also mead specialists. Wines comprise Chardonnay, Rhine Riesling, Frontignac, Adelaide Nouveau, Cabernet Merlot, Old Tawny Port and Maxwell Meads (various).

Distribution: Principally cellar door sales and mailing list. Cellar door sales 10 a.m. to 5 p.m. 7 days; Mailing list enquiries as above. Limited retail distribution services, principally direct ex-winery all states. For information phone winery as above. UK imports through Gullin & Co.

Prices: Table wines $5 to $14; Maxwell Mead $6 to $14 cellar door.

Vintage Rating 1986–89: White: '86, '89, '88, '87. Red: '86, '89, '87, '88.

Outstanding Prior Vintages: White: '82. Red: '82, '80.

Tasting Notes:

1989 CHARDONNAY [CS] Colour: light to medium straw-yellow. *Bouquet:* subdued melon/fig fruit aromas and some slightly smelly, leesy characters. *Palate:* strong melon/fig fruit flavours, still a little hard on the finish; if cleaned up and softened prior to bottling will score in the mid to high 70's.

1988 CHARDONNAY [80] Colour: medium yellow-green. *Bouquet:* smooth, buttery/honey aromas with some weight. *Palate:* clean, smooth honeyed/butter fruit, with nice mouth-feel and smooth oak; varietal character is somewhat muted. Drink '90–'92.

1989 ADELAIDE NOUVEAU [75] Colour: very good purple-red. *Bouquet:* clean and quite firm; full berry/cherry fruit with light maceration character. *Palate:* fresh cherry/berry carbonic maceration style, with that typical, ever so slightly furry finish. Drink '90.

1987 CABERNET SAUVIGNON MERLOT [77] Colour: medium purple-red. *Bouquet:* shows some elegance and style, with clean leafy/tobacco aromas showing pronounced merlot varietal character. *Palate:* light to medium in weight, with leafy berry flavours, and a touch of astringency evident in both the bouquet and palate; once again strong varietal influence from the merlot. Drink '90–'93.

Summary: An interesting winery that makes wine for half of the year and mead for the other half; the meads are outstanding. The table wines reviewed for this edition were impressive, although the other '87 red wines were spoilt by sulphide.

❦ MIDDLEBROOK

Location: Sand Road, McLaren Vale, 5171;
4 km east of McLaren Vale.
(08) 383 0004.

Winemaker: Nick Holmes

Principal Wines: A carefully chosen range of
varietal wines, principally made from locally
grown grapes, including Rhine Riesling,
Chardonnay, Late Harvest Rhine Riesling,
Sauvignon Blanc, Shiraz, Cabernet Sauvignon,
Tawny Port and, finally, Durus, a marvellous
cumquat-flavoured wine fortified with old
brandy and sweetened with honey.

Summary: Middlebrook is now part of the Ryecroft
group, and the label is presently in recess. It is
likely to reappear in the future, however.

❦ MOUNT HURTLE

Location: Mount Hurtle Winery, cnr Pimpala and
Byards Road, Reynella, 5161. Restoration of
old Mount Hurtle Winery (est. 1897).
(08) 271 2267.

Winemakers: Joe Di Fabio and Geoff Merrill.

1989 Production: 8000 cases.

Principal Wines: Sauvignon Blanc/Semillon,
Grenache (rosé style) and Cabernet Sauvignon.

Distribution: Fine wine retail and restaurant
distribution through Tucker & Co. (NSW, Qld
and ACT); Rutherglen Wine Co. (Vic.); Caon
Tucker (SA & WA). UK imports through
Atkinson Baldwin & Co. Ltd. Also mailing list;
enquiries to PO Box 386, McLaren Vale, 5171.
Cellar door sales 10 a.m. to 4 p.m. Monday to
Friday; noon to 4 p.m. weekends.

Prices: $9 to $14 cellar door.

Vintage Rating 1986–89: White: '86, '87, '88 ('89
not rated). Red: '87, '88, '89, '86.

Outstanding Prior Vintages: White: '87. Red: '85.

Tasting Notes:

1989 SAUVIGNON BLANC SEMILLON [75]
Colour: light green-yellow. *Bouquet:* light,
herbaceous tobacco leaf aromas. *Palate:* almost
identical light, fresh herbaceous/tobacco fruit
but an attractive counter-balancing touch of
honey on the finish, no doubt coming from the
semillon component. Drink '90–'92.

1988 GRENACHE [82] Colour: brilliant crimson-red.
Bouquet: vibrantly fresh and fruity, and
wonderfully clean, with none of those distracting
maceration characters. *Palate:* a brilliantly
constructed and flavoured wine with fruity/
strawberry flavours, and a crisp, clean finish.
Should have been drunk by now, but any still
around should be consumed '90.

1987 CABERNET SAUVIGNON [69] Colour: very
light red. *Bouquet:* very clean but very light,
particularly in the context of the far more
masculine reds typical of the region. *Palate:*
again, seems very light in comparison to the
other reds, with pronounced slightly pencilly/
lemony oak and light fruit. Assessed on its own
would almost certainly be pointed higher, but
that's how the cookie crumbles. Drink '90–'91.

Summary: Mount Hurtle is the alter ego of Geoff
Merrill, but the wine styles are as deliberately
different from those under the Geoff Merrill
banner as are the brightly coloured Mount
Hurtle labels from the understated Merrill
labels.

❦ NOON'S

Location: Rifle Range Road, McLaren Vale, 5171;
5 km south-east of township.
(08) 323 8290.

Winemaker: David Noon.

1989 Production: 2850 cases.

Principal Wines: Red wine specialists, also producing a number of whites. Only locally-grown grapes are used, and all wines are entirely made, matured and bottled at the winery. As well as being available in their (regular) filtered form, most reds are available in unfiltered form. Wines comprise Burgundy, Cabernet Sauvignon, Dry Red, Grenache-Shiraz, Hill-side Red, Maceration Carbonique, Mulled Red, Rosé, Shiraz-Cabernet, Traditional Red, Vintage Port, Chablis and Semillon. Most reds sold with 2 or 3 years' bottle-age.

Distribution: Exclusively cellar door sales and mailing list; mailing list enquiries to PO Box 88, McLaren Vale, 5171. Cellar door sales 9 a.m. to 5 p.m. 7 days.

Prices: $9 to $12 cellar door, with a discount for dozens.

Vintage Rating 1986–89: '86, '88, '87, '89.

Outstanding Prior Vintages: '76, '80, '84.

Summary: It grieves me to say it, but I simply could not find a wine worthy of review in the substantial number of 1987 reds submitted in the district tasting; sulphide seems to have run rampant. In years gone by, I have greatly admired the massively constructed reds of this winery, and I do hope others do not find the extreme bitterness that struck down all of the reds in a large blind tasting, with the Noon wines sprinkled throughout yet invariably failing.

❦NORMAN'S

Location: Grants Gully Road, Clarendon, 5157. (08) 383 6138; Fax (08) 383 6089.

Winemakers: Brian Light, chief winemaker; Gregory O'Keefe, winemaker.

1989 Production: 120,000 cases.

Principal Wines: Chardonnay, Sauvignon Blanc, Rhine Riesling, Chenin Blanc, Shiraz, Pinot Noir, Cabernet Sauvignon, Conquest Brut, Pinot and Chardonnay Brut Premier, 1066 Tawny, 12-year-old King William Tawny and XO 30-Year-Old Tawny Port. The grapes are sourced from the company's vineyards at Evanston Estate, Adelaide Plains and Clarendon in the Adelaide Hills. Additionally, grapes are purchased from selected growers at McLaren Vale and Coonawarra. Norman's also produces a top quality range of limited-release table wines under the Norman's Chais Clarendon label.

Distribution: National retail distribution through Concorde Liquor Pty Ltd, (03) 894 2555. Cellar door sales and mailing list.

Prices: Around $7 to $12 retail for the Norman's releases; Chais Clarendon at significantly higher prices.

Vintage Rating 1986–89: White: '87, '89, '88, '86. Red: '89, '87, '86, '88.

Outstanding Prior Vintages: White: '85, '82. Red: '82, '80.

Tasting Notes:

1989 SAUVIGNON BLANC **[TS]** _Colour:_ medium yellow-green. _Bouquet:_ strong herbal/tobacco varietal aroma, albeit a fraction thin. _Palate:_ strong herbal tobacco flavours showing a particular manifestation of varietal character; really headed towards a chablis style and around 75 points.

1989 CHARDONNAY **[CS]** _Colour:_ medium to full yellow-green, very advanced and suggesting skin contact. _Bouquet:_ extremely attractive and sophisticated toasty oak with very good fruit balance. _Palate:_ beautiful fruit and oak; great fruit/melon flavours, tangy and lively; tremendous length and style. Absolutely outstanding as a cask sample; if it lives up to this potential will merit up to 90 points.

1987 CLARENDON CHARDONNAY **[79]** _Colour:_ full golden-yellow. _Bouquet:_ very complex bottle-developed aromas with excellent oak handling; has real style/bite and racy breed. _Palate:_ a very complex, oak-driven wine with strong secondary bottle-developed vanillan/honeyed/camphor flavours developing. I have the suspicion that this wine may already be at or past its peak. Drink '90.

1989 PINOT NOIR **[CS]** _Colour:_ very good strong purple-red. _Bouquet:_ clean and firm, showing obvious winemaking skills but only moderate pinot varietal character. _Palate:_ firm and clean; some cherry/plum pinot fruit and evidence of some stalk character; once again, a real effort has been made to handle the variety. It should rate in the 70's.

1988 CLARENDON SHIRAZ [87] Colour: dense purple-red. *Bouquet:* clean, dense and strong fruit, teetering on the edge of being extractive. *Palate:* a very richly structured and high-flavoured dark berry wine with soft but persistent tannins, and very good oak handling. Drink ' 93–'98.

1988 CLARENDON CABERNET SAUVIGNON [90] Colour: full purple-red. *Bouquet:* solid, concentrated cassis/berry aromas with an appropriate touch of cabernet-derived astringency. *Palate:* beautiful rich berry/cassis fruit with exemplary oak handling, and an exceedingly long future. Drink '94–2000.

Summary: Right across the range, Norman's is producing wines of excellent and at times down-right exciting quality. The Clarendon range certainly deserves its high profile and relatively high price.

🍇 OLIVERHILL WINES

Location: Seaview Road, McLaren Vale, 5171; 4 km north of township. (08) 323 8922.

Winemaker: Vincenzo Berlingieri.

Principal Wines: Fortified wine specialist offering Tawny Port, Liqueur Muscat, Oloroso Sherry and, in the future, a range of vintage ports. New releases include Cabernet Sauvignon and Frontignac Spatlese.

Distribution: Exclusively cellar door sales and mailing list. Cellar door sales 10 a.m. to 5 p.m. 7 days. Mailing list enquiries to PO Box 22, McLaren Vale, 5171. Lunchtime restaurant with Italian and Chinese cuisine from chefs Berlingieri and Kiaw Ngo.

Summary: Vincenzo Berlingieri was once a tireless promoter of his wines, but these days seems to shun publicity.

🍇 PIRRAMIMMA VINEYARDS

Location: Johnston Road, McLaren Vale, 5171; 2 km south-west of township. (08) 323 8205.

Winemaker: Geoff Johnston.

1989 Production: Approximately 50,000 cases.

Principal Wines: Chardonnay, Rhine Riesling, Rhine Riesling Spatlese, Cabernet Sauvignon, Shiraz, Special Selection Shiraz, Vintage Port, Tawny Port and Liqueur Port. Shiraz and Shiraz Grenache sold in 20-litre packs and in 205-litre drums; 5-Year-Old Tawny Port also sold in 205-litre drums.

Distribution: Limited fine wine retail distribution in Sydney, Melbourne and Adelaide through wholesalers L. Laforgia, Adelaide; Yarra Valley Wine Consultants, Melbourne and Tucker & Co., Sydney. UK imports through Fortis Ltd. Significant cellar door sales 8.30 a.m. to 5 p.m. Monday to Friday; 10 a.m. to 5 p.m. Saturday; and noon to 4 p.m. Sunday. Mailing list enquiries to PO Box 7, McLaren Vale, 5171.

Prices: $8.50 to $15 cellar door.

Vintage Rating 1986–89: White: '88, '87, '86, '89. Red: '86, '88, '87, '89.

Outstanding Prior Vintages: White: '79, '80. Red: '66, '70, '72, '80, '82, '84.

Tasting Notes:

1988 CHARDONNAY [63] Colour: light to medium straw-yellow. *Bouquet:* a fraction dull, seemingly due to rather plain, green oak. *Palate:* again, varietal fruit is not done justice by rather green, hard oak. Drink '91–'92.

1987 RHINE RIESLING [79] Colour: light to medium yellow-green. *Bouquet:* broad and full pineapple/lime aromas showing some bottle development and softness. *Palate:* full, soft, high flavoured lime/pineapple tastes with plenty of flavour, and a clean, soft finish. Drink '90.

1987 HILLSVIEW CABERNET SAUVIGNON [61] Colour: light red-purple. *Bouquet:* very light and rather thin, leafy berry aromas, suggesting over-cropped vines. *Palate:* again, peculiar watered/leafy fruit flavours, strongly suggestive of excess cropping or over-zealous irrigation. Drink '90–'92.

1985 CABERNET SAUVIGNON [77] Colour: bright red-purple of medium depth. *Bouquet:* spotlessly clean and surprisingly undeveloped, light red berry aromas. *Palate:* clean, sweet cassis berry fruit of light to medium weight, and low tannin; a veritable Peter Pan of a wine. Drink '90–'96.

Summary: I have always had great respect for the Johnston family and their wines; Pirramimma led the way in the early days of the renaissance of McLaren Vale in the second half of the '70s as it moved from a producer of over-extracted red wines and fortified wines to the premium district it is today. Somehow or other, however, I suspect those who have come after have tended to leave Pirramimma in their wake.

RICHARD HAMILTON

Location: Willunga Vineyards, Main South Road, Willunga, 5172; 2 km north of township. (085) 56 2288.

Winemaker: John Innes.

1989 Production: 10,000 cases.

Principal Wines: A range of white table wines, with Cabernet Sauvignon reintroduced in 1987. Wines include Chardonnay, Rhine Riesling, Chenin Blanc, Semillon, Sauvignon Blanc, Cabernet Sauvignon and *Méthode champenoise* Sparkling wine. Chardonnay accounts for the major part of the output, with new plantings of chardonnay in Coonawarra to provide the base material both for Chardonnay and *Méthode champenoise.*

Distribution: Significant retail distribution through wholesale distributors in NSW (Regional Wines Pty Ltd), Vic. (The Wine Broker) and through direct distribution in SA. Cellar door sales

9.30 a.m. to 5 p.m. Monday to Saturday; Sundays and holidays 11 a.m. to 5 p.m. Mailing list enquiries to PO Box 421, Willunga, 5172.

Prices: \$8.50 to \$12.50 cellar door.

Vintage Rating 1986–89: '87, '86, '88, '89.

Outstanding Prior Vintages: '72, '73, '75, '76.

Tasting Notes:

1988 CHENIN BLANC [74] Colour: medium straw-yellow. *Bouquet:* solid and slightly broad, with some bottle-developed aromas including an echo of seaweed. *Palate:* full flavoured, mouth-filling sweet fruit, rounded and fleshy, with a touch of residual sugar; a good commercial wine. Drink '90.

1988 SEMILLON [53] Colour: light straw-brown. *Bouquet:* slightly dull varnishy/green oak. *Palate:* hard green oak spoils whatever varietal character is present, but the wine may con-ceivably soften with one or two years in the bottle. Drink '90–'91.

1988 CHARDONNAY [60] Colour: medium yellow-green. *Bouquet:* rather closed and slightly sour/stripped, suggesting problems at bottling. *Palate:* slightly sour coarse edges, with plenty of honeyed fruit underneath; something went wrong somewhere along the line with some good base material. Drink '90–'91.

Summary: The Hamilton family has a winemaking lineage second to none, and with the Richard Hamilton and Leconfield wineries in its care, intends to be winemakers for years to come.

ROSS McLAREN ESTATE

Location: Cnr Main South Road and Budgen Road, McLaren Vale, 5171. (08) 323 8614.

Winemaker: Darryl Ross.

Principal Wines: Red table and fortified wines made chiefly from Shiraz, Malbec and Cabernet Sauvignon.

Distribution: Largely cellar door and through mail order. Cellar door sales 9 a.m. to 5 p.m. Monday to Friday and 10 a.m. to 5 p.m. weekends.

Summary: Little is known about the present operations of Ross McLaren Estate which is, nonetheless, a substantial producer and very visible as one drives along the main South Road to McLaren Vale.

RYECROFT

Location: Ingoldby Road, McLaren Flat, 5171; 1 km north-east of township. (08) 383 0001.

Winemaker: Nick Holmes.

1989 Production: Approximately 30,000 cases.

Principal Wines: A full range of varietal table wines including Wood Matured Semillon, Chardonnay, Sauvignon Blanc, Cabernet Sauvignon and Shiraz; wine of special quality and greater bottle age released under the Reserve label.

Distribution: National retail through Australian Vineyard Distributors Pty Ltd, NSW, Vic. and Adelaide; National Liquor, WA; Auspac Marketing, Qld.; Consolidated Liquor, NT; Harry Williams & Co., ACT; and David Johnstone, Tas. UK imports through S.Wines Ltd., 21 Burnaby Street, Chelsea.

Prices: $7.99 to $18.50 recommended retail.

Tasting Notes:

1989 RHINE RIESLING [71] Colour: light yellow-green. _Bouquet:_ soft, clean and pretty tutti-frutti aromas. _Palate:_ soft, full cocktail-type rhine riesling with soft toasty characters and fleshy fruit. No doubt very commercial. Drink '90.

1988 WOOD MATURED SEMILLON [68] Colour: straw-yellow. _Bouquet:_ good fruit but rather flawed by undistinguished green oak. _Palate:_ once again, slightly aggressive oily/green oak detracts somewhat from the wine. Drink '90-'92.

1988 SAUVIGNON BLANC [64] Colour: light yellow-green. _Bouquet:_ of medium weight with fruit somewhat dulled by oak; a hint of matchbox, too. _Palate:_ soft, medium weight fruit with

muted varietal character dulled by common, slightly oily oak. Drink '90-'91.

1988 CHARDONNAY [75] Colour: medium yellow-green. _Bouquet:_ clean and smooth, of medium to full intensity with butter/peachy fruit. _Palate:_ abundant sweet peachy fruit flavours; the residual sugar is just a little obvious for my taste, but will have commercial appeal. Drink '90-'91.

1987 HERMITAGE [74] Colour: medium purple-red. _Bouquet:_ slightly sawdusty/pencilly/green oak with clean fruit underneath. _Palate:_ much better with strong vanillan American oak of the kind one finds in lightweight American barrels; allied with warm, berry fruit it does work far better on the palate than the bouquet. Drink '90-'94.

1987 CABERNET SAUVIGNON [65] Colour: medium red, with just a touch of purple. _Bouquet:_ clean, but with rather raw pencilly oak. _Palate:_ the oak is overdone and somewhat raw; the wine has masses of flavour, but seems to have been overworked and certainly over-oaked. Drink '90-'93.

Summary: The Ryecroft Wines outside of the Reserve range are not expensive, and offer value for money. Personally, I wish that an extra $1 per bottle were charged, and the money put back into purchasing better oak.

ST FRANCIS

Location: Bridge Street, Old Reynella, 5161; on northern outskirts of Reynella township. (08) 381 1925.

Winemakers: Rob Dundon (consultant) and James Irvine (consultant).

1989 Production: Approximately 25,000 cases.

Principal Wines: The St Francis wines are offered in two ranges: one under the St Francis label, featuring premium varietals made from grapes grown in various South Australian districts; and the second under the Governor Phillip label, once again made from grapes grown in various South Australian regions. The varieties offered cover the full range of the premium varieties in vogue today, including Rhine Riesling, Fumé Blanc, Chardonnay, Late Harvest Frontignac, Chablis, Pinot Noir, Hermitage, Shiraz Cabernet and Cabernet Sauvignon. A range of sparkling wines and ports is also offered.

Distribution: Largely cellar door and through the very substantial on-site restaurant. St Francis deliberately caters to the tourist trade, providing a full range of facilities 9 a.m. to 5 p.m. 7 days. Increasing retail distribution through Appellation Wines, Wayne Leicht Wines, Consolidated Liquor and Standard Distillers.

Prices: $6.90 to $14.50 cellar door.

Tasting Notes:

1988 CLASSIC DRY WHITE [75] Colour: medium yellow-green. _Bouquet:_ smooth, clean, gently honeyed/buttery fruit. _Palate:_ a clean, attractive honeyed/rounded wine with good balance, good length and little or no oak. Drink '90–'91.

1988 COONAWARRA CHARDONNAY [63] Colour: full yellow. _Bouquet:_ some toasty oak with complex camphor/bottle-developed characters and the fruit starting to drop out. _Palate:_ an altogether prematurely aged wine starting to break up. Drink '90.

1984 COONAWARRA CLASSIC RHINE RIESLING [87] Colour: deep gold. _Bouquet:_ rich, developed toasty aromas with some lime fruit lingering, and not drying out. _Palate:_ a lovely old wine with strong Germanic overtones; flavours of lime and camphor. Drink '90.

1987 BAROSSA VALLEY HERMITAGE [74] Colour: medium red-purple. _Bouquet:_ clean and full berry fruit, with good depth. _Bouquet:_ big, strong berry fruit with a touch of meaty astringency and a faint whisper of aldehyde. Drink '90–'93.

1986 CABERNET MERLOT [78] Colour: medium full red. _Bouquet:_ clean, full and smooth dark cherry/berry fruits. _Palate:_ strong, sweet cherry/berry fruit; developing slowly, with soft but persistent tannins; a fruit rather than oak driven wine of real quality. Drink '90–'95.

1986 BAROSSA VALLEY CABERNET SAUVIGNON

[74] Colour: medium purple-red. _Bouquet:_ very clean; some red berry aromas of medium weight. _Palate:_ pleasant, sweet berry fruit and soft vanilla bean American oak; soft persistent tannins towards the finish. Drink '90–'94.

Summary: As was the case with the wines reviewed in the last edition of this book, the St Francis consultants have done an outstanding job in selecting wines purchased in bulk (usually already bottled) for release under the St Francis label. One wonders how the quality and price is maintained, indeed, but there is no sign yet of it slipping.

❦ _SCARPANTONI ESTATES_

Location: Scarpantoni Drive, McLaren Flat, 5171; directly opposite post office. (08) 383 0186.

Winemakers: Domenico Scarpantoni and Michael Filippo.

1989 Production: 5000 cases.

Principal Wines: Block 1 Rhine Riesling, Sauvignon Blanc, Late Harvest Rhine Riesling, Botrytis Rhine Riesling, Chardonnay, Shiraz, Cabernet Merlot, Gamay (a red maceration style), Cabernet Sauvignon, Liqueur Riesling (fortified) and Vintage Port.

Distribution: Almost entirely cellar door and mailing list. Cellar door sales 10 a.m. to 5 p.m. 7 days. Mailing list enquiries to PO Box 84, McLaren Vale, 5171. Limited retail distribution through S. & V. Distributors, Adelaide. UK imports through Peter Watts Wines, Essex.

Prices: Table wines $7.50 to $15 cellar door.

Vintage Rating 1986–89: White: '88, '89, '87, '86. Red: '86, '88, '87, '89.

Outstanding Prior Vintages: White: '84, '80, '82, '85. Red: '80, '84, '82, '85.

Tasting Notes:

1989 RHINE RIESLING [80] Colour: light straw-green. *Bouquet:* light clean and crisp herbaceous/lime aromas. *Palate:* very intense, pungent herbaceous style with a very long finish; altogether most interesting, and should age well. Much better than the '88. Drink '90–'93.

1989 SAUVIGNON BLANC [90] Colour: light straw-green. *Bouquet:* enormous, potent gooseberry/passionfruit aromas of exceptional intensity. *Palate:* lively, fragrant and fresh gooseberry passionfruit characters showing perfect fruit ripeness and outstanding length; tasted only four weeks after it was bottled, when theoretically it should have taken something of a knock. Drink '90–'91.

1988 CHARDONNAY [70] Colour: medium yellow-green. *Bouquet:* clean and quite complex, with pronounced lemony/vanillan oak. *Palate:* once again, strong vanillan/lemony oak tends to sit on top of the fruit; I do not find this oak style entirely satisfactory, but others have rated this wine highly, evidently accepting the oak style. Drink '90–'91.

1987 BOTRYTIS RHINE RIESLING [74] Colour: deep orange-yellow. *Bouquet:* raisined, rich and sweet apricot/coconut aromas. *Palate:* strong, coconut/vanilla bean/apricot flavours, almost suggesting some oak, although there is none; very concentrated, but the acid is pleasantly soft. Drink '90.

1987 SHIRAZ [83] Colour: medium purple-red. *Bouquet:* firm and structured, with ripe dark berry fruits. *Palate:* full, clean and smooth, with ripe dark berry flavours; a rounded wine with controlled tannins. Drink '90–'94.

1988 VINTAGE PORT [89] Colour: full red, with a touch of purple. *Bouquet:* complex and fragrant brandy spirit with strong, spicy/dark chocolate fruit. *Palate:* exceptionally rich dark chocolate fruit flavours with a chewy mid-palate; once again, fine brandy spirit used to fortify the wine; finishes long and clean. A wine that takes on Hardys at its own game.

Summary: Scarpantoni Estates may not be an especially romantic or trendy winery, but the quality of its young wines is absolutely outstanding. Nor are these wines any flash in the pan: prior tastings have also unearthed some excellent wines.

❧ SEAVIEW

Location: Chaffeys Road, McLaren Vale, 5171. (08) 323 8250.

Winemakers: Robin Moody (production manager) and Mike Farmilo (winemaker).

Principal Wines: Seaview is a somewhat schizophrenic label: some of the wines produced under it are strictly brands, with the grapes coming from many parts of South Australia, but the red wines—and in particular the cabernet sauvignon—are almost entirely sourced from McLaren Vale, with a substantial part of the production coming from Seaview's own vineyards. The wines comprise Rhine Riesling, Traminer Riesling, Chardonnay, White Burgundy, Cabernet Sauvignon (one of the bottled-wine brand leaders in Australia), Cabernet Shiraz and Tawny Port.

Distribution: National retail through all types of liquor outlets.

Prices: $6.99 to $9.99 gives some idea of discount pricing range.

Vintage Rating 1986–89: White: '87, '89, '88, '86. Red: '86, '88, '89, '87.

Outstanding Prior Vintages: Red: '82, '84, '72, '76.

Tasting Notes:

1989 WHITE BURGUNDY [TS] Colour: light to medium green-yellow. *Bouquet:* broad, with good fruit, and ever so slight wet dog aromas that will almost certainly be cleared up prior to bottling. *Palate:* very full and rich fruit salad/honeyed fruit with masses of flavour; tasted prior to cold stabilisation and bottling; promises to perform extremely well given its price.

1989 RHINE RIESLING [TS] Colour: light yellow-green. *Bouquet:* firm, strong and clean toasty/lime aromas, quite classic. *Palate:* lovely and intense lime fruit with an exceptionally long palate and equally good balance; very good varietal definition, and an outstanding achievement given the vintage. If it ends up in bottle looking like this, could rate as high as 90 points; certainly a wine to watch.

1988 WHITE BURGUNDY [77] Colour: medium to full yellow-green. *Bouquet:* very pleasant bottle-developed aromas with nicely integrated lemony oak. *Palate:* attractive bottle-developed flavours; smooth, and quite oaky, but with fruit to carry that oak. Drink '90.

1988 CHARDONNAY [90] Colour: glowing medium green-yellow. *Bouquet:* clean and smooth citric/grapefruit aromas with good intensity and beautifully balanced and integrated oak. *Palate:* a wonderfully flavoured, balanced and constructed wine with intense grapefruit peach flavours and soft oak. To be honest, I do not know how the wine came to score so highly, but I did taste it with extreme care. Drink '90–'92.

1988 CABERNET SHIRAZ [CS] Colour: medium to full purple-red. *Bouquet:* smooth and clean with full, sweet berry aromas. *Palate:* clean, full chewy/ripe sweet fruit with great texture. Headed towards 80 points or more.

1988 CABERNET SAUVIGNON [CS] Colour: medium to full purple-red. *Bouquet:* strong, full, concentrated and clean ripe cabernet aroma with great depth and style. *Palate:* superbly rich fruit with strong vanillan oak; a thick, chewy Penfolds style (the comments were made before I knew the identity of the wine) with beautiful tannin balance. Absolutely outstanding and, if it shows this character in bottle, will merit 90 points.

Summary: The astonishing quantity of the upcoming Seaview table wines was sufficient to shut out all of the sparkling wines; these performed well enough, but paled into insignificance against the reviewed wines. There certainly has been some shaking and moving in recent times throughout the Penfold group companies.

THE SETTLEMENT WINE COMPANY

Location: Temporary premises at Torresan Wine Estates, Martins Road, McLaren Vale; 0.5 km west of McLaren Vale. (08) 323 8808.

Winemaker: Janis Gesmanis.

Principal Wines: Full-bodied red wines and port wines. The port wine range includes the controversial Dr David's Plasma Port and Koala Port, the latter being available in a cloth gift bag. Cabernet releases feature a label design with paintings by Australian artist Tom Gleghorn.

Distribution: Principally cellar door sales and mailing list; mailing list enquiries as above. Agents distributing in NSW, Qld serviced direct from winery.

Prices: $6 to $12.

Tasting Notes:

1987 CABERNET SAUVIGNON [74] Colour: medium to full red-purple. *Bouquet:* very strong, rich vanillan American oak with full, red berry fruit underneath. *Palate:* follows the bouquet, except that the vanilla bean American oak really does hang around and tend to submerge the fruit. May settle down with further time in bottle. Drink '93–'96.

Summary: The Settlement Wine Company has had a hard time of things since a fire destroyed the winery in February 1987. Owner Dr David Mitchell is however confident that Settlement will return to its old home and once again "be able to provide the public with the quality, style and range of products that it was noted for".

SHOTTESBROOKE

Location: Ryecroft Vineyard, Ingoldby Road, McLaren Flat, 5171; 3 km east of McLaren Vale. (08) 383 0001.

Winemaker: Nick Holmes.

1989 Production: 4000 cases.

Principal Wines: Sauvignon Blanc, and a cabernet

sauvignon merlot cabernet franc (or malbec) blend simply labelled Shottesbrooke.

Distribution: Cellar door sales, mailing list and limited retail and restaurant distribution. Cellar door sales by appointment only. UK exports through Gullin & Co.

Prices: $13.50 to $17.25 retail.

Vintage Rating 1986–89: Red: '86, '88, '87 ('89 not rated).

Outstanding Prior Vintages: Red: '84.

Tasting Notes:

1989 SAUVIGNON BLANC [CS] _Colour:_ light straw-green. _Bouquet:_ clean, medium weight with relatively subdued fruit showing little varietal character. _Palate:_ clean, quite soft and seemingly retaining some residual sugar; yet to develop positive varietal fruit. The wine is free from fault, and may well ultimately reach 70 or more points.

1988 CABERNET MERLOT MALBEC [CS] _Colour:_ medium to full red-purple. _Bouquet:_ strong vanillan oak and some casky aromas. _Palate:_ very rich and textured with strong vanillan oak, almost into a Penfold style, and far richer than the usually fairly light Shottesbrook wines; perhaps due to the inclusion of malbec at the expense of cabernet franc. Indicative points in the high 70's.

Summary: As I have said before, Shottesbrooke shows that mercaptan is not inevitable, and is not regional character. The wines are invariably clean, and have tended to be unusually elegant; the '88 suggests a move towards the fuller bodied style typical of the district. I should add in passing that I was not particularly taken by the 1987 vintage.

🍇SIMON HACKETT

Location: Off McMurtrie Road, McLaren Vale, 5171. (08) 331 7348.

Winemaker: Simon Hackett.

Principal Wines: Made at various wineries under Simon Hackett's personal direction. An oak maturation and packaged-wine storage facility is being established in McMurtrie Road, McLaren Vale.

Distribution: Exclusively retail with SA, WA, NSW, ACT and export serviced direct by Simon Hackett Wines; telephone as above. Vic., through The Wine Company and Qld through Samuel Smith & Sons Pty Ltd. Enquiries to PO Box 166, Walkerville, 5081.

Tasting Notes:

1987 CHARDONNAY [74] _Colour:_ medium to full yellow-green, with good brightness. _Bouquet:_ slightly dull with a distinct matchbox/wet dog edge, possibly from some re-used oak barrels. _Palate:_ infinitely better on the fore and mid-palate, with strong melon/grapefruit flavours, before toughening off slightly on the finish, perhaps a legacy of that errant bouquet. Nonetheless, a wine with lots of flavour. Drink '90–'92.

1987 CABERNET SAUVIGNON [74] _Colour:_ medium red-purple. _Bouquet:_ scented sweet berry aromas, and a touch of spice, reminiscent of shiraz. _Palate:_ almost essence sweetness to the spicy fruit flavours, possibly oak derived; a wine that consumers will either love or hate, and the points are something of a compromise between the two extremes. Certainly not short of character. Drink '91–'95.

Summary: In the 1988 edition I suggested that The Simon Hackett wines lacked flair or colour. No such accusation could be made about these wines, which are guaranteed to polarise opinions.

🍇SOUTHERN VALES WINERY

Location: 151 Main Road, McLaren Vale, 5171. (08) 323 8656.

Winemakers: Roland Wahlquist and Jane Paull.

Principal Wines: The wines are sold under the Tatachilla name. Wines under the newly released "The Wattles" range include Semillon, Rhine Riesling, Chenin Blanc, Frontignac and Dry Red.

Distribution: Retail, cellar door and export sales; cellar door sales 10 a.m. 4 p.m. Monday to Saturday; noon to 4 p.m. Sundays and public holidays.

Prices: $6 to $15 retail.

Vintage Rating 1986–89: '89, '88, '86, '87.

Outstanding Prior Vintages: '72, '76, '77, '80.

Tasting Notes:

1989 THE WATTLES SEMILLON [CS] Colour: light yellow-green. *Bouquet:* light, clean quite herbaceous fruit aromas with some fermentation characters lingering. *Palate:* a strong herbaceous style with very good fruit intensity, and clearly very well made. Headed towards the high 70's, low 80's.

1989 THE WATTLES RHINE RIESLING [64] Colour: light to medium straw-yellow. *Bouquet* slightly dull and hard, lacking fruit aroma. *Palate:* again, slightly dull, but with some residual sugar to prop up the total flavour; it could be that the fruit had been knocked around in the sample tasted, and the wine may merit a higher rating. Drink '90–'91.

1989 CHARDONNAY [CS] Colour: light to medium yellow-straw. *Bouquet:* firm, slightly herbaceous fruit aroma of light to medium intensity. *Palate:* quite different to that which the bouquet would suggest; much riper, but with a rather hard alcohol burn to the finish; very early days, but it does at least have flavour. Difficult to determine where it will end up.

1989 THE WATTLES DRY RED [CS] Colour: crimson purple. *Bouquet:* clean, very spicy aromas with a touch of leafy maceration character, but showing very good style. *Palate:* lovely lively spicy shiraz, fresh and tingling; full of promise as a fresh early drinking style at 85 points or thereabouts.

Summary: There has not only been a change of ownership at Tatachilla, but a complete restaff, with an extremely competent winemaking team now in charge. Some lovely wines seem likely to materialise.

❦ *THOMAS FERNHILL ESTATE*

Location: Ingoldby Road, McLaren Flat, 5171; on northern outskirts of township. (08) 383 0167.

Winemaker: Wayne Thomas.

1989 Production: 40,000 litres.

Principal Wines: Chardonnay, Sauvignon Blanc, Rhine Riesling, Shiraz, Cabernet Sauvignon, Old Tawny Port and Fernhill Brut.

Distribution: Substantial cellar door sales 10 a.m. to 5 p.m. 7 days; mailing list enquiries as above. Limited fine wine retail distribution through wholesalers in NSW, De Bono Pty Ltd; SA, Fern Hill Estate; Vic., Harvey Long Winebrokers; and Qld, Barrique Fine Wines.

Prices: $5 to $16 cellar door.

Vintage Rating 1986–89: White: '86, '89, '88, '87. Red: '88, '86, '87, '89.

Outstanding Prior Vintages: White: '85. Red: '82, '79.

Tasting Notes:

1989 SAUVIGNON BLANC [CS] Colour: light green-yellow. *Bouquet:* some burnt/medicinal fermentation characters tending to obscure fruit. *Palate:* full flavoured but seemingly very sweet; a wine needing considerable work.

Summary: Wayne Thomas is a very experienced winemaker who produces small batches sold chiefly to a loyal mailing list. The two cask samples (one not reviewed) were very difficult to evaluate.

❦ *THOMAS HARDY*

Location: Reynella Road, Reynella, 5161; on southern outskirts of township. Also at Main Road, McLaren Vale, 5171 (Tintara Cellars). (08) 381 2266; Fax (08) 381 1968; cellar door (08) 381 7397; McLaren Vale (08) 323 8676.

Winemakers: Fortified—Bill Hardy; red—David O'Leary; white—Tom Newton; sparkling–Tom Newton.

1989 Production: Not for publication.

Principal Wines: Hardy's produces a full range of wines including Australia's greatest vintage and tawny ports, the principal source being McLaren Vale shiraz. The majority of the premium table wine produced comes from Padthaway, with Chardonnay, Rhine Riesling and Semillon being the backbone of the whites, and Pinot Noir and Cabernet Sauvignon leading the resurgence in quality of the dry reds. Hardy's leading brand-seller, Siegersdorf, is basically made from Padthaway and Clare material. The two principal lines are the Collection Series (premium quality) and the Bird Series (mid-range commercial). The Padthaway Collection series wines are separately dealt with under the Padthaway Thomas Hardy entry.

Distribution: National retail distribution at all levels through own distribution network.

Prices: $4.99 to $30 (for Classic Cuvee Vintage) retail.

Vintage Rating 1986–89: White: '88, '89, '86, '87. Red: '87, '89, '86, '88.

Outstanding Prior Vintages: White: '80, '78, '76. Red: '79, '80, '82.

Tasting Notes:

1988 SIEGERSDORF RHINE RIESLING [82] Colour: bright green-yellow. *Bouquet:* clean, with attractive soft fruit aromas with an underlying touch of tighter toasty character. *Palate:* has very good structure and likewise balance; the fruit flavours are building, and will continue to do so; has length and power on the finish. Drink '90–'93.

1988 EDEN TRAMINER RIESLING [71] Colour: light green-yellow. *Bouquet:* clean, light floral aromas with a touch of classic lychee. *Palate:* appreciably sweet, but a most attractive example of commercial traminer riesling and even better at its very modest price. Drink '90.

1988 COLLECTION CHARDONNAY (PADTHAWAY/ CLARE) [92] Colour: light green-yellow. *Bouquet:* elegant and harmonious with beautiful fruit/oak balance; the fruit with aromas of melon, fig and grapefruit. *Palate:* a beautifully made, balanced and constructed wine; exceptionally good grapefruit/melon fig flavours. Drink '90 –'92.

1987 EILEEN HARDY SHIRAZ (PADTHAWAY/ McLAREN VALE) [90] Colour: vivid purple-red. *Bouquet:* highly aromatic spotless red berry/ cherry fruit complexed by exotic silver cashew/ musk/spice oak. *Palate:* superbly textured, rich fruit with exotic clove/spice oak that does not, however, burn; excellent tannin on the finish. Due for release mid to late 1990. Drink '93–2000.

1982 VINTAGE PORT [90] Colour: medium to full red, starting to show some bottle development. *Bouquet:* very complex, rich, dark fruit aromas with fine brandy spirit. *Palate:* full, rich and deep dark chocolate flavours; superb texture and structure throughout, and a lingering finish that does not cloy. Drink '90–2000.

Summary: While I think that many of the finest of the very large Thomas Hardy table wines come from Padthaway, it is also producing some superb wines with regional blends, particularly now that it is able to draw upon the Clare Valley vineyards of Stanley Leasingham; and, of course, its vintage ports remain supreme. Overall, however, the most significant changes have been in red winemaking style, culminating in the winning of the 1988 Jimmy Watson Trophy with the 1987 Padthaway Collection Cabernet Sauvignon, but with other great red wines coming through the system: one has to look no further than the forthcoming '87 Eileen Hardy Shiraz.

TINLINS WINERY

Location: Kangarilla Road, McLaren Flat, SA, 5171.
(08) 323 8649.

Winemaker: W. D. Tinlin.

1989 Production: Approximately 300 tonnes crushed.

Principal Wines: A full range of white and red table wine, sparkling wine, flavoured wine and fortified wine available both under the Tinlin Winery label and in bulk; substantial bulk sales either in customer-supplied containers (two litres and above) or ex-winery in 27 litre containers.

Distribution: Principally cellar door sales 8 a.m. to 5 p.m. Monday to Friday; 8 a.m. to 4.30 p.m. weekends.

Summary: A family owned and operated winery where the accent is on value for money; the wines offered in bulk are some of the cheapest available anywhere in Australia.

❦ *TORRESAN ESTATE*

Location: Manning Road, Flagstaff Hill, 5159.
(08) 270 2500; Fax (08) 270 3848.

Winemakers: Amelio Torresan and Tim Mortimer.

1989 Production: The equivalent of 28,000 cases.

Principal Wines: Rhine Riesling, Kabinett Rhine Riesling, Shiraz, Cabernet Shiraz, Cabernet Sauvignon and "The Godfather" ports.

Distribution: Limited retail distribution, cellar door sales and mail order. Enquiries to PO Box 110, St Mary's, 5042.

Prices: $6.50 to $25.

Vintage Rating 1986–89: White: '89, '86, '87, '88. Red: '86, '88, '89, '87.

Summary: The 1989 samples submitted for this edition were simply not reviewable; it is difficult to tell whether this was due to difficulties that always confront preparation of samples of unbottled wines, or something more serious. I can therefore give no assistance on the quality of upcoming wines, although it is true to say that prior vintages have been of variable quality.

❦ *WIRRA WIRRA VINEYARDS*

Location: McMurtrie Road, McLaren Vale, 5171; 2 km south-east of township.
(08) 323 8414; Fax (08) 323 8596.

Winemaker: Ben Riggs.

1989 Production: 25,000 cases.

Principal Wines: A limited range of very high-quality table wines, made from grapes grown predominantly within the McLaren Vale region, the majority of this being estate grown or grown on associated vineyards. Wines include Hand Picked Rhine Riesling, Late Picked Rhine Riesling, Chardonnay, Sauvignon Blanc, Semillon-Sauvignon Blanc, Cabernet Sauvignon, Church Block (Cabernet-Shiraz-Merlot) and The Cousins (Pinot Noir-Chardonnay) *Méthode champenoise.*

Distribution: Substantial cellar door sales 10 a.m. to 5 p.m. Monday to Saturday; 11 a.m. to 5 p.m. Sunday. Also significant fine wine retail distribution through Rutherglen Wine Co., Vic., and Tas; I. H. Baker, NSW, WA, and Qld; Tim Seats Pty Ltd, NT; The Oak Barrel, ACT; and La Forgia Wine Agencies, SA. UK imports through Boxford Wine Co, Essex.

Prices: $11 to $18 retail.

Vintage Rating 1986–89: White: '86, '88, '87, '89. Red: '87, '86, '88, '89.

Outstanding Prior Vintages: White: '79, '82, '84. Red: '80, '82, '84.

Tasting Notes:

1988 RHINE RIESLING [85] Colour: glowing bright green-yellow. *Bouquet:* stylish, clean and fresh passionfruit of medium intensity. *Palate:* a complete and harmonious balanced wine with lovely feel in the mouth; again passionfruit flavours dominate on a lingering finish. Drink '90–'91.

1988 SAUVIGNON BLANC [89] Colour: light to medium yellow-green. *Bouquet:* superb, rich varietal character showing strong gooseberry aromas and no oak. *Palate:* a beautifully balanced and constructed wine showing exemplary varietal character; lovely tangy finish. Drink '90–'92.

1988 CHARDONNAY [85] Colour: light to medium straw-yellow. *Bouquet:* complex, stylish aromas with charred oak and some zip to the fruit. *Palate:* high-toned, rich flavours with sweet fruit on the mid-palate followed by a tangy finish. Drink '90–'92.

1987 CHURCH BLOCK [73] Colour: medium purple-red. *Bouquet:* pleasant red berry fruits, with what I first took to be a slightly leathery edge but then decided was in fact nothing more than a touch of charred oak. *Palate:* clean, firm cherry fruit of light to medium weight, with a pleasant low tannin finish. A wine constructed for early consumption. Drink '90–'91.

Summary: As the tasting notes indicate, I have an enormous regard for the white wines of Wirra Wirra, but have never been able to really relate to its light-bodied reds. I have also deliberately opted to give tasting notes for the '88 vintage (rather than incomplete '89 vintage wines taken from cask or tank) simply because prior experience show that these wines improve out of all recognition with time in bottle. You will in fact be lucky to find the '88 whites still available on retail shelves, but they will be worth the effort if you succeed.

❦ WOODSTOCK

Location: Douglas Gully Road, McLaren Flat, 5171; 5 km north-east of township. (08) 383 0156.

Winemaker: Scott Collett.

1989 Production: 25,000 cases.

Principal Wines: A range of very high-quality table and fortified wines comprising Rhine Riesling, Sauvignon Blanc, Semillon, Chardonnay, Botrytis Sweet White, Cabernet Sauvignon, Shiraz, Tawny Port and Vintage Port. Tawny Port also sold in 25-litre containers.

Distribution: Substantial cellar door sales 9 a.m. to 5 p.m. Monday to Friday; and noon to 5 p.m. weekends and holidays. High-quality mailing list; enquiries to PO Box 151, McLaren Vale, 5171. National distribution through Southern Districts Wine Merchants, NSW; Van Cooth & Co., Vic.; La Forgia Agency, SA; Premium Wine Company, WA; Tallerman Wine and Spirits, Qld; and Camperdown Cellars at the Mount, Tas. UK imports through Lay & Wheeler Ltd.

Prices: $6 to $20 cellar door.

Vintage Rating 1986–89: White: '88, '89, '87, '86. Red: '89, '87, '88, '86.

Outstanding Prior Vintages: White: '83, '85. Red: '82, '84, '85.

Tasting Notes:

1988 RHINE RIESLING [71] Colour: light yellow, with just a touch of green. *Bouquet:* fairly light fruit lacking varietal intensity, without any winemaking fault. *Palate:* light passionfruit/ lime fruit; fairly soft on both mid-palate and finish and a little one dimensional. Drink '90–'91.

1988 SAUVIGNON BLANC [79] Colour: light straw-yellow. *Bouquet:* attractive, complex bottle-developed aromas with some gooseberry fruit still evident. *Palate:* quite complex, with attractive fruit, but the oak constantly threatens to overtake the other flavour components; needed just that little bit of extra richness to carry the oak. Drink '90.

1988 CHARDONNAY [69] Colour: medium yellow, with a hint of straw. *Bouquet:* of medium weight, with slightly sour/burnt characters from what appears to be a hint of sulphide. *Palate:* smooth, honeyed fruit lurks under a touch of bitterness; I almost wonder whether this was a poor bottle of what in reality is a better wine. Drink '90.

1987 CABERNET SAUVIGNON [82] Colour: medium full red-purple. *Bouquet:* very clean and smooth with red fruit cherry/berry aromas. *Palate:* most attractive rounded sweet cherry/ berry fruit; a very clean and soft wine with low tannins. Drink '90–'94.

Summary: A somewhat eclectic range of wines were submitted for the tasting for this book with the magnificent Botrytis Sweet White a notable omission, presumably because Woodstock is between vintages. I would not therefore regard the notes as giving a full indication of both the quality and consistency that has been the hallmark of the Woodstock label over the past five years.

Western Australia

Lower Great Southern Area

1988 VINTAGE

The Lower Great Southern Area is by far the largest wine district in Australia. Should the rate of development continue, it will undoubtedly be divided into six distinct regions: Mount Barker, Frankland River, Denmark, Albany, The Porongurups and Manjimup/Pemberton. The overview given in these vintage reports is therefore somewhat generalised.

The winter and spring continued the six year winter drought pattern, with little or no surface run-off to fill the all-important dams. However, there was sufficient moisture to promote a satisfactory budburst, and some late November rain came at a critical time. That rain became all the more important following a dry summer with none of the thunderstorms which the area can usually rely on.

While conditions were very dry, they were also very mild, with only three or four days on which the temperature exceeded 34° C. Mild, warm conditions and cool nights gave rise to an early start to vintage, but the usual extended finish. Thus the harvest started with the early varieties at Albany picked in early March and finished with the last of the cabernet sauvignon on 30 April, the day prior to the onset of a 100 mm deluge.

Overall yields were slightly down; by and large it was a more successful year for white wines than for reds, with riesling, chardonnay and sauvignon blanc above average in quality, and red wines average.

1989 VINTAGE

The rain which commenced on the day following the last day of the 1988 vintage continued through the calendar year, breaking the six year drought in no uncertain fashion. By the end of the year it reached 1100 mm compared with the average 750 mm. All of the dams filled, and soil moisture reserves were likewise at capacity. It was in fact the wettest year since 1937.

Not surprisingly, the vines reacted with enthusiasm to the conditions, with very strong budburst and abundant flowering, coupled with excellent set. The greatest problem during the growing season came from mildew, prevalent because of the very moist growing conditions and the abundant vine canopies. Spray programmes by and large controlled the mildews, and two bursts of very hot weather between 18 January and 23 January, and again between 1 February and 5 February likewise helped the control.

The rain returned in April, leading to problems with some botrytis. While this intensified flavour in the rhine riesling, it required constant vigilance to prevent it spreading to the red varieties.

It should be an excellent year for rhine riesling; a moderately good year for chardonnay and sauvignon blanc, where flavours are down on intensity; a good year for shiraz with strong peppery spice flavours; and a quite outstanding year for cabernet sauvignon, with the wines showing intense mulberry/blackberry flavours.

THE CHANGES

There is considerable activity across the span of the Lower Great Southern Area. The new entries are Blackwood Crest, Dalyup River Estate, Karri View and Lefroy Brook, but these represent only the tip of the iceberg. Under the wing of the fast developing Goundrey Wines Limited, Catherine Hill, Scottsdale Brook, Mount Shadforth Estate, and a vineyard owned by Dr and Mrs Ian McGlew in Redman Road, Denmark, will all come into production over the next year or so, all with significant output.

Goundrey Wines itself has been converted into a public company and has not only built a large new winery, but engaged on a massive planting programme which will see output increase in leaps and bounds from the already substantial 18,000 cases in 1989.

Blackwood Crest has in fact been in existence for some considerable time; it is one of the most northerly vineyards, being 70 km north of Alkoomi. It has had a relatively low profile, with some emphasis on fortified wines, but has retained Rob Bowen as consultant winemaker, leading to a marked increase in the quality of the currently available table wines. Blackwood Crest also offers a restaurant which specialises in by-appointment dinners and catering; it is not open other than by appointment. The owners, Max and Ros Fairbrass, are third generation wool growers for whom grape growing and winemaking is a much needed diversification.

Another major development has been the establishment of two large plantings masterminded by Perth wine identity Stewart Van Raalte; over 80 hectares are already planted, with more than half subject to a long term supply contract with Houghton Wines. Houghton is also the future off-taker of another very large and exciting development in the Manjimup region. Both of these have been financed by tax-based schemes similar to those employed by Wyndham Estate. The Manjimup area is very cool indeed, and a number of the purchasers in both developments are intending to take early picked pinot noir and chardonnay as base wine for *Méthode champenoise* styles.

It is at Pemberton, near Manjimup, that the third of the new entries, Lefroy Brook, has its vineyard. Patrick and Barbara Holt commenced planting pinot noir and chardonnay six years ago on ultra-close one metre by 0.5 metre spacing. As yet, they only have 6000 vines established, but intend to increase this to 25,000 vines over the next few years. The quality of their pinot noir is said to have Dr Bill Panell and his co-owners of the famous Burgundy vineyard Pousse d'Or most excited. I am not surprised: I tasted the 1989 Pinot Noir reviewed in this edition and wrote the tasting notes before I had heard of the Burgundian interest: Pousse d'Or is situated in Volnay and my ascription of Volnay character was entirely in ignorance of and unprompted by the Burgundians.

Another major change came in the sale of Forest Hill to the Holmes á Court interest for a reported $1.3 million. The sale was consummated on a walk-in walk-out basis, with all stock therefore remaining with the purchaser. Forest Hill will in future produce only white wines, which will henceforth be made at Vasse Felix. Chatsfield, too, has changed hands with Dr Ken Lynch and wife Joyce the incoming owners.

Dalyup River's owner, Tom Murray, hopes to build a small winery on site in one to two years, and to gradually take over winemaking responsibilities from John Wade as he completes a wine science degree from the Riverina Murray Institute of Higher Education in 1992 (all going to plan).

Finally, Chateau Barker has disappeared: the vineyard has been sold to the Goundrey Wines Limited group and, apart from back stocks, the label will disappear from sight.

Overall wine quality is good. The district came second to Margaret River at the 1989 Sheraton Wine Awards, but nonetheless performed creditably and underlined the fact that the real future for winemaking in the West lies in its southern regions.

ALKOOMI

Location: Wingeballup Road, Frankland, 6396; 11 km west of township.
(098) 55 2229.

Winemakers: Kim Hart and Merv Lange.

1989 Production : 8000 cases.

Principal Wines: Rhine Riesling, Semillon, Sauvignon Blanc, Chardonnay, Shiraz, Malbec and Cabernet Sauvignon.

Distribution: Mailing list, cellar door sales and retail through wholesale distributors. Limited exports. Mailing list enquiries to RMB 234, Frankland, 6396. Cellar door sales 10 a.m. to 5 p.m. Monday to Saturday and 1 p.m. to 5 p.m. Sunday.

Prices: $10.90 to $23.80 retail.

Vintage Rating 1986–89: '86, '89, '87, '88.

Outstanding Prior Vintages: '77, '80, '82, '83, '84.

Tasting Notes:

1989 SAUVIGNON BLANC [85] Colour: light straw-green. *Bouquet:* clean, with excellent varietal character and weight, pronounced soft gooseberry aromas. *Palate:* no less excellent varietal definition, with good mid-palate richness and weight; a most attractive non-oaked style. Drink '90–'92.

1989 CHARDONNAY [78] Colour: very good green-yellow of medium depth. *Bouquet:* complex lemony/honeyed bouquet, already showing development and completeness. *Palate:* full bodied, rich and complex, with toasty oak and very stylish grapefruit underneath; pointed because it was so complete, but even these points may be on the low side. Drink '90–'92.

1988 RHINE RIESLING [81] Colour: medium yellow-green. *Bouquet:* rich bottle-developed toasty/lime aromas. *Palate:* very attractive bottle-developed lime flavours, with very good acid; again, shows some development but, in the style of the region, will undoubtedly live for many years. Drink '90–'93.

1988 CABERNET SAUVIGNON [85] Colour: strong, deep purple-red *Bouquet:* concentrated, deep and rich textured cabernet aroma; very clean and showing excellent varietal definition. *Palate:* potent, concentrated and perfectly ripened cabernet in a classic mould; all this wine requires is a great deal of patience. Drink '96–2010.

1987 MALBEC [81] Colour: light to medium purple-red. *Bouquet:* clean, firm berry fruit, with excellent oak and fruit balance and integration. *Palate:* very fragrant fruity/red berry/cherry tastes, precisely as one should expect from malbec; the wine has excellent balance and structure, and finishes with soft tannin. Drink '92–'95.

Summary: Alkoomi loses nothing in comparison with Goundrey or Plantagenet; both red and white wines have marvellous flavour, varietal definition and the capacity to repay extended cellaring.

BLACKWOOD CREST

Location: RMB 404A Boyup Brook, 6244; 40 km east of Boyup Brook and 53 km west of the Perth/Albany Highway, Kojonup.

Winemakers: Max Fairbrass and Rob Bowen (contract).

1989 Production : Approximately 600 cases.

Principal Wines: Rhine Riesling, Semillon Sauvignon Blanc, Hermitage, Cabernet Sauvignon and Ruby Port.

Distribution: Principally cellar door sales and mailing list; cellar door sales 10 a.m. to 5 p.m. 7 days. Limited local retail and hotel distribution.

Prices: $8 to $12 cellar door.

Tasting Notes:

1988 RHINE RIESLING **[60]** *Colour:* light straw-yellow. *Bouquet:* full, broad and soft lime/pineapple fruit,. *Palate:* broad and flavoursome, but rather phenolic, with some rather hard, cheesey characters. Drink '90.

1987 HERMITAGE **[58]** *Colour:* extraordinarily dense purple-red. *Bouquet:* concentrated and rich dark berry fruit, with minty overtones, and then a distinct touch of sulphide. *Palate:* a huge, rather over-extracted wine, with strong fruit, high tannin and then some sulphidic bitterness. A wine with such massive flavour that it may in fact overcome that bitterness, and if it does, would rate much higher points. Drink '93–'97.

1986 CABERNET SAUVIGNON **[80]** *Colour:* dense purple-red. *Bouquet:* clean, with strong, attractive sweet minty fruit. *Palate:* full, concentrated fleshy/juicy/minty fruit flavours and good tannins; a striking and high flavoured wine. Drink '91–'98.

1986 RUBY PORT **[75]** *Colour:* light to medium purple-red. *Bouquet:* clean and rich spicy fruit with clean spirit. *Palate:* attractive spicy fruit to a wine of medium weight and traditional sweetness; a cellar door special. Drink '90–'93.

Summary: Blackwood Crest makes a quite auspicious, even if overdue, entry. Max Fairbrass tells me the '88 and '89 reds are even stronger and richer, in which case we have something quite remarkable to look forward to. Production, too, will increase quite rapidly from its present modest level.

CASTLE ROCK ESTATE

Location: Porongurup Road, Porongurup, 6324; (098) 41 1037 or 53 1035 (vineyard).

Winemaker: Angelo Diletti.

Principal Wines: Rhine Riesling, Late Harvest Riesling and Cabernet Sauvignon.

Distribution: Principally mailing list and "vineyard door" sales. Mailing list enquiries to PO Box 891, Albany, 6330. Vineyard sales 10 a.m. to 4 p.m. Wednesday, weekends and public holidays. Selected retail outlets Perth, Sydney and Melbourne.

Prices: $10 to $15 retail.

Tasting Notes:

1989 RHINE RIESLING **[CS]** *Colour:* light green-yellow. *Bouquet:* closed and a little hard, showing the distinct effects of an only just-completed fermentation. *Palate:* again, very youthful, closed and rather hard when tasted July 1989. Will undoubtedly improve once it has got through the after-effects of fermentation.

1987 CABERNET SAUVIGNON **[70]** *Colour:* vivid red-purple. *Bouquet:* exceptionally youthful, if not sharp, fruit bouquet; very fresh, but lacking complexity. *Palate:* extremely youthful, crying out for time in bottle to gain complexity, and in fact giving the impression it was bottled too early. In the long haul could come good, for the essential fruit flavour is certainly there. Drink '94–'98.

Summary: The two Castle Rock wines tasted for this edition suffered from extreme youth; the track record of Angelo Diletti's vineyard and wines leaves me in no doubt that patience will be its own reward.

CHATSFIELD

Location: 34 Albany Highway, Mount Barker, 6324; at township.
(098) 51 1266 or (098) 51 1721.

Winemaker: Rodney Hooper (contract).

Principal Wines: Rhine Riesling, Traminer, Chardonnay and Shiraz.

Distribution: Principally cellar door sales and mailing list; cellar door sales 10.30 a.m. to 4.30 p.m. Tuesday to Friday, 11 a.m. to 3 p.m. Saturday and Sunday. Mailing list enquiries to PO Box 1417, Albany, 6330. Limited retail distribution through restaurants and liquor stores in Perth.

Prices: $9 to $12.50 retail.

Vintage Rating 1986–89: White: '86, '88, '87 ('89 not yet rated). Red: '86, '88, '87 ('89 not yet rated).

Tasting Notes:

1989 RHINE RIESLING [67] Colour: medium yellow-green. _Bouquet:_ soft and surprisingly broad lime/pineapple aromas, already showing some development. _Palate:_ a soft, easy drinking and exceptionally forward style for Chatsfield, with similar lime/pineapple flavours to those of the bouquet. Drink '90.

1989 TRAMINER [65] Colour: medium yellow-green. _Bouquet:_ much more reserved than the rhine riesling, rather hard, with some spicy characters just evident. _Palate:_ some of those typical oily, almost greasy, characters that can be found in traminer; again very soft and rather bland. Drink '90.

1988 SHIRAZ [90] Colour: full purple-red. _Bouquet:_ strong and firm dark berry/plum fruit, with smooth oak in support. _Palate:_ extremely attractive rich and smooth berry plum fruit, crammed with flavour, and with excellent structure from soft supporting tannins. Drink '92–'97.

Summary: The white wines represent a startling turn around in the Chatsfield style; these are usually extremely fine and reserved in their youth. It is possible they may have been unrepresentative samples shortly prior to bottling. The shiraz, however, is quite simply superb.

DALYUP RIVER ESTATE

Location: Murray's Road, Esperance, 6450. (090) 76 5027 (vineyard only).

Winemaker: John Wade (contract).

1989 Production : 350 cases.

Principal Wines: Riesling, Shiraz, Sauvignon Blanc (as from 1990) and Cabernet Sauvignon (as from 1991).

Distribution: Principally by mail order; enquiries to PO Box 253, Esperance, 6450.

Prices: $8.50 to $10.50.

Tasting Notes:

1988 RHINE RIESLING [69] Colour: pale straw-green. _Bouquet:_ clean and firm, though tending to hardness; young vine material well handled. _Palate:_ clean, but very light bodied, possibly reflecting young vines; again, clever winemaking is evident and the balance is good. Drink '90.

Summary: Tom Murray's Dalyup River Estate was in fact first planted in 1976 (as cuttings), but the vines have grown slowly and early indications are that the red wines may be the best in the long term.

FOREST HILL

Location: 142 km peg, Muir Highway, Forest Hill via Mount Barker, 6324. (098) 51 1724 or (098) 51 1971.

Winemaker: Plantagenet Wines (contract) up to 1989; 1990 and subsequent at Vasse Felix.

Principal Wines: A specialised range of white wines comprising Rhine Riesling, Traminer and Chardonnay.

Distribution: Chiefly mailing list. Retail distribution through I. H. Baker Wines & Spirits, Perth; Fesq & Co., Vic.; Specialist Wine Co., NSW. Mailing list enquiries to PO Box 49, Mount Barker, 6324.

Prices: $9 to $14.

Tasting Notes:

1988 RHINE RIESLING [93] Colour: medium yellow-green. _Bouquet:_ classic toasty riesling with no extravagant fruit flavours; lime vanillan characters coming through high aromatics. _Palate:_ a fine intense toasty riesling, with some passionfruit flavours in exceptional style. This bottle bore absolutely no resemblance to that exhibited at the 1989 Sheraton Wine Awards,; the latter has to have been a bad bottle. Drink '90–'92.

1988 SAUVIGNON BLANC [72] Colour: light green-yellow. *Bouquet:* unusual aroma, flower-like, and not obviously varietal. *Palate:* much more fruit flavour and varietal character than the bouquet promises, with a touch of gooseberry; the finish falters slightly. Drink '90.

1988 TRAMINER [59] Colour: distinct traces of pink-brown. *Bouquet:* rather blousy and soft, with minimal spice. *Palate:* relies strictly on residual sugar for flavour, with some rather common and slightly oxidised/oily fruit flavours. A major disappointment. One wonders whether there were some bottling problems. Drink '90.

1987 CABERNET SAUVIGNON [75] Colour: medium red-purple. *Bouquet:* fresh, clean and fragrant light fruit, with appropriately judged spicy oak. *Palate:* very clean, fresh and modern style light-bodied cabernet; once again the oak is not over played and the wine finishes with low tannin. Drink '90–'93.

Summary: One cannot be certain where Forest Hills is headed, but it would be a shame if the substantial goodwill attached to the name built up with such devotion by Betty Pearse over the years were allowed to die.

GALAFREY

Location: 145 Lower Sterling Terrace, Albany, 6330; in township.
(098) 41 6533.

Winemaker : Ian Tyrer.

1989 Production: 1600 cases (50% reduction due to hail in December).

Principal Wines: Rhine Riesling, Chardonnay, Muller Thurgau, Shiraz, Pinot Noir and Cabernet Sauvignon.

Distribution: Principally cellar door sales and mail order; cellar door sales 10 a.m. to 5 p.m. Monday to Saturday; also long weekends. Public holidays weekends only. Mailing list

address as above. Wholesale distribution through Premium Wine Co, Perth ((09) 479 3976).

Prices: $7 to $15 cellar door.

Tasting Notes:

1988 RHINE RIESLING [83] Colour: medium yellow-green. *Bouquet:* very full, with strong lime/pineapple bottle-developed characters, and even a touch of camphor apparent. *Palate:* soft, bottle-developed camphor lime flavours; nice style, but very slightly hollow, suggesting the fruit may drop out quickly from this point onwards. Drink '90.

Summary: Galafrey is situated in an attractive and spacious ex-wool store in Albany; however, Ian and Linda Tyrer are making efforts to expand the sales-base in the eastern states, and we may see more of Galafrey in the future.

GOUNDREY

Location: Muir Highway, Mount Barker, 6324 (winery).
(098) 511 777; Fax (098) 511 997.
Cellar door sales 11 North Street, Denmark, 6333 (in township).
(098) 48 1525.

Winemaker: Michael Goundrey.

1989 Production: 18,000 cases.

Principal Wines: Rhine Riesling, Chardonnay, Sauvignon Blanc, Pinot Noir, Cabernet Shiraz and Cabernet Sauvignon.

Distribution: Mailing list and cellar door sales; extensive retail distribution through I. H. Baker Wines & Spirits (eastern states) and own sales representative (Perth); WA country through H. M. Beigew & Co. Cellar door sales 10 a.m. to 4 p.m. Monday to Saturday, 12 to 4 p.m. Sunday. Mailing-list enquiries as above.

Prices: $13.45 to $18.99 retail.

Vintage Rating 1986–89: White: '89, '88, '87, '86. Red: '88, '87, '89, '86.

Outstanding Prior Vintages: White: '82, '85. Red: '81, '85.

Tasting Notes:

1988 RHINE RIESLING [89] Colour: very good

green-yellow. *Bouquet:* rich and very full, with strong lime/passionfruit aromas. *Palate:* firm, concentrated and powerful, with very rich, sweet fruit and a markedly long finish. Drink '90–'93.

1988 CHARDONNAY [87] Colour: medium green-yellow. *Bouquet:* tangy grapefruit and toasty charred oak. *Palate:* an extremely stylish wine, with ultra-sophisticated oak handling, fine structure and long flavour to the fruity finish. Drink '90–'92.

1988 SAUVIGNON BLANC [85] Colour: light green-yellow. *Bouquet:* smoky/spicy oak, beautifully integrated and balanced, with light to medium herbaceous fruit. *Palate:* fresh, crisp fruit flavours; spicy oak tends to dominate, but is well handled and will come into perfect balance with a little more time; a wine of very good overall weight. Drink '90–'91.

1988 SHIRAZ [83] Colour: full purple-red. *Bouquet:* spotlessly clean with full, rich and dense concentrated fruit. *Palate:* rich and concentrated red berry flavours with a touch of pepper in the background, and soft persistent tannins. Drink '93–'97.

1987 CABERNET SHIRAZ [86] Colour: medium purple-red. *Bouquet:* clean, with nicely balanced and integrated fruit and oak, and some faint tobacco-leaf aromas. *Palate:* most attractive clean, sweet red berry fruits, with a light touch of vanillan/charred oak; a wine of real elegance. Drink '91–'95.

1987 CABERNET SAUVIGNON [80] Colour: medium purple-red. *Bouquet:* very clean; red berry fruit of medium weight surrounded by soft lemony/vanillan oak. *Palate:* once again, the oak is quite evident, but it is complex and well integrated and balanced; textured red berry fruit rounds off another very good red wine. Drink '92–'96.

Summary: Goundrey is throwing out the challenge to Plantagenet as the senior winery in the Mount Barker district: both are producing some superb wines in quantities which will ensure Australia-wide recognition.

🍇 *HAY RIVER*

Location: Denmark Road, Mount Barker, 6324; 30 km west of Mount Barker (vineyard only).

Winemaker: Goundrey (contract).

1989 Production: 1100 cases.

Principal Wines: Only one grape is grown and only one wine is made: Cabernet Sauvignon.

Distribution: Limited Perth retail distribution. No cellar door sales nor eastern states distribution.

Prices: $12 retail.

Vintage Rating 1986–89: '89, '88, '86, '87.

Tasting Notes:

1987 CABERNET SAUVIGNON [82] Colour: medium to full-red purple. *Bouquet:* clean, light fruit with most attractive spicy oak. *Palate:* once again, lovely spicy oak is the main feature of the wine, which is of medium body and a clean soft finish. Drink '91–'94.

Summary: The beautiful and remote vineyard of Hay River has, right from the first vintage, produced remarkably soft and luscious cabernet that is quite distinct from most of the Mount Barker vineyards.

🍇 *HOWARD PARK*

Location: Lot 11, Little River Road, Denmark, 6333.
(098) 48 1261.

Winemaker: John Wade.

1989 Production: 850 cases.

Principal Wines: Riesling and Cabernet Sauvignon.

Distribution: Fine wine retail and restaurant distribution New South Wales and Victoria through Tucker, Seabrook, Caon Group; otherwise by mail order.

Prices: Riesling $165 per case; Cabernet Sauvignon $250 per case (mail order).

Vintage Rating 1986–89: White: '89, '87, '86, '88.

Red: '89, '87, '88, '86.

Tasting Notes:

1988 RHINE RIESLING [81] Colour: light green-yellow. *Bouquet:* fine, tight and reserved, with some floral citrus/lime aromas. *Palate:* pronounced lime flavours with a toasty/chalky overlay, and a slightly hard finish; will benefit from cellar age. Drink '91–'95.

1987 CABERNET SAUVIGNON [86] Colour: medium purple-red. *Bouquet:* very clean; light to medium red berry/cassis fruit with soft charred/vanillan oak. *Palate:* a fine, elegant and complex wine, with cassis red berry flavours and a touch of charred oak replicating the bouquet; despite its gentle tannins, has very good structure and is still extremely youthful. Drink '93–'99.

Summary: John Wade is a vastly experienced winemaker, and it is hardly surprising that the tiny quantities of wines produced under the Howard Park label are of exemplary quality.

Vintage Rating 1986–89: White: '86, '89, '88, '87. Red: '86, '87 ('88 and '89 not yet rated).

Tasting Notes:

1987 CABERNET SAUVIGNON [59] Colour: medium to full red. *Bouquet:* concentrated berry aromas and strong charred oak, with some bottle development evident. *Palate:* raw oak entirely overwhelms some very good fruit underneath; the oak comes as a surprise after the bouquet, but unfortunately unbalances what might have been a very good wine. Presumably limited production made oak handling difficult. Drink '92–'95.

Summary: Some lovely wines have been made, albeit in small quantities, under the Jingalla label; the 1986 Cabernet Sauvignon won the gold medal and trophy for Best Dry Red in the open classes of the Mount Barker Wine Show, and this is far more typical of what the winery has to offer.

JINGALLA

Location: RMB 114 Bolganup Dam Road, Porongurup, 6324; 24 km east of Mount Barker.
(098) 53 1023 or 53 1014

Winemakers: Geoff Clarke and Rodney Hooper (contract).

1989 Production: 1500 cases.

Principal Wines: Rhine Riesling, Late Harvest Riesling, Verdelho, Cabernet Sauvignon and Port.

Distribution: Almost exclusively cellar door sales and mailing list; cellar door sales 10.30 a.m. to 5 p.m. 7 days; limited retail distribution in Perth and Western Australian country disticts.

Prices: $8 to $15.50 cellar door.

KARRELEA ESTATE

Location: Duck Road, Mount Barker, 6324; (vineyard only).
(098) 511 838.

Winemaker: Plantagenet Wines (contract).

1989 Production: Approximately 500 cases.

Principal Wines: Rhine Riesling, Sauvignon Blanc, Pinot Noir, and Cabernet Sauvignon Cabernet Franc Merlot.

Distribution: Chiefly mailing list and very limited retail distribution in Perth and through Sutherland Cellars, Melbourne; mailing list enquiries to PO Box 3, Karrelea Estate, Mount Barker, 6324. Cellar door sales (weekends only) planned for 1989–90.

Prices: $10 to $15 cellar door.

Vintage Rating 1986–89: White: '89, '87, '88, '86.

Red: '89, '87, '88, '86.

Tasting Notes:

1989 RHINE RIESLING [70] Colour: light to medium yellow-green. *Bouquet:* voluminous broad lime/pineapple aromas, with a very slight cosmetic overtone. *Palate:* strong pineapple/passionfruit flavours, presumably fleshed out by a degree of botrytis; may come together well in the short term and merit higher points. Drink '90–'91.

1988 RHINE RIESLING [74] Colour: light green-yellow. *Bouquet:* very clean with floral lime aromas of some intensity. *Palate:* clean and light, with gentle acid; the fruit is soft, but the wine has been well made. Drink '90.

1988 SAUVIGNON BLANC [77] Colour: light green-yellow. *Bouquet:* soft, clean and smoky; not particularly varietal, but clean and well made. *Palate:* more varietal character evident than the bouquet would suggest; firm and rich; has length to tropical gooseberry flavours. Drink '90–'91.

Summary: The initial releases from Karrelea Estate have all been full of promise; the vineyard clearly produces fruit of above average quality thanks to the combined efforts of the Shearer family.

🍇 *KARRI VIEW*

Location: Scotsdale Road, Denmark, 6333; (vineyard only). (098) 40 9381.

Winemaker: John Wade (contract).

1989 Production : 60 cases.

Principal Wines: Presently only Pinot Noir and Chardonnay, but 1989 plantings of shiraz, cabernet sauvignon and sauvignon blanc will extend the range.

Distribution: Initially ex-cellar only; cellar door sales area under construction and should be open 1990.

Prices: $8 to $15 cellar door.

Summary: A family operation of the Mansor family; the vineyard is surrounded by wonderful karri trees, providing a picturesque setting for the cellar door sales facility.

🍇 *LEFROY BROOK VINEYARD*

Location: Cascades Road, Pemberton, near Manjimup, 6258 (vineyard only).

Winemaker: Peter Fimmell (contract).

1989 Production : Of miniscule proportions.

Principal Wines: Pinot Noir and Chardonnay.

Distribution: 1989 Pinot Noir to be released early 1991; available at selected outlets in Perth and by mail order. 1989 Chardonnay will be available by mail order only.

Prices: Chardonnay $17 and Pinot Noir $26 mail order.

Tasting Notes:

1989 PINOT NOIR [CS] Colour: medium purple-red. *Bouquet:* rather neutral, soft and clean slightly sweet fruit with some strawberry aromas. *Palate:* far more expressive than the bouquet, with attractive sweet cherry/strawberry fruit showing very good varietal character in a Volnay style. Headed towards 75 points or above.

Summary: Patrick and Barbara Holt have established a no-holds-barred Burgundian approach to vine spacing and planting, aiming at one to two bottles of wine per vine. They say "like a number of others, we are chasing the holy grail of a truly Burgundian Pinot". As the introduction to this chapter indicates, they may well bring the Burgundians to Manjimup, even if they do not take Manjimup to Burgundy.

🍇 *NARANG WINES*

Location: Woodlands, Porongurup, 6324; 19km east of Mount Barker. (098) 53 1009.

Winemaker: John Wade (contract).

1989 Production: 550 cases.

Principal Wines: Rhine Riesling only release to date; new plantings of chardonnay and shiraz will increase the range in future years.

Distribution: Principally cellar door sales and mailing list. Cellar door sales 10 a.m. to 5 p.m. weekends and public holidays, and at other times by appointment. Mailing list enquiries to PO Box 146, Mount Barker, 6324. Limited retail distribution serviced direct ex-winery.

Prices: $11 cellar door.

Vintage Rating 1987–89: '89, '88, '87.

Tasting Notes:

1987 RHINE RIESLING [76] Colour: very good light green-yellow. *Bouquet:* potent and fine, with a faint but not unattractive seaweed aroma. *Palate:* very elegant, fine and long, with gently toasty fruit, excellent balance and finishing with soft acid. Now sold out, but was a relatively recent tasting. Drink '90.

Summary: The McGready family is gradually extending the plantings on its spectacularly situated vineyard nestling at the base of the towering rocks of the Porongurups. Quality is excellent, and the small production is worth seeking out.

PLANTAGENET

Location: Albany Highway, Mount Baker, 6324; on northern outskirts of township.
(098) 51 1150; Fax (098) 51 1839.

Winemaker: John Wade.

1989 Production: 11,200 cases.

Principal Wines: An ever-expanding range of table and foritifed wines is made, produced from a variety of grapes partly estate grown, partly purchased from other vineyards in the district, but also coming from the Bindoon region. The source of all the grapes is clearly stated on the label. Small releases of high-quality table

wines, restricted to cellar door and mailing list sales, appear under the Kings Reserve Series; others simply under the Plantagenet label, but indicating both the district and vineyard of source. Wines include Rhine Riesling, Chenin Blanc, Chardonnay, Frontignac, Fleur, Shiraz, Cabernet Sauvignon and Cabernet Hermitage.

Distribution: Significant retail distribution through wholesale agents in each State; also active mailing list and cellar door sales. Cellar door sales 9 a.m. to 5 p.m. Monday to Saturday; mailing list enquiries to PO Box 122, Mount Barker, 6324. Wholesale distributors are West Coast Wines, Perth; Fesq & Co., Sydney; Rutherglen Wine Co., Melbourne; Tallerman & Co. Pty Ltd, Brisbane; and B. H. MacLachlan Pty Ltd, Adelaide.

Prices: $10 to $18 retail.

Vintage Rating 1986–89: White: '89, '87, '86, '88. Red: '89,. '86, '88, '87.

Outstanding Prior Vintages: '77, '83, '85.

Tasting Notes:

1989 FRONTIGNAC [70] Colour: light green-yellow. *Bouquet:* light, spicy/grapy/toasty aromas. *Palate:* fresh and fruity, with the accent on crispness rather than sweetness; very well made, even though an unashamedly commercial style. Drink '90.

1988 CHARDONNAY [77] Colour: medium to full yellow-green. *Bouquet:* strong barrel ferment characters allied with complex fruit flavours; strong, lemony oak. *Palate:* very rich and complex fruit and barrel ferment characters, but held back by slightly hessiany oak and a touch of hardness in the finish. A wine that I have tasted on a number of occasions, and that always seems different. Drink '90–'93.

1988 PINOT NOIR [75] Colour: very good light red-purple. *Bouquet:* light, clean cherry plum fruit aromas. *Palate:* clean and pleasant fruit, with a touch of strawberry plum flavour and a nice twist of spice; a well handled wine, and the best pinot noir to come from the district other than Wignall's. Drink '90–'91.

1987 SHIRAZ [80] Colour: medium red. *Bouquet:* complex fruit, without the peppery spice one often finds in Plantagenet wines; some lemony oak. *Palate:* a beautifully textured and structured wine, with attractive red berry fruit set against strong lemony oak; will mature well. Drink '92–'96.

1987 CABERNET SAUVIGNON [81] Colour: medium to full red-purple. *Bouquet:* rather closed, but does have the latent fruit to develop with bottle age. *Palate:* much more accessible, rich and textured, with good mouth-feel and a nice touch of lemony oak. Drink '92–'95.

Summary: The 1987 reds of Plantagenet are something of a soft landing after the absolutely brilliant '86 wines. It is worth noting that with great honesty Plantagenet rates the '87s least of the last four vintages, even though it is the vintage currently on offer. Certainly, the overall quality of wines under the Plantagenet label is first-class.

SHEMARIN

Location: 19 Third Avenue, Mount Lawley, 6050. (098) 51 1682.

Winemaker: Rob Bowen.

1989 Production: 1250 cases.

Principal Wines: Shemarin is the label for the very small quantities of wine which former Plantagenet winemaker Rob Bowen has made on his own account on and off since 1980. The 1985 vintage was the first vintage from estate-grown grapes; intermittently since 1980 parcels of wine have been made from grapes purchased in from other growers in the region. The estate will concentrate on Sauvignon Blanc, Chardonnay and Hermitage. Other releases (largely made from purchased grapes) have included and will in the future include Chenin Blanc, Chardonnay, Hermitage, Zinfandel and Cabernet Sauvignon.

Distribution: By mailing list and through The Oak Barrel, Sydney; Tallerman & Co., Brisbane; and numerous retail outlets, Perth.

Prices: $13 Sauvignon Blanc.

Vintage Rating 1986–89: '88, '89, '87, '86.

Tasting Notes:

1989 SAUVIGNON BLANC [CS] Colour: light to medium straw-yellow. *Bouquet:* very rich, full honeyed/tropical fruity aromas, not altogether typical of variety but attractive nonetheless. *Palate:* rich, full honeyed style; very forward with some tangy gooseberry flavours on the finish. Certainly has potential; a low sulphur sample, and it will be freshened and tightened up prior to bottling.

Summary: With Rob Bowen's move to Perth and involvement in extensive consultancy work, the range for Shemarin is likely to open up and quantities increase. Some lovely wines have appeared under the label in the past, and will no doubt do so in the future.

 TINGLE-WOOD WINES

Location: Glenrowan Road, Denmark, 6333; 8 km north-west of town; (handbill/map available from Denmark Tourist Bureau). (098) 40 9218.

Winemaker: Plantagenet (contract).

1989 Production: Not stated but sufficient for cellar door sales.

Principal Wines: Rhine Riesling and Cabernet Shiraz.

Distribution: Exclusively cellar door sales and mailing list; cellar door sales 9 a.m. to 5 p.m. 7 days. Mailing list enquiries to PO Box 160, Denmark, 6333.

Prices: $9 cellar door.

Summary: Tingle-wood is truly one of the most extraordinary vineyards, established on the very edge of a massive tingle-wood forest, which had to be cleared for the vineyard, with massive rocks surfacing along the vine rows. However, the concentration of flavour in the wines makes up for all the difficulties in persuading the vines to grow in the first place.

WIGNALLS KING RIVER

Location: Chester Pass Road (Highway 1), Albany, 6330; 6km north-east of Albany.
(098) 41 2848.

Winemaker: John Wade (contract).

1989 Production: 2000 cases.

Principal Wines: Chardonnay, Sauvignon Blanc and Pinot Noir.

Distribution: Principally mailing list and cellar door sales. Limited retail distribution through Barrique Fine Wines Agency, Brisbane; Sutherland Cellars, Melbourne; and Oddbins, Sydney. Mailing list enquiries to PO Box 248, Albany, 6330. Cellar door sales 10 a.m. to 4 p.m. Monday to Saturday. Closed July and August except by appointment.

Prices: $8 to $16 cellar door.

Tasting Notes:

1989 SAUVIGNON BLANC [CS] Colour: very light straw-green. *Bouquet:* clean, with strong passionfruit/peach aromas. *Palate:* light, clean passionfruit peach fruit with soft acid; unusual varietal flavours showing early in its life, and may have been yeast influenced, but none-theless very attractive and highly commercial. Should merit high points.

1988 CHARDONNAY [83] Colour: medium yellow-green. *Bouquet:* smooth and quite solid tangy grapefruit aromas. *Palate:* complex melon/fig/grapefruit flavours with some honeyed bottle development; slightly more oak might have given greater structure. Nonetheless, a good wine. Drink '90–'92.

Summary: Bill and Pat Wignall's King River vineyard is situated on the outskirts of the town

of Albany, which has a strong maritime influence resulting in budburst coming exceptionally early and yet vintage finishing late. The long ripening season is obviously beneficial for fruit quality, and some exciting wines (especially pinot noir) have come from what are still relatively young vines. The future looks very promising indeed.

Margaret River

1988 VINTAGE

1988 was a year the vignerons of the Margaret River would by and large prefer to forget. Long used to problems with the flowering and setting of rhine riesling and chardonnay, this year spring hail and strong winds brought havoc among the later flowering varieties, cabernet sauvignon and merlot.

An initially mild summer gave way to a heatwave in February, with record temperatures over a prolonged period. Harvest was brought forward very rapidly, but the early ripening varieties such as chardonnay and pinot noir suffered least and came into the wineries in good condition. Yields were slightly below average.

The vines reacted adversely to the extreme stress of the hot spell, and the much reduced crops of cabernet sauvignon (merlot was non-existent in some vineyards) ripened unevenly, and, in some instances, inadequately.

Acids are accordingly low, and soft, fleshy early maturing red wines can be expected. White wine styles are varied: there are some herbaceous semillons in typical Margaret River style, but overall the white wines will be more delicate and less aromatic than usual.

1989 VINTAGE

Once again, it was a tortuous and troubled spring. Budburst was up to one week later than usual, but strong winds and hail storms again stunted growth, and caused very erratic set in chardonnay, riesling and pinot noir. In this respect the year was the reverse of 1988, because the later varieties set well.

The season continued to be very difficult. Persistent rains arrived at the end of February and continued through into March, causing substantial rot problems in some vineyards. Others, with different canopy management schemes and better spray programmes, largely escaped these problems, and although yields were down, quality was very high in some instances. Both Cullens and Evans and Tate, for example, rate the year as outstanding for white wines.

Overall the red wines were somewhat disappointing, with a tendency to low acid and high pH. But the greatest threat of all came from birds, which attacked in unprecedented numbers and with unprecedented ferocity, thanks to a total failure in the flowering of the gum trees.

THE CHANGES

There are three new entries: Eagle Bay Estate, Lenton Brae and Woody Nook. Fermoy Estate, a very short entry last year (in its infancy), has a sharply raised profile thanks to its success at the hotly contested 1989 Sheraton Wine Awards.

These awards are unusual in that only one gold and one silver medal are awarded in each class, and Fermoy Estate won the gold medal in competition with 44 other wines in the light bodied red class, accounting for the most distinguished names in so doing. It was a fairytale start for Perth-based chartered accountant and Western Mining director John Anderson and for his youthful winemaker Michael Kelly, who learnt his trade at Mount Mary in the Yarra Valley.

Eagle Bay Estate, the future retirement hobby of Perth lawyer Jim Mazza, Lenton Brae and Woody Nook (the name chosen by its English owners) are all low key operations as yet, although Woody Nook has the advantage of a qualified and experienced winemaker, John Smith.

With 26 entries, Margaret River is an important winemaking region by any standard. Its importance was underlined by the fact that it won top spot in the four dry table wine classes at the 1989 Sheraton Wine Awards. Willespie took out the gold medal in the Full Bodied Dry Red class, while Evans and Tate won the gold medal in the Light Bodied White class, and came first in the Full Bodied White class with a silver medal. Given the fairly troubled vintages in 1988 and 1989, that is no mean achievement.

AMBERLEY ESTATE

Location: Wildwood and Thornton Road, Yallingup, 6282; 7 km south of Dunsborough (vineyard only).

Winemaker: To be appointed.

1989 Production: All grapes sold.

Principal Wines: Will be made from semillon and sauvignon blanc, chardonnay, chenin blanc, shiraz, and a blend of cabernet sauvignon, cabernet franc and merlot.

Summary: The first Amberley Estate Wines will be made in 1990 in a new winery to be erected on site prior to that vintage. It will be a substantial crush, as 50 tonnes of grapes were produced in 1989.

ASHBROOK ESTATE

Location: Harman's South Road, Willyabrup, 6284; 10 km north-east of Margaret River. (097) 55 6262.

Winemakers: The Devitt family.

1989 Production: 3500 to 4000 cases.

Principal Wines: A limited range of varietal table wines including Semillon, Chardonnay, Verdelho, Rhine Riesling, Sauvignon Blanc and Cabernet Sauvignon.

Distribution: Principally cellar door sales and mailing list; cellar door sales 11 a.m. to 5 p.m. weekends and public holidays. Mailing list enquiries to PO Box 263, West Perth, 6005; telephone (09) 481 0977. Distribution through The Specialist Wine Company, Sydney; Caon Tucker & Co. (WA) Pty Ltd, Perth; and Sutherland Cellars, Melbourne.

Prices: $11 to $18 cellar door.

Summary: Ashbrook Estate does not participate in the show judging system and prefers, in Tony

Devitt's words, "to let the client make up his or her mind". He continues "the business is very small and we deal with our clients on a very personal basis". Accordingly, no wines were available for tasting.

CAPE CLAIRAULT

Location: Henry Road, Willyabrup, 6284; 19 km north-east of Margaret River. (097) 55 5229 or (097) 55 6225.

Winemakers: Ian Lewis, Jan and Mike Davies.

1989 Production: 2500 cases.

Principal Wines: Semillon Sauvignon Blanc, Sauvignon Blanc, Rhine Riesling, Cabernet Sauvignon and Vintage Port.

Distribution: Principally cellar door and mailinglist. Cellar door sales 10 a.m. to 5 p.m. Monday to Saturday (and Sunday during school holidays). Limited retail sales distribution through Sutherland Cellars, Melbourne; Carol-Ann Classic Wines, Sydney; and Lionel Samson & Son, Perth. Mailing list enquiries to CMB Carbunup River, 6280.

Prices: $9 to $19 cellar door.

Vintage Rating 1986–89: White: '89, '88, '87, '86. Red: '86, '87, '89, '88.

Tasting Notes:

1989 SAUVIGNON BLANC [CS] Colour: medium straw yellow-green. *Bouquet:* full flavoured, with good varietal character but distinct fermentation characters persisting early in its life (before bottling). *Palate:* again, strong primary fruit flavours showing considerable potential provided the wine is cleaned up.

1989 SEMILLON SAUVIGNON BLANC [CS] Colour: light to medium yellow-green. *Bouquet:* very full fruit with considerable potential; some bitter fermentation/sulphide characters evident early in its life. *Palate:* strong melon/grapefruit/ herbaceous fruit, again with obvious potential, but needing work.

Summary: Cape Clairault has enjoyed great success with its white and red wines over the years, winning a gold medal at the 1988 Sheraton Wine Awards for its Sauvignon Blanc and the Trophy for Best Red of Show at the 1987 Lord Forrest competition. On its track record, there should be no problems with the 1989 white wines once they are bottled and come onto the market, even if the 1987 Cabernet Sauvignon is disappointing.

🍇 CAPE MENTELLE

Location: Off Wallcliffe Road, Margaret River, 6285; 3 km west of town.
(097) 57 2070; Fax (097) 57 2770.

Winemakers: David Hohnen and John Durham.

1989 Production: 13,000 cases.

Principal Wines: Now famous as a Cabernet Sauvignon specialist, but offers an eclectic choice of Semillon (which includes a touch of sauvignon blanc and chenin blanc), Rhine Riesling, Zinfandel, Hermitage and Cabernet Sauvignon.

Distribution: Retail, cellar door and mailing list sales. Cellar door sales 10 a.m. to 4.30 p.m. 7 days. Substantial sales through fine wine retailers with wholesale distributors in each State. For mailing list (and regular handsome bulletins) write to PO Box 110, Margaret River, 6285.

Prices: $10 to $18.60 cellar door.

Vintage Rating 1986–89: '88, '89, '87, '86.

Outstanding Prior Vintages: '82, '83.

Tasting Notes:

1988 CHARDONNAY [77] Colour: medium straw-green. *Bouquet:* very complex, bottle-developed aromas, with some distinctly burgundian overtones. *Palate:* rich, lemony, tangy oak set against full fruit; some smoky characters still lingering; long finish. Drink '90–'92.

1988 SEMILLON SAUVIGNON BLANC [87] Colour: light straw-green. *Bouquet:* voluminous herbal/grassy fruit, very clean and by far the best wine of this style to come out under the Cape Mentelle label. *Palate:* a lovely tangy wine with high quality, rich herbal/gooseberry flavours; quite delicious. Drink '90–'93.

1987 ZINFANDEL [90] Colour: bright medium to full purple-red. *Bouquet:* spotlessly clean, with lovely peppery fruit in the style of a top quality Rhone Valley shiraz. *Palate:* a lovely, lively spicy wine with touches of cherry fruit; fresh and vibrant, with excellent structure and balance. Utterly belies its 14 degrees of alcohol. Drink '90–'92.

1987 CABERNET SAUVIGNON [82] Colour: medium red-purple. *Bouquet:* fragrant, leafy cabernet aromas, showing less richness and density than some of the earlier wines. *Palate:* very clean leafy/herbal/cassis fruit; nicely balanced tannins; simply lacks the fruit flesh of the very best Cape Mentelle cabernets. Drink '91–'95.

Summary: Cape Mentelle is, without question, one of the great names of the Margaret River. Owner/winemaker David Hohnen is a dedicated, indeed passionately dedicated, winemaker with a fierce pride in his wines, and a better than average idea about marketing them. Cape Mentelle deserves every bit of success and recognition it gets.

🍇 CHATEAU XANADU

Location: Railway Terrace, off Wallcliffe Road, Margaret River, 6285; 4 km west of town.
(097) 57 2581.

Winemaker: Conor Lagan.

1989 Production: 5000 cases.

Principal Wines: Chardonnay, Semillon, Semillon II, Sauvignon Blanc, Cabernet Sauvignon and Cabernet Franc.

Distribution: Principally cellar door sales and mailing list. Significant retail sales in Perth; eastern States limited. Cellar door sales 10 a.m. to 4.30 p.m. Monday to Saturday, 11 a.m. to 4.30 p.m. Sunday. Mailing list enquiries to PO Box 144, Margaret River, 6285.

Prices: $11 to $24 cellar door.

Vintage Rating 1986–89: White: '87, '86, '89, '88. Red: '86, '87, '89, '88.

Tasting Notes:

1989 SEMILLON [76] Colour: light green-yellow. _Bouquet:_ clean, soft sweet peachy fruit. _Palate:_ light, soft peachy/vanillan fruit in a most attractive yet unusual style for Margaret River, and which seems to be the hallmark of the best whites of the year. Drink '90–'93.

1988 CHARDONNAY [75] Colour: medium yellow-green. _Bouquet:_ clean, smooth and soft rounded vanillan oak and fruit. _Palate:_ smooth, rich and rounded structure, with soft buttery fruit and ever so slightly hessiany oak. An early maturing style. Drink '90–'91.

Summary: As was the case last year, Chateau Xanadu is producing some very attractive white wines, but what I can only describe as aberrational red wines. The 1986 Cabernet Sauvignon had absolutely an unacceptable degree of volatility. Fresh from Roseworthy, Conor Lagan took over winemaking responsibilities at short notice for the 1989 vintage, and seems to have more than successfully met the challenge.

🍇 CULLENS WILLYABRUP

Location: Caves Road, Willyabrup via Cowaramup, 6284; 15 km north-west of Margaret River. (097) 55 5277.

Winemaker: Vanya Cullen.

1989 Production: Approximately 8000 cases.

Principal Wines: Classic range of white and red

table wines: Chardonnay, Semillon, Sauvignon Blanc, Rhine Riesling (dry), Sauvignon Blanc Sauternes style, Pinot Noir and Cabernet Merlot.

Distribution: National fine wine retail distribution. Cellar door and mailing list. Cellar door sales 10 a.m. to 4 p.m. Monday to Saturday. Mailing list, PO Box 17, Cowaramup, 6284. UK distributors, Heyman Bros,130 Ebury Street, London.

Prices: $8 to $18 cellar door.

Vintage Rating 1986–89: White: '89, '86, '88, '87. Red: '89, '86, '88, '87.

Outstanding Prior Vintages: '76, '82.

Tasting Notes:

1988 SEMILLON [78] Colour: medium yellow-green. _Bouquet:_ intense tobacco herbal aromas in a style often encountered in the Margaret River. _Palate:_ similar strong herbal/tobacco fruit; light oak background; a wine which raises the question when is a semillon not a semillon, and also suggests that it is possible to make a vinous virtue of necessity. Drink '90–'91.

1988 CHARDONNAY [84] Colour: medium to full yellow-green. _Bouquet:_ warm, sweet vanillan/ coconut oak with soft, clean fruit. _Palate:_ quite complex, with pronounced sweet/butterscotch oak and soft peachy fruit; very full-flavoured, and cloys fractionally on the finish. Drink '90–'91.

1988 SAUVIGNON BLANC [74] Colour: light straw-yellow. _Bouquet:_ quite pronounced spicy/ lemony oak with good fruit weight and some varietal character. _Palate:_ strong, spicy lemony oak; light but lively fruit does not quite carry the oak as yet; a wine with some future in front of it. Drink '90–'92.

1987 CABERNET SAUVIGNON MERLOT [85] Colour: medium purple-red. _Bouquet:_ strong, concentrated, classic cabernet aroma, ripe but not over-ripe; good supporting oak. _Palate:_ a fine, elegant wine; lighter and more accessible than many of the young Cullen reds; soft but persistent tannins. Drink '92–'97.

Summary: I have noticed a fairly marked degree of bottle variation amongst the Cullen white wines, suggesting that there may be one or two intermittent bottling problems. The cabernet sauvignon merlot blend is, as ever, absolutely reliable.

EAGLE BAY ESTATE

Location: Eagle Bay Road, Eagle Bay ;
6 km west of Dunsborough.
(09) 325 7488 or (097) 55 3346.

Winemaker: Dorham Mann (consultant).

1989 Production: Less than 200 cases (devastated by birds).

Principal Wines: Rhine Riesling, Sauvignon Blanc, Semillon, Chardonnay, Shiraz and Merlot.

Distribution: Exclusively by cellar door sales; winery open during school holidays and on public holidays 9 a.m. to 5 p.m. No mailing list.

Prices: $14.50.

Tasting Notes:

1988 SHIRAZ [55] Colour: vibrant light purple-red. *Bouquet:* very light, with strong free SO₂ muffling fruit. *Palate:* again, high SO₂ adds a sharp edge to very attractive underlying fruit. Drink '92–'94.

Summary: Eagle Bay Estate will always remain a small operation as the retirement hobby of Perth lawyer James Mazza.

EVANS AND TATE REDBROOK ESTATE

Location: Metricup Road, Willyabrup, 6284.
(097) 55 6244.

Winemaker: Krister Jonsson

1989 Production: 11,000 cases.

Principal Wines: A limited range of fine varietal table wines comprising Semillon, Sauvignon Blanc, Chardonnay, Hermitage, Merlot and Cabernet Sauvignon.

Distribution: National fine wine retail distribution through wholesale agents Caon & Co., SA; I. H. Baker and Co., NSW and Qld; The Wine Co., Vic. Distributed direct in WA Cellar door sales 11 a.m. to 4 p.m 7 days, and mailing list; mailing list address: Evans and Tate, PO Cowaramup, 6284.

Prices: $11 to $25 recommended retail.

Vintage Rating 1986–89: White: '89, '88, '87, '86. Red: '88, '87, '89, '86.

Outstanding Prior Vintages: '81, '82, '84.

Tasting Notes:

1989 MARGARET RIVER SEMILLON [93] Colour: strong green-yellow. *Bouquet:* complex, smoky/tangy concentrated fruit. *Palate:* an exceptionally fine, fruit driven wine; gorgeous, soft, mouth-filling tangy grapefruit flavours with perfect sugar/acid balance. None of those Margaret River green/grassy characters, yet there is a citric character to the fruit that is no doubt a regional/vintage manifestation. Drink '90–'94.

1989 TWO VINEYARDS CHARDONNAY [CS] Colour: medium to full yellow-green. *Bouquet:* a cask sample tasted in July '89 was exceptionally forward, rich and complex, but may have needed sulphur adjusting. *Palate:* again, exceptionally rich forward and complex; if it realises its full potential is headed towards 90 points or more.

1989 MARGARET RIVER CLASSIC [81] Colour: very light green-yellow. *Bouquet:* highly floral, lifted tropical fruit salad/peach fruit aromas, possibly yeast-influenced. *Palate:* striking peachy/fruit salad flavours; a truly fascinating wine; extremely commercial and seductive, and continuing the fruit salad style for Evans and Tate from 1989. A blend of sauvignon blanc and chenin blanc. Drink '90–'91.

1988 SEMILLON [80] Colour: light green-yellow. *Bouquet:* fragrant grassy/ tobacco fruit, typical of Margaret River in some vintages, and reminiscent of New Zealand semillon, with all of its sauvignon blanc connotations. *Palate:* quite elegant; clean herbal/tobacco flavours, but does have some richness and mouthfeel; crisp, light finish. Drink '90.

1987 HERMITAGE [74] Colour: medium purple-red. *Bouquet:* that haunting, fascinating and inexplicable aroma that one minute smells of sulphide and the next minute of vibrantly fresh crushed pepper and spice. *Palate:* very light, clean youthful and crisp peppery shiraz, which proves beyond doubt that what appears to be sulphide on the nose is in fact pepper spice, although many very experienced judges can find this difficult to believe or accept. At the end of the day, the wine does lack sufficient fruit richness and weight to lift it into the highest class. Drink '90–'91.

1987 CABERNET SAUVIGNON [74] Colour: light to medium red-purple. *Bouquet:* firm, leathery astringent cabernet sauvignon, seemingly lacking full fruit ripeness. *Palate:* light to medium fruit with tangy lemony oak and just a suggestion of cassis/red berry fruit; low tannin and a fraction one dimensional. Drink '90–'93.

Summary: Evans and Tate have done quite magical things with their 1989 whites, which were the stars of the 1989 Sheraton Wine Awards in Perth. The red wine styles are slightly more controversial, increasingly looking as if they are made from grapes that are picked a fraction early, and that a desire for elegance has led to a loss of that all important ingredient—fruit richness.

FERMOY ESTATE

Location: Metricup Road, Willyabrup via Cowaramup, 6284; 20 km north-west of Margaret River.
(097) 55 6285.

Winemaker: Michael Kelly.

1989 Production: 1000 cases.

Principal Wines: Semillon/Sauvignon Blanc and Cabernet Sauvignon.

Distribution: Presently exclusively by mailing list to PO Box 123, Cowaramup, 6284. Cellar door sales planned from the summer of 1990–91 with hours yet to be determined. Winery and vineyard tours by appointment in the meantime.

Prices: $11.80 to $13.

Vintage Rating 1988–89: White: '89, '88. Red: '89, '88.

Tasting Notes:

1988 CABERNET SAUVIGNON [90] Colour: excellent medium to full purple-red. *Bouquet:* clean and fragrant, with complex leafy/berry fruit aromas and a suggestion of some slightly gamey characters. *Palate:* clean and fragrant spicy berry flavours; lively fruit with exceptionally good balance and length. Not a heavyweight wine by any standards, but a brilliantly structured one nonetheless. Will develop early. Drink '92–'95.

Summary: Fermoy Estate had a dream debut, winning the gold medal (and the only gold medal) in the Light Bodied Red class at the 1989 Sheraton Wine Awards, beating a class of 44 West Australian red wines in so doing.

FREYCINET

Location: Lot 1, Gnarawary Road, Margaret River, 6285; 6 km south-west of town.
(097) 57 6358.

Winemaker: Peter Gherardi.

Principal Wines: Varietal wines comprise Sauvignon Blanc, Semillon, Chenin Blanc, Chardonnay and Cabernet Sauvignon/Merlot/Cabernet Franc blend.

Distribution: Retail and restaurant distribution in Western Australia. Wholesale distribution in Sydney, Melbourne, Brisbane and ACT.

Prices: $13 to $16.50.

Vintage Rating 1986–89: White: '88, '86, '89, '87. Red: '86, '87, '88, '89.

Tasting Notes:

1987 CABERNET SAUVIGNON [64] Colour: very good red-purple. *Bouquet:* firm cabernet fruit, with some rather leathery/gravelly astringency. *Palate:* very firm and rather hard cabernet sauvignon; some charred oak showing; light to medium tannin; a wine that seems to have been bottled too early, needing softening and handling to bring out the best of the powerful underlying fruit. Drink '92–'95.

1986 CABERNET SAUVIGNON [70] Colour: medium purple-red. *Bouquet:* firm, slightly astringent cabernet, but with nice red berry aromas. *Palate:* pleasant light red berry fruit, fresh and crisp; low tannin; rather simple oak lets the structure of the wine down. Drink '91–'94.

Summary: I have substantial reservations about the current Freycinet white wines, not-withstanding some very pleasant earlier vintages. The cabernets are very firm, slightly astringent, typically gravelly Margaret River styles that are quite austere but that will repay cellaring.

GILLESPIE VINEYARDS

Location: Davis Road, Witchcliffe, 6286; 10 km south of Margaret River.
(097) 57 6281.

Winemaker: Alastair Gillespie.

Principal Wines: Three wines only marketed: Semillon Sauvignon Blanc, Cabernet Sauvignon and Rhine Riesling.

Distribution: Principally cellar door and mailing list. Cellar door sales 10 a.m. to 4 p.m. Saturday or by appointment. Mailing list enquiries as above. Very limited retail distribution in Sydney and through Sutherland Cellars, Melbourne. Reasonable Perth retail and restaurant distribution.

Summary: Gillespie is adopting a relatively low profile; previous releases have provided very strong, robust cabernet sauvignon and less impressive white wines.

GRALYN CELLARS

Location: Caves Road, Willyabrup via Cowaramup, 6284; 15 km north-west of Margaret River.
(097) 44 6245.

Winemakers: Graham and Merilyn Hutton.

Principal Wines: Vintage Port specialists, also offering Rhine Riesling, Beaujolais, Hermitage, Cabernet Sauvignon, Hermitage Port, Cabernet Port and White Port (made from rhine riesling).

Distribution: Exclusively cellar door and mailing list. Cellar door sales 10.30 a.m. to 4.30 p.m. 7 days. Mailing list, c/o PO Box Cowaramup, 6284.

Tasting Notes:

1989 BEAUJOLAIS [70] Colour: very good crimson-purple. *Bouquet:* fresh fragrant plummy/berry fruit. *Palate:* wonderful fresh berry fruit, but with very pronounced residual sugar. The sweetness may upset the unwary, and might equally cause problems in the bottle if the wine has not been sterile filtered. Drink '90.

Summary: In recent years the Huttons have sold almost all the grapes from their excellent vineyard, one of the best in the Margaret River, but have cautiously re-entered the market with a limited range of wines, including the very attractive if rather eccentric 1989 Beaujolais.

HAPP'S

Location: Commonage Road, Dunsborough, 6281; 5 km south of Dunsborough.
(097) 55 3300.

Winemaker: Erland Happ.

1989 Production: Not stated, but usually around 5000 cases.

Principal Wines: Chardonnay, Cabernet Merlot, Merlot, Shiraz, Verdelho Muscat and Port.

Distribution: Principally cellar door and mailing list. Cellar door sales 10 a.m. to 5 p.m. 7 days. Mailing list, PO Dunsborough, 6281. Perth wholesale, Westel; UK imports through Horseshoe Wines.

Prices: $10 to $20 cellar door.

Vintage Rating 1986–89: '88, '86, '87 ('89 not yet rated).

Tasting Notes:

1987 MERLOT [64] Colour: light to medium purple-red. *Bouquet:* light but quite complex, with gently leafy/herbaceous aromas, a touch of mint and then some slightly gravelly characters. *Palate:* some unexpected spicy characters to the fruit, which is light and a fraction simple, lacking structure and oak. Drink '90–'92.

1987 CABERNET MERLOT [63] Colour: medium to full red-purple. *Bouquet:* of medium weight with red berry fruit tinged with some leathery/gravel characters. *Palate:* shows more fruit and structure than the bouquet, but a distinct mercaptan-derived bitterness mars a potentially excellent wine. Drink '90–'91.

1986 MERLOT [78] Colour: medium red, still with a touch of purple. *Bouquet:* quite complex secondary bottle-developed characters with a touch of typical merlot tobacco. *Palate:* a lovely elegant wine with strong merlot varietal character; complex leafy/tobacco flavours, yet not green; already close to its peak. Drink '90–'92.

1986 VINTAGE PORT [77] Colour: medium to full red-purple. *Bouquet:* clean, spicy fruit with light spirit; attractive style. *Palate:* most attractive spicy fruit, not too sweet and certainly not heavy; yet another light and lively vintage port from this region. Drink '90–'93.

Summary: Erl Happ cares greatly and thinks very deeply about his wines. He will not be particularly pleased with my review of some of them, but I have tasted the wines in several circumstances and come up with almost identical results.

🍇 *LEEUWIN ESTATE*

Location: Gnaraway Road, Margaret River, 6285; 5 km south of town.
(097) 57 6253.

Winemaker: Bob Cartwright.

1989 Production: 18,000 cases.

Principal Wines: Chardonnay, Rhine Riesling, Sauvignon Blanc, Pinot Noir and Cabernet Sauvignon. All wines offered with significant bottle-age and immaculate packaging. The Art Series labels added a new dimension to Australian wine marketing when first introduced.

Distribution: Extensive fine wine retail distribution (wholesale agents I. H. Baker & Co.). Cellar door sales 10 a.m. to 4.30 p.m. 7 days. Mailing list, PO Box 7441, Cloisters Square, Perth, 6000.

Prices: $16 to $42 retail.

Vintage Rating 1986–89: White: '87, '86, '88, '89. Red: '88, '87, '89, '86.

Outstanding Prior Vintages: '82, '85.

Tasting Notes:

1988 RHINE RIESLING [81[Colour: light green-yellow. *Bouquet:* very clean, aromatic/floral toasty lime aromas. *Palate:* flavourful and fruity with lime/toast characters; light to medium weight overall, with good balance. A very successful riesling for the district. Drink '90–'92.

1988 SAUVIGNON BLANC [83] Colour: light green-yellow. *Bouquet:* clean and smooth; quite concentrated varietal character, with overtones of gooseberry and considerable depth. *Palate:* clean and very smooth, with concentrated, soft, slightly sweet gooseberry fruit; soft acid finish. Drink '90–'93.

1988 GEWURZTRAMINER [73] Colour: bright light green-straw. *Bouquet:* clean but very light, with relatively subdued varietal character. *Palate:* really too light for top points; a beautifully made wine, but neither the fruit nor the varietal character is there. Drink '90.

1985 CHARDONNAY [84] Colour: very good, bright green-yellow of medium depth. *Bouquet:* exceedingly complex with strong burgundian (slightly cabbagey) overtones; tight, deep and rich. *Palate:* has rather less weight and richness than the bouquet would suggest, but the same very distinctive French style, with a pleasant dry finish; one of the rare Australian chardonnays to genuinely benefit from bottle-age. Drink '90–'92.

1985 CABERNET SAUVIGNON [85] Colour: medium red-purple. *Bouquet:* clean and classic leafy/tobacco/dark fruit aromas, concentrated and smooth; once again, comparisons with France are inevitable. *Palate:* fine and concentrated, with pronounced herbal/leafy fruit; good oak handling, but needs a fraction more flesh and sweet berry characters to move into the very highest class.

Summary: Leeuwin Estate is the showpiece of the Margaret River in more ways than one. Its wines are very expensive, but nothing is spared either in their production or marketing, and at the end of the day, the price simply indicates the excellence that Leeuwin strives for – and with its current releases has by and large achieved.

🍇LENTON BRAE

Location: Caves Road, Willyabrup, 6280. (097) 55 6255.

Winemaker: Tim Hallyburton.

Principal Wines: Semillon, Chardonnay, Sauvignon Blanc and Cabernet Merlot.

Distribution: Cellar door sales and mailing list; cellar door sales 8 a.m. to 5 p.m. 7 days. Mailing list enquiries to PO Box 30, South Perth, 6151.

Tasting Notes:

1988 SAUVIGNON BLANC [59] Colour: medium straw. *Bouquet:* very strong and rather unintegrated raw, oily lemony oak dominates fruit. *Palate:* raw, lemony oak dominates and lingers on the finish of a light bodied wine apparently made with grapes from young vines. Drink '90.

Summary: Lenton Brae is making its first tentative steps towards commercial production; the very limited volume of the wines produced so far makes winemaking difficult.

🍇MOSS BROTHERS

Location: Caves Road, Willyabrup, 6280. (097) 55 6290.

Principal Wines: Semillon, Chardonnay, Sauvignon Blanc, Cabernet Sauvignon/ Merlot/Cabernet Franc.

Distribution: Cellar door sales and mailing list; cellar door sales and mailing list enquiries to Carbunup Store, Carbunup, 6282.

Summary: A winery in its infancy, with several wines entered in the 1989 Sheraton Wine Award's competition. However they were not reviewable.

🍇MOSS WOOD

Location: Metricup Road, Willyabrup via Cowaramup, 6284; 18 km north-east of Margaret River. (097) 55 6266.

Winemaker: Keith Mugford.

1989 Production: 4000 cases.

Principal Wines: Chardonnay, Semillon, Pinot Noir and Cabernet Sauvignon.

Distribution: Fine wine retail distribution, cellar door and mailing list. Cellar door sales 10 a.m. to 4 p.m. (preferably by appointment). Mailing list, PO Box 52, Busselton, 6280.

Prices: $15 to $22 cellar door.

Vintage Rating 1986–89: White: '88, '89, '87, '86. Red: '87, '88, '89, '86.

Outstanding Prior Vintages: '77, '81, '83, '85.

Tasting Notes:

1987 PINOT NOIR [72] Colour: light red. *Bouquet:* light, with faint sappy/tobacco varietal character evident, but seemingly a little tired. *Palate:* again light bodied, but with more style evident; simply lacks intensity and fruit sweetness; there is also a suggestion of some volatility present. Drink '90.

1987 CABERNET SAUVIGNON [90] Colour: medium full red-purple. *Bouquet:* full and complex, with a near perfect amalgam of berry and leafy aromas; perfect weight and style.

Palate: a very stylish, elegant wine that utterly belies its 13.3% alcohol; a most attractive blend of dark fruits, cassis and a touch of tobacco; the finish is very long and clean. Drink '92–'96.

Summary: The '89 Moss Wood whites were not ready for tasting, and the '88s had sold out. Had they been available, I feel sure they would have rated very highly; Keith Mugford has hardly missed a beat in recent years. As ever, the Moss Wood Cabernet Sauvignon is quite superb, and it is little wonder that Moss Wood has such a high reputation.

PIERRO

Pierro
CHARDONNAY
H427   Product of Australia   750ml.

Location: Caves Road, Willyabrup via Cowaramup, 6284; 17.5 km north-west of Margaret River. (097) 55 6220.

Winemaker: Michael Peterkin.

1989 Production: 2500 cases.

Principal Wines: Les Trois Cuvees (a blend of sauvignon blanc, semillon and chardonnay), Chardonnay and Pinot Noir.

Distribution: Cellar door, mailing list and limited fine wine retail sales through Sutherland Cellars, Melbourne; Fesq & Co., Sydney; Fiorelli (Cairns) Pty Ltd, Queensland. Cellar door sales 10 a.m. to 5 p.m. 7 days, including school holidays and public holidays. Mailing list, PO Box 522, Busselton, 6280.

Prices: $10.90 to $19.90 cellar door.

Vintage Rating 1986–89: White: '87, '88, '89, '86. Red: '87, '89, '88, '86.

Outstanding Prior Vintages: '80, '82.

Tasting Notes:

1989 LES TROIS CUVEES [77] Colour: light green-yellow. *Bouquet:* soft clean and fruity, with some herbaceous/smoky overtones; well made. *Palate:* crisp, tangy fruit with good weight and length; little or no oak, but good mouthfeel. Drink '90–'92.

1988 CHARDONNAY [72] Colour: light to medium yellow-green. *Bouquet:* soft, with coconut/vanillan oak and light to medium fruit. *Palate:* a clean, rather one-dimensional wine, with vanillan/coconut oak again quite evident; could conceivably develop further complexity with greater bottle age. Drink '90 –'92.

1986 CHARDONNAY [88] Colour: medium yellow-green. *Bouquet:* very complex, intense and concentrated tangy grapefruit aroma with nicely integrated oak. *Palate:* high quality, rich and complex fruit augmented by some barrel fermentation characters; some burgundian overtones, and a remarkably long finish. Has fulfilled the promise it showed two years ago. Drink '90–'92.

1988 PINOT NOIR [58] Colour: light red, with just a touch of purple remaining. *Bouquet:* soft slightly sappy/jammy aromas with some varietal character, but lacking fruit intensity. *Palate:* light fruit and a rather sharp, slightly volatile edge leading to some hardness; does not give the impression that it will improve with age. Drink '90.

Summary: Dr Michael Peterkin is consistently making excellent white wines of considerable complexity; he is commited to pinot noir, but I really feel the climate is against him.

REDGATE

REDGATE
of MARGARET RIVER
Cabernet–Shiraz
1987
Produced & Bottled by
Redgate Wines Pty. Ltd. Margaret River W.A.
750ml PRODUCE OF AUSTRALIA ALC / VOL

Location: Boodjidup Road, Margaret River, 6285; 8 km south-west of town. (097) 57 6208.

Winemakers: Bill and Paul Ullinger.

1989 Production: 5000 cases.

Principal Wines: Semillon, Chenin Blanc, Sauvignon Blanc, Spatlese Riesling, Pinot Noir, Cabernet Shiraz and Cabernet Sauvignon.

Distribution: Principally cellar door sales and

mailing list; limited wholesale distribution through Premium Wine Co., Perth; Carol-Ann Martin Classic Wines, Sydney, Canberra and Brisbane; exports to the United Kingdom, Singapore and New Zealand. Cellar door sales 10 a.m. to 4.30 p.m. 7 days. Mailing list enquiries to PO Box 117, Margaret River, 6285.

Prices: $9.85 to $15 cellar door.

Vintage Rating 1986–89: White: '89, '88, '86, '87. Red: '86, '87 ('88, '89 not yet rated).

Tasting Notes:

1989 CHENIN BLANC [72] Colour: very pale green-straw. *Bouquet:* light to medium, quite well made, with a touch of honeyed/slightly chalky aromas showing recognisable varietal character in the mould of Vouvray. *Palate:* an attractive, commercial style bordering on spatlese sweetness, again a throw-back to Vouvray; an easy, soft wine that has been well put together. Drink '90.

1988 RHINE RIESLING [65] Colour: light straw-green. *Bouquet:* full, broad and slightly phenolic, with some spicy overtones. *Palate:* again, rather broad and slightly oily, with some pressings characters; high-flavoured, and should go well with food. Drink '90–'91.

1988 SAUVIGNON BLANC [65] Colour: bright, light green-yellow. *Bouquet:* fresh, fragrant and aromatic with a nice touch of grassy sauvignon blanc varietal character. *Palate:* fresh and crisp herbal/grassy varietal flavour, and a clean crisp finish. Drink '90.

1988 SAUVIGNON BLANC OAK MATURED [72] Colour: good green-yellow. *Bouquet:* strong, slightly oily/cosmetic oak, but the overall impression is not unpleasant. *Palate:* light to medium fruit, with a slightly herbaceous varietal edge; smooth, slightly oily oak. Better oak selection could have resulted in an outstanding wine. Drink '90–'91.

1987 CABERNET SHIRAZ [78] Colour: medium red-purple. *Bouquet:* clean, light to medium leafy berry aromas, with a distinct hint of tobacco; good bottle development and style. *Palate:* an extremely attractive wine, with nice fruit/oak balance and integration; some almost chewy characters on the mid-palate on the leafy/red berry spectrum; dips marginally on the back-palate, but then finishes with pleasant tannin. Drink '90–'94.

1987 CABERNET SAUVIGNON [88] Colour: medium to full red-purple. *Bouquet:* concentrated, strong, deep tobacco/berry/ gravelly fruit, in forceful Margaret River style. *Palate:* excellent varietal character throughout; firm, classic, slightly leafy (though not excessively so) cabernet sauvignon; good structure with lingering tannins. Failed at the 1989 Sheraton Show Awards because it was entered in the light bodied class, and light bodied the wine is not. Drink '92–'97.

Summary: Redgate is producing a range of mainstream Margaret River styles, full and firm. Many require bottle age, and likewise an understanding of the fairly unyielding characteristics of many of the young wines from the region.

RIBBON VALE ESTATE

Location: Lot 5 Caves Road, Willyabrup via Cowaramup, 6284; 19 km north of Margaret River.
(097) 55 6272.

Winemaker: John James.

1989 Production: Not stated, but normally around 1500 cases.

Principal Wines: Semillon, Sauvignon Blanc, Semillon Sauvignon Blanc, Cabernet Sauvignon and Merlot.

Distribution: Through cellar door and mailing list. Wines available through fine wine retailers in Perth, Adelaide, Melbourne and Sydney. Wholesale agents are Seabrook & Seabrook, 13 College Street, Tanunda, SA, 5352; Vintners Pty Ltd, PO Box 165, Rosanna, Vic., 3084; and Regional Wines Pty Ltd, 76 Regent Street, Redfern, NSW, 2016. Mailing list, PO Box 127, Cowaramup, 6284.

Prices: $9 to $14 cellar door.

Vintage Rating 1986–89: White: '89, '88, '87, '86.

Red: '86, '89 ('87, '88 not rated).

Tasting Notes:

1989 SAUVIGNON BLANC [CS] Colour: bright light green-yellow. *Bouquet:* fragrant and aromatic, with light but clearly defined grassy/gooseberry varietal aroma. *Palate:* very light and crisp early in its life, with youthful herbal/grassy flavour; should develop very nicely in bottle.

1987 CABERNET SAUVIGNON [74] Colour: good strong and bright medium to full purple-red. *Bouquet:* pronounced astringent cabernet sauvignon aroma, with a slightly leathery edge. *Palate:* strong, clean fruit of light to medium weight set against complex vanillan/coconut oak, with a touch of char. Drink '92–'96.

Summary: Some of the Ribbon Vale wines tasted for this edition were decidedly uncertain, although a number were not bottled and any final judgement seemed premature. The flavour is certainly there, although once again one has the feeling that some fairly raw and aggressive fruit needs more handling and softening in the winemaking process. John James' use of consultants should achieve this in due course.

 SANDALFORD MARGARET RIVER ESTATE

Location: Metricup Road, Willyabrup via Cowaramup, 6284; 20 km north-west of Margaret River (vineyard only). (097) 55 6213.

Winemakers: Christian Morlaes, Tony Rowe and Candy Jonsson.

1989 Production: 25,000 cases.

Principal Wines: Semillon, Rhine Riesling, Verdelho, Late Harvest Rhine Riesling, Auslese Rhine Riesling, Cabernet Sauvignon, Shiraz and Vintage Port.

Distribution: National retail through Caldbecks; cellar door sales and tasting facility 11 a.m. to 4 p.m. 7 days.

Prices: $11 to $22.50 cellar door.

Vintage Rating 1986–89: '89, '88, '87, '86.

Tasting Notes:

1989 VERDELHO [80] Colour: light yellow-green. *Bouquet:* highly aromatic, pungent and estery fruit with considerable style; a touch of free SO2 evident which will settle down. *Palate:* a youthful, balanced and harmonious wine showing very strong fruit flavour, with a touch of grapefruit, possibly yeast derived, which may diminish with time. Drink '90–'91.

1988 SEMILLON [70] Colour: medium yellow-green. *Bouquet:* very strong lemony oak, with not enough fruit-weight to give balance at this juncture. *Palate:* a tangy, lemony oaky style strongly reminiscent of Mitchelton Wines of Victoria; the oak may soften, and the wine would certainly be pleasant with food. Drink '90–'92.

1988 VERDELHO [66] Colour: medium yellow-green. *Bouquet:* quite firm, but already exhibiting some toasty bottle-developed characters in a manner of a riesling. *Palate:* soft, clean and toasty, with good mid-palate fruit; falls away slightly on the finish. Drink '90.

1988 RHINE RIESLING [75] Colour: medium yellow-green. *Bouquet:* full, soft and rich lime/pineapple aromas. *Palate:* clean and very soft bottle-developed pineapple fruit, with a touch of toast; easy drinking, fleshy, forward style. Drink '90.

1987 CABERNET SAUVIGNON [64] Colour: light to medium red, showing surprising development. *Bouquet:* clean, bottle-developed herbal/spice aromas of light to medium weight. *Palate:* marked herbal/aniseed flavours take the wine out of the usual spectrum; however, none of the sulphide characters of earlier vintages are evident. Drink '90–'92.

Summary: So far as I am concerned, at least, a very welcome change for the better at Sandalford, which has entirely thrown off the sulphide problems of by-gone years, and is showing some real style with its white wines.

❦ SUSSEX VALE

Location: Harmans Mill Road, Willyabrup via Cowaramup, 6284; 23 km north of Margaret River.
(097) 55 6234.

Winemaker: Gerry Middleton.

Principal Wines: Semillon, Sauvignon Blanc, Chardonnay, Cabernet Rosé and Cabernet Sauvignon.

Distribution: Principally cellar door sales and mailing list. Cellar door sales 10 a.m. to 4.30 p.m. 7 days; mailing list enquiries to RMB 398, Willyabrup via Cowaramup, 6284.

Summary: Sussex Vale is adopting a very low profile; wine quality is not good.

❦ VASSE FELIX

Location: Cnr Caves Road and Harmans South Road, Cowaramup, 6284; 7 km west of town.
(097) 55 5242; Fax (097) 55 5425.

Winemaker: Bernard Abbott.

1989 Production: 10,000 cases.

Principal Wines: Rhine Riesling, Verdelho, Classic Dry White, Hermitage, Cabernet Sauvignon and Classic Dry Red.

Distribution: Cellar door, mailing list and fine wine retailers in all capital cities (The Oak Barrel, Sydney; Fesq & Co., Melbourne; McLachlan & Co., Adelaide; Barrique Fine Wines, Brisbane); also exports. Cellar door sales 10 a.m. to 4.30 p.m. 7 days. Mailing list as above.

Prices: $13.60 to $24.

Vintage Rating 1986–89: White: '89, '86, '87, '88.
Red: '87, '86, ('88, '89 not rated).

Outstanding Prior Vintages: '76, '78, '79, '84, '85.

Summary: The oldest of the Margaret River wineries, now owned by Robert Holmes á Court and family; samples were not submitted nor did it enter the Sheraton Wine Awards competition. Nonetheless, the quality of the finely sculptured and extremely elegant cabernets is well known.

❦ WILLESPIE WINES

Location: Harmans Mill Road, Willyabrup via Cowaramup, 6284; 24 km north of Margaret River.
(097) 55 6248.

Winemakers: Kevin Squance; J. and M. Davies (consultants).

Principal Wines: Rhine Riesling, Semillon, Verdelho, Cabernet Sauvignon and Vintage Port.

Distribution: Principally cellar door sales and through restaurants. Cellar door sales 10 a.m. to 4.30 p.m. 7 days. Limited fine wine distribution through select retailers in Perth, Sydney and Melbourne.

Prices: $14 to $18 cellar door.

Vintage Rating 1986–89: White: '89, '88, '87, '86.
Red: '87, '89, '88, '86.

Tasting Notes:

1989 VERDELHO [70] Colour: light to medium yellow-green. *Bouquet:* smooth, well balanced fruit, quite rich and almost suggesting some oak. *Palate:* crisp, clean and youthful, with pleasant weight; very slightly grassy overtones, and an obvious future. Drink '90–'92.

1988 SEMILLON [64] Colour: medium to full yellow-green. *Bouquet:* strong and complex fruit and oak, with just a touch of sulphide. *Palate:* complex lemony fruit and oak, but again a faint twist of bitterness on the finish deriving from that sulphide. Drink '90–'92.

1987 CABERNET SAUVIGNON [90] Colour: outstanding medium full purple-red. *Bouquet:*

firm and potent, with beautifully accented cool cabernet sauvignon; some herbaceous/capsicum notes. *Palate:* firm concentrated and long lived herbaceous/capsicum style, with exceptional concentration and rich texture. Drink '93–2000.

Summary: The husband and wife Davies wine consulting team has done its work very well; the 1987 Cabernet Sauvignon was a fully deserving winner of the gold medal at the 1989 Sheraton Wine Awards, and is a wine with a tremendous future.

WOODLANDS

Location: Cnr Caves Road and Metricup Road, Willyabrup via Cowaramup, 6284; 19 km north-east of Margaret River.
(09) 294 1869 (home), (097) 55 6226 (vineyard), (09) 274 6421 or (09) 274 6155 (office).

Winemaker: David Watson

1989 Production: 1400 litres.

Principal Wines: Pinot Noir and Cabernet Sauvignon; the Pinot Noir is available in only minute quantities.

Distribution: Cellar door by appointment. By mailing list and through selected retail outlets in Perth, Sydney and Melbourne. Substantial Perth retail distribution; Camperdown Cellars, North Shore Fine Wines in Sydney; Sutherland Cellars, Melbourne. Mailing list enquiries to 29 Spring Park Road, Midland, 6056.

Prices: $20 retail; $15 cellar door

Vintage Rating 1986–89: '86, '87 ('88, '89 not yet rated).

Outstanding Prior Vintages: '79, '81, '82.

Tasting Notes:

1987 CABERNET SAUVIGNON [68] Colour: medium red-purple. *Bouquet:* pleasant, albeit somewhat light minty/leafy fruit, with just a

touch of astringency. *Palate:* soft caramel/ vanilla bean oak; light cherry flavoured fruit; low tannins. Drink '91–'94.

Summary: Woodlands remains very much a part time occupation for owner/ winemaker David Watson; nonetheless, the 1987 Cabernet Sauvignon does represent a partial return to form of the outstanding wines of the early 1980s.

WOODY NOOK WINES

Location: Metricup Road, Metricup, 6280.

Winemaker: John Russell Smith.

1989 Production: 500 cases.

Principal Wines: Semillon, Sauvignon Blanc, Chenin Blanc, Cabernet Merlot and Merlot.

Distribution: Principally through cellar door sales and mailing list; cellar door sales 9 a.m. to 5 p.m. Thursday, Saturday and Sunday. Limited retail distribution through local retailers and restaurants. Mailing list enquiries to winery at above address.

Prices: $10 to $13.50.

Tasting Notes:

1989 CHENIN BLANC/SAUVIGNON BLANC [76] Colour: medium straw-yellow. *Bouquet:* complex, full, slightly blousy but very rich fruit, with some tropical fruit salad characters. *Palate:* once again, abundant fruit in the fruit salad/ pineapple spectrum, and a long finish. Drink '90–'91.

1989 CABERNET MERLOT [CS] Colour: bright but fairly light purple-red. *Bouquet:* strong, ripe cassis/berry fruit. *Palate:* while relatively light bodied, is very clean and does have most attractive young berry fruit flavours; the tannin is in balance. Should be headed towards the 80 point mark.

Summary: John Smith, formerly winemaker at Chateau Xanadu, has now formed a wine consultancy business with his wife Dina, and the Woody Nook wines are the first practical results of that consultancy.

🍇 WRIGHTS

Location: Harmans South Road, Cowaramup, 6284; 18 km north-west of Margaret River. (097) 55 5314.

Winemaker: Henry Wright.

1989 Production: 2600 cases.

Principal Wines: Sauvignon Blanc, Semillon, Chardonnay, Hermitage, Cabernet Sauvignon and Vintage Port.

Distribution: Principally cellar door and mailing list. Cellar door sales 10 a.m. to 4.30 p.m. 7 days. Mailing list, PO Box 25, Cowaramup, 6284. Limited fine wine retail merchants in eastern states; substantial Perth retail sales.

Prices: $10 to $14 cellar door.

Vintage Rating 1986–89: White: '89, '88, '87, '86. Red: '89, '88, '87 ('86 not rated).

Outstanding Prior Vintages: '80, '82, '84.

Tasting Notes:

1987 HERMITAGE [58] Colour: medium purple-red. *Bouquet:* light, slightly herbaceous fruit, with rather astringent, leathery overtones. *Palate:* once again, the fruit is diminished by some bitter, leathery flavours, which one can only assume to be derived from sulphide. Drink '90–'92.

1987 CABERNET SAUVIGNON [59] Colour: medium red, with just a touch of purple remain-0ing. *Bouquet:* very light and rather leathery, with varietal character very subdued. *Palate:* unfortunately follows the bouquet, with rather empty and slightly bitter flavours. Drink '90–'92.

Summary: In common with the vast majority of Margaret River winemakers, the Wrights are the most delightful and pleasant people, and a friendly welcome is always assured when you visit the cellar door. I only wish I could be more enthusiastic about the wines.

Perth Hills

1988 VINTAGE

The spring and early summer conditions were problem free; temperatures were mild with average spring rainfall. However, in late January, temperatures rose well above average and remained high for four weeks. The vines were subjected to extreme stress, resulting in fruit dehydration and some defoliation. Rapid sugar accumulation persuaded many growers to pick, but a sudden change in the weather saw baumes drop quite rapidly, with the consequence that some vineyards were in fact picked too early.

Overall, yields were down 15 per cent to 20 per cent, with pinot reduced as much as 50 per cent. Wine quality was average, with the white wine showing slightly more flavour and body than the reds.

1989 VINTAGE

Above average spring and early summer rains resulted in moist soil conditions throughout the growing season. Small creeks that run through the region and that almost always stop flowing by January continued to carry water flow throughout the summer and autumn.

Flowering was even and uninterrupted, and with the ideal growing conditions crops were large. However, in the year when every-thing else went right, birds (silver eyes) caused immense destruction. All varieties suffered, but semillon, chardonnay and cabernet sauvignon were the prime targets, with up to 30 per cent loss.

Wine quality is above average; the pinots have good colour with good levels of dry extract, while both chardonnays and cabernets show very concentrated flavours.

THE CHANGES

There are many changes, the most obvious being the change of name from Darling Ranges to Perth Hills, a name decided on by the local vignerons under the energetic direction of Hainault's Peter Fimmel.

The new entries are Avalon and Scarp Valley; Brookside has abandoned ideas of making wine, and is simply selling its grapes, so disappears from the book; Woodhenge has changed its name to Piesse Brook; and Woodthorpe has likewise discontinued winemaking, and has been leased for 10 years to the rapidly growing Darlington Vineyard.

Avalon is owned by local magistrate David Brown and his wife Catherine; when they decided to move to the Perth Hills and acquire a 8-hectare block, they agreed they should do something with it. After flirting with the idea of establishing a cherry orchard, they opted for vines, albeit without any prior experience. Scarp Valley has in fact been in existence for some years now, but the minuscule production of Bob and Doris Duncan (whose wines are made by contract at Hainault) has hitherto meant that they are not commercially available. Even now, the production must be close to the smallest in Australia.

The Perth Hills is a very pretty area; much of the native vegetation is typically West Australian and hence quite different to anything found in the eastern states. However, the complex hill and valley pattern is quite reminiscent of a scaled down version of the Adelaide Hills. The climate is distinctly warmer than the Adelaide Hills, although far cooler than that of the Swan Valley. It seems to be an area suited to semillon, chardonnay, shiraz and cabernet sauvignon; I feel the aromatic varieties and pinot noir are less suited, although various makers (including Peter Fimmel) seem determined to prove me wrong on that view. Wine quality is extremely variable, but the retention of Rob Bowen as a consultant at Darlington Vineyard has brought forth spectacular results. One can only hope that other makers in the region will take a close look at the 1989 Darlington wines and perhaps band together to obtain some technical assistance.

Finally, there is something of an inter-loper: Chittering Estate. Chittering is not a member of the Perth Hills Vignerons Association and in fact comes from a distinct region all on its own. It does, however, share some common features with the Perth Hills: the vineyard is established at a height of up to 300 metres above sea level; vintage is very much later than the Swan Valley; and Chittering Valley is north-east of Perth. Finally, the brand- new winery has been established in a most beautiful setting which would do any of the Perth Hills' vineyards proud. No expense has been spared in establishing Chittering Estate; the funds come from George Kailis (one of the well-known Perth fishing magnates) and the entrepreneurial skill and technical input from South African-born Steven Shapira. Immaculate packaging, special bottlings of wines labelled with hand-made paper fabricated from vine leaves grown on the estate, and an overall approach reminiscent of Leeuwin Estate will signal a significant arrival on the scene.

AVALON

Location: Lot 156, Bailey Road, Glen Forrest, 6071.
(09) 298 8049.

Winemaker: Jim Elson (contract).

1989 Production: 20 cases (chardonnay).

Principal Wines: Semillon, Chardonnay and
Cabernet Merlot.

Distribution: Cellar door only at present; by
appointment.

Summary: The 1989 Chardonnay from Avalon had
suffered badly in being taken from cask and
could not be properly assessed; a subsequent
sample seemed far better on a brief view. In
any event, it is not until 1990 (with a projected
production of 350 cases, and 1991, 950 cases)
that the wines will become available in
meaningful commercial quantities.

CAROSA VINEYARD

Location: Lot 3, Houston Street, Mount Helena,
6555; in Mount Helena township, 3 km east of
Mundaring, and 35 km east of Perth.
(09) 572 1603.

Winemaker: Jim Elson.

1989 Production: Approximately 400 cases.

Principal Wines: Chardonnay, Cabernet Merlot
blend, Rhine Riesling and Champagne
(chardonnay and pinot noir).

Distribution: Initially will be cellar door sales and
by mail order, with limited retail sales in Perth;
mailing list enquiries to the above address.

Prices: $12 to $16.

Summary: The 1989 Carosa samples tasted were not
in fit condition to be properly judged.
Winemaker Jim Elson spent many years working
for Seppelt in Victoria and South Australia, and
accordingly has the necessary expertise to
produce wine of commercial quality.

CHIDLOW BROOK

Location: Lot 318, Lakeview Road, Chidlow, 6556;
1 km north-west of Chidlow and 43 km east of
Perth.
(09) 572 4021.

Winemaker: Les Johnston.

Principal Wines: Chardonnay and Cabernet
Sauvignon.

Distribution: Cellar door sales (by appointment),
mailing list (address as above) and through
Chidlow Tavern.

Summary: A tiny operation with exclusively local
sales, and nothing known of the quality.

CHITTERING ESTATE

Location: Chittering Valley Road, Lower
Chittering, 6084; 22 km north-east of
Bullsbrook (on the Great Northern Highway).
(09) 571 8144; Fax (09) 571 8007.

Winemaker: Steven Shapira.

1989 Production: 2000 cases.

Principal Wines: Semillon/Sauvignon Blanc,
Chardonnay, and Cabernet Sauvignon/ Merot.

Distribution: Significant Perth distribution and
exports through G. Kailis; cellar door sales,
wine tastings and light meals by appointment,
chiefly weekends.

Prices: $18 to $22 cellar door.

Tasting Notes:

1987 SEMILLON SAUVIGNON BLANC [67] Colour:
medium yellow-green. _Bouquet:_ strong and quite
complex, but with distinct hot ferment/ solids
aromas which I simply do not like. _Palate:_ quite
complex in terms of structure and with some
mouthfeel; however, fruit flavour has been
stripped out of the wine, which will appeal to

some, but is not to my liking. Will be long lived. Drink '90–'94.

1987 CHARDONNAY [74] Colour: medium to full yellow-green. *Bouquet:* complex and rich in terms of structure, again showing some hot solids fermentation characters. *Palate:* has much greater weight and richness than the bouquet would suggest; honeyed and almost monolithic; a strong Californian influence at work in the fashioning of this wine. Once again will be long lived, and once again will greatly appeal to some. Drink '90–'93.

1987 CABERNET SAUVIGNON MERLOT [80] Colour: deep purple-red. *Bouquet:* concentrated firm cassis red berry fruit; oak in restraint. *Palate:* huge, concentrated dark cassis/berry fruit flavours on a very full to mid-palate; strong tannins finish off the wine. Once again, very long-lived style. Drink '93–2000.

Summary: Chittering is setting itself up as a tall poppy from the word go, and is bound to cause both jealousy and misunderstanding. Winemaker and co-proprietor Steven Shapira does not welcome this but is realistic enough to understand the consequences of the high marketing profile.

DARLINGTON VINEYARD

Location: Lot 39, Nelson Road, Glen Forrest; 6071; 35 km east of Perth.
(09) 299 6268; Fax (09) 386 3083.

Winemakers: Balt Van der Meer (proprietor) and Rob Bowen (contract).

1989 Production: In excess of 15,000 cases.

Principal Wines: Chardonnay, Semillon, Sauvignon Blanc, Gamay, Beaujolais, Shiraz, Cabernet Sauvignon, Merlot and Port.

Distribution: Principally cellar door sales and mailing list, with limited local and Perth retail and restaurant distribution. Retailers serviced

direct ex-winery. Cellar door sales Wednesday to Saturday 10 a.m. to 5 p.m., Sunday 11 a.m. to 4 p.m. Mailing list enquiries, Lot 39, Nelson Road, Glen Forrest, 6071.

Prices: $6 to $15 cellar door.

Tasting Notes:

1989 PRELUDE SEMILLON SAUVIGNON BLANC [CS] Colour: light to medium green-yellow. *Bouquet:* attractive spicy oak with clean, light fruit showing good varietal character. *Palate:* attractive light fruit with beautifully handled spicy oak; a very well made wine with good mouthfeel and pleasant citric/grassy flavours. Almost certain to score in excess of 80 points once bottled.

1989 CHARDONNAY [CS] Colour: strong green-yellow. *Bouquet:* clean, complex and rich with excellent fruit weight oak balance and integration; great fruit tinged with spicy oak. *Palate:* superb fruit and oak balance and integration; has already obtained lovely richness; very good balance and style. A 90 point wine in the making.

1989 VIN PRIMEUR LIGHT RED [CS] Colour: light to medium purple-red. *Bouquet:* clean with some biscuity carbonic maceration characters overlying sweet berry fruit. *Palate:* very peculiar rather empty entry to the mouth, carrying through to the mid-palate; a hollow, shell-like wine; the after-taste is, however, quite good. Difficult to determine where the wine is headed in terms of points.

1988 PARKERVILLE VINEYARD CABERNET SAUVIGNON [74] Colour: medium red-purple. *Bouquet:* pronounced minty/leafy fruit aromas; clean, with light oak influence. *Palate:* fairly light wine, less structured than the main cabernet sauvignon of the year, and finishes a fraction hard. Drink '92–'95.

1988 CABERNET SAUVIGNON [79] Colour: medium red-purple. *Bouquet:* strong leafy/minty aromas of medium weight. *Palate:* a very clean wine of strong ripe cassis/berry fruit with some meaty overtones; soft lingering tannins. Drink '93–'98.

1986 SHIRAZ [79] Colour: medium to full red. *Bouquet:* clean with quite complex velvety/earthy varietal fruit in traditional ripe style. *Palate:* very attractive, rich and concentrated sweet dark berry/dark chocolate fruit flavours; well balance and structured, with soft lingering tannins. Drink '91–'95.

Summary: Darlington is comprehensively showing the way to the vignerons of the Perth Hills; if Darlington can achieve this standard of excellence, there is surely no reason why others should not do so.

HAINAULT

Location: Walnut Road, Bickley, 6076;
30 km east of Perth.
(09) 293 8339.

Winemaker: Peter Fimmel.

1989 Production: Approximately 1500 cases.

Principal Wines: Chardonnay, Gewurztraminer, Semillon, Pinot Noir and Cabernet Merlot.

Distribution: Principally by mailing list and cellar door sales. Mailing list enquiries as above. Limited retail distribution in Perth, Melbourne and Sydney. Cellar door sales noon to 5 p.m. Saturday and Sunday or by appointment.

Prices: $13 to $25 retail.

Vintage Rating 1986–89: White: '87, '89, '86, '88. Red: '89, '87, '88, '86.

Outstanding Prior Vintages: '84.

Tasting Notes:

1989 GEWURZTRAMINER [TS] *Colour:* medium yellow-green. *Bouquet:* soft with some lychee spice, and some fermentation characters still lingering. *Palate:* full and strong varietal spice lychee flavours with a rather hard phenolic finish; if it is fined before being bottled, will merit in excess of 70 points.

1989 PINOT NOIR [CS] *Colour:* good purple-red. *Bouquet:* sweet fruit with faint tobacco/sappy/ leather varietal characters. *Palate:* some cherry/plum varietal fruit flavours; quite tannic; would be

enormously improved with some new oak treatment. 70 points or thereabouts is the most likely range.

1988 GEWURZTRAMINER [65] *Colour:* medium yellow-green. *Bouquet:* clean and soft, with slightly caramel/coffee overtones and a touch of varietal spice. *Palate:* soft, blurred caramel/ lychee flavours; very soft, and with both the bouquet and palate evidencing a little oxidation at work. Drink '90.

Summary: Peter Fimmel is the perfect ambassador for any emerging district; he works harder in semi-retirement than he did as a biochemist, and has a very clear idea as to how the district should promote and present itself. If dedication counts, Hainault will succeed.

PIESSE BROOK
(formerly Woodhenge Wines)

Location: Lot 731, Aldersyde Road, Bickley, 6076;
30 km east of Perth.
(09) 386 7872.

Winemaker: B. D. Murphy.

Principal Wines: Cabernet Sauvignon and Shiraz.

Distribution: Exclusively cellar door; cellar door sales 2 p.m. to 5 p.m. Sunday.

Tasting Notes:

1988 CABERNET SHIRAZ [80] *Colour:* medium to full red-purple. *Bouquet:* clean, with most attractive minty fruit with a touch of vanillan oak. *Palate:* once again, very clean and well structured with very attractive minty fruit balanced by some tannins on a long, clean finish. Drink '92–'95.

Summary: A very small operation, but with wine of exemplary quality.

❦ *SCARP VALLEY*

Location: 6 Robertson Road, Gooseberry Hill, 6076.
(09) 454 5748.

Winemaker: Peter Fimmel (contract Hainault).

1989 Production: Approximately 25 cases.

Principal Wines: Only Hermitage made.

Distribution: Mail order only.

Prices: $10 to $12.50 (depending on vintage).

Tasting Notes:

1988 HERMITAGE [63] Colour: light to medium red-purple. *Bouquet:* light, leafy herbal/minty aromas suggesting slightly unripe fruit despite the 12.5° alcohol. *Palate:* pronounced light/leafy minty fruit with fairly high acid; a somewhat unfinished, rather jumpy palate. May settle down with more time. Drink '92–'94.

1987 HERMITAGE [71] Colour: medium red-purple. *Bouquet:* soft tobacco edges to slightly edgy fruit, which is, however, distinctly richer than the '88. *Palate:* pleasant red berry flavours with some minty leafy characters, evidently typical of the vineyard; clean but lacks structure; low tannin. Drink '90–'92.

Summary: With production of around 25 dozen per year, Scarp Valley must surely be the smallest winery in Australia; however, Robert Duncan is prepared to make available 200 or so bottles "to selected persons who, like us, think it is rather special".

South-West Coastal Plain

1988 VINTAGE

It has to be stressed that the South-west Coastal Plain is an area united not by close physical boundaries but by common geology—the fine tuart sands upon which all of the vineyards are planted. The region in fact extends for several hundred kilometres along the coast, and climatic conditions can thereby vary widely.

Accordingly, in the south it was a difficult year, with poor flowering and set followed by a very hot and dry growing season, leading to stress, particularly in the red varieties. In the outcome, both quantity and quality were down.

In the north, the pattern was very different. Flowering and set was far less affected, and while the end of the growing season was marked by hot weather, it was no hotter than usual. Some first-class white and red wines resulted.

1989 VINTAGE

The year was very much more successful for all subdistricts. Particularly in the south, the set for chardonnay and pinot noir was reduced somewhat, but the growing season conditions from this point on were very much more favourable. Rainfall kept moisture reserves in the soil up, but did necessitate increased spraying against mildews. Those vineyards which successfully coped with this challenge produced some of the best material seen for years.

The other problem was a burst of wet weather just after the commencement of harvest. Once again, decisions on picking were critical in determining the outcome of the year. Those who waited for conditions to dry out again did best.

THE CHANGES

The one new entry is Baldivis Estate, a most interesting new development which may well have a major influence on the district in years to come. The vineyard was established in 1982 as part of a large orchard business, the main thrust of which is the production of avocadoes, limes and mangoes. By the time the development is complete, $4 million will have been invested. The vineyards account for a little under eight hectares, but may be expanded.

Jeffrey Grosset comes all the way from the Clare Valley to assist John Galatis with vintage each year; the introduction was arranged through Dr Bryce Rankin, and the arrangement works well from Grosset's viewpoint as he is able to finish the vintage before the first grapes are harvested in the Clare Valley.

One other behind-the-scenes has taken place at Leschenault; the Killerbys have decided against selling, and have taken consultancy advice that has dramatically transformed the quality of their white wines. Thanks to Capel Vale and Leschenault, the southern end of the Coastal Plain is producing some of the very best white wines to come from Western Australia.

BALDIVIS ESTATE

Location: Lot 165, River Road, Baldivis, 6171;
10 km east of Manandurah Highway.
(09) 525 2066; Fax (09) 525 2411.

Winemaker: John Galatis (Geoffrey Grossett
consultant).

1989 Production: Approximately 2500 cases.

Principal Wines: Chardonnay, Sauvignon Blanc,
Semillon, Cabernet Sauvignon and Merlot.

Distribution: Principally mail order (enquiries to
RMB 249A River Road, Baldivis, 6171) and
through Liquorland and John Jens, Perth;
Melbourne distribution through Greg Tootell.
No cellar door sales yet established.

Prices: $10.99 to $11.99 Perth retail; $120 per case
mail order.

Tasting Notes:

1989 CHARDONNAY [CS] Colour: very light
straw-yellow. *Bouquet:* light smoky/lemony oak
with subdued fruit yet to throw off the effects of
fermentation. *Palate:* light smoky/ spicy oak;
clean crisp fruit; attractive wood handling and
likewise of the base material. Should develop
well to a 75 plus wine.

1988 CABERNET MERLOT [65] Colour: very good
light purple-red. *Bouquet:* cherry fruit flavours
marred by just a touch of bitterness. *Palate:*
very good fruit flavours; there is a bitter taste
which may be charred oak, or may be sulphide;
time will tell.

Summary: With unlikely consultancy help from
Geoffrey Grossett, who makes the long trip
from Clare Valley before the start of his own
vintage, Baldivis Estate will certainly produce
very good wines in the years to come. Indeed,
there are already touches of style in the as yet
unbottled wines reviewed in this edition.

CAPEL VALE

Location: Lot 5, Capel North West Road, Sterling
Estate, Capel, 6271; 1 km west of town.
(097) 27 2439; Fax (097) 21 8339.

Winemakers: Dr Peter Pratten and Alan Johnson.

1989 Production: Approximately 170 tonnes.

Principal Wines: A full range of varietal table wines
comprising Rhine Riesling, Gewurztraminer,
Traminer Riesling, Semillon-Sauvignon Blanc,
Chardonnay, Shiraz and Cabernet Sauvignon,
and Baudin, a blend of cabernet shiraz and
merlot.

Distribution: Cellar door sales, mailing list and fine
wine retailers through the Fine Wine
Wholesalers, WA; Haviland Wine Company,
NSW; I. H. Baker Wines & Spirits, Vic.; and
Barrique Fine Wines, Qld. Cellar door sales
10 a.m. to 4.30 p.m. 7 days. Mailing list
enquiries to PO Box 692, Bunbury, 6230.

Prices: $10 to $16 cellar door.

Tasting Notes:

1989 RHINE RIESLING [84] Colour: light green-
yellow. *Bouquet:* crisp clean toasty/lime/
passionfruit aromas, beautifully made. *Palate:*
again, exemplary winemaking with crisp clean
and fragrant lime/passionfruit flavours; as
should be the case, very low phenolics. Drink
'90–'91.

1989 TRAMINER [74] Colour: light green-yellow.
Bouquet: clean, fragrant, slightly herbaceous/
grassy edge, unusual for the variety, but
probably still developing. *Palate:* light, clean
and crisp non-phenolic style; should develop
very well over the next 12 months. Drink '90.

1989 SAUVIGNON BLANC SEMILLON [80]
Colour: light green-yellow. *Bouquet:* clean,
youthful, stylish with strong herbaceous
sauvignon blanc flavours and a touch of slightly
smoky overtones. *Palate:* light, crisp and clean
with excellent tangy gooseberry/herbaceous

varietal fruit; has the feel and weight to go on. Drink '90–'92.

1987 SHIRAZ [80] Colour: very good purple-red, strong and deep. _Bouquet:_ clean, fragrant lively berry/cassis, with attractive spicy oak. _Palate:_ very youthful fresh spicy/cassis varietal fruit with excellent flavour; yet to build structure and complexity, but will do so with bottle-age when it could become quite outstanding. Drink '92–'96.

1987 BAUDIN [75] Colour: medium full red-purple. _Bouquet:_ soft, very slightly leathery fruit with some minty characters. _Palate:_ follows on with quite pronounced eucalypt minty flavours; of medium weight, smooth and with soft tannins in the finish. Drink '91–'94.

1987 CABERNET SAUVIGNON [62] Colour: deep purple-red. _Bouquet:_ dense, chocolatey fruit with some leathery/biscuity sulphide edges. _Palate:_ very strong berry fruit, tending towards over-extraction, and then some sulphide bitterness on the finish. Drink '92–'95.

Summary: Capel Vale consistently makes some of Australia's finest white wines, with a series of quite brilliant rieslings and chardonnays. I have criticised its red wines for sulphides in the past, but most (though not all) seem to have thrown off that problem.

HARTRIDGE

Location: Lot 36, 35 km peg, Wanneroo Road, Wanneroo, 6065.
(09) 407 5117.

Winemaker: Perry Sandow.

Principal Wines: Chenin Blanc, Pinot Noir and Cabernet Sauvignon.

Distribution: Almost exclusively cellar door sales and mailing list. Cellar door sales 10 a.m. to 6 p.m. Monday to Saturday. Mailing list enquiries to PO Box 37, Wanneroo, 6065.

Summary: Little or nothing is known of the current activities of Hartridge.

LESCHENAULT

Location: Minninup Road, off Lakes Road, Gelorup, 6230; 10 km south of Bunbury. (097) 95 7222.

Winemaker: Dr Barry Killerby.

Principal Wines: Traminer, Semillon, Chardonnay, April Red, Shiraz, Cabernet Sauvignon, Pinot Noir and Crystal Dessert Wine.

Distribution: Principally cellar door sales and mailing list; limited retail distribution in eastern States, either serviced direct from winery or through a local agent. Cellar door sales 10 a.m. to 5 p.m. Monday to Friday, 10 a.m. to 6 p.m. weekends and holidays. Mailing list enquiries, PO Box 1058, Bunbury, 6230.

Prices: $8.50 to $12.50 retail.

Vintage Rating 1986–89: White: '89, '88, '86, '87. Red: '89, '87, '86, '88.

Outstanding Prior Vintages: '81, '82, '84.

Tasting Notes:

1989 SEMILLON [78] Colour: light green-yellow. _Bouquet:_ light and clean, with slightly herbaceous/powdery overtones. _Palate:_ shows much more at an early stage that the bouquet; beautifully handled light spicy oak with clean, fresh herbaceous fruit; very good balance and style, and will mature well. Drink '90–'92.

1988 CHARDONNAY [89] Colour: light to medium yellow-green. _Bouquet:_ discrete, restrained cool fruit characters with quite pronounced spicy/lemony oak. _Palate:_ again, lemony/spicy oak is well balanced and set against fine, understated fruit with a long, crisp acid finish. A wine with time in front of it. Drink '90–'92.

1988 TRAMINER [71] Colour: light to medium green-yellow. _Bouquet:_ soft clean fruity aromas with good spicy/lychee varietal character. _Palate:_ soft, full-flavoured traminer grapy and pungent; the only criticism is a slightly oily finish, so hard to avoid with this variety. Drink '90.

1989 APRIL RED [72] Colour: light crimson-purple. *Bouquet:* light, fragrant and fruity. *Palate:* a light, fruity and fresh rosé style with a perfectly judged flick of residual sugar; highly commercial. Drink '90.

1987 SHIRAZ [70] Colour: bright purple-red of medium depth. *Bouquet:* light to medium intensity with fresh but slightly leafy/herbal overtones. *Palate:* clean, fresh red berry fruits, again with a faint herbal background; unobtrusive oak and light to medium tannin. Drink '91–'94.

Summary: There has been a veritable revolution in the style and quality of Leschenault's white wines, so disappointing in previous years. Both making and bottling techniques have improved out of sight, doing justice to the obviously very good fruit grown in the now fully-mature vineyards. Red wine quality, too, has taken a turn for the better, and the Killerbys now have no thought of selling out.

🍇 *LUISINI*

Location: 17 km peg, Wanneroo Road, Wanneroo, 6065; 17 km north of Perth.
(09) 409 9007.

Principal Wines: Chablis, Chenin Blanc, Late Picked Chenin Blanc, Shiraz, Shiraz Cabernet, and a wide range of fortified wines including Liqueur Verdelho, Ruby Port, Liqueur Port, Tawny Port and Muscat Constantia.

Distribution: Principally cellar door sales 8.30 a.m. to 5.30 p.m. 7 days. Mailing orders filled, enquiries as above. Limited retail distribution including Summer Hill Liquor Store, Sydney.

Summary: Luisini is a substantial operation operating in a winery which can only be charitably described as antiquated, and which markets its products almost exclusively to local and Perth-based trade.

🍇 *PAUL CONTI*

Location: 529 Wanneroo Road, Wanneroo, 6065; 19 km north of Perth.
(09) 409 9160.

Winemaker: Paul Conti.

Principal Wines: Rhine Riesling, Chenin Blanc, Chardonnay, Late Picked Frontignac, Mariginiup Hermitage, Cabernet Sauvignon, Vintage Port and a small amount of Pinot Noir from new plantings. Almost all wines are now sourced from estate-grown grapes, although Conti has (after a break of several years) once again produced a Mount Barker Rhine Riesling.

Distribution: Principally cellar door sales 9.30 a.m. to 5.30 p.m. Monday to Saturday. Extensive Perth retail distribution through I. H. Baker Wines & Spirits; limited retail distribution in eastern States through Wayne Leicht, Melbourne, and Hayes Fine Wines, Sydney.

Prices: $8.37 to $15 retail.

Vintage Rating 1986–89: White: '88, '86, '87 ('89 not yet rated). Red: '88, '87, '86 ('89 not yet rated).

Outstanding Prior Vintages: White: '85. Red: '84.

Tasting Notes:

1988 RHINE RIESLING [76] Colour: medium yellow-green. *Bouquet:* of light to medium weight, with faint plasticine characters over fine, penetrating lime fruit. *Palate:* excellent fruit depth and flavour, with lime/passionfruit flavours and some fruit-sweetness; long finish. Drink '90–'91.

1988 CHENIN BLANC [72] Colour: medium yellow-straw. *Bouquet:* soft fruit salad aromas with some toasty bottle-developed characters starting to appear. *Palate:* soft, round and fleshy fruit, smooth and easy drinking; low acid. Drink '90.

1988 BEAU ROUGE [70] Colour: light red. _Bouquet:_ light clean strawberry fruit. _Palate:_ clean fresh strawberry fruit flavours with a very slight confection edge; highly commercial and attractive. Drink '90

1987 MARIGINIUP HERMITAGE [80] Colour: purple-red. _Bouquet:_ clean, smooth cherry fruit with very good oak. _Palate:_ clean fresh and smooth with good fruit; a nice touch of soft vanillan oak is both well integrated and well balanced. A lovely drinking style. Drink '90–'93.

Summary: Paul Conti is now one of the elder statesmen of the west. He continues to produce wines of remarkably consistent quality, with the white wines starring one year, the reds the next. This time it was basically the turn of the red wines, and in particular the ever-reliable Mariginiup Hermitage.

PEEL ESTATE

Location: Fletcher Road, Baldivis, 6171; 15 km north of Mandurah and 60 km south of Perth, off Main Coastal Highway. (095) 24 1221.

Winemaker: Will Nairn.

Principal Wines: Chenin Blanc, Wood Matured Chenin Blanc, Sauvignon Blanc, Chardonnay, Verdelho, Zinfandel, Shiraz, Cabernet Sauvignon and Vintage Port.

Distribution: Substantial cellar door sales and mailing list sales; cellar door sales 10 a.m. to 5 p.m. 7 days. Mailing list enquiries to PO Box 37, Mandurah, 6210. Limited retail distribution through wholesalers in Perth, Chateau Barnard; Melbourne, Van Cooth and Co.; Sydney, Bill Graham; and Brisbane, Barrique Fine Wines.

Tastings Notes:

1986 CABERNET SAUVIGNON [75] Colour: excellent bright red-purple of medium to full depth. _Bouquet:_ strong charred oak together with good dark berry fruit. _Palate:_ once again, some lemony charred barrel-ferment type oak characters evident; fresh, clean fruit runs underneath, with low tannin. Will develop into an elegant wine. Drink '90–'94.

Summary: Peel Estate has been a consistent producer of elegant red wines based on shiraz and cabernet sauvignon, but has also produced some interesting wooded chenin blanc styles from time to time. It is a pity that more wines were not available for tasting for this edition.

THOMAS WINES

Location: 23-24 Crowd Road, Gelorup, 6230. (097) 21 7228.

Winemaker: Gill Thomas.

1989 Production: Not stated.

Principal Wines: Pinot Noir (produced from grapes grown on Briar Holme Vineyard) and Cabernet Sauvignon (from high-country vineyard at Donnybrook).

Distribution: By mailing list and through NZA Marketing (wholesale) to most fine wine retailers in Western Australia. Mailing list enquiries to PO Box 286, Bunbury, 6230. Cellar door sales and tastings by appointment.

Prices: $14.95 cellar door.

Vintage Rating 1986–89: Red: '88, '89, '87, '86.

Summary: No new wines have been released since the last edition of this book, in which the Pinot Noir and Cabernet Sauvignon both rated well. Gill Thomas is particularly enthusiastic about the quality of the up-coming '88 and '89 Pinot Noirs which he sees as a marked improvement on earlier wines and which he believes will be "of classic style and dimension".

Swan Valley

1988 VINTAGE

Winter rainfall was below average, and the drier than normal conditions prevailed right through spring and early summer. Most vineyards have supplementary irrigation from underground water supplies, so the absence of rainfall was not critical. Slightly cooler weather in December and January also assisted, although once vintage commenced, a prolonged spell of extremely hot weather led to rapid ripening of all varieties and an extremely compressed vintage.

All varieties were picked in prime condition, free of disease. By and large both colour and flavour was intense, and acid levels were reasonably good. For most wineries it was a good vintage providing wines in typical style.

1989 VINTAGE

Budburst was interrupted by an unseasonable spell of cold weather which, while not unduly affecting set, did lead to uneven ripening. Apart from that one week period, the growing season was mild right through to the end of January, when the first grapes were harvested for sparkling wines. A week of very hot weather at the start of February brought maturities on quickly, and the main harvest then commenced. Picking no sooner got underway than a week of heavy rain led to outbreaks of black rot, with chenin blanc particularly affected.

Conditions then returned to normal with 30° C plus temperatures and wind, which dried out the rot and mould, and led to the best red wines (shiraz and cabernet sauvignon) for 20 years or more. Verdelho was very uneven, but chardonnay was by and large excellent, while the botrytis in the chenin blanc led to some attractive, high-flavoured wines.

THE CHANGES

The Swan Valley continues much as ever, utterly dominated by Houghton. The quality of its wines, and the success of its winemaking, means that it is able to readily absorb every tonne of available grapes and every litre of bulk wine offered by other growers and makers in the district. It has also been very active in encouraging farmers to plant vineyards, supplying the planting material and contracting to buy the grapes for long periods. Its most successful wine, Houghton White Burgundy, represents 30% of all the wine made in Western Australia, and is a national brand leader.

Former Plantagenet winemaker Rob Bowen moved to Perth and provided consultancy services to a number of the small wineries, leading to sharp improvement in quality in many instances.

As ever, the region breaks into two camps: numerous small cellar door operations selling wine of mediocre quality in bulk (principally to the Yugoslav community), and the dozen or so more professional operations providing bottled and branded table wine of real quality.

Henley Park wines has been acquired by Danish interests, while Glenalwyn has also been sold and has changed its name to Little River Wines. Finally, on a sad note, that great man of the Australian wine industry, Jack Mann, died, but his memory will live on at Lamonts, where his daughter and son-in-law will always make wine in the fashion that Jack Mann would have approved of. Lamonts, incidentally, has opened a very good restaurant which is run by their daughter Kate.

ADRIATIC WINES

Location: Great Northern Highway, Herne Hill, 6056.
(09) 296 4518.

Winemaker: P. Jurjevich.

Principal Wines: Bulk red and white table wines for home bottling, and a vintage port specialist. Varieties grown include chenin blanc, shiraz, pedro, grenache and muscat.

Distribution: Cellar door sales 8 a.m. to 5 p.m. Monday to Saturday.

BANARA WINES

Location: Banara Road, Caversham, 6055.
(09) 279 6823.

Winemaker: Charles Knezovic.

Principal Wines: Fortified wine specialist producing a range of ports and muscats from estate-grown shiraz and muscat.

Distribution: Exclusively cellar door sales 8.30 a.m. to 6 p.m. Monday to Saturday, 10 a.m. to 6 p.m. Sunday.

BASSENDEAN

Location: 147 West Road, Bassendean, 6054; 7 km east of Perth GPO on the Swan River.
(09) 276 1734.

Winemaker: Laurie Nicoletto.

Principal Wines: A red wine specialist who magically creates soft and clean burgundy-style wines without the aid of any form of oak maturation and very often from fruit of humble variety and origin. Wines include Shiraz, Burgundy, Cabernet Shiraz, Chenin Blanc and Vintage Port. Wine usually available cellar door with up to five years bottle-age.

Distribution: Has now largely shrunk to cellar door sales and mailing list; principal retail distribution in Perth metropolitan area. Cellar door sales 5.15 p.m. to 6.30 p.m. Monday to Friday, 9 a.m. to 5 p.m. Saturday. Other hours by appointment.

BONANNELLA & SONS

Location: 3 Pinjar Road, Wanneroo, 6065.
(09) 405 1084.

Winemaker: Immacolata Bonannella

Principal Wines: Dry white table wine, dry red table wine, and Rosé, Sherry, Port and Marsala.

Distribution: Cellar door sales 8.30 a.m. to 8 p.m. 7 days.

COBANOV

Location: Lot 1, Stock Road, Herne Hill, 6056.
(09) 296 4210.

Winemaker: Steve Cobanov.

Principal Wines: White and red table wine and fortified wine.

Distribution: Wines sold in bulk only by direct sales methods; cellar door sales by appointment only.

COORINJA

Location: Box 99, Toodyay Road, Toodyay, 6566; 50 km north-east of the Swan Valley.
(096) 26 2280.

Winemakers: Doug and Hector Wood.

Principal Wines: A basic range of non-vintage red and fortified table wines is made which, despite their lack of vintage date and unpretentious packaging, often provide surprising value for money. Not truly part of the Swan Valley, and having no viticultural neighbours, Coorinja has remained largely unchanged for half a century or more.

Distribution: Cellar door sales and mail order; local retail distribution only. Cellar door sales 8 a.m. to 5 p.m. Monday to Saturday.

ELLENDALE ESTATE WINES

Location: 18 Ivanhoe Street, Bassendean, 6054; in Bassendean township, 0.5 km north of Bassendean railway station.
(09) 279 1007.

Winemaker: John Barrett-Leonard.

Principal Wines: A wide range of table and fortified wines sold either in bottle or flagon, with special emphasis on young, lightly fortified wines. The 28 wines available at cellar door include Riesling, Shiraz, Cabernet Sauvignon, Sauterne, White Liqueur Muscat, Vintage Port and Cabernet Port.

Distribution: Exclusively cellar door sales and mail order. Cellar door sales 8.30 a.m. to 6 p.m. Monday to Saturday. Mailing list enquiries as above.

Tasting Notes:

1986 SAUTERNE [70] Colour: very good green-yellow. *Bouquet:* pungent honeysuckle aromas, suggestive of late picked verdelho. *Palate:* strong, honeysuckle fruit; rich and smooth; simply lacks the structural complexity of botrytised wine. Drink '90–'92.

1985 CABERNET SAUVIGNON [61] Colour: medium developed red. *Bouquet:* rich, ripe roasted porty/jammy fruit. *Palate:* old traditional style of cabernet sauvignon made from very ripe fruit and showing full jammy/porty characters; there are certainly those who still admire the style. Drink '90–'93.

Summary: Ellendale is a quite substantial operation and although its products never find their way to eastern states, John Barrett-Leonard does know how to produce good wine.

❦EVANS AND TATE

Location: Swan Street, Henley Brook, 6055; 28 km north-east of Perth.
(09) 296 4666.

Winemakers: Bill Crappsley (chief winemaker) and Krister Jonsson (winemaker).

1989 Production: 5000 cases.

Principal Wines: High-quality table wines made from two vineyards: Redbrook in the Margaret River (see separate entry) and Gnangara Estate in the Swan Valley. The latter produces Gnangara Shiraz (a blend of 80% shiraz and 20% cabernet sauvignon); a wider range of wines comes from Redbrook.

Distribution: National fine wine retail distribution through I. H. Baker & Co., NSW and Q'd.; The Wine Co. Pty. Ltd., Vic.; Caon & Co., SA; in WA distributed direct to quality restaurants and retailers. Cellar door sales 10 a.m. to 5 p.m. Monday to Friday, noon to 4 p.m. Saturday, Sunday and public holidays. High-quality mailing list; special wine offered to mailing list subscribers.

Prices: $12 recommended retail.

Vintage Rating 1986–89: Red: '88, '87, '89, '86.

Outstanding Prior Vintages: '77, '82, '84.

Tasting Notes:

1988 GNANGARA SHIRAZ [73] Colour: medium red. *Bouquet:* soft and complex, with suggestions of a touch of carbonic maceration, and light oak. *Palate:* soft, clean, fruity and easily accessible red wine, again with just a faint suspicion of carbonic maceration; the balance is extremely good. Drink '91–'94.

Summary: Evans and Tate have been one of the driving forces in Western Australian viticulture and oenology over the last 10 years, thanks to a unique combination of marketing drives and skill provided by John and Toni Tate, and a new approach in the vineyard and winery by Bill Crappsley. The latter involved a move away from the late-picked, high-alcohol styles to far earlier picking and fresher fruit. Inevitably, there was a degree of experimentation, and some observers—myself included—felt this process was taken too far for a time. However, recent vintages under the Evans and Tate label show a return to top form, particularly in the Margaret River.

❦FARANDA WINES

Location: Wanneroo Road, Wanneroo, 6061.
(09) 405 1025.

Winemaker: Basil Faranda.

Principal Wines: Flagon table wine made from chasselas, muscat and grenache.

Distribution: Exclusively cellar door sales 8 a.m. to 6 p.m. 7 days.

GLENORA WINES

Location: Lot 38, Nelson Road, Glen Forrest, WA, 6071.

Winemaker: David Cooper.

Principal Wines: Semillon, Chardonnay, Sauvignon Blanc, Verdelho, Cabernet Sauvignon and Cabernet Merlot.

Distribution: Chiefly through Perth retailers; distributed through WA wine brokers. Cellar door sales and tasting by appointment only. Mail order enquiries to above address.

HENLEY PARK WINES

Location: Swan Street, West Swan, 6055; near Henley Brook, 22 km north of Perth. (09) 296 4328.

Winemaker: Vincent Desplat.

1989 Production: Approximately 3500 cases.

Principal Wines: Rhine Riesling, Semillon, Chardonnay, Chenin Blanc, Muscadelle, Muscat Gordo Blanco, Shiraz and Cabernet Sauvignon.

Distribution: Principally cellar door sales and mailing list; cellar door sales 9 a.m. to 6 p.m. Monday to Saturday and 10 a.m. to 6 p.m. Sunday. Perth retail service direct; NSW distributors Ricrowe Pty Ltd.

Tasting Notes:

1989 RHINE RIESLING [65] Colour: very good medium yellow-green. *Bouquet:* quite potent and concentrated rhine riesling with a faint seaweed edge to the aroma. *Palate:* very intense and rich riesling, with masses of fruit, and again a slightly odd edge to the flavour that may well simply represent the last effects of fermentation yet to settle down. Drink '90–'91.

1989 BEAUJOLAIS [65] Colour: light, bright purple-red. *Bouquet:* light fruit with accented pie and peas carbonic maceration characters. *Palate:* light and fresh, again showing carbonic maceration spicy/meaty flavours; well-made example of its style. Drink '90.

Summary: The new Danish owners of Henley Park Wines have radically reshaped the production, and wine quality has also significantly improved.

HIGHWAY WINES

Location: Great Northern Highway, Herne Hill, 6056; 17 km north-east of Perth. (09) 296 4353.

Winemaker: Anthony Bakranich.

Principal Wines: A wide range of traditional table and fortified wines available, chiefly sold in flagons.

Distribution: Exclusively cellar door sales, 8 a.m. to 6 p.m. Monday to Saturday.

HOUGHTON

Location: Dale Road, Middle Swan, 6055; 22 km north-east of Perth. (09) 274 5100; Fax (09) 274 5372.

Winemaker: Peter Dawson.

1989 Production: 300,000 cases.

Principal Wines: More than half the fruit crushed at Houghton comes from the company's own vineyard in the Swan Valley and near Gingin, where grapes such as verdelho, chardonnay, chenin blanc and cabernet sauvignon are grown. The remaining fruit derives largely from the company's third vineyard at Frankland River in the cool south-west of Western Australia, which is an important source of cabernet sauvignon, rhine riesling, pinot noir and chardonnay. Further supplies of semillon, verdelho, chardonnay, cabernet and merlot are contracted in the Margaret River, Manjimup and Mt Barker regions. In recent years, wines made at Houghton have been re-organised into three distinct ranges:

the Line range (which includes Houghton White Burgundy), the Wildflower Ridge range (which includes some wines sourced or blended with wines grown outside Western Australia) and the Gold Reserve range (reserved for the company's very finest wines). The Houghton Line range includes Chablis, Rhine Riesling, Late Picked Verdelho, Verdelho, Cabernet, Shiraz/Malbec and Cabernet Rosé in addition to the White Burgundy. Wildflower Ridge includes Rhine Riesling and Chablis, together with Fumé Blanc, Frontignac, Cabernet/Shiraz, Shiraz and a Soft Red. The current Gold Reserve range includes Verdelho, Chardonnay, Sauvignon Blanc, Rhine Riesling, Beerenauslese and Margaret River Cabernet. Recent additions include the re-release of successful fully matured wines such as the 1983 Houghton White Burgundy and 1984 Houghton Chardonnay as Show Reserve Wines and the 1982 Shiraz, 1982 Cabernet Sauvignon and 1983 Rhine Riesling Cellar Reserves. Each of the Houghton ranges includes wines made from or blended with grapes grown on the company's different vineyards and the source or sources of fruit for each wine is clearly noted on each label.

Distribution: National wholesale by the Houghton Wine Company in Western Australia and the Hardy Wine Company in other states.

Prices: $9.59 to $13.49 recommended retail for table wines; Champagne, Show Reserve wines and Centenary Port $11.42 to $18.88.

Vintage Rating 1986–89: White: '89, '88, '86, '87. Red: '89, '88, '86, '87.

Outstanding Prior Vintages: '82, '83.

Tasting Notes:

1989 WHITE BURGUNDY [85] Colour: light yellow-green. *Bouquet:* fragrant, clean and tangy with some passionfruit aromas. *Palate:* exceptionally fragrant and lively fruit with flavours of peach and passionfruit, and a long finish; it may well prove to be the best release ever under this label, thanks in part to the inclusion of a significant percentage of chardonnay for the first time. Drink '90–'94.

1989 CABERNET ROSE [78] Colour: bright crimson-purple. *Bouquet:* very clean, with that typical touch of grassy cabernet fruit. *Palate:* lively, fresh and tingling; a beautifully balanced wine, with subliminal residual sugar and very good fruit; to be hypercritical, there is the slightest touch of furriness in the after-taste. Drink '90.

1989 NEW LEAF SOFT RED [80] Colour: brilliant purple-red. *Bouquet:* fresh, clean and fragrant spicy/berry fruit. *Palate:* lovely fresh cherry fruit, clean and flavoursome; excellent crisp finish; one of the best nouveaus of 1989. Drink '90.

1989 GOLD RESERVE SAUVIGNON BLANC [81] Colour: light straw-yellow. *Bouquet:* light, crisp smoky/herbal/gooseberry varietal fruit that will grow deliciously in bottle. *Palate:* lively, crisp, clean and tangy, with very well-balanced gooseberry fruit flavours; not a particularly big wine, but a stylish one. Drink '90–'92.

1987 FRANKLAND RIVER CABERNET SAUVIGNON [71] Colour: medium purple-red. *Bouquet:* clean, gently sweet red berry and a faint touch of tobacco; the oak is slightly dull. *Palate:* pleasant bottle development showing a touch of herbaceous/tobacco varietal character with some astringency; once again, better oak would have lifted the wine. Drink '90–'93.

CENTENARY TAWNY PORT [72] Colour: red-brown of medium depth. *Bouquet:* rich and ripe caramel liqueur style rather than classic tawny. *Palate:* soft, round and sweet liqueur style that has plenty of flavour, a little too much oak, and again is not a classic tawny.

Summary: Houghton continues to break the tyranny of distance between Perth and the eastern states' markets thanks to a combination of winemaking skills, adept promotion and marketing and superb packaging right across the range.

🍇 JADRAN WINES

Location: 445 Reservoir Road, Orange Grove, 6109; 13 km south-east of Perth (winery not in the Swan Valley). (09) 459 1110.

Winemaker: Stephen Radojkovich.

Principal Wines: Substantial but unstated production of table wine, sparkling wine and fortified wines produced from a variety of sources and sold in containers of all sizes.

Distribution: Exclusively cellar door sales 8.30 a.m. to 8.30 p.m. Monday to Saturday.

JANE BROOK ESTATE

Location: Toodyay Road, Middle Swan, 6056; 3 km north of Midland.
(09) 274 143; Fax (09) 274 1211.

Winemaker: David Atkinson.

1989 Production: 10,000 cases.

Principal Wines: A range of table wines from the Swan Valley comprising Wood Aged Chenin Blanc, Chardonnay, Sauvignon Blanc, Late Harvest Frontignan, Cabernet Merlot, Tawny Port, Vintage Port, Liqueur Tokay, Liqueur Muscat and Liqueur Verdelho.

Distribution: Principally cellar door sales and mailing list; limited exports through Hicks and Hayes; Perth retail distribution. Cellar door sales 10 a.m. to 5 p.m. Monday to Saturday, noon to 5 p.m. Sunday and public holidays. NSW distribution through Camperdown Cellars.

Prices: Table wines $7.50 to $11 cellar door; fortified $9.50 to $27.

Vintage Rating 1986–89: White: '88, '89, '87, '86. Red: '89, '88, '87, '86.

Tasting Notes:

1988 CHARDONNAY [75] Colour: medium full yellow-green. Bouquet: clean and smooth, gently honeyed/buttery fruit; typical warm area style, not particularly fragrant; oak in restraint. Palate: a well-made wine with smooth honeyed/butter fruit with light to medium weight and the oak held well in restraint. Drink '90–'91.

1988 CHENIN BLANC [78] Colour: light to medium yellow-green. Bouquet: pungent tangy/ tropical gooseberry/grapefruit aromas, fruit rather than oak driven, and still very youthful. Palate: good fruit, again with overtones of sauvignon blanc rather than chenin blanc; rather less luscious than the bouquet suggests, and finishes quite dry. A very unusual style of chenin blanc. Drink '90.

1988 SAUVIGNON BLANC [74] Colour: medium yellow-green. Bouquet: quite unusual fruit aromas, slightly oily and over-ripe into honey/ peach characters. Palate: full, ripe honey/ peach fruit with just a touch of gooseberry; good mouth-feel and balance; an interesting if unusual wine that almost seems to play a role reversal with the chenin blanc. Drink '90.

Summary: The Atkinsons work hard at Jane Brook, and the winery is well ordered and well equipped. The major problem with the wines lies in the not terribly pleasant flavours of the German oak which seems to have been used extensively; as this is outside the control of the winemaker once the oak has been chosen, it seems unfair to be so critical, but the appeal of the wines must necessarily be diminished by that oak.

LAKEVILLE VINEYARDS

Location: 1921 Albany Highway, Maddington, 6109; 16 km south of Perth.
(09) 459 1637.

Winemakers: Jose and Mate Maras.

Principal Wines: Limited range of table and fortified wines, made from estate-grown grapes and sold exclusively to local clientele.

Distribution: Cellar door sales 8.30 a.m. to 8 p.m. 7 days.

LAMONT WINES

Location: Bisdee Road, Millendon, 6056; 17 km north-east of Perth.
(09) 296 4485.

Winemaker: Corin Lamont.

1989 Production: 3300 cases.

Principal Wines: Limited range of table and fortified wines including White Burgundy, Chardonnay, Cabernet Rosé, Cabernet Sauvignon, Vintage Port and a marvellous and exclusive fortified wine called Navera, the latter made in minuscule quantities.

Distribution: Almost exclusively cellar door/mail order sales; cellar door sales 10 a.m. to 5 p.m. Wednesday to Sunday. Two retail outlets in Perth.

Prices: $6 to $10 cellar door.

Vintage Rating 1986–89: '88, '86, '87, '89.

Tasting Notes:

1989 CHENIN BLANC [74] Colour: medium to full yellow-green. *Bouquet:* rich, soft slightly tropical fruit with abundant weight. *Palate:* soft and flavoursome, with touches of peach and honey; a soft, easy finish. Drink '90–'91.

1988 WHITE BURGUNDY [69] Colour: medium yellow-green. *Bouquet:* very complex, with some burgundian, slightly sulphidic, characters. *Palate:* again, a very complex wine with strong "French" flavours in the inimitable Lamont style. Drink '90–'91.

1988 CABERNET ROSE [72] Colour: light pink red. *Bouquet:* sweet fruit aromas with a slightly caramel/fruit cake edge. *Palate:* unmistakable cabernet varietal character; crisp and tart slightly herbaceous fruit; made bone-dry. Drink '90.

1988 HERMITAGE [77] Colour: medium to full red-purple. *Bouquet:* clean and smooth concentrated ripe berry aromas. *Palate:* lovely soft, ripe red berry/plum/cherry fruit; no oak influence evident; finishes with soft tannins. Drink '91–'95.

1988 CABERNET [75] Colour: medium to full red-purple. *Bouquet:* clean with fairly ripe black currant/cassis cabernet varietal fruit. *Palate:* of light to medium structure, but with ripe slightly jammy cassis fruit on the mid-palate followed by a hint of astringent herbal characters on the finish; tannin in restraint. Drink '91–'94.

Summary: 1989 was Jack Mann's last vintage; he has taken his beloved three C's to a higher place where cricket, christianity and chablis are no doubt being no less appreciated. He can rest assured that his daughter, Corin Lamont, will keep the faith.

LITTLE RIVER WINES
(formerly Glenalwyn)

Location: Corner of West Swan and Forrest Swan Streets, West Swan, 6055; 10 km north of Guildford.
(09) 296 4462.

Winemaker: Rob Bowen (contract 1989).

1989 Production: Approximately 5500 cases

Principal Wines: Prince Regent Riesling, Late Harvest Frontignac, Chenin Blanc, Verdelho, Shiraz, Cabernet Sauvignon, White Port, Vintage Port and Tawny Port.

Distribution: Exclusively cellar door sales and mail order; cellar door sales 10 a.m. to 6 p.m. 7 days. Mailing order enquiries as above.

Prices: $9.90 to $12 cellar door.

Tasting Notes:

1989 RHINE RIESLING [64] Colour: light straw-green. *Bouquet:* highly scented floral fruit with a faint hint of spice. *Palate:* very clean, fresh and floral, again with a slight traminer-like spice; should develop well in bottle and may well merit higher points. Drink '90–'91.

1989 CHENIN BLANC [60] Colour: medium yellow-green. *Bouquet:* quite broad and fleshy, with typical fruit salad aromas. *Palate:* again, somewhat broad with light toasty characters; just lacking a little intensity and weight. Drink '90.

Summary: Previous vintages of Little River wines were not attractive and not really of commercial quality; however, the retention of Rob Bowen as a consultant in 1989 has led to a marked improvement in style and quality.

MOONDAH BROOK ESTATE

Location: Mooliabeenie Road, Gingin, 6503; (vineyard only).
(09) 279 4944.

Winemaker: Paul Lapsley.

1989 Production: 30,000 cases.

Principal Wines: Verdelho, Chenin Blanc, Chardonnay and Cabernet Sauvignon. A number of successful fully mature wines have been re-released this year under the Moondah Brook Estate Show Reserve label.

Distribution: National wholesale by the Houghton Wine Company in Western Australia and the Hardy Wine Company in other states.

Prices: $11.24 to $17.08 recommended retail.

Vintage Rating 1986–89: White: '89, '88, '87, '86. Red: '86, '89, '88, '87.

Outstanding Prior Vintages: '80, '83.

Tasting Notes:

1989 VERDELHO [71] Colour: light green-yellow. *Bouquet:* highly aromatic fruit with some smoky fermentation characters still lingering, but very well made. *Palate:* a young wine with quite remarkably intense fruit which should be drinking very well by 1990. Drink '90–'91.

1989 CHARDONNAY [CS] Colour: light to medium green-yellow. *Bouquet:* fine, complex rich grapefruit aromas with very good oak. *Palate:* a wine showing absolutely outstanding character flavour and balance in July 1989; if it fulfils its promise, will rate between 85 and 90.

1987 CABERNET SAUVIGNON [74] Colour: medium red, with a touch of purple. *Bouquet:* of light to medium weight, spotlessly clean, soft red currant fruit and slightly dusty oak. *Palate:* clean soft pleasant cherry berry fruit slightly one dimensional; better oak would have made all the difference. Drink '90–'93.

Summary: The Moondah Brook is the other arm of Houghton, with a quite distinct vineyard some distance away from the Swan Valley proper. The wines are invariably generously flavoured; occasional releases of the Verdelho and Chenin Blanc, in particular, have been outstanding.

OLIVE FARM

Location: 77 Great Eastern Highway, South Guildford, 6055; 3 km north of Perth Airport.
(09) 277 2989.

Winemaker: Ian Yurisich.

Principal Wines: A substantial range of table, sparkling and fortified wines is made; wines include Verdelho, Chenin Blanc, Semillon, Late Harvest Semillon, Chardonnay, Cabernet Shiraz, Cabernet Sauvignon, Oloroso Sherry, Old Madeira, Vintage Port and Tawny Port.

Distribution: Limited retail distribution outside of Perth; principally cellar door sales and mailing list. Mailing list enquiries to PO Box 98, Guildford, 6055. Cellar door sales 10 a.m. to 5.30 p.m. Monday to Friday, 9 a.m. to 3 p.m. Saturday and public holidays.

Summary: Olive Farm is the oldest winery in Australia to have remained in continuous use, and is now surrounded by urban sprawl. The Yurisich family, however, guards its inheritance jealously, consistently making some of the better wines in the Swan Valley. However, neither wines for tasting nor information was forthcoming for this edition.

REVELRY

Location: 200 Argyle Street, Herne Hill, 6056; 5 km south of Midland.
(09) 296 4271.

Winemaker: Stephen Illich.

Principal Wines: A range of table wines sold chiefly in flagon.

Distribution: Exclusively cellar door to local clientele; cellar door sales 2 p.m. to 8 p.m. Monday to Saturday.

SANDALFORD

Location: West Swan Road, Caversham, 6055; 5 km north of Guildford.
(09) 274 5922.

Winemakers: Christian Morlaes (managing director), Tony Roe and Candy Jonsson.

1987 Production: 5000 cases.

Principal Wines: Chenin/Verdelho, Semillon/ Chardonnay, Matilda Rosé, Caversham Estate Cabernet Sauvignon and Zinfandel, Liqueur Port, Liqueur Sandalera and St Nicolas Tawny Port.

Distribution: National retail through Caldbecks; cellar door sales and tasting facilities 10 a.m. to 5 p.m. Monday to Saturday and noon to 3 p.m. Sunday.

Prices: $10 to $21 cellar door.

Vintage Rating 1986–89: '89, '88, '87, '86.

Tasting Notes:

1989 ZINFANDEL [66] *Colour:* light red-purple. *Bouquet:* light, sweet slightly jammy fruit which does however show quite good varietal character in that ripe mould. *Palate:* light cherry/spicy zinfandel varietal fruit flavours again quite pronounced; as with all of the 1988 and 1989 Sandalford wines, spotlessly clean and free of sulphide. Drink '91–'93.

ST NICOLAS TAWNY PORT [60] *Colour:* medium red, with some tawny on the rim. *Bouquet:* biscuity/caramel aromas, though not absolutely fresh. *Palate:* quite rich and full, with some real pretensions to tawny style.

LIQUEUR SANDALERA [73] *Colour:* tawny-brown of medium depth. *Bouquet:* aged rich and complex with the fruit drying out ever so slightly. *Palate:* quite complex blend of predominantly old material freshened by some younger wine; the component parts have not absolutely come together, but the wine certainly has breeding and potential.

Summary: There has been a radical change for the better right across the Sandalford range, with the mercaptan problems of by-gone years entirely laid to rest.

TALIJANCICH WINES

Location: 121 Hyem Road, Herne Hill, 6056; just off Great Northern Highway, 8 km north of Midland.
(09) 296 4289.

Winemakers: Peter and James Talijancich (consultant Rob Bowen).

Principal Wines: Wooded Verdelho, Wooden Semillon, Grenache Rosé, Late Picked Verdelho, Shiraz, Vintage Port, Liqueur Tokay, Liqueur Muscat, Vintage Port and Tawny Port.

Distribution: Principally cellar door sales (50%), hotels and restaurants (25%) and mailing list (25%). Cellar door sales 8.30 a.m. to 5.30 p.m. 7 days. Mailing list enquiries to address above.

Prices: $9 to $38.

Vintage Rating 1986–89: White: '89, '87, '88, '86. Red: '89, '87, '88, '86.

Tasting Notes:

1989 GRENACHE ROSE [80] *Colour:* glorious light crimson-purple. *Bouquet:* fruity and soft with strawberry aromas, though not quite as expressive as the palate. *Palate:* excellent fruit flavours; very fresh and clean, with perfect sugar acid balance giving a lovely feel in the mouth; an exceedingly commercial and beautifully structured wine. Drink '90.

1989 LATE PICKED VERDELHO [65] *Colour:* very good light green-yellow. *Bouquet:* attractive smoky/honeyed fruit with some fermentation characters still lingering July 1989. *Palate:* strong, sweet fruit with good intensity and well made; simply one dimensional compared to botrytis style. Drink '90–'91.

1989 SHIRAZ [CS] Colour: vibrant purple-red. *Bouquet:* spotlessly clean, rich and concentrated youthful red berry/plum aromas. *Palate:* youthful, concentrated ripe plum berry fruit ; has very good potential if it receives good oak and goes safely to bottle—rating 80 points or above.

TAWNY PORT [85] Colour: dark brown with an olive rim. *Bouquet:* very aged, concentrated and rich, with strong rancio characters. *Palate:* aged and concentrated; exceptionally rich dark chocolate flavours; pronounced rancio and good acid; nothing whatsoever to do with a tawny port, but a great deal to do with a super-rich liqueur port style.

SHOW BLEND TOKAY [75] Colour: golden tawny-brown. *Bouquet:* aged, concentrated tea leaf rancio characters. *Palate:* concentrated dark chocolate/raisined fruit balanced by good acid; shows every bit of its average age of 13 years. Stylish and potent.

Summary: As from 1989 there has been a complete change of emphasis at Talijancich. Trickle irrigation in the vineyards and the retention of Rob Bowen as consultant has seen the production of some excellent table wines to complement the luscious, aged fortified wines for which Talijancich is deservedly famous. In my view, those fortified wines were somewhat harshly treated at the 1989 Sheraton Wine Awards.

❦ TWIN HILLS

Location: Great Northern Highway, Baskerville, 6056; 10 km north of Midland. (09) 296 4272.

Winemakers: Mark and Eddie Kraljevich.

Principal Wines: A wide range of table and fortified wines, each one of which is offered in bulk, in flagons or in bottles, without differentiation.

Distribution: Exclusively cellar door sales 8.30 a.m. to 6 p.m. Monday to Saturday.

❦ VINDARA

Location: Great Northern Highway, Herne Hill, 6065; 7 km north of Midland.

Winemaker: Ivan Viskovich.

Principal Wines: Limited range of table wines, usually offered non-vintage and by generic descriptions such as Dry White and Burgundy.

Distribution: Exclusively cellar door sales 8 a.m. to 6 p.m. Monday to Saturday.

❦ WESTFIELD

Location: Cnr Memorial Avenue and Great Northern Highway, Baskerville, 6056; 10 km north of Midland. (09) 296 4356.

Winemaker: John Kosovich.

1989 Production: Approximately 3500 cases.

Principal Wines: Chardonnay, Verdelho, Chenin Blanc, Semillon, Cabernet Blanc, Riesling, Shiraz, Merlot and Cabernet Sauvignon.

Distribution: 50% sold through cellar door, 20% through mailing list and 30% to Perth restaurants and liquor stores. Cellar door sales 8.30 a.m. to 5 p.m. Monday to Saturday. Mailing list address as above.

Prices: $8.50 to $13.50 cellar door.

Vintage Rating 1986–89: '87, '86, '89, '88.

Tasting Notes:

1989 VERDELHO [75] Colour: light to medium yellow-green. *Bouquet:* clean, soft and smooth with a slight herbaceous/honeysuckle edge. *Palate:* well-balanced harmonious fruit with an almost nutty richness in the mid-palate and then echoes of the grassy characters evident on the bouquet. Drink '90–'91.

1988 CHARDONNAY [70] Colour: medium yellow-green. *Bouquet:* strong, complex tangy fruit and oak. *Palate:* the oak threatens to dominate the wine, being slightly raw and hessiany; the fruit is there, and the wine should improve with bottle-age. Drink '91–'94.

1987 SHIRAZ [68] Colour: medium red, with a touch of purple. *Bouquet:* quite stylish firm leafy/berry fruit. _Palate:_ much softer and riper than the bouquet would suggest, with soft ripe and slightly jammy berry fruit; the wine is clean and does have more than adequate flavour. Drink '91–'94.

Summary: John Kosovich is one of the most respected and best-liked winemakers in Swan Valley, quietly producing some very good table wines at very modest prices. More than most, he knows that great wine starts in the vineyard, and pays great attention his wines.

Canberra District, Queensland and Tasmania

Canberra District

1988 VINTAGE

In an area in which many of the vineyards are not drip-irrigated, and in which the summer is usually dry, winter spring rains are all-important. The 1988 vintage got off to a good start with a mild, wet winter and an unusually early budburst. Cool conditions in spring then slowed growth, and the vignerons crossed their fingers as the frost danger period at the end of October arrived. Frost is one of the problems the Canberra District faces, and when the devastating frosts struck Coonawarra and Padthaway, it seemed inevitable that Canberra would feel the lash. Instead, it simply snowed, and the danger passed.

Flowering was completed only slightly ahead of time, with all varieties through before the end of December. Isolated patches of hail caused minor, localised damage in that month, but by early January the warm weather had arrived and continued through to the commencement of harvest, one of the earliest recorded by many vineyards. The chemical composition of the grapes was very good, producing full-flavoured, well-balanced wines. Yet for some vineyards in the Murrimbateman area there was next to no vintage: the vines had been defoliated or deformed by drift from aerial spraying of a hormone herbicide.

1989 VINTAGE

Good sub-soil moisture from winter rainfall was followed by a warm spring. Conditions at flowering and fruit set were good, and potential crops were larger than normal with more bunches of generally smaller berries. A cooler than normal summer with evenly spaced follow-up rain led to an ideally slow ripening season, and when warm weather arrived at the beginning of March it was welcomed with open arms, as it lifted lagging sugar levels.

Just as vintage began with the early varieties in the warmer sites, the rain started. as much as 400 mm, two-thirds of the annual average, fell in March and April, initially in several large downpours of 100 to 150 mm, and then as intermittent lighter showers during April. Varieties such as pinot noir and chardonnay, picked before the rain in the earlier maturing vineyards, were of good quality and flavour, and some good wines are expected.

For the remaining varieties and vineyards, the year was one of the most difficult on record. Botrytis, bunch rot and powdery mildew, compounded by bird damage, combined to play havoc with the crops. Some vineyards suffered 50 per cent loss, and several left most of their riesling and thin-skinned varieties like semillon on the vine. Some material was salvaged by selective picking at generally low baumes; reds picked after the rain are of a light style, with less dense colour and lighter tannins and flavours than usual. All in all, a year the district would prefer to forget.

THE CHANGES

After four new entries in the last edition, there is only one this time around. However, on the basis of the district tasting, Brindabella Hills Winery is going to make a major contribution to the production of quality wine in the area. Roger Harris, who owns and runs Brindabella was formerly principal research scientist at the CSIRO division of plant industry. He graduated with distinction B.App.Sc (Wine Science) from the Riverina-Murray Institute of Higher Education (now the Charles Sturt University) in 1988. Although he is now fully engaged at Brindabella Hills, Roger Harris has continued to collaborate with Dr N. S. Allen in his award-winning research into the active flavour compounds in sauvignon blanc and cabernet sauvignon.

Brindabella Hills Winery was built in time for the 1989 vintage, but Roger Harris had made some wine in 1988 on an experimental basis. Brindabella Hills, which had its own 3.5 hectare vineyard, was then supplemented by two neighbouring properties, providing a total area of 10 hectares planted to cabernet sauvignon, cabernet franc, merlot, pinot noir, chardonnay, sauvignon blanc, semillon and rhine riesling.

Overall, the quality of the wines from the Canberra district is disconcertingly—indeed unacceptably—variable. A number of the wines submitted for tasting for this edition were so grossly faulty as to render them totally unfit for consumption. Some were samples taken from tank or barrel, and it may be that the commercially bottled wine will be better, but others had already been bottled—and never should have been. At the other end of the spectrum, the good wines are getting better, with wineries such as Doonkuna, Lark Hill and now Brindabella Hills showing just what can be achieved. I hasten to add that some of the other wineries are also producing some good wines, although not quite with the consistency of the top three.

AFFLECK VINEYARD

Location: RMB 244, Gundaroo Road,
  Bungendore, 2621.
  (062) 36 9276.

Winemakers: I. A. and S. G. Hendry.

1989 Production: 100 cases.

Principal Wines: Pinot Noir, Chardonnay and
  Cabernet Shiraz.

Distribution: Principally mailing list; enquiries as
  above. Limited Canberra retail distribution.
  Cellar door sales by appointment only.

Prices: $7 to $10 retail.

Vintage Rating 1986–89: White: '87, '89, '86, '88.
  Red: '86, '88, '87, '89.

Tasting Notes:

1988 CHARDONNAY [55] Colour: straw-yellow.
  Bouquet: attractive spicy oak underneath rather
  plain, oily and slightly oxidised fruit. *Palate:*
  once again, some attractive spicy oak flavours,
  but the wine shows oily, oxidised character,
  most probably acquired when the wine was
  being bottled. Drink '90.

1988 LATE PICKED SAUVIGNON BLANC [68]
  Colour: light green-yellow. *Bouquet:* intense and
  lingering passionfruit/lime aromas. *Palate:*
  soft and quite complex with fruit salad/vanillan/
  coconut flavours, finishing fractionally hard.
  Impressive winemaking for a difficult style.
  Drink '90–'92.

1987 PINOT NOIR [60] Colour: dark red-purple.
  Bouquet: strong, with fair depth but rather
  roasted, and lacking any varietal character.
  Palate: strong, vanillan American oak is
  entirely unsuited to pinot noir, and obliterates
  whatever varietal character may be present; by
  no means a bad wine, but says nothing about
  pinot noir. Drink '90–'92.

1987 CABERNET SHIRAZ [78] Colour: medium
  red-purple. *Bouquet:* clean, quite complex, with
  bottle-developed leafy/berry fruit and soft

American oak. *Palate:* quite strong vanilla
  bean American oak goes well with quite full,
  sweet fruit; has plenty of weight and good total
  flavour and balance. Drink '90–'94.

Summary: Ian and Sue Hendry live busy
  professional lives, and are determined to keep
  Affleck's production at a level where they can
  comfortably handle it during weekends and
  holidays. Living on-site is a decided advantage,
  and the wines show real promise.

BENFIELD ESTATE

Location: Fairy Hole Road, Yass, 2582; off Wargeila
  Road, 8 km south of Yass.
  (062) 26 2427.

Winemaker: David Fetherston.

Principal Wines: Most of the Benfield Estate wines
  released to date have been made from grapes
  grown in other districts, including the Hunter
  Valley and Mudgee. The original ambitious
  plans for a large-scale home vineyard have
  been substantially scaled down, and the scale of
  commercial operations likewise. Estate grown
  and made wines include Semillon, Rhine
  Riesling, Merlot and Cabernet Sauvignon.

Distribution: Almost exclusively cellar door sales
  and mailing list. Cellar door sales 10 a.m. to
  5 p.m. weekends, other times by appointment.
  Mailing-list enquiries, PO Box 336, Yass, 2582.

Tasting Notes:

1988 YASS MERLOT [61] Colour: dense purple-
  red. *Bouquet:* solid, deep fruit with some
  leathery/gravelly astringency. *Palate:* a huge
  wine, basically undermade, and which should
  have been fined down before bottling. Time in
  bottle may help the softening process. Drink
  '92–'95.

Summary: David Fetherston commenced Benfield
  Estate with all the right aims and ambitions,
  coupled with some excellent wines which are
  still drinking very well. Since that time, he
  seems to have faltered somewhat, and one can
  only hope that he regains that early
  momentum.

BRINDABELLA HILLS WINERY

Location: Woodgrove Close, via Hall, 2618.
(062) 302 583.

Winemaker: Roger Harris.

1989 Production: 800 cases.

Principal Wines: Rhine Riesling, Chardonnay, Sauvignon Blanc, Pinot Noir and Cabernet (Bordeaux blend), most produced from grapes grown on the Hercynia and Nioka Ridge vineyards in the Hilltops region.

Distribution: Cellar door sales 9 a.m. to 5 p.m. 7 days (while wines last—advisable to telephone first).

Prices: $7 to $14 cellar door.

Tasting Notes:

1989 HERCYNIA CHARDONNAY [CS] Colour: light green. *Bouquet:* complex barrel-ferment characters allied with cool climate melon/grapefruit aromas; sophisticated winemaking. *Palate:* much lighter than the bouquet would suggest, but again, all of the signs of very competent winemaking. Should progressively build flavour and depth and head to points above 75.

1989 HERCYNIA PINOT NOIR [CS] Colour: medium red-purple. *Bouquet:* lively, spicy oak with fresh strawberry fruit, and a touch of sappiness; good varietal character. *Palate:* lively, fresh strawberry pinot fruit, with slightly sawdusty oak still to finally integrate. Quite outstanding and almost certainly headed towards 85 or above.

1989 HERCYNIA CABERNET MERLOT [CS] Colour: medium to full purple-red. *Bouquet:* spotlessly clean, super-sophisticated spicy oak with light to medium berry fruit. *Palate:* once again, very strong, spicy Troncais/Allier oak characters, slightly out of balance with the fruit; great potential if back-blended with less-oaked material, and once again headed above 85 points.

1989 CABERNET SAUVIGNON CABERNET FRANC MERLOT [CS] Colour: very good purple-red. *Bouquet:* clean, youthful ripe berry fruit. *Palate:* clean, rich cherry/ berry fruit with quite persistent tannins; yet another wine of outstanding potential.

1989 NIOKA PICNIC CREEK CABERNET SAUVIGNON [CS] Colour: medium purple-red. *Bouquet:* clean, relatively light leafy berry fruit. *Palate:* of light to medium weight, with leafy/berry fruit almost identical to the bouquet, and a touch of charred oak. Will rate more than 75.

Summary: It is difficult to think how Roger Harris could have made a more impressive start. If these wines live up to even half their promise, Brindabella Hills will not only become a major player in the Canberra District, but a significant small producer in the total Australian context.

CLONAKILLA

Location: Crisps Lane, off Gundaroo Road, Murrumbateman, 2582.
(062) 51 1938 (after hours).

Winemaker: John Kirk.

1989 Production: 350 cases.

Principal Wines: Cabernet Sauvignon, Semillon, Riesling, Late Picked Sauvignon Blanc, Pinot Noir, Cabernet-Shiraz, Muscat and Vintage Port.

Distribution: Cellar door sales only, 10.30 a.m. to 5 p.m. Saturday and Sunday.

Prices: $7 to $12 cellar door.

Vintage Rating 1986–89: '87, '86, '88, '89.

Tasting Notes:

1988 RHINE RIESLING [64] Colour: medium yellow-green. *Bouquet:* quite good fruit expression, albeit broad and slightly blowsy, suggesting the inclusion of some pressings. *Palate:* again, a very full-flavoured, soft wine with quite spicy fruit but tending to broadness; reasonably high residual sugar in cellar door style. Drink '90–'91.

1988 SEMILLON [73] Colour: very good light green-yellow. *Bouquet:* nice, clean, herbaceous varietal fruit, still quite undeveloped. *Palate:* fragrant, tangy herbaceous fruit, vaguely reminiscent of New Zealand semillon; faint bitterness may soften with further age. A well-made wine. Drink '91–'94.

1987 CABERNET SAUVIGNON [60] Colour: medium red. *Bouquet:* very closed and undeveloped, with slightly dull, old oak. *Palate:* once again, old oak characters do not help, and the wine seems to lack varietal character, having a vaguely roasted taste; may open up with more bottle-age. Drink '92–'95.

Summary: Clonakilla is one of the better-equipped wineries in the district, and Dr John Kirk brings a highly trained scientific mind to the operation. Wine quality is consistent and, if a little more money were spent on oak, could be very good indeed.

🍇 *DOONKUNA ESTATE*

Location: Barton Highway, Murrumbateman, 2582; 20 km south-east of Yass. (06) 227 5885.

Winemaker: Sir Brian Murray.

1989 Production: 1200 cases.

Principal Wines: Rhine Riesling, Chardonnay, Sauvignon Blanc, Pinot Noir, Shiraz and Cabernet Sauvigon.

Distribution: By mail order; mailing list enquiries as above. Cellar door sales 10 a.m. to 4 p.m. weekdays and by appointment. Some retail and restaurant outlets.

Prices: $9.50 to $17 cellar door and mailing list.

Vintage Rating 1986–89: '88, '87, '86, '89.

Tasting Notes:

1988 CHARDONNAY [80] Colour: bright and strong green-yellow. *Bouquet:* quite pronounced

lemony oak with light, citric/grassy fruit. *Palate:* light but very elegant, understated cool climate style; a classic chablis in the French sense. Drink '90–'92.

1988 FUME BLANC [87] Colour: light green-yellow. *Bouquet:* clean, and of light to medium intensity, with well-balanced lemony/spicy oak. *Palate:* beautifully handled oak combines well with light, crisp fruit; the wine is very fresh, yet harmonious, in the mouth. Drink '90–'92.

1988 CABERNET SAUVIGNON [87] Colour: full purple-red. *Bouquet:* clean, complex and full with dark berry fruit neatly set against a touch of toasty charred oak. *Palate:* extremely fresh, clean and stylish; the structure is excellent, with soft but persistent tannins. Drink '92–'97.

1987 SHIRAZ [79] Colour: medium red, with just a touch of purple. *Bouquet:* soft and sappy, almost pinot-like. *Palate:* attractive spicy/sappy fruit which is fresh, light and once again with all the feel of a French Burgundy; an unusual wine, to say the least. Drink '90–'93.

Summary: The retention of professional consultants on the winemaking side continues to pay huge dividends for Doonkuna.

🍇 *HELM'S*

Location: Butts Road, Murrumbateman, 2582; off Barton Highway, 20 km south-east of Yass and 35km north of Canberra, off Yass River Road. (06) 227 5536.

Winemaker: Ken Helm.

1989 Production: 1400 cases.

Principal Wines: Rhine Riesling, Traminer, Chardonnay, Muller Thurgau, Cabernet Sauvignon and Hermitage.

Distribution: Cellar door sales and mailing list; cellar door sales 10 a.m. to 5 p.m. daily,

Tuesdays and Wednesdays appointment required. Limited retail outlets. Selected restaurants and hotel groups. Mailing list enquiries as above .

Prices: $10 to $15 cellar door.

Vintage Rating 1986–89: White: '89, '88, '86, '87. Red: '88, '86, '87, '89.

Outstanding Prior Vintages: '83, '84 (particularly for reds).

Tasting Notes:

1988 HERMITAGE [65] Colour: dense blackish-red. *Bouquet:* clean, solid but very closed, with almost no fruit aromas escaping. *Palate:* a huge, dense, slightly extractive wine, with many indications of very low SO_2, a situation which can have unexpected and undesirable consequences. Drink '92–'94.

Summary: Ken Helm took early retirement from the CSIRO in September 1988 to concentrate on the development of his winery, which had the largest crush in the 1989 vintage, and which will be producing 3000 cases by 1991. The 1986 Cabernet Sauvignon won a gold medal at the Royal Sydney Wine Show in 1988 in the New South Wales Small Producers Class, so Ken Helm clearly knows how to make red wine. I continue to have problems with the white wines from this winery.

 JEIR CREEK WINES

Location: Gooda Creek Road, Murrumbateman, 2582.
(062) 58 8292 (A/H) or (06) 227 5999 (winery).

Winemaker: Rob Howell.

1989 Production: 450 cases.

Principal Wines: Rhine Riesling, Chardonnay, New Shiraz, Shiraz Cabernet Sauvignon and Cabernet Sauvignon.

Distribution: Exclusively cellar door sales and mailing list; cellar door sales 10 a.m. to 5 p.m. weekends and public holidays; other times by appointment. Mailing list enquiries to PO Box 5, Murrumbateman, 2582.

Prices: $9 to $14 cellar door.

Vintage Rating 1986–89: White: '87, '88, '89 ('86 not rated). Red: '87, '89, '88 ('86 not rated).

Tasting Notes:

1988 SHIRAZ CABERNET [82] Colour: medium to full purple-red. *Bouquet:* clean, concentrated and youthful dark berry/plum fruit in good style. *Palate:* very rich, ripe and full cassis/ dark plum/berry fruits with a faint touch of aniseed spice; high-toned flavours throughout. Drink '92–'97.

Summary: Rob Howell has the requisite technical knowledge and dedication to quality to succeed with Jeir Creek; I have the feeling he will be one of the survivors, and his wines worth following. The single white wine, a 1989 Chardonnay, was not reviewable thanks to very raw and nasty oak. Time and back-blending may or may not redeem it.

 KYEEMA

KYEEMA
1988
CHARDONNAY
A dry, well balanced and persistently flavoured varietal with added complexity from fermentation in French oak. Made from grapes grown by R. McKenzie, Murrumbateman, NSW.

A J & M K McEwin
Enquiries P.O. Box 282 BELCONNEN ACT 2616
PRODUCE OF AUSTRALIA 750ml 12.5% ALC/VOL
PRESERVATIVE 220 ADDED

Location: Canberra; enquiries to PO Box 282, Belconnen, ACT, 2616.
(062) 54 7557 or (062) 49 9392 (B/H).

Winemaker: Andrew McEwin.

1989 Production: 400 cases.

Principal Wines: Semillon (unwooded and wooded), Cabernet Sauvignon, Shiraz and Chardonnay.

Distribution: Canberra fine wine retail outlets such as La Copita (Narrabundah) and Kegs Stores, and selected local restaurants. Mail order available.

Prices: $10 to $18 retail.

Vintage Rating 1986–89: White: '88, '87, '86, '89.
  Red: '87, '88, '86, '89.

Tasting Notes:

1988 SEMILLON [52] Colour: light straw.
Bouquet: the fruit appears to have been
stripped, either by warm fermentation or by
oxidation at bottling. *Palate:* similar problems
exist; the wine is rather hard, backing fruit and
richness in the mouth. Time may help a little.
Drink '91–'93.

Summary: Andrew McEwin has had a long affair
with every aspect of wine, amongst other
things, being a dedicated consumer and part-
time judge. Kyeema is a backyard winery
operating out of a suburban house, and
utilising grapes purchased chiefly from the
Hilltops region. I have always found quality
variable, and continue to do so.

▼ *LAKE GEORGE*

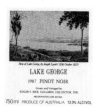

Location: Federal Highway, Collector, 2581;
  50 km north-east of Canberra.
  (048) 48 0039 or (062) 48 6302.

Winemaker: Dr Edgar Riek.

1989 Production: 550 cases.

Principal Wines: Chardonnay, Pinot Noir,
  Semillon, Cabernet Sauvignon and Merlot.

Distribution: Canberra vineyard visits can be
  arranged for those appreciative of wine, but by
  appointment only.

Prices: $75 to $140 per case (wholesale only to
  licensed outlets).

Vintage Rating 1986–89: White: '88, '87, '86, '89.
  Red: '86, '88, '87, '89.

Tasting Notes:

1988 CHARDONNAY [61] Colour: light straw.
Bouquet: rather plain, oily oak and light fruit.
Palate: poor oily/green oak mars some pleasant,

light melon/peach chardonnay fruit; there has
been no problem with the winemaking or
handling other than the indifferent oak. Drink
'90–'92.

1987 PINOT NOIR [60] Colour: light red-brown.
Bouquet: slightly burnt with some Chinese five
spice characters. *Palate:* interesting Chinese
roast duck flavours, but not those of pinot noir;
I can only assume the roast duck comes from
oak of a kind outside my prior experience.
Drink '90.

1987 MERLOT [60] Colour: medium purple-red,
slightly dull. *Bouquet:* clean enough, but with
somewhat squashy/soapy fruit aromas
suggesting high pH. *Palate:* similar slightly
soapy edge to the fruit, again indicative of a
high pH wine; at the finish there is a touch of
the Chinese five spice evident in the pinot.
Drink '90–'91

Summary: Dr Riek is the godfather of the district,
having done most if not all of the pioneering
work. He is a decided iconoclast and seems to
revel in a love–hate relationship with the
district as a whole and with his own wines. He
cannot resist experimentation, something
which he seems to have taken to a new level
with his '87 dry reds.

▼ *LARK HILL*

Location: RMB 281, Gundaroo Road,
  Bungendore, 2621; 30 km north-east of
  Canberra.
  (062) 38 1393.

Winemakers: Dr Dave Carpenter and Sue
  Carpenter.

1989 Production: 1200 cases.

Principal Wines: Chardonnay, Rhine Riesling,
  Semillon, Cabernet Sauvignon/Merlot blends,
  Pinot Noir. All wines made from estate-grown
  or Canberra district grapes. Botrytis styles in
  some years.

Distribution: Cellar door sales, mailing list, retail outlets Canberra, Sydney, Melbourne and selected restaurants in Canberra. Cellar door sales 10 a.m. to 5 p.m. weekends and public holidays, otherwise by appointment. Mailing list enquiries as above. UK imports through Mitchells of Lancaster.

Prices: $8 to $17 cellar door.

Vintage Rating 1986–89: White: '88, '89, '87, '86. Red: '88, '87, '89, '86.

Tasting Notes:

1988 RHINE RIESLING [82] Colour: light yellow-green. *Bouquet:* clean, toasty, dry but classic fruit of light to medium weight. *Palate:* delicate, crisp bone-dry riesling showing perfect handling of the variety. Drink '90–'91.

1988 CHARDONNAY [86] Colour: light green-yellow. *Bouquet:* light, spotlessly clean, with finely balanced oak. *Palate:* beautifully made and constructed; a delicate wine of exceptional finesse showing a hint of spicy oak and finishing with gentle acid. Totally belies its 13° of alcohol. Drink '90–'92.

1988 AUSLESE RHINE RIESLING [85] Colour: medium to full yellow-green. *Bouquet* extremely concentrated and striking, with intense and pungent lime aroma. *Palate:* strong lime flavours with great weight and intensity; by far the best late harvest riesling to have been made in the district. Drink '90–'93.

1988 CABERNET MERLOT [76] Colour: medium red-purple. *Bouquet:* strong minty/leafy aromas, partially reflecting the merlot and partially the climate. *Palate:* similar minty/spicy fruit flavours, clean and fresh, with light oak. Drink '91–'94.

1987 CABERNET MERLOT [81] Colour: medium to full red-purple. *Bouquet:* clean, soft and smooth with a trace of mint. *Palate:* full, smooth and quite complex fruit and mint flavours with soft tannins; good balance and structure, with more depth than the '88. Drink '92–'96.

Summary: Lark Hill was the only winery to supply consistently faultless wines. In every other instance, at least one wine was not reviewable. The dedication and experience of the Carpenters is evident for all to see, and Lark Hill can only go from strength to strength.

❦ MADEW WINES

Location: Furlong Road, Queanbeyan, 2620; on the outskirts of Queanbeyan and 8 km from Canberra.
(062) 97 2742.

Winemaker: Dr David Madew.

Principal Wines: Rhine Riesling, Semillon, Chardonnay and Cabernet Sauvignon.

Distribution: Almost exclusively cellar door sales and mailing list; cellar door sales 9 a.m. to 5 p.m. weekends and public holidays; at other times by appointment. Mailing list enquiries, PO Box 295, Queanbeyan, 2620.

Prices: $7 to $10 mailing list.

Summary: No wines were submitted for tasting for this edition; wine tasted previously showed considerable variation in quality, but I can only assume the learning curve is continuing.

❦ MIDDLETONS

Location: Barton Highway, Murrumbateman, 2582; 30 km north of Canberra.
(062) 27 5584.

Winemaker: Geoffrey B. Middleton.

Principal Wines: Rhine Riesling, Traminer and Shiraz principally using grapes from other districts, including Young and Griffith; Rhine Riesling, Sauvignon Blanc, Chardonnay, Shiraz and Cabernet Sauvignon using Murrumbateman grapes; Mead.

Distribution: Cellar door sales 10 a.m. to 5 p.m. 7 days, and mail order. Licensed restaurant open Friday and Saturday nights and Sunday lunch.

Summary: Middletons has been on the market for sale for some time, and may well have been sold by the time of publication. Winemaking activities have run down to a low level in recent years.

❦ SHINGLE HOUSE

Location: RMB 209, Brooks Road, Bungendore, 2621; 35 km north-east of Canberra.
(062)

Winemakers: Max and Yvonne Blake.

1989 Production: Very small.

Principal Wines: Vineyard planted to mataro, cinsaut, cabernet sauvignon, malbec and chardonnay. Mataro is the only wine so far produced in sufficient quantity to justify commercial sale.

Distribution: Unless and until a licence is granted, not available for sale to the public.

Summary: Max and Yvonne Blake have learnt the hard way about the problems of frost in the Canberra District; the rather unusual plantings simply represent the survivors of an originally far larger vineyard which included other more conventional grapes. However, although the production is tiny, Max and Yvonne Blake are both very careful and exceptionally talented winemakers. It is a pity that the tiny production will prevent these wines reaching a wider audience.

❦ SIMONS WINES

Location: RMB 274 Badgery Road, Burra Creek, 2620; 30 km south of Queanbeyan/Canberra. (062) 36 3216.

Winemaker: Lloyd Simons.

1989 Production: 330 cases.

Principal Wines: Small quantities of hand-made wines including Wood Fermented Chardonnay, Traminer, Semillon, Pinot Noir and Merlot.

Distribution: Cellar door sales 10 a.m. to 5 p.m. weekends and public holidays. Mailing list enquiries to address above.

Prices: $6 to $10 cellar door.

Vintage Rating 1986–89: White: '89, '88, '86, '87. Red: '89, '88, '87 ('86 not made).

Tasting Notes:

1989 TRAMINER [55] Colour: light green-yellow. *Bouquet:* slightly burnt, medicinal overtones with light, spicy fruit underneath. *Palate:* light, spicy varietal fruit, but again a touch of those burnt medicinal characters evident in the bouquet. May settle down with time in bottle. Drink '90.

1987 MERLOT [52] Colour: dense purple-black. *Bouquet:* rather over-ripe fruit with slightly leathery oak. *Palate:* strong, over-ripe and over-

extracted wine with very high tannin; if picked earlier, and less enthusiastically made, could have had some potential. Drink '92–'95.

Summary: The tiny quantities of hand-crafted wines apparently sell well enough through the cellar door, even if they fall somewhat short of conventional wine quality standards.

❦ WESTERING VINEYARD

Location: Federal Highway, Collector, 2581; 10 km south of town. (062) 95 8075.

Winemaker: Captain G. P. Hood.

1989 Production: Approximately 200 cases.

Principal Wines: Chardonnay, Lake Picked Rhine Riesling, Shiraz, Cabernet Sauvignon and Dry Sherry.

Distribution: Exclusively mail order. Enquiries to 97 Jansz Crescent, Griffith, ACT, 2603.

Tasting Notes:

1988 CHARDONNAY [88] Colour: light to medium yellow-green. *Bouquet:* clean, light peachy/melon/fig fruit and oak. *Palate:* fresh, tangy melon/peach/grapefruit flavours, lively and stylish; the oak and fruit balance and integration are perfect. Drink '90–'93.

1987 CHARDONNAY [65] Colour: medium yellow-green. *Bouquet:* complex oak and fruit with abundant character, but with a few extraneous glue paste/sulphide characters. *Palate:* complex charred oak and then some rather odd biscuity/brandy snap flavours; what appears to have been a good wine let down by slightly errant oak. Drink '90–'91.

Summary: Westering is doing very good things with chardonnay: the '88 is a tour de force. It is simply a pity there is not more of it.

❦ YASS VALLEY WINES

Location: Crisps Lane, Murrumbateman, 2582; 30 km north of Canberra. (062) 27 1592.

Winemaker: Peter J. Griffiths.

Principal Wines: Rhine Riesling, Semillon, Rosé and Shiraz. 1983 Rhine Riesling only estate-grown wines so far released: other wines made from grapes grown at Barwang Vineyard, Young.

Distribution: Exclusively cellar door sales and mailing list. Cellar door sales 10 a.m. to 5 p.m. weekends, or by appointment. Mailing list enquiries to PO Box 18, Murrumbateman, 2582.

Granite Belt

1988 VINTAGE

Budburst was uniform and the set generally good for all varieties. Late frosts, always a threat in this high-altitude region, stayed away, as did the other great threat: hail. Overall, the growing season was cool and cloudy; above average rainfall in January threatened to cause problems, but stopped just when growers started to become concerned. The combined effect of the cloud cover and the periods of rain resulted in a low heat summation index (under 1700 day degrees) and all of the early ripening varieties were harvested in prime condition.

The only significant problems of the year came in April, normally a dry month, but this year hit by continuous heavy rain, causing significant problems for later harvested varieties. Shiraz was once again the most successful variety, producing another good Ballandean Nouveau, but also making a fuller bodied style with later picked grapes. Semillon also did well, continu-ing the reputation which this variety has in the Granite Belt.

1989 VINTAGE

A mild winter led to budburst around two to three weeks earlier than normal, setting the pattern for a season which remained two to three weeks in advance of the normal sched-ule right through to the end of harvest. The spring was mild, and flowering took place in mild conditions. For the second year in a row, neither frost nor hail caused any damage.

Two periods of abnormally warm and dry weather, the first in October, the second in February, caused quite severe stress. The October weather led to very poor fruit in some vineyards, and the yield was also depressed by the very dry summer. Some vignerons received less than 25mm of rain during the entire ripening period. The effect was very unpredictable: the red varieties were down by as much as 50% in some vineyards, while chardonnay, semillon and sauvignon blanc were up to 20% in excess of normal. It seems probable that the shiraz will be very concentrated and peppery; the cabernet sauvignon medium bodied; chardonnay will be of average weight; sauvignon blanc with an herbaceous bite; and semillon rich and full-flavoured.

THE CHANGES

The air of optimism that I referred to in the 1988 edition of this book may have taken something of a knock in the wake of the 1989 Brisbane Wine Show. For the first time, the special Queensland classes were abandoned, and all of the Queensland wines were entered in the general classes, using the system adopted in Perth. In other words, the volume requirements for entry for Queensland wines are very much lower, but in other respects they compete equally with interstate wines. The Queensland entries failed to gain a single bronze medal between them, with the result that there were no trophies of any description awarded, not even the Most Successful Exhibitor: even a single point for a bronze medal would have sufficed, but it was not to be.

Luck is always a component of wine shows, and it is certain that luck did not run with the Queensland wineries. There are some wineries in the Granite Belt which are producing wines of medal standard, but the results do emphasise just how embryonic the local industry still is. To put this into some perspective, the 1989 crush in the Granite Belt produced a total of 300 tonnes of wine grapes, significantly less than the amount of grapes any of the large Australian companies would handle during any one day in vintage.

There are no new entries, but there have been some changes behind the scenes. Rodney Hooper has left what was in the last edition called Sundown Valley Vineyards and which has now been renamed Ballandean Estate Winery; Hooper spent two vintages with Goundrey in Western Australia before joining Charles Sturt University (formerly the Riverina College of Advanced Education) as winemaker. Peter Scudamore-Smith, noted Queensland wine identity and food technologist, has become consultant winemaker. Bald Mountain has joined forces with Cassegrain in the Hastings Valley of New South Wales; Cassegrain now contract-makes all of the Bald Mountain wines, keeping half and returning half.

BALD MOUNTAIN

Location: Old Wallangarra Road, Wallangarra, Qld,4383; off New England Highway 6 km north of Wallangarra. (076) 84 3186.

Winemakers: Denis Parsons and John Cassegrain (contract).

1989 Production: Approximately 1000 cases.

Principal Wines: Sauvignon Blanc, Chardonnay, Shiraz and Cabernet Sauvignon.

Distribution: Initially exclusively cellar door sales and mailing list; cellar door sales 9 a.m. to 5 p.m. Monday to Saturday. Mailing list enquiries as above.

Tasting Notes:

1988 SAUVIGNON BLANC [62] Colour: medium to full yellow. *Bouquet:* quite full and clean; has weight, yet little or no varietal character. *Palate:* an odd wine, which shows almost nothing until one comes to the finish, which is crisp, clean and with very good acid; earlier in the palate there are all the signs of oxidation at work, and once again varietal character is absent. Drink '90–'91.

1988 SHIRAZ [73] Colour: medium to full purple-red. *Bouquet:* quite complex, with some vanillan oak and a faint aroma of hand lotion; spice lurks in the background. *Palate:* spicy fruit comes to the fore; the wine has lots of flavour, although it dips slightly on the back-palate; light oak and low tannin. Drink '92–'95.

Summary: The Parsons are dedicated, skilled and meticulous viticulturists and John Cassegrain a very experienced winemaker. It is only a question of time before some teething problems are surmounted, and Bald Mountain starts to produce first class wines. A 1988 Chardonnay, incidentally, was destroyed by mouldy oak.

BALLANDEAN ESTATE WINERY
(formerly Sundown Valley Vineyards)

Location: Sundown Road, Ballandean, 4382; 4 km west of town, and 18 km south of Stanthorpe. (076) 84 1226.

Winemaker: Peter Scudamore-Smith (consultant).

1989 Production: 5000 cases.

Principal Wines: There are two distinct ranges: Ballandean Estate and Sundown Valley Vineyards. Ballandean Estate offers a varietal range of Print Label Sauvignon Blanc, Semillon, Chardonnay, Print Label Shiraz, Cabernet Sauvignon and Light Red Shiraz. The Sundown Valley Vineyards is a generic range of Moselle, Rhine Riesling, White Burgundy, Sylvaner Auslese, Lambrusco and Dry Red. There is also a range of fortified wines: Goldminers Liqueur Muscat, Tinminers Rum Port, Pioneer Tawny Port and Vintage Port.

Distribution: Ballandean Estate national through Tucker-Seabrook-Caon group; cellar door for Sundown Valley Vineyard range and mailing list. Cellar door sales 9 a.m. to 5 p.m. 7 days. Mailing list as above.

Prices: Ballandean Estate $8.50 to $15.50 and Sundown Valley Vineyards $5 to $15.

Vintage Rating 1986–89: White: '89, '87, '88, '86. Red: '89, '87, '86, '88.

Outstanding Prior Vintages: White: '83, '81, '79. Red: '83, '80, '74.

Tasting Notes:

1989 BALLANDEAN ESTATE SAUVIGNON BLANC [74] Colour: medium green-yellow. *Bouquet:* quite rich, with gooseberry fruit and a hint of tobacco; soft vanillan oak. *Palate:* strong vanilla bean American oak is far more evident than in the bouquet, and is not entirely suited to the variety; a wine with plenty of depth of flavour, and would have merited higher points still if a more suitable oak type had been used; the actual handling of the oak cannot be faulted. Drink '90–'91.

1989 SUNDOWN VALLEY RHINE RIESLING [71] *Colour:* light to medium yellow-green. *Bouquet:* full, broad with some slightly oily pressings character. *Palate:* big, full, broad and high-flavoured style, again showing some pressings characters; good acid on the finish helps. An adequate, indeed good, cellar door wine. Drink '90–'91.

1988 BALLANDEAN ESTATE SEMILLON [64] *Colour:* light to medium green-yellow. *Bouquet:* clean fruit, but slightly smelly glue paste/oily old oak. *Palate:* much better than the bouquet, with some herbaceous tang and length to the varietal fruit flavour; perhaps fractionally sweet and tending to cloy every so slightly on the finish. Drink '90–'92.

1988 BALLANDEAN ESTATE LIGHT RED SHIRAZ [68] Colour: very good light purple-red. *Bouquet:* very curious steam roller/peppermint/ aniseed fruit aromas. *Palate:* jumpy, early picked shiraz with flavours of mint, spice and leaf; clean, but with a curious corrected acid feel. Drink '90.

1985 BALLANDEAN ESTATE CABERNET SAUVIGNON [75] Colour: medium to full red-purple. *Bouquet:* clean, quite rich with soft vanillan oak. *Palate:* soft, full, sweet vanillan/ coconut American oak with soft and sweet fruit and fine tannins. Drink '90–'93.

1983 BALLANDEAN ESTATE SHIRAZ [85] *Colour:* medium red. *Bouquet:* clean, soft and sweet velvety shiraz showing classic bottle-developed varietal character. *Palate:* very attractive, sweet, velvety shiraz, very similar to a top-class Hunter; has developed beautifully in bottle with lovely balance. Drink '90–'93.

Summary: Ballandean Estate is the largest winery in the district, and has the distinction of commercial distribution through the Tucker-Seabrook-Caon group. Its 1983 Shiraz is a first-class wine by any standards, and there is absolutely no reason why it cannot produce wines of similar stature in the future.

BUNGAWARRA

Location: Bents Road (formerly Marshalls Crossing Road), Ballandean, Qld, 4382. (076) 84 1128.

Winemaker: Philip Christensen.

Principal Wines: Chardonnay, Late Harvest Semillon, Balandean Nouveau, Shiraz, Cabernet Sauvignon, Vintage Port and Liqueur Muscat.

Distribution: Principally cellar door sales and mailing list; cellar door sales 9 a.m. to 5 p.m. 7 days. Mailing list enquiries to PO Box 10, Ballandean, 4382. Very limited eastern states retail distribution through Bob Thompson, Barrique Fine Wines, Brisbane.

Summary: Bungawarra has been particularly successful in local shows in recent years, receiving the *Courier Mail*–Sheraton Hotel Award for Best Queensland Dry White Wine in both 1986 and 1987 with its then current vintage Chardonnay. Philip Christensen has now assumed majority ownership, and the earlier winemaking-by-committee approach has been abandoned, which should see far greater consistency.

ELSINORE WINES

Location: Kerridges Road, Glen Aplin, 4381; 10 km south of Stanthorpe. (076) 83 4234 (winery) or (07) 848 6733 (Brisbane Office).

Winemaker: Peter Love.

Principal Wines: Three non-vintage table wines (Chablis, Riesling and Lambrusco) with several releases of vintage-dated Hermitage; Tawny Port and Tarragon Wine Vinegar also.

Distribution: Mostly cellar door sales and mail order; cellar door sales 9 a.m. to 5 p.m. weekends and public holidays. Coaches and groups welcome to use barbeque and picnic grounds. Mailing list enquiries to PO Box 106, Coorparoo, 4151.

Prices: $8 to $12.

Summary: Elsinore is a tourist-oriented operation with the estate-made wines being of modest quality.

FELSBERG

Location: Newman Road, Glen Aplin, 4381;
   1.5 km south of Glen Aplin, just off New
   England Highway.
   (076) 300 1946.

Winemaker: Otto Haag.

Principal Wines: Chardonnay, Rhine Riesling,
   Traminer and Shiraz.

Distribution: Initially will be exclusively cellar door
   sales and mailing list. Cellar door sales
   planned for Saturday and Sunday only during
   early years.

Summary: Felsberg promises to be one of the
   showpieces of the Granite Belt, with the house
   and winery commanding sweeping views of the
   surrounding countryside.

FOSTERS

Location: Kalunga, Flaggy Creek via
   Herberton, 4872; 9 km south of Herberton.
   (07) 96 2359.

Winemaker: Christopher Foster.

Principal Wines: Moselle, Riesling, Isabel, Rosé,
   Mataro, Shiraz, Claret and Medium Muscat.
   Wine sold both in bottle and in bulk to
   purchasers providing own container.

Distribution: Exclusively cellar door, daylight until
   dark, 7 days.

Summary: Fosters enjoys a substantial local trade,
   particularly among the Italian community,
   providing bulk wine at very low prices.

KOMINOS WINES

Location: New England Highway, Severnlea, 4352;
   8 km south of Stanthorpe.
   (076) 83 4311.

Winemaker: Tony Comino.

1989 Production: Approximately 25,000 cases.

Principal Wines: Chenin Blanc, Semillon,
   Chardonnay, Balandean Nouveau, Cabernet
   Sauvignon, Shiraz and Light Red.

Distribution: Principally cellar door sales and
   mailing list. Cellar door sales 9 a.m. to 4.30
   p.m. 7 days. Mailing list enquiries to PO Box
   225, Stanthorpe, 4380.

Prices: $7 to $9.

Vintage Rating 1986–89: White: '89, '86, '87, '88.
   Red: '89, '86, '87, '88.

Tasting Notes:

1989 RHINE RIESLING [65] Colour: bright green-
   yellow. _Bouquet:_ lush, opulent fruit with hints of
   lime and toast, albeit with a very slightly cosmetic
   edge. _Palate:_ high-flavoured, rich and slightly
   broad, with quite pronounced residual sugar
   aimed fairly and squarely at the cellar door.
   Drink '90–'91.

1989 CHENIN BLANC [59] Colour: strong, bright
   green-yellow. _Bouquet:_ remarkably intense and
   penetrating fruit salad aroma with a slightly
   herbaceous edge. _Palate:_ comes as a disappointment after the bouquet, because while the fruit
   salad/herbaceous flavours are there, so is a
   great deal of residual sugar—more than is
   necessary or appropriate. Drink '90.

1989 SEMILLON [75] Colour: straw-yellow.
   Bouquet: clean, well made with pronounced
   herbaceous/tobacco characters in the style of
   Margaret River or New Zealand. _Palate:_ again,
   strong herbaceous/tobacco fruit dominates,
   with a light touch of spicy oak; a wine in the
   modern style, with mid-palate flavour, length
   and good acid on the finish. Drink '90–'92.

1989 LIGHT RED [60] Colour: light to medium
   purple-red. _Bouquet:_ strong, biscuity carbonic
   maceration characters with a distinct leafy edge.
   Palate: partially successful maceration style,
   with that slightly furry character which you
   often find and which is very distracting. Drink
   '90.

1989 CABERNET SAUVIGNON [CS] Colour: full
   purple-red. _Bouquet:_ rich, complex and full
   berry fruit. _Palate:_ ripe, full berry fruit with a
   pleasant touch of charred oak; full of promise.

Summary: With the new winery now fully bedded down, Tony Comino should lead Kominos towards the top of the Granite Belt producers. He has the technical qualifications, the dedication and the knowledge to produce wines of high quality.

🍇 MOUNT MAGNUS

Location: Donnelly's Castle Road, off New England Highway, Severnlea, 4352; 4km south of Pozieres.
(076) 85 3213.

Principal Wines: Semillon, Traminer, Balandean Nouveau and Shiraz are top releases. Granite Hills White and Western Hills Moselle also sold.

Distribution: Exclusively cellar door and mailing list for the time being. Cellar door sales 9 a.m. to 5 p.m. 7 days.

Summary: Mount Magnus provides both wine and apple juice. It was planned for winemaking activities to recommence, but I am not certain whether this has in fact transpired.

🍇 OLD CAVES WINERY

Location: New England Highway, Stanthorpe, 4380; on northern outskirts of town.
(076) 81 1494.

Winemaker: David Zanatta.

1989 Production: 30,000 litres.

Principal Wines: A wide range of wines, from premium varietals through to generic table wines, including Chardonnay, Chardonnay/Semillon, Cabernet Shiraz, Armchair Port, and Tawny Port.

Distribution: Exclusively cellar door sales and by mail order; cellar door sales 9 a.m. to 5 p.m. 7 days. Mail order enquiries to PO Box 368, Stanthorpe, 4380.

Prices: $6 to $11.50.

Vintage Rating 1986–89: '88, '89, '86, '87.

Outstanding Prior Vintages: Red: '84.

Tasting Notes:

1988 CHARDONNAY [77] Colour: medium to full yellow-green. Bouquet: surprisingly complex and stylish, with soft buttery fruit together with some slightly cabbagey/citric characters. Palate: rich, full, honeyed/butterscotch flavours showing attractive bottle development; perhaps the wine is fractionally sweet, but that is a quibble. Excellent wine for the region. Drink '90–'91.

1988 CABERNET SHIRAZ [57] Colour: medium red, with a slightly dull purple edge. Bouquet: fair fruit marred by some bitter sulphides. Palate: pleasant, light fruit, but the wine falls away sadly on the finish, which is furry and biscuity. Drink '90.

ARMCHAIR PORT (BOTTLING NO. 2) [65] Colour: light tawny-red. Bouquet: strong muscat characters, attractive but nothing to do with port. Palate: similar attractive, fresh liqueur muscat style, nothing whatsoever to do with any traditional concept of port, but a certain success at the cellar door.

Summary: Old Caves Winery is a substantial operation run under the cheerful direction of David Zanatta; dry table wines are far less important to the substantial cellar door trade than the wide range of flavoured and fortified wines on offer. The 1988 Chardonnay was a most pleasant surprise; if it can be repeated, Old Caves is well on the way to better things.

🍇 ROBINSONS FAMILY

Location: New England Highway, Lyra, 4352; south of Ballandean.
(076) 32 8615.

Winemakers: Rod McPherson and Philippa Hambleton.

1989 Production: 3000 cases.

Principal Wines: Chardonnay, Cabernet Sauvignon, Shiraz, Pinot Noir, Méthode champenoise—chardonnay, pinot noir blend (to be released in 1990), Ballandean Nouveau Light Red (maceration carbonique).

Distribution: Cellar door, mailing list, nationally through Auspac Marketing Pty Ltd, Qld. Cellar door sales 9 a.m. to 5 p.m. 7 days. Mailing list, PO Box 613, Toowoomba, 4350.

Prices: $10 to $15 retail.

Vintage Rating 1986–89: White: '89, '88, '86, '87. Red: '86, '87, '89, '88.

Outstanding Prior Vintages: White: '76, '82. Red: '81, '82, '83, '84.

Tasting Notes:

1989 CHARDONNAY [CS] Colour: light straw-yellow. *Bouquet:* fragrant, youthful fruit with slightly raw oak still to fully integrate, but has style. *Palate:* fresh, stylish with attractive grapefruit/melon fruit and some barrel-ferment characters; if it lives up to its potential, will be the best Robinson chardonnay to date and will rate in the mid to high 70s.

1989 SHIRAZ [CS] Colour: deep purple-red. *Bouquet:* youthful, concentrated red cassis/berry fruits. *Palate:* extremely youthful and concentrated; both bouquet and palate are clean, and the wine has very good potential.

1989 SHIRAZ [78] Colour: medium to full red-purple. *Bouquet:* clean, with a touch of sweet oak; the fruit was initially unexpressive but came up in the glass. *Palate:* fresh, crisp and clean berry fruits, with a nice touch of oak and high acid; needs time to soften and gain complexity, but should do so. Drink '93–'98.

1985 CABERNET SAUVIGNON [65] Colour: full red-purple. *Bouquet:* strong, lemony/vanillan oak with extractive fruit. *Palate:* an extremely tannic wine, with pronounced lemony oak; the tannins are out of balance with the fruit, and it is exceedingly unlikely that they will ever come back into full balance. Drink '93–'96.

Summary: Robinsons is one of the major wineries in the Granite Belt region; despite upwards of 10 years experience, John Robinson is still having considerable difficulty in deciding on style. In the outcome, wine style is very unpredictable and, it must be said, quality likewise. As the tasting notes indicate, the better wines are quite attractive.

ROMAVILLA

Location: Northern Road, Roma, 4455; on northern outskirts of township. (076) 22 1822.

Winemaker: David Wall.

Principal Wines: A full range of table wine and fortified wine is produced, with fortified wines a long-standing speciality of the winery but table wines assuming increasing importance.

Distribution: Exclusively cellar door sales and mail order; cellar door sales 8 a.m. to 5 p.m. Monday to Friday and 9 a.m. to noon Saturday. Mailing list enquiries to PO Box 38, Roma, 4455.

Tasting Notes:

MARANOA MADEIRA [85] Colour: clear tawny, with no red hues remaining. *Bouquet:* extremely complex with strong muscat overtones and obvious age. *Palate:* very high-flavoured and intense wine, with a fair degree of volatility (but only what one would expect from an old, cask-aged wine); superb, lingering finish.

Summary: Romavilla caters basically to its local market, but is still noted for some of its high-quality fortified wines, based upon old blending stocks.

RUMBALARA

Location: Fletcher Road, Fletcher, 4381; 15 km south of Stanthorpe. (076) 84 1206.

Winemaker: Bob Gray.

Principal Wines: Rhine Riesling, Semillon, Rosé, Cabernet Sauvignon, Pinot Noir, Shiraz, Vintage Port and Muscat. The Girrawheen and Rumbalara labels are now merged into Rumbalara as the sole label of the Granite Belt Vignerons Partnership.

Distribution: Principally cellar door sales and mail order; cellar door sales 9 a.m. to 5 p.m. 7 days. Mailing list enquiries as above.

Prices: $7 to $12.50.

Vintage Rating 1986–89: White: '86, '87, '88 ('89 not rated). Red: '86, '87, '88 ('89 not rated).

Outstanding Prior Vintages: White: '84, '83, '79. Red: '84, '85.

Tasting Notes:

1987 SEMILLON **[61]** Colour: very light yellow-green. _Bouquet:_ clean, but extraordinarily backward, with a touch of melon/honey. _Palate:_ has some weight, but there is some evidence of warm fermentation, and the wine is still rather hard on the finish. On the evidence of earlier releases, may well improve with bottle-age. Drink '90–'92.

1987 CABERNET SAUVIGNON **[90]** Colour: full purple-red. _Bouquet:_ clean, firm dark berry/cassis fruit with unusual depth and richness. _Palate:_ strong, deep smooth berry/cassis/plum fruit flavours of exceptional weight and concentration; a textured wine which relies purely on its fruit, rather than on oak, for its truly excellent quality. Drink '93–'98.

1986 CABERNET SAUVIGNON **[87]** Colour: medium red-purple. _Bouquet:_ complex bottle-developed aromas with lemony/vanillan oak and sweet fruit. _Palate:_ complex, rich and full, with superb bottle-developed characters starting to emerge; sweet oak, and the overall impression is almost like a Bordeaux from a very warm year. Drink '92–'97.

Summary: I would have to say that the two Rumbalara Cabernet Sauvignons were the most surprising wines of the 5000 or so tasted for this edition of the book. Rumbalara has always had a (fully deserved) reputation for its semillon, and how these two lovely cabernets came into being I do not know. I find it difficult to believe that if they were entered in shows they would fail to win medals.

STONE RIDGE

Location: Limberlost Road, Glen Aplin, 4381; 12.9 km south of Stanthorpe. (076) 83 4211.

Winemaker: Jim Lawrie.

1989 Production: Approximately 500 cases.

Principal Wine: Shiraz.

Distribution: Cellar door sales and mailing list; cellar door sales 10 a.m. to 5 p.m. Mailing list enquiries, PO Box 412, Stanthorpe, 4380.

Prices: $12.50 cellar door.

Vintage Rating 1986–89: Red: '87, '89, '88, '86.

Tasting Notes:

1988 SHIRAZ **[74]** Colour: medium purple-red. _Bouquet:_ strong, clean peppery/spice with good weight and style. _Palate:_ strong spicy fruit flavours, although the texture of the wine is not heavy; light tannin and then an ever so slightly bitter finish. Drink '92–'94.

Summary: Jim Lawrie and Ann Kennedy are making lovely shiraz in a new but Lilliputian-sized winery on weekends and holidays. Production is tiny but well worth seeking out.

WINEWOOD

Location: Sundown Road, Ballandean, 43821; 17 km south of Stanthorpe. (076) 84 1187.

Winemaker: Ian Davis.

1989 Production: 200 cases.

Principal Wines: Semillon, Balandean Nouveau, Shiraz, Shiraz Mataro and Cabernet Sauvignon.

Distribution: Exclusively cellar door sales and mailing list at this juncture; cellar door sales 9 a.m. to 5 p.m. weekends, unless front gate is closed; weekdays by appointment. Mailing list enquiries to PO Box 84, Ballandean, 4382.

Prices: $7 to $12 cellar door.

Vintage Rating 1986–89: White: '88, '86, '87 ('89 not rated). Red: '88, '87, '86 ('89 not rated).

Summary: Ian and Janet Davis add to the array of young and dedicated talent in the Granite Belt; their small but spotlessly clean and well-ordered winery should produce exciting wines in the future.

Tasmania

1988 VINTAGE

1988 was the vintage of the decade. Indeed, in regard to the development of the Tasmanian industry, it was truly the vintage of the century. For once, everything went right from start to finish, and by the time the wines had finished fermentation, expectations were sky-high. Calm and mild weather at the critical times of flowering and berry set ensured a record crop of 316 tonnes, an increase of 55% on 1987, and almost three times the 1985 yield of 110 tonnes.

Of equal importance was the warm growing season, which lifted sugar levels to heights seldom achieved, notwithstanding the larger than usual crop. All varieties were harvested in perfect condition. The breakdown between districts showed that the north-east (Pipers Brook) produced 185 tonnes of grapes, the Tamar Valley 80 tonnes and the south 52 tonnes.

1989 VINTAGE

The season got off to an uncertain start, with October being the windiest and wettest month on record for Tasmania. However, the weather then turned, and most varieties flowered between mid and late December in ideal conditions—still, dry, sunny days—which resulted in excellent set. Cabernet sauvignon faired particularly well, and the largest crops on record eventuated.

The season then turned once again, with rain falling intermittently throughout January and February, necessitating constant spraying against powdering mildew, with occasional outbreaks of downy mildew also experienced. The degree to which vineyards were affected varied substantially between the east coast, the south and the north, but in all districts, vignerons were kept on their toes.

On 31 March heavy rain commenced to fall, and continued for two weeks. Pinot and chardonnay harvested before the rain were of excellent quality, and late harvest cabernet sauvignon and merlot picked after the rain were likewise good. Even here, the north-east and the east coast were more affected by rain than was the south. Riesling suffered the most, with heavy infections of botrytis, while some vineyards even reported plagues of snails arriving during the rain. A difficult vintage, to be sure, but not without its bright spots.

THE CHANGES

The Tasmanian industry continues to grow apace. Plantings during the winter increased the area under vine to 180 hectares, but only half of this (93 hectares) bore fruit in 1989, underlining both the rate of expansion and the still tiny scale of grape growing and winemaking.

There are two new entries in this edition, although in many ways they represent the tip of the iceberg. What is more, one of the entries, La Provence, lays claim to being the oldest vineyard in Tasmania. It was established between 1956 and 1960 by Jean Miguet, a Frenchman working on a civil engineering project near Launceston. After Miguet returned to France in the mid 1970s, the vineyard fell on hard times, but was purchased by Stuart Bryce and family in 1890. Stuart Bryce, a retired Wing Commander, successfully undertook the wine science degree at Charles Sturt University, and plans to establish his own on-site winery once the existing vineyard has doubled in size (to 3.5 hectares) and some neighbourhood plantings come into bearing. In the meantime, the wine is made at Heemskerk.

Elsewhere Vineyard was established by Eric and Jette Phillips in 1985 as an extension of their flower business at Galziers Bay, south of Hobart. Elsewhere lays claim to being one of the most southerly vineyards in the world, challenged only by those in Argentina.

Other changes have been the acquisition of Glengarry by Buchanan Wines, and the first release of wines from the latter operation. Buchanan wines is destined to become one of the larger Tasmanian producers: Don Buchanan has now planted 10 hectares on the home vineyard (known as Loira), and with the acquisition of the Glengarry vineyard in August 1988, Buchanan is one of the largest single vineyard holders in Tasmania. Don Buchanan graduated from Roseworthy College in 1973, and had 12 years' experience with major South Australian wineries before moving to Tasmania in 1985.

There are a number of other significant developments. Clover Hill Vineyard was established in 1987 by Taltarni with the objective of supplying Taltarni with material for sparkling wine. Twelve hectares are now under vine, and in the long term an on-site winery is planned.

There is substantial overseas interest in Tasmania. Bernard Rochaix heads a Swiss-based syndicate that is establishing Idlewilde Vineyard in the Pipers River district; 6.5 hectares is under vine, with further plantings planned. Stoney Vineyard, too, has passed into Swiss ownership: Peter and Ruth Althause of Zurich fell in love with Stoney and purchased it from George Park almost on impulse. Their plans are to expand the vineyard to around 8 hectares. The Roederer joint venture with Heemskerk continues, albeit at a leisurely pace and with what has so far been a relatively low profile. A syndicate headed by Mornington Peninsula vigneron and viticulturist Garry Crittenden has established a vineyard to supply material for sparkling wines, with Domaine Chandon the principal purchaser.

The next edition is likely to see entries for Dallas and Julie Targett's Bellingham Vineyard (in the Pipers River district) Cliff House Vineyard (in the Tamar Valley, with the wines being made under contract by Julian Alcorso) and Panorama Vineyard, operated by Steve Ferencz in the Huon Valley, not far from Elsewhere Vineyard.

Finally, just as the book was going to print, news came of the sale of the Gawiths' vineyard at Pipers Brook to Andrew Pirie. The Gawiths' will retain the Wattley Creek label (and all stock) and will develop a new vineyard in southern Tasmania

Despite all of this, and despite the 1988 vintage, Tasmania still progresses slowly. I have to admit to some disappointment with the wines from the 1988 vintage: they were tasted in July 1989 and may well have been going through a quiet phase of their development. I certainly hope so, because if Tasmania is ever going to seriously compete with the mainland, it must do so with wines made in years such as 1988.

BUCHANAN WINES

Location: Glendale Road, Loira, West Tamar, 7275. (003) 94 7488; Fax (003) 94 7581.

Winemaker: Don Buchanan.

1989 Production: 2000 cases.

Principal Wines: Chardonnay, Sauvignon Blanc, Pinot and Cabernet Blend.

Distribution: Chiefly by mail order and through selected Tasmanian outlets; distributed by David Johnstone and Associates. Small quantities available at Crittendens, Melbourne. Cellar door tasting by appointment only; mail order enquiries to above address.

Prices: $17.50 to $19.90 retail.

Vintage Rating 1986–89: '89, '88, '86, '87.

Tasting Notes:

1988 CHARDONNAY [77] Colour: light straw-green. *Bouquet:* has some weight and style, even if lemony oak does make a major impact. *Palate:* strong, vanillan/coconut influence, with light, clean fruit underneath; crisp acid gives balance and life to the wine. Drink '90–'92.

1988 PINOT NOIR [69] Colour: deep purple-red, remarkably intense and strong. *Bouquet:* utterly dominated by new, lemony, Nevers oak. *Palate:* once again, absolutely swamped by Nevers oak; it is very difficult to tell how much varietal character and style the underlying fruit has. I do not think that time will bring the wine back into balance. Drink '92–'94.

Summary: The 1989 samples submitted by Buchanan Wines were not reviewable, presumably due to sampling problems. The 1988 wines show promise, particularly once expanded volume permits a balance between new and old oak.

DELAMERE

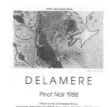

Location: Bridport Road, Pipers Brook, 7254. (003) 82 7190.

Winemaker: Richard Richardson.

1989 Production: 7 tonnes.

Principal Wines: Pinot Noir and Chardonnay.

Distribution: Principally mailing list; address as above; limited retail outlets, including Melbourne Airport Fine Wines.

Prices: $14 to $20.

Vintage Rating 1986–89: White: '89, '88 ('86 and '87 not rated). Red: '88, '87, '89, '86.

Tasting Notes:

1988 CHARDONNAY [72] Colour: very light green-yellow. *Bouquet:* clean, but very light and restrained; yet to develop any real character. *Palate:* extremely light in body and intensity, with faint lemony/melon flavours; the wine has been well made, but the fruit does not appear to have been there in the first place. Certainly an extreme cool climate style, and it may be that I will be surprised in the longer term. Drink '90–'92.

1987 CHARDONNAY [68] Colour: medium yellow-green. *Bouquet:* very neutral and restrained, with a faint touch of spice. *Palate:* a developed version of the 1988, but the fruit simply isn't there, and it seems unlikely that it will ever develop. Drink '90–'92.

1988 PINOT NOIR [76] Colour: excellent purple-red. *Bouquet:* spotlessly clean, with strong minty aromas proclaiming its cool climate origin. *Palate:* extremely powerful and concentrated wine with surprising tannins, and, once again, minty flavours dominating. Normally these are associated with low alcohol pinot noir, but this wine has 12.9%. Obviously, a strong regional influence at work. Drink '90–'92.

Summary: Delamere stands tall among the producers of Tasmanian pinot noir, and Richard Richardson has the zeal of a true pinot missionary. I am intrigued by the flavours in the 1988 pinot, but would prefer to see more of the characters shown by the '86. I shall watch the future releases of Delamere with great interest.

ELSEWHERE VINEYARD

Location: Glaziers Bay, Tasmania, 7112. (002) 95 1509.

Winemaker: Julian Alcorso (contract).

Principal Wines: Rhine Riesling, Chardonnay, Pinot Noir and Cabernet Sauvignon.

Distribution: Solely by mail order; enquiries as above.

Tasting Notes:

1988 PINOT NOIR [70] Colour: strong purple-red. *Bouquet:* clean, concentrated but rather closed, with faint minty fruit. *Palate:* clean, solid, minty wine with plenty of fruit flavour and quite good balance; these strong minty characters are in no way representative of conventional pinot noir, but it may be others are more tolerant of them than I. Drink '90–'92.

Summary: There are mainland parallels for the peppermint character which seems to dominate many Tasmanian pinot noirs; sometimes these characters derive from imperfectly ripened fruit, but not always. Modern analysis techniques will no doubt lead to the compound responsible for the flavour being identified, and we may then understand more about it. In the meantime, I have difficulty in accepting it as a desirable face for pinot noir.

FREYCINET VINEYARD

Location: Tasman Highway via Bicheno, 7215. (002) 57 8384.

Winemaker: Geoffrey Bull.

1989 Production: Approximately 1000 cases.

PrincipalWines: Riesling Muller Thurgau, Chardonnay, Sauvignon Blanc, Pinot Noir and Cabernet Sauvignon.

Dietribution: Cellar door sales 10 a.m. to 4 p.m. 7 days. Mailing list enquiries welcome; address as above.

Prices: $12 to $17 cellar door.

Tasting Notes:

1989 RIESLING MULLER THURGAU [73] Colour: light green-straw. *Bouquet:* soft, clean, fragrant fruit of light to medium intensity, and well made. *Palate:* clean and crisp, with light fruit and very well-judged residual sugar; like the bouquet, of light to medium weight. Drink '90–'91.

1989 SAUVIGNON BLANC [70] Colour: light to medium straw-yellow. *Bouquet:* strong herbal/tobacco fruit in pronounced cool climate style. *Palate:* pungent and penetrating herbal/tobacco flavours of extraordinary intensity, with an almost chemical after-taste. Tasted immediately after bottling, and will presumably settle down with time. Drink '90–'91.

1989 CABERNET SAUVIGNON [CS] Colour: full purple-red. *Bouquet:* quite rich red berry/cassis fruit with some slightly gamey, barrel-ferment overtones. *Palate:* rich and complex on the fore-palate, but hollow on the back-palate; if that dip in flavour fills out will rate well into the 70's.

1988 CABERNET SAUVIGNON [60] Colour: medium red, with a tinge of brown. *Bouquet:* quite complex tobacco leaf/briary aromas. *Palate:* slightly varnishy oak, and the fruit is diminished through the apparent effects of some oxidation. Drink '90–'92.

Summary: Geoff Bull has produced some quite excellent wines from Freycinet over the years. The 1988 wines submitted suffered from a variety of problems, including volatility and over-extraction, disappointing given the reputation of the vintage. However, the 1989s by and large (though not even here universally) show signs of being back on track.

GLENGARRY VINEYARD

Location: Loop Road, Glengarry, West Tamar, 7275. (003) 96 1141 or (003) 94 7488.

Winemaker: Don Buchanan.

1989 Production: Incorporated in Buchanan Wines.

Principal Wines: Pinot Noir, Cabernet and Merlot.

Summary: The Glengarry label is currently in recession, but Don Buchanan intends re-establishing the label in 12 to 18 months for a select range of premium reds.

 HEEMSKERK

Location: Pipers Brook, 7254; 20 km west of Bridport and 50 km north of Launceston.
(003) 82 7133 (winery) or (003) 31 6795 (office).

Winemaker: Graham Wiltshire.

1989 Production: The equivalent of 13,000 cases (including contract work).

Principal Wines: Chardonnay, Pinot Noir, Cabernet Sauvignon and Sparkling wines.

Distribution: Exclusively fine wine retailers; distributed by Fesq & Co. in NSW, Vic., and Hedges & Lawson, Tas. No cellar door sales or mailing lists; winery visits by appointment only. UK imports through Maisons Marques et Domaines, London.

Prices: $12 to $30 retail.

Vintage Rating 1986–89: White: '88, '86, '87, '89. Red: '89, '88, '86, '87.

Outstanding Prior Vintages: White: '82, '85. Red: '82.

Tasting Notes:

1988 CHARDONNAY [70] Colour: very light straw-green. _Bouquet:_ biscuity/bready oak tends to dominate and the fruit lacks intensity. _Palate:_ super bready/biscuity flavours, and a slightly hard finish; the middle palate is still conspicuous by its absence, but may develop with time. Drink '91–'93.

1987 CHARDONNAY [75] Colour: light straw-green. _Bouquet:_ clean, with light melon fruit developing slowly but pleasantly. _Palate:_ light melon fruit with very pronounced acid running throughout in a distinctly European style; there are some of those biscuity characters of the '88, and the wine is still developing. Drink '90–'92.

1986 CABERNET SAUVIGNON [79] Colour: medium purple-red. _Bouquet:_ complex aromas of mulberry and spice, together with a touch of mint; reminiscent of Coonawarra. _Palate:_ complex minty/leafy/berry flavours, with surprising tannin; will be long lived. Drink '92–'97.

Summary: Heemskerk is now the largest winery in Tasmania, producing wines both on its own account and for a number of other producers. Once the vineyards dedicated to the production of sparkling wine for the joint venture with Roederer come into full production, output will increase further. Because of its size, much of the success or failure of Tasmania will be gauged by the wines of Heemskerk.

LA PROVENCE VINEYARDS

Location: Lalla, Tasmania, 7267.
(003) 95 1290.

Winemaker: Heemskerk (contract).

1989 Production: 400 cases.

Principal Wines: Pinot Noir and Chardonnay.

Distribution: Almost exclusively through mailing list; also available through Hedges & Lawson, 85 Elizabeth Street, Launceston. Mailing list enquiries to PO Box 99, Lilydale, Tasmania, 7268.

Prices: $17 to $21 mail order.

Vintage Rating 1986–89: '86, '88, '87 ('89 not rated).

Tasting Notes:

1987 CHARDONNAY [79] Colour: medium yellow-green. _Bouquet:_ strong hessiany oak with pronounced biscuity aromas. _Palate:_ has quite exceptional mouthfeel and weight, with honeyed/peach fruit and a powerful finish, balanced by good acid. Drink '90–'92.

1987/88 PINOT NOIR **[75]** *Colour:* medium purple-red. *Bouquet:* soft, with slightly burnt characters evident, but plummy fruit coming up progressively in the glass. *Palate:* rich, plummy fruit in good burgundian style, and might have been outstanding with better oak; however, it does fall away slightly on the finish. Drink '90–'92.

Summary: The wines of La Provence came as a pleasant surprise. One assumes that the now thoroughly mature vineyards are responsible for that extra dimension of fruit-weight apparent in both wines.

☙ *MARIONS VINEYARD*

Location: Foreshore Road, Deviot, 7251; 25 km north of Launceston.

Winemakers: Mark and Marion Semmens.

Principal Wines: Muller Thurgau, Chardonnay, Pinot Noir and Cabernet Sauvignon.

Distribution: Cellar door sales 10 a.m. to 5 p.m. 7 days; wines also available retail through Aberfeldy Cellars and Websters Wines; limited Melbourne fine wine distribution.

Summary: A beautifully situated winery on the banks of the Tamar River, producing wines of considerable strength and individual style. Winemakers Mark and Marion Semmens will not tolerate any criticism of these wines.

☙ *MEADOWBANK*

Location: Glenora, Derwent Valley, 7410; 75 km north-west of Hobart (vineyard only).

Winemaker: Andrew Pirie (contract).

Principal Wines: Rhine Riesling and Cabernet Sauvignon.

Distribution: Principally through mailing list; enquiries to Meadowbank Wines, Glenora, Tasmania, 7410. Also available through Aberfeldy Cellars, Hobart.

Prices: $14 retail.

Tasting Notes:

1988 RHINE RIESLING **[77]** *Colour:* light green-yellow. *Bouquet:* clean, fragrant with good varietal character showing some passionfruit and a light touch of toast. *Palate:* clean and well-balanced with light lime/passionfruit flavours; very well made, but lacking the richness one might have hoped for in this vintage. Drink '90–'91.

1988 CABERNET SAUVIGNON **[CS]** *Colour:* dark purple-red. *Bouquet:* ripe, with gamey/ mulberry/plum/spice fruit of good depth. *Palate:* once again, has good concentration and depth, with obvious adequately ripened fruit and good tannins; one of the few immediately obvious successes for the vintage, and should rate in the 80's.

1987 CABERNET SAUVIGNON **[63]** *Colour:* medium red. *Bouquet:* in total contrast to the '88, with light, slightly leafy/minty aromas more akin to merlot than cabernet sauvignon. *Palate:* very light and thin, with washed-out flavour like a poor year wine from St Emilion. Drink '90–'91.

Summary: Meadowbank was one of the undoubted successes in the 1988 vintage, most obviously with cabernet sauvignon. It does have a long history of producing fine riesling, and the new ownership must be well pleased with its investment.

☙ *MOORILLA ESTATE*

Location: 655 Main Road, Berriedale, 7011; 10 km north of Hobart. (002) 49 2949; Fax (002) 49 4093.

Winemaker: Julian Alcorso.

1989 Production: 8000 cases.

Principal Wines: Pinot Noir, Rhine Riesling, Gewurztraminer, Chardonnay and Cabernet Sauvignon.

Distribution: Reasonably extensive retail distribution through David Johnstone & Associates, Tasmania and Dorado Wine Co., Australian mainland. Significant mailing list custom with an annual bulletin and release in October of each year. Winery visits by appointment until September 1990, when a cellar door sales facility will open.

Prices: $17 to $30 retail.

Vintage Rating 1986–89: White: '88, '89, '87, '86. Red: '88, '89, '87, '86.

Outstanding Prior Vintages: Red: '84.

Tasting Notes:

1988 RHINE RIESLING [80] Colour: light green-yellow. *Bouquet:* some estery lift with some fractionally hard citrus characters. *Palate:* pronounced estery fruit that has the intensity that so many of the other Tasmanian rieslings lack; slightly edgy acid needs time to settle down, but the wine has an undoubted future. Drink '90–'93.

1988 GEWURZTRAMINER [72] Colour: light straw-green. *Bouquet:* very soft, with faintly sweet tobacco overtones, lacking varietal character. *Palate:* clean and well balanced, but lacking varietal flavour and intensity; finishes with pleasantly crisp acidity. Drink '90–'91.

1987 CHARDONNAY [74] Colour: medium yellow-green. *Bouquet:* rich, full, complex melon fruit, textured and quite burgundian. *Palate:* high acid tends to throw the wine out of balance, and there are some slightly bitter flavours not evident in the bouquet; at least the wine makes a positive statement. Drink '90–'92.

1987 PINOT NOIR [83] Colour: bright, light to medium purple-red. *Bouquet:* light and clean, with excellent sappy pinot noir varietal aroma. *Palate:* light-bodied but very fine pinot flavours with a touch of sappiness; the wine has lovely flavour throughout, although it is not particulary long on the finish. Drink '90–'92.

1987 CABERNET SAUVIGNON [74] Colour: medium red-purple. *Bouquet:* very complex, leafy/tobacco/gamey fruit amalgam. *Palate:* an extreme style with almost discordant gamey/tobacco flavours; extreme manifestation of cool climate cabernet that is not easy to point. Drink '90–'94.

Summary: Moorilla Estate is breathing down the neck of Heemskerk, with substantial additional associated vineyards still to come into full production. Julian Alcorso has set his heart on making first class pinot noir, and the '87 suggests he may well achieve that aim.

☙ PIPERS BROOK

PIPERS BROOK VINEYARD
1988 CHARDONNAY
Tasmania

Location: Bridport Road, Pipers Brook, 7254; 20 km west of Bridport and 50 km north-east of Launceston.
(003) 82 7197; Fax (003) 82 7226.

Winemaker: Andrew Pirie.

Principal Wines: Riesling Traminer, Chardonnay, Pinot Noir and Cabernet Sauvignon.

Distribution: A complex distribution arrangement with restaurants only being serviced by I. H. Baker Wines & Spirits, NSW; Dorado Wine Co., Vic.; Classic Wine Merchants, SA; David Johnstone & Associates, Hobart; and Chancellors, Launceston. Retail outlets in each capital city serviced direct ex-winery. Much of the production is in fact sold direct ex-winery by mailing list; address as above.

Vintage Rating 1986–89: White: '88, '86, '89, '87. Red: '88, '87, '86, '89.

Outstanding Prior Vintages: Red: '81 Pinot Noir, '82.

Tasting Notes:

1988 RHINE RIESLING [76] Colour: light yellow-green. *Bouquet:* clean but rather soft, and lacking fruit intensity. *Palate:* very soft and light; clean and very well made; it is the fruit rather than the winemaking that lets the wine down at this juncture, but the track record of Pipers Brook Riesling suggests substantial improvement in the bottle. Drink '90–'93.

1988 TRAMINER [72] Colour: light green-yellow. *Bouquet:* clean, light lychee fruit with good varietal character. *Palate:* clean but simply too light in body; faint lychee spice flavours, lacking any intensity and seemingly lacking the potential for development in bottle. Drink '90.

1988 CHARDONNAY [82] Colour: light to medium yellow-green. *Bouquet:* rounded fruit with a pronounced grapefruit tang and good intensity. *Palate:* complex melon/grapefruit flavours with excellent texture, balance and weight; should develop well. Drink '90–'93.

1988 PINOT NOIR [74] Colour: light purple-red. *Bouquet:* light minty/cherry fruit with an attractive touch of spice. *Palate:* clean, light, smooth minty/cherry fruit with light oak; needs more structure and intensity for top points. Drink '90–'92.

Summary: For many, Tasmania is synonymous with Pipers Brook, and Pipers Brook with Tasmania. Andrew Pirie is a tireless worker and great ambassador for Tasmanian wine, but then so is the wine in the bottle and the Pipers Brook label itself—surely the most beautiful in Australia.

POWERCOURT VINEYARDS

Location: McEwans Road, Legana, 7251;
10 km north of Launceston on the West Tamar Highway.
(003) 30 1700.

Winemaker: Ralph Power.

1989 Production: 100 cases (but increasing).

Principal Wines: Chardonnay, Pinot Noir, Cabernet Sauvignon and Cabernet Sauvignon Pinot Noir Blend.

Distribution: Exclusively mailing list and cellar door (by appointment).

Prices: $14 to $18 cellar door.

Tasting Notes:

1985 CABERNET PINOT [64] Colour: light to medium red-purple. *Bouquet:* light, with faint leafy/leather characters. *Palate:* light-bodied and, as one might expect from this unusual blend, no particular varietal character; faintly leafy flavours throughout, with low tannin. Drink '90–'91.

Summary: Powercourt's minuscule production will increase in future years following the expansion of the vineyard. Some powerful wines have appeared from earlier vintages; some marred by sulphide, however.

ROTHERHYTHE

Location: Hendersons Lane, Gravelly Beach, Exeter, 7251.
(003) 34 0188.

Winemaker: Steven Hyde.

1989 Production: Very small.

Principal Wines: Pinot Noir and Cabernet Sauvignon.

Distribution: Exclusively mailing list; enquiries to Dr S. Hyde, 9 Frederick Street, Launceston, 7250.

Tasting Notes:

1986 PINOT NOIR [80] Colour: good purple-red. *Bouquet:* ripe, with some stylish plummy characters in a quite distinct burgundian mould. *Palate:* strong pinot varietal flavour throughout in a sappy/plummy spectrum; the wine is slightly disjointed, but shows exciting potential. Drink '90–'93.

1986 CABERNET SAUVIGNON [77] Colour: medium red-purple. *Bouquet:* strong, tobacco/leafy characters, very like Bordeaux merlot. *Palate:* light to medium leafy characters, again reminiscent of merlot more than cabernet sauvignon; the wine has good balance, with soft, integrated tannins. Drink '90–'94.

Summary: A tiny operation relying exclusively on cellar door sales to friends and acquaintances. Wine quality can be exemplary, as witnessed by the quite lovely 1986 reds.

ST MATTHIAS

Location: Rosevears Drive, Rosevears, 7251;
4 km south of Rosevears.
(003) 30 1700.

Winemaker: Graham Wiltshire (contract).

1989 Production: 2000 cases

Principal Wines: Pinot Noir, Rhine Riesling, Chardonnay and Cabernet Merlot Blend.

Distribution: Mailing list, cellar door sales and limited restaurant distribution. Cellar door sales 11 a.m. to 5 p.m. 7 days, September to May; June to August by appointment only. Sales facility also offers the wines of Heemskerk, Moorilla, Pipers Brook, Freycinet, Meadowbank and Buchanan.

Prices: $10 to $16 cellar door.

Vintage Rating 1986–89: White: '89, '88, '86, '87. Red: '89, '88, '87, '86.

Tasting Notes:

1988 CHARDONNAY [69] Colour: very light straw-green. *Bouquet:* extremely light with slightly biscuity characters and a touch of volatile lift. *Palate:* strong bready/biscuity characters which seem to run through every chardonnay made at Heemskerk; whether it is malolactic fermentation or oak I am not sure, but it is certainly made in a particular style, with the fruit apparently deliberately down-played Drink '91–'93.

1988 PINOT NOIR [80] Colour: strong purple-red. *Bouquet:* of light to medium weight, but with stylish cherry/plum fruit. *Palate:* attractive cherry flavours of light to medium weight; the wine is a fraction one-dimensional but does show good, fully ripened pinot fruit. Drink '90–'92.

1988 KINBURN CABERNET MERLOT [81] Colour: excellent purple-red. *Bouquet:* clean, with fresh, red berry aromas showing ripe fruit; the oak has been well handled. *Palate:* fresh, clean red berry flavours, again demonstrating ripe fruit in a cool climate mould; low tannins. Drink '91–'95.

1987 KINBURN CABERNET MERLOT [75] Colour: medium purple-red. *Bouquet:* distinctly lighter than the '88, with faint minty overtones; smooth and well made. *Palate:* light, fresh and clean with some red berry fruit touched by mint; simply lacks the richness and depth of the '88. Drink '90–'92.

Summary: St Matthias has come a long way in a very short space of time, showing just what can be done with adequate capital and a sound business plan. Wine quality is, as one would expect, good, and St Matthias is certain to go from strength to strength.

ST PATRICKS WATTLEY CREEK

Location: Hills Road, Pipers Brook, 7254. (003) 82 7184.

Winemaker: Leigh Gawith.

Principal Wines: Montage Semillon Blend, Vignette Pinot Noir and Montage Cabernet Blend.

Distribution: Chiefly through mailing list; mail order enquiries as above, with active mailing list maintained. Limited retail distribution through Aberfeldy Cellars, Hobart.

Prices: $12 to $16.

Tasting Notes:

1988 MONTAGE SEMILLON BLEND [62] Colour: light straw-green. *Bouquet:* clean but very light grassy/tobacco characters. *Palate:* light fruit with a somewhat hard and slightly oily finish; the fruit weight on the mid-palate is conspicuous by its absence; others have enjoyed this wine more than I. Drink '90–'91.

1988 VIGNETTE PINOT NOIR [75] Colour: light to medium purple-red. *Bouquet:* clean, with sweet vanillan oak dominant although well integrated. *Palate:* again, sweet vanillan oak flavours tend to dominate the light, sweet cherry fruit; a more sympathetic choice of oak could have made a truly excellent pinot noir. Drink '90–'91.

1988 MONTAGE CABERNET BLEND [65] Colour: light red-purple. *Bouquet:* clean, light and with pronounced minty/toothpaste aromas. *Palate:* light and delicate minty fruit with a slightly rough-sawn oak aftertaste. Drink '90–'92.

Summary: St Patricks swept all before it at the 1988 Royal Hobart Wine Show, winning the Tasmanian Fine Wine Distributors Trophy for the Most Successful Tasmanian Exhibitor, the Trophy for the Best Tasmanian Red, and the Trophy for the Best Tasmanian Wine (white or red). The award winning wines were the 1988 Semillon and 1988 Pinot Noir. However, as the introduction to this chapter notes, the Gawiths have sold the vineyard (but not the name) and are moving south.

❦ STONEY VINEYARD

Location: Campania, 7202; 35 km north-east of
    Hobart.
    (002) 62 4174.

Winemaker: To be appointed.

Principal Wines: Rhine Riesling, Cabernet
    Sauvignon and Pinot Noir.

Distribution: New distribution arrangement yet to
    be determined.

Tasting Notes:

1988 RHINE RIESLING [65] Colour: light yellow-
    green. _Bouquet:_ clean, very well made with light
    passionfruit aroma. _Palate:_ the wine enters the
    mouth very pleasantly, but the fruit is not there
    on the mid-palate, and hard phenolics toughen
    the finish. Time may help. Drink '90–'92.

1988 PINOT NOIR [76] Colour: strong purple-red.
    Bouquet: spotlessly clean, with subdued oak and
    pleasant plum fruit. _Palate:_ smooth, rounded
    dark cherry/plum flavours with good intensity;
    just a little short on fragrance and lift. Drink
    '90–'93.

1988 CABERNET SAUVIGNON [78] Colour: dense
    purple-red. _Bouquet:_ very concentrated and deep
    minty fruit, bordering on the extractive. _Palate:_
    strong, clean and smooth minty flavours with
    adequate berry fruit; soft but persistent tannins,
    and the oak is in balance. Drink '92–'96

Summary: George Park has left a generous legacy
    in the form of the 1988 wines. It will be
    interesting to see how the new Swiss owners
    develop Stoney in the years to come.

Glossary

The *Australian Wine Compendium* contains a large glossary of common wine terms, grape varieties and the like. The glossary which follows is intended to supplement that of the *Compendium,* and is directed mainly to the at-times arcane terminology of the tasting notes. It also covers in a little more detail some of the background to wine faults.

Acetic: A wine with an excess of acetic acid, a volatile acid present in virtually all table wines in small quantities. Acetic volatility, and volatile acidity, are alternative terms.

Aggressive: An unpleasantly obvious component of wine flavour, e.g., aggressive tannin.

Aldehyde: A volatile fluid deriving from the oxidation of alcohol, present in most wines but undesirable in any appreciable quantity; hence, aldehydic.

Armpit: A colloquial term used to describe the rather sweaty and stuffy smell of a wine which is showing the after-effects of a highly controlled fermentation and maturation in which oxygen has been rigorously excluded. It is a condition which usually passes after the wine has spent a year or so in bottle. For some reason, sauvignon blanc seems to suffer particularly from the character.

Aroma: The scent or smell of the grape variety; aroma decreases with age as bouquet builds; hence, aromatic.

Astringent; Astringency: Sharpness or bitterness deriving usually from tannin and sometimes from acid; particularly evident in a young wine, and can be an indication of the keeping potential of such a wine. Can also be associated with mercaptan, and overall is not a desirable characteristic.

Autolysis; Autolysed: The breakdown of internal barriers within dead cells to allow enzymes present in those cells to digest components of the cell, producing both flavour and structure changes in the wine; a marmite-toast flavour is often noted, while the surface tension of the wine is decreased, leading to smaller bubbles in the sparkling wine in which the process of autolysis occurs.

Backbone: A term used to describe a wine with a core of strength, which derives from acid (in the case of white wine) or from tannin and/or acid (in the case of red wine).

Back-palate: The point in the tasting cycle shortly before or shortly after the wine is swallowed.

Balance: The harmony or equilibrium between the different flavour components of wine, and the first requirement of a great wine.

Barrel Fermentation: The practice of conducting the primary fermentation in the small oak barrels in which wine is normally stored at the end of fermentation; a common practice in making French white burgundy, but of recent introduction in Australia.

Body: A term used to describe the weight or substance of a wine in the mouth and deriving from alcohol and tannin. Softens and mellows with age.

Bottle-development: A reference to the secondary characters and flavours which develop after a wine has been cellared for some years.

Botrytis; Botrytised: Reference to the effect on the taste of the wine of *Botrytis cinerea*, a microscopic fungus or mould and which leads to the great sweet wines of the world. It tends to impose a lime/tropical fruit aroma and, in high concentrations, to mask substantially the natural varietal aroma and flavour of the grape it attacks once made into wine.

Bouquet: The smell of the wine (as opposed to simply the aroma of the grape) produced by the volatile esters present in any wine. Bouquet becomes more complex during the time the wine needs to reach full maturity and finally softens and dissipates with extreme age. Much work still remains to be done to understand fully the very complex chemical changes which take place in a wine as it matures and which contribute to the changing bouquet.

Bready: Literally the smell of freshly baked bread, often associated with the influence of yeast, and probably, but by no means necessarily, a pleasant aroma.

Broad: A term used to describe wine which is soft or coarse, lacking in refinement.

Camphor: A smell which can develop after a wine has spent a number of years in bottle; usually quite pleasant unless it becomes too marked.

Caramel: Literally, a caramel flavour found in wine, usually white wine, and often indicating either oxidation or over-ripe fruit.

Carbonic Maceration: A winemaking method which involves a substantial portion of the primary fermentation taking place within whole berries, which have not been crushed in the usual method. It results in very soft wines with a distinctive aroma of spice and well-hung meat.

Cassis: A dark purple liquor made from blackcurrants, chiefly near Dijon in Burgundy. The aroma of cassis is often found in high-quality cabernet sauvignon as the smell of sweet blackcurrants.

Cedar: An oak-derived aroma or taste reminiscent of the smell of cedar, usually developed in older red wines.

Chalky: A rather dry, dusty aroma or taste, often found in young wines made from chenin blanc in the Loire Valley of France; may also be due to solids fermentation (see hereunder).

Character: The overall result of the combination of vinosity, balance and style of a wine.

Charred Oak: A particular taste deriving from oak which has been deliberately charred during the heating process needed to shape the wooden staves into barrel form. A complex, pleasantly smoky/toasty aroma and flavour is often the result.

Cheesy: A smell (and very occasionally a taste) which principally occurs in white wines and which tends to diminish fruit aromas. Its most likely cause is a degree of oxidation or perhaps yeast problems. Not particularly desirable.

Chewy: A term used to denote the structure (rather than the flavour) of a wine which just stops short of being thick or heavy; generally a term of qualified approval.

Cigar-box: Literally the smell of an empty cigar-box, usually manifesting itself in older red wines and deriving from oak. Sometimes present in young wines. Usually a term of approbation.

Clean: The absence of any foreign (or "off") odour or flavour; an important aspect of a wine of quality.

Closed: A wine lacking fruit aroma and possibly flavour; normally affects young wines and diminishes with age.

Cloying: The characteristic of a wine which lacks acid.

Coarse: Indicates a wine with excessive extract of solids, particularly tannins, and probably affected by oxidation during the making process.

Coffee: An undesirable taste or aroma reminiscent of coffee, normally indicating oxidation.

Complex: A term of commendation, but otherwise having its normal English meaning.

Corked; Corkiness: Refers to a wine affected by microscopic moulds (chiefly of the penicillin family) which penetrate corks in the cork factory and which subsequently impart a sour, mouldy taste in the wine.

Cosmetic: A somewhat imprecise term used to indicate a foreign, and often faintly sickly, aroma (or possibly flavour).

Creamy: A term used particularly in relation to sparkling wine and intended to denote texture more than flavour.

Crisp: A term of commendation, but otherwise having its normal English meaning.

Dull: Denotes a wine either cloudy or hazy in colour, or with a muted or flawed bouquet or palate.

Dumb: A wine showing either no aroma or distinct varietal taste, or no development; closed.

Dusty: Used to describe both the bouquet and taste of red wine, and normally denoting a character caused by long storage in big, old (but sound) oak casks.

Earthy: Bouquet and flavour reminiscent of certain soil types; a smell of fresh earth can often be identified in young vintage port.

Extractive: A coarse or heavy wine with excessive extract from skins and pips.

Fading: A wine past its peak, losing its bouquet, flavour and character.

Finesse: A term denoting a wine of elegance and subtlety.

Finish: The flavour or taste remaining after the wine leaves the mouth.

Firm: A term usually applied to the finish of a wine, and denoting the impact of tannin and possibly acid.

Flat: Similar to dull and flabby; a lack of freshness, character or acid.

Fleshy: A youthful wine with full-bodied varietal flavour.

Flowery: The aroma reminiscent of flowers contributed by certain aromatic grape varieties. Thus also floral; usually a term of commendation.

Fore-palate: Used to describe that part of the tasting cycle as the wine is first taken into the mouth.

Fresh: An aroma or taste free from any fault or bottle-developed characters, usually characteristic of a young wine but occasionally of older wines.

Furry: A term used to denote a particular aspect of the texture (rather than the taste) of a red wine, almost invariably deriving from tannin and akin to the sensation of soft fur on the side of the tongue.

Generic: A term used to denote a wine falling within a general style (e.g. chablis, white burgundy, claret) and not made from any particular grape variety or from any particular region.

Grassy; Grassiness: Literally the smell of freshly cut or partially dried grass, found very frequently in sauvignon blanc and in cabernet sauvignon grown in cooler areas or in cooler vintages. Can also occur occasionally in other varieties, particularly semillon. Provided it is present in moderation, is more likely to be desirable than not.

Gravel; Gravelly: Denotes a slightly flinty, slightly sour, taste akin to the taste (or sensation) of sucking a pebble.

Green: Term applied to a young wine which is unbalanced because of excess malic acid deriving from unripe grapes.

Green-yellow: The colour of white wine in which green tones predominate over yellow, but both are present. Highly desirable.

Grip: A component of the structure of a wine which probably has marked acid, but usually a term of qualified approval.

Hard: An unbalanced and unyielding wine suffering from an excess of tannin and/or acid (if red) and acid (if white).

Harsh: Usually applied to red wine suffering from excess tannin, often when young.

Herbaceous: Similar to grassy, but indicating a slightly broader spectrum of grass and herb-like flavours, usually a little richer and more complete. As in the case of a grassy wine, should not be excessively marked.

Hollow: Applies to a wine with initial taste and with finish, but with little or no flavour on the mid-palate.

Honeyed: Denotes both the flavour and the structure (or feel in the mouth) of a mature white wine, particularly aged semillon but also sauternes.

Integrated; Integration: Used in relation to a wine in which (most probably) fruit and oak flavours have blended harmoniously and merged imperceptibly into each other; a most desirable characteristic.

Intensity: Applied in particular in relation to fruit aroma or flavour; very different from weight; normally used in relation to a high-class wine.

Jammy: Excessively ripe and heavy red grape flavours, sweet but cloying.

Lactic: Refers to lactic acid, seldom present in grapes but formed during the alcoholic and malolactic fermentations. Also occurs in faulty wines as a result of bacterial decomposition of sugars; the slightly sickly, sour-milk aroma is very unpleasant.

Leafy: Yet another variant of the grassy/herbaceous spectrum of flavours, usually the lightest in weight. May or may not be pleasant.

Leathery: A slightly sour, astringent smell or taste, almost certainly deriving from small concentrations of mercaptan.

Lift; Lifted: Usually applied in relation to a wine with a degree of volatility, but in which that volatility is not excessive.

Lime: A lime-juice flavour commonly encountered in rhine riesling, and often (but not invariably) indicating that the fruit has been affected by botrytis.

Limousin: A particular type of French oak with a distinctive spicy aroma and taste.

Malic: A rather tart, green flavour deriving from higher than normal levels of malic acid, an acid found in all grapes but usually converted to lactic acid during the secondary fermentation.

Malty: Literally, the taste of malt; not a particularly desirable wine characteristic.

Matchbox: Literally the smell of a box of matches, a slightly sulphurous/wood smell; not at all desirable.

Meaty: The smell of slightly aged, raw meat, usually although not inevitably a form of mercaptan.

Medicinal: A somewhat vague term used to describe childhood recollections of cough mixture; not desirable.

Mercaptan: Produced by ethyl mercaptan and ethyl sulphides in wine, deriving from hydrogen sulphide produced during the fermentation. It manifests itself in a range of unpleasant odours ranging from burnt rubber to garlic, onion, gamy meat, stale cabbage and asparagus. While hydrogen sulphide can easily be removed, once mercaptan is formed it is much more difficult to eliminate.

Mid-palate: The mid-point of the tasting cycle, as the wine rests in the centre of the mouth.

Millerandage: Obviously enough, a French term, which has been colloquially translated as "hen-and-chicken", a vivid description of bunches containing both full-sized and stunted or unformed berries. The very small berries, if formed at all, carry no seeds as they are unfertilised. The condition is due to wind and/or rain at flowering.

Mint; Minty: An aroma and flavour of red wine in the eucalypt/peppermint spectrum, and not garden mint.

Modulated: A wine in which varietal aroma or flavour is very well-balanced between the extremes such aroma or flavour can on occasions take.

Mouldy: Off flavours and aromas derived from mouldy grapes or storage in a mouldy cask or from a bad cork.

Mousy: A peculiar flat, or biscuity, undesirable taste resulting from bacterial growth in wines, most evident after the wine leaves the mouth. Its precise cause is not yet known.

Mouth-feel: Literally, the feel rather than the taste of the wine in the mouth; a wine with good mouth-feel will be pleasantly round and soft.

Must: Fermenting wine which in the case of white wine is simply grape juice, and in the case of red wine comprises the juice, skins and pips of the grapes.

Nevers: An important French oak which imparts a slightly lemony taste, frequently used to mature Cabernet Sauvignon.

Nose: The scents and odours of a wine, encompassing both aromas and bouquet.

Oily: Oils deriving from grape pips or stalks and not desirable in wine. May also derive from poor oak.

Oxidised; Oxidation: Used in respect of a wine which has been exposed to too much oxygen, resulting in coarseness and loss of flavour.

Pastille: The flavour of a fruit pastille, not totally unpleasant but nonetheless undesirable.

Pencil Shavings: A rather bitter and raw oak aroma or flavour caused by the use of poor oak or unskilled use of oak maturation.

Phenolic: Deriving from phenols, important flavour contributors to wine, but denoting a hard or heavy coarse character; not desirable.

Powdery: Similar to dusty, and almost inevitably deriving from prolonged old oak storage. Can be quite attractive.

Pressings: Wine recovered from pressing the skins, stalks and pips after fermentation. It is higher in tannin and may be deeper coloured. Often back-blended into free run wine to add strength and colour.

Pungent: A characteristic of a very aromatic wine with a high level of volatiles.

Purple-red: A red wine colour in which the purple hues dominate the red; usually a young wine colour, and desirable.

Rancio: Distinctive, developed wood character of an old dessert wine stemming from a degree of oxidation. Highly desirable.

Raw: A term used to describe a sharp and aggressive oak flavour, due either to poor, unseasoned oak or to wine which has been removed from new oak barrels too quickly.

Red-purple: Applies to wine in which the red hues are more dominant than the purple; usually the first stage of colour change.

Reductive: A term used to describe a wine which has been rigorously protected from oxygen, and in which the fruit aroma may well be suppressed.

Residual Sugar: Unfermented grape sugar remaining in white wine in the form of glucose and fructose. Can be tasted in levels in excess of 5 grams per litre. Many so-called dry white wines have 6 to 7 grams per litre of residual sugar.

Robust: Usually applied to a young red wine which needs further time in bottle.

Rough: Astringent, coarse tannin taste in red wines indicating lack of balance and maturity.

Round: A well-balanced, smooth wine showing good balance of flavours, and particularly of acid.

Rubbery: The most common manifestation of hydrogen sulphide in the form of mercaptan.

Sappy; Sappiness: A touch of herbaceous or stalky character often found in young wines, particularly pinot noir, and usually a sign of potential quality.

Scented: Characteristic of a wine having a highly aromatic smell usually associated with flowers or fruits.

Smooth: Agreeable and harmonious; opposite of astringent, harsh or rough.

Soft: Refers to a wine with a pleasing finish, neither hard nor aggressive. May indicate fairly low acid levels, but not necessarily so.

Solid: Unrelated to solids (see below); used in relation to aroma or flavour that is full or ample, but which possibly lacks subtlety.

Solids: Literally, suspended particles of skin and flesh in grape juice; when not removed from white grape juice prior to fermentation (by cold settling or filtration) may cause the finished wine to have a harsh, hard aroma, flavour and/or structure.

Sorbate: A chemical used to control oxidation but which imparts an unpleasant aroma and flavour.

Spice: A term used to denote any one of the numerous spice flavours which can occur in wines, deriving either from oak or from the grape itself. Most spicy characters are very pleasant and add to complexity. The actual spectrum is as broad as the name suggests, running from nutmeg to black pepper.

Spritz; Spritzig: A German term indicating the presence of some carbon dioxide bubbles in the wine, frequently encountered in Australian white wine and occasionally in reds. Often an unintended consequence of protecting the wine from oxidation during storage and/or bottling. Can be felt as a slight prickle on the tongue.

Stalky: Bitter character deriving from grape stalks, mainly appearing in red wines and indicative of poor winemaking.

Straw: Refers either to colour (self-explanatory) or to taste; in the latter context usually denotes a degree of oxidation.

Structure: An all-encompassing term covering all aspects of a wine other than its primary flavours, and includes alcohol, body, weight, tannin and acid, even though some of these also manifest themselves as flavours.

Stylish: A somewhat imprecise and subjective term to denote a wine which attractively conforms to varietal or generic style.

Sulphide; Sulphidic: The generic term given to hydrogen sulphide and mercaptans.

Sulphur Dioxide (SO_2): An anti-oxidant preservative used in virtually every wine, red, white or sparkling. In excessive quantities imparts a disagreeable odour and may artificially retard the development of the wine. Dissipates with age.

Supple: Denotes a lively, yet round and satisfying, wine.

Sweaty saddle: A description most frequently accorded to aged Hunter Valley reds, probably indicating the presence of some mercaptan, but curiously a term of commendation more than condemnation.

Tannin: A complex organic constituent of wine deriving chiefly from grape pips and stalks, and occurring in greater quantities in reds than in whites. Plays an important part in the self-clearing of young wines after fermentation, and thereafter in the period of maturation the wine requires: a full-bodied red, high in tannin, requires a longer period than does a lighter-bodied wine. Easily perceived in the taste of the wine by the slightly mouth-puckering, drying, furry sensation, particularly on the side of the tongue and on the gums. Some red winemakers add powdered tannin to wine to increase the tannin level artificially.

Tart: Characteristic of a wine with excess acid.

Thick: Denotes an excessively heavy, and probably jammy, wine.

Thin: Lacking in body, almost watery and probably excessively acid.

Toast; Toasty: Literally the smell of fresh toast, occurring almost exclusively in white wines, and usually developing with bottle-age. Applies particularly to Hunter Valley semillon, but curiously, also to many rieslings.

Tobacco: Literally, the smell of tobacco.

Vanilla; Vanillin: A sweet aroma usually derived from American oak, but also occuring in old bottle-developed white wines.

Varietal: (i) Character of wine derived from the grape.
(ii) Term for wines made from a single or dominant variety and identified by reference to that variety.

Vegetative: Normally indicates a rather dank, vegetable-like aroma, sometimes reminiscent of cabbage, and seldom desirable.

Velvety: The softly rich and smooth feel of an aged wine which has retained strong fruit flavour.

Veraison: The point at which the grapes start to change colour from green to red in the case of red grapes, and from green to translucent green/yellow in the case of white grapes. A critical stage in the evolution of the vintage.

Vinosity; Vinous: A term relating to the strength of the grape character in a wine (though not necessarily the varietal character) and linked to the alcoholic strength of the wine. Denotes a desirable characteristic.

Volatile: A characteristic of a wine spoiled by an excess of acetic acid.

Volatile Acid: A group of acids comprising acetic, carbonic, butyric, propionic and formic.

Volatility: Relating to the release of acetic acid and other esters, and may be present to excess in a faulty wine.

Weight: Normally a measure of the strength of the wine in terms of alcohol and possibly tannin.

Yeasty: A smell or aroma deriving from the action of the yeast used to ferment the wine; except in the case of sparkling wine, should not be discernible to any degree.

Yellow-green: A white wine colour in which the yellow hues are more dominant than the green.

Zest; Zesty: Used in relation to a wine which is very fresh and pleasantly lively and acidic.

Index